I CAN'T REMEMBER IF WE'RE CHEAP OR SMART

Other DILBERT® books from Andrews McMeel Publishing

Teamwork Means You Can't Pick the Side That's Right
ISBN: 978-1-4494-1018-6

How's That Underling Thing Working Out for You?
ISBN: 978-1-4494-0819-0

Your Accomplishments Are Suspiciously Hard to Verify
ISBN: 978-1-4494-0102-3

Problem Identified and You're Probably Not Part of the Solution
ISBN: 978-0-7407-8534-4

I'm Tempted to Stop Acting Randomly
ISBN: 978-0-7407-7806-3

14 Years of Loyal Service in a Fabric-Covered Box
ISBN: 978-0-7407-7365-5

Freedom's Just Another Word for People Finding Out You're Useless
ISBN: 978-0-7407-7815-5

Dilbert 2.0: 20 Years of Dilbert
ISBN: 978-0-7407-7735-6

This Is the Part Where You Pretend to Add Value
ISBN: 978-0-7407-7227-6

Cubes and Punishment
ISBN: 978-0-7407-6837-8

Positive Attitude
ISBN: 978-0-7407-6379-3

Try Rebooting Yourself
ISBN: 978-0-7407-6190-4

What Would Wally Do?
ISBN: 978-0-7407-5769-3

Thriving on Vague Objectives
ISBN: 978-0-7407-5533-0

The Fluorescent Light Glistens Off Your Head
ISBN: 978-0-7407-5113-4

It's Not Funny If I Have to Explain It
ISBN: 978-0-7407-4658-1

Don't Stand Where the Comet Is Assumed to Strike Oil
ISBN: 978-0-7407-4539-3

Words You Don't Want to Hear During Your Annual Performance Review
ISBN: 978-0-7407-3805-0

When Body Language Goes Bad
ISBN: 978-0-7407-3298-0

What Do You Call a Sociopath in a Cubicle? Answer: A Coworker
ISBN: 978-0-7407-2663-7

Another Day in Cubicle Paradise
ISBN: 978-0-7407-2194-6

When Did Ignorance Become a Point of View?
ISBN: 978-0-7407-1839-7

Excuse Me While I Wag
ISBN: 978-0-7407-1390-3

Dilbert—A Treasury of Sunday Strips: Version 00
ISBN: 978-0-7407-0531-1

Random Acts of Management
ISBN: 978-0-7407-0453-6

Dilbert Gives You the Business
ISBN: 978-0-7407-0003-3

Don't Step in the Leadership
ISBN: 978-0-8362-7844-6

Journey to Cubeville
ISBN: 978-0-8362-6745-7

I'm Not Anti-Business, I'm Anti-Idiot
ISBN: 978-0-8362-5182-1

Seven Years of Highly Defective People
ISBN: 978-0-8362-3668-2

Casual Day Has Gone Too Far
ISBN: 978-0-8362-2899-1

Fugitive from the Cubicle Police
ISBN: 978-0-8362-2119-0

It's Obvious You Won't Survive by Your Wits Alone
ISBN: 978-0-8362-0415-5

Still Pumped from Using the Mouse
ISBN: 978-0-8362-1026-2

Bring Me the Head of Willy the Mailboy!
ISBN: 978-0-8362-1779-7

Shave the Whales
ISBN: 978-0-8362-1740-7

Dogbert's Clues for the Clueless
ISBN: 978-0-8362-1737-7

Always Postpone Meetings with Time-Wasting Morons
ISBN: 978-0-8362-1758-2

Build a Better Life by Stealing Office Supplies
ISBN: 978-0-8362-1757-5

For ordering information, call 1-800-223-2336.

I CAN'T REMEMBER IF WE'RE CHEAP OR SMART

by SCOTT ADAMS

Andrews McMeel
Publishing, LLC

Kansas City • Sydney • London

Andrews McMeel Publishing, LLC
an Andrews McMeel Universal company
1130 Walnut Street, Kansas City, Missouri 64106
www.andrewsmcmeel.com

12 13 14 15 16 BAM 10 9 8 7 6 5 4 3 2 1

ISBN: 978-1-4494-2309-4

Library of Congress Control Number: 2012936729

www.dilbert.com

For Shelly

Introduction

If you've ever owned a dog, you probably thought it was less intelligent than you. For example, a dog can't do algebra, whereas you have a clear memory of having once taken a class by that name. Or maybe you heard someone else talking about the class. Or it's the name of a band. Whatever. The point is that humans are way smarter than dogs, as far as we know.

But here's the interesting part: I'm certain dogs think they are smarter than humans. The stuff that we know—the knowledge that makes us feel so smart—is irrelevant to dogs. They don't care about finding a good Wi-Fi signal or knowing how to redeem their airline miles. What they *do* know is how a cat's ass smells, and frankly they pity you for your ignorance in that domain. I mean, I assume you're ignorant in that domain. But I'm not judging.

I used a dog in my example, but I think you see the same phenomenon in human-to-human interactions. We always think we're smarter than everyone else in the room, at least in the ways that seem important to *us*. Sure, you might know more than I do about artisanal cheese, but I think that's a totally douchey thing to know. How much do you know about the truly important things in life, such as writing introductions to *Dilbert* books? Okay, sure, you probably *do* know how to write one page of rambling, poorly constructed prose. But that's only 80 percent of what I do. The other 20 percent is hoping no one reads it.

We'll never know for sure if humans are smarter than dogs in any way that matters. But if we ever find an objective way to compare dog intelligence to human intelligence I don't like our odds of coming out on top. If you consider how quickly an average dog can find a bone in the backyard versus how long it takes you to find your cell phone in your house, I think it would be generous to call that a tie.

Sometimes we humans like to label our character flaws as "smart." We're funny that way. For example, you don't say you're too frightened to go rock climbing; you say you're too smart to engage in risky sports. You're not a hoarder; you're too smart to discard things you might need later. And you don't say you're a cheap bastard; you say you're a smart shopper.

If you repeat your smartness mantra long enough, you'll actually forget whether you're damaged or brilliant. And maybe that's a good thing. It's hard to be self-aware and have a good day at the same time. I think Buddha said that before I did, which probably means it's smart. On the other hand, he didn't spend much on his wardrobe, so . . .

S.Adams

Scott Adams

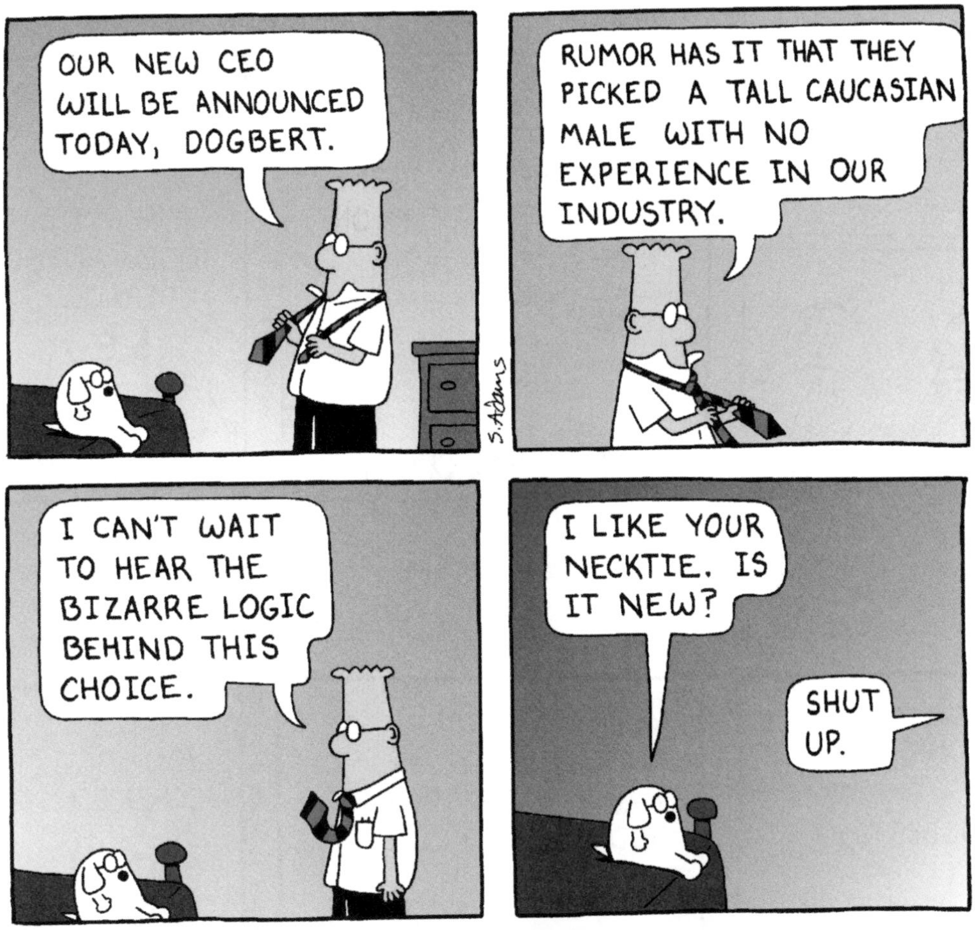
OUR NEW CEO WILL BE ANNOUNCED TODAY, DOGBERT.
RUMOR HAS IT THAT THEY PICKED A TALL CAUCASIAN MALE WITH NO EXPERIENCE IN OUR INDUSTRY.
I CAN'T WAIT TO HEAR THE BIZARRE LOGIC BEHIND THIS CHOICE.
I LIKE YOUR NECKTIE. IS IT NEW?
SHUT UP.

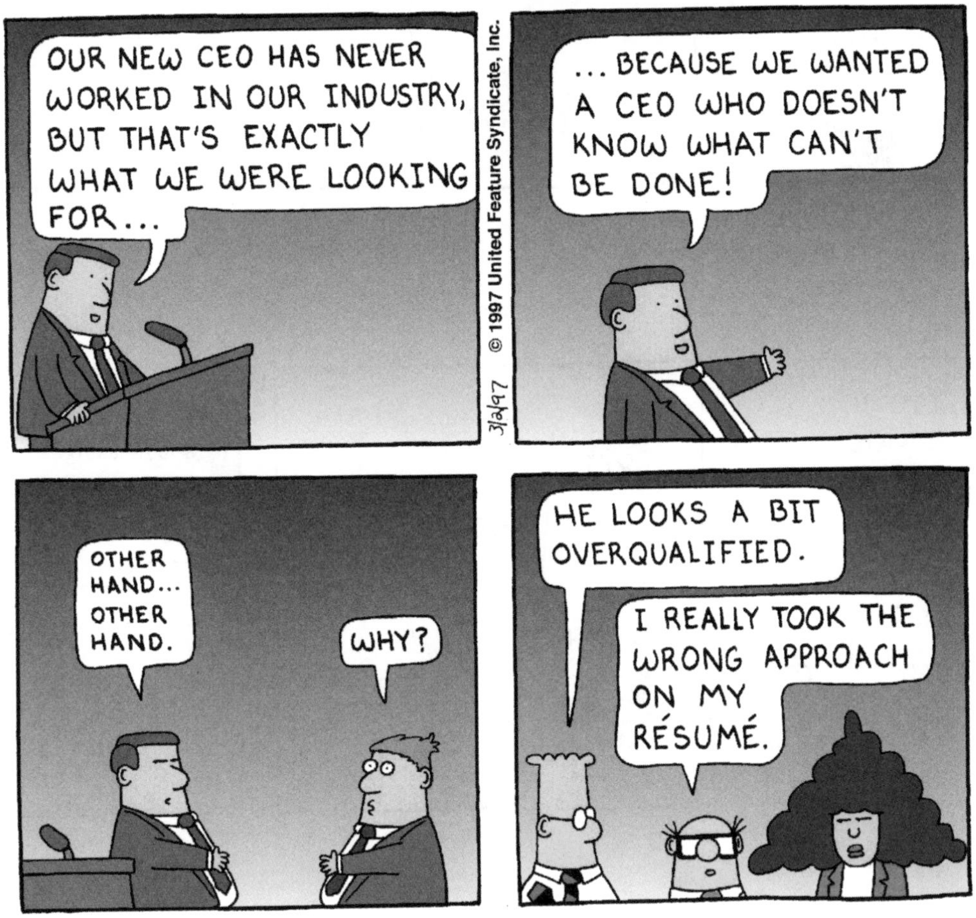
OUR NEW CEO HAS NEVER WORKED IN OUR INDUSTRY, BUT THAT'S EXACTLY WHAT WE WERE LOOKING FOR...
... BECAUSE WE WANTED A CEO WHO DOESN'T KNOW WHAT CAN'T BE DONE!
OTHER HAND... OTHER HAND.
WHY?
HE LOOKS A BIT OVERQUALIFIED.
I REALLY TOOK THE WRONG APPROACH ON MY RÉSUMÉ.

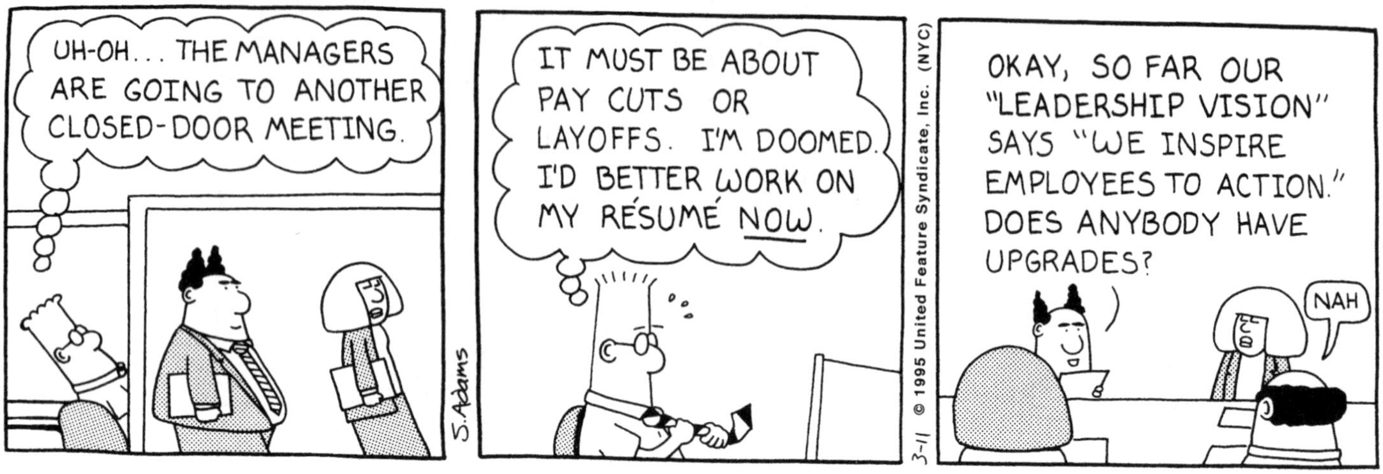
UH-OH... THE MANAGERS ARE GOING TO ANOTHER CLOSED-DOOR MEETING.
S. Adams
IT MUST BE ABOUT PAY CUTS OR LAYOFFS. I'M DOOMED. I'D BETTER WORK ON MY RÉSUMÉ NOW.
3-11 © 1995 United Feature Syndicate, Inc. (NYC)
OKAY, SO FAR OUR "LEADERSHIP VISION" SAYS "WE INSPIRE EMPLOYEES TO ACTION." DOES ANYBODY HAVE UPGRADES?
NAH

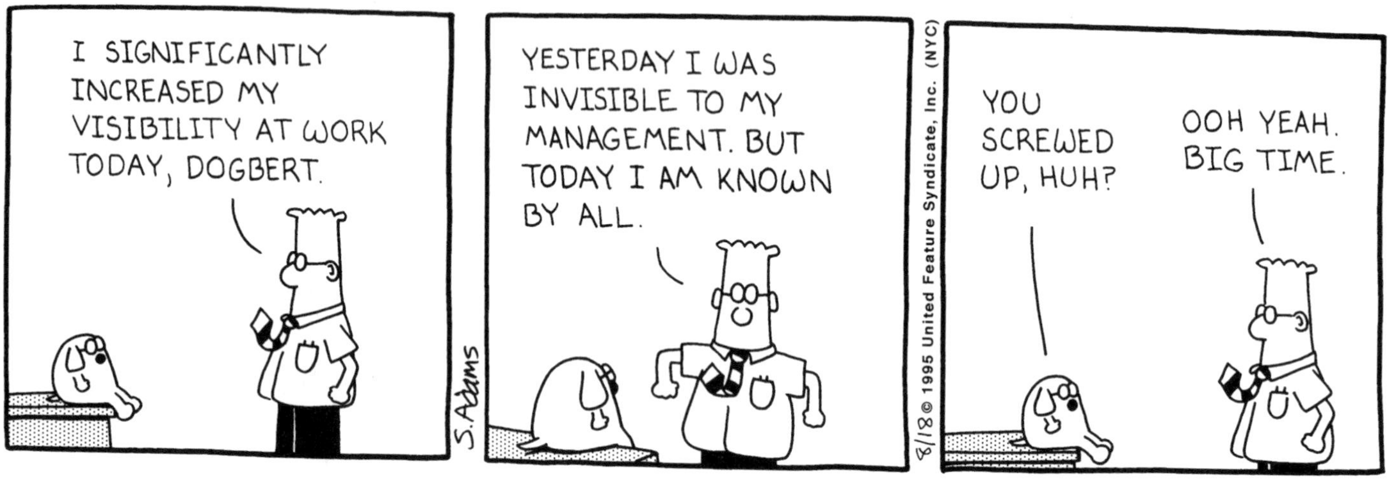
I SIGNIFICANTLY INCREASED MY VISIBILITY AT WORK TODAY, DOGBERT.
S. Adams
YESTERDAY I WAS INVISIBLE TO MY MANAGEMENT. BUT TODAY I AM KNOWN BY ALL.
8/18 © 1995 United Feature Syndicate, Inc. (NYC)
YOU SCREWED UP, HUH?
OOH YEAH. BIG TIME.

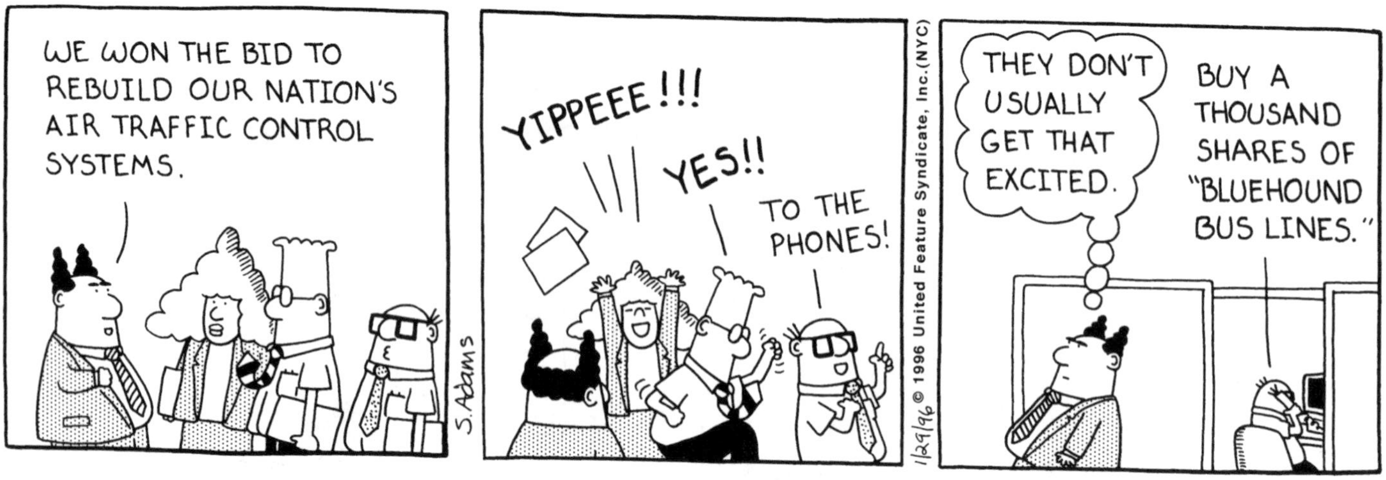
WE WON THE BID TO REBUILD OUR NATION'S AIR TRAFFIC CONTROL SYSTEMS.
S. Adams
YIPPEEE!!!
YES!!
TO THE PHONES!
1/29/96 © 1996 United Feature Syndicate, Inc. (NYC)
THEY DON'T USUALLY GET THAT EXCITED.
BUY A THOUSAND SHARES OF "BLUEHOUND BUS LINES."

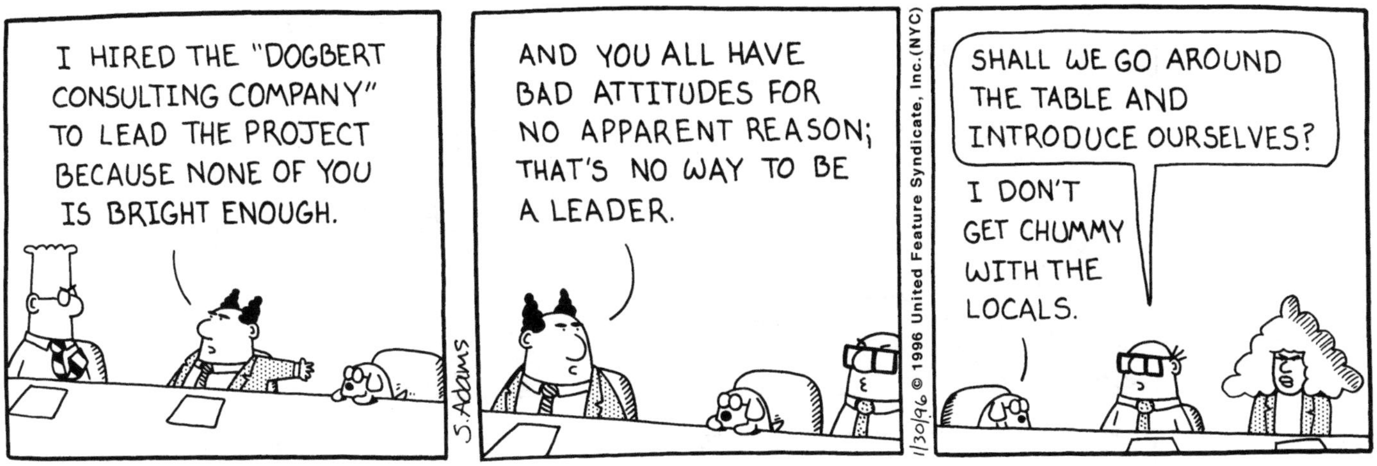
I HIRED THE "DOGBERT CONSULTING COMPANY" TO LEAD THE PROJECT BECAUSE NONE OF YOU IS BRIGHT ENOUGH.
S. Adams
AND YOU ALL HAVE BAD ATTITUDES FOR NO APPARENT REASON; THAT'S NO WAY TO BE A LEADER.
1/30/96 © 1996 United Feature Syndicate, Inc.(NYC)
SHALL WE GO AROUND THE TABLE AND INTRODUCE OURSELVES?
I DON'T GET CHUMMY WITH THE LOCALS.

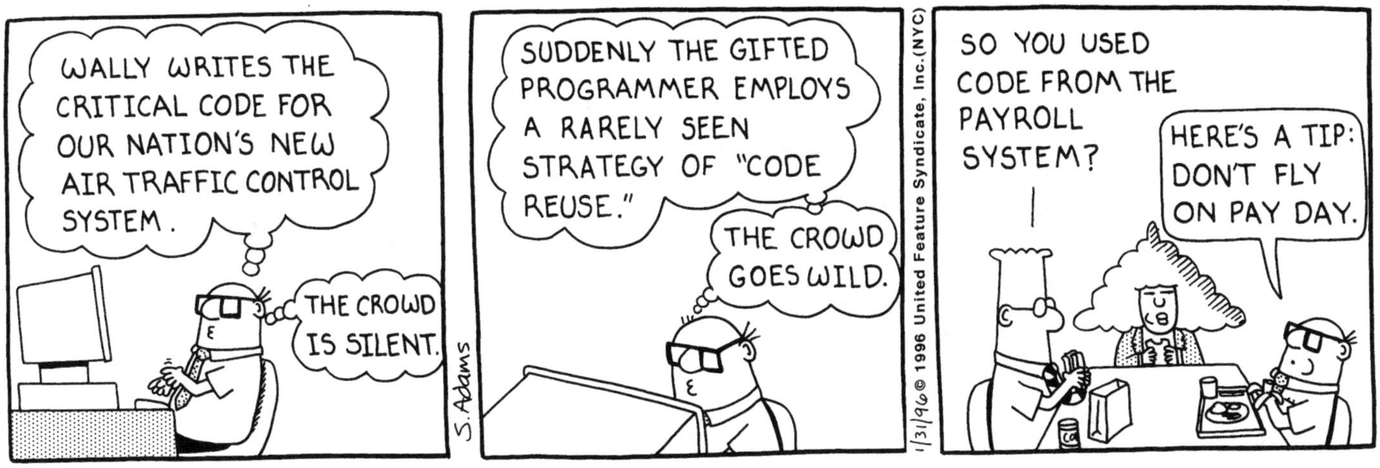
WALLY WRITES THE CRITICAL CODE FOR OUR NATION'S NEW AIR TRAFFIC CONTROL SYSTEM.
THE CROWD IS SILENT.
S. Adams
SUDDENLY THE GIFTED PROGRAMMER EMPLOYS A RARELY SEEN STRATEGY OF "CODE REUSE."
THE CROWD GOES WILD.
1/31/96 © 1996 United Feature Syndicate, Inc.(NYC)
SO YOU USED CODE FROM THE PAYROLL SYSTEM?
HERE'S A TIP: DON'T FLY ON PAY DAY.

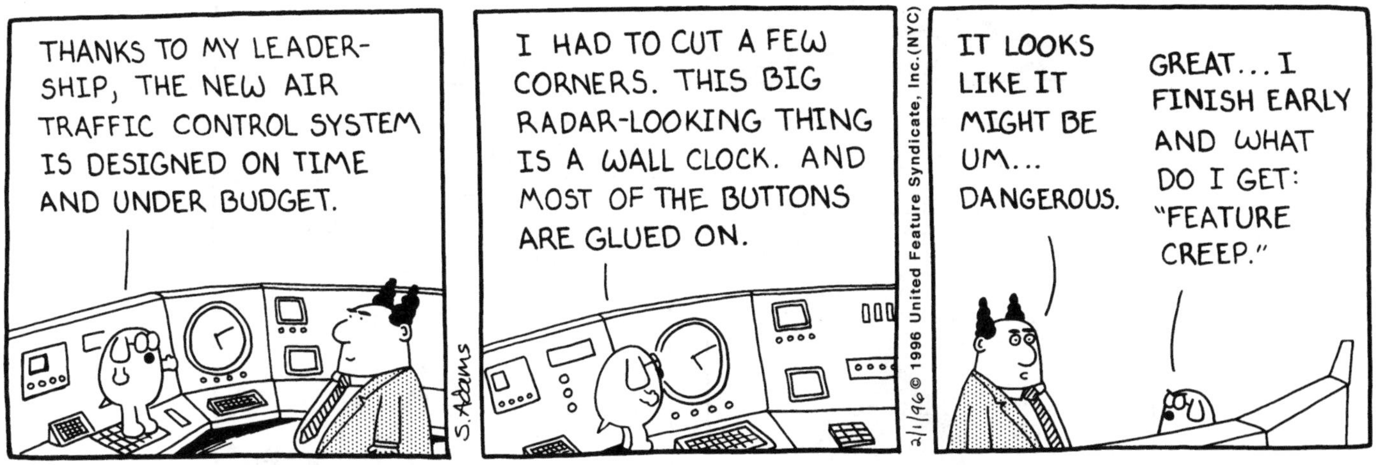
THANKS TO MY LEADERSHIP, THE NEW AIR TRAFFIC CONTROL SYSTEM IS DESIGNED ON TIME AND UNDER BUDGET.
S. Adams
I HAD TO CUT A FEW CORNERS. THIS BIG RADAR-LOOKING THING IS A WALL CLOCK. AND MOST OF THE BUTTONS ARE GLUED ON.
2/1/96 © 1996 United Feature Syndicate, Inc.(NYC)
IT LOOKS LIKE IT MIGHT BE UM... DANGEROUS.
GREAT... I FINISH EARLY AND WHAT DO I GET: "FEATURE CREEP."

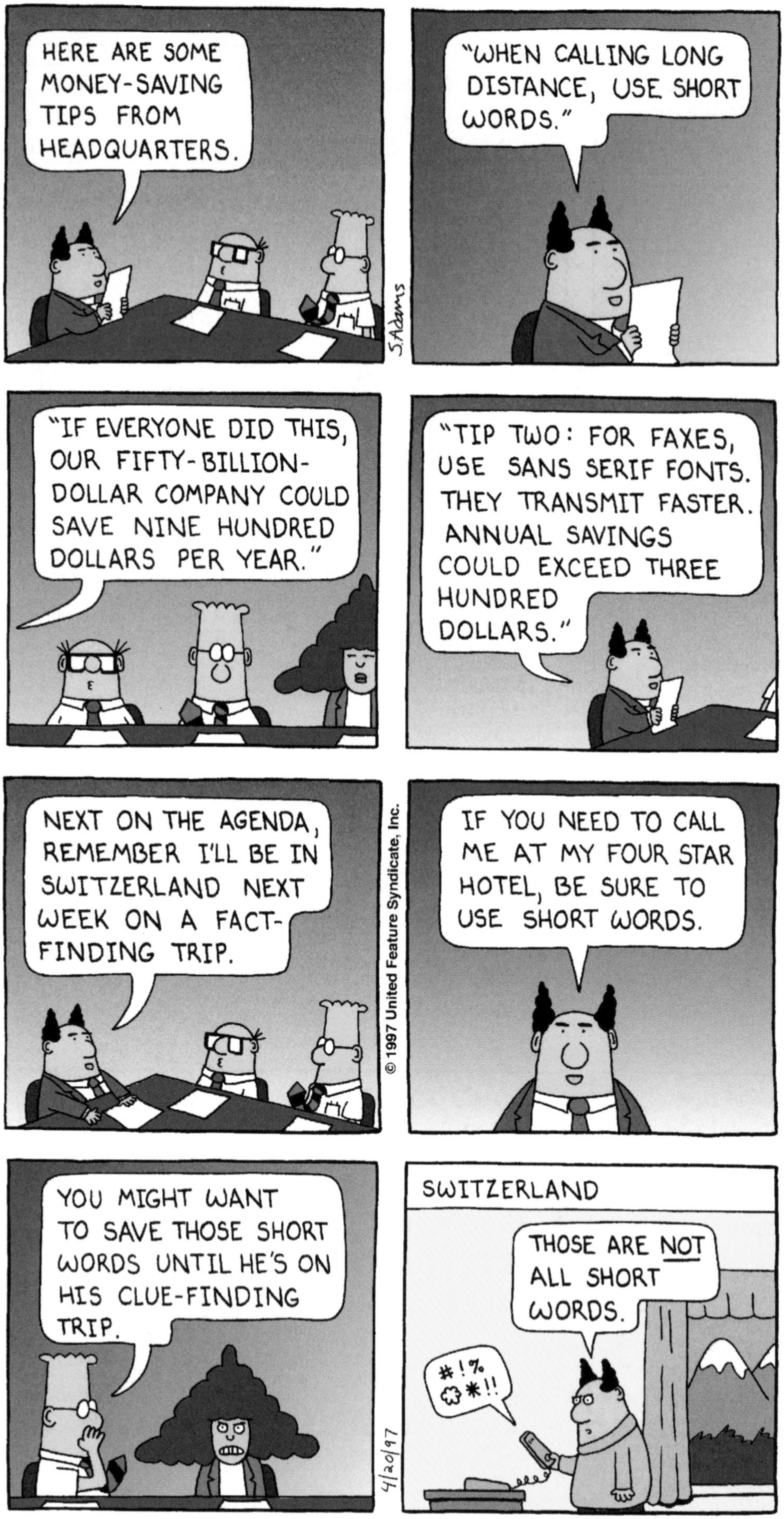
HERE ARE SOME MONEY-SAVING TIPS FROM HEADQUARTERS.
"WHEN CALLING LONG DISTANCE, USE SHORT WORDS."
S. Adams
"IF EVERYONE DID THIS, OUR FIFTY-BILLION-DOLLAR COMPANY COULD SAVE NINE HUNDRED DOLLARS PER YEAR."
"TIP TWO: FOR FAXES, USE SANS SERIF FONTS. THEY TRANSMIT FASTER. ANNUAL SAVINGS COULD EXCEED THREE HUNDRED DOLLARS."
NEXT ON THE AGENDA, REMEMBER I'LL BE IN SWITZERLAND NEXT WEEK ON A FACT-FINDING TRIP.
© 1997 United Feature Syndicate, Inc.
IF YOU NEED TO CALL ME AT MY FOUR STAR HOTEL, BE SURE TO USE SHORT WORDS.
YOU MIGHT WANT TO SAVE THOSE SHORT WORDS UNTIL HE'S ON HIS CLUE-FINDING TRIP.
4/20/97
SWITZERLAND
THOSE ARE NOT ALL SHORT WORDS.
#!% ✿*!!

AN EXECUTIVE SEARCH FIRM IS TRYING TO FIND A NEW C.E.O. FOR US.
IT'LL BE TOUGH.
S.Adams
NO ETHICAL PERSON WOULD BOARD A SINKING SHIP JUST TO PLUNDER ITS TREASURE.
6/20/98 © 1998 United Feature Syndicate, Inc.
ARE YOU READY TO TAKE THE CHALLENGE?
OH, I'LL TAKE MORE THAN THAT!

MISTER DOGBERT HAS RETURNED AS OUR C.E.O. BECAUSE NO ONE ELSE WANTS THE JOB.
S.Adams
I CAN'T TELL YOU MY PLAN FOR THE ASSETS OF THIS COMPANY ... BUT IT RHYMES WITH "VILLAGE."
6/22/98 © 1998 United Feature Syndicate, Inc.
I HOPE IT'S "FILLAGE."

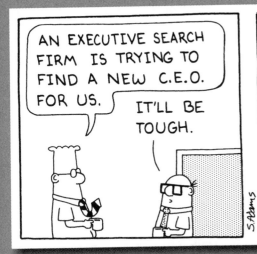

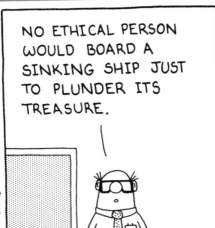

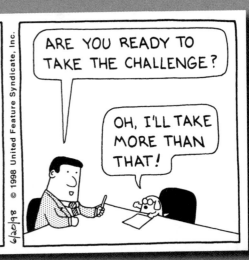

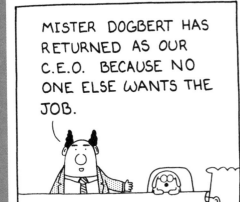

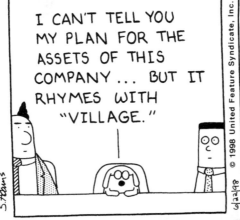

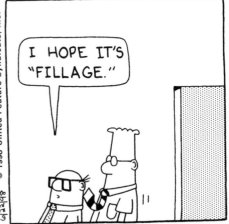

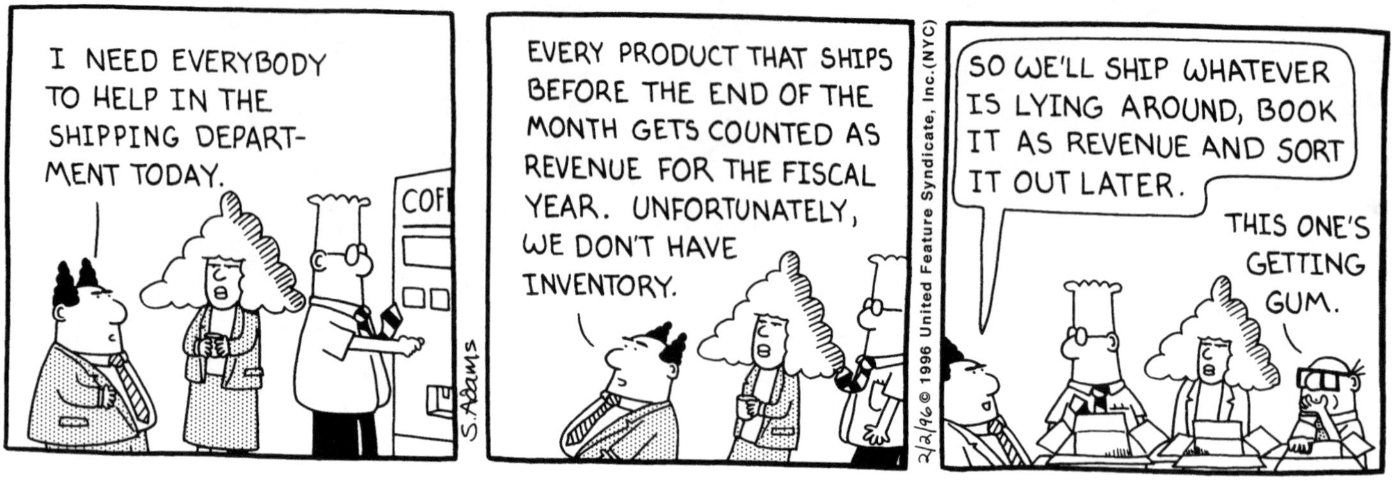
I NEED EVERYBODY TO HELP IN THE SHIPPING DEPARTMENT TODAY.
COF
S. Adams
EVERY PRODUCT THAT SHIPS BEFORE THE END OF THE MONTH GETS COUNTED AS REVENUE FOR THE FISCAL YEAR. UNFORTUNATELY, WE DON'T HAVE INVENTORY.
2/2/96 © 1996 United Feature Syndicate, Inc.(NYC)
SO WE'LL SHIP WHATEVER IS LYING AROUND, BOOK IT AS REVENUE AND SORT IT OUT LATER.
THIS ONE'S GETTING GUM.

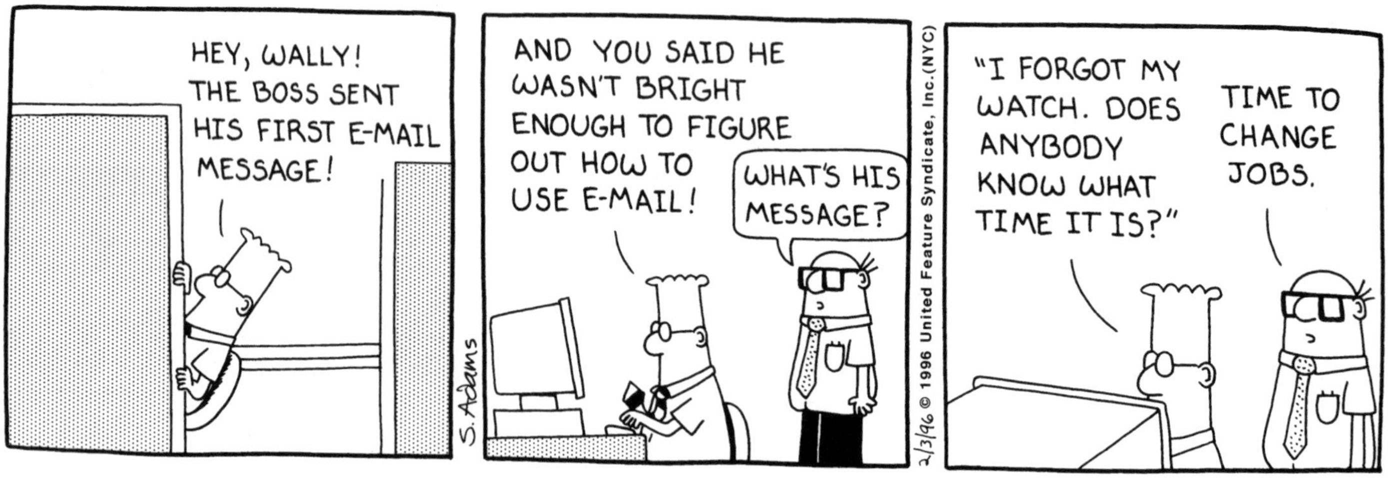
HEY, WALLY! THE BOSS SENT HIS FIRST E-MAIL MESSAGE!
S. Adams
AND YOU SAID HE WASN'T BRIGHT ENOUGH TO FIGURE OUT HOW TO USE E-MAIL!
WHAT'S HIS MESSAGE?
2/3/96 © 1996 United Feature Syndicate, Inc.(NYC)
"I FORGOT MY WATCH. DOES ANYBODY KNOW WHAT TIME IT IS?"
TIME TO CHANGE JOBS.

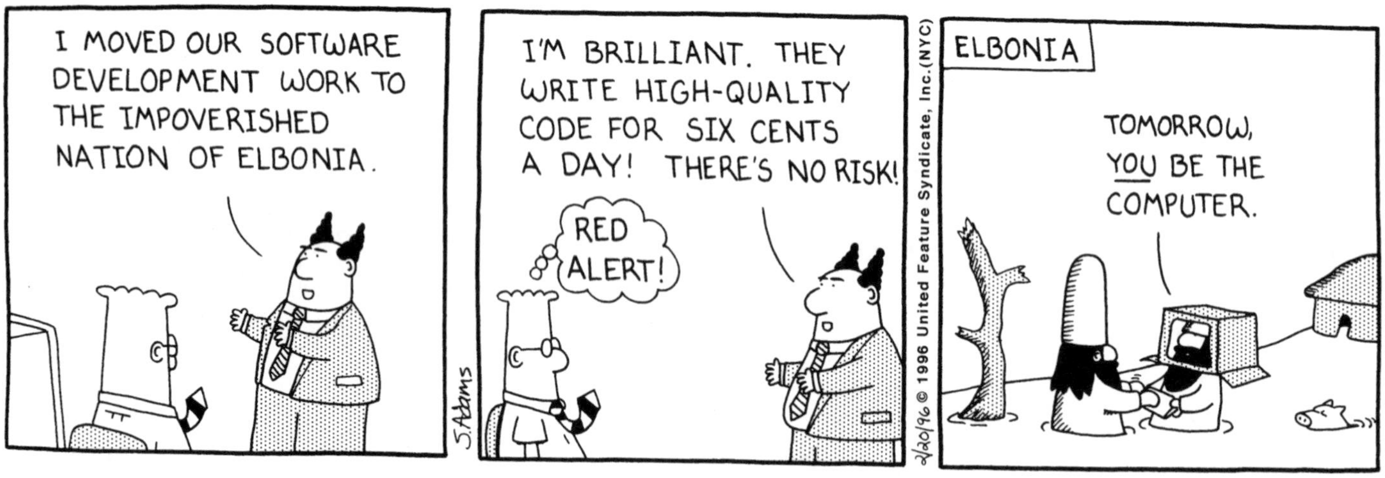
I MOVED OUR SOFTWARE DEVELOPMENT WORK TO THE IMPOVERISHED NATION OF ELBONIA.
S. Adams
I'M BRILLIANT. THEY WRITE HIGH-QUALITY CODE FOR SIX CENTS A DAY! THERE'S NO RISK!
RED ALERT!
2/20/96 © 1996 United Feature Syndicate, Inc.(NYC)
ELBONIA
TOMORROW, YOU BE THE COMPUTER.

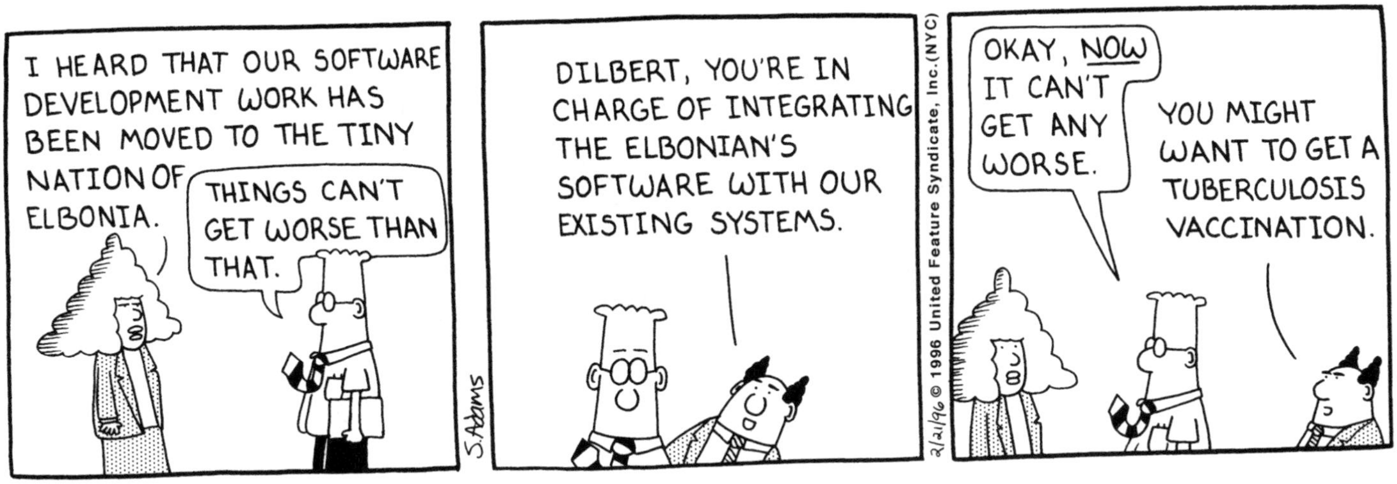
I HEARD THAT OUR SOFTWARE DEVELOPMENT WORK HAS BEEN MOVED TO THE TINY NATION OF ELBONIA.
THINGS CAN'T GET WORSE THAN THAT.
DILBERT, YOU'RE IN CHARGE OF INTEGRATING THE ELBONIAN'S SOFTWARE WITH OUR EXISTING SYSTEMS.
OKAY, NOW IT CAN'T GET ANY WORSE.
YOU MIGHT WANT TO GET A TUBERCULOSIS VACCINATION.
S. Adams

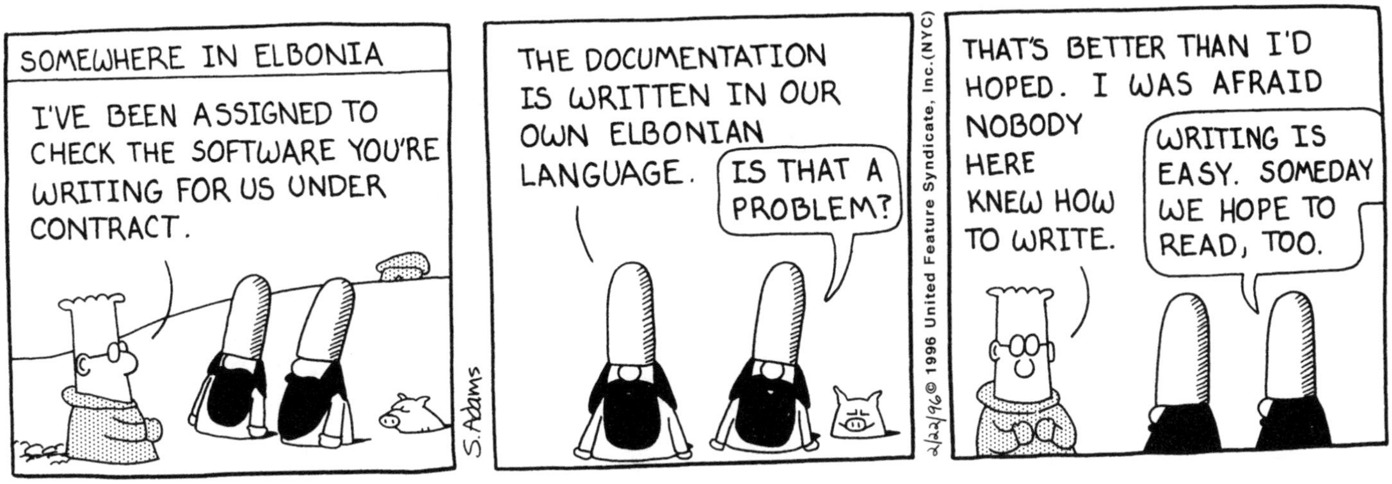
SOMEWHERE IN ELBONIA
I'VE BEEN ASSIGNED TO CHECK THE SOFTWARE YOU'RE WRITING FOR US UNDER CONTRACT.
THE DOCUMENTATION IS WRITTEN IN OUR OWN ELBONIAN LANGUAGE.
IS THAT A PROBLEM?
THAT'S BETTER THAN I'D HOPED. I WAS AFRAID NOBODY HERE KNEW HOW TO WRITE.
WRITING IS EASY. SOMEDAY WE HOPE TO READ, TOO.
S. Adams

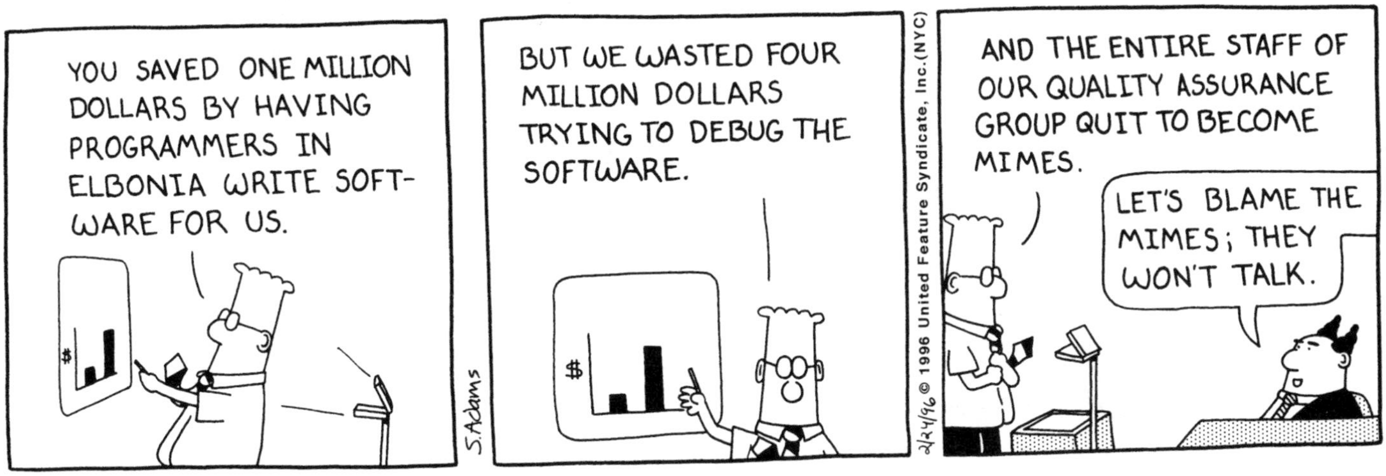
YOU SAVED ONE MILLION DOLLARS BY HAVING PROGRAMMERS IN ELBONIA WRITE SOFT-WARE FOR US.
$
BUT WE WASTED FOUR MILLION DOLLARS TRYING TO DEBUG THE SOFTWARE.
$
AND THE ENTIRE STAFF OF OUR QUALITY ASSURANCE GROUP QUIT TO BECOME MIMES.
LET'S BLAME THE MIMES; THEY WON'T TALK.
S. Adams

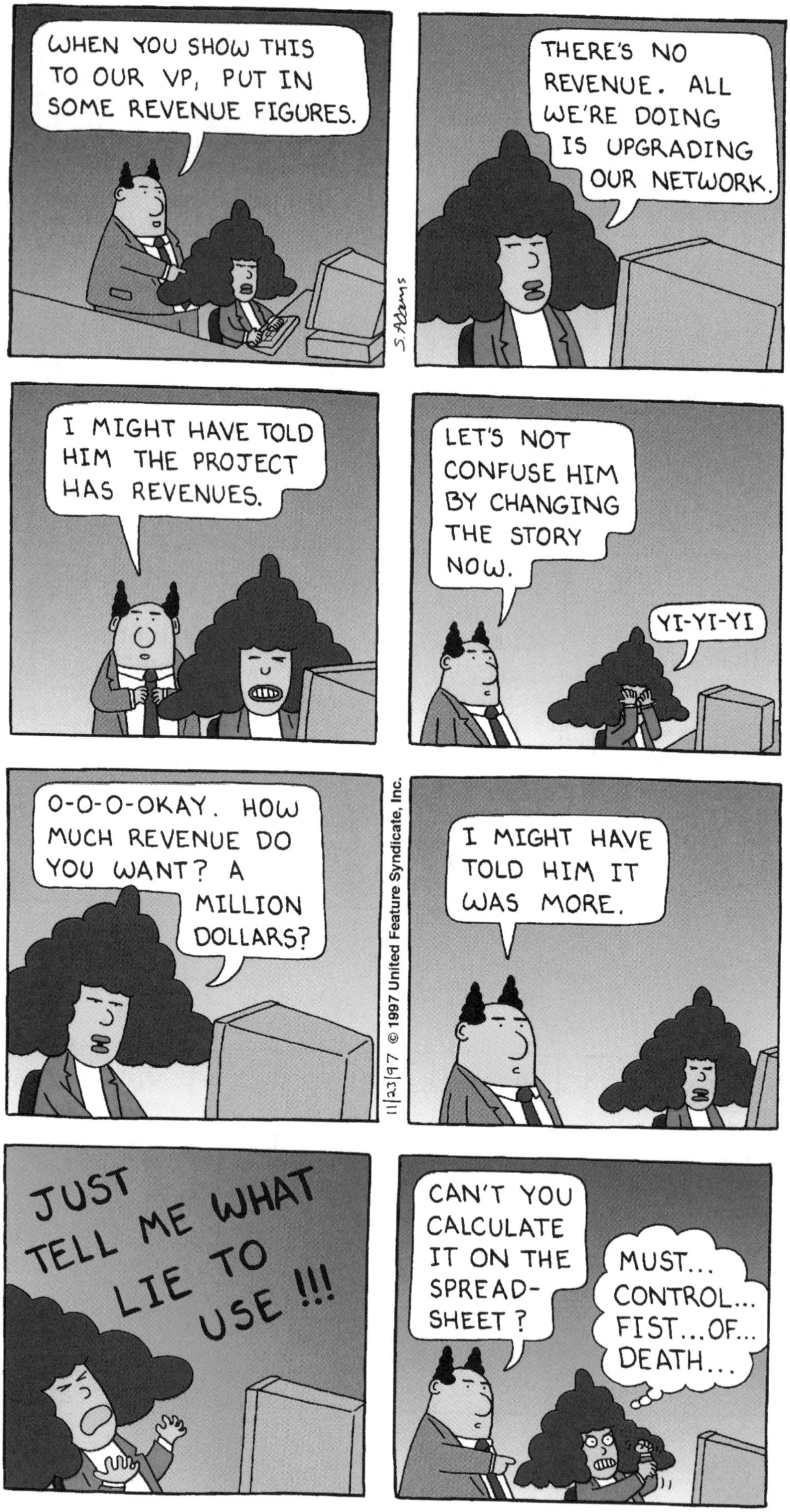
WHEN YOU SHOW THIS TO OUR VP, PUT IN SOME REVENUE FIGURES.
S. Adams
THERE'S NO REVENUE. ALL WE'RE DOING IS UPGRADING OUR NETWORK.
I MIGHT HAVE TOLD HIM THE PROJECT HAS REVENUES.
LET'S NOT CONFUSE HIM BY CHANGING THE STORY NOW.
YI-YI-YI
O-O-O-OKAY. HOW MUCH REVENUE DO YOU WANT? A MILLION DOLLARS?
11/23/97 © 1997 United Feature Syndicate, Inc.
I MIGHT HAVE TOLD HIM IT WAS MORE.
JUST TELL ME WHAT LIE TO USE !!!
CAN'T YOU CALCULATE IT ON THE SPREAD-SHEET?
MUST... CONTROL... FIST... OF... DEATH...

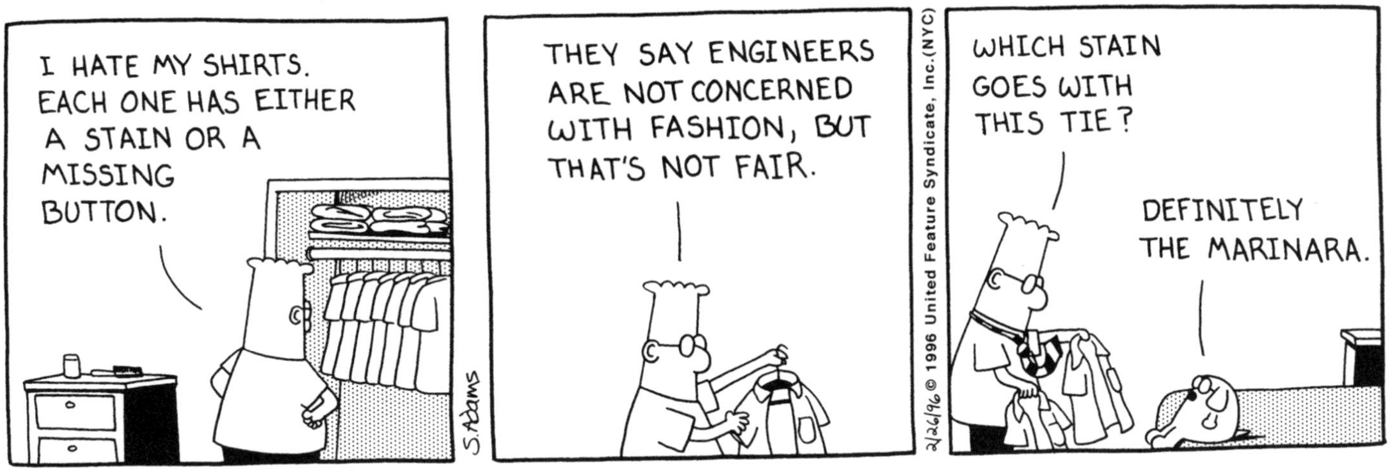
I HATE MY SHIRTS. EACH ONE HAS EITHER A STAIN OR A MISSING BUTTON.
S. Adams
THEY SAY ENGINEERS ARE NOT CONCERNED WITH FASHION, BUT THAT'S NOT FAIR.
2/26/96 © 1996 United Feature Syndicate, Inc.(NYC)
WHICH STAIN GOES WITH THIS TIE?
DEFINITELY THE MARINARA.

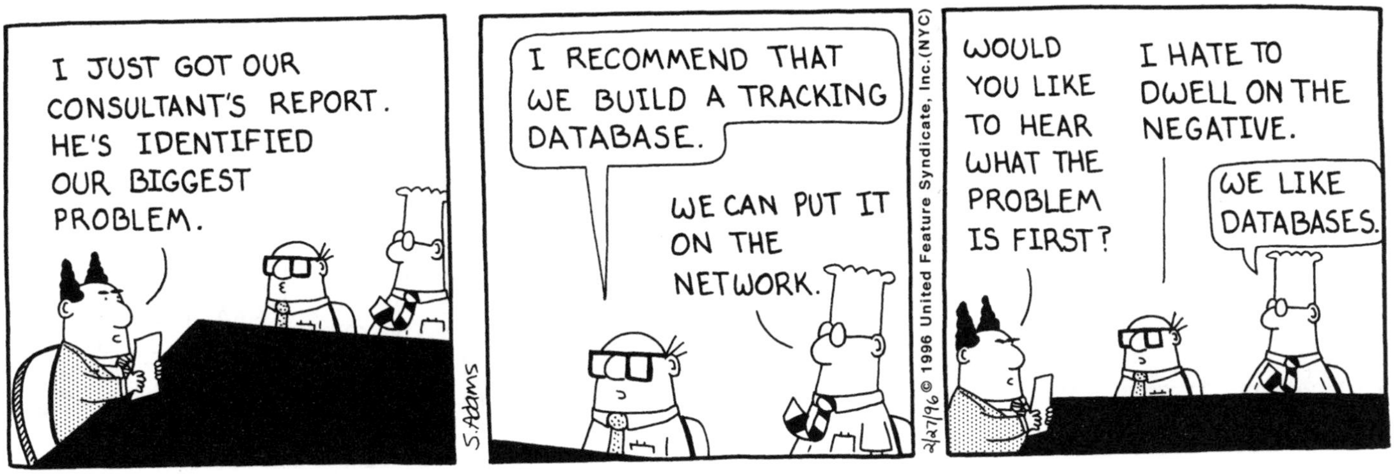
I JUST GOT OUR CONSULTANT'S REPORT. HE'S IDENTIFIED OUR BIGGEST PROBLEM.
S. Adams
I RECOMMEND THAT WE BUILD A TRACKING DATABASE.
WE CAN PUT IT ON THE NETWORK.
2/27/96 © 1996 United Feature Syndicate, Inc.(NYC)
WOULD YOU LIKE TO HEAR WHAT THE PROBLEM IS FIRST?
I HATE TO DWELL ON THE NEGATIVE.
WE LIKE DATABASES.

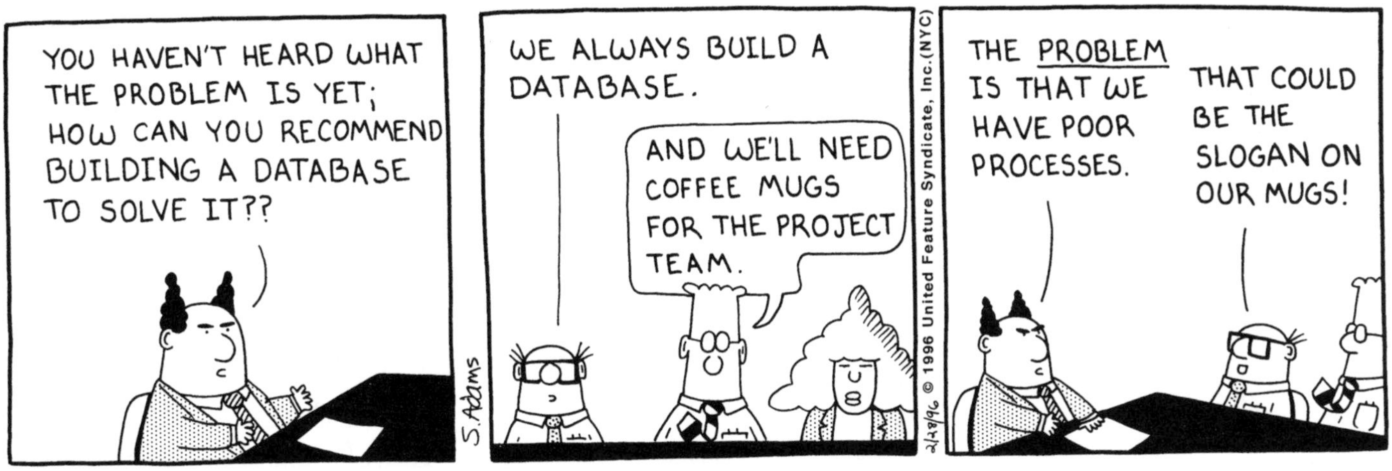
YOU HAVEN'T HEARD WHAT THE PROBLEM IS YET; HOW CAN YOU RECOMMEND BUILDING A DATABASE TO SOLVE IT??
S. Adams
WE ALWAYS BUILD A DATABASE.
AND WE'LL NEED COFFEE MUGS FOR THE PROJECT TEAM.
2/28/96 © 1996 United Feature Syndicate, Inc.(NYC)
THE PROBLEM IS THAT WE HAVE POOR PROCESSES.
THAT COULD BE THE SLOGAN ON OUR MUGS!

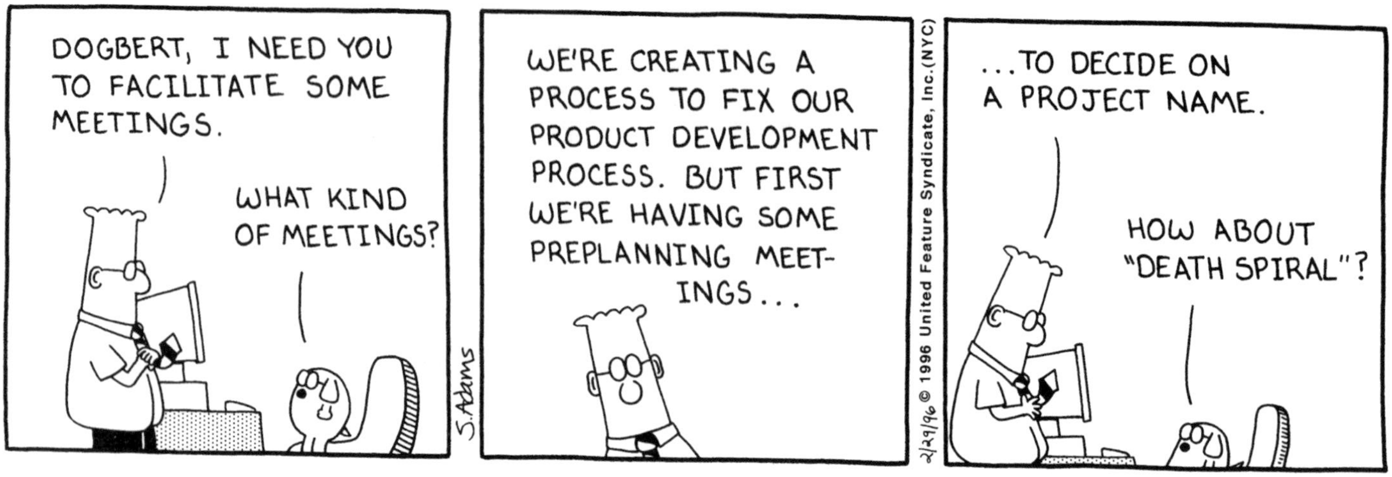
DOGBERT, I NEED YOU TO FACILITATE SOME MEETINGS.
WHAT KIND OF MEETINGS?
S. Adams
WE'RE CREATING A PROCESS TO FIX OUR PRODUCT DEVELOPMENT PROCESS. BUT FIRST WE'RE HAVING SOME PREPLANNING MEET-INGS...
2/29/96 © 1996 United Feature Syndicate, Inc.(NYC)
...TO DECIDE ON A PROJECT NAME.
HOW ABOUT "DEATH SPIRAL"?

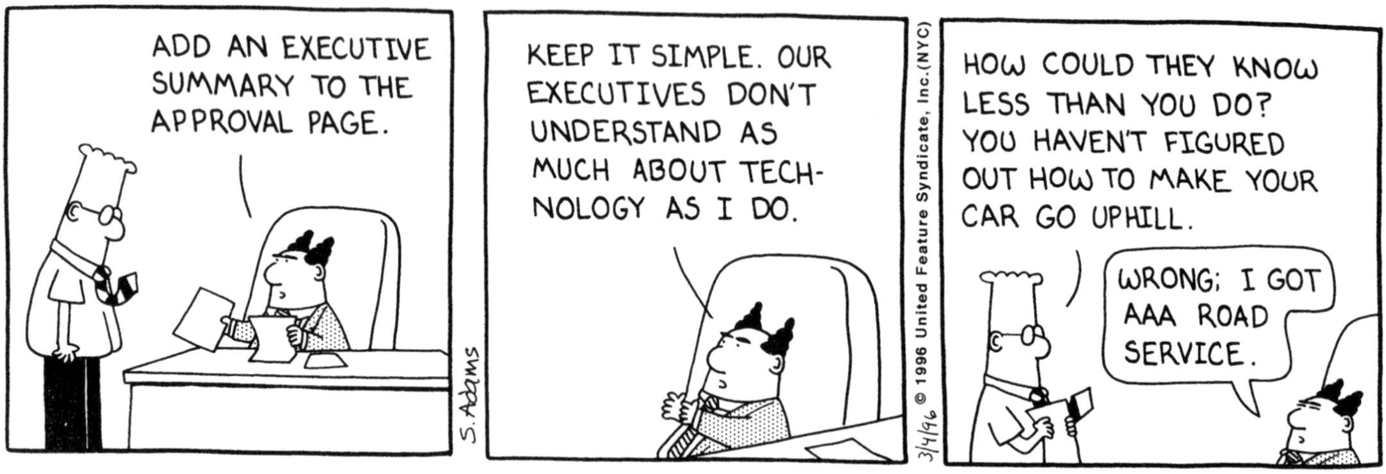
ADD AN EXECUTIVE SUMMARY TO THE APPROVAL PAGE.
S. Adams
KEEP IT SIMPLE. OUR EXECUTIVES DON'T UNDERSTAND AS MUCH ABOUT TECH-NOLOGY AS I DO.
3/4/96 © 1996 United Feature Syndicate, Inc.(NYC)
HOW COULD THEY KNOW LESS THAN YOU DO? YOU HAVEN'T FIGURED OUT HOW TO MAKE YOUR CAR GO UPHILL.
WRONG; I GOT AAA ROAD SERVICE.

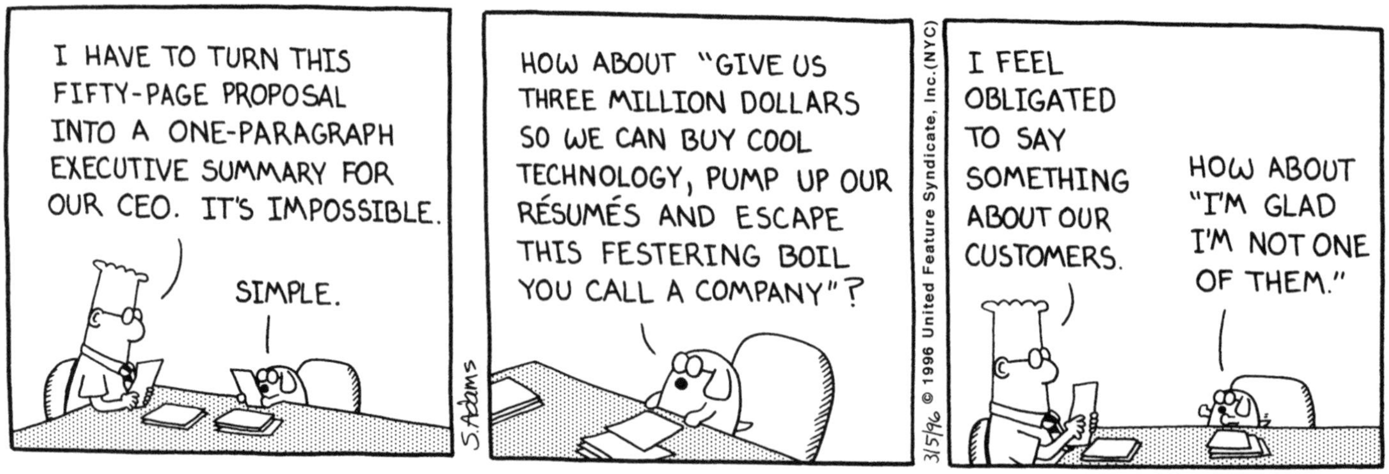
I HAVE TO TURN THIS FIFTY-PAGE PROPOSAL INTO A ONE-PARAGRAPH EXECUTIVE SUMMARY FOR OUR CEO. IT'S IMPOSSIBLE.
SIMPLE.
S. Adams
HOW ABOUT "GIVE US THREE MILLION DOLLARS SO WE CAN BUY COOL TECHNOLOGY, PUMP UP OUR RÉSUMÉS AND ESCAPE THIS FESTERING BOIL YOU CALL A COMPANY"?
3/5/96 © 1996 United Feature Syndicate, Inc.(NYC)
I FEEL OBLIGATED TO SAY SOMETHING ABOUT OUR CUSTOMERS.
HOW ABOUT "I'M GLAD I'M NOT ONE OF THEM."

DOGBERT THE C.E.O.
I NEED A PERSONAL "GOPHER." ARE YOU INTERESTED?
SURE!
GOOD. YOU'LL WEAR A SPECIAL UNIFORM AND HAVE A SPECIAL OFFICE TO SHOW YOUR STATUS.
SHEESH. I HAVEN'T MADE A BANK SHOT YET.
S. Adams
6/23/98
© 1998 United Feature Syndicate, Inc.

DOGBERT THE C.E.O.
I'VE DECIDED TO MANIPULATE OUR STOCK PRICE FOR PERSONAL GAIN.
I'LL SPIN OFF A FEW DIVISIONS, BUY BACK SOME OF OUR STOCK AND ANNOUNCE MASSIVE BUDGET CUTS.
UM... DO YOU EVEN KNOW WHAT PRODUCTS WE MAKE?
HOW WOULD THAT BE RELEVANT?
S. Adams
6/24/98
© 1998 United Feature Syndicate, Inc.

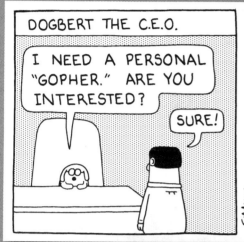

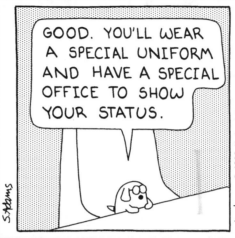

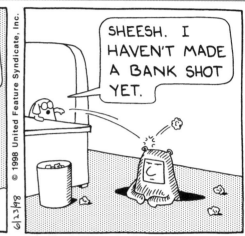

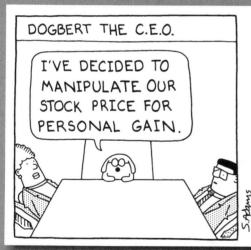

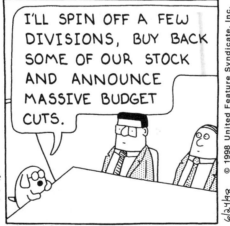

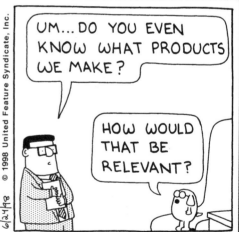

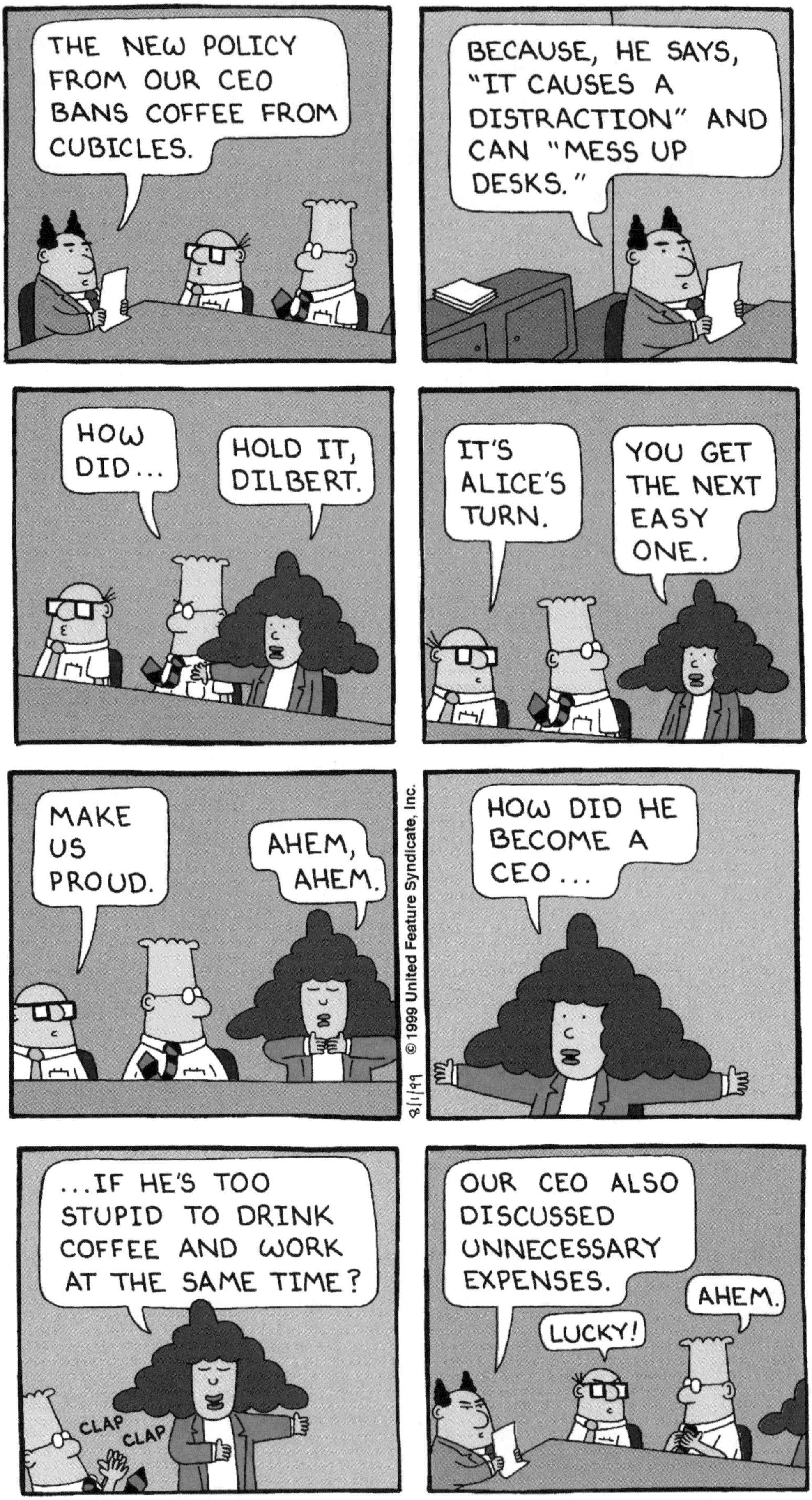
THE NEW POLICY FROM OUR CEO BANS COFFEE FROM CUBICLES.
BECAUSE, HE SAYS, "IT CAUSES A DISTRACTION" AND CAN "MESS UP DESKS."
HOW DID...
HOLD IT, DILBERT.
IT'S ALICE'S TURN.
YOU GET THE NEXT EASY ONE.
MAKE US PROUD.
AHEM, AHEM.
© 1999 United Feature Syndicate, Inc.
8/1/99
HOW DID HE BECOME A CEO...
...IF HE'S TOO STUPID TO DRINK COFFEE AND WORK AT THE SAME TIME?
CLAP
CLAP
OUR CEO ALSO DISCUSSED UNNECESSARY EXPENSES.
LUCKY!
AHEM.

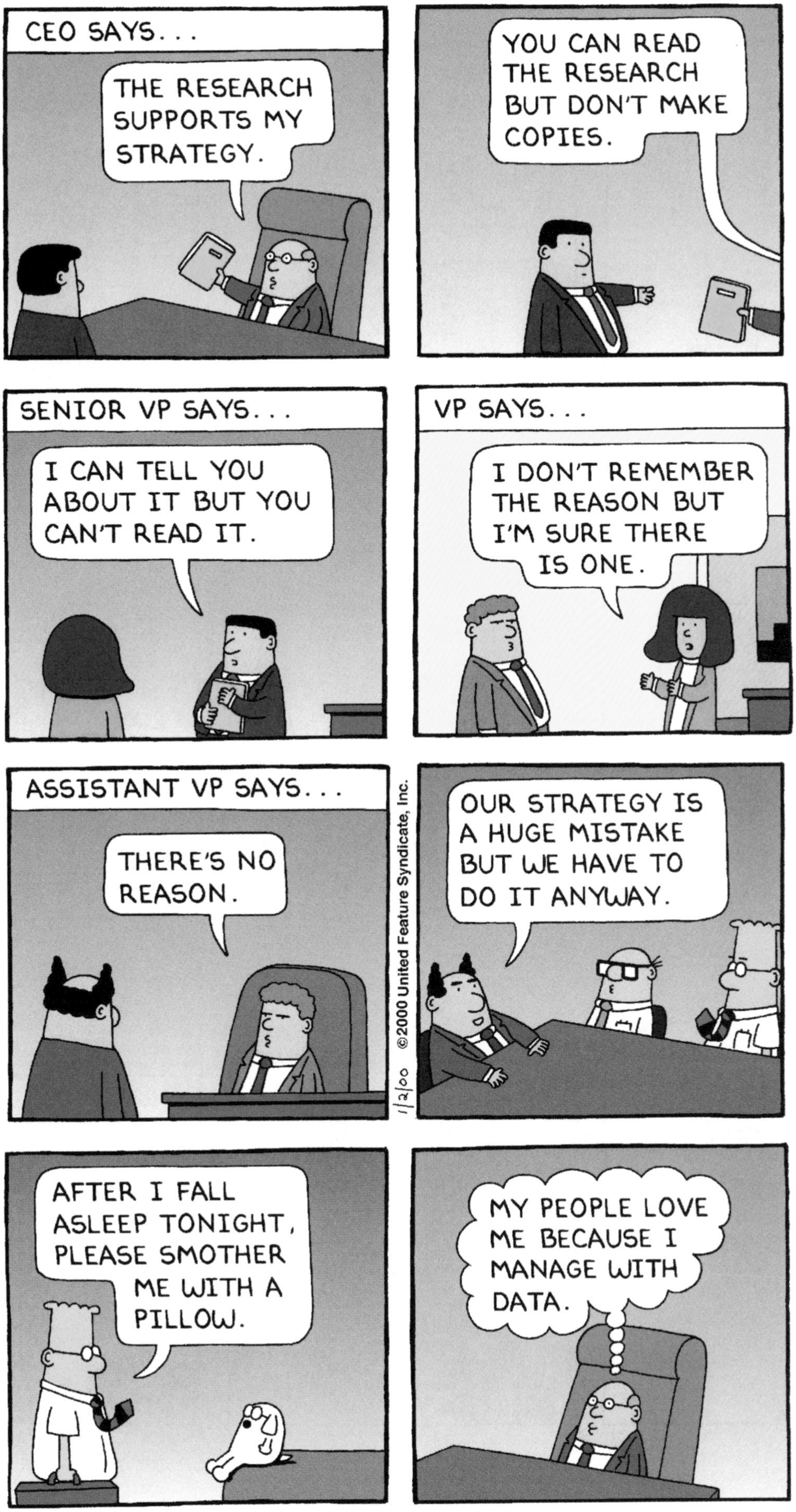
CEO SAYS...
THE RESEARCH SUPPORTS MY STRATEGY.
YOU CAN READ THE RESEARCH BUT DON'T MAKE COPIES.
SENIOR VP SAYS...
I CAN TELL YOU ABOUT IT BUT YOU CAN'T READ IT.
VP SAYS...
I DON'T REMEMBER THE REASON BUT I'M SURE THERE IS ONE.
ASSISTANT VP SAYS...
THERE'S NO REASON.
©2000 United Feature Syndicate, Inc.
1/2/00
OUR STRATEGY IS A HUGE MISTAKE BUT WE HAVE TO DO IT ANYWAY.
AFTER I FALL ASLEEP TONIGHT, PLEASE SMOTHER ME WITH A PILLOW.
MY PEOPLE LOVE ME BECAUSE I MANAGE WITH DATA.

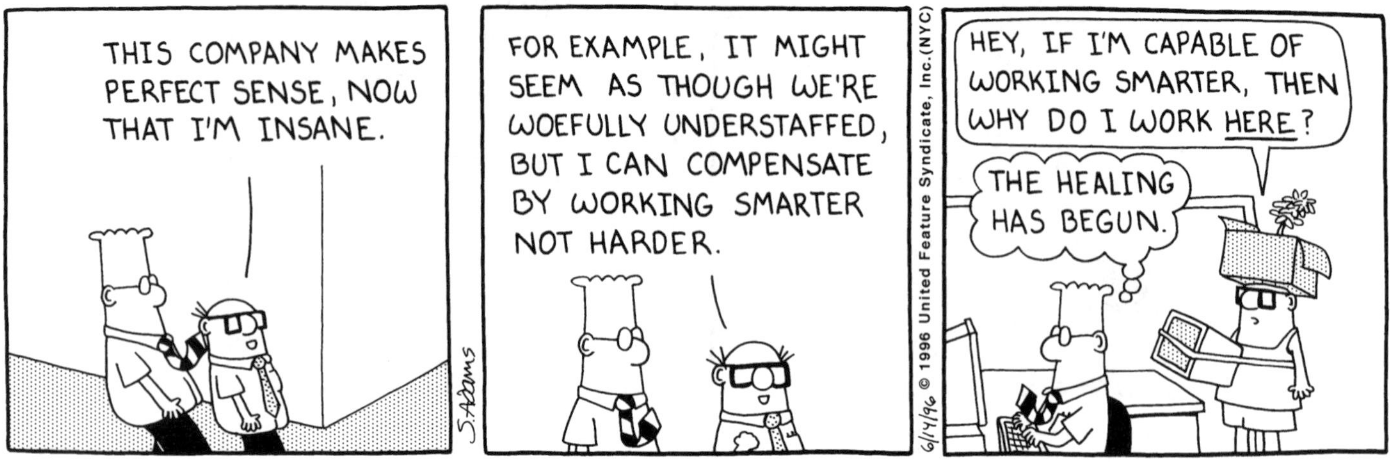
THIS COMPANY MAKES PERFECT SENSE, NOW THAT I'M INSANE.
FOR EXAMPLE, IT MIGHT SEEM AS THOUGH WE'RE WOEFULLY UNDERSTAFFED, BUT I CAN COMPENSATE BY WORKING SMARTER NOT HARDER.
6/1/96 © 1996 United Feature Syndicate, Inc.(NYC)
HEY, IF I'M CAPABLE OF WORKING SMARTER, THEN WHY DO I WORK HERE?
THE HEALING HAS BEGUN.

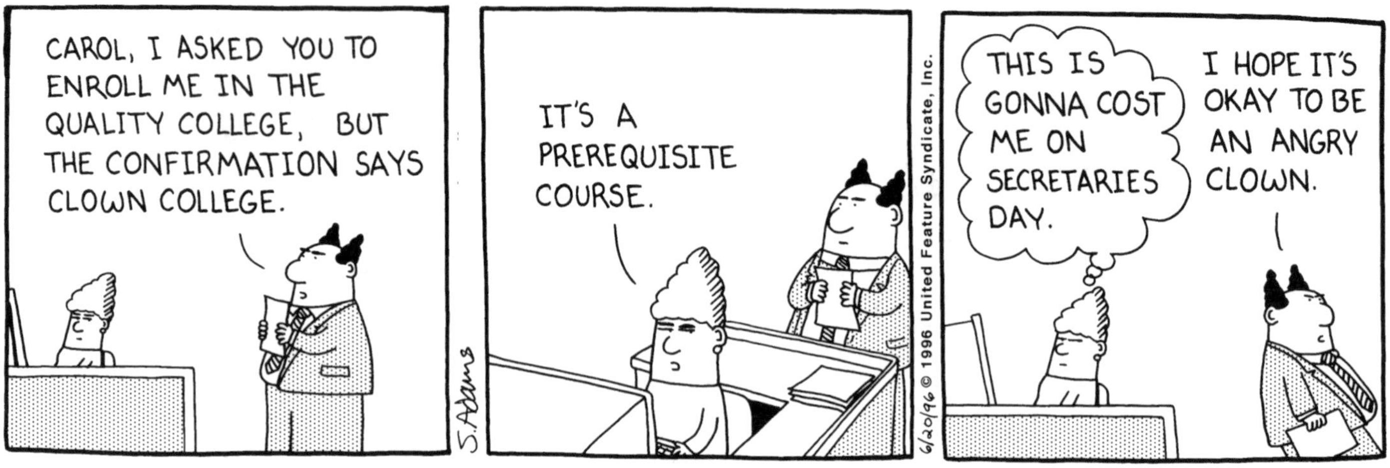
CAROL, I ASKED YOU TO ENROLL ME IN THE QUALITY COLLEGE, BUT THE CONFIRMATION SAYS CLOWN COLLEGE.
IT'S A PREREQUISITE COURSE.
6/20/96 © 1996 United Feature Syndicate, Inc.
THIS IS GONNA COST ME ON SECRETARIES DAY.
I HOPE IT'S OKAY TO BE AN ANGRY CLOWN.

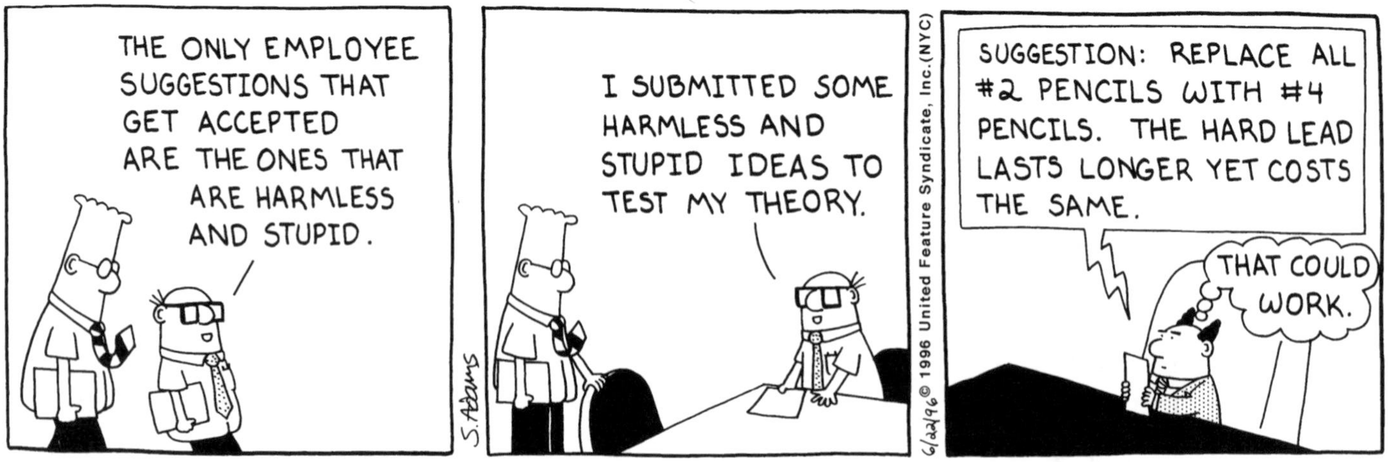
THE ONLY EMPLOYEE SUGGESTIONS THAT GET ACCEPTED ARE THE ONES THAT ARE HARMLESS AND STUPID.
I SUBMITTED SOME HARMLESS AND STUPID IDEAS TO TEST MY THEORY.
6/22/96 © 1996 United Feature Syndicate, Inc.(NYC)
SUGGESTION: REPLACE ALL #2 PENCILS WITH #4 PENCILS. THE HARD LEAD LASTS LONGER YET COSTS THE SAME.
THAT COULD WORK.

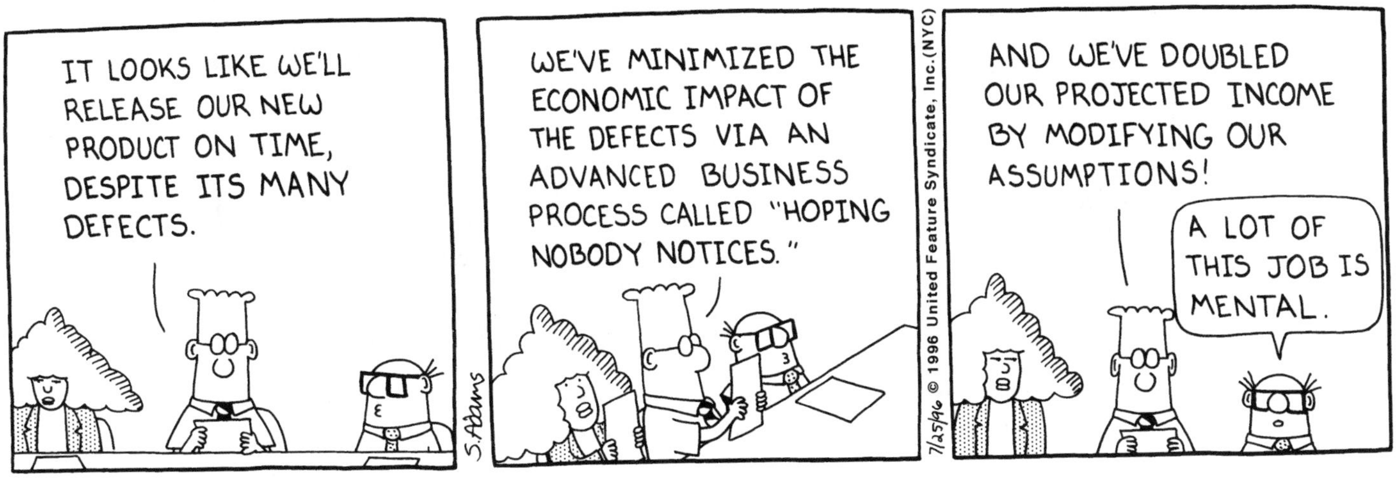
IT LOOKS LIKE WE'LL RELEASE OUR NEW PRODUCT ON TIME, DESPITE ITS MANY DEFECTS.
WE'VE MINIMIZED THE ECONOMIC IMPACT OF THE DEFECTS VIA AN ADVANCED BUSINESS PROCESS CALLED "HOPING NOBODY NOTICES."
AND WE'VE DOUBLED OUR PROJECTED INCOME BY MODIFYING OUR ASSUMPTIONS!
A LOT OF THIS JOB IS MENTAL.
S. Adams
7/25/96 © 1996 United Feature Syndicate, Inc.(NYC)

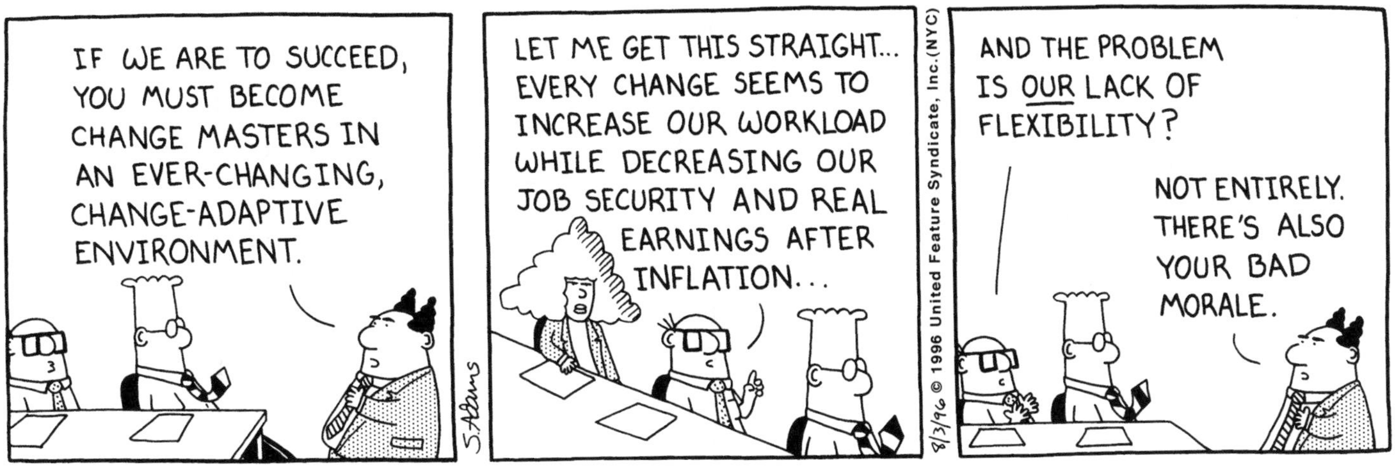
IF WE ARE TO SUCCEED, YOU MUST BECOME CHANGE MASTERS IN AN EVER-CHANGING, CHANGE-ADAPTIVE ENVIRONMENT.
LET ME GET THIS STRAIGHT... EVERY CHANGE SEEMS TO INCREASE OUR WORKLOAD WHILE DECREASING OUR JOB SECURITY AND REAL EARNINGS AFTER INFLATION...
AND THE PROBLEM IS OUR LACK OF FLEXIBILITY?
NOT ENTIRELY. THERE'S ALSO YOUR BAD MORALE.
S. Adams
8/3/96 © 1996 United Feature Syndicate, Inc.(NYC)

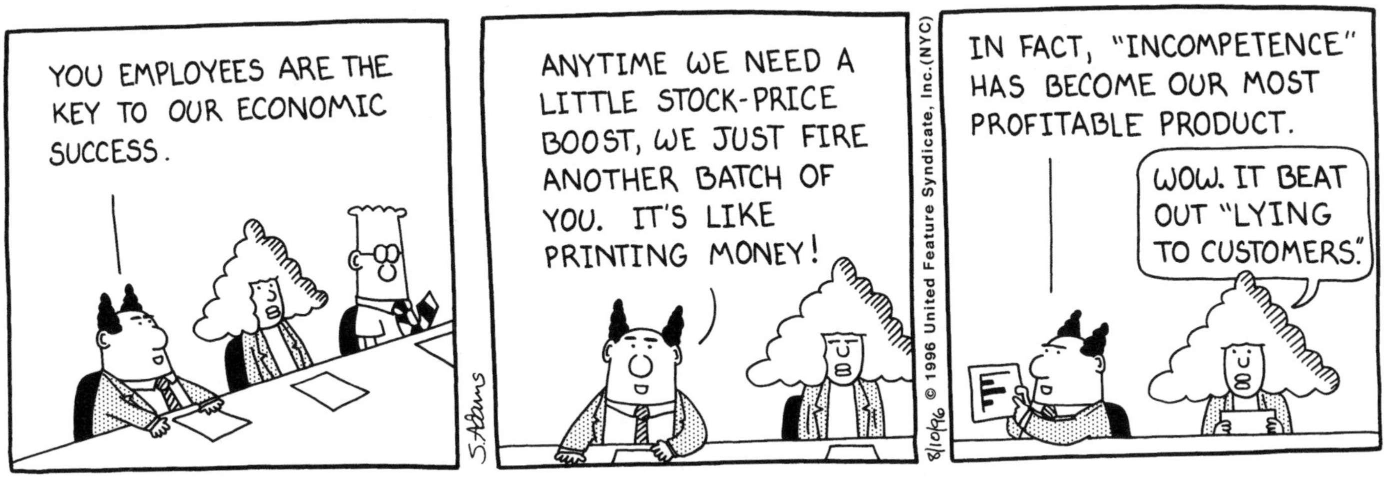
YOU EMPLOYEES ARE THE KEY TO OUR ECONOMIC SUCCESS.
ANYTIME WE NEED A LITTLE STOCK-PRICE BOOST, WE JUST FIRE ANOTHER BATCH OF YOU. IT'S LIKE PRINTING MONEY!
IN FACT, "INCOMPETENCE" HAS BECOME OUR MOST PROFITABLE PRODUCT.
WOW. IT BEAT OUT "LYING TO CUSTOMERS."
S. Adams
8/10/96 © 1996 United Feature Syndicate, Inc.(NYC)

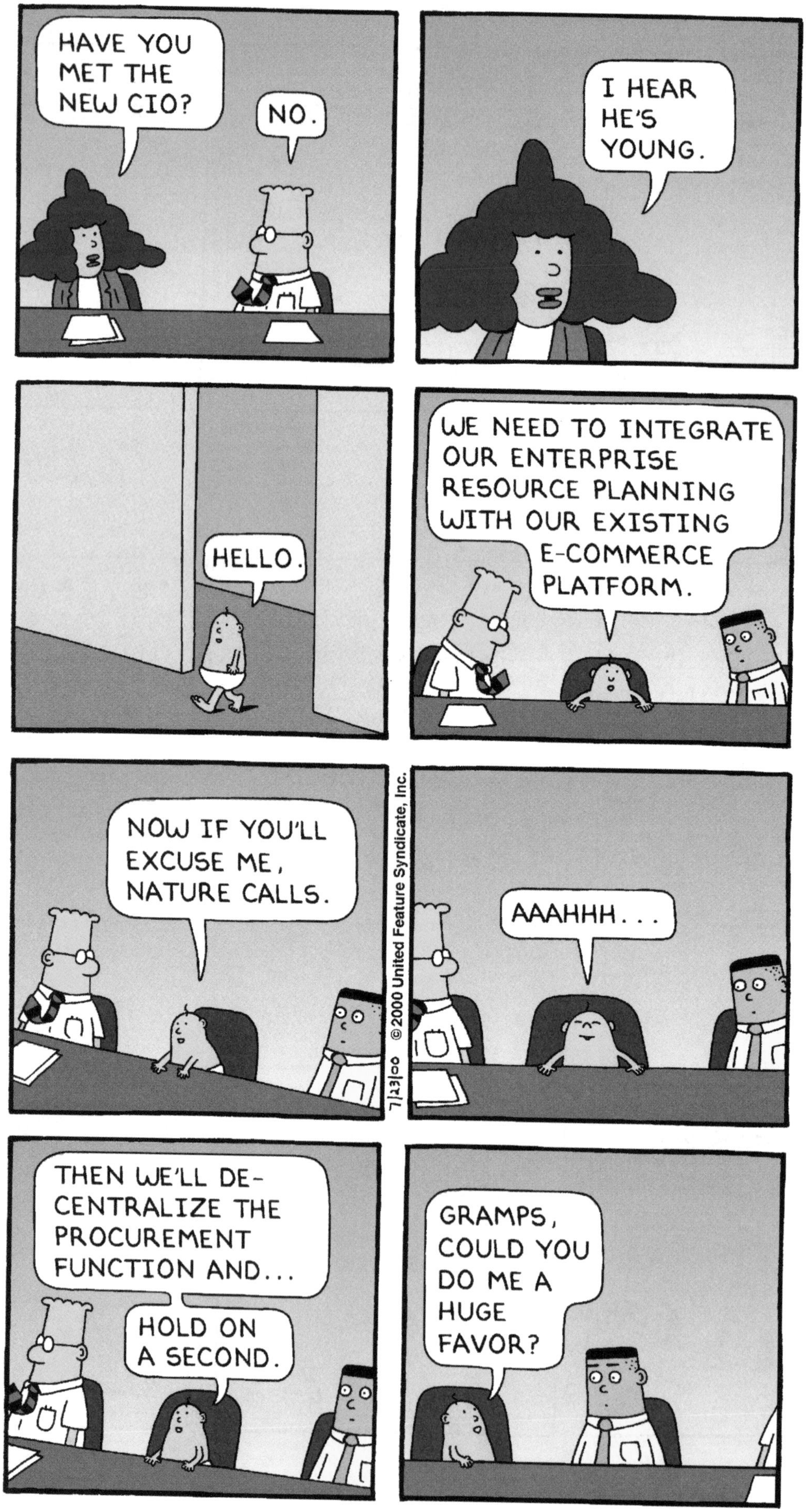
HAVE YOU MET THE NEW CIO?
NO.
I HEAR HE'S YOUNG.
HELLO.
WE NEED TO INTEGRATE OUR ENTERPRISE RESOURCE PLANNING WITH OUR EXISTING E-COMMERCE PLATFORM.
NOW IF YOU'LL EXCUSE ME, NATURE CALLS.
7/23/00 ©2000 United Feature Syndicate, Inc.
AAAHHH...
THEN WE'LL DE-CENTRALIZE THE PROCUREMENT FUNCTION AND...
HOLD ON A SECOND.
GRAMPS, COULD YOU DO ME A HUGE FAVOR?

DOGBERT THE C.E.O.
I MAKE A MOTION THAT THE BOARD OF DIRECTORS DOUBLE MY PAY.
ALL IN FAVOR, BLEAT LIKE SHEEP.
BA-A-A
BA-A-A
BA-A-A
I THINK WE'RE MISSING A CHECK OR A BALANCE SOMEWHERE.
S. Adams
6/25/98
© 1998 United Feature Syndicate, Inc.

DOGBERT THE C.E.O.
THE "UNITED CHARITIES" WOULD LIKE YOU TO BE CHAIRMAN THIS YEAR.
I'D BE HONORED.
OH, AND WHILE YOU'RE UP, CANCEL THE COMPANY HEALTH PLAN.
ONE WEEK LATER
UNDER HIS LEADERSHIP, OUR FREE CLINICS HAVE HANDLED TWICE AS MANY PEOPLE.
UNITED CHARITIES
THANKS.
S. Adams
6/26/98
© 1998 United Feature Syndicate, Inc.

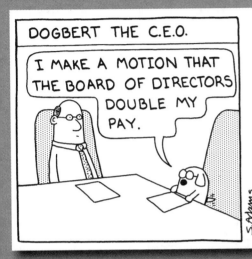

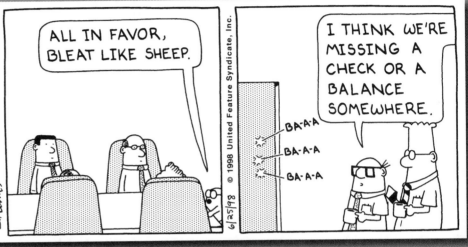

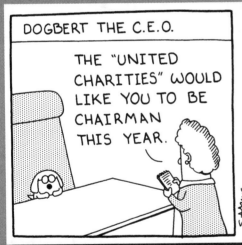

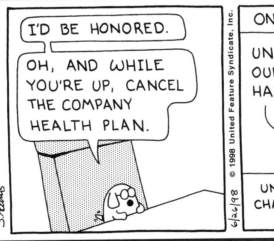

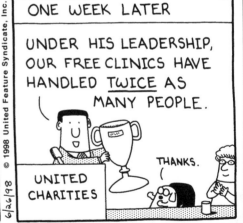

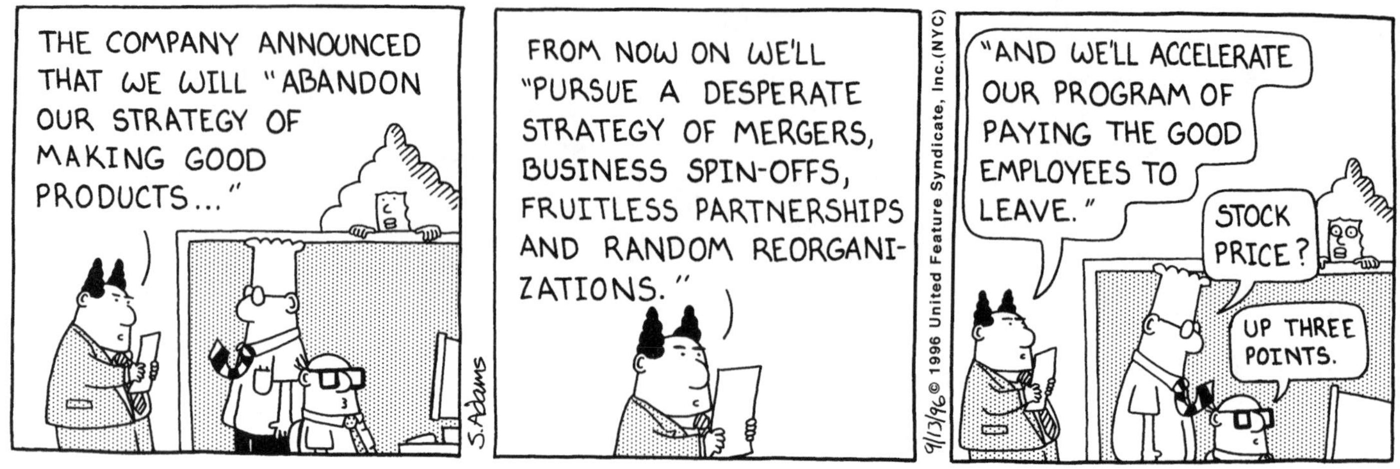
THE COMPANY ANNOUNCED THAT WE WILL "ABANDON OUR STRATEGY OF MAKING GOOD PRODUCTS..."
S. Adams
FROM NOW ON WE'LL "PURSUE A DESPERATE STRATEGY OF MERGERS, BUSINESS SPIN-OFFS, FRUITLESS PARTNERSHIPS AND RANDOM REORGANIZATIONS."
9/13/96 © 1996 United Feature Syndicate, Inc.(NYC)
"AND WE'LL ACCELERATE OUR PROGRAM OF PAYING THE GOOD EMPLOYEES TO LEAVE."
STOCK PRICE?
UP THREE POINTS.

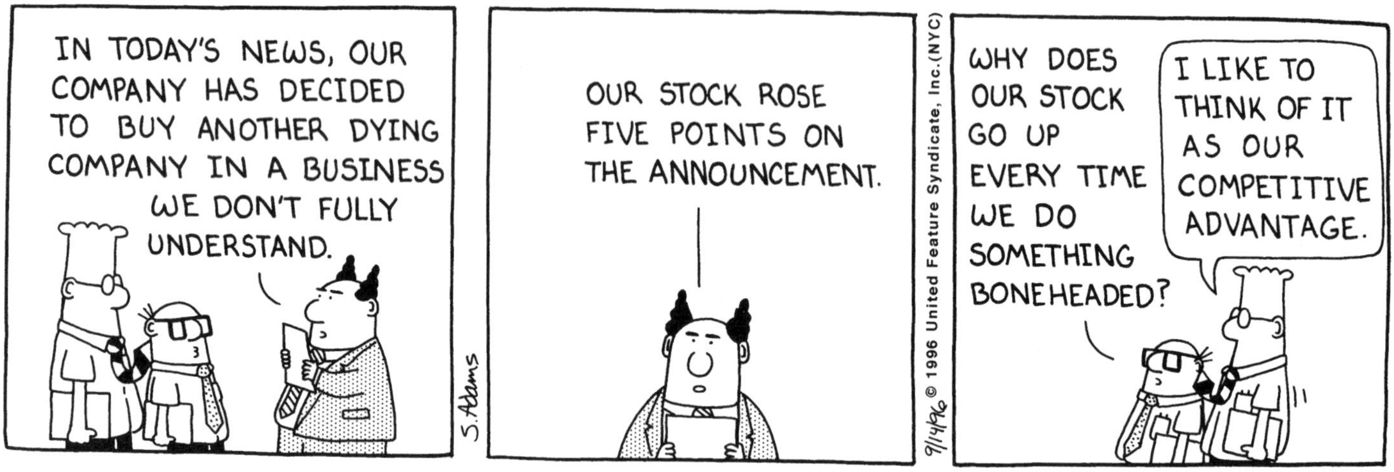
IN TODAY'S NEWS, OUR COMPANY HAS DECIDED TO BUY ANOTHER DYING COMPANY IN A BUSINESS WE DON'T FULLY UNDERSTAND.
S. Adams
OUR STOCK ROSE FIVE POINTS ON THE ANNOUNCEMENT.
9/14/96 © 1996 United Feature Syndicate, Inc.(NYC)
WHY DOES OUR STOCK GO UP EVERY TIME WE DO SOMETHING BONEHEADED?
I LIKE TO THINK OF IT AS OUR COMPETITIVE ADVANTAGE.

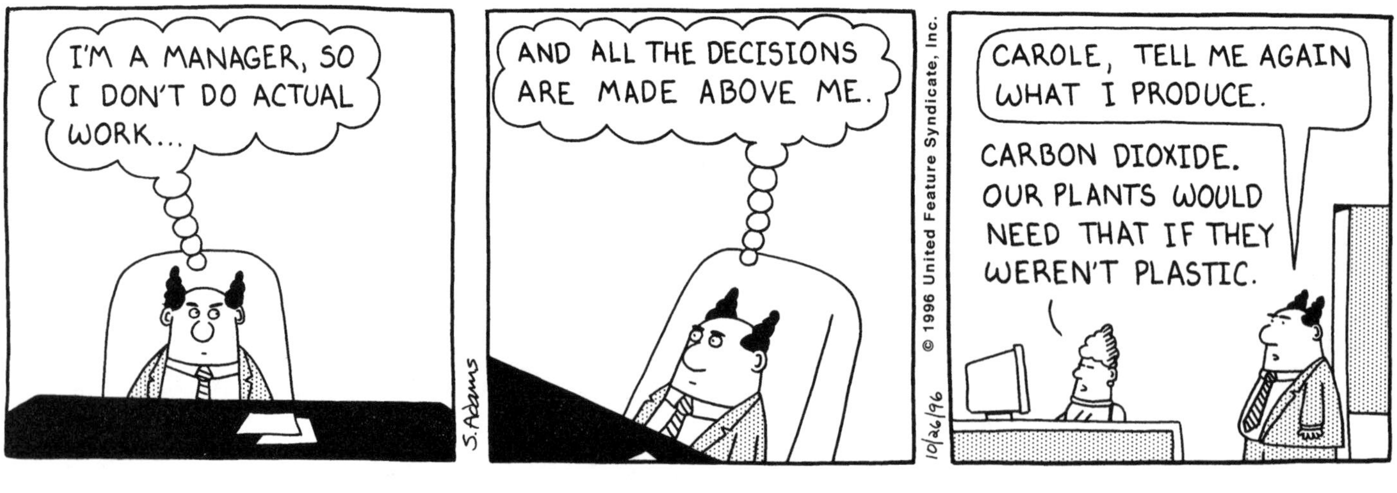
I'M A MANAGER, SO I DON'T DO ACTUAL WORK...
S. Adams
AND ALL THE DECISIONS ARE MADE ABOVE ME.
10/26/96 © 1996 United Feature Syndicate, Inc.
CAROLE, TELL ME AGAIN WHAT I PRODUCE.
CARBON DIOXIDE. OUR PLANTS WOULD NEED THAT IF THEY WEREN'T PLASTIC.

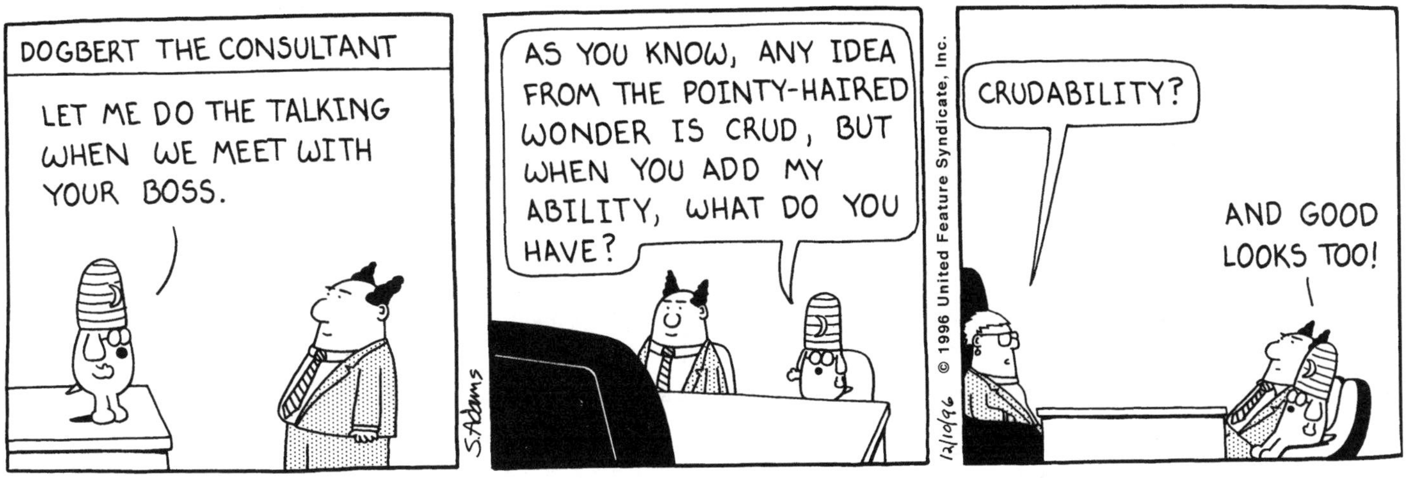
DOGBERT THE CONSULTANT
LET ME DO THE TALKING WHEN WE MEET WITH YOUR BOSS.
S.Adams
AS YOU KNOW, ANY IDEA FROM THE POINTY-HAIRED WONDER IS CRUD, BUT WHEN YOU ADD MY ABILITY, WHAT DO YOU HAVE?
12/10/96 © 1996 United Feature Syndicate, Inc.
CRUDABILITY?
AND GOOD LOOKS TOO!

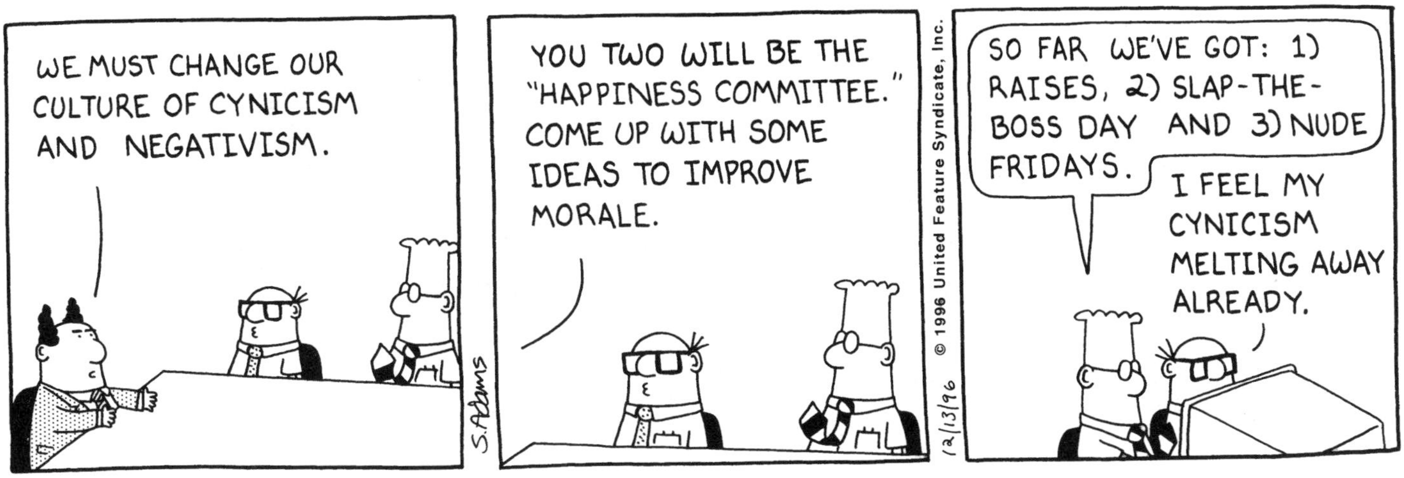
WE MUST CHANGE OUR CULTURE OF CYNICISM AND NEGATIVISM.
S.Adams
YOU TWO WILL BE THE "HAPPINESS COMMITTEE." COME UP WITH SOME IDEAS TO IMPROVE MORALE.
12/13/96 © 1996 United Feature Syndicate, Inc.
SO FAR WE'VE GOT: 1) RAISES, 2) SLAP-THE-BOSS DAY AND 3) NUDE FRIDAYS.
I FEEL MY CYNICISM MELTING AWAY ALREADY.

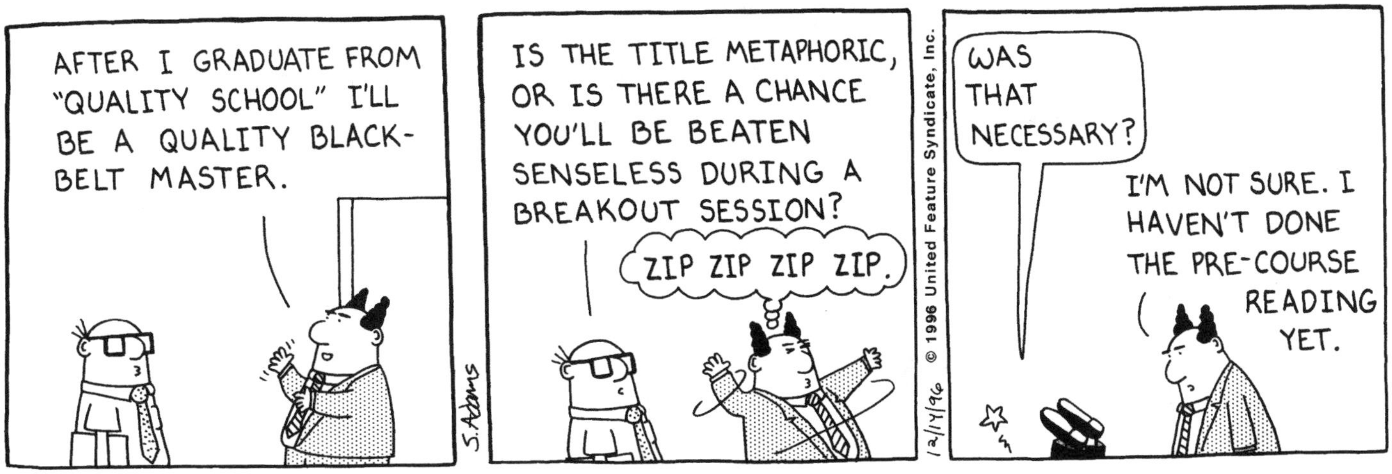
AFTER I GRADUATE FROM "QUALITY SCHOOL" I'LL BE A QUALITY BLACK-BELT MASTER.
S.Adams
IS THE TITLE METAPHORIC, OR IS THERE A CHANCE YOU'LL BE BEATEN SENSELESS DURING A BREAKOUT SESSION?
ZIP ZIP ZIP ZIP.
12/14/96 © 1996 United Feature Syndicate, Inc.
WAS THAT NECESSARY?
I'M NOT SURE. I HAVEN'T DONE THE PRE-COURSE READING YET.

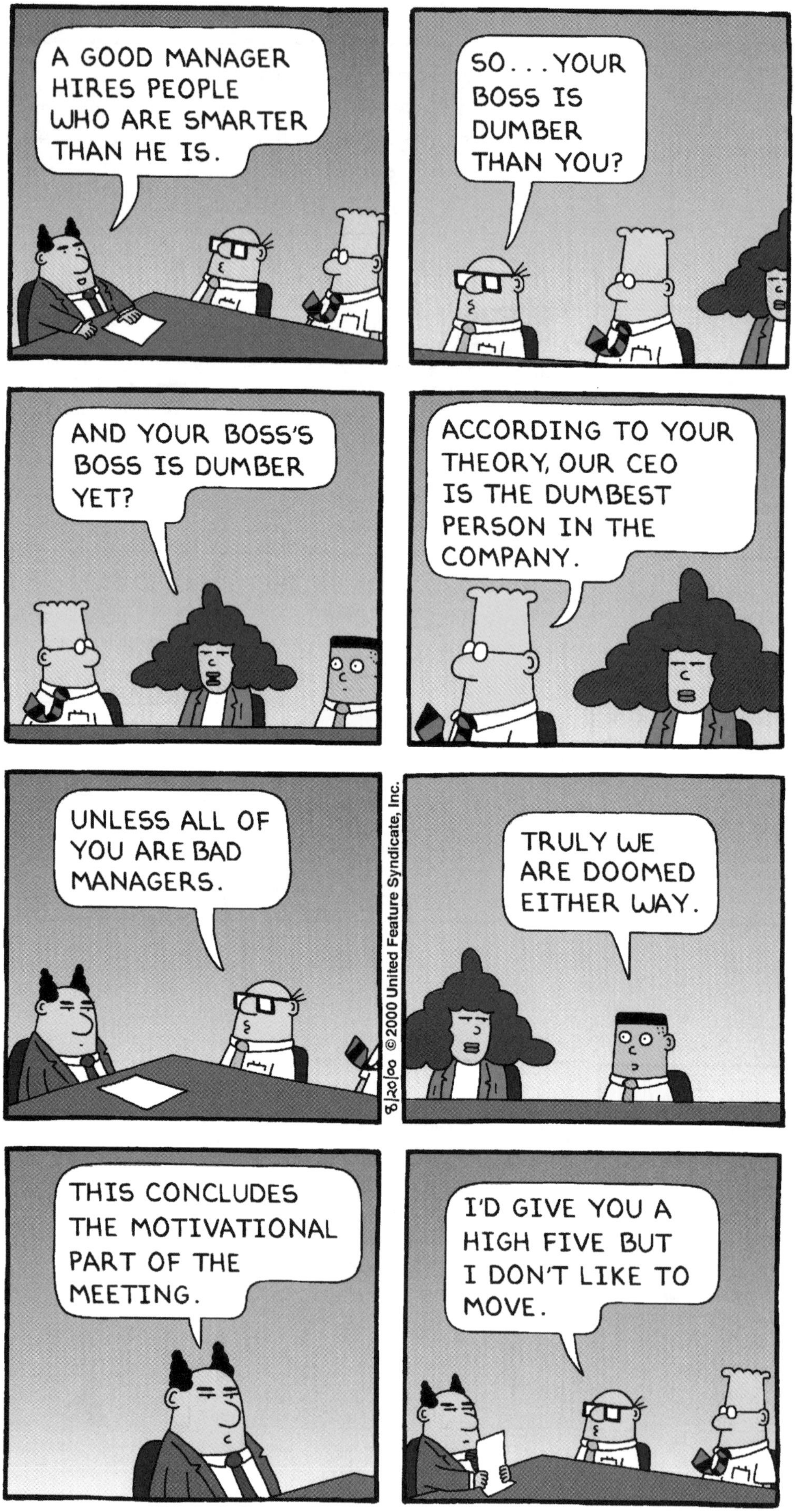
A GOOD MANAGER HIRES PEOPLE WHO ARE SMARTER THAN HE IS.
SO... YOUR BOSS IS DUMBER THAN YOU?
AND YOUR BOSS'S BOSS IS DUMBER YET?
ACCORDING TO YOUR THEORY, OUR CEO IS THE DUMBEST PERSON IN THE COMPANY.
UNLESS ALL OF YOU ARE BAD MANAGERS.
TRULY WE ARE DOOMED EITHER WAY.
THIS CONCLUDES THE MOTIVATIONAL PART OF THE MEETING.
I'D GIVE YOU A HIGH FIVE BUT I DON'T LIKE TO MOVE.
8/20/00 © 2000 United Feature Syndicate, Inc.

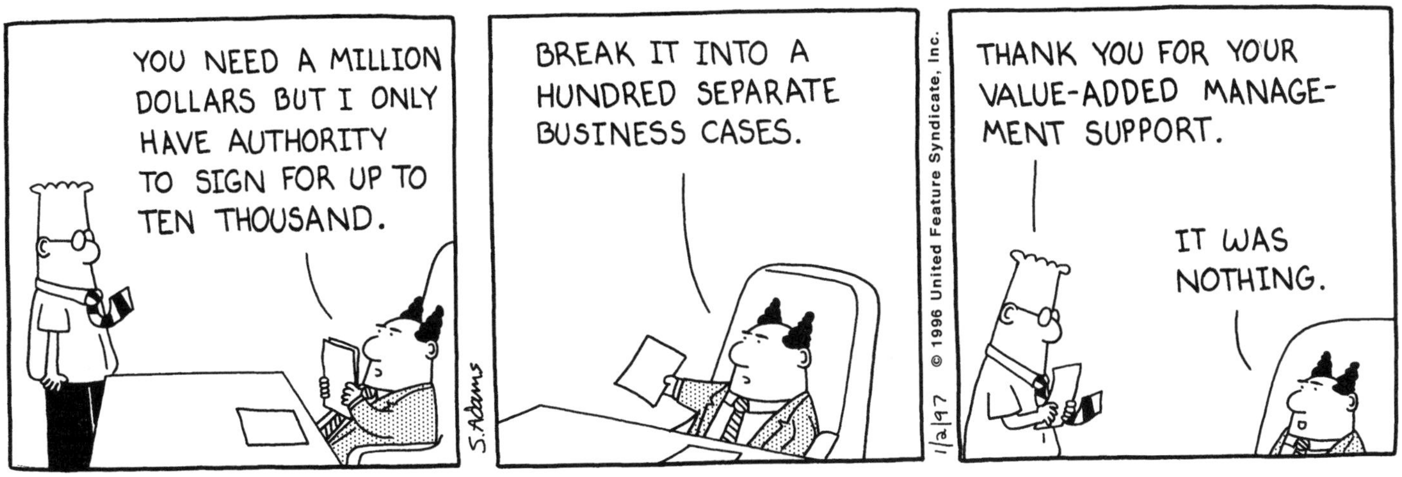
YOU NEED A MILLION DOLLARS BUT I ONLY HAVE AUTHORITY TO SIGN FOR UP TO TEN THOUSAND.
S. Adams
BREAK IT INTO A HUNDRED SEPARATE BUSINESS CASES.
1/2/97
© 1996 United Feature Syndicate, Inc.
THANK YOU FOR YOUR VALUE-ADDED MANAGEMENT SUPPORT.
IT WAS NOTHING.

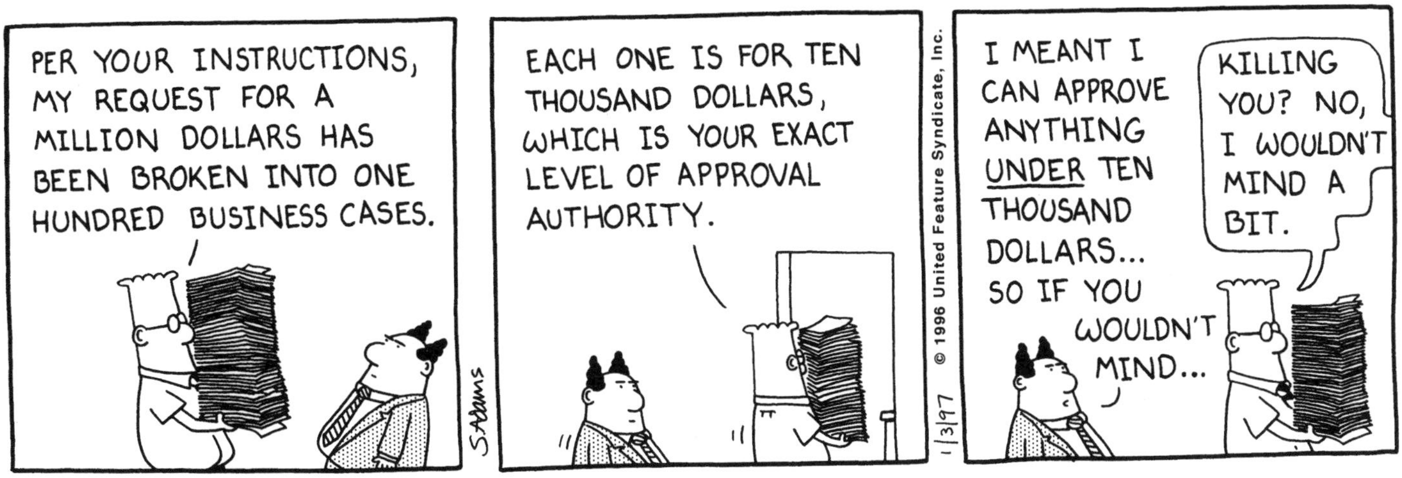
PER YOUR INSTRUCTIONS, MY REQUEST FOR A MILLION DOLLARS HAS BEEN BROKEN INTO ONE HUNDRED BUSINESS CASES.
S. Adams
EACH ONE IS FOR TEN THOUSAND DOLLARS, WHICH IS YOUR EXACT LEVEL OF APPROVAL AUTHORITY.
1/3/97
© 1996 United Feature Syndicate, Inc.
I MEANT I CAN APPROVE ANYTHING UNDER TEN THOUSAND DOLLARS... SO IF YOU WOULDN'T MIND...
KILLING YOU? NO, I WOULDN'T MIND A BIT.

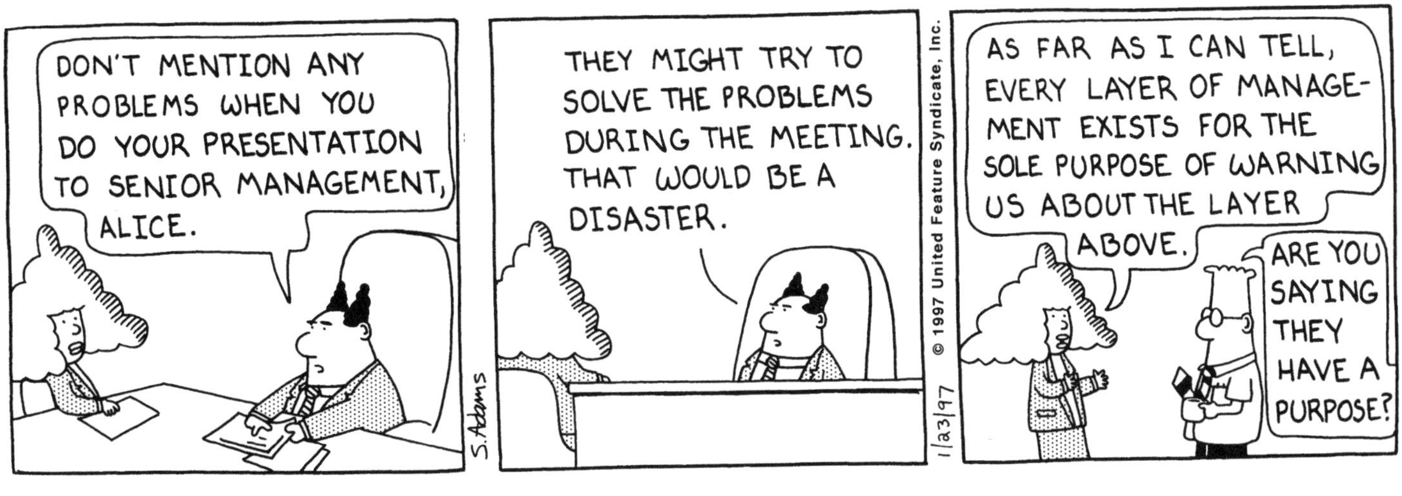
DON'T MENTION ANY PROBLEMS WHEN YOU DO YOUR PRESENTATION TO SENIOR MANAGEMENT, ALICE.
S. Adams
THEY MIGHT TRY TO SOLVE THE PROBLEMS DURING THE MEETING. THAT WOULD BE A DISASTER.
1/23/97
© 1997 United Feature Syndicate, Inc.
AS FAR AS I CAN TELL, EVERY LAYER OF MANAGEMENT EXISTS FOR THE SOLE PURPOSE OF WARNING US ABOUT THE LAYER ABOVE.
ARE YOU SAYING THEY HAVE A PURPOSE?

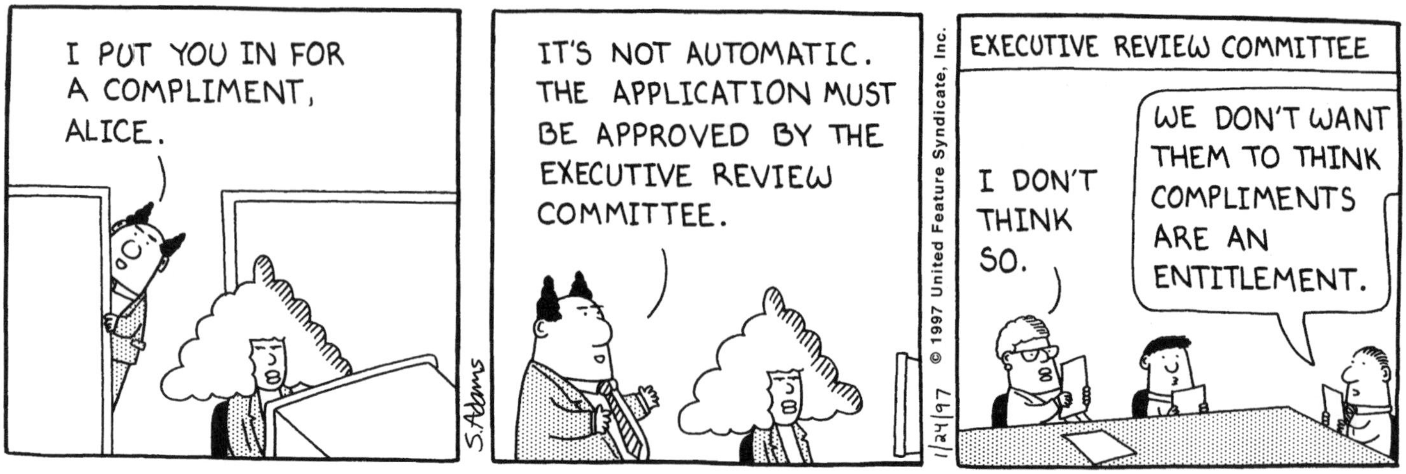
I PUT YOU IN FOR A COMPLIMENT, ALICE.
IT'S NOT AUTOMATIC. THE APPLICATION MUST BE APPROVED BY THE EXECUTIVE REVIEW COMMITTEE.
EXECUTIVE REVIEW COMMITTEE
I DON'T THINK SO.
WE DON'T WANT THEM TO THINK COMPLIMENTS ARE AN ENTITLEMENT.
S. Adams
1/24/97
© 1997 United Feature Syndicate, Inc.

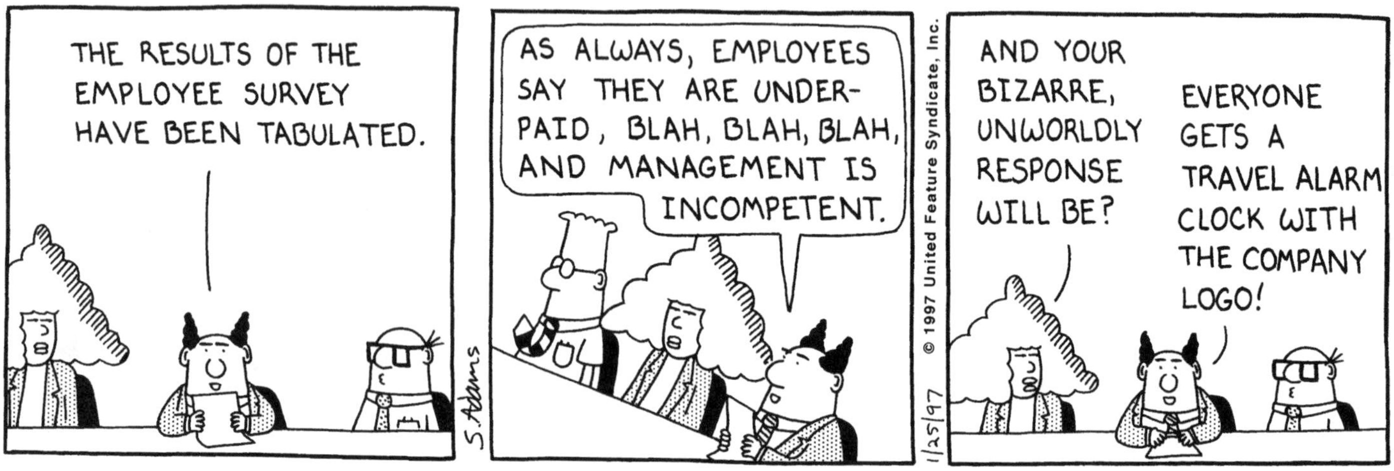
THE RESULTS OF THE EMPLOYEE SURVEY HAVE BEEN TABULATED.
AS ALWAYS, EMPLOYEES SAY THEY ARE UNDERPAID, BLAH, BLAH, BLAH, AND MANAGEMENT IS INCOMPETENT.
AND YOUR BIZARRE, UNWORLDLY RESPONSE WILL BE?
EVERYONE GETS A TRAVEL ALARM CLOCK WITH THE COMPANY LOGO!
S. Adams
1/25/97
© 1997 United Feature Syndicate, Inc.

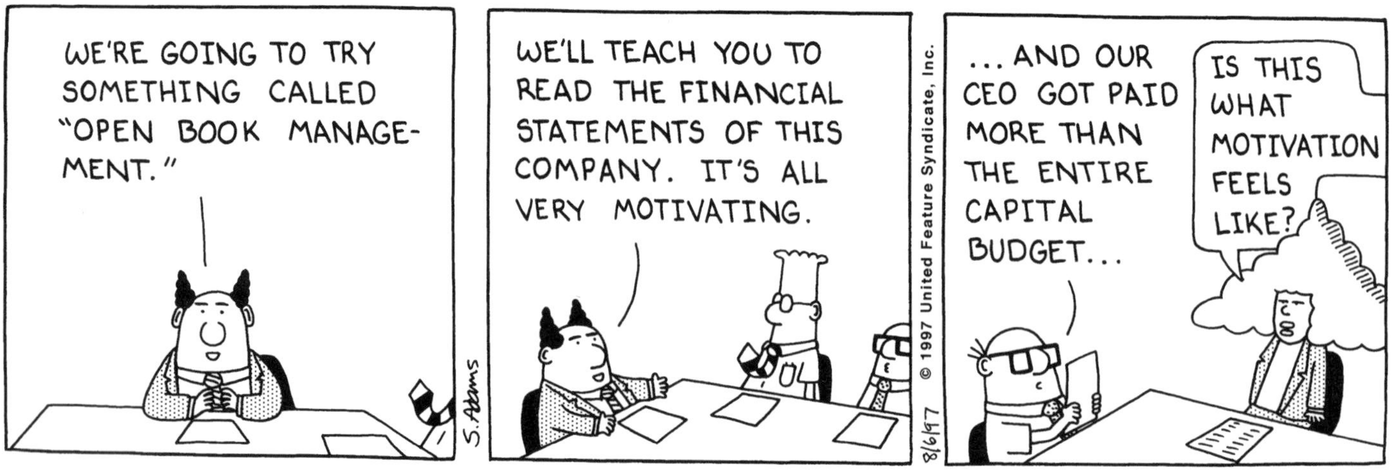
WE'RE GOING TO TRY SOMETHING CALLED "OPEN BOOK MANAGEMENT."
WE'LL TEACH YOU TO READ THE FINANCIAL STATEMENTS OF THIS COMPANY. IT'S ALL VERY MOTIVATING.
... AND OUR CEO GOT PAID MORE THAN THE ENTIRE CAPITAL BUDGET...
IS THIS WHAT MOTIVATION FEELS LIKE?
S. Adams
8/6/97
© 1997 United Feature Syndicate, Inc.

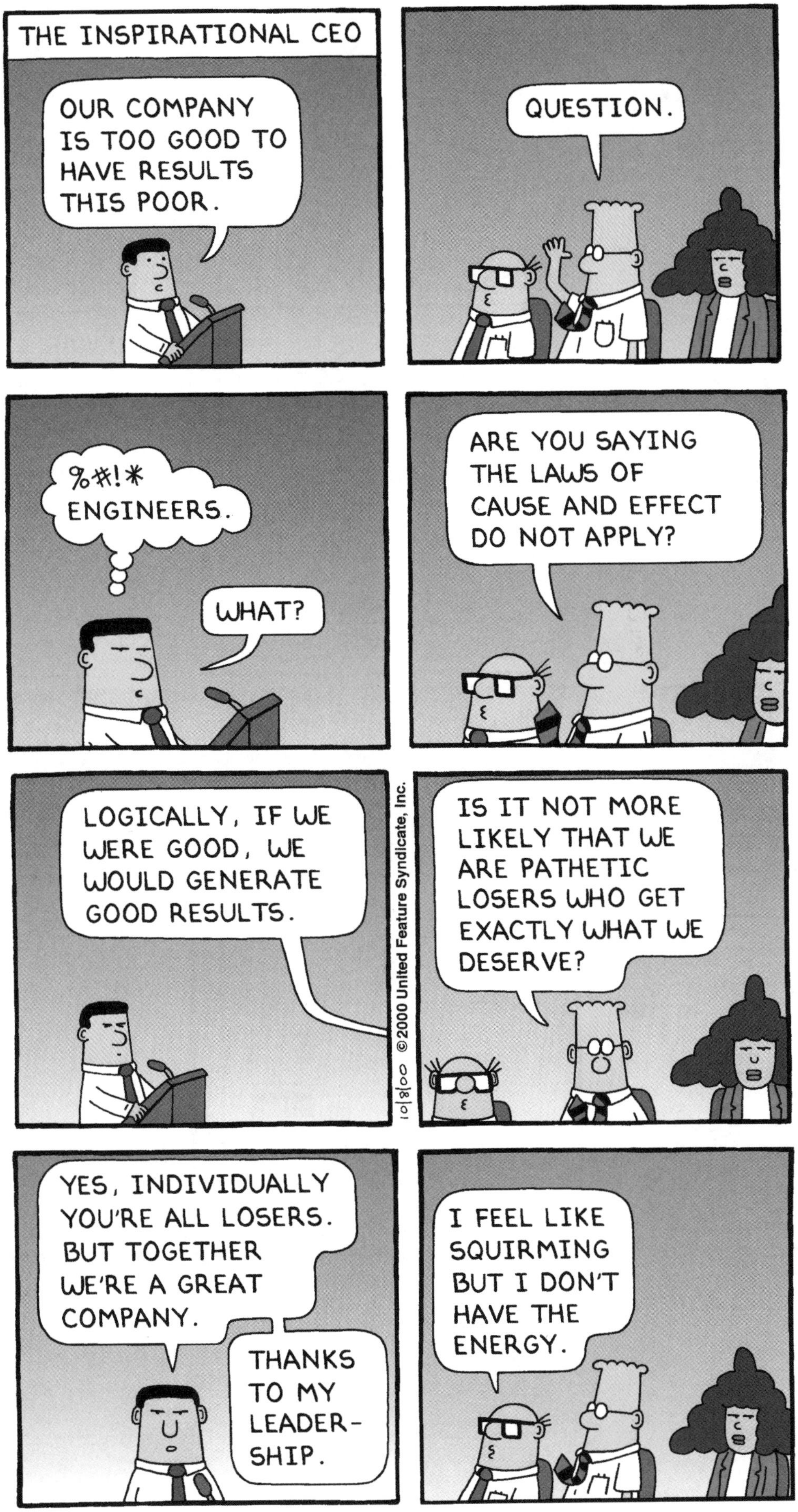
THE INSPIRATIONAL CEO
OUR COMPANY IS TOO GOOD TO HAVE RESULTS THIS POOR.
QUESTION.
%#!* ENGINEERS.
WHAT?
ARE YOU SAYING THE LAWS OF CAUSE AND EFFECT DO NOT APPLY?
LOGICALLY, IF WE WERE GOOD, WE WOULD GENERATE GOOD RESULTS.
IS IT NOT MORE LIKELY THAT WE ARE PATHETIC LOSERS WHO GET EXACTLY WHAT WE DESERVE?
YES, INDIVIDUALLY YOU'RE ALL LOSERS. BUT TOGETHER WE'RE A GREAT COMPANY.
THANKS TO MY LEADER-SHIP.
I FEEL LIKE SQUIRMING BUT I DON'T HAVE THE ENERGY.
10/8/00 ©2000 United Feature Syndicate, Inc.

DOGBERT THE C.E.O.
I'M AN INVESTMENT BANKER. I CAN HELP YOU LOOT THIS PLACE AND ESCAPE.
S. Adams
YOU'LL MERGE WITH MY OTHER CLIENT COMPANY. YOUR GOLDEN PARA-CHUTE KICKS IN. THEN YOU EXERCISE YOUR STOCK OPTIONS ON THE UPTICK.
6/27/98 © 1998 United Feature Syndicate, Inc.
YOU RARELY SEE A MERGER ANNOUNCE-MENT WITH THE PHRASE, "SO LONG, SUCKERS."
OUCH.

DOGBERT THE CEO
MY SALARY IS 400 TIMES MORE THAN YOURS.
S. Adams
MY GOAL IS TO JACK THAT UP TO 410, MAYBE 420.
10-13-08 ©2008 Scott Adams, Inc./Dist. by UFS, Inc.
I HATE YOU FOR THIS.
SO YOU ADMIT YOU'RE SELFISH?

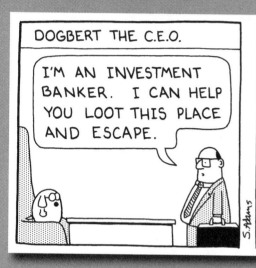

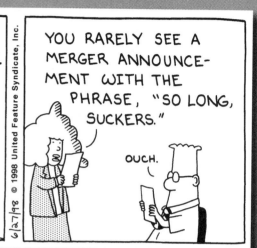

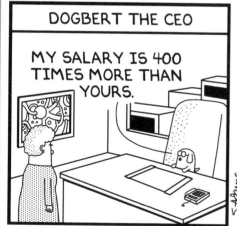

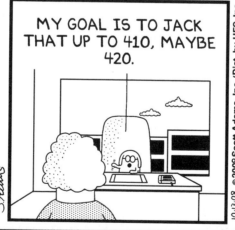

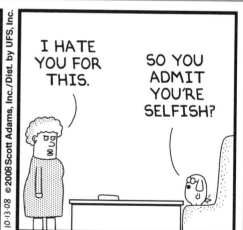

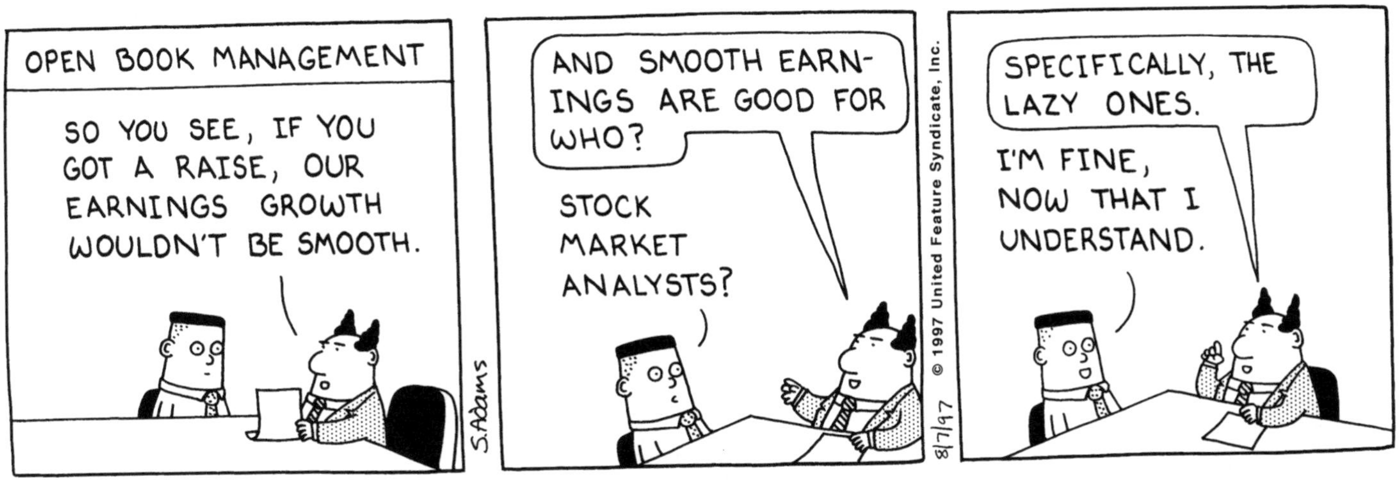
OPEN BOOK MANAGEMENT
SO YOU SEE, IF YOU GOT A RAISE, OUR EARNINGS GROWTH WOULDN'T BE SMOOTH.
S. Adams
AND SMOOTH EARNINGS ARE GOOD FOR WHO?
STOCK MARKET ANALYSTS?
© 1997 United Feature Syndicate, Inc.
8/7/97
SPECIFICALLY, THE LAZY ONES.
I'M FINE, NOW THAT I UNDERSTAND.

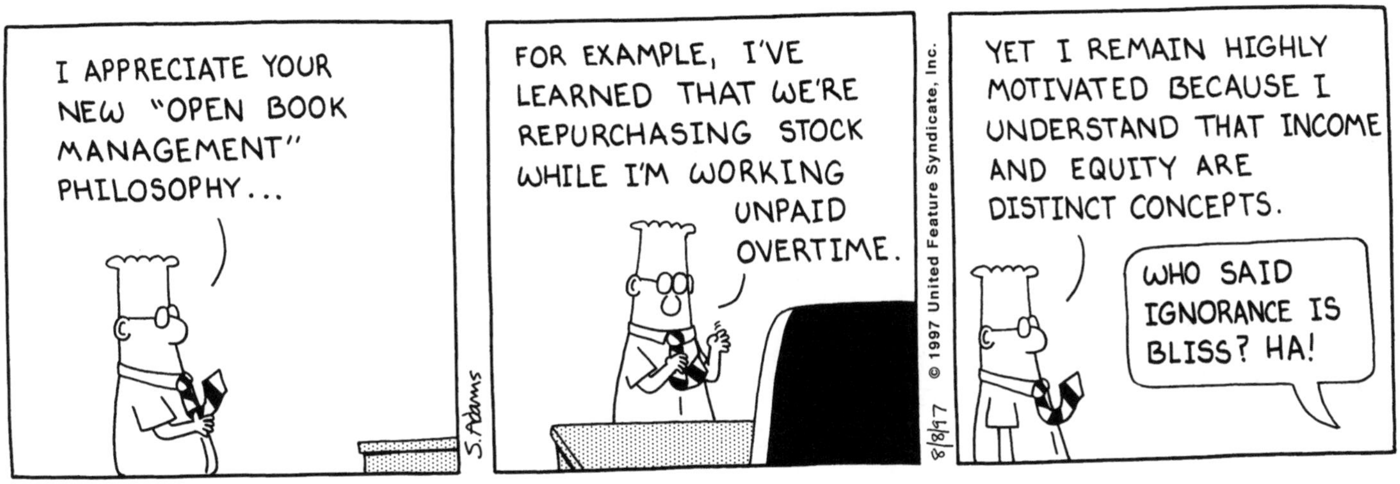
I APPRECIATE YOUR NEW "OPEN BOOK MANAGEMENT" PHILOSOPHY...
S. Adams
FOR EXAMPLE, I'VE LEARNED THAT WE'RE REPURCHASING STOCK WHILE I'M WORKING
UNPAID OVERTIME.
© 1997 United Feature Syndicate, Inc.
8/8/97
YET I REMAIN HIGHLY MOTIVATED BECAUSE I UNDERSTAND THAT INCOME AND EQUITY ARE DISTINCT CONCEPTS.
WHO SAID IGNORANCE IS BLISS? HA!

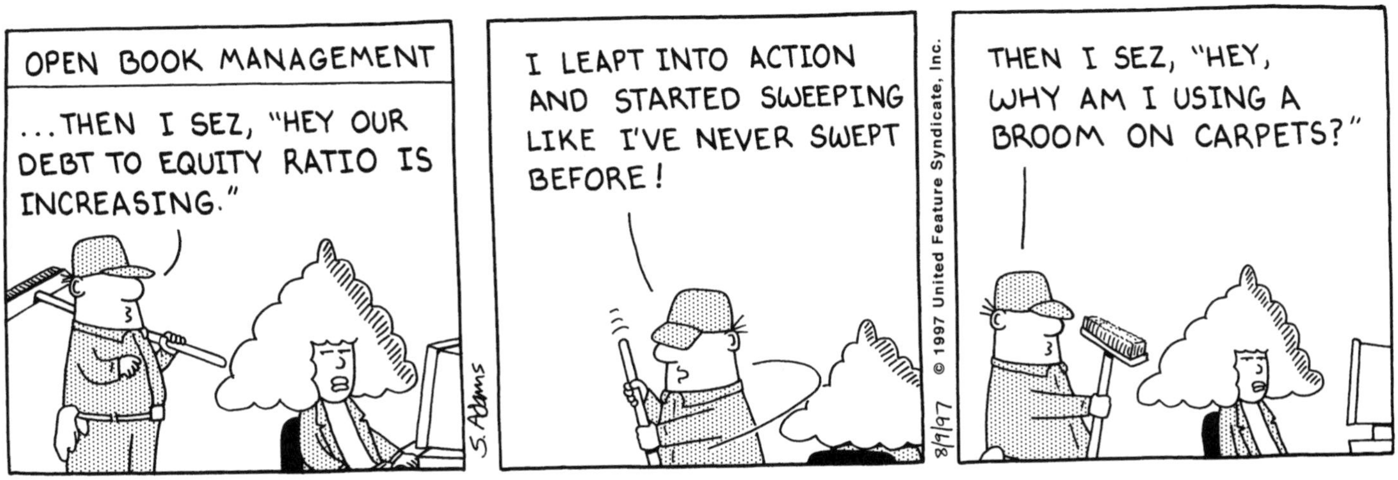
OPEN BOOK MANAGEMENT
...THEN I SEZ, "HEY OUR DEBT TO EQUITY RATIO IS INCREASING."
S. Adams
I LEAPT INTO ACTION AND STARTED SWEEPING LIKE I'VE NEVER SWEPT BEFORE!
© 1997 United Feature Syndicate, Inc.
8/9/97
THEN I SEZ, "HEY, WHY AM I USING A BROOM ON CARPETS?"

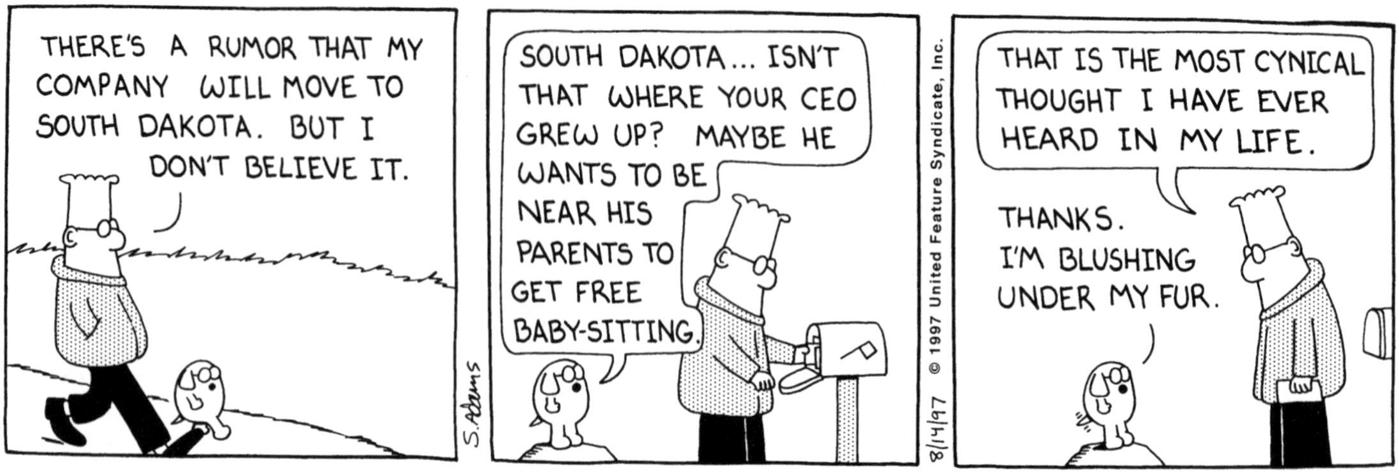
THERE'S A RUMOR THAT MY COMPANY WILL MOVE TO SOUTH DAKOTA. BUT I DON'T BELIEVE IT.
SOUTH DAKOTA... ISN'T THAT WHERE YOUR CEO GREW UP? MAYBE HE WANTS TO BE NEAR HIS PARENTS TO GET FREE BABY-SITTING.
THAT IS THE MOST CYNICAL THOUGHT I HAVE EVER HEARD IN MY LIFE.
THANKS. I'M BLUSHING UNDER MY FUR.
S. Adams
8/14/97
© 1997 United Feature Syndicate, Inc.

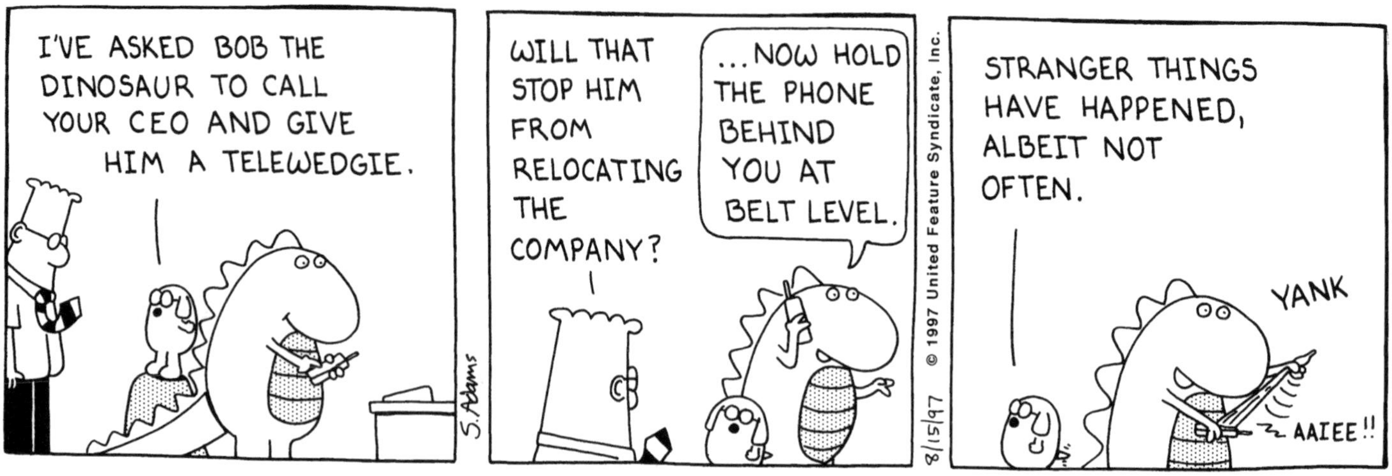
I'VE ASKED BOB THE DINOSAUR TO CALL YOUR CEO AND GIVE HIM A TELEWEDGIE.
WILL THAT STOP HIM FROM RELOCATING THE COMPANY?
...NOW HOLD THE PHONE BEHIND YOU AT BELT LEVEL.
STRANGER THINGS HAVE HAPPENED, ALBEIT NOT OFTEN.
YANK
AAIEE!!
S. Adams
8/15/97
© 1997 United Feature Syndicate, Inc.

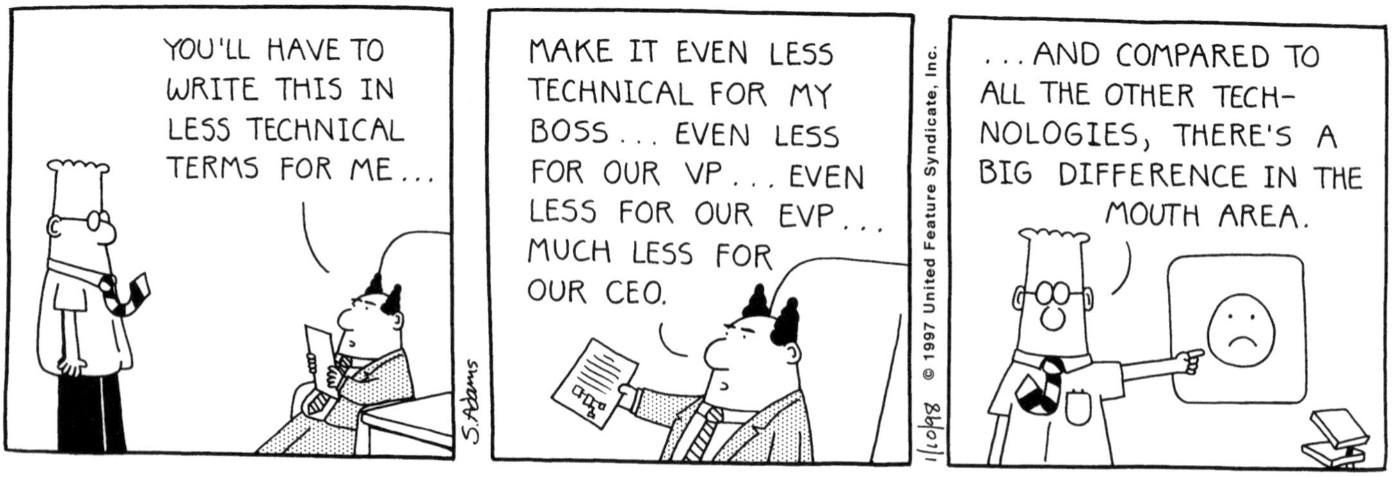
YOU'LL HAVE TO WRITE THIS IN LESS TECHNICAL TERMS FOR ME...
MAKE IT EVEN LESS TECHNICAL FOR MY BOSS... EVEN LESS FOR OUR VP... EVEN LESS FOR OUR EVP... MUCH LESS FOR OUR CEO.
...AND COMPARED TO ALL THE OTHER TECH-NOLOGIES, THERE'S A BIG DIFFERENCE IN THE MOUTH AREA.
S. Adams
1/10/98
© 1997 United Feature Syndicate, Inc.

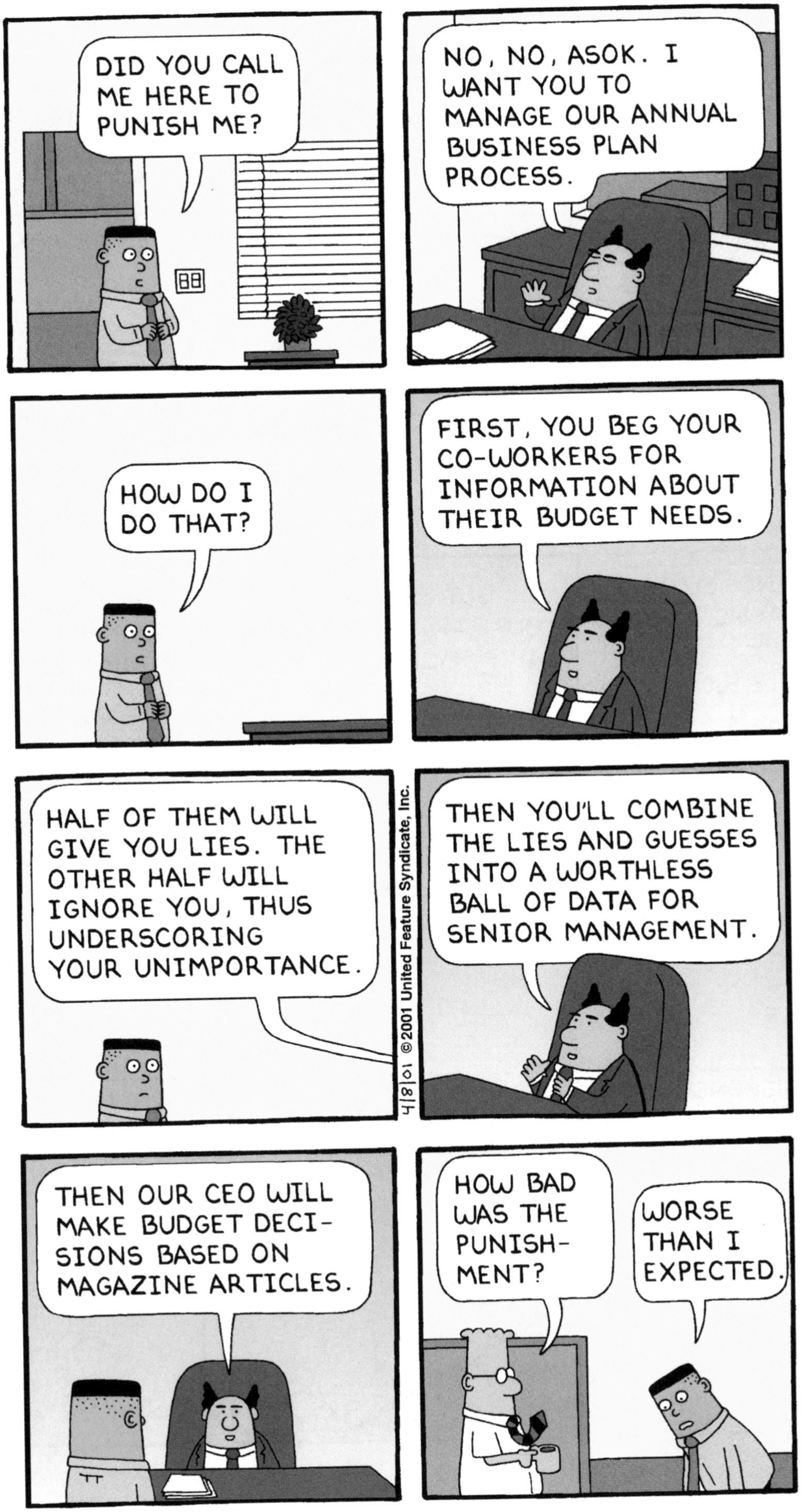
DID YOU CALL ME HERE TO PUNISH ME?
NO, NO, ASOK. I WANT YOU TO MANAGE OUR ANNUAL BUSINESS PLAN PROCESS.
HOW DO I DO THAT?
FIRST, YOU BEG YOUR CO-WORKERS FOR INFORMATION ABOUT THEIR BUDGET NEEDS.
HALF OF THEM WILL GIVE YOU LIES. THE OTHER HALF WILL IGNORE YOU, THUS UNDERSCORING YOUR UNIMPORTANCE.
4/8/01 ©2001 United Feature Syndicate, Inc.
THEN YOU'LL COMBINE THE LIES AND GUESSES INTO A WORTHLESS BALL OF DATA FOR SENIOR MANAGEMENT.
THEN OUR CEO WILL MAKE BUDGET DECI- SIONS BASED ON MAGAZINE ARTICLES.
HOW BAD WAS THE PUNISH- MENT?
WORSE THAN I EXPECTED.

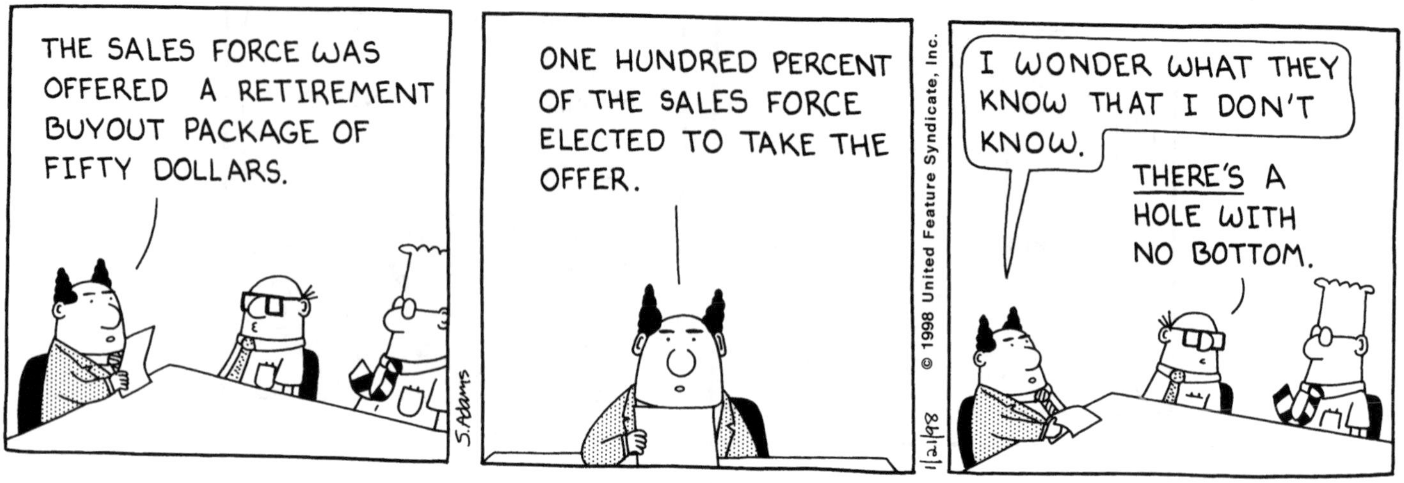
THE SALES FORCE WAS OFFERED A RETIREMENT BUYOUT PACKAGE OF FIFTY DOLLARS.
S. Adams
ONE HUNDRED PERCENT OF THE SALES FORCE ELECTED TO TAKE THE OFFER.
1/21/98 © 1998 United Feature Syndicate, Inc.
I WONDER WHAT THEY KNOW THAT I DON'T KNOW.
THERE'S A HOLE WITH NO BOTTOM.

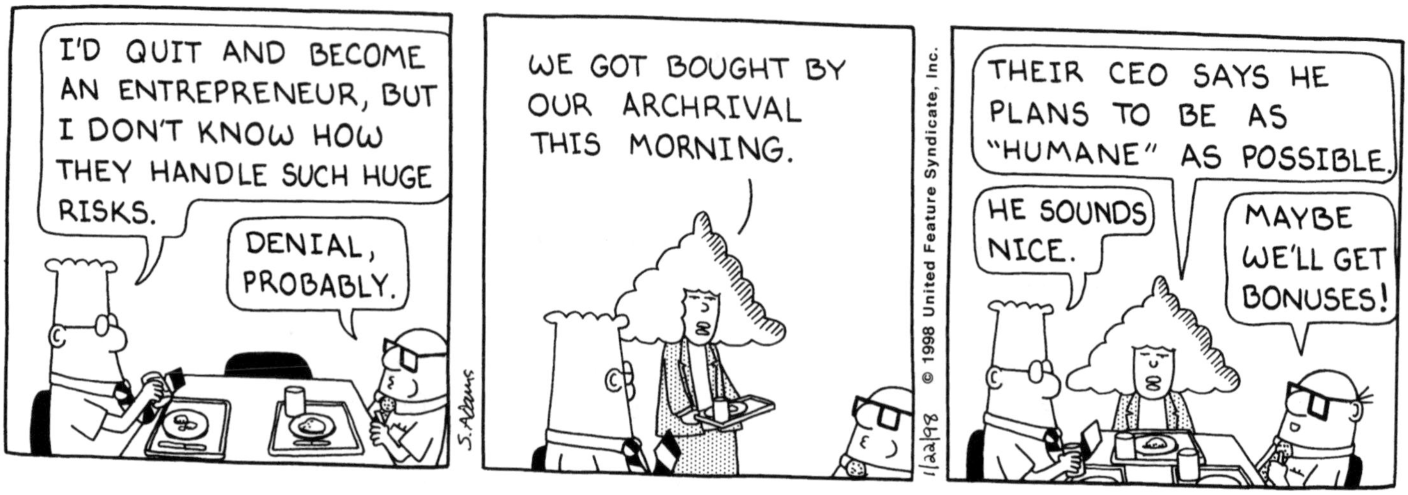
I'D QUIT AND BECOME AN ENTREPRENEUR, BUT I DON'T KNOW HOW THEY HANDLE SUCH HUGE RISKS.
DENIAL, PROBABLY.
S. Adams
WE GOT BOUGHT BY OUR ARCHRIVAL THIS MORNING.
1/22/98 © 1998 United Feature Syndicate, Inc.
THEIR CEO SAYS HE PLANS TO BE AS "HUMANE" AS POSSIBLE.
HE SOUNDS NICE.
MAYBE WE'LL GET BONUSES!

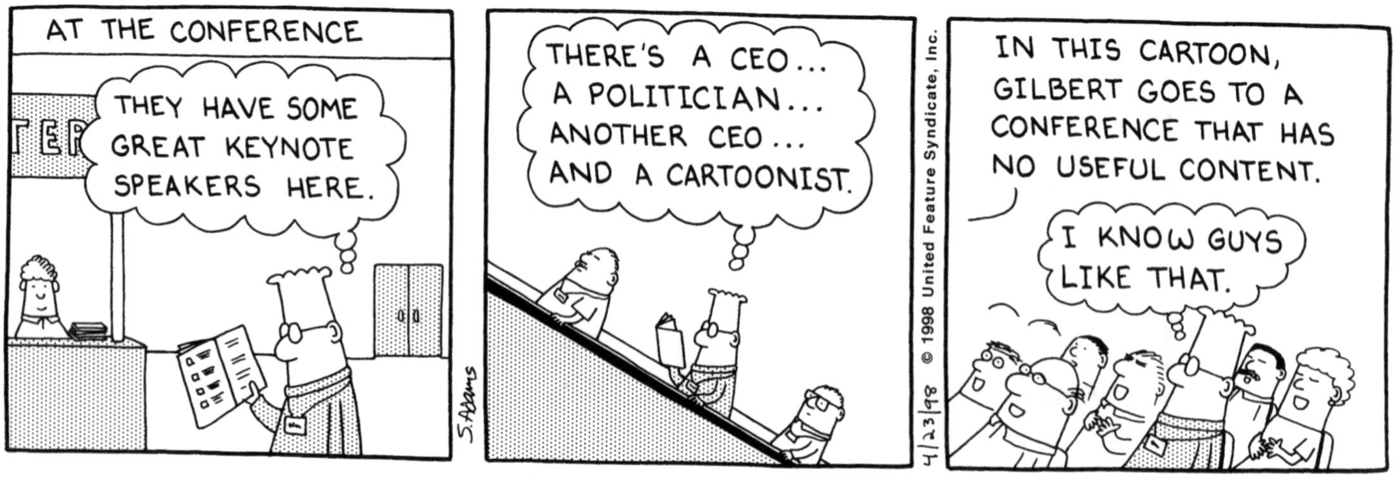
AT THE CONFERENCE
THEY HAVE SOME GREAT KEYNOTE SPEAKERS HERE.
S. Adams
THERE'S A CEO... A POLITICIAN... ANOTHER CEO... AND A CARTOONIST.
4/23/98 © 1998 United Feature Syndicate, Inc.
IN THIS CARTOON, GILBERT GOES TO A CONFERENCE THAT HAS NO USEFUL CONTENT.
I KNOW GUYS LIKE THAT.

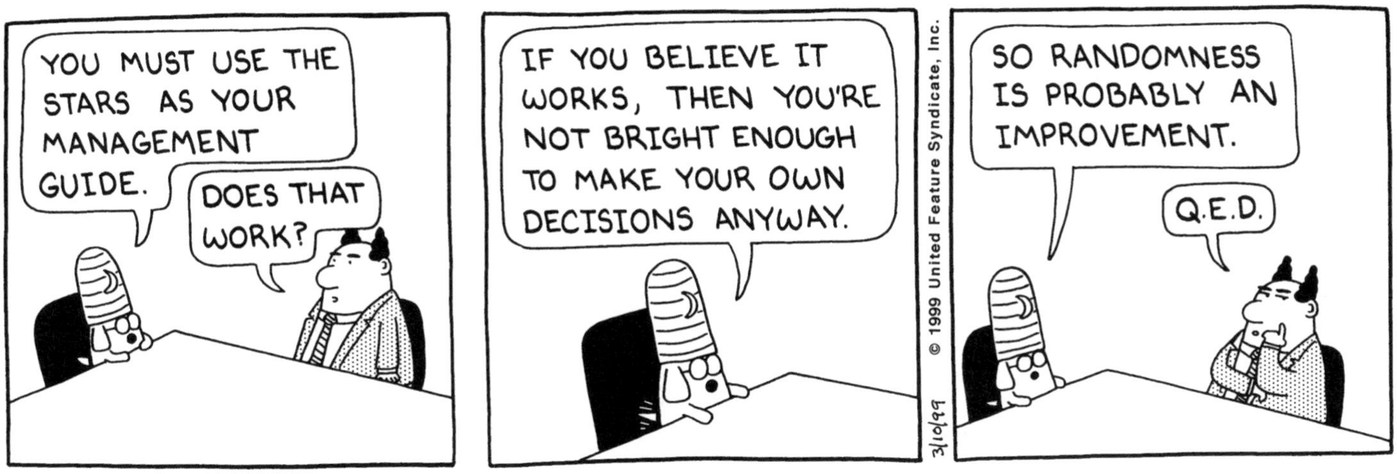
YOU MUST USE THE STARS AS YOUR MANAGEMENT GUIDE.
DOES THAT WORK?
IF YOU BELIEVE IT WORKS, THEN YOU'RE NOT BRIGHT ENOUGH TO MAKE YOUR OWN DECISIONS ANYWAY.
© 1999 United Feature Syndicate, Inc.
3/10/99
SO RANDOMNESS IS PROBABLY AN IMPROVEMENT.
Q.E.D.

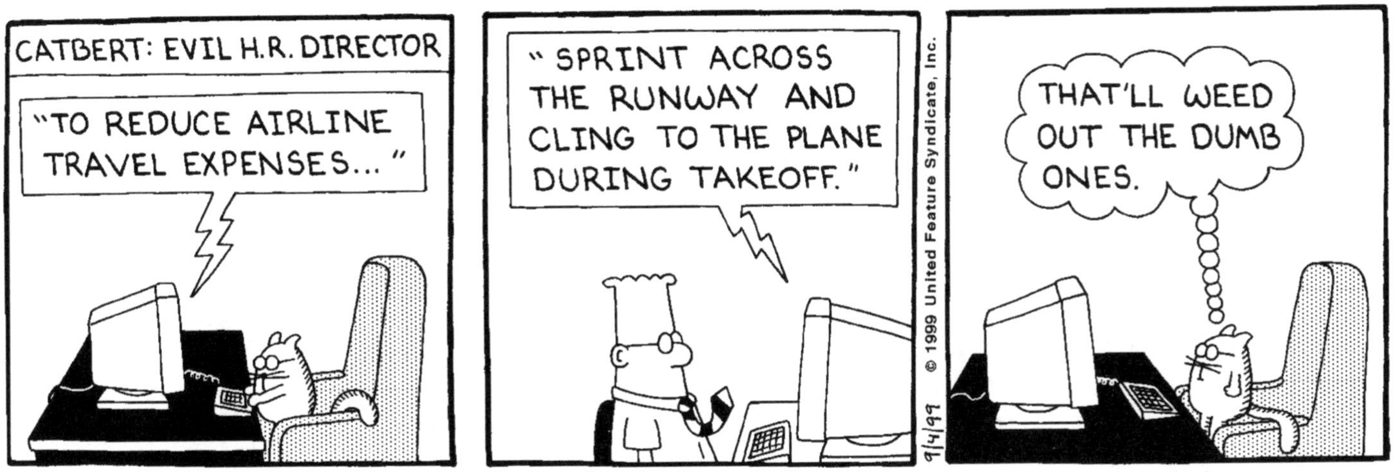
CATBERT: EVIL H.R. DIRECTOR
"TO REDUCE AIRLINE TRAVEL EXPENSES..."
"SPRINT ACROSS THE RUNWAY AND CLING TO THE PLANE DURING TAKEOFF."
© 1999 United Feature Syndicate, Inc.
9/4/99
THAT'LL WEED OUT THE DUMB ONES.

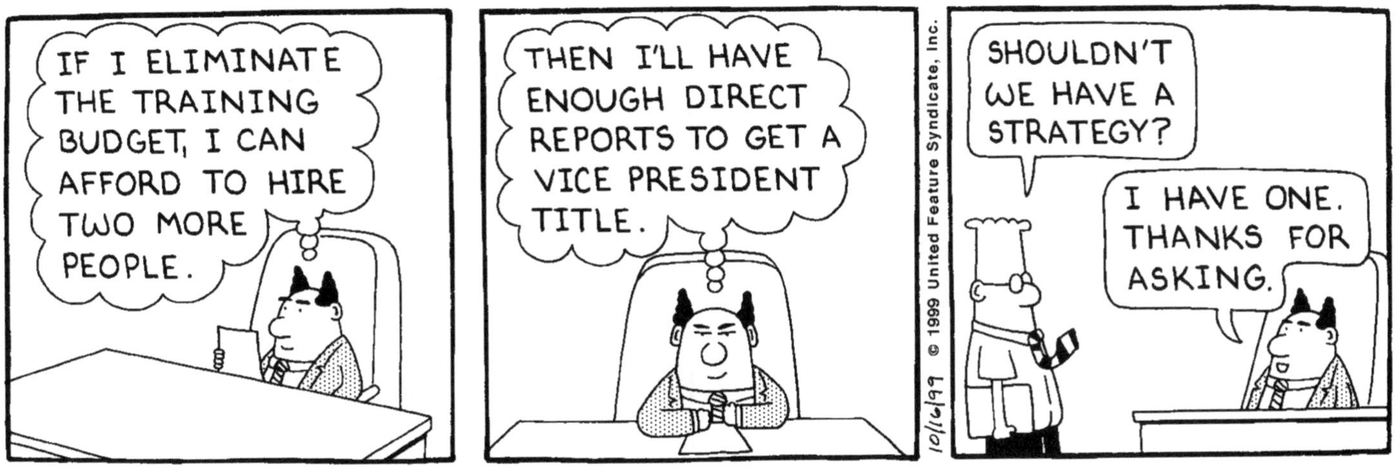
IF I ELIMINATE THE TRAINING BUDGET, I CAN AFFORD TO HIRE TWO MORE PEOPLE.
THEN I'LL HAVE ENOUGH DIRECT REPORTS TO GET A VICE PRESIDENT TITLE.
© 1999 United Feature Syndicate, Inc.
10/16/99
SHOULDN'T WE HAVE A STRATEGY?
I HAVE ONE. THANKS FOR ASKING.

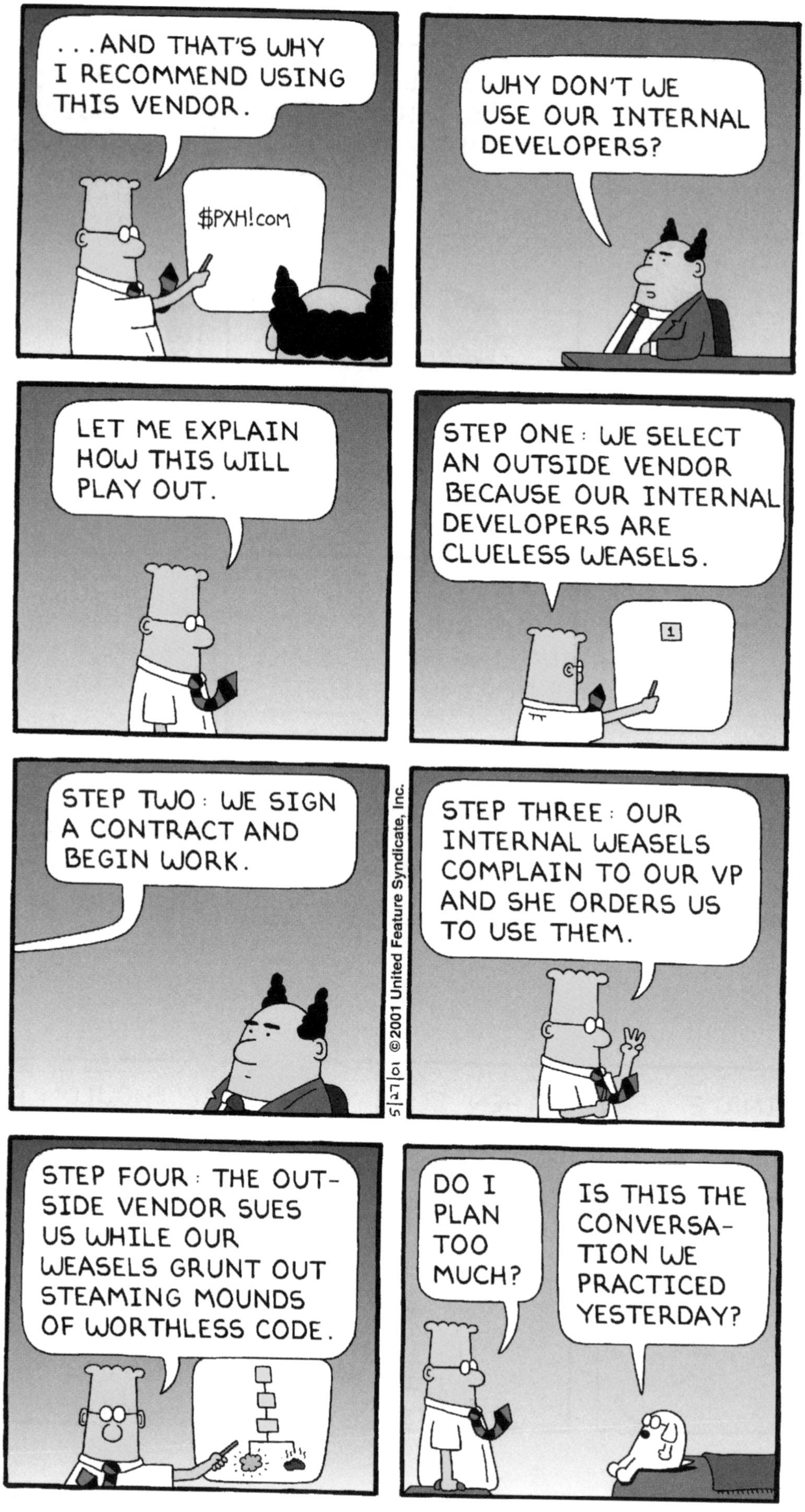
...AND THAT'S WHY I RECOMMEND USING THIS VENDOR.
$PXH!com
WHY DON'T WE USE OUR INTERNAL DEVELOPERS?
LET ME EXPLAIN HOW THIS WILL PLAY OUT.
STEP ONE: WE SELECT AN OUTSIDE VENDOR BECAUSE OUR INTERNAL DEVELOPERS ARE CLUELESS WEASELS.
1
STEP TWO: WE SIGN A CONTRACT AND BEGIN WORK.
5/27/01 ©2001 United Feature Syndicate, Inc.
STEP THREE: OUR INTERNAL WEASELS COMPLAIN TO OUR VP AND SHE ORDERS US TO USE THEM.
STEP FOUR: THE OUT-SIDE VENDOR SUES US WHILE OUR WEASELS GRUNT OUT STEAMING MOUNDS OF WORTHLESS CODE.
DO I PLAN TOO MUCH?
IS THIS THE CONVERSA-TION WE PRACTICED YESTERDAY?

DOGBERT THE CEO
I EARN 420 TIMES WHAT YOU MAKE. THAT MEANS I'M 420 TIMES SMARTER.
ACTUALLY, IT MEANS THE SYSTEM IS DEEPLY FLAWED.
IF YOU WERE 420 TIMES SMARTER, YOU WOULDN'T BE CONTRADICTING YOUR BOSS RIGHT NOW.
10-14-08
© 2008 Scott Adams, Inc./Dist. by UFS, Inc.

DOGBERT THE CEO
OUR INVESTORS ARE NOT HAPPY THAT YOU BOUGHT A HELICOPTER.
OR THAT YOU ONLY USE IT TO KEEP BIRDS OFF THE BUILDING.
OR THAT THE PARKING LOT IS FILLING UP WITH BEAKS AND FEATHERS.
I CAN'T PLEASE EVERY-ONE.
10-15-08
© 2008 Scott Adams, Inc./Dist. by UFS, Inc.

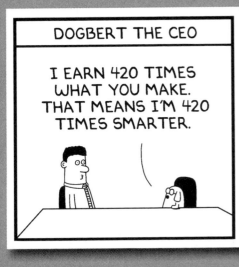

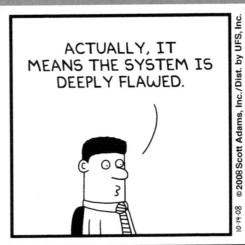

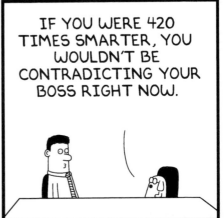

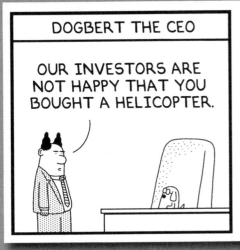

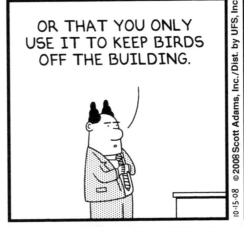

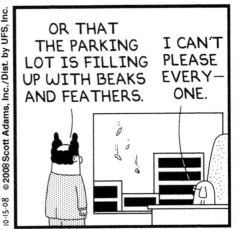

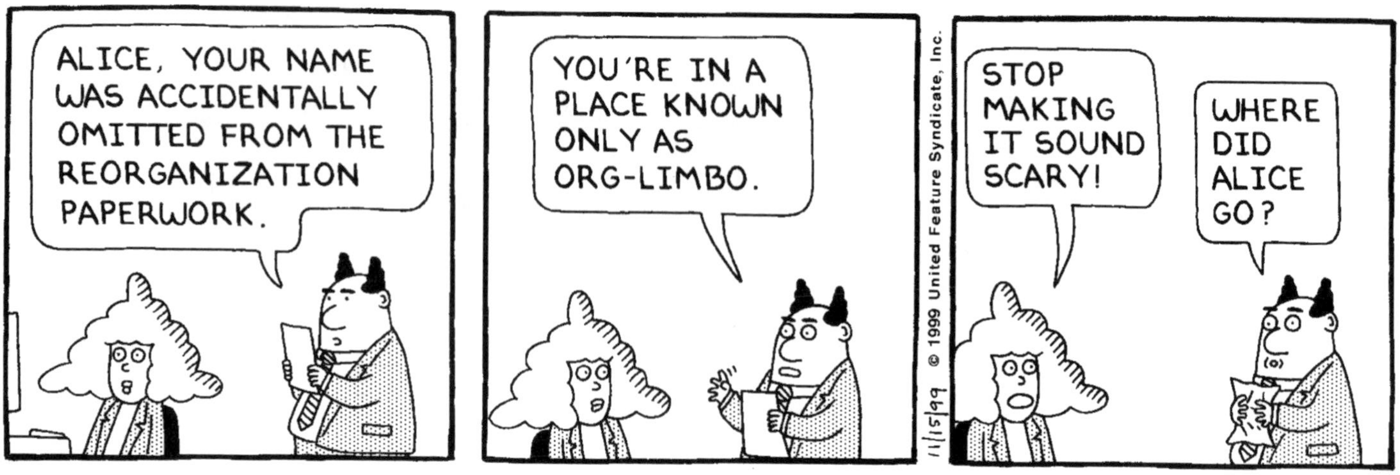
ALICE, YOUR NAME WAS ACCIDENTALLY OMITTED FROM THE REORGANIZATION PAPERWORK.
YOU'RE IN A PLACE KNOWN ONLY AS ORG-LIMBO.
11/15/99 © 1999 United Feature Syndicate, Inc.
STOP MAKING IT SOUND SCARY!
WHERE DID ALICE GO?

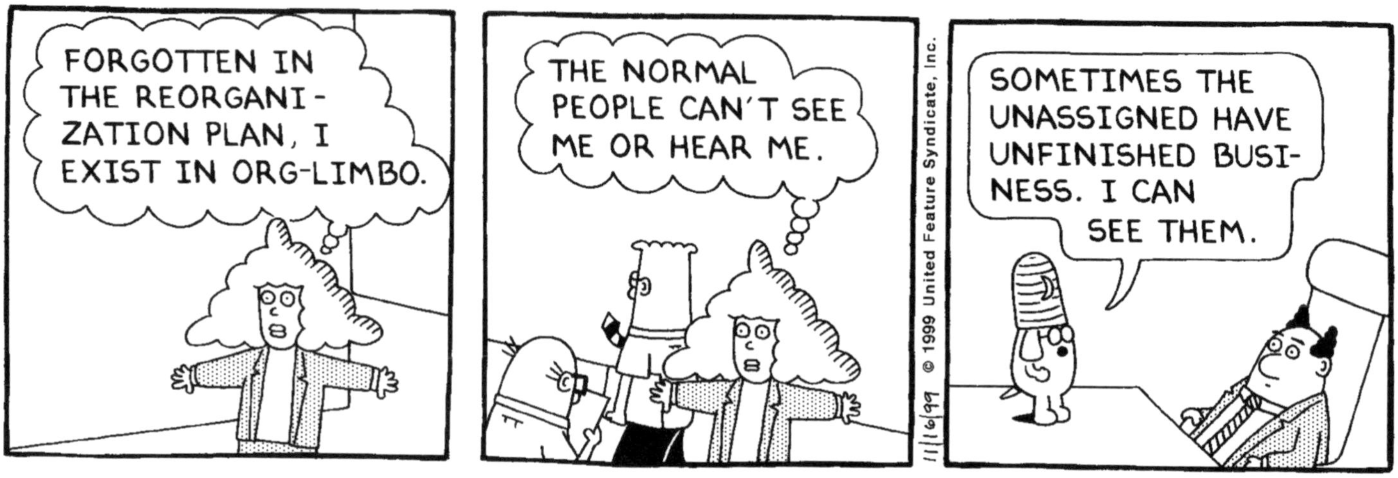
FORGOTTEN IN THE REORGANIZATION PLAN, I EXIST IN ORG-LIMBO.
THE NORMAL PEOPLE CAN'T SEE ME OR HEAR ME.
11/16/99 © 1999 United Feature Syndicate, Inc.
SOMETIMES THE UNASSIGNED HAVE UNFINISHED BUSINESS. I CAN SEE THEM.

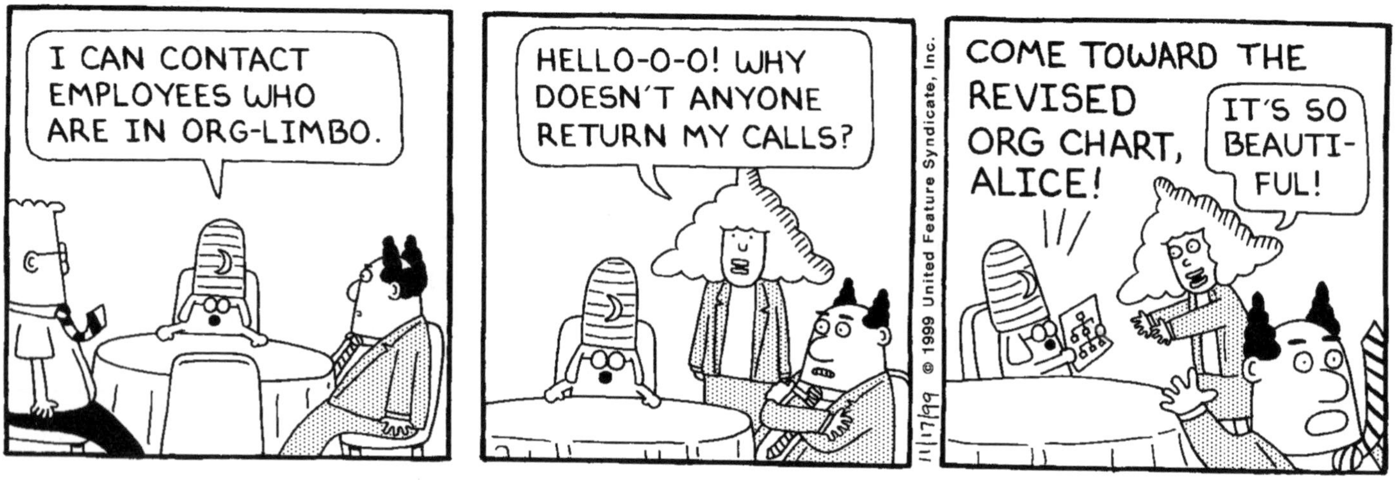
I CAN CONTACT EMPLOYEES WHO ARE IN ORG-LIMBO.
HELLO-O-O! WHY DOESN'T ANYONE RETURN MY CALLS?
11/17/99 © 1999 United Feature Syndicate, Inc.
COME TOWARD THE REVISED ORG CHART, ALICE!
IT'S SO BEAUTIFUL!

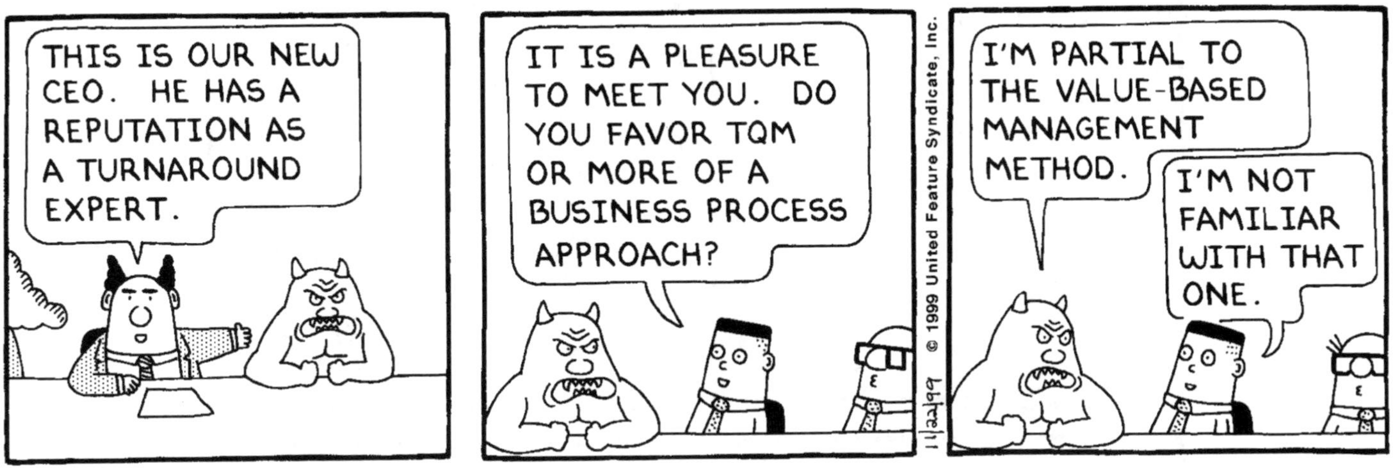
THIS IS OUR NEW CEO. HE HAS A REPUTATION AS A TURNAROUND EXPERT.
IT IS A PLEASURE TO MEET YOU. DO YOU FAVOR TQM OR MORE OF A BUSINESS PROCESS APPROACH?
11/22/99 © 1999 United Feature Syndicate, Inc.
I'M PARTIAL TO THE VALUE-BASED MANAGEMENT METHOD.
I'M NOT FAMILIAR WITH THAT ONE.

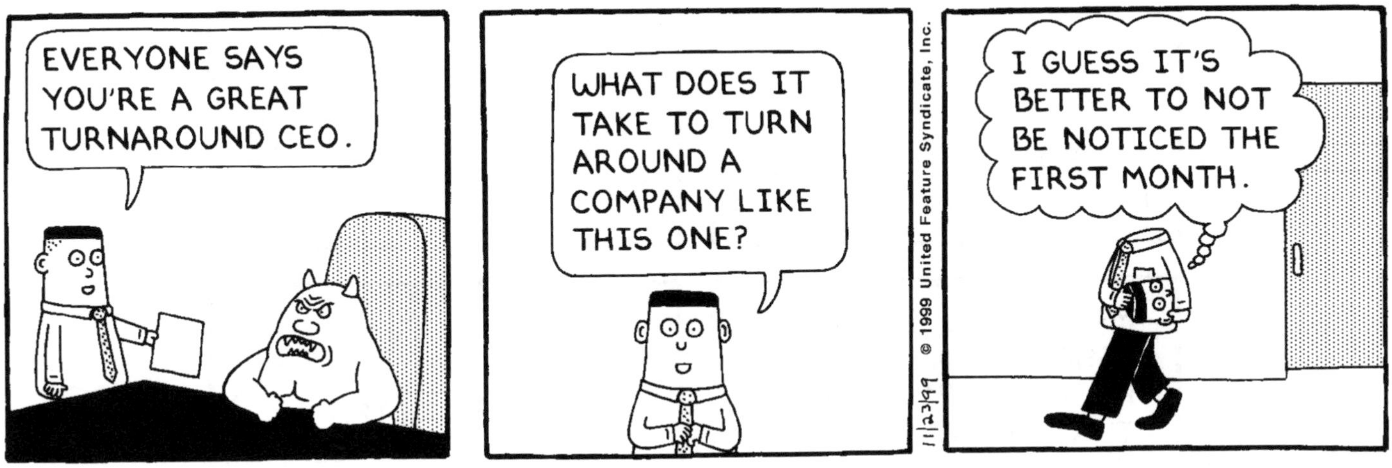
EVERYONE SAYS YOU'RE A GREAT TURNAROUND CEO.
WHAT DOES IT TAKE TO TURN AROUND A COMPANY LIKE THIS ONE?
11/23/99 © 1999 United Feature Syndicate, Inc.
I GUESS IT'S BETTER TO NOT BE NOTICED THE FIRST MONTH.

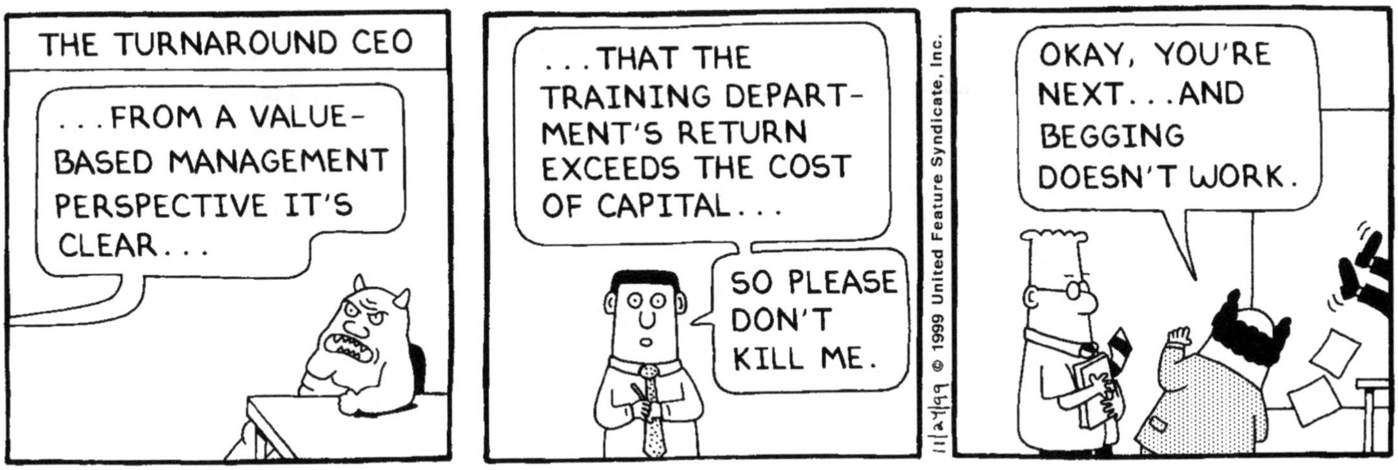
THE TURNAROUND CEO
...FROM A VALUE-BASED MANAGEMENT PERSPECTIVE IT'S CLEAR...
...THAT THE TRAINING DEPARTMENT'S RETURN EXCEEDS THE COST OF CAPITAL...
SO PLEASE DON'T KILL ME.
11/24/99 © 1999 United Feature Syndicate, Inc.
OKAY, YOU'RE NEXT...AND BEGGING DOESN'T WORK.

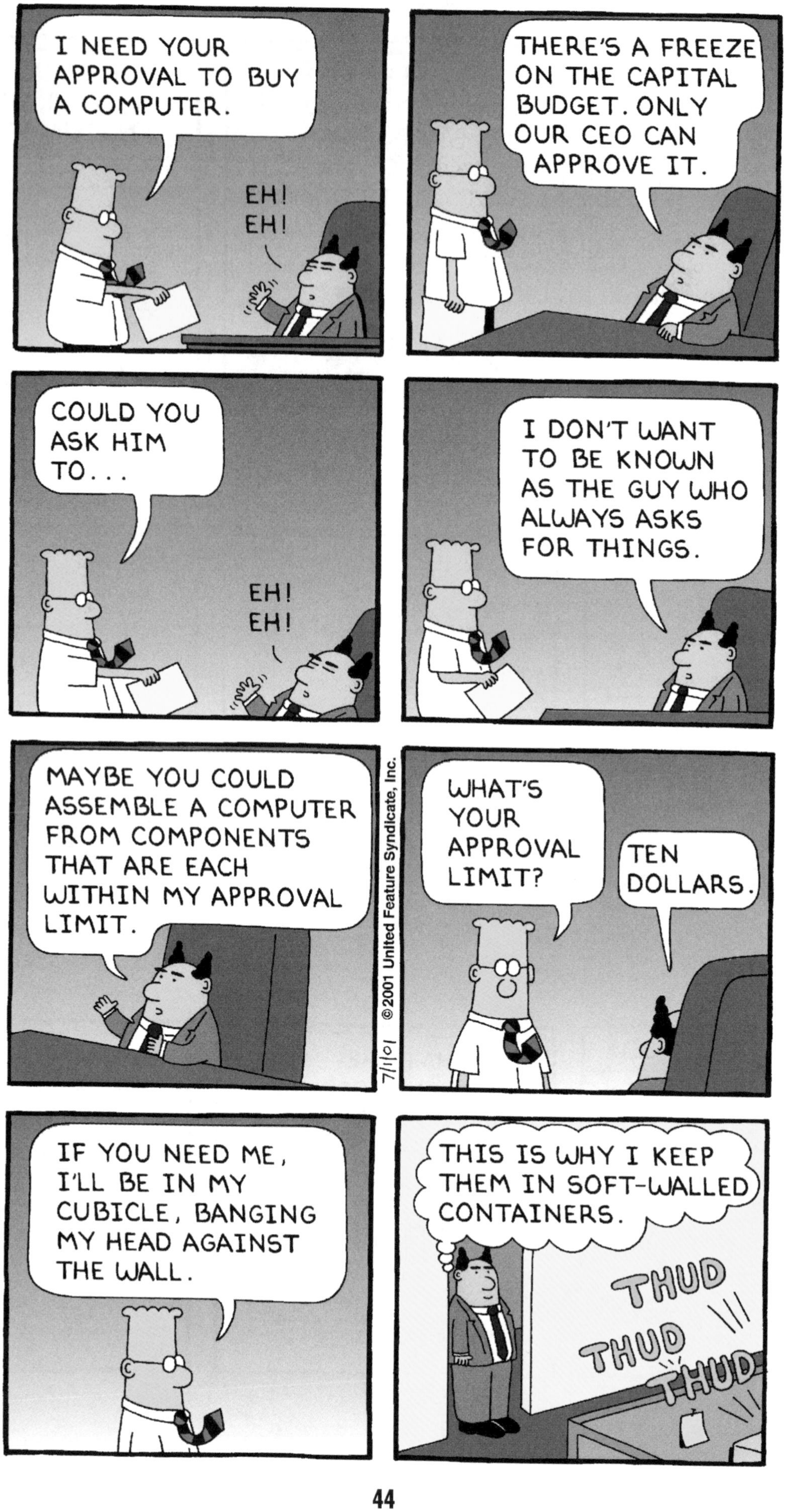
I NEED YOUR APPROVAL TO BUY A COMPUTER.
EH! EH!
THERE'S A FREEZE ON THE CAPITAL BUDGET. ONLY OUR CEO CAN APPROVE IT.
COULD YOU ASK HIM TO . . .
EH! EH!
I DON'T WANT TO BE KNOWN AS THE GUY WHO ALWAYS ASKS FOR THINGS.
MAYBE YOU COULD ASSEMBLE A COMPUTER FROM COMPONENTS THAT ARE EACH WITHIN MY APPROVAL LIMIT.
7/1/01 ©2001 United Feature Syndicate, Inc.
WHAT'S YOUR APPROVAL LIMIT?
TEN DOLLARS.
IF YOU NEED ME, I'LL BE IN MY CUBICLE, BANGING MY HEAD AGAINST THE WALL.
THIS IS WHY I KEEP THEM IN SOFT-WALLED CONTAINERS.
THUD
THUD
THUD

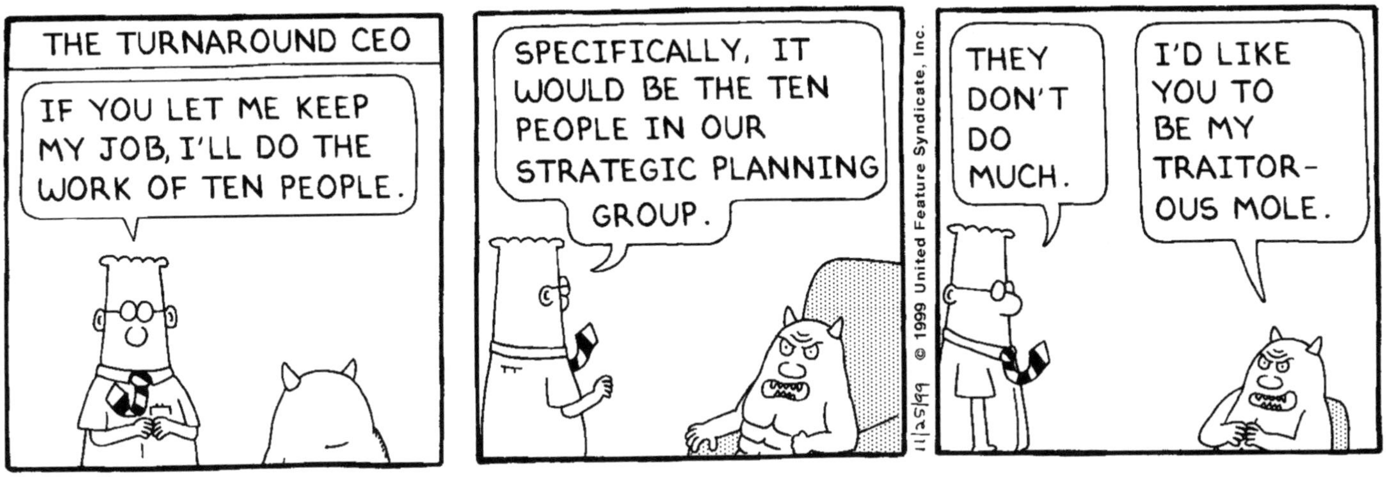
THE TURNAROUND CEO
IF YOU LET ME KEEP MY JOB, I'LL DO THE WORK OF TEN PEOPLE.
SPECIFICALLY, IT WOULD BE THE TEN PEOPLE IN OUR STRATEGIC PLANNING GROUP.
THEY DON'T DO MUCH.
I'D LIKE YOU TO BE MY TRAITOR-OUS MOLE.
11/25/99 © 1999 United Feature Syndicate, Inc.

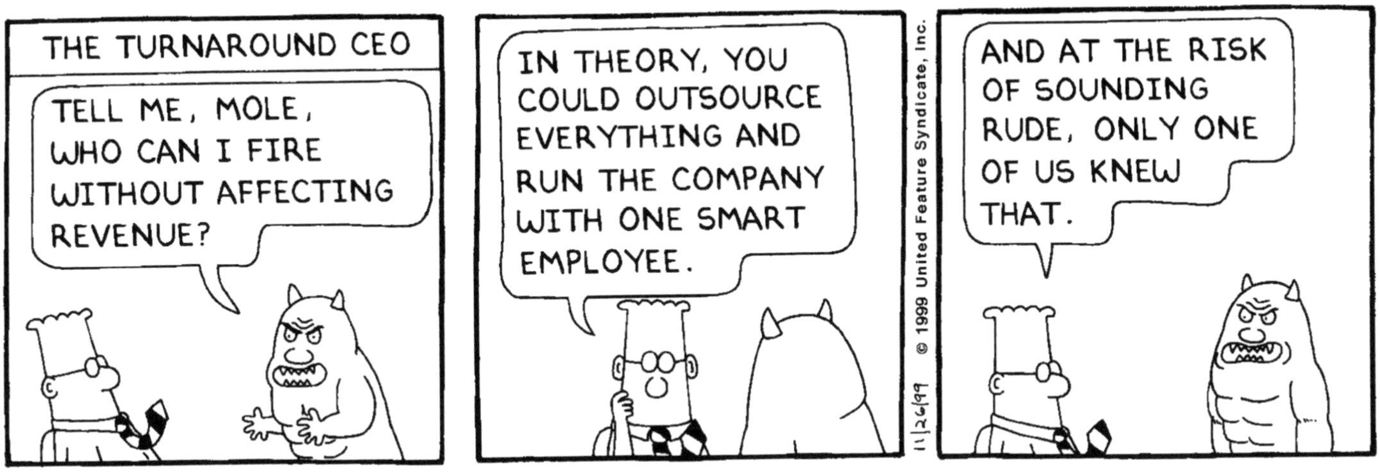
THE TURNAROUND CEO
TELL ME, MOLE, WHO CAN I FIRE WITHOUT AFFECTING REVENUE?
IN THEORY, YOU COULD OUTSOURCE EVERYTHING AND RUN THE COMPANY WITH ONE SMART EMPLOYEE.
AND AT THE RISK OF SOUNDING RUDE, ONLY ONE OF US KNEW THAT.
11/26/99 © 1999 United Feature Syndicate, Inc.

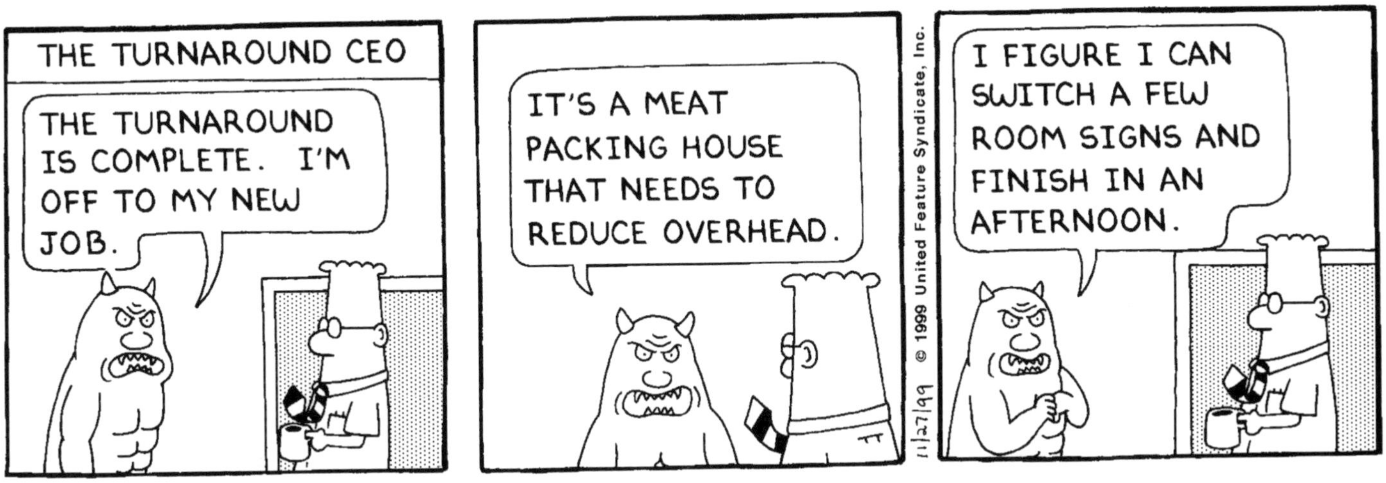
THE TURNAROUND CEO
THE TURNAROUND IS COMPLETE. I'M OFF TO MY NEW JOB.
IT'S A MEAT PACKING HOUSE THAT NEEDS TO REDUCE OVERHEAD.
I FIGURE I CAN SWITCH A FEW ROOM SIGNS AND FINISH IN AN AFTERNOON.
11/27/99 © 1999 United Feature Syndicate, Inc.

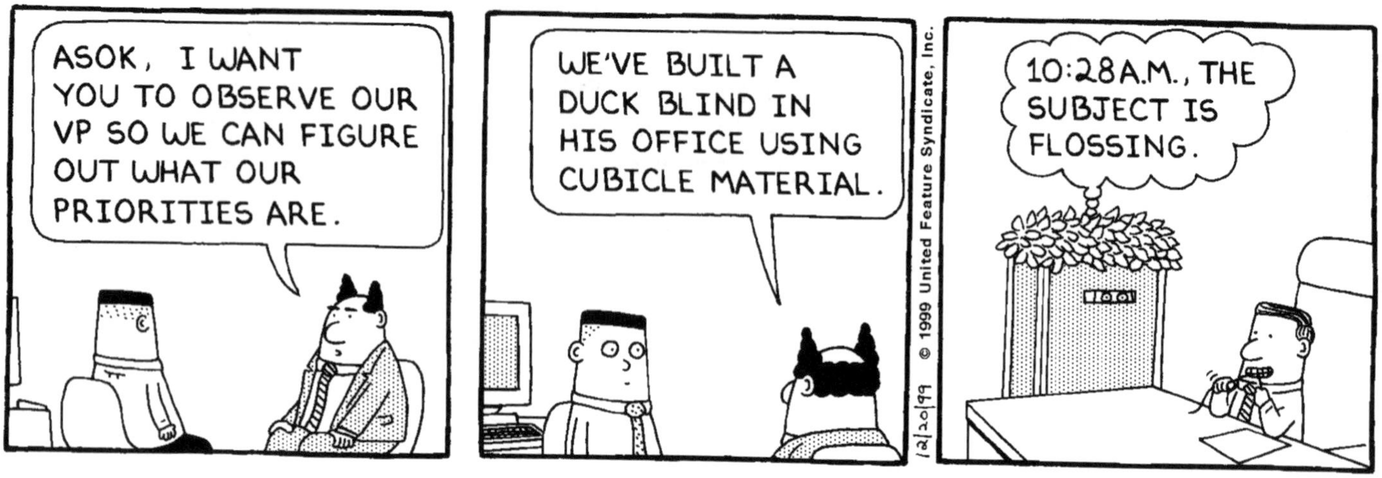
ASOK, I WANT YOU TO OBSERVE OUR VP SO WE CAN FIGURE OUT WHAT OUR PRIORITIES ARE.
WE'VE BUILT A DUCK BLIND IN HIS OFFICE USING CUBICLE MATERIAL.
12/20/99 © 1999 United Feature Syndicate, Inc.
10:28 A.M., THE SUBJECT IS FLOSSING.

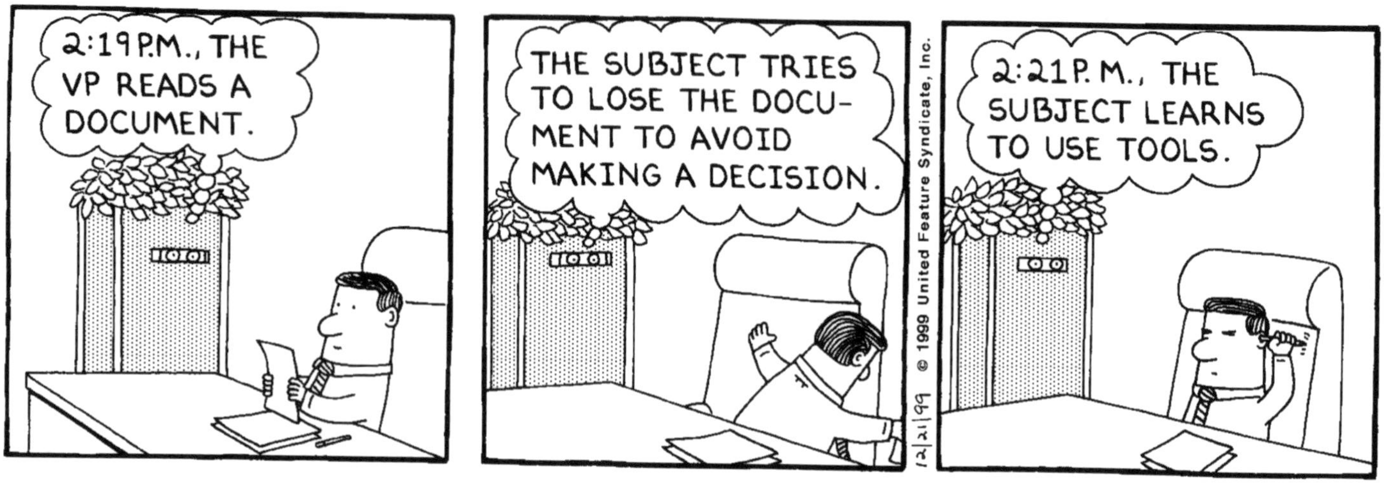
2:19 P.M., THE VP READS A DOCUMENT.
THE SUBJECT TRIES TO LOSE THE DOCUMENT TO AVOID MAKING A DECISION.
12/21/99 © 1999 United Feature Syndicate, Inc.
2:21 P.M., THE SUBJECT LEARNS TO USE TOOLS.

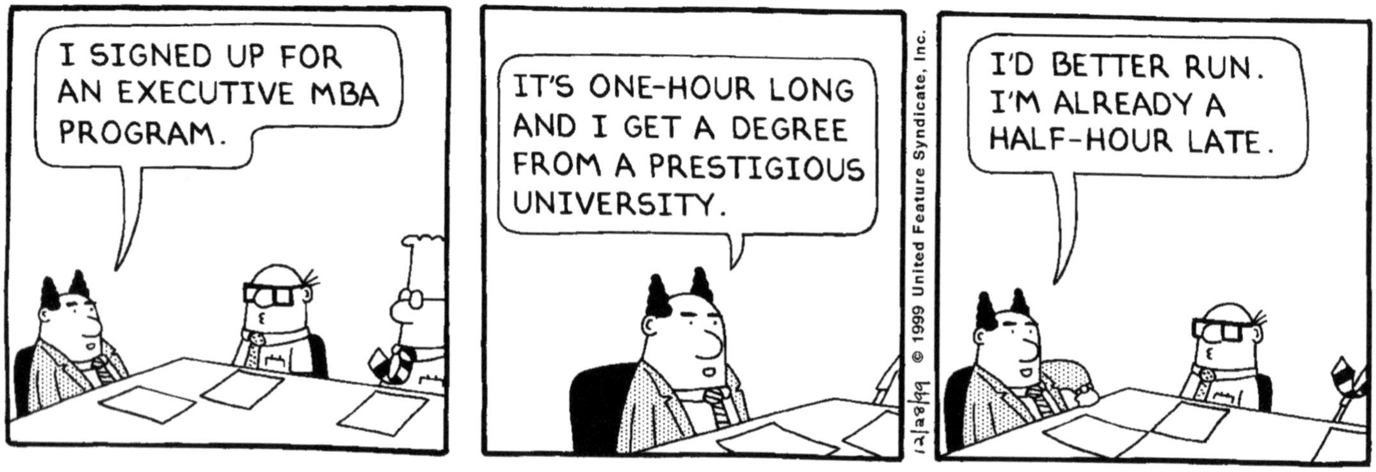
I SIGNED UP FOR AN EXECUTIVE MBA PROGRAM.
IT'S ONE-HOUR LONG AND I GET A DEGREE FROM A PRESTIGIOUS UNIVERSITY.
12/28/99 © 1999 United Feature Syndicate, Inc.
I'D BETTER RUN. I'M ALREADY A HALF-HOUR LATE.

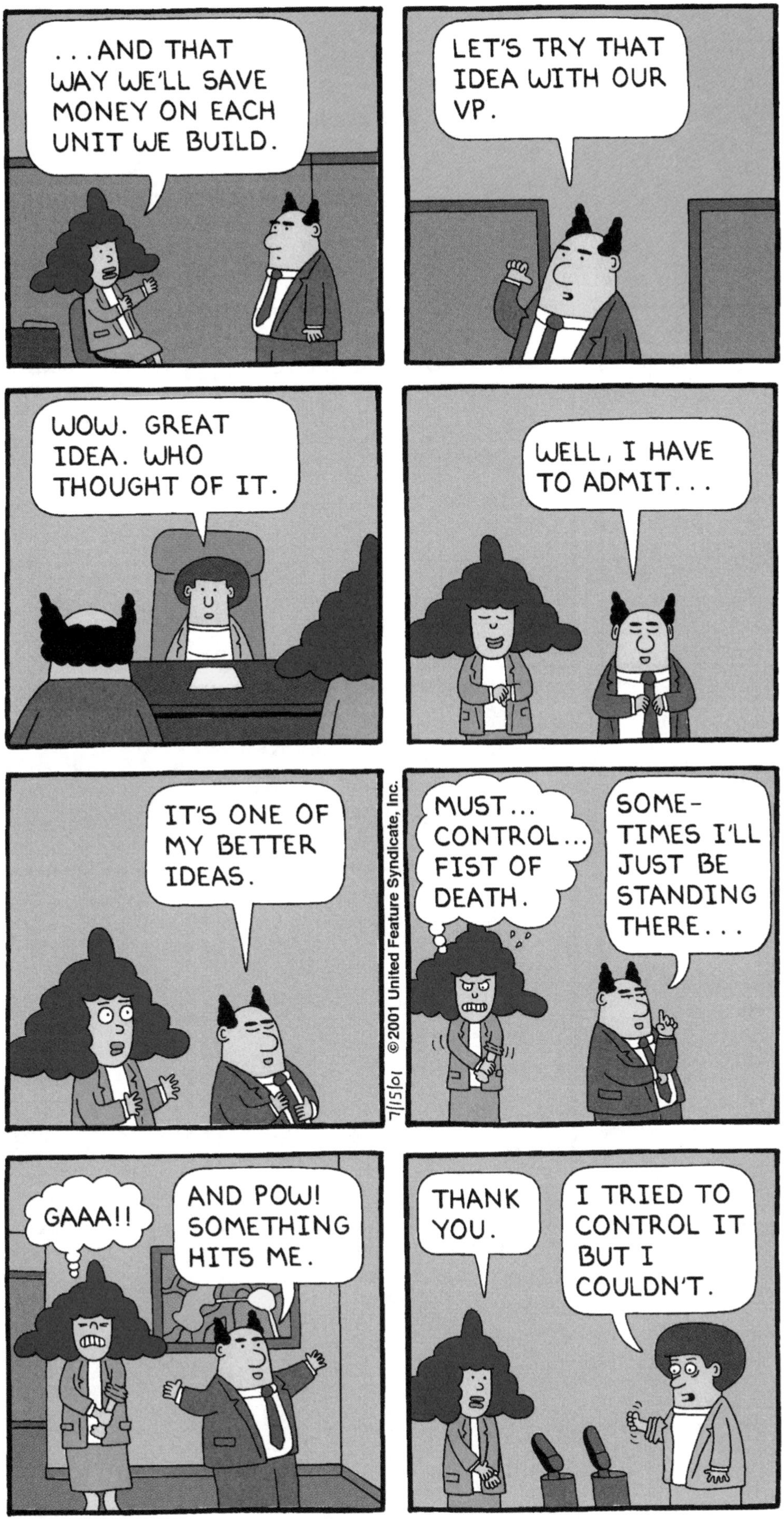
...AND THAT WAY WE'LL SAVE MONEY ON EACH UNIT WE BUILD.
LET'S TRY THAT IDEA WITH OUR VP.
WOW. GREAT IDEA. WHO THOUGHT OF IT.
WELL, I HAVE TO ADMIT...
IT'S ONE OF MY BETTER IDEAS.
©2001 United Feature Syndicate, Inc.
7/15/01
MUST... CONTROL... FIST OF DEATH.
SOME-TIMES I'LL JUST BE STANDING THERE...
GAAA!!
AND POW! SOMETHING HITS ME.
THANK YOU.
I TRIED TO CONTROL IT BUT I COULDN'T.

DOGBERT THE CEO
START SOME RUMORS, SPREAD SOME LIES. . .
WAIT FOR THE STOCK TO POP UP. . . EXERCISE MY STOCK OPTIONS. . .
BANG!
10-16-08 © 2008 Scott Adams, Inc./Dist. by UFS, Inc.
HOW DID PEOPLE STEAL BEFORE COMPUTERS?

I AM STEPPING DOWN AS CEO SO I CAN SPEND MORE TIME WITH THE MONEY I STOLE FROM THIS HELLHOLE.
I NEED YOU AND YOU TO CARRY HUGE BAGS OF CASH TO MY HELICOPTER.
10-17-08 © 2008 Scott Adams, Inc./Dist. by UFS, Inc.
THE WORST PART IS THAT IF HE EVER WRITES A BOOK, I'LL PROBABLY BUY IT.
$
$

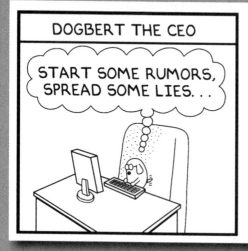

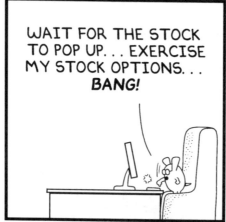

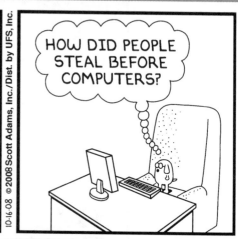

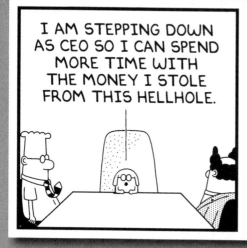

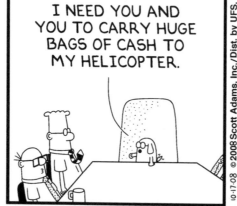

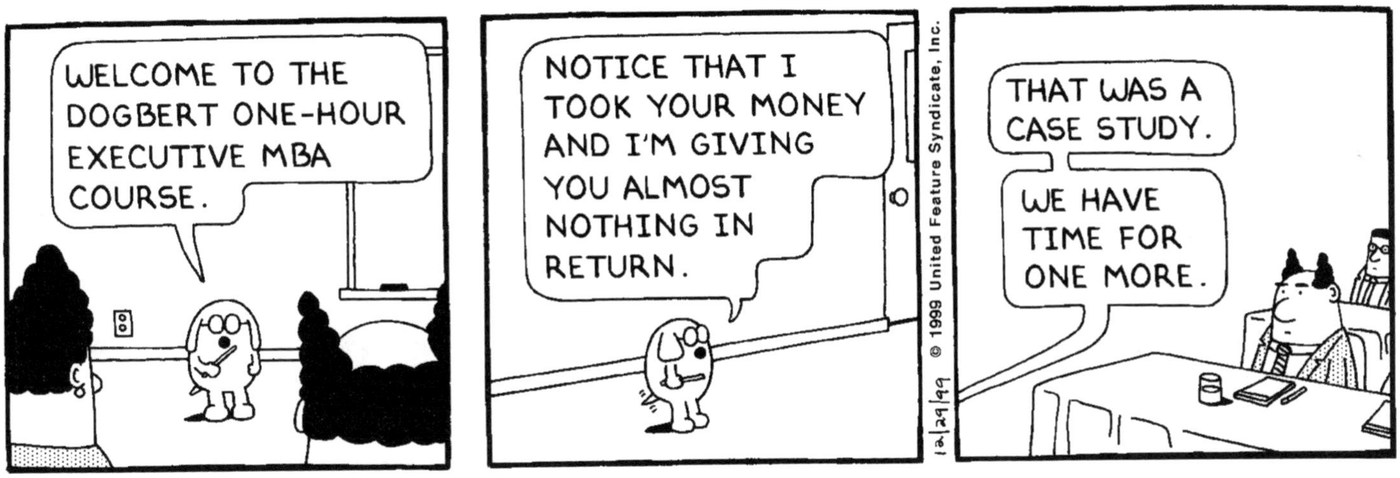
WELCOME TO THE DOGBERT ONE-HOUR EXECUTIVE MBA COURSE.
NOTICE THAT I TOOK YOUR MONEY AND I'M GIVING YOU ALMOST NOTHING IN RETURN.
12/29/99 © 1999 United Feature Syndicate, Inc.
THAT WAS A CASE STUDY.
WE HAVE TIME FOR ONE MORE.

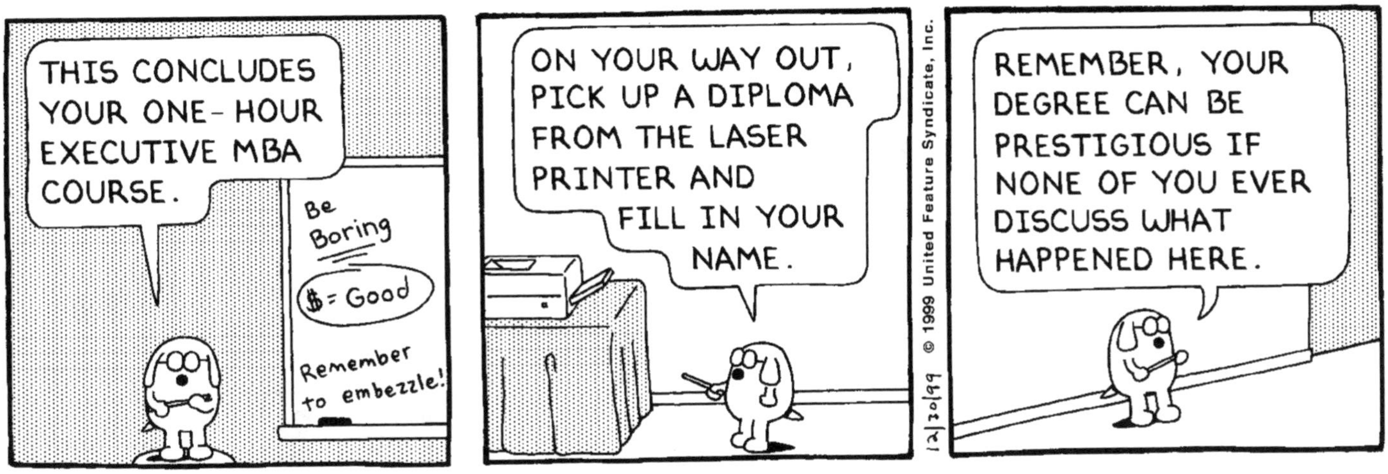
THIS CONCLUDES YOUR ONE-HOUR EXECUTIVE MBA COURSE.
Be Boring
$ = Good
Remember to embezzle!
ON YOUR WAY OUT, PICK UP A DIPLOMA FROM THE LASER PRINTER AND FILL IN YOUR NAME.
12/30/99 © 1999 United Feature Syndicate, Inc.
REMEMBER, YOUR DEGREE CAN BE PRESTIGIOUS IF NONE OF YOU EVER DISCUSS WHAT HAPPENED HERE.

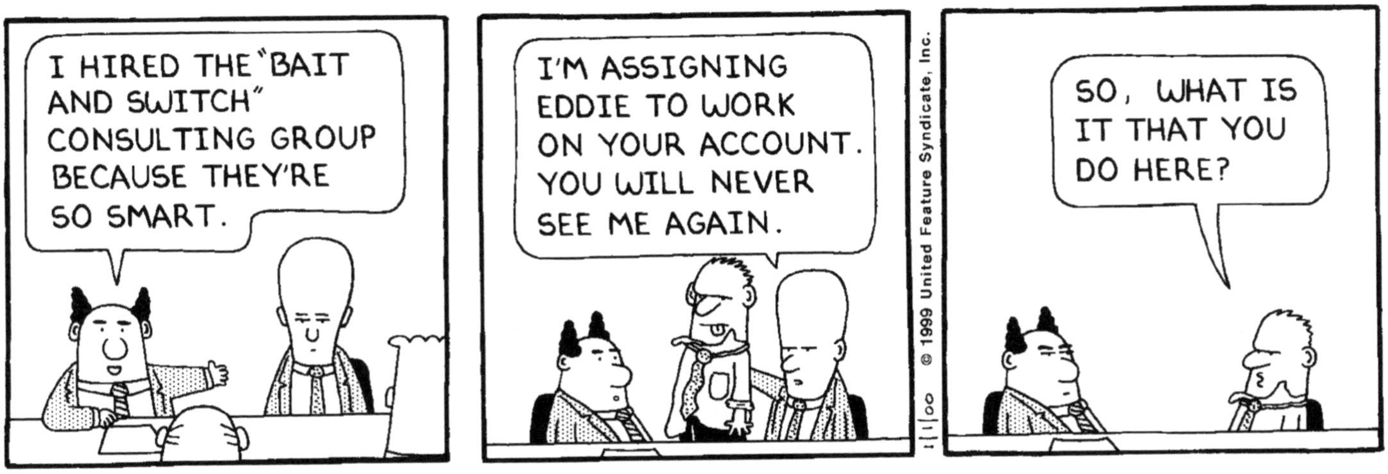
I HIRED THE "BAIT AND SWITCH" CONSULTING GROUP BECAUSE THEY'RE SO SMART.
I'M ASSIGNING EDDIE TO WORK ON YOUR ACCOUNT. YOU WILL NEVER SEE ME AGAIN.
1/1/00 © 1999 United Feature Syndicate, Inc.
SO, WHAT IS IT THAT YOU DO HERE?

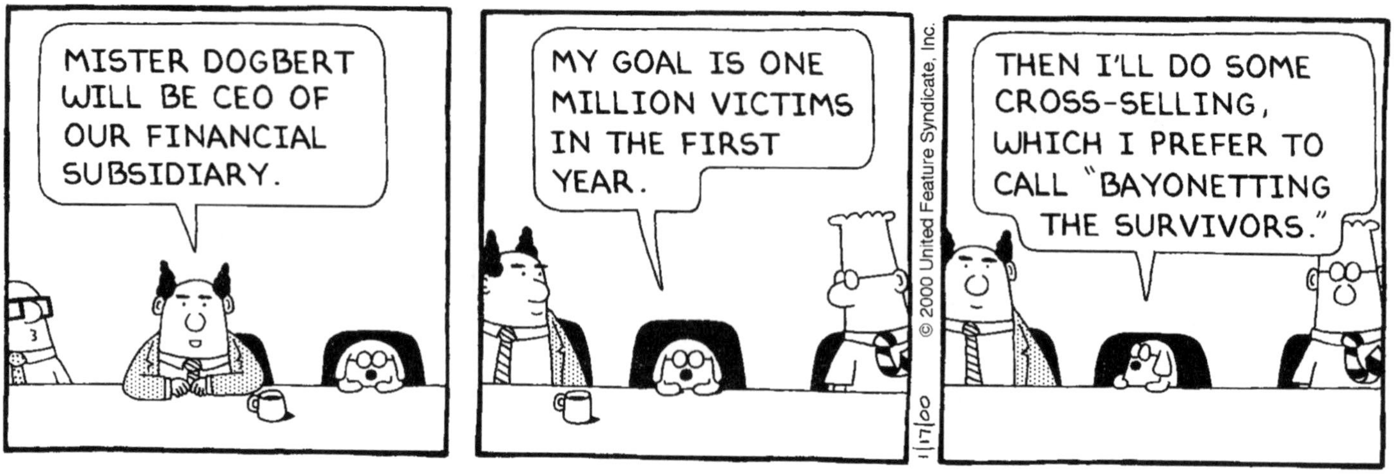
MISTER DOGBERT WILL BE CEO OF OUR FINANCIAL SUBSIDIARY.
MY GOAL IS ONE MILLION VICTIMS IN THE FIRST YEAR.
THEN I'LL DO SOME CROSS-SELLING, WHICH I PREFER TO CALL "BAYONETTING THE SURVIVORS."
© 2000 United Feature Syndicate, Inc.
1/17/00

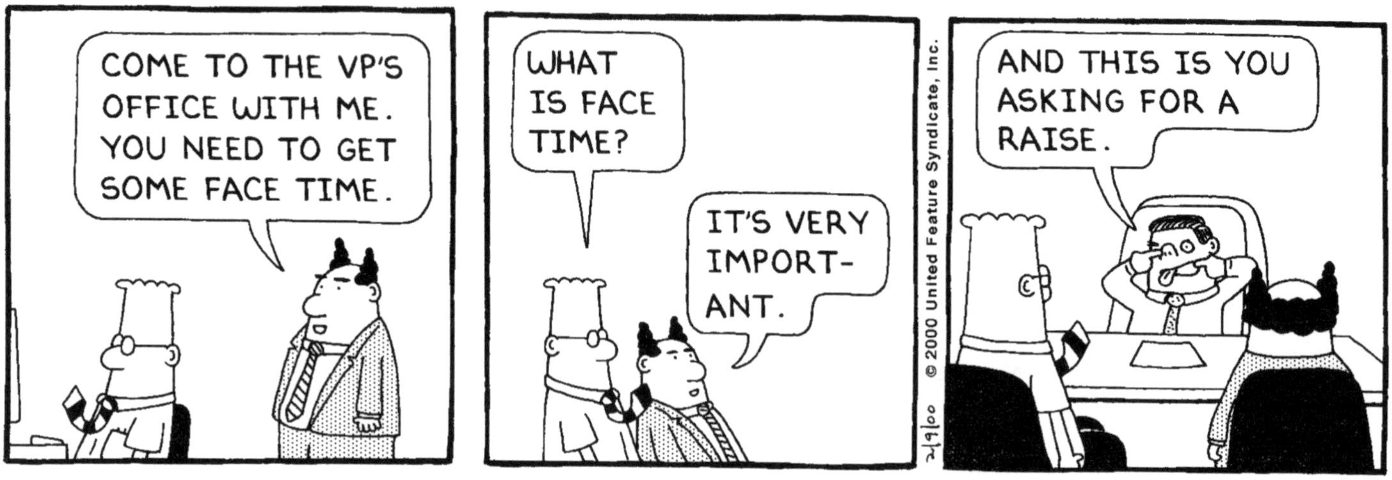
COME TO THE VP'S OFFICE WITH ME. YOU NEED TO GET SOME FACE TIME.
WHAT IS FACE TIME?
IT'S VERY IMPORT-ANT.
AND THIS IS YOU ASKING FOR A RAISE.
© 2000 United Feature Syndicate, Inc.
2/9/00

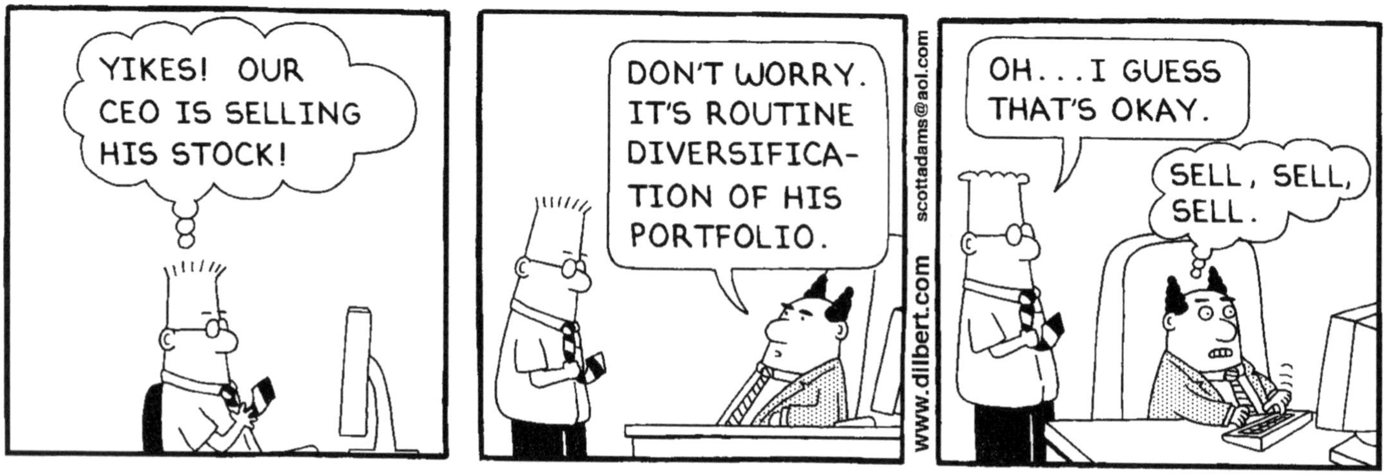
YIKES! OUR CEO IS SELLING HIS STOCK!
DON'T WORRY. IT'S ROUTINE DIVERSIFICA-TION OF HIS PORTFOLIO.
OH...I GUESS THAT'S OKAY.
SELL, SELL, SELL.
scottadams@aol.com
www.dilbert.com

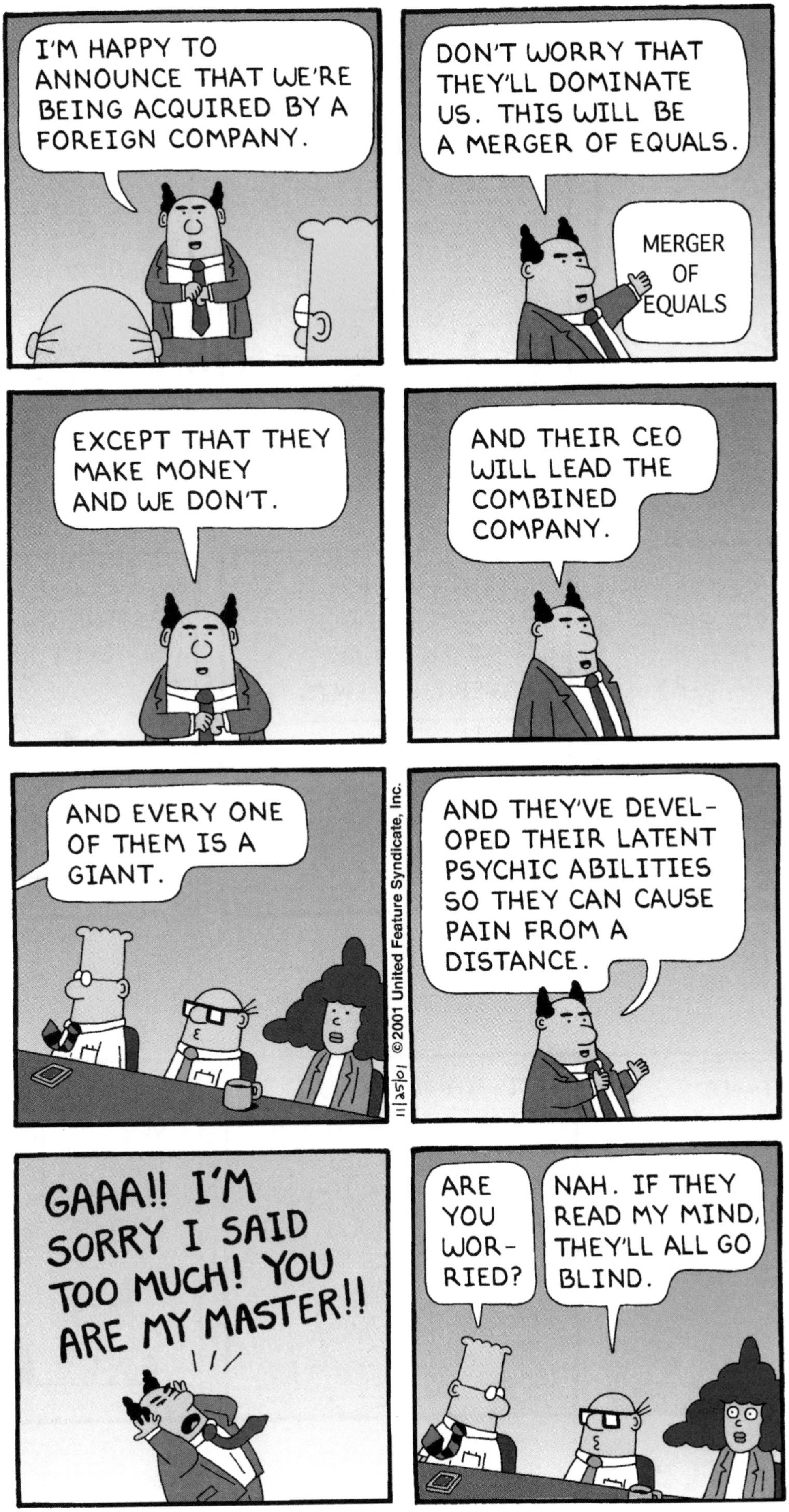
I'M HAPPY TO ANNOUNCE THAT WE'RE BEING ACQUIRED BY A FOREIGN COMPANY.
DON'T WORRY THAT THEY'LL DOMINATE US. THIS WILL BE A MERGER OF EQUALS.
MERGER OF EQUALS
EXCEPT THAT THEY MAKE MONEY AND WE DON'T.
AND THEIR CEO WILL LEAD THE COMBINED COMPANY.
AND EVERY ONE OF THEM IS A GIANT.
AND THEY'VE DEVEL-OPED THEIR LATENT PSYCHIC ABILITIES SO THEY CAN CAUSE PAIN FROM A DISTANCE.
GAAA!! I'M SORRY I SAID TOO MUCH! YOU ARE MY MASTER!!
ARE YOU WOR-RIED?
NAH. IF THEY READ MY MIND, THEY'LL ALL GO BLIND.

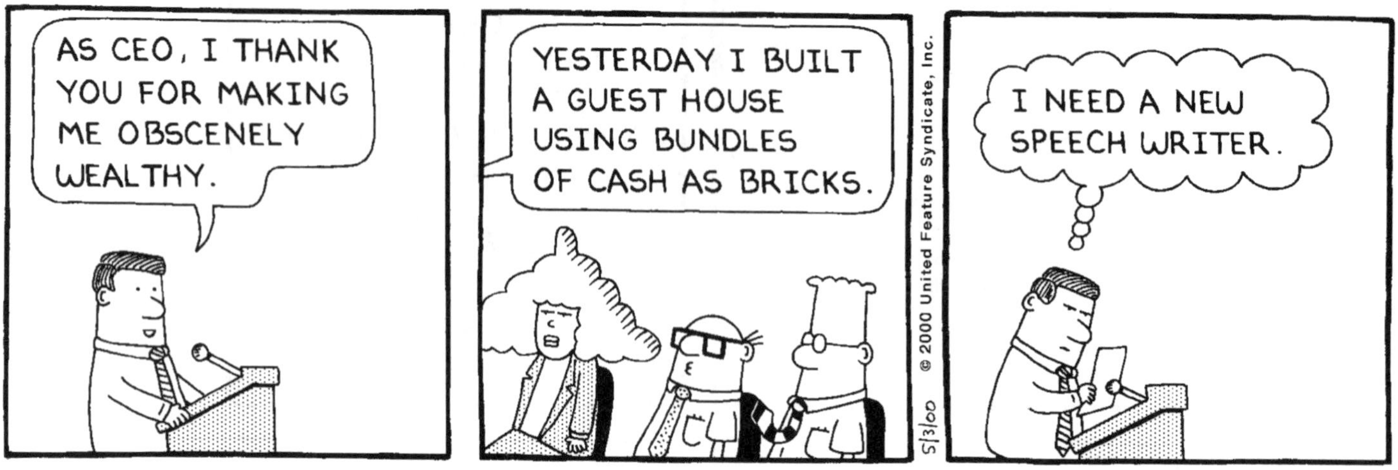
AS CEO, I THANK YOU FOR MAKING ME OBSCENELY WEALTHY.
YESTERDAY I BUILT A GUEST HOUSE USING BUNDLES OF CASH AS BRICKS.
5/3/00 © 2000 United Feature Syndicate, Inc.
I NEED A NEW SPEECH WRITER.

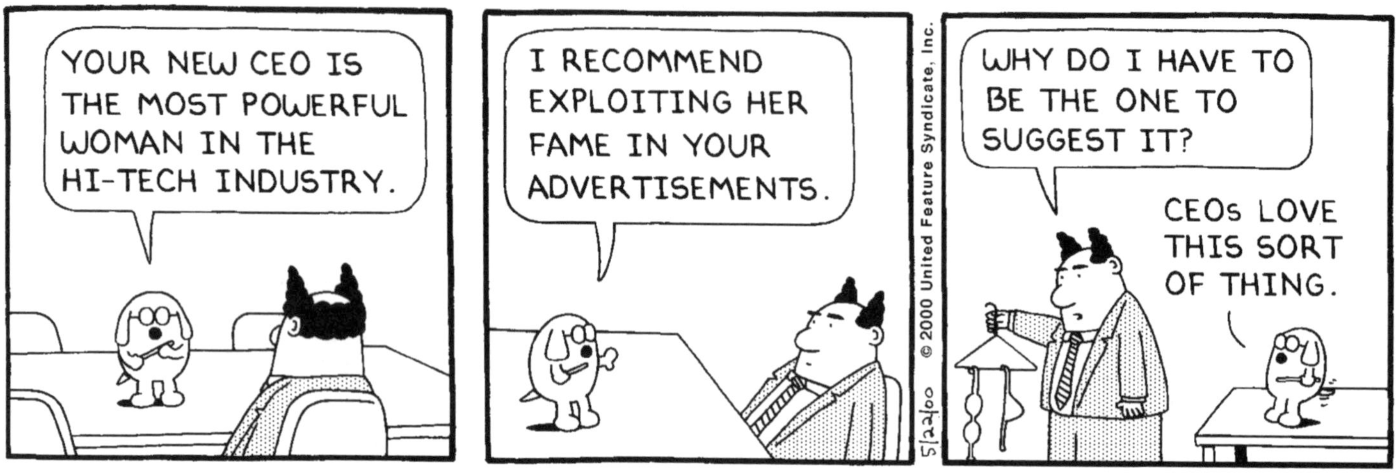
YOUR NEW CEO IS THE MOST POWERFUL WOMAN IN THE HI-TECH INDUSTRY.
I RECOMMEND EXPLOITING HER FAME IN YOUR ADVERTISEMENTS.
5/22/00 © 2000 United Feature Syndicate, Inc.
WHY DO I HAVE TO BE THE ONE TO SUGGEST IT?
CEOs LOVE THIS SORT OF THING.

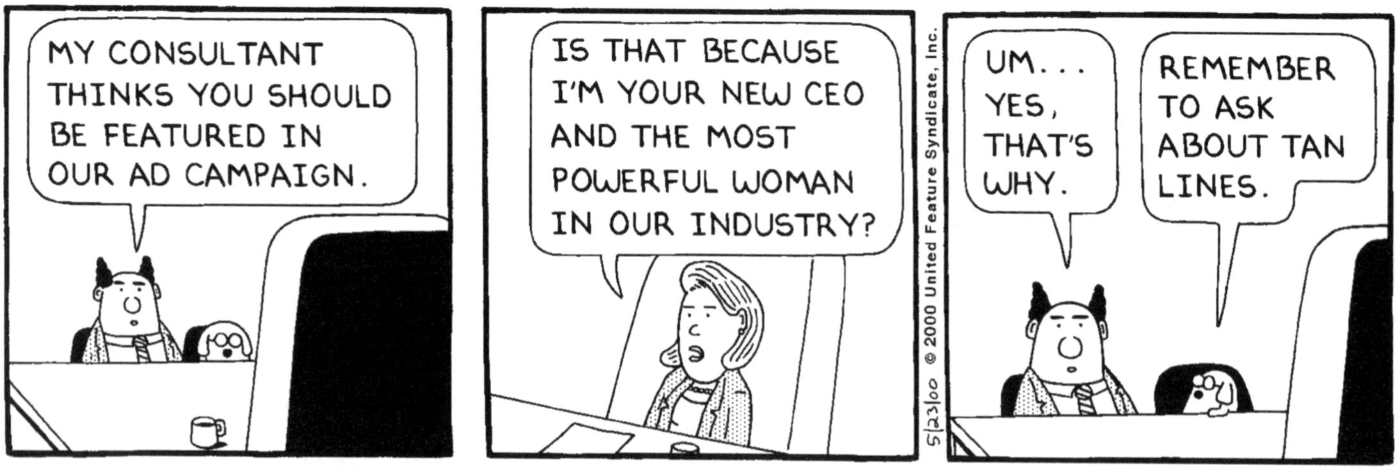
MY CONSULTANT THINKS YOU SHOULD BE FEATURED IN OUR AD CAMPAIGN.
IS THAT BECAUSE I'M YOUR NEW CEO AND THE MOST POWERFUL WOMAN IN OUR INDUSTRY?
5/23/00 © 2000 United Feature Syndicate, Inc.
UM... YES, THAT'S WHY.
REMEMBER TO ASK ABOUT TAN LINES.

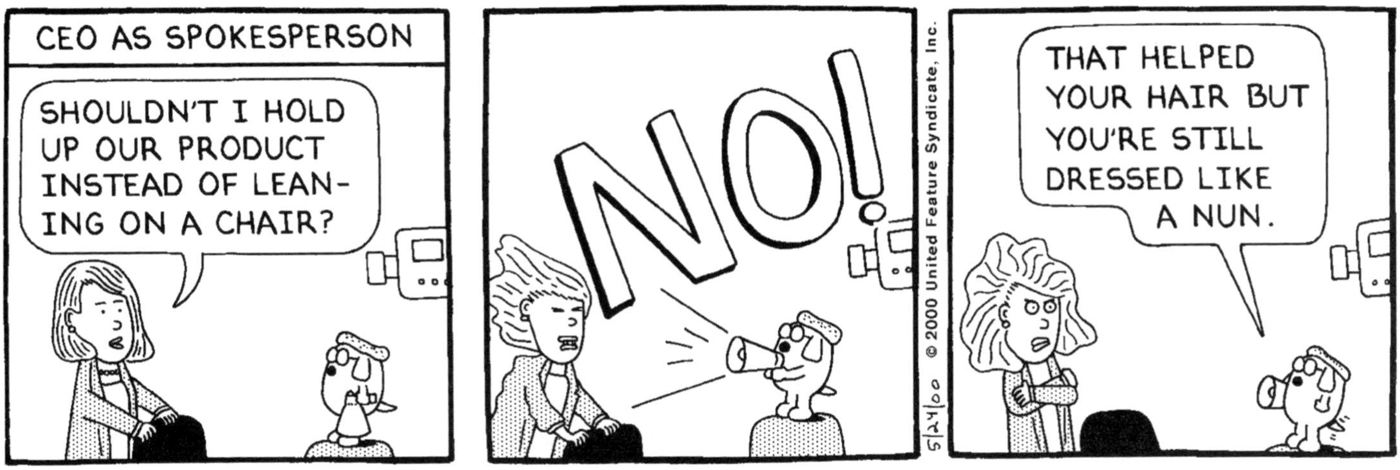
CEO AS SPOKESPERSON
SHOULDN'T I HOLD UP OUR PRODUCT INSTEAD OF LEAN-ING ON A CHAIR?
NO!
THAT HELPED YOUR HAIR BUT YOU'RE STILL DRESSED LIKE A NUN.
5/24/00
© 2000 United Feature Syndicate, Inc.

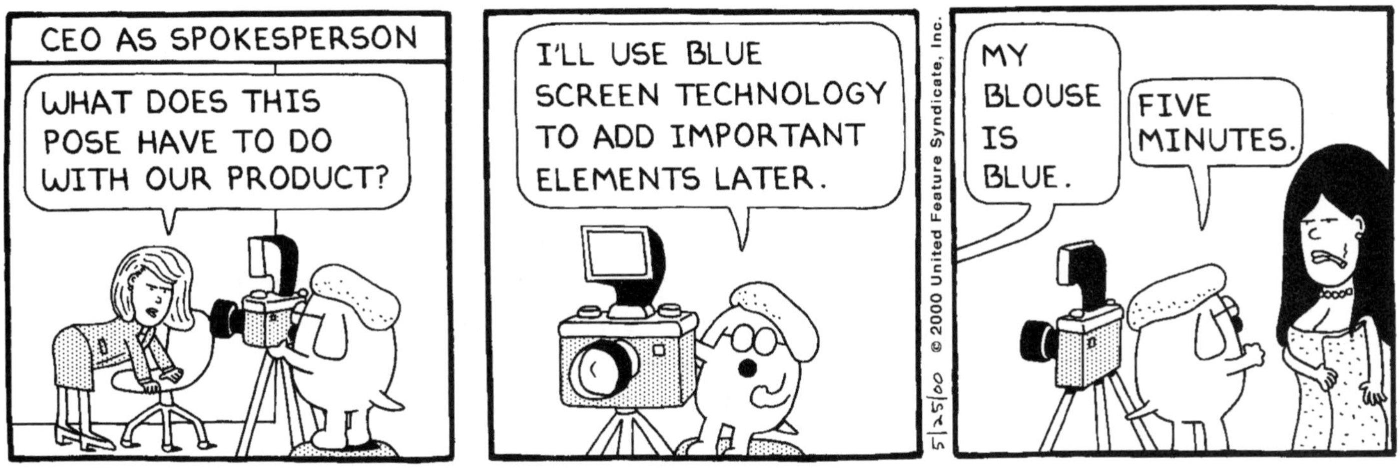
CEO AS SPOKESPERSON
WHAT DOES THIS POSE HAVE TO DO WITH OUR PRODUCT?
I'LL USE BLUE SCREEN TECHNOLOGY TO ADD IMPORTANT ELEMENTS LATER.
MY BLOUSE IS BLUE.
FIVE MINUTES.
5/25/00
© 2000 United Feature Syndicate, Inc.

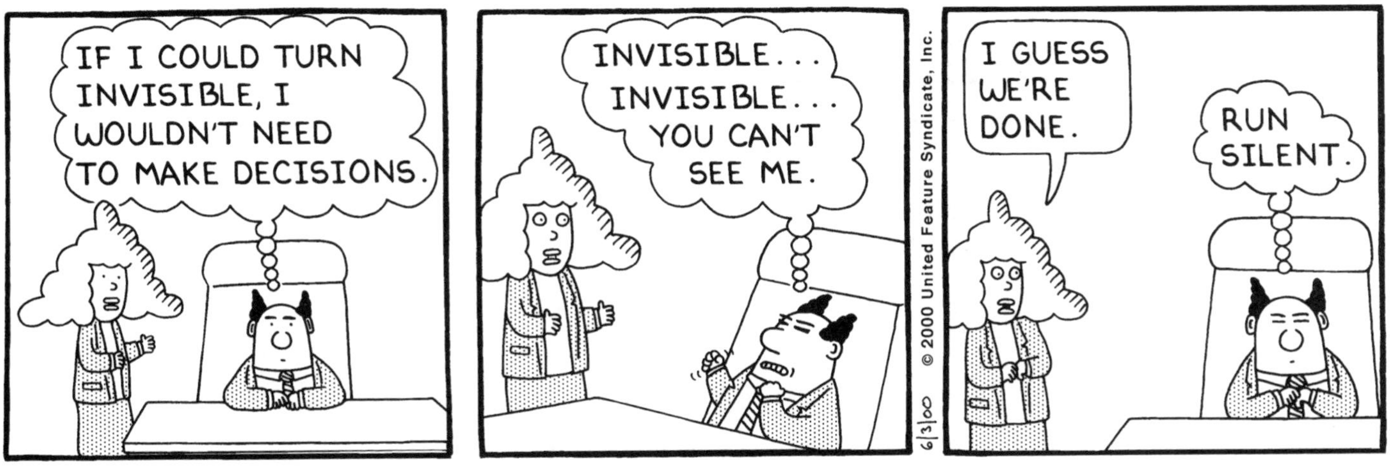
IF I COULD TURN INVISIBLE, I WOULDN'T NEED TO MAKE DECISIONS.
INVISIBLE... INVISIBLE... YOU CAN'T SEE ME.
I GUESS WE'RE DONE.
RUN SILENT.
6/3/00
© 2000 United Feature Syndicate, Inc.

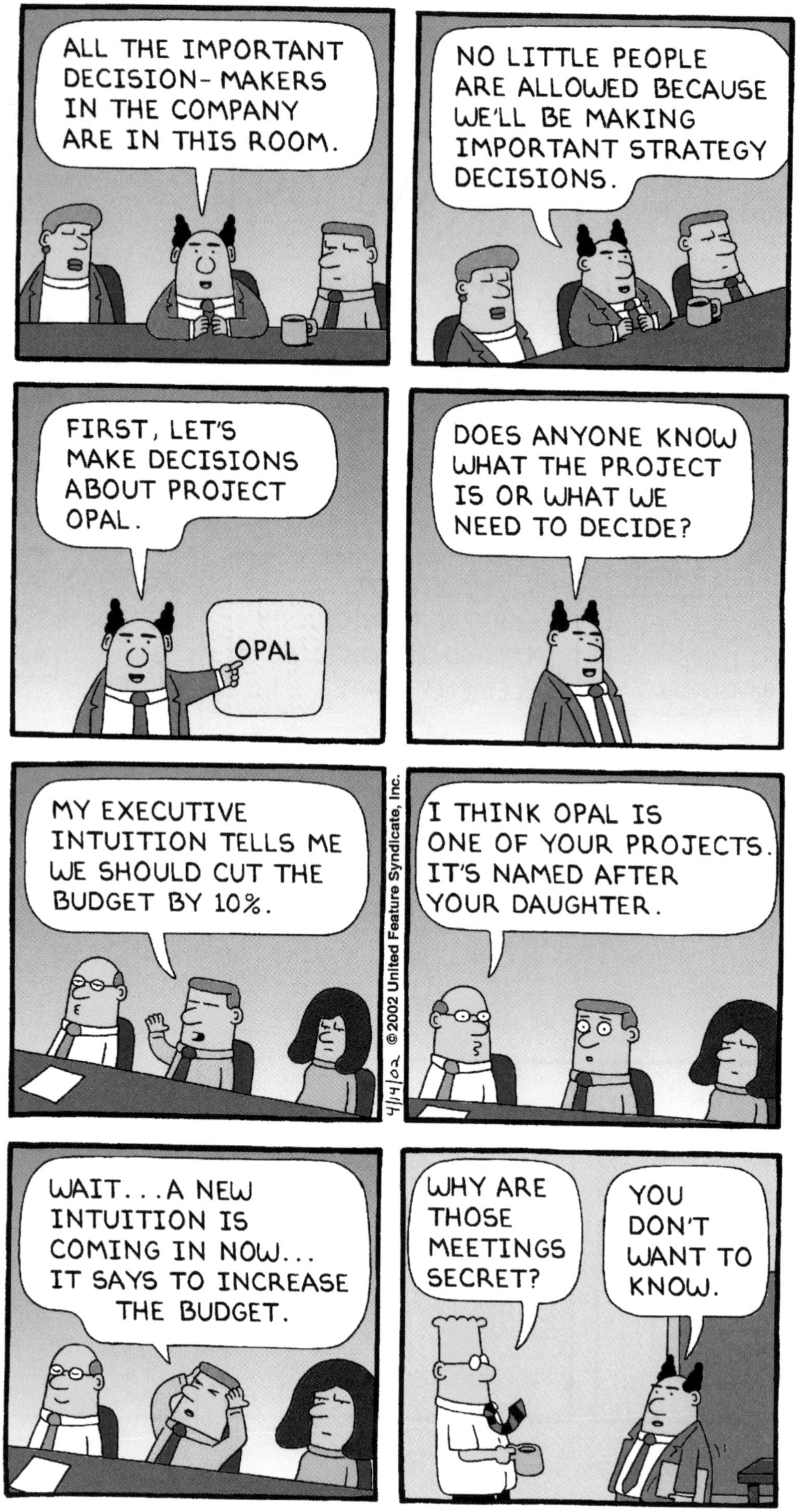
ALL THE IMPORTANT DECISION-MAKERS IN THE COMPANY ARE IN THIS ROOM.
NO LITTLE PEOPLE ARE ALLOWED BECAUSE WE'LL BE MAKING IMPORTANT STRATEGY DECISIONS.
FIRST, LET'S MAKE DECISIONS ABOUT PROJECT OPAL.
OPAL
DOES ANYONE KNOW WHAT THE PROJECT IS OR WHAT WE NEED TO DECIDE?
MY EXECUTIVE INTUITION TELLS ME WE SHOULD CUT THE BUDGET BY 10%.
4/14/02 ©2002 United Feature Syndicate, Inc.
I THINK OPAL IS ONE OF YOUR PROJECTS. IT'S NAMED AFTER YOUR DAUGHTER.
WAIT. . . A NEW INTUITION IS COMING IN NOW. . . IT SAYS TO INCREASE THE BUDGET.
WHY ARE THOSE MEETINGS SECRET?
YOU DON'T WANT TO KNOW.

DOGBERT THE CEO
I'M HAPPY TO ANNOUNCE THAT THE GOVERNMENT GAVE US A BAILOUT LOAN OF $25 BILLION.
I'M EVEN HAPPIER TO ANNOUNCE THAT I KEPT THE ENTIRE AMOUNT FOR MY BONUS.
WHO WANTS TO SEE A PICTURE OF MY ISLAND FORTRESS?
2-26-09 © 2009 Scott Adams, Inc./Dist. by UFS, Inc.

DOGBERT THE CEO
YOU WANT A RAISE? I HAVE ONE WORD FOR YOU.
GOINK!
I LOVE HAVING A NEW FAVORITE WORD.
3-23-09 © 2009 Scott Adams, Inc./Dist. by UFS, Inc.

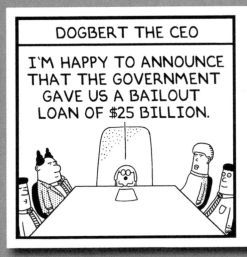

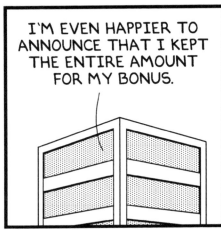

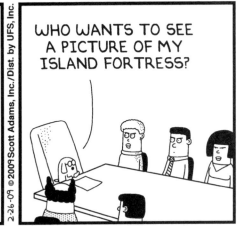

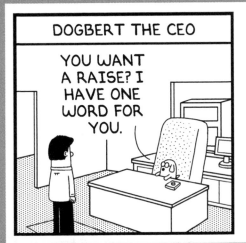

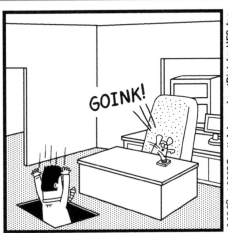

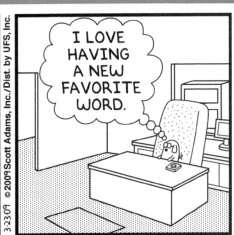

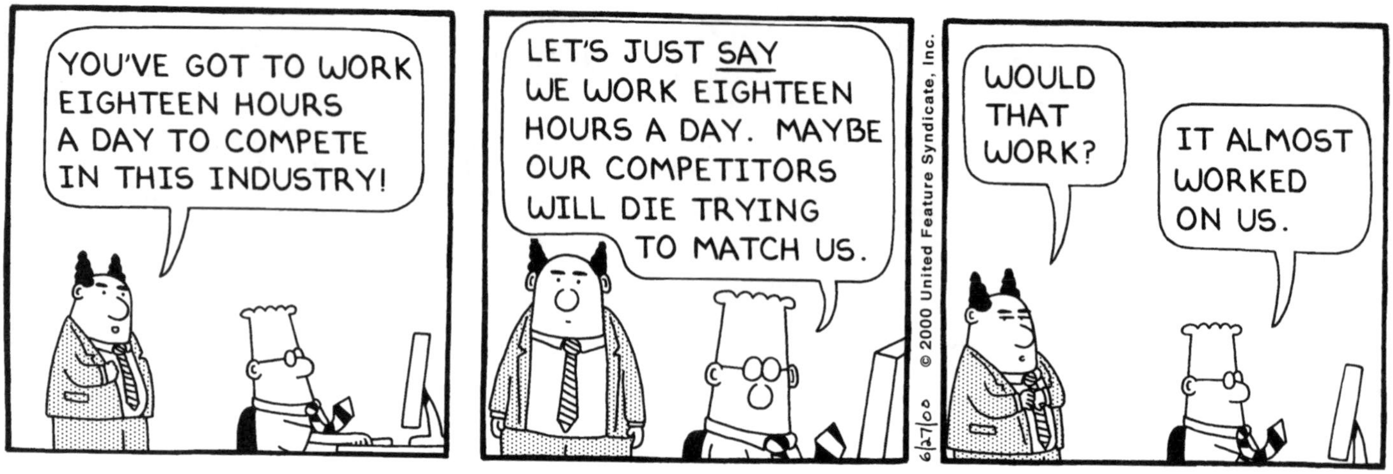
YOU'VE GOT TO WORK EIGHTEEN HOURS A DAY TO COMPETE IN THIS INDUSTRY!
LET'S JUST SAY WE WORK EIGHTEEN HOURS A DAY. MAYBE OUR COMPETITORS WILL DIE TRYING TO MATCH US.
6/27/00 © 2000 United Feature Syndicate, Inc.
WOULD THAT WORK?
IT ALMOST WORKED ON US.

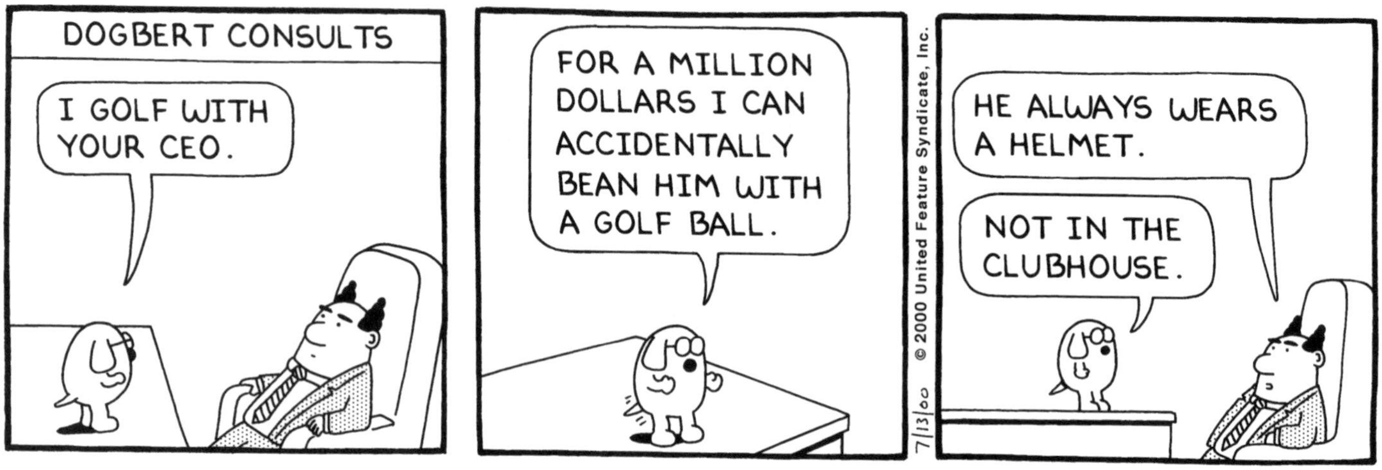
DOGBERT CONSULTS
I GOLF WITH YOUR CEO.
FOR A MILLION DOLLARS I CAN ACCIDENTALLY BEAN HIM WITH A GOLF BALL.
7/13/00 © 2000 United Feature Syndicate, Inc.
HE ALWAYS WEARS A HELMET.
NOT IN THE CLUBHOUSE.

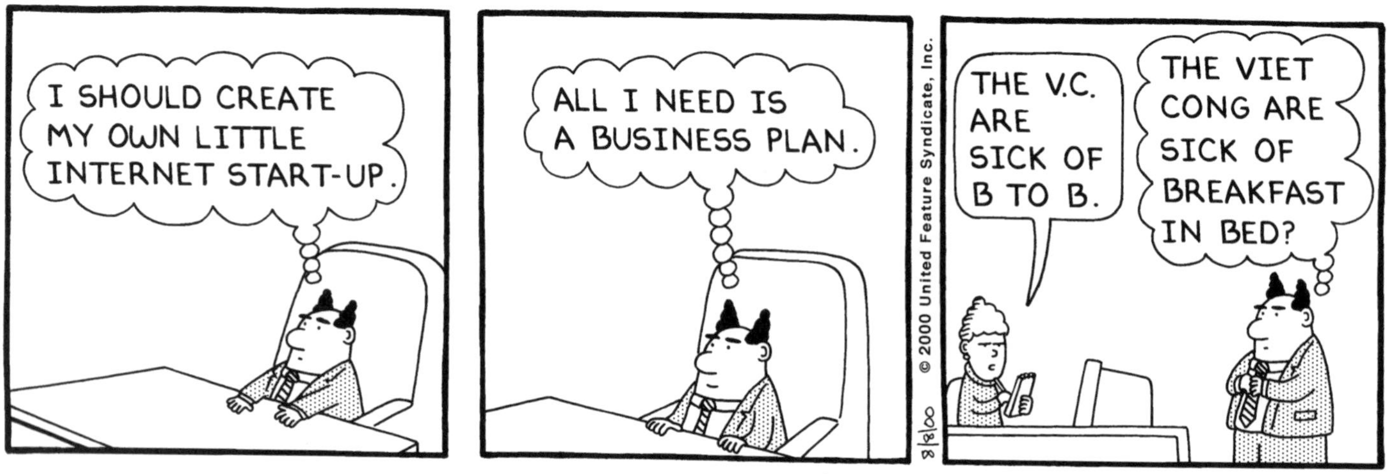
I SHOULD CREATE MY OWN LITTLE INTERNET START-UP.
ALL I NEED IS A BUSINESS PLAN.
8/8/00 © 2000 United Feature Syndicate, Inc.
THE V.C. ARE SICK OF B TO B.
THE VIET CONG ARE SICK OF BREAKFAST IN BED?

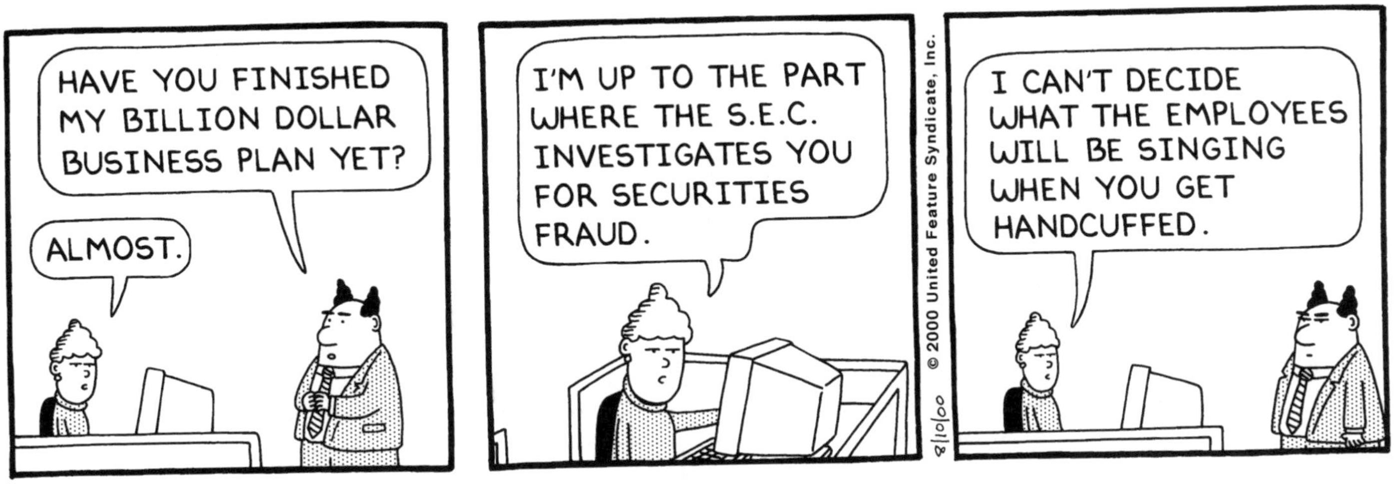
HAVE YOU FINISHED MY BILLION DOLLAR BUSINESS PLAN YET?
ALMOST.
I'M UP TO THE PART WHERE THE S.E.C. INVESTIGATES YOU FOR SECURITIES FRAUD.
8/10/00
© 2000 United Feature Syndicate, Inc.
I CAN'T DECIDE WHAT THE EMPLOYEES WILL BE SINGING WHEN YOU GET HANDCUFFED.

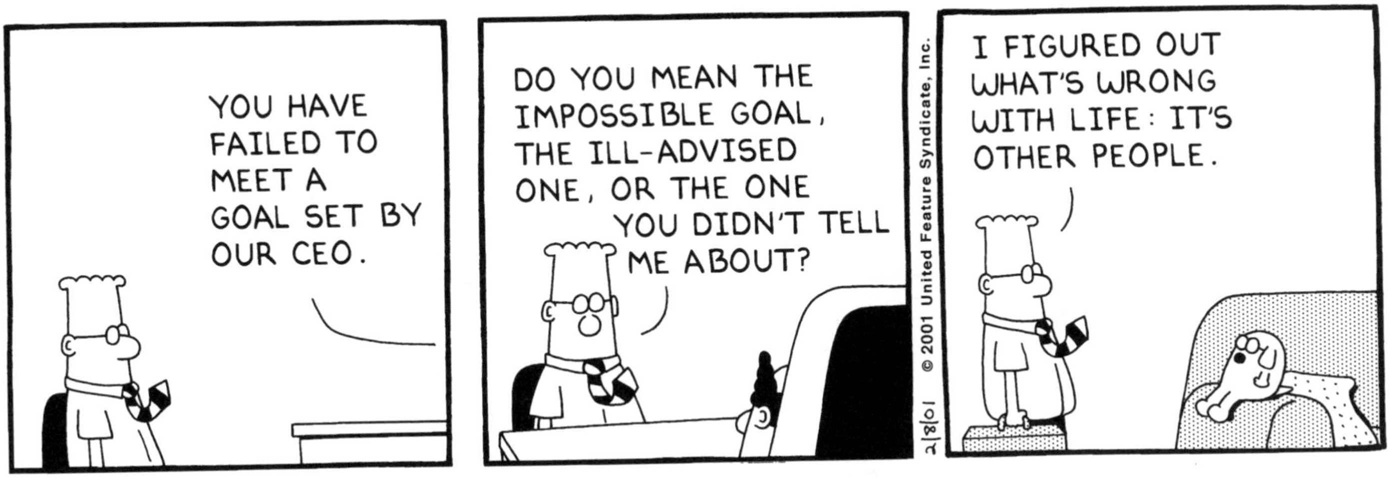
YOU HAVE FAILED TO MEET A GOAL SET BY OUR CEO.
DO YOU MEAN THE IMPOSSIBLE GOAL, THE ILL-ADVISED ONE, OR THE ONE YOU DIDN'T TELL ME ABOUT?
2/8/01
© 2001 United Feature Syndicate, Inc.
I FIGURED OUT WHAT'S WRONG WITH LIFE: IT'S OTHER PEOPLE.

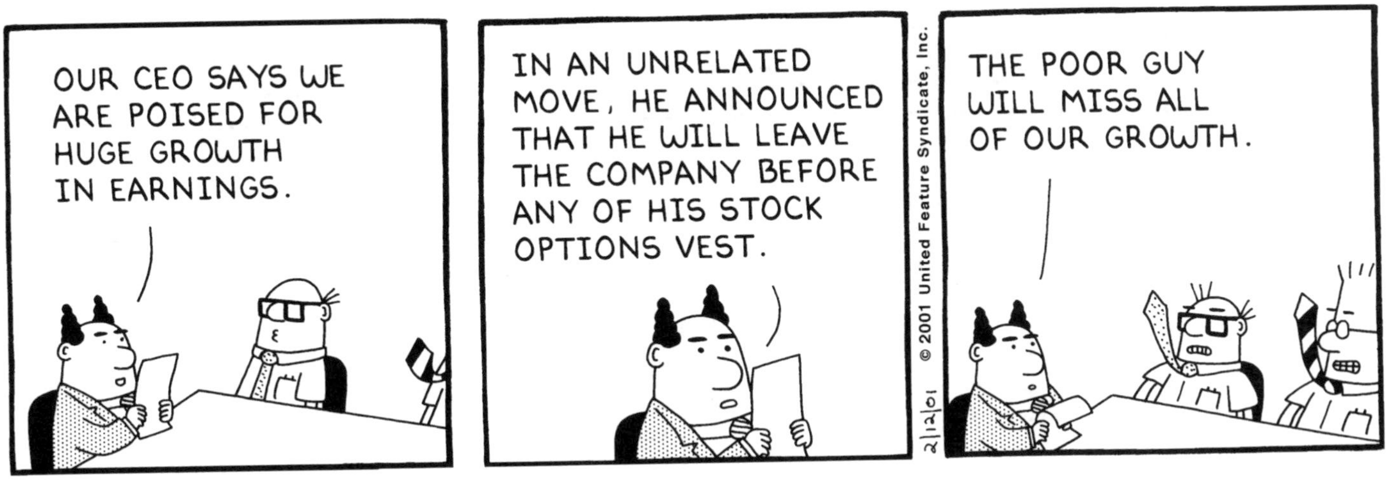
OUR CEO SAYS WE ARE POISED FOR HUGE GROWTH IN EARNINGS.
IN AN UNRELATED MOVE, HE ANNOUNCED THAT HE WILL LEAVE THE COMPANY BEFORE ANY OF HIS STOCK OPTIONS VEST.
2/12/01
© 2001 United Feature Syndicate, Inc.
THE POOR GUY WILL MISS ALL OF OUR GROWTH.

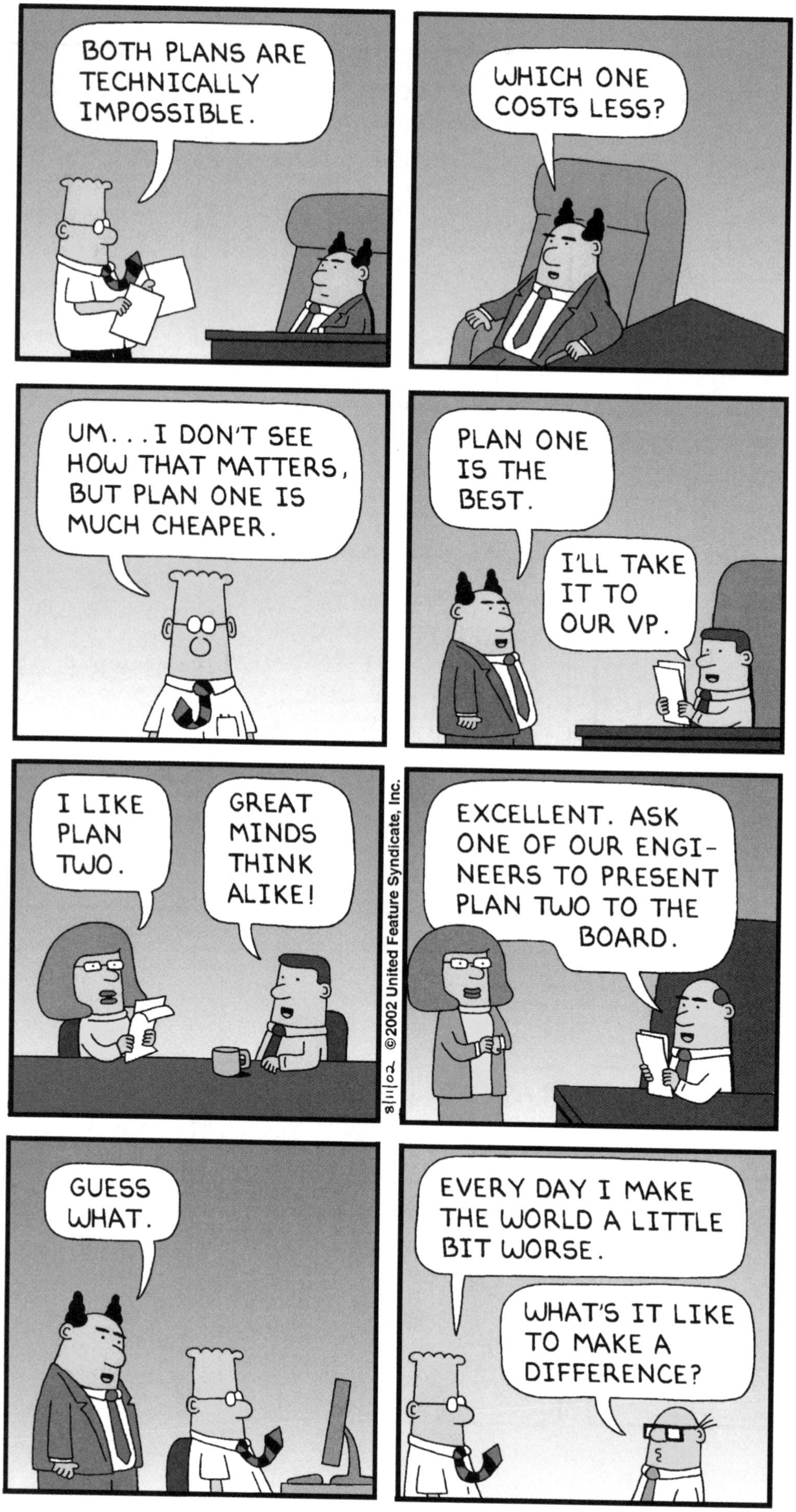
BOTH PLANS ARE TECHNICALLY IMPOSSIBLE.
WHICH ONE COSTS LESS?
UM. . . I DON'T SEE HOW THAT MATTERS, BUT PLAN ONE IS MUCH CHEAPER.
PLAN ONE IS THE BEST.
I'LL TAKE IT TO OUR VP.
I LIKE PLAN TWO.
GREAT MINDS THINK ALIKE!
©2002 United Feature Syndicate, Inc.
8/11/02
EXCELLENT. ASK ONE OF OUR ENGI- NEERS TO PRESENT PLAN TWO TO THE BOARD.
GUESS WHAT.
EVERY DAY I MAKE THE WORLD A LITTLE BIT WORSE.
WHAT'S IT LIKE TO MAKE A DIFFERENCE?

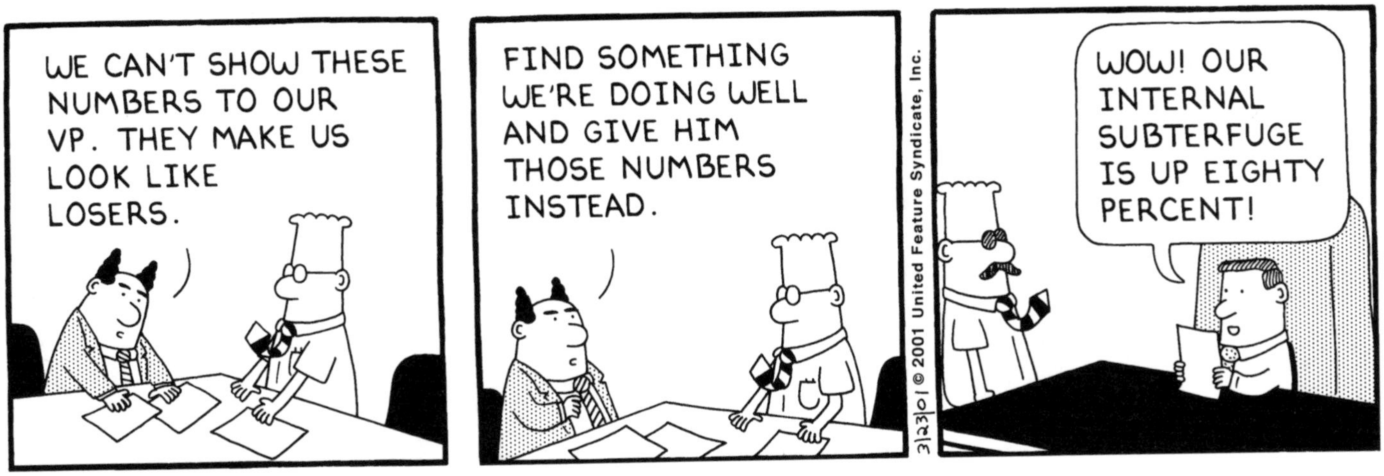
WE CAN'T SHOW THESE NUMBERS TO OUR VP. THEY MAKE US LOOK LIKE LOSERS.
FIND SOMETHING WE'RE DOING WELL AND GIVE HIM THOSE NUMBERS INSTEAD.
3/23/01 © 2001 United Feature Syndicate, Inc.
WOW! OUR INTERNAL SUBTERFUGE IS UP EIGHTY PERCENT!

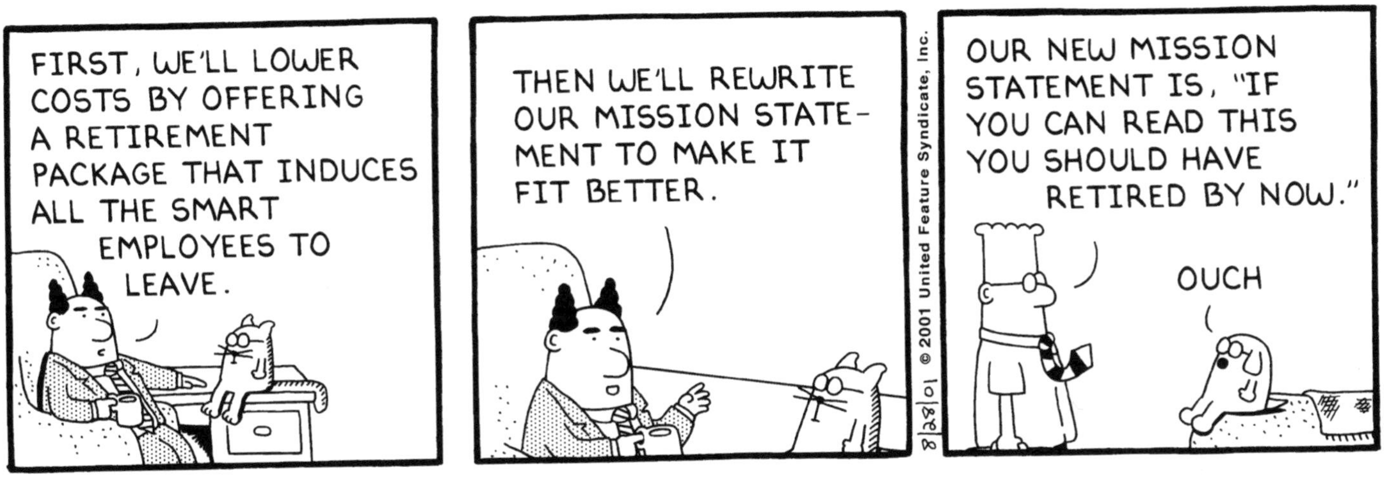
FIRST, WE'LL LOWER COSTS BY OFFERING A RETIREMENT PACKAGE THAT INDUCES ALL THE SMART EMPLOYEES TO LEAVE.
THEN WE'LL REWRITE OUR MISSION STATEMENT TO MAKE IT FIT BETTER.
8/28/01 © 2001 United Feature Syndicate, Inc.
OUR NEW MISSION STATEMENT IS, "IF YOU CAN READ THIS YOU SHOULD HAVE RETIRED BY NOW."
OUCH

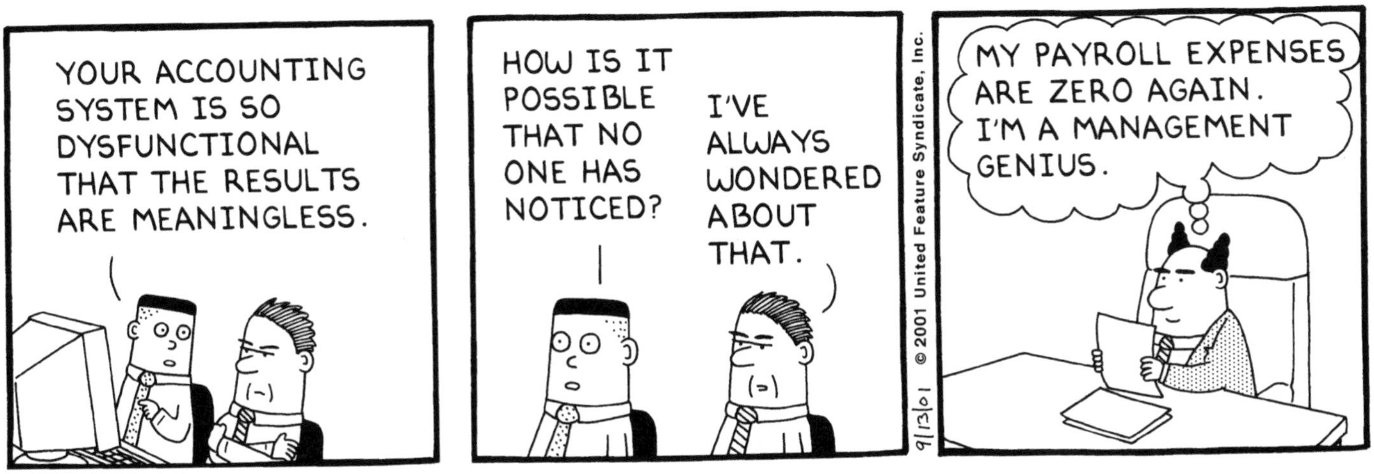
YOUR ACCOUNTING SYSTEM IS SO DYSFUNCTIONAL THAT THE RESULTS ARE MEANINGLESS.
HOW IS IT POSSIBLE THAT NO ONE HAS NOTICED?
I'VE ALWAYS WONDERED ABOUT THAT.
9/13/01 © 2001 United Feature Syndicate, Inc.
MY PAYROLL EXPENSES ARE ZERO AGAIN. I'M A MANAGEMENT GENIUS.

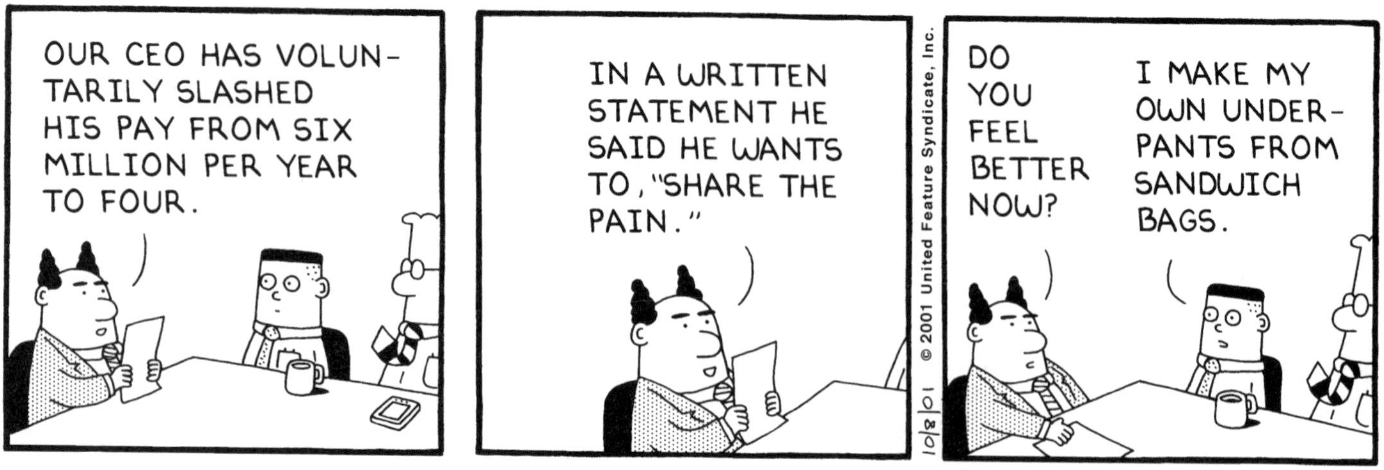
OUR CEO HAS VOLUNTARILY SLASHED HIS PAY FROM SIX MILLION PER YEAR TO FOUR.
IN A WRITTEN STATEMENT HE SAID HE WANTS TO, "SHARE THE PAIN."
10/8/01 © 2001 United Feature Syndicate, Inc.
DO YOU FEEL BETTER NOW?
I MAKE MY OWN UNDERPANTS FROM SANDWICH BAGS.

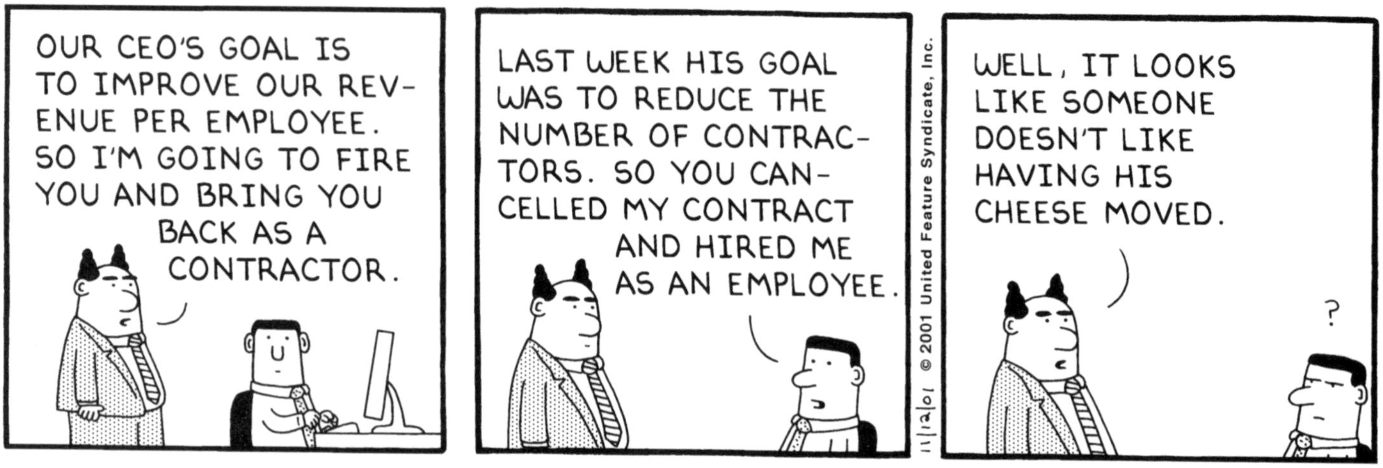
OUR CEO'S GOAL IS TO IMPROVE OUR REVENUE PER EMPLOYEE. SO I'M GOING TO FIRE YOU AND BRING YOU BACK AS A CONTRACTOR.
LAST WEEK HIS GOAL WAS TO REDUCE THE NUMBER OF CONTRACTORS. SO YOU CANCELLED MY CONTRACT AND HIRED ME AS AN EMPLOYEE.
11/12/01 © 2001 United Feature Syndicate, Inc.
WELL, IT LOOKS LIKE SOMEONE DOESN'T LIKE HAVING HIS CHEESE MOVED.
?

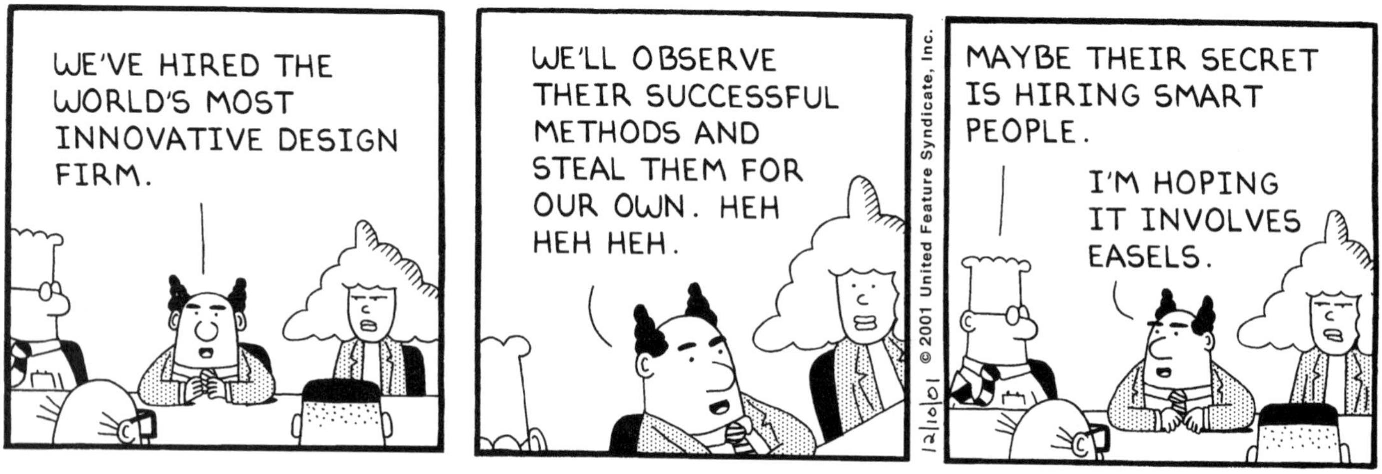
WE'VE HIRED THE WORLD'S MOST INNOVATIVE DESIGN FIRM.
WE'LL OBSERVE THEIR SUCCESSFUL METHODS AND STEAL THEM FOR OUR OWN. HEH HEH HEH.
12/10/01 © 2001 United Feature Syndicate, Inc.
MAYBE THEIR SECRET IS HIRING SMART PEOPLE.
I'M HOPING IT INVOLVES EASELS.

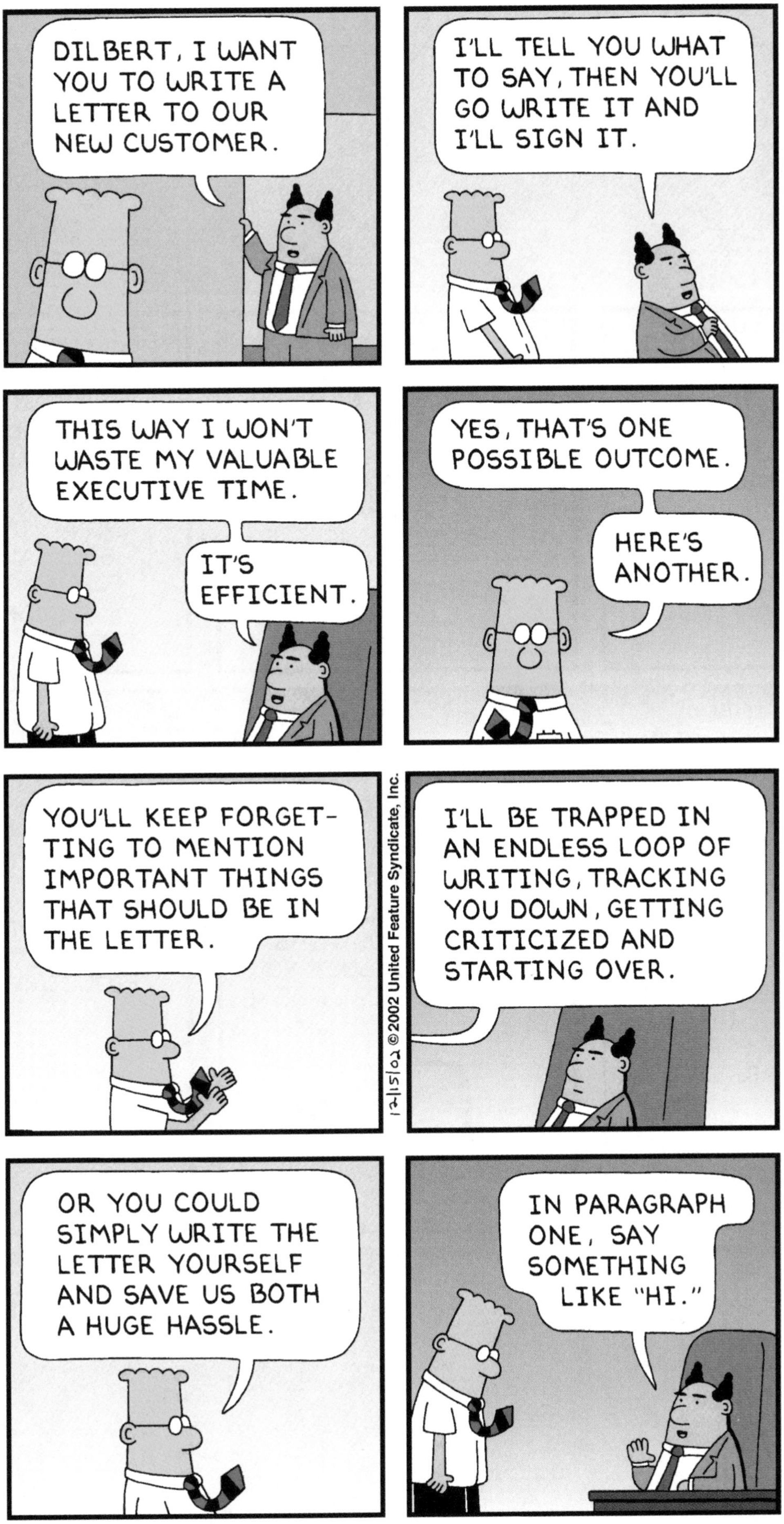
DILBERT, I WANT YOU TO WRITE A LETTER TO OUR NEW CUSTOMER.
I'LL TELL YOU WHAT TO SAY, THEN YOU'LL GO WRITE IT AND I'LL SIGN IT.
THIS WAY I WON'T WASTE MY VALUABLE EXECUTIVE TIME.
IT'S EFFICIENT.
YES, THAT'S ONE POSSIBLE OUTCOME.
HERE'S ANOTHER.
YOU'LL KEEP FORGET-TING TO MENTION IMPORTANT THINGS THAT SHOULD BE IN THE LETTER.
I'LL BE TRAPPED IN AN ENDLESS LOOP OF WRITING, TRACKING YOU DOWN, GETTING CRITICIZED AND STARTING OVER.
OR YOU COULD SIMPLY WRITE THE LETTER YOURSELF AND SAVE US BOTH A HUGE HASSLE.
IN PARAGRAPH ONE, SAY SOMETHING LIKE "HI."
12/15/02 ©2002 United Feature Syndicate, Inc.

DOGBERT THE CEO
UNTIL THE COMPANY RETURNS TO PROFIT–ABILITY I WILL ONLY FLY COACH.
I'LL BOOK THREE COACH SEATS IN A ROW SO I CAN STRETCH OUT.
ONE OF YOU WILL BE A SHERPA FOR MY BEDDING.
I'LL BRING MY OWN AIR MARSHAL TO PUNCH ANYONE WHO TALKS WHILE I'M NAPPING.
AND A VIDEOGRAPHER SO I CAN SEE THE PLAYBACK WHEN I WAKE UP.
3-24-09 © 2009 Scott Adams, Inc./Dist. by UFS, Inc.

DOGBERT THE CEO
NOW THAT YOU'VE RUN YOUR BANK INTO THE GROUND, I PLAN TO BUY IT FOR A DOLLAR.
IN PHASE TWO I'LL USE COMMON BUSINESS WORDS TO INSULT YOU FOR A JOB POORLY DONE.
WHAT DO YOU THINK OF THAT, YOU BIG FIDUCIARY BAG?
3-25-09 © 2009 Scott Adams, Inc./Dist. by UFS, Inc.

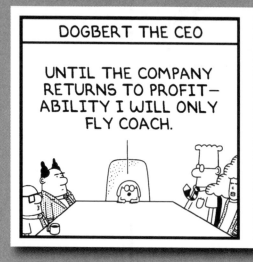

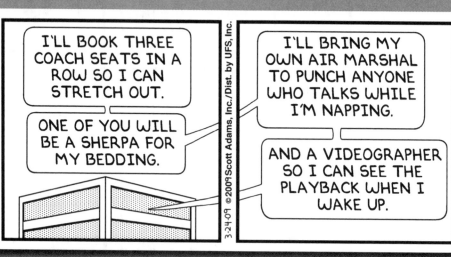

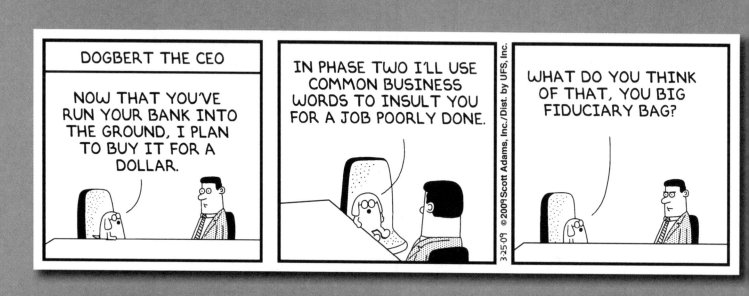

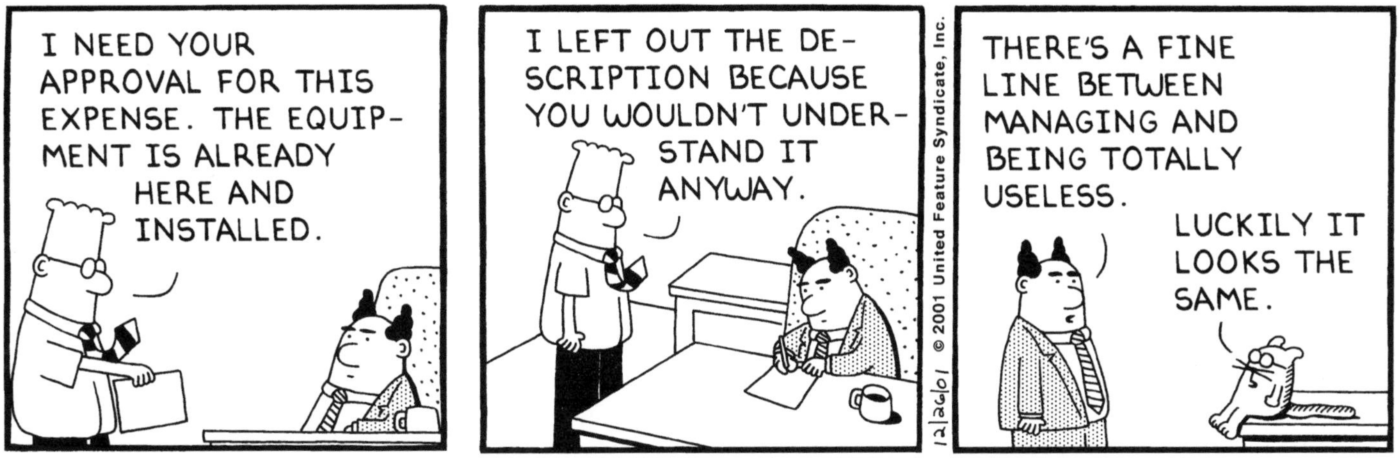
I NEED YOUR APPROVAL FOR THIS EXPENSE. THE EQUIPMENT IS ALREADY HERE AND INSTALLED.
I LEFT OUT THE DESCRIPTION BECAUSE YOU WOULDN'T UNDERSTAND IT ANYWAY.
12/26/01 © 2001 United Feature Syndicate, Inc.
THERE'S A FINE LINE BETWEEN MANAGING AND BEING TOTALLY USELESS.
LUCKILY IT LOOKS THE SAME.

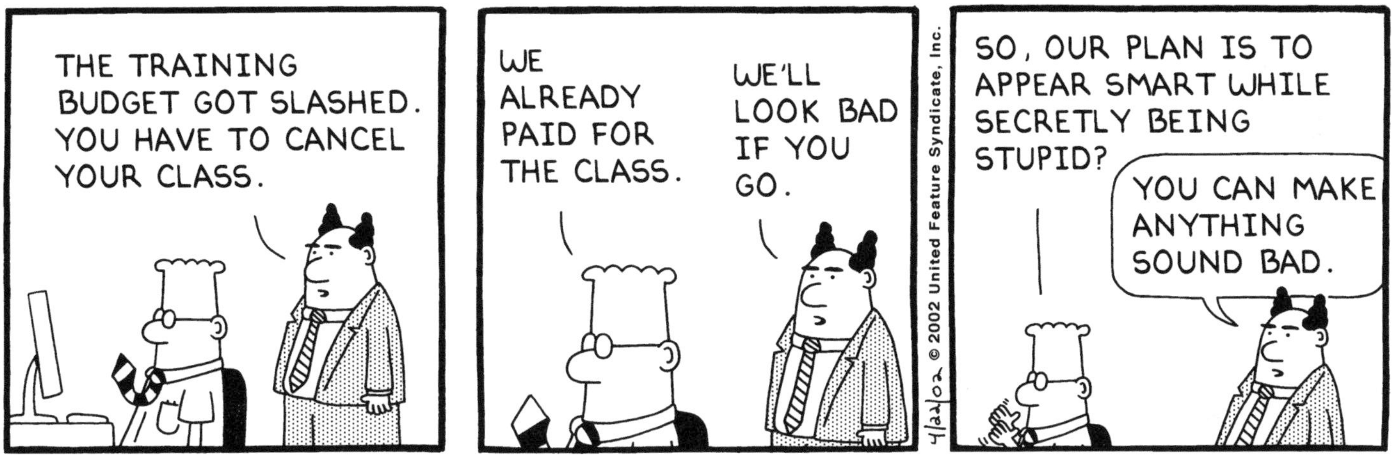
THE TRAINING BUDGET GOT SLASHED. YOU HAVE TO CANCEL YOUR CLASS.
WE ALREADY PAID FOR THE CLASS.
WE'LL LOOK BAD IF YOU GO.
4/22/02 © 2002 United Feature Syndicate, Inc.
SO, OUR PLAN IS TO APPEAR SMART WHILE SECRETLY BEING STUPID?
YOU CAN MAKE ANYTHING SOUND BAD.

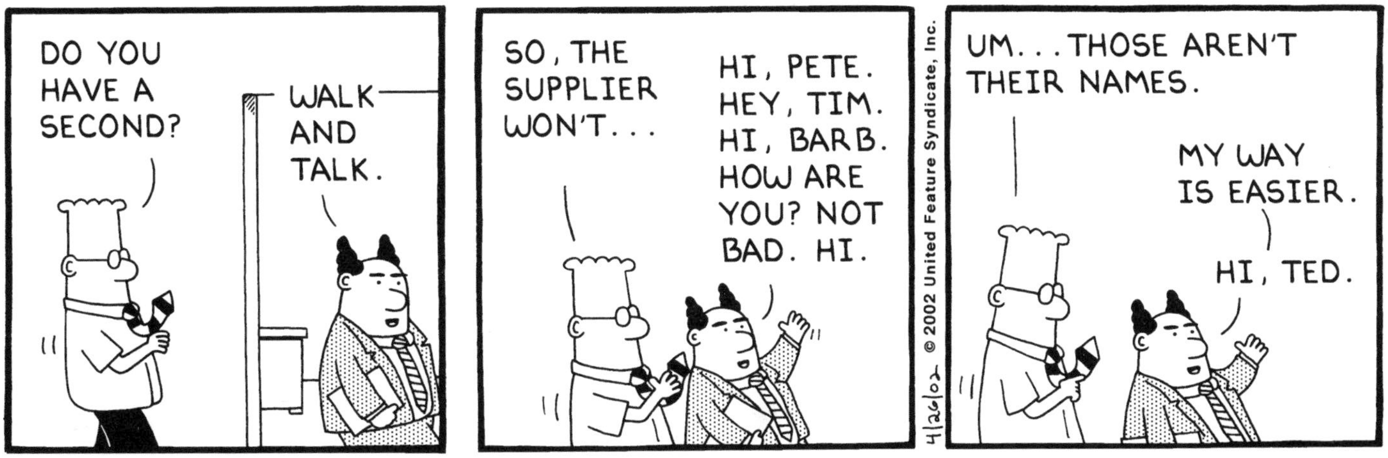
DO YOU HAVE A SECOND?
WALK AND TALK.
SO, THE SUPPLIER WON'T...
HI, PETE. HEY, TIM. HI, BARB. HOW ARE YOU? NOT BAD. HI.
4/26/02 © 2002 United Feature Syndicate, Inc.
UM...THOSE AREN'T THEIR NAMES.
MY WAY IS EASIER.
HI, TED.

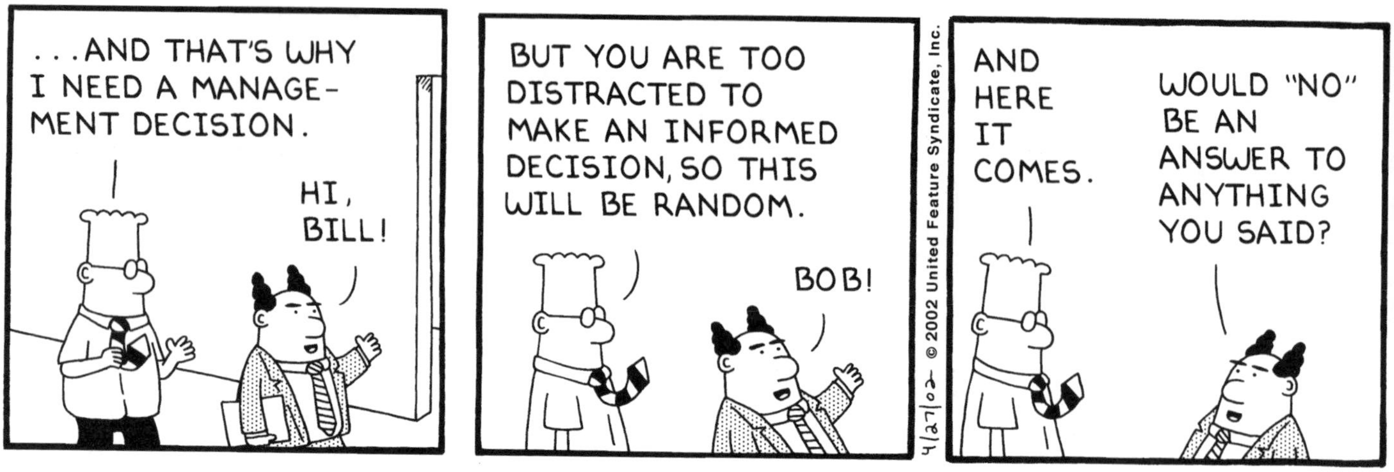
...AND THAT'S WHY I NEED A MANAGEMENT DECISION.
HI, BILL!
BUT YOU ARE TOO DISTRACTED TO MAKE AN INFORMED DECISION, SO THIS WILL BE RANDOM.
BOB!
4/27/02 © 2002 United Feature Syndicate, Inc.
AND HERE IT COMES.
WOULD "NO" BE AN ANSWER TO ANYTHING YOU SAID?

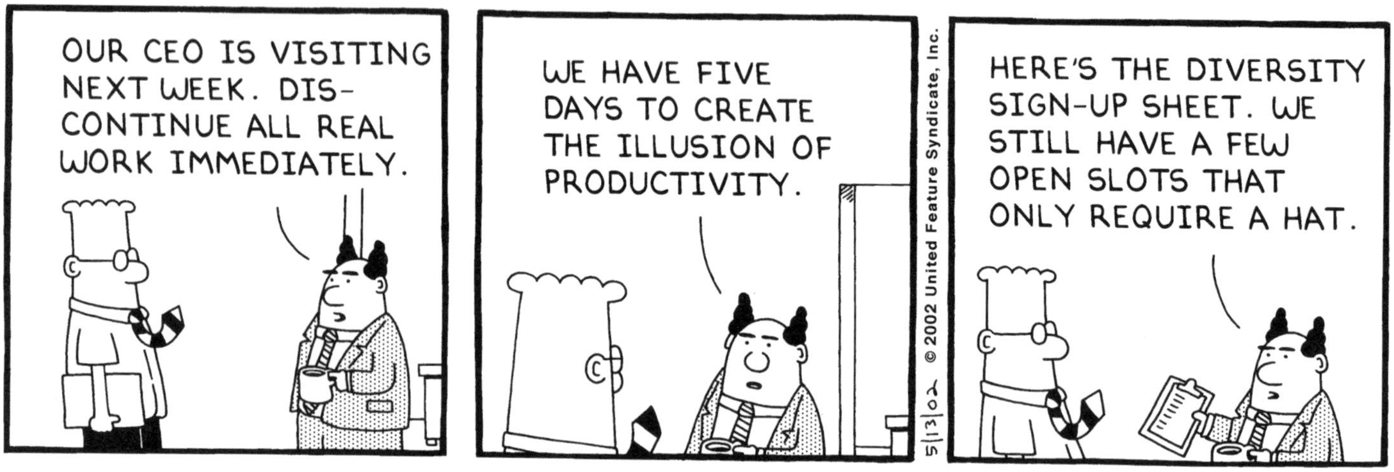
OUR CEO IS VISITING NEXT WEEK. DISCONTINUE ALL REAL WORK IMMEDIATELY.
WE HAVE FIVE DAYS TO CREATE THE ILLUSION OF PRODUCTIVITY.
5/13/02 © 2002 United Feature Syndicate, Inc.
HERE'S THE DIVERSITY SIGN-UP SHEET. WE STILL HAVE A FEW OPEN SLOTS THAT ONLY REQUIRE A HAT.

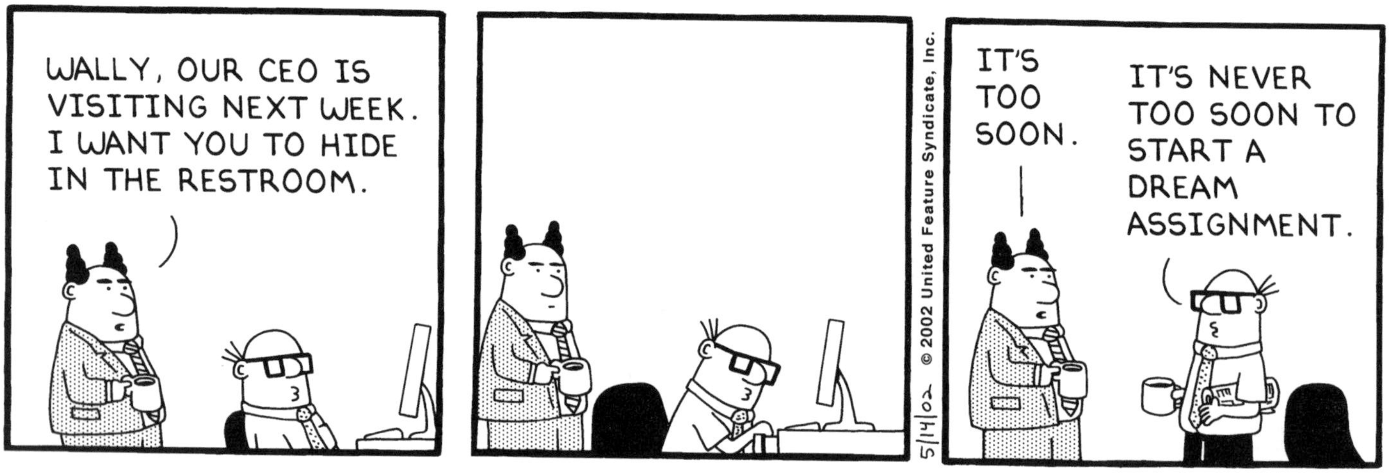
WALLY, OUR CEO IS VISITING NEXT WEEK. I WANT YOU TO HIDE IN THE RESTROOM.
5/14/02 © 2002 United Feature Syndicate, Inc.
IT'S TOO SOON.
IT'S NEVER TOO SOON TO START A DREAM ASSIGNMENT.

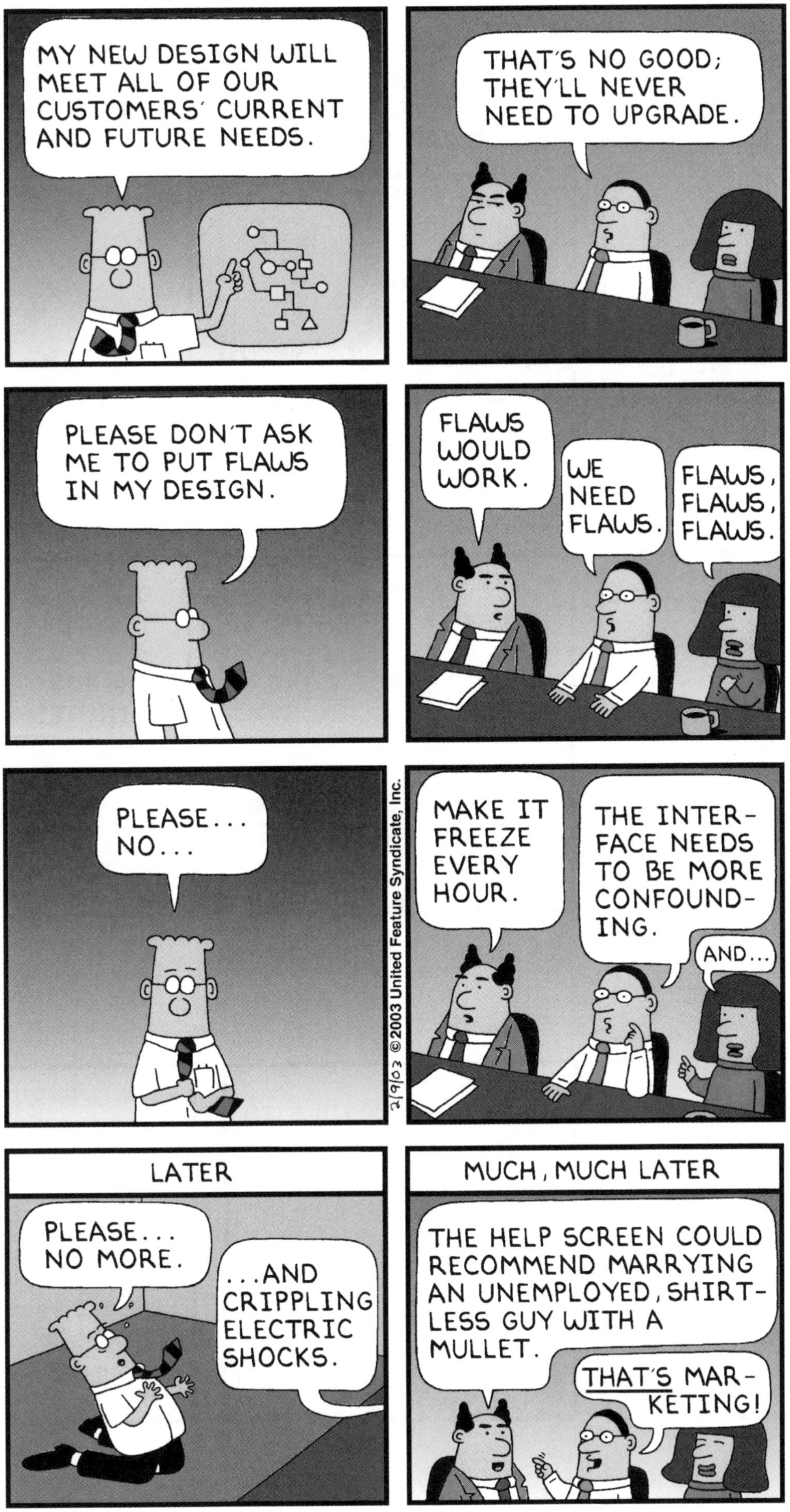
MY NEW DESIGN WILL MEET ALL OF OUR CUSTOMERS' CURRENT AND FUTURE NEEDS.
THAT'S NO GOOD; THEY'LL NEVER NEED TO UPGRADE.
PLEASE DON'T ASK ME TO PUT FLAWS IN MY DESIGN.
FLAWS WOULD WORK.
WE NEED FLAWS.
FLAWS, FLAWS, FLAWS.
PLEASE... NO...
MAKE IT FREEZE EVERY HOUR.
THE INTER-FACE NEEDS TO BE MORE CONFOUND-ING.
AND...
LATER
PLEASE... NO MORE.
...AND CRIPPLING ELECTRIC SHOCKS.
MUCH, MUCH LATER
THE HELP SCREEN COULD RECOMMEND MARRYING AN UNEMPLOYED, SHIRT-LESS GUY WITH A MULLET.
THAT'S MAR-KETING!

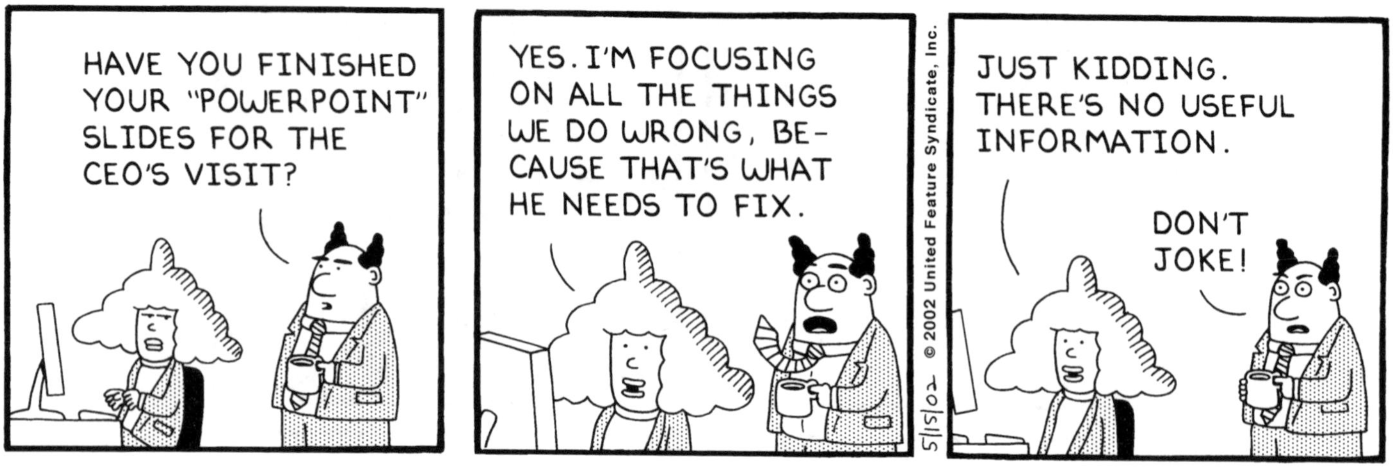
HAVE YOU FINISHED YOUR "POWERPOINT" SLIDES FOR THE CEO'S VISIT?
YES. I'M FOCUSING ON ALL THE THINGS WE DO WRONG, BE-CAUSE THAT'S WHAT HE NEEDS TO FIX.
5/15/02 © 2002 United Feature Syndicate, Inc.
JUST KIDDING. THERE'S NO USEFUL INFORMATION.
DON'T JOKE!

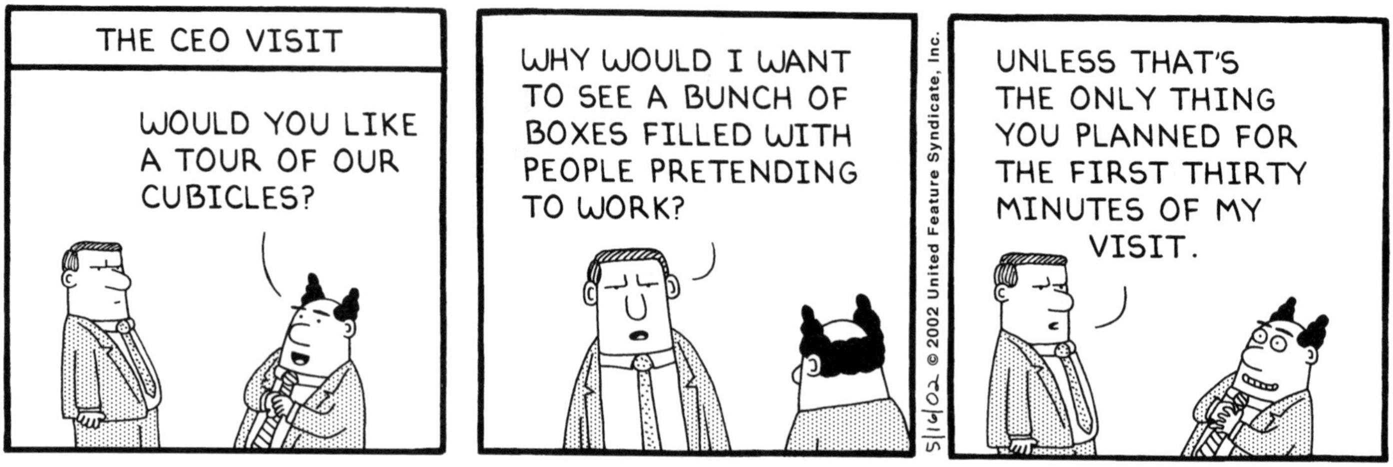
THE CEO VISIT
WOULD YOU LIKE A TOUR OF OUR CUBICLES?
WHY WOULD I WANT TO SEE A BUNCH OF BOXES FILLED WITH PEOPLE PRETENDING TO WORK?
5/16/02 © 2002 United Feature Syndicate, Inc.
UNLESS THAT'S THE ONLY THING YOU PLANNED FOR THE FIRST THIRTY MINUTES OF MY VISIT.

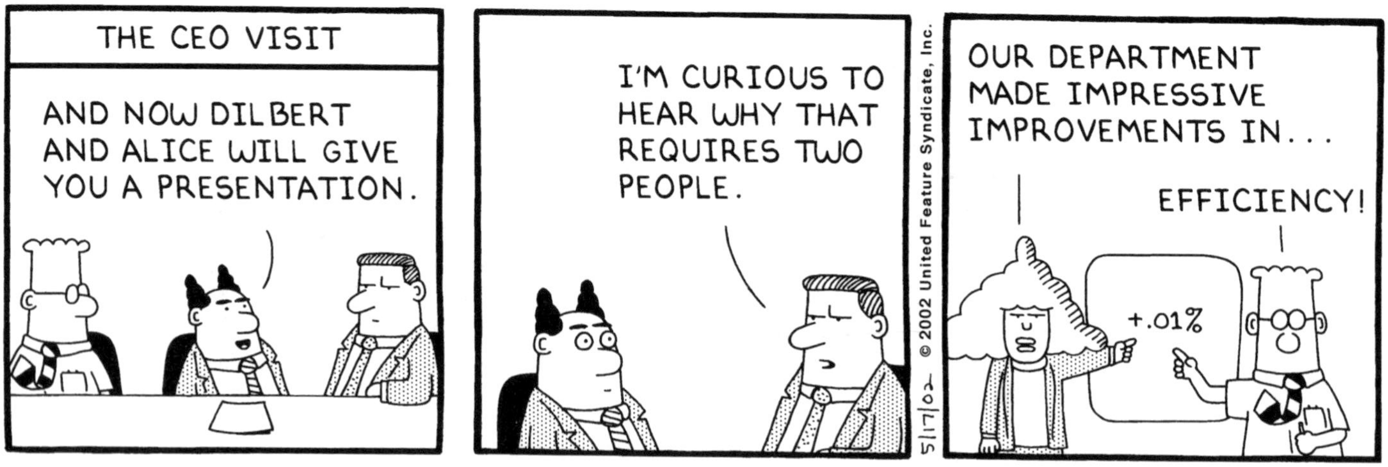
THE CEO VISIT
AND NOW DILBERT AND ALICE WILL GIVE YOU A PRESENTATION.
I'M CURIOUS TO HEAR WHY THAT REQUIRES TWO PEOPLE.
5/17/02 © 2002 United Feature Syndicate, Inc.
OUR DEPARTMENT MADE IMPRESSIVE IMPROVEMENTS IN...
EFFICIENCY!
+.01%

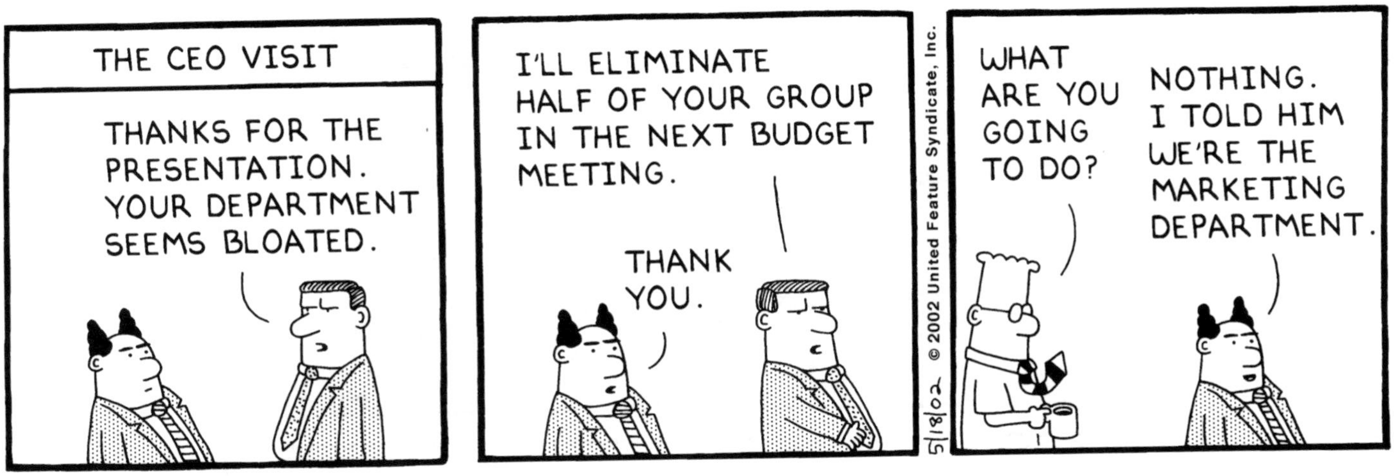
THE CEO VISIT
THANKS FOR THE PRESENTATION. YOUR DEPARTMENT SEEMS BLOATED.
I'LL ELIMINATE HALF OF YOUR GROUP IN THE NEXT BUDGET MEETING.
THANK YOU.
WHAT ARE YOU GOING TO DO?
NOTHING. I TOLD HIM WE'RE THE MARKETING DEPARTMENT.
5/18/02 © 2002 United Feature Syndicate, Inc.

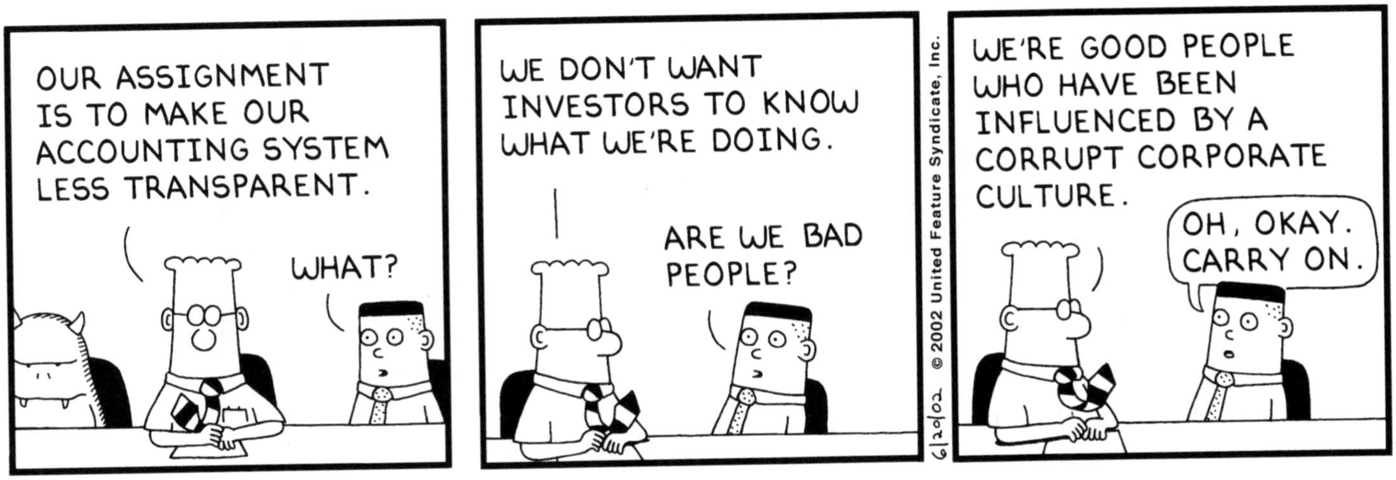
OUR ASSIGNMENT IS TO MAKE OUR ACCOUNTING SYSTEM LESS TRANSPARENT.
WHAT?
WE DON'T WANT INVESTORS TO KNOW WHAT WE'RE DOING.
ARE WE BAD PEOPLE?
WE'RE GOOD PEOPLE WHO HAVE BEEN INFLUENCED BY A CORRUPT CORPORATE CULTURE.
OH, OKAY. CARRY ON.
6/20/02 © 2002 United Feature Syndicate, Inc.

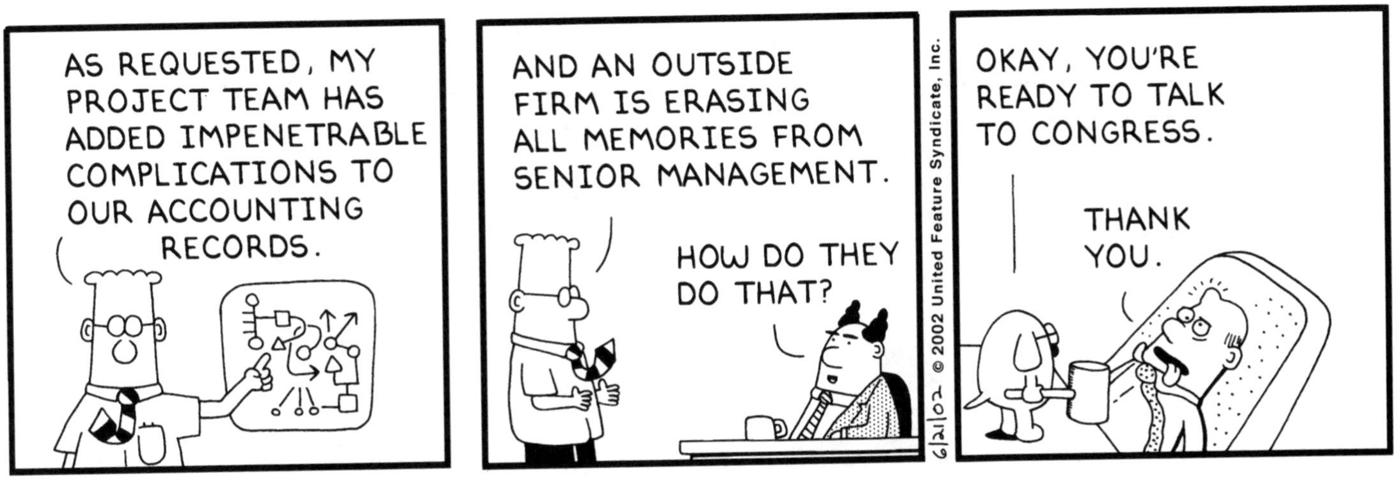
AS REQUESTED, MY PROJECT TEAM HAS ADDED IMPENETRABLE COMPLICATIONS TO OUR ACCOUNTING RECORDS.
AND AN OUTSIDE FIRM IS ERASING ALL MEMORIES FROM SENIOR MANAGEMENT.
HOW DO THEY DO THAT?
OKAY, YOU'RE READY TO TALK TO CONGRESS.
THANK YOU.
6/21/02 © 2002 United Feature Syndicate, Inc.

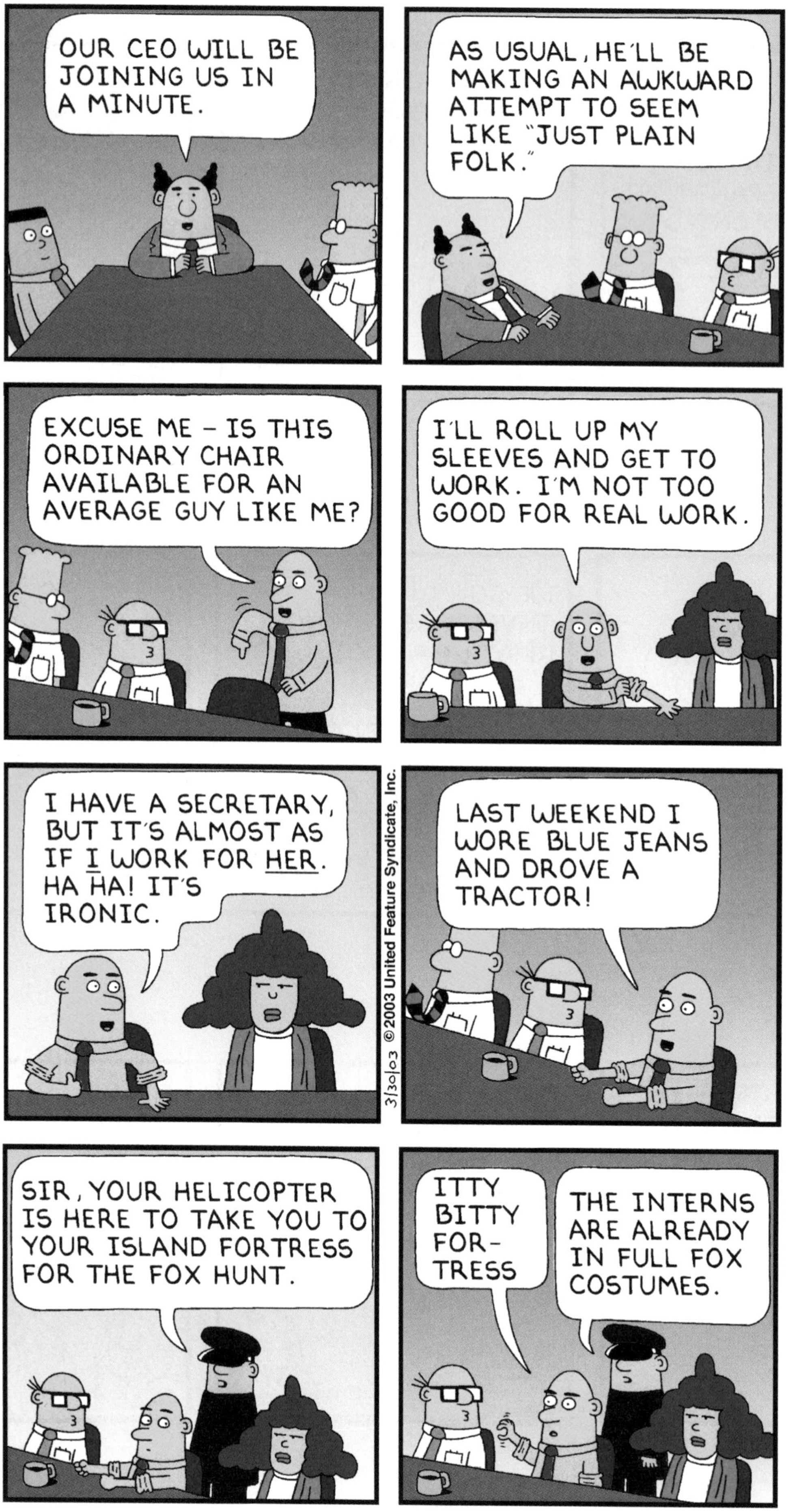
OUR CEO WILL BE JOINING US IN A MINUTE.
AS USUAL, HE'LL BE MAKING AN AWKWARD ATTEMPT TO SEEM LIKE "JUST PLAIN FOLK."
EXCUSE ME – IS THIS ORDINARY CHAIR AVAILABLE FOR AN AVERAGE GUY LIKE ME?
I'LL ROLL UP MY SLEEVES AND GET TO WORK. I'M NOT TOO GOOD FOR REAL WORK.
I HAVE A SECRETARY, BUT IT'S ALMOST AS IF I WORK FOR HER. HA HA! IT'S IRONIC.
3/30/03 © 2003 United Feature Syndicate, Inc.
LAST WEEKEND I WORE BLUE JEANS AND DROVE A TRACTOR!
SIR, YOUR HELICOPTER IS HERE TO TAKE YOU TO YOUR ISLAND FORTRESS FOR THE FOX HUNT.
ITTY BITTY FOR-TRESS
THE INTERNS ARE ALREADY IN FULL FOX COSTUMES.

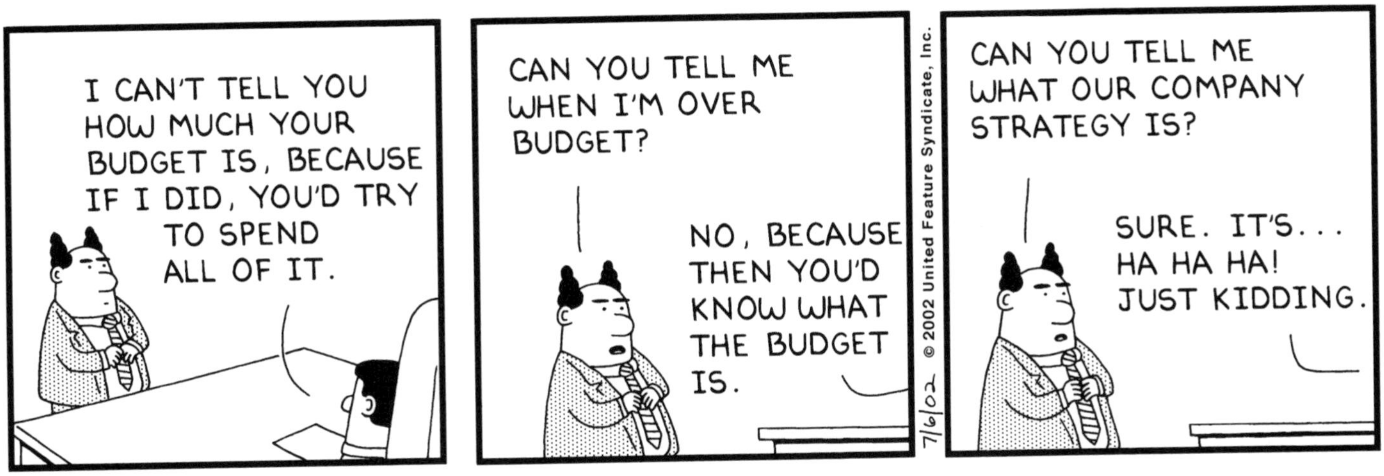
I CAN'T TELL YOU HOW MUCH YOUR BUDGET IS, BECAUSE IF I DID, YOU'D TRY TO SPEND ALL OF IT.
CAN YOU TELL ME WHEN I'M OVER BUDGET?
NO, BECAUSE THEN YOU'D KNOW WHAT THE BUDGET IS.
7/6/02 © 2002 United Feature Syndicate, Inc.
CAN YOU TELL ME WHAT OUR COMPANY STRATEGY IS?
SURE. IT'S... HA HA HA! JUST KIDDING.

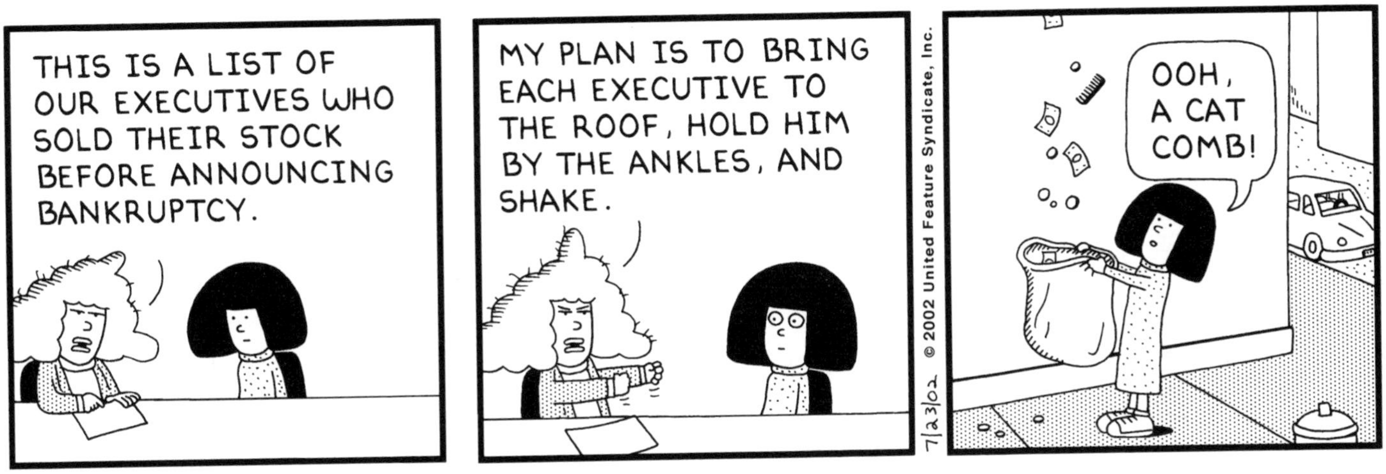
THIS IS A LIST OF OUR EXECUTIVES WHO SOLD THEIR STOCK BEFORE ANNOUNCING BANKRUPTCY.
MY PLAN IS TO BRING EACH EXECUTIVE TO THE ROOF, HOLD HIM BY THE ANKLES, AND SHAKE.
7/23/02 © 2002 United Feature Syndicate, Inc.
OOH, A CAT COMB!

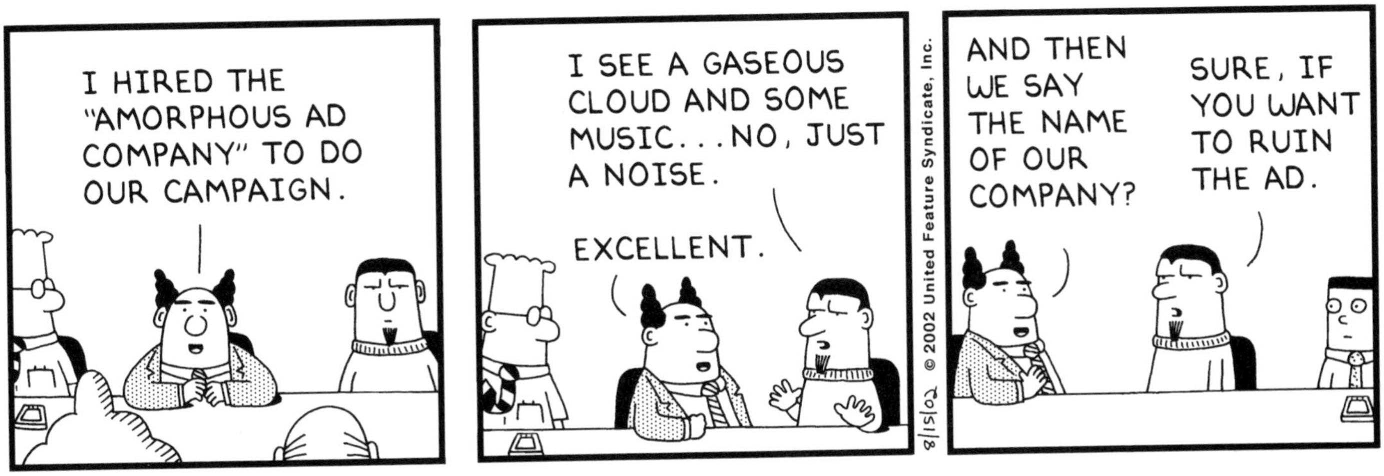
I HIRED THE "AMORPHOUS AD COMPANY" TO DO OUR CAMPAIGN.
I SEE A GASEOUS CLOUD AND SOME MUSIC... NO, JUST A NOISE.
EXCELLENT.
8/15/02 © 2002 United Feature Syndicate, Inc.
AND THEN WE SAY THE NAME OF OUR COMPANY?
SURE, IF YOU WANT TO RUIN THE AD.

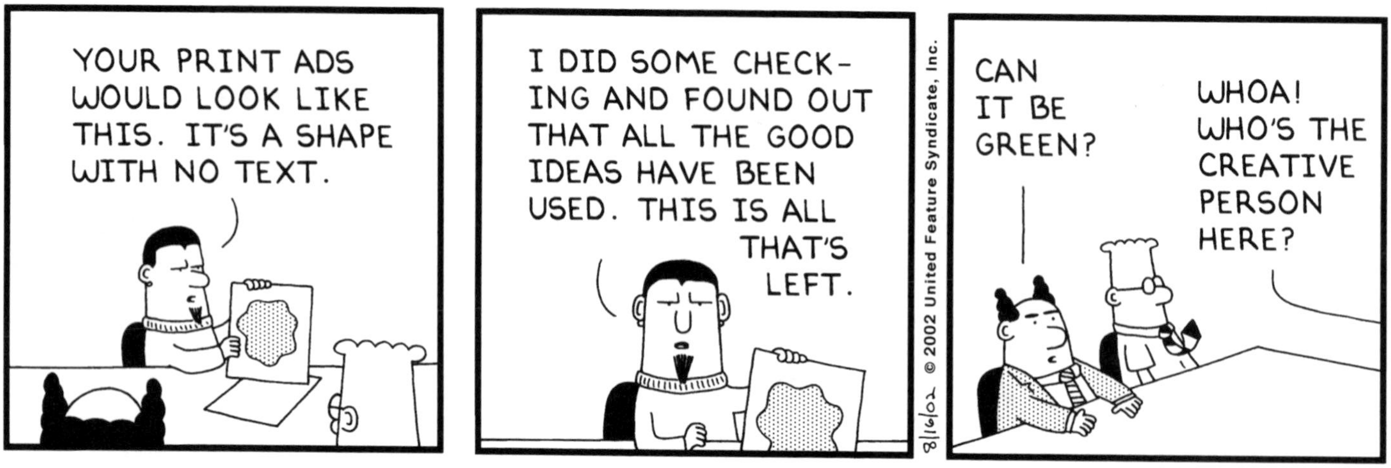
YOUR PRINT ADS WOULD LOOK LIKE THIS. IT'S A SHAPE WITH NO TEXT.
I DID SOME CHECKING AND FOUND OUT THAT ALL THE GOOD IDEAS HAVE BEEN USED. THIS IS ALL THAT'S LEFT.
8/16/02 © 2002 United Feature Syndicate, Inc.
CAN IT BE GREEN?
WHOA! WHO'S THE CREATIVE PERSON HERE?

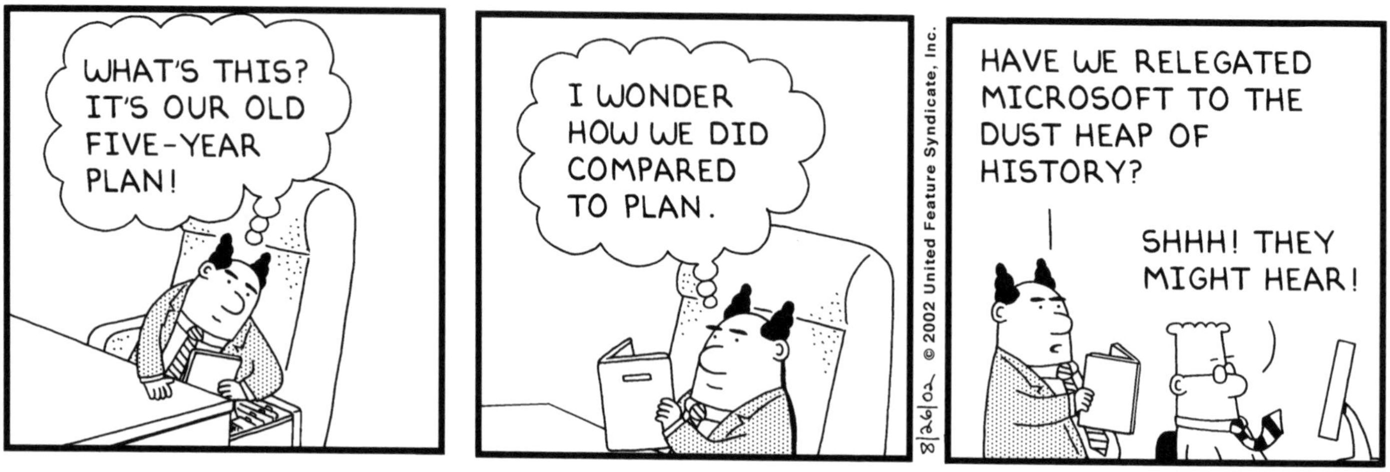
WHAT'S THIS? IT'S OUR OLD FIVE-YEAR PLAN!
I WONDER HOW WE DID COMPARED TO PLAN.
8/26/02 © 2002 United Feature Syndicate, Inc.
HAVE WE RELEGATED MICROSOFT TO THE DUST HEAP OF HISTORY?
SHHH! THEY MIGHT HEAR!

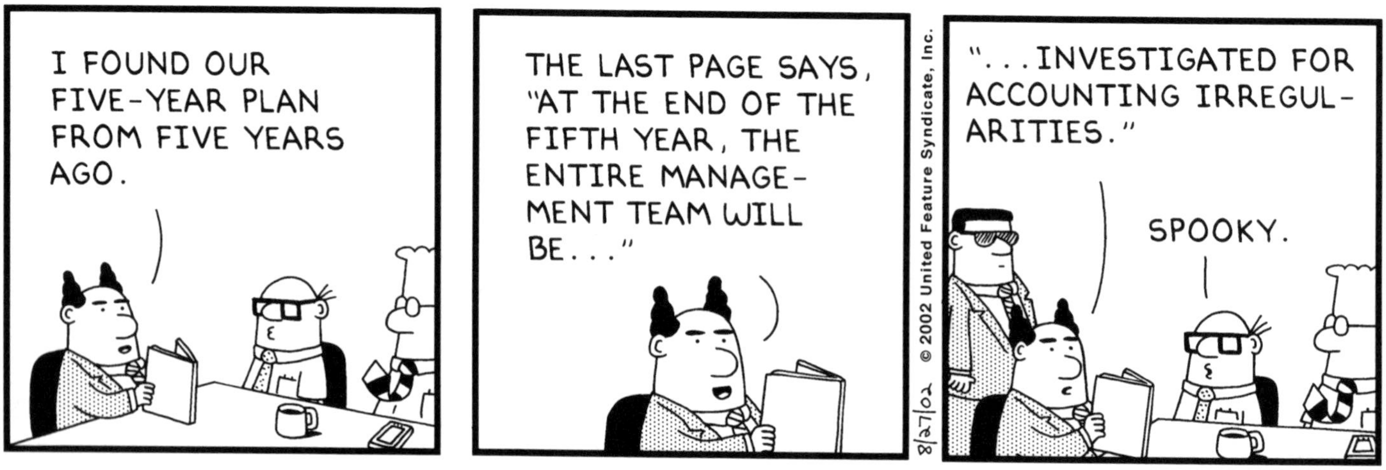
I FOUND OUR FIVE-YEAR PLAN FROM FIVE YEARS AGO.
THE LAST PAGE SAYS, "AT THE END OF THE FIFTH YEAR, THE ENTIRE MANAGEMENT TEAM WILL BE..."
8/27/02 © 2002 United Feature Syndicate, Inc.
"...INVESTIGATED FOR ACCOUNTING IRREGULARITIES."
SPOOKY.

I'D LIKE YOU TO MEET BRADLEY, OUR NEW MANAGER OF EXECUTIVE COMPENSATION.

BRADLEY'S JOB IS TO RECOMMEND TO OUR BOARD HOW MUCH TO PAY COMPANY EXECUTIVES SUCH AS ME.

BRADLEY IS TOTALLY OBJECTIVE.

TOTALLY.

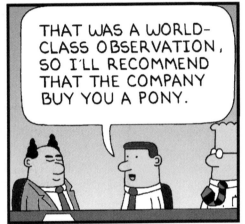

THAT WAS A WORLD-CLASS OBSERVATION, SO I'LL RECOMMEND THAT THE COMPANY BUY YOU A PONY.

...A STRONG PONY TO CARRY THE HUGE BAGS OF CASH I RECOMMEND FOR YOU.

GOOD WORK, BRADLEY. I'LL RECOMMEND TO THE BOARD THAT YOU GET A HUGE RAISE!

GAAA!!! STOP PRETENDING TO HAVE REASONS!! JUST STEAL THE STUPID MONEY!!!

SEE WHAT I HAVE TO DEAL WITH EVERY DAY?

WOULD AN EXTRA MONTH OF VACATION REDUCE THE STING?

11-30-03 © 2003 United Feature Syndicate, Inc.

71

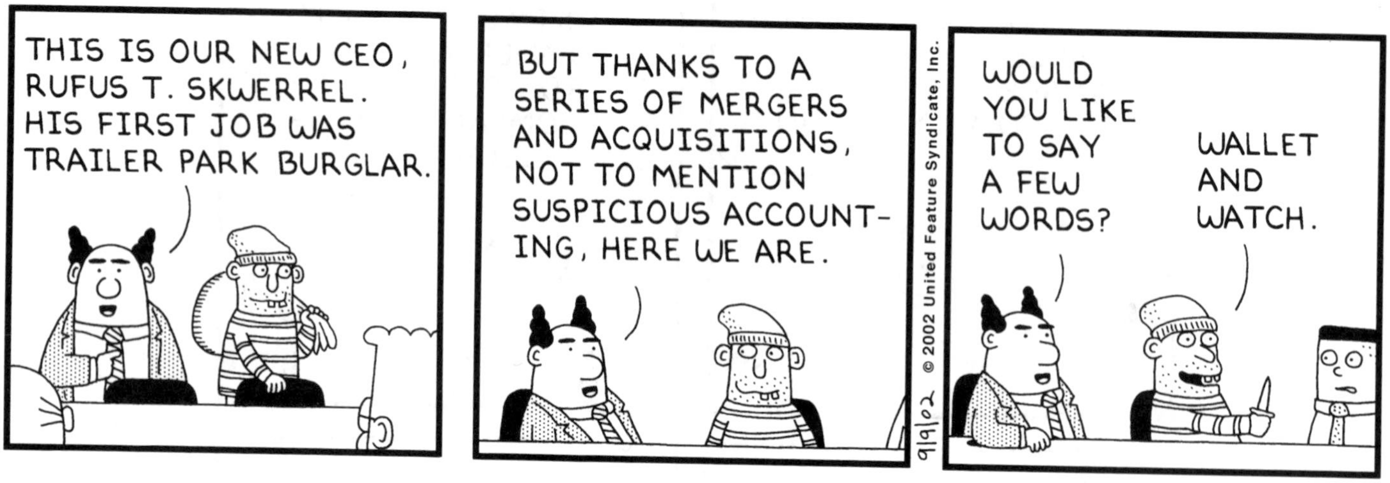
THIS IS OUR NEW CEO, RUFUS T. SKWERREL. HIS FIRST JOB WAS TRAILER PARK BURGLAR.
BUT THANKS TO A SERIES OF MERGERS AND ACQUISITIONS, NOT TO MENTION SUSPICIOUS ACCOUNTING, HERE WE ARE.
9/9/02 © 2002 United Feature Syndicate, Inc.
WOULD YOU LIKE TO SAY A FEW WORDS?
WALLET AND WATCH.

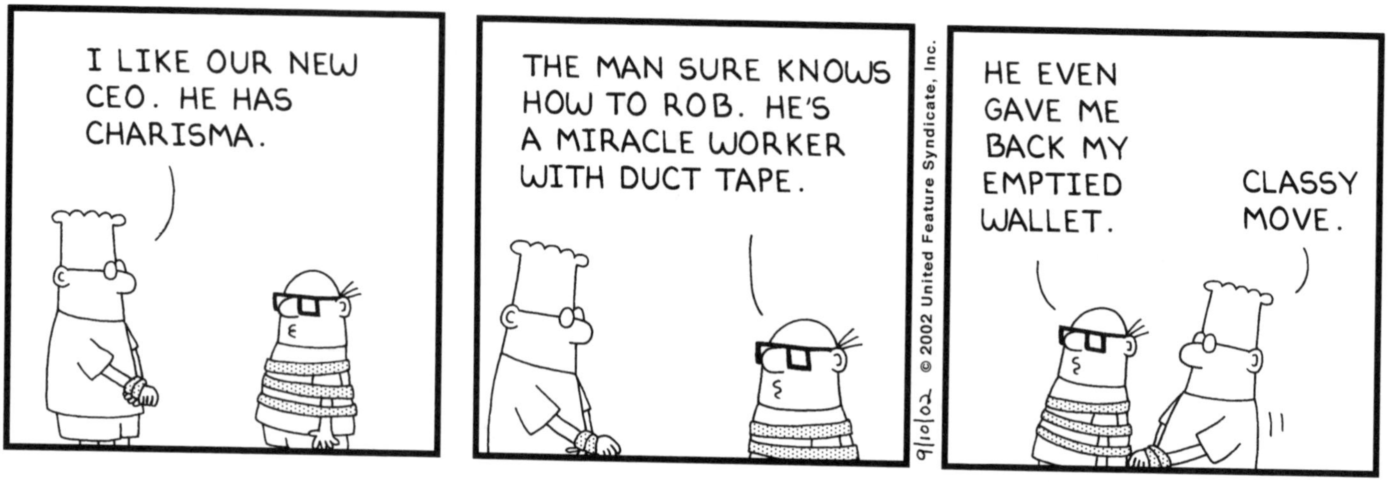
I LIKE OUR NEW CEO. HE HAS CHARISMA.
THE MAN SURE KNOWS HOW TO ROB. HE'S A MIRACLE WORKER WITH DUCT TAPE.
9/10/02 © 2002 United Feature Syndicate, Inc.
HE EVEN GAVE ME BACK MY EMPTIED WALLET.
CLASSY MOVE.

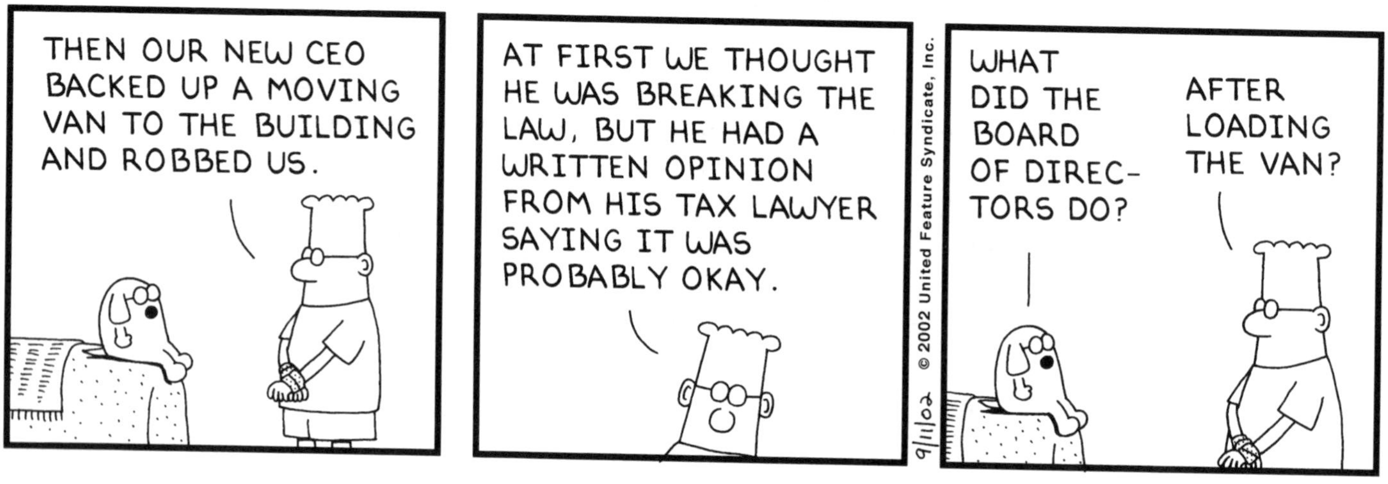
THEN OUR NEW CEO BACKED UP A MOVING VAN TO THE BUILDING AND ROBBED US.
AT FIRST WE THOUGHT HE WAS BREAKING THE LAW, BUT HE HAD A WRITTEN OPINION FROM HIS TAX LAWYER SAYING IT WAS PROBABLY OKAY.
9/11/02 © 2002 United Feature Syndicate, Inc.
WHAT DID THE BOARD OF DIRECTORS DO?
AFTER LOADING THE VAN?

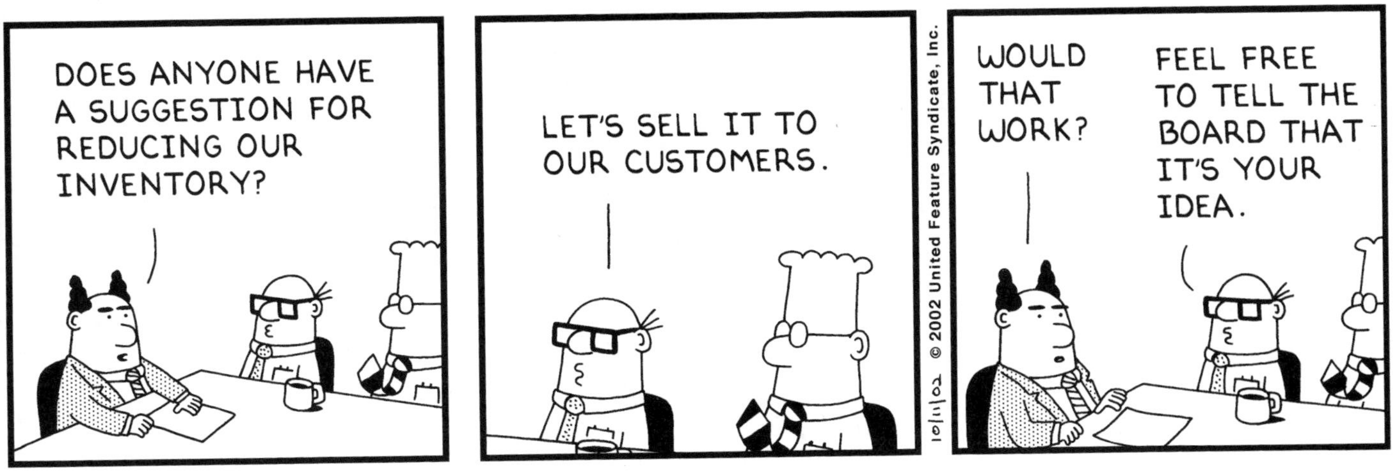
DOES ANYONE HAVE A SUGGESTION FOR REDUCING OUR INVENTORY?
LET'S SELL IT TO OUR CUSTOMERS.
10/11/02 © 2002 United Feature Syndicate, Inc.
WOULD THAT WORK?
FEEL FREE TO TELL THE BOARD THAT IT'S YOUR IDEA.

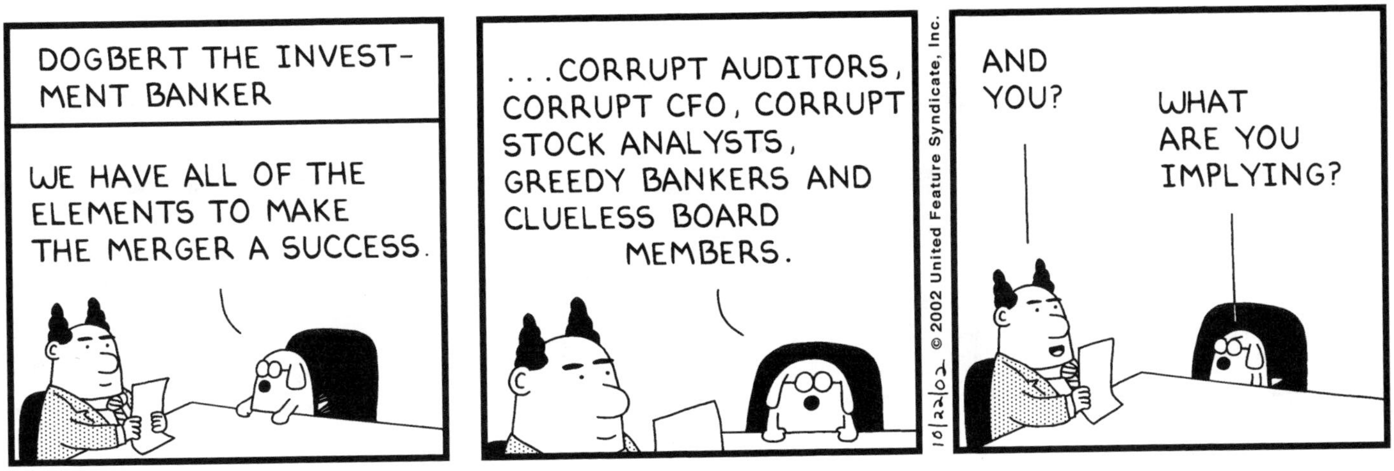
DOGBERT THE INVESTMENT BANKER
WE HAVE ALL OF THE ELEMENTS TO MAKE THE MERGER A SUCCESS.
...CORRUPT AUDITORS, CORRUPT CFO, CORRUPT STOCK ANALYSTS, GREEDY BANKERS AND CLUELESS BOARD MEMBERS.
10/22/02 © 2002 United Feature Syndicate, Inc.
AND YOU?
WHAT ARE YOU IMPLYING?

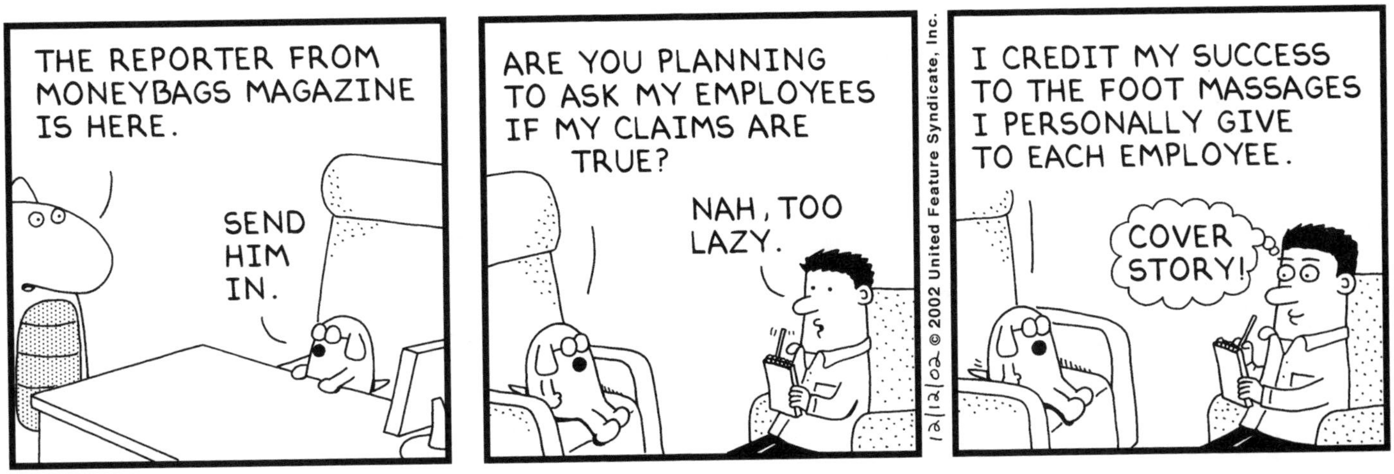
THE REPORTER FROM MONEYBAGS MAGAZINE IS HERE.
SEND HIM IN.
ARE YOU PLANNING TO ASK MY EMPLOYEES IF MY CLAIMS ARE TRUE?
NAH, TOO LAZY.
12/12/02 © 2002 United Feature Syndicate, Inc.
I CREDIT MY SUCCESS TO THE FOOT MASSAGES I PERSONALLY GIVE TO EACH EMPLOYEE.
COVER STORY!

DOGBERT THE CEO
OUR NEW FINANCIAL PRODUCT IS A HYBRID OF RISKY MORTGAGE LOANS AND A PONZI SCHEME.
WE'LL COVER OUR BAD LOAN LOSSES WITH OUR PROFITS FROM MAKING EVEN WORSE LOANS.
3-26-09 ©2009 Scott Adams, Inc./Dist. by UFS, Inc.
I'LL NEED SOME WAGGING ROOM WHILE I TELL YOU HOW THIS TIES INTO MY BONUS STRUCTURE.

DOGBERT THE CEO
DOES ANYONE HAVE ANY QUESTIONS ABOUT MY STRATEGIES?
YES, I. . .
BONK!
ZING!
3-27-09 ©2009 Scott Adams, Inc./Dist. by UFS, Inc.
THIS ISN'T THE DOTCOM ERA.

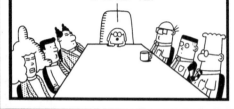

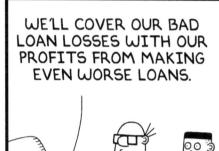

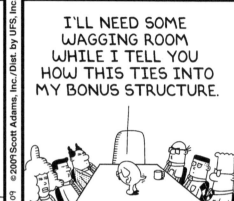

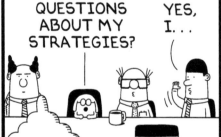

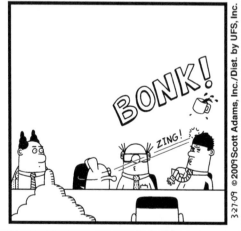

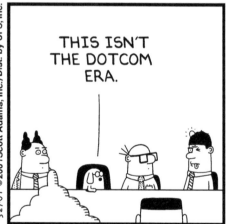

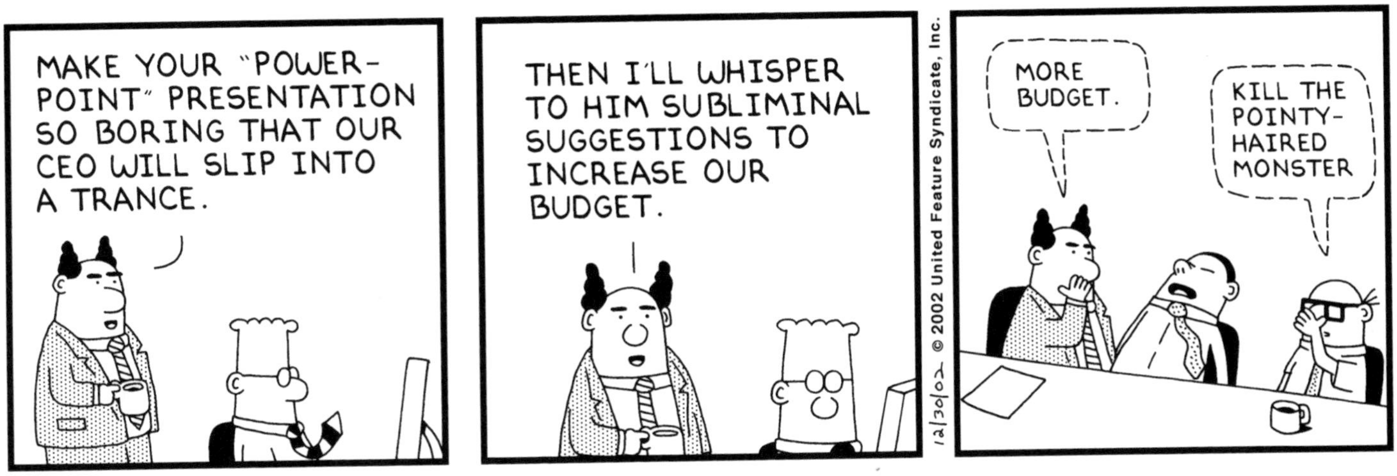
MAKE YOUR "POWER-POINT" PRESENTATION SO BORING THAT OUR CEO WILL SLIP INTO A TRANCE.
THEN I'LL WHISPER TO HIM SUBLIMINAL SUGGESTIONS TO INCREASE OUR BUDGET.
MORE BUDGET.
KILL THE POINTY-HAIRED MONSTER
12/30/02 © 2002 United Feature Syndicate, Inc.

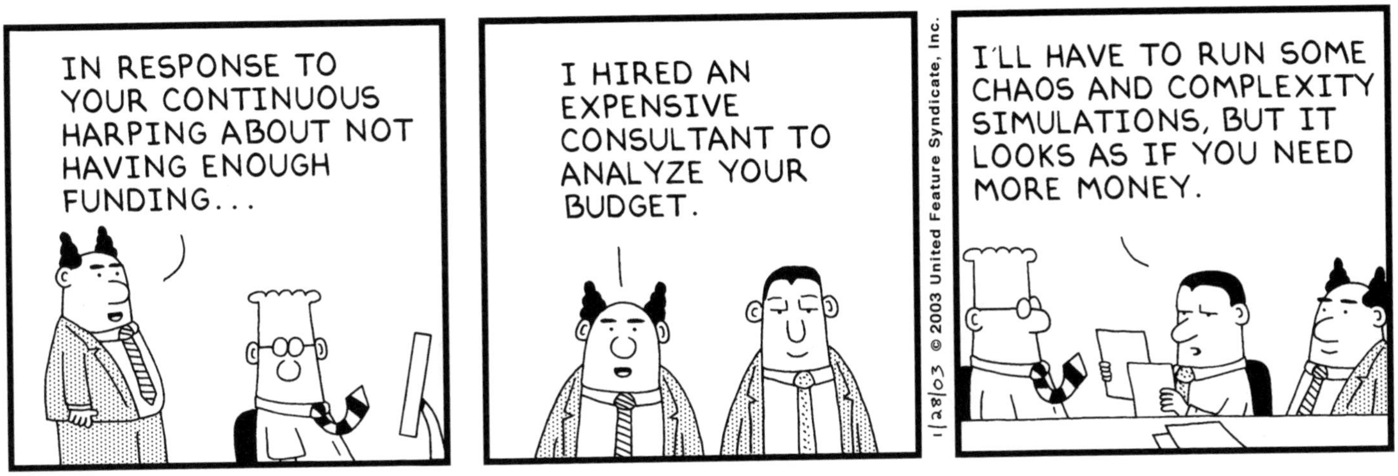
IN RESPONSE TO YOUR CONTINUOUS HARPING ABOUT NOT HAVING ENOUGH FUNDING...
I HIRED AN EXPENSIVE CONSULTANT TO ANALYZE YOUR BUDGET.
I'LL HAVE TO RUN SOME CHAOS AND COMPLEXITY SIMULATIONS, BUT IT LOOKS AS IF YOU NEED MORE MONEY.
1/28/03 © 2003 United Feature Syndicate, Inc.

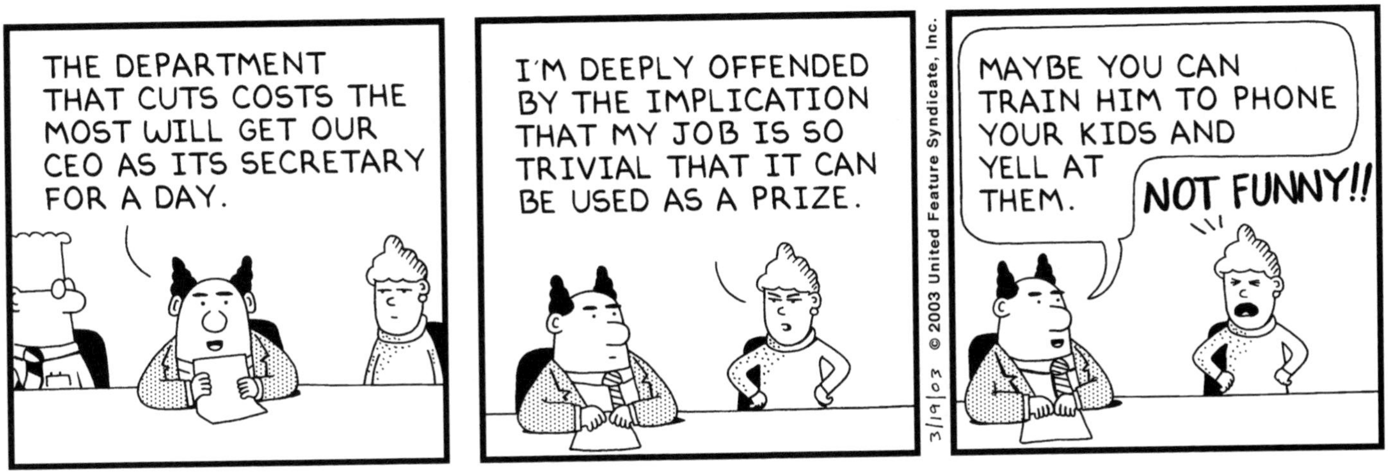
THE DEPARTMENT THAT CUTS COSTS THE MOST WILL GET OUR CEO AS ITS SECRETARY FOR A DAY.
I'M DEEPLY OFFENDED BY THE IMPLICATION THAT MY JOB IS SO TRIVIAL THAT IT CAN BE USED AS A PRIZE.
MAYBE YOU CAN TRAIN HIM TO PHONE YOUR KIDS AND YELL AT THEM.
NOT FUNNY!!
3/19/03 © 2003 United Feature Syndicate, Inc.

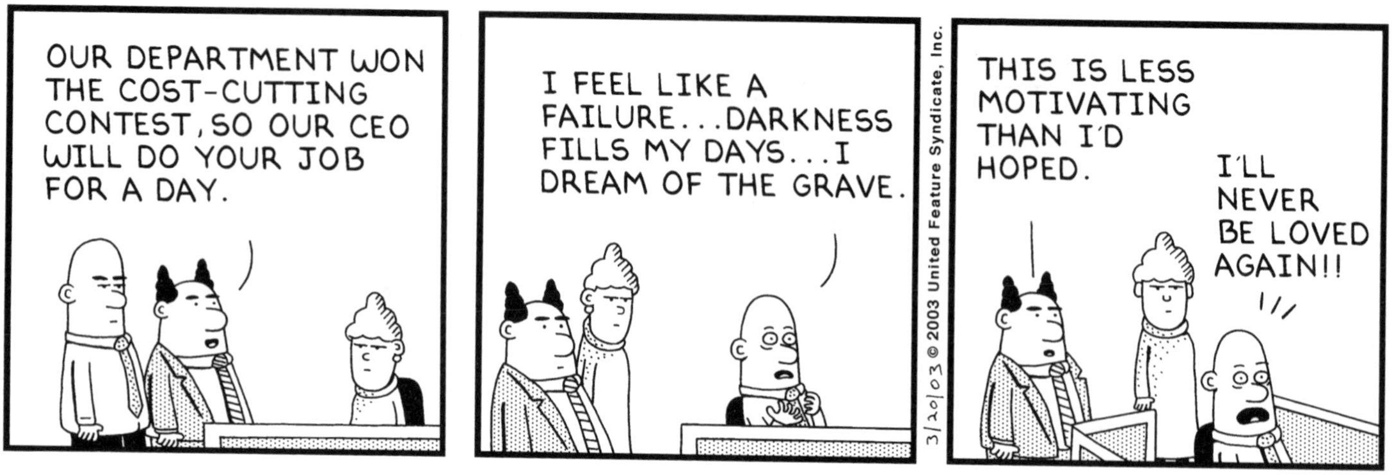
OUR DEPARTMENT WON THE COST-CUTTING CONTEST, SO OUR CEO WILL DO YOUR JOB FOR A DAY.
I FEEL LIKE A FAILURE...DARKNESS FILLS MY DAYS...I DREAM OF THE GRAVE.
3/20/03 © 2003 United Feature Syndicate, Inc.
THIS IS LESS MOTIVATING THAN I'D HOPED.
I'LL NEVER BE LOVED AGAIN!!

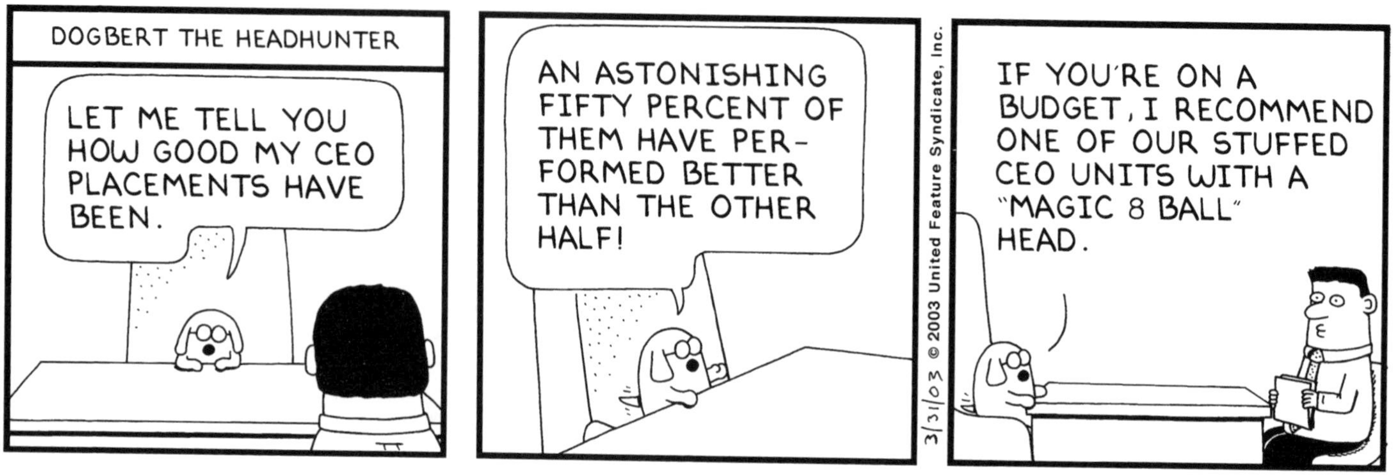
DOGBERT THE HEADHUNTER
LET ME TELL YOU HOW GOOD MY CEO PLACEMENTS HAVE BEEN.
AN ASTONISHING FIFTY PERCENT OF THEM HAVE PER-FORMED BETTER THAN THE OTHER HALF!
3/31/03 © 2003 United Feature Syndicate, Inc.
IF YOU'RE ON A BUDGET, I RECOMMEND ONE OF OUR STUFFED CEO UNITS WITH A "MAGIC 8 BALL" HEAD.

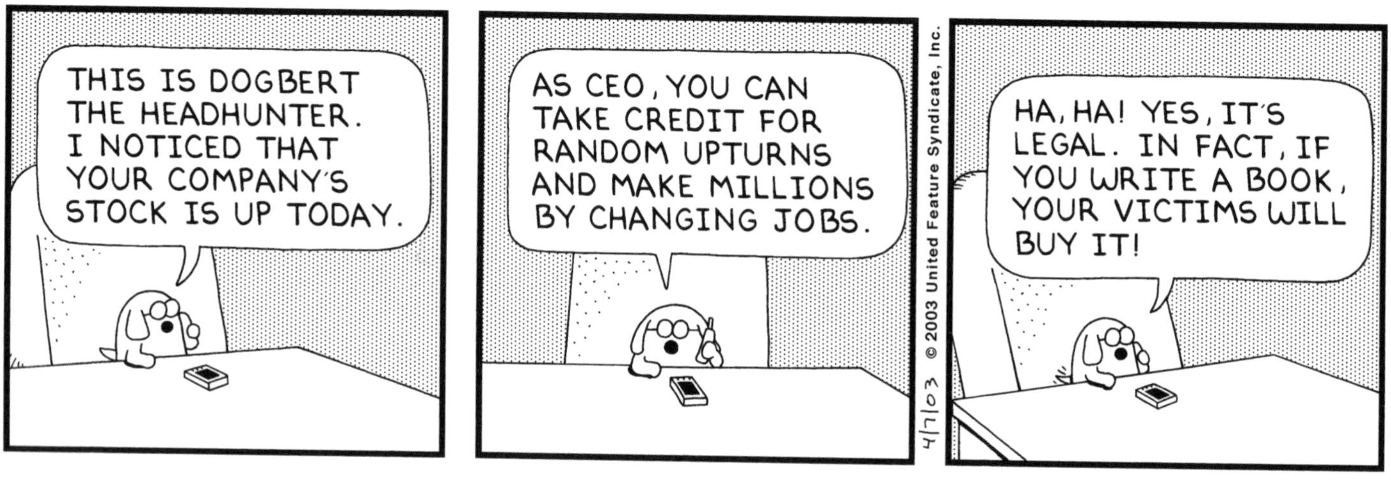
THIS IS DOGBERT THE HEADHUNTER. I NOTICED THAT YOUR COMPANY'S STOCK IS UP TODAY.
AS CEO, YOU CAN TAKE CREDIT FOR RANDOM UPTURNS AND MAKE MILLIONS BY CHANGING JOBS.
4/7/03 © 2003 United Feature Syndicate, Inc.
HA, HA! YES, IT'S LEGAL. IN FACT, IF YOU WRITE A BOOK, YOUR VICTIMS WILL BUY IT!

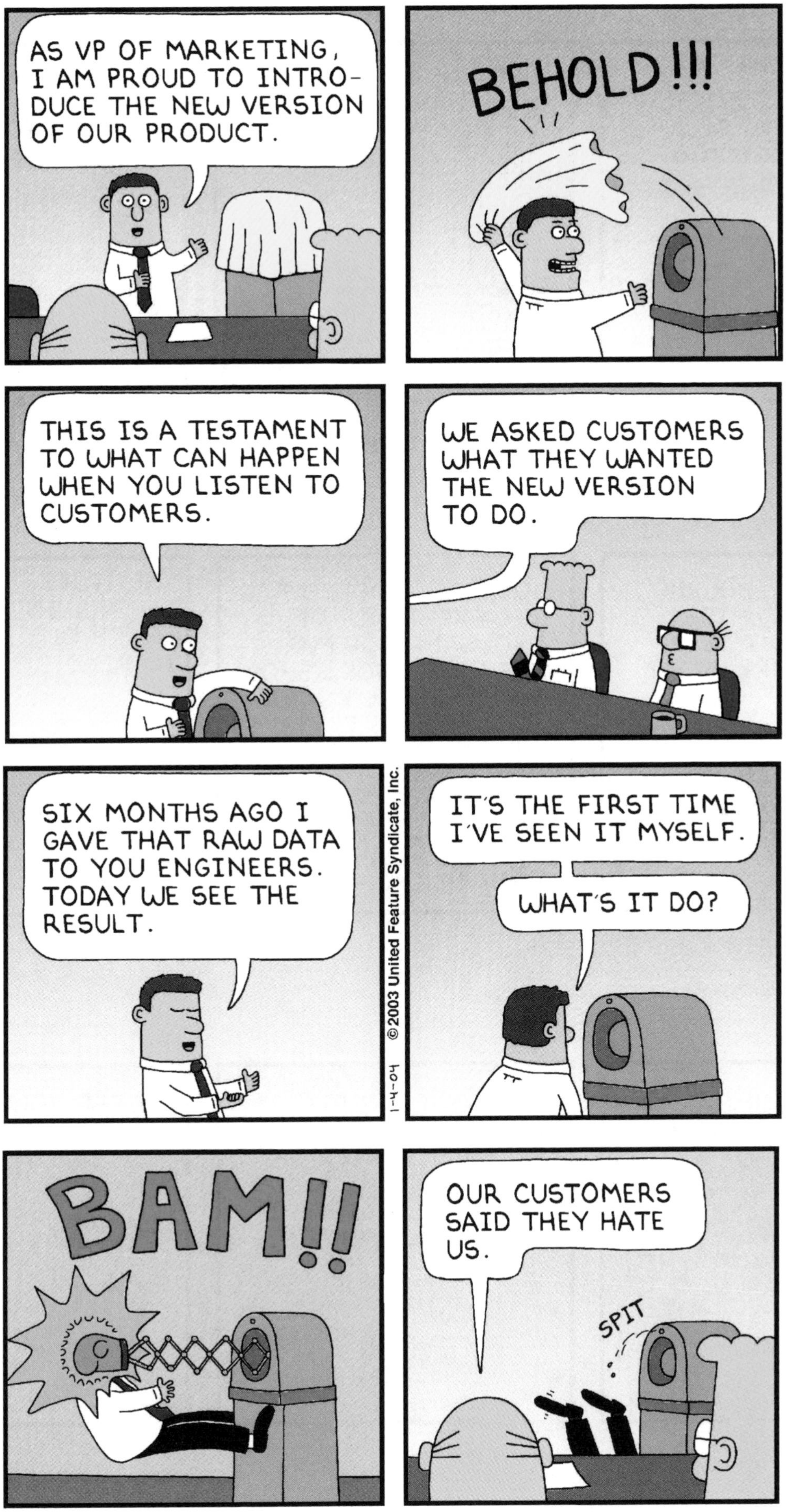
AS VP OF MARKETING, I AM PROUD TO INTRO- DUCE THE NEW VERSION OF OUR PRODUCT.
BEHOLD!!!
THIS IS A TESTAMENT TO WHAT CAN HAPPEN WHEN YOU LISTEN TO CUSTOMERS.
WE ASKED CUSTOMERS WHAT THEY WANTED THE NEW VERSION TO DO.
SIX MONTHS AGO I GAVE THAT RAW DATA TO YOU ENGINEERS. TODAY WE SEE THE RESULT.
©2003 United Feature Syndicate, Inc.
1-4-04
IT'S THE FIRST TIME I'VE SEEN IT MYSELF.
WHAT'S IT DO?
BAM!!
OUR CUSTOMERS SAID THEY HATE US.
SPIT

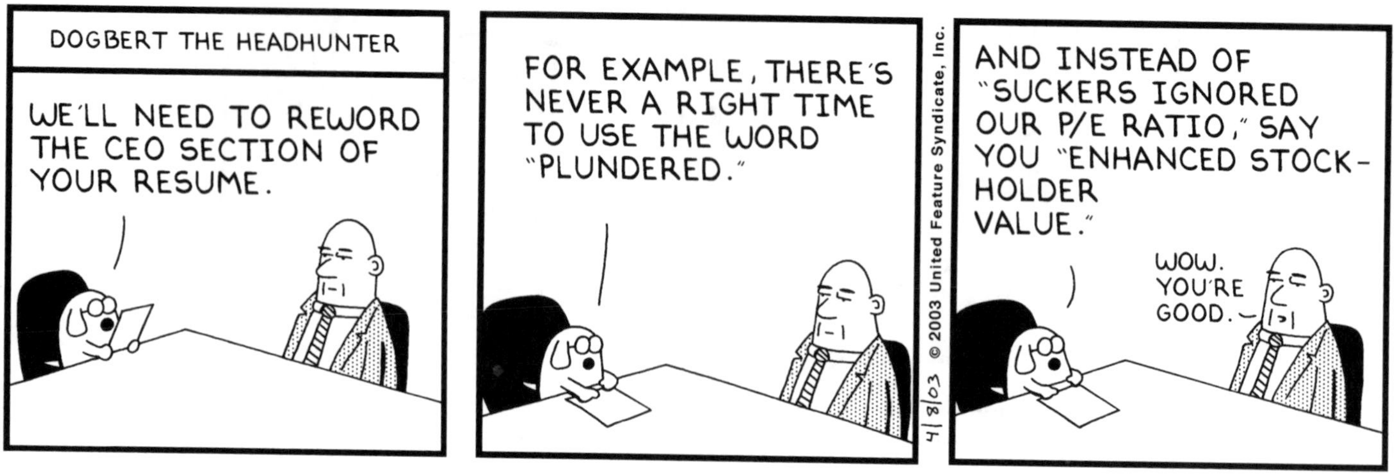
DOGBERT THE HEADHUNTER
WE'LL NEED TO REWORD THE CEO SECTION OF YOUR RESUME.
FOR EXAMPLE, THERE'S NEVER A RIGHT TIME TO USE THE WORD "PLUNDERED."
© 2003 United Feature Syndicate, Inc.
4/8/03
AND INSTEAD OF "SUCKERS IGNORED OUR P/E RATIO," SAY YOU "ENHANCED STOCK-HOLDER VALUE."
WOW. YOU'RE GOOD.

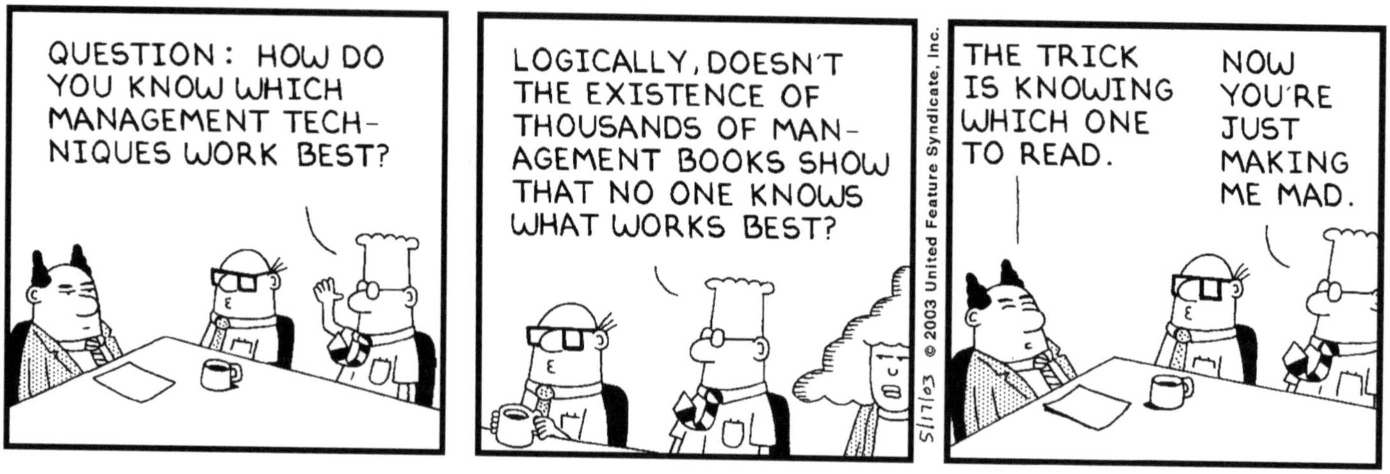
QUESTION: HOW DO YOU KNOW WHICH MANAGEMENT TECHNIQUES WORK BEST?
LOGICALLY, DOESN'T THE EXISTENCE OF THOUSANDS OF MANAGEMENT BOOKS SHOW THAT NO ONE KNOWS WHAT WORKS BEST?
© 2003 United Feature Syndicate, Inc.
5/17/03
THE TRICK IS KNOWING WHICH ONE TO READ.
NOW YOU'RE JUST MAKING ME MAD.

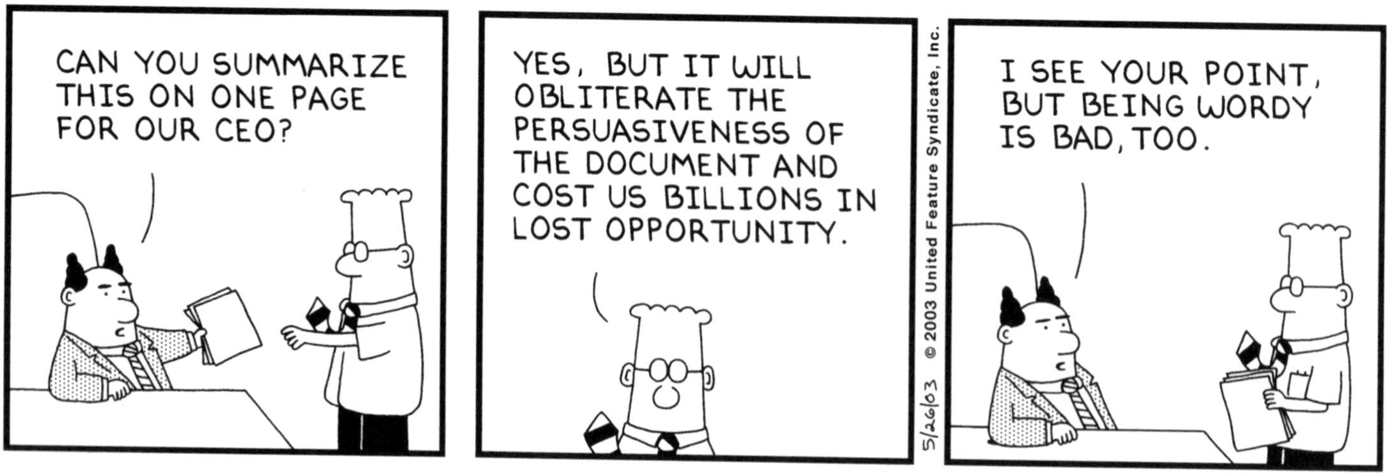
CAN YOU SUMMARIZE THIS ON ONE PAGE FOR OUR CEO?
YES, BUT IT WILL OBLITERATE THE PERSUASIVENESS OF THE DOCUMENT AND COST US BILLIONS IN LOST OPPORTUNITY.
© 2003 United Feature Syndicate, Inc.
5/26/03
I SEE YOUR POINT, BUT BEING WORDY IS BAD, TOO.

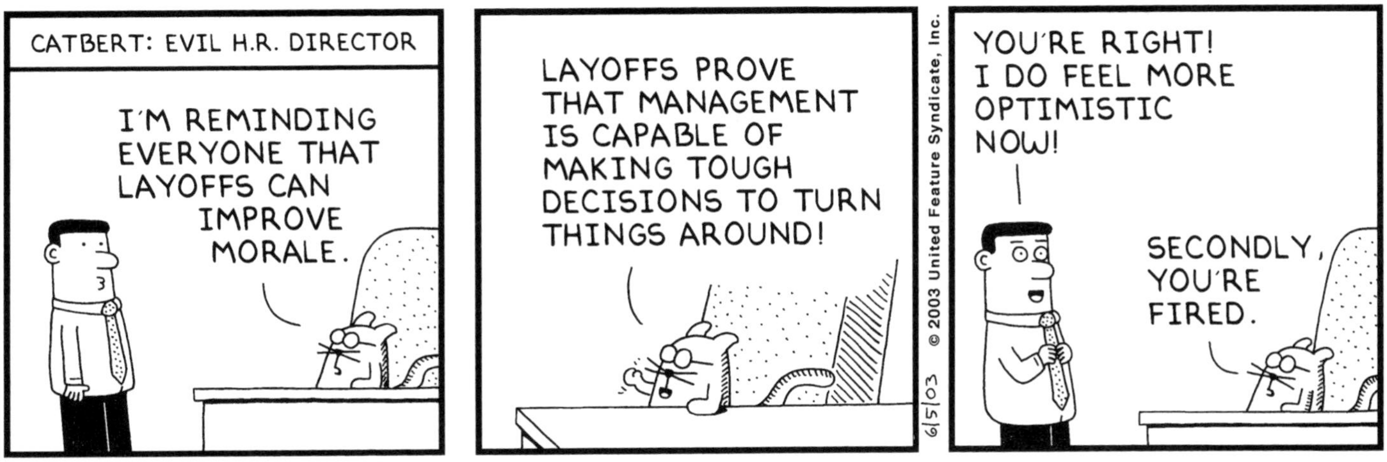
CATBERT: EVIL H.R. DIRECTOR
I'M REMINDING EVERYONE THAT LAYOFFS CAN IMPROVE MORALE.
LAYOFFS PROVE THAT MANAGEMENT IS CAPABLE OF MAKING TOUGH DECISIONS TO TURN THINGS AROUND!
6/5/03 © 2003 United Feature Syndicate, Inc.
YOU'RE RIGHT! I DO FEEL MORE OPTIMISTIC NOW!
SECONDLY, YOU'RE FIRED.

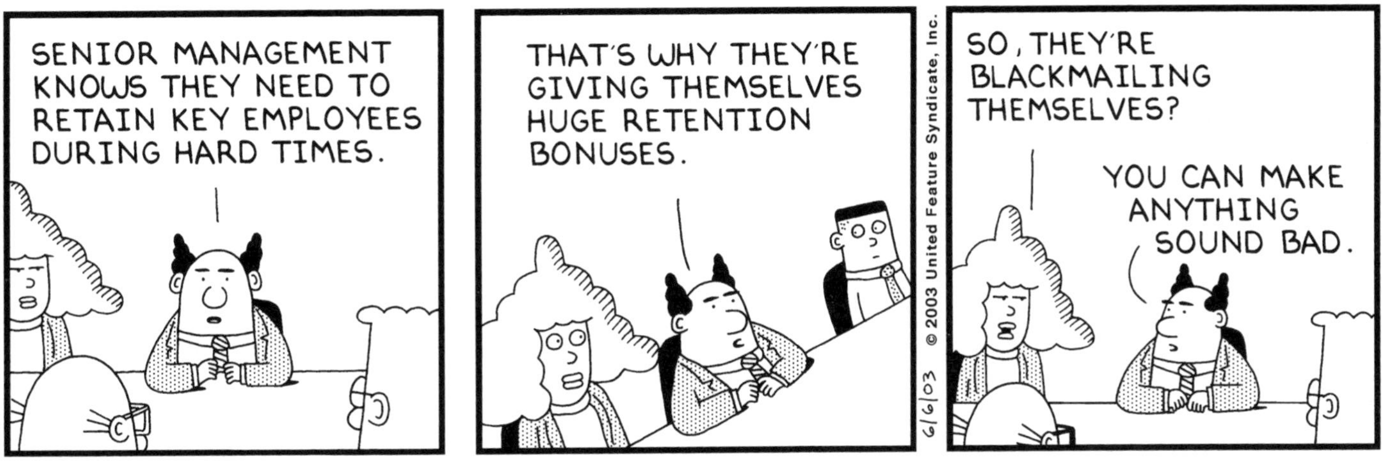
SENIOR MANAGEMENT KNOWS THEY NEED TO RETAIN KEY EMPLOYEES DURING HARD TIMES.
THAT'S WHY THEY'RE GIVING THEMSELVES HUGE RETENTION BONUSES.
6/6/03 © 2003 United Feature Syndicate, Inc.
SO, THEY'RE BLACKMAILING THEMSELVES?
YOU CAN MAKE ANYTHING SOUND BAD.

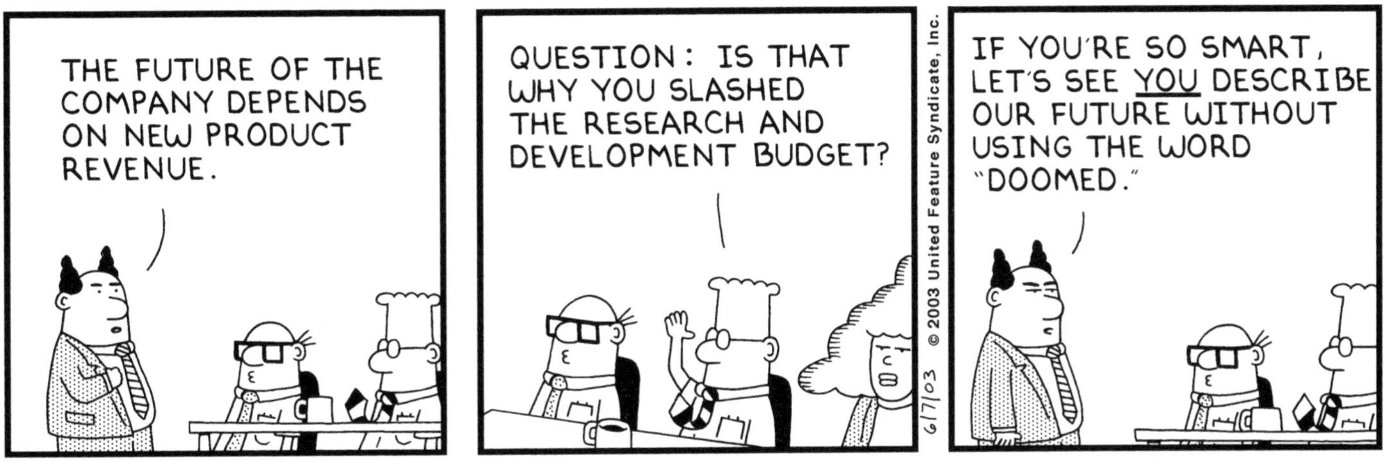
THE FUTURE OF THE COMPANY DEPENDS ON NEW PRODUCT REVENUE.
QUESTION: IS THAT WHY YOU SLASHED THE RESEARCH AND DEVELOPMENT BUDGET?
6/7/03 © 2003 United Feature Syndicate, Inc.
IF YOU'RE SO SMART, LET'S SEE YOU DESCRIBE OUR FUTURE WITHOUT USING THE WORD "DOOMED."

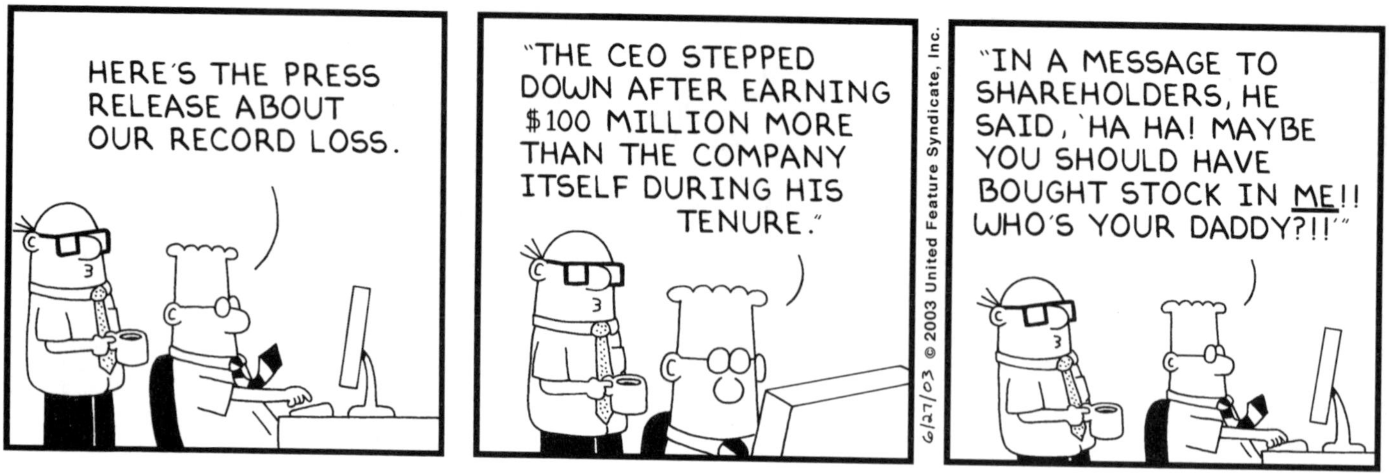
HERE'S THE PRESS RELEASE ABOUT OUR RECORD LOSS.
"THE CEO STEPPED DOWN AFTER EARNING $100 MILLION MORE THAN THE COMPANY ITSELF DURING HIS TENURE."
© 2003 United Feature Syndicate, Inc.
6/27/03
"IN A MESSAGE TO SHAREHOLDERS, HE SAID, 'HA HA! MAYBE YOU SHOULD HAVE BOUGHT STOCK IN ME!! WHO'S YOUR DADDY?!!'"

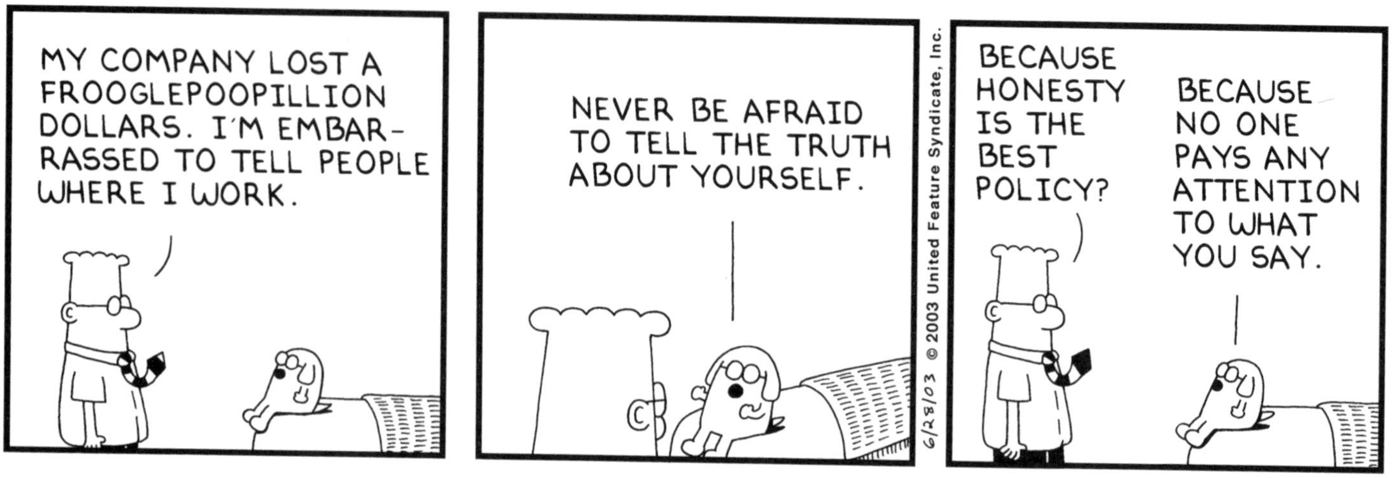
MY COMPANY LOST A FROOGLEPOOPILLION DOLLARS. I'M EMBARRASSED TO TELL PEOPLE WHERE I WORK.
NEVER BE AFRAID TO TELL THE TRUTH ABOUT YOURSELF.
© 2003 United Feature Syndicate, Inc.
6/28/03
BECAUSE HONESTY IS THE BEST POLICY?
BECAUSE NO ONE PAYS ANY ATTENTION TO WHAT YOU SAY.

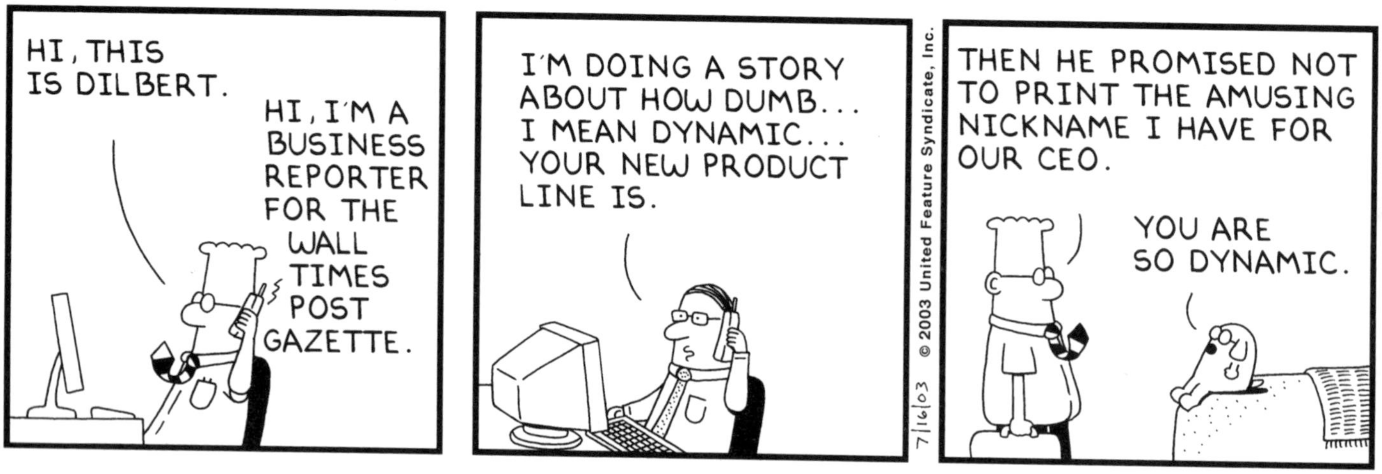
HI, THIS IS DILBERT.
HI, I'M A BUSINESS REPORTER FOR THE WALL TIMES POST GAZETTE.
I'M DOING A STORY ABOUT HOW DUMB... I MEAN DYNAMIC... YOUR NEW PRODUCT LINE IS.
© 2003 United Feature Syndicate, Inc.
7/16/03
THEN HE PROMISED NOT TO PRINT THE AMUSING NICKNAME I HAVE FOR OUR CEO.
YOU ARE SO DYNAMIC.

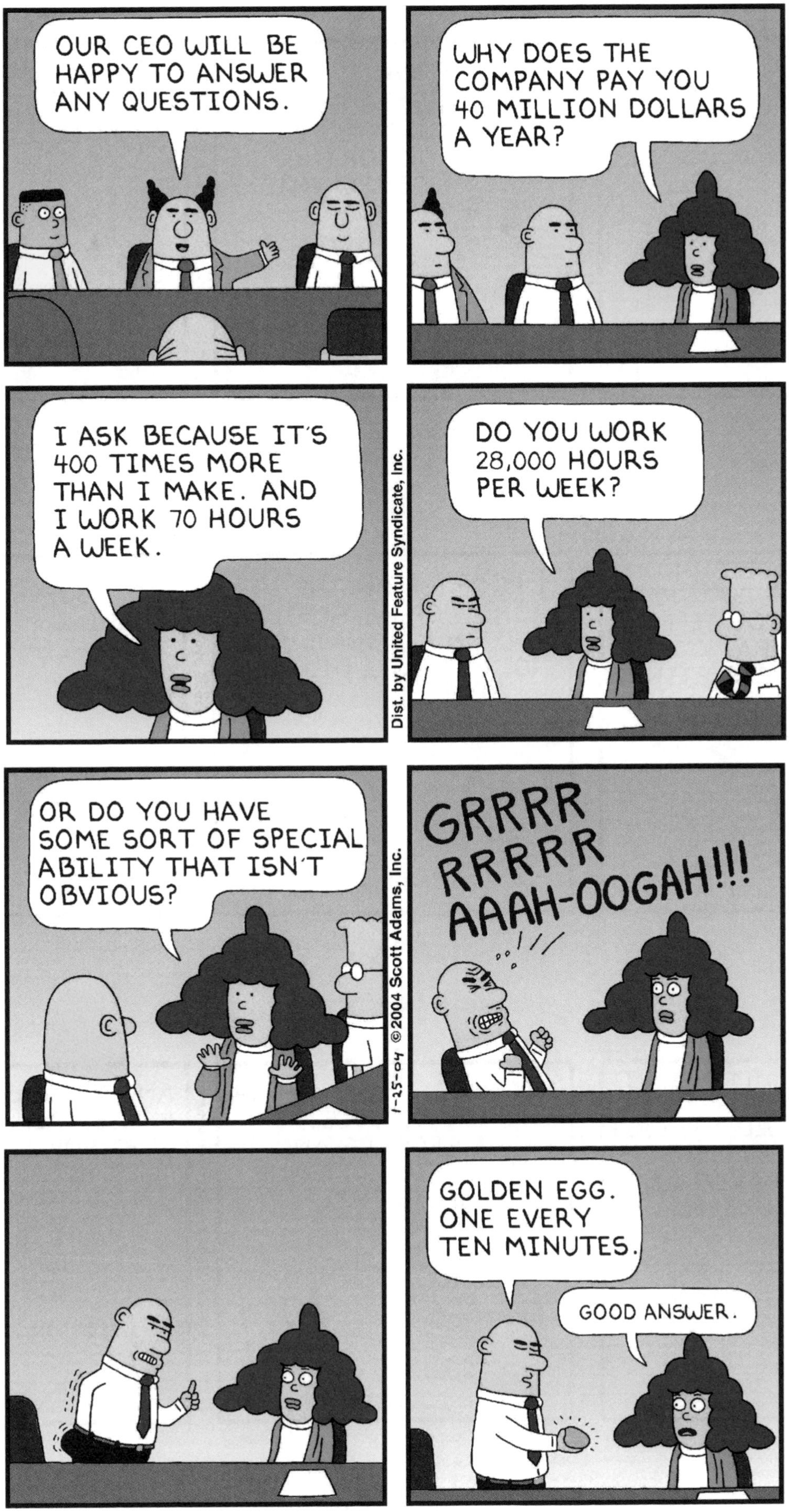
OUR CEO WILL BE HAPPY TO ANSWER ANY QUESTIONS.
WHY DOES THE COMPANY PAY YOU 40 MILLION DOLLARS A YEAR?
I ASK BECAUSE IT'S 400 TIMES MORE THAN I MAKE. AND I WORK 70 HOURS A WEEK.
DO YOU WORK 28,000 HOURS PER WEEK?
OR DO YOU HAVE SOME SORT OF SPECIAL ABILITY THAT ISN'T OBVIOUS?
GRRRR RRRRR AAAH-OOGAH!!!
GOLDEN EGG. ONE EVERY TEN MINUTES.
GOOD ANSWER.
Dist. by United Feature Syndicate, Inc.
1-25-04 ©2004 Scott Adams, Inc.

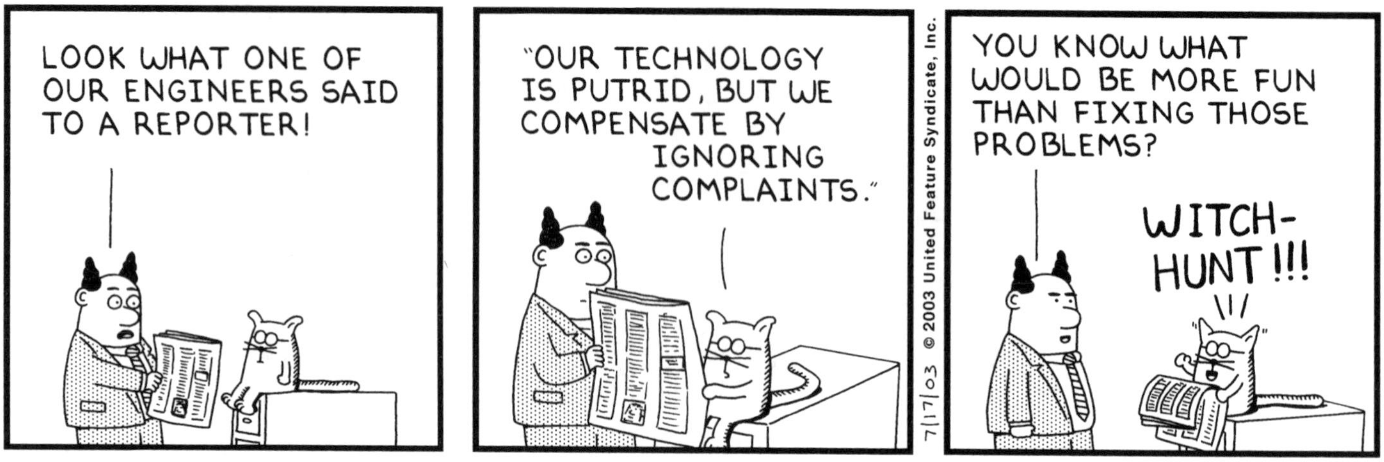
LOOK WHAT ONE OF OUR ENGINEERS SAID TO A REPORTER!
"OUR TECHNOLOGY IS PUTRID, BUT WE COMPENSATE BY IGNORING COMPLAINTS."
© 2003 United Feature Syndicate, Inc.
7/17/03
YOU KNOW WHAT WOULD BE MORE FUN THAN FIXING THOSE PROBLEMS?
WITCH-HUNT!!!

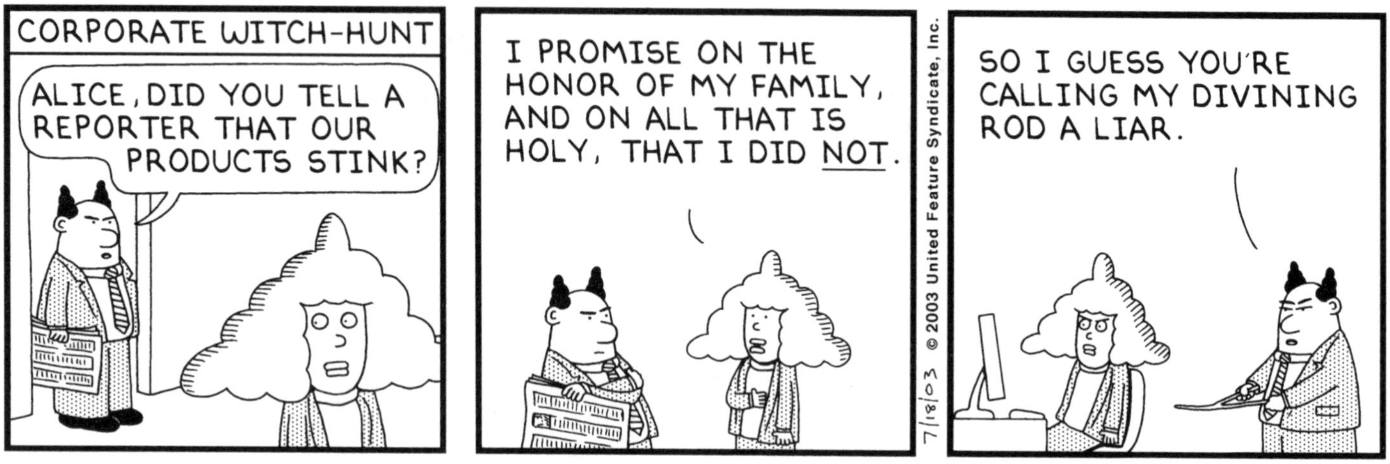
CORPORATE WITCH-HUNT
ALICE, DID YOU TELL A REPORTER THAT OUR PRODUCTS STINK?
I PROMISE ON THE HONOR OF MY FAMILY, AND ON ALL THAT IS HOLY, THAT I DID NOT.
© 2003 United Feature Syndicate, Inc.
7/18/03
SO I GUESS YOU'RE CALLING MY DIVINING ROD A LIAR.

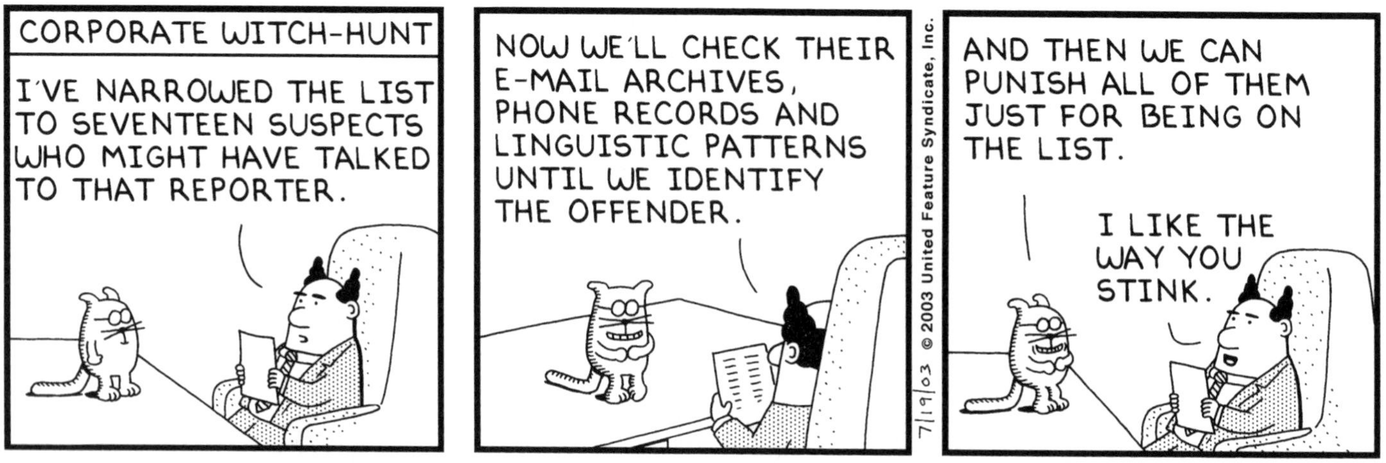
CORPORATE WITCH-HUNT
I'VE NARROWED THE LIST TO SEVENTEEN SUSPECTS WHO MIGHT HAVE TALKED TO THAT REPORTER.
NOW WE'LL CHECK THEIR E-MAIL ARCHIVES, PHONE RECORDS AND LINGUISTIC PATTERNS UNTIL WE IDENTIFY THE OFFENDER.
© 2003 United Feature Syndicate, Inc.
7/19/03
AND THEN WE CAN PUNISH ALL OF THEM JUST FOR BEING ON THE LIST.
I LIKE THE WAY YOU STINK.

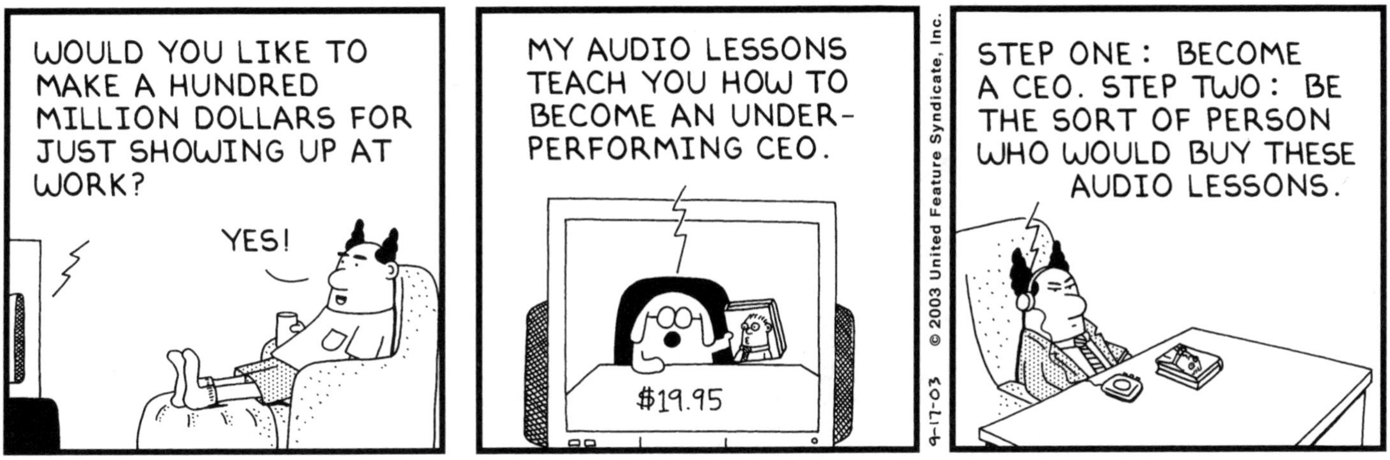
WOULD YOU LIKE TO MAKE A HUNDRED MILLION DOLLARS FOR JUST SHOWING UP AT WORK?
YES!
MY AUDIO LESSONS TEACH YOU HOW TO BECOME AN UNDER-PERFORMING CEO.
$19.95
9-17-03
© 2003 United Feature Syndicate, Inc.
STEP ONE: BECOME A CEO. STEP TWO: BE THE SORT OF PERSON WHO WOULD BUY THESE AUDIO LESSONS.

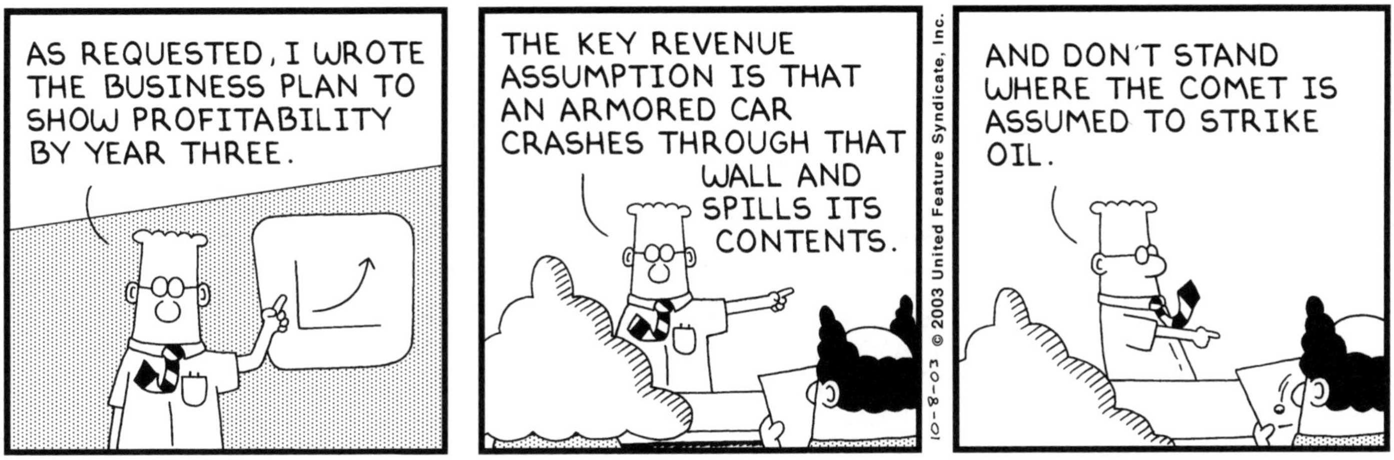
AS REQUESTED, I WROTE THE BUSINESS PLAN TO SHOW PROFITABILITY BY YEAR THREE.
THE KEY REVENUE ASSUMPTION IS THAT AN ARMORED CAR CRASHES THROUGH THAT WALL AND SPILLS ITS CONTENTS.
10-8-03
© 2003 United Feature Syndicate, Inc.
AND DON'T STAND WHERE THE COMET IS ASSUMED TO STRIKE OIL.

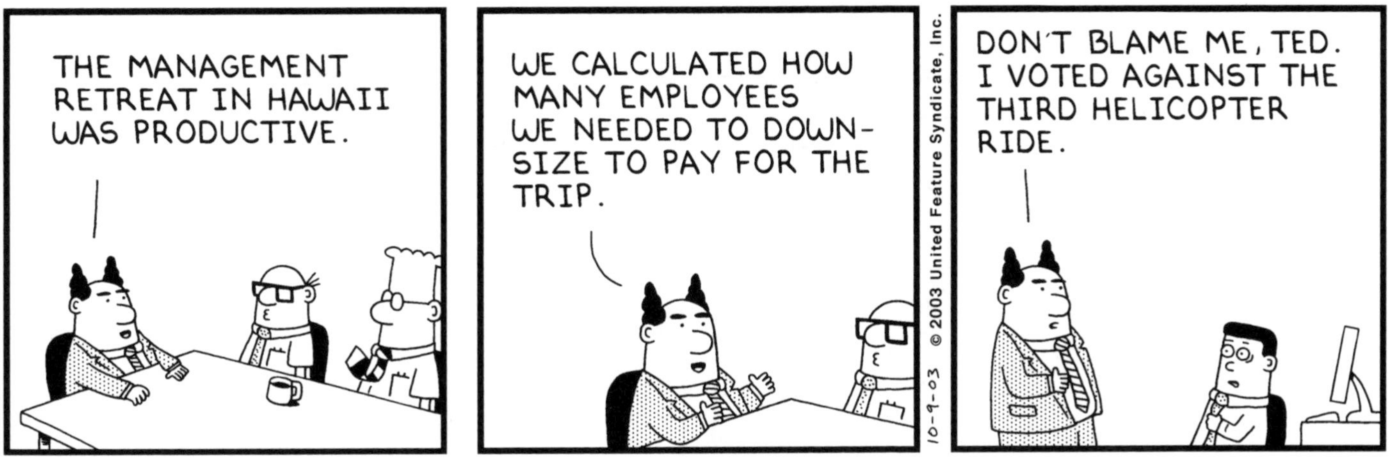
THE MANAGEMENT RETREAT IN HAWAII WAS PRODUCTIVE.
WE CALCULATED HOW MANY EMPLOYEES WE NEEDED TO DOWN-SIZE TO PAY FOR THE TRIP.
10-9-03
© 2003 United Feature Syndicate, Inc.
DON'T BLAME ME, TED. I VOTED AGAINST THE THIRD HELICOPTER RIDE.

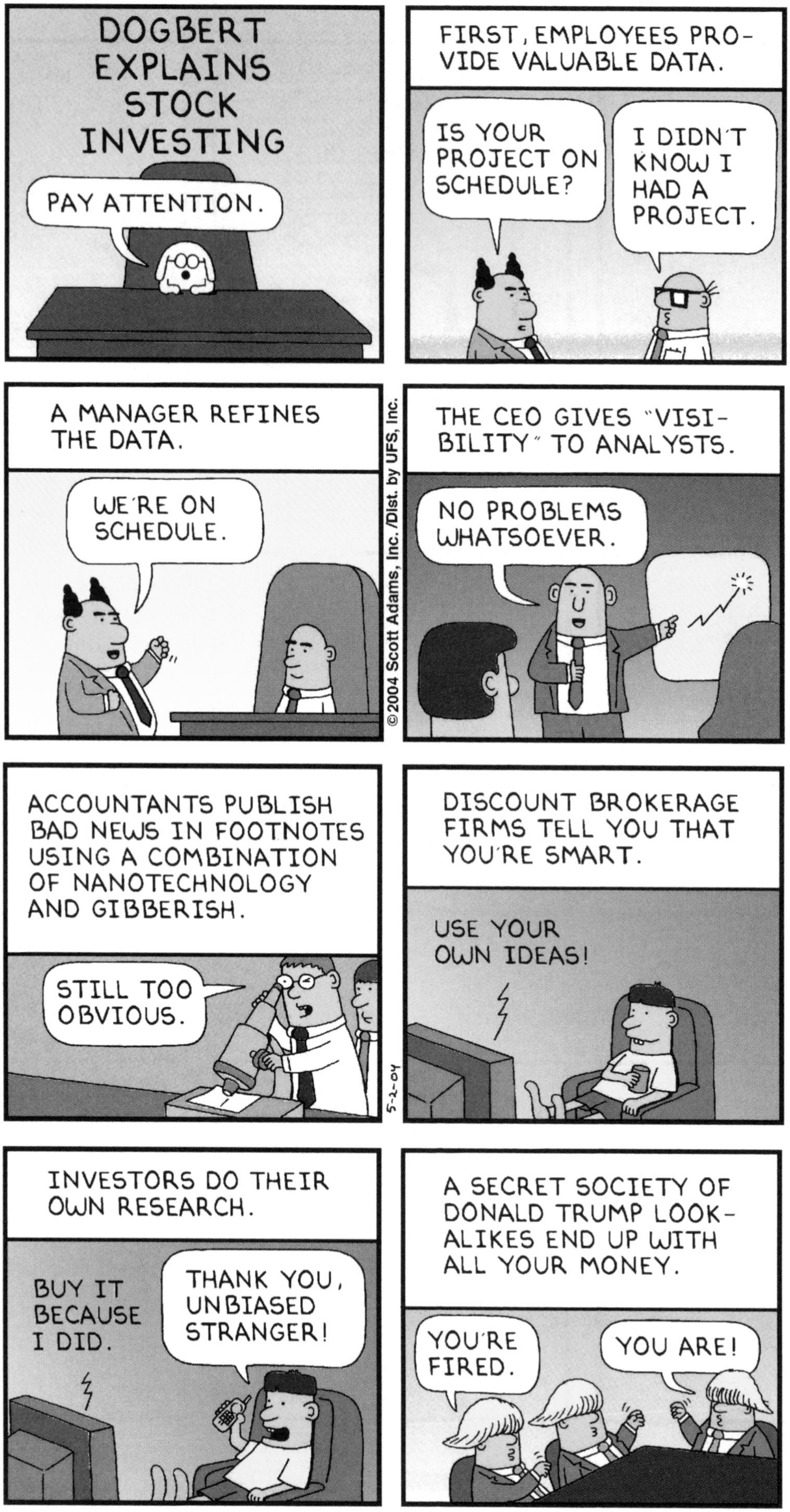
DOGBERT EXPLAINS STOCK INVESTING
PAY ATTENTION.
FIRST, EMPLOYEES PROVIDE VALUABLE DATA.
IS YOUR PROJECT ON SCHEDULE?
I DIDN'T KNOW I HAD A PROJECT.
A MANAGER REFINES THE DATA.
WE'RE ON SCHEDULE.
©2004 Scott Adams, Inc./Dist. by UFS, Inc.
THE CEO GIVES "VISIBILITY" TO ANALYSTS.
NO PROBLEMS WHATSOEVER.
ACCOUNTANTS PUBLISH BAD NEWS IN FOOTNOTES USING A COMBINATION OF NANOTECHNOLOGY AND GIBBERISH.
STILL TOO OBVIOUS.
5-2-04
DISCOUNT BROKERAGE FIRMS TELL YOU THAT YOU'RE SMART.
USE YOUR OWN IDEAS!
INVESTORS DO THEIR OWN RESEARCH.
BUY IT BECAUSE I DID.
THANK YOU, UNBIASED STRANGER!
A SECRET SOCIETY OF DONALD TRUMP LOOK-ALIKES END UP WITH ALL YOUR MONEY.
YOU'RE FIRED.
YOU ARE!

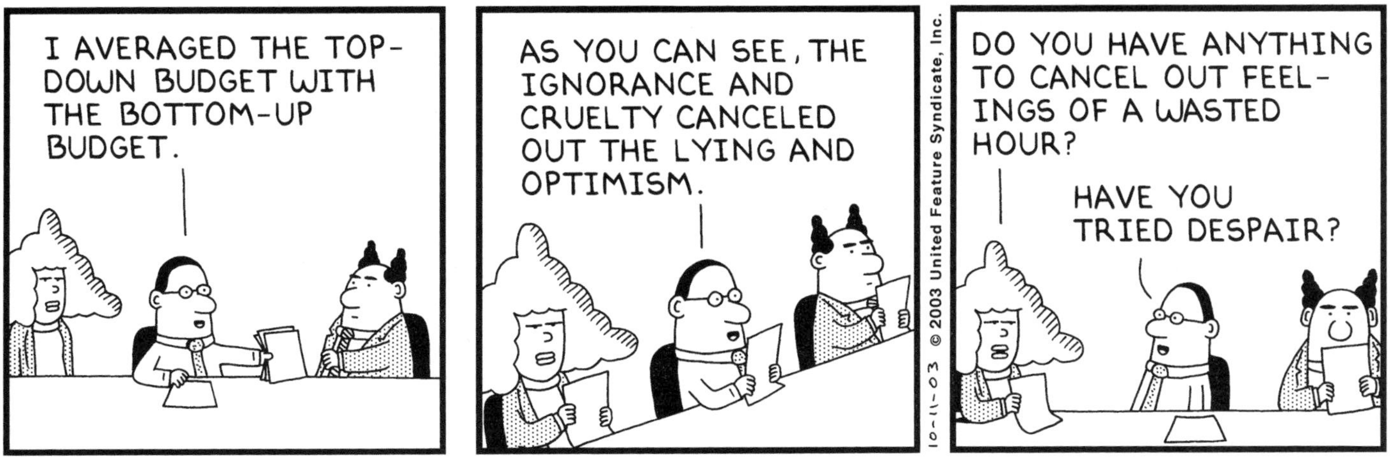
I AVERAGED THE TOP-DOWN BUDGET WITH THE BOTTOM-UP BUDGET.
AS YOU CAN SEE, THE IGNORANCE AND CRUELTY CANCELED OUT THE LYING AND OPTIMISM.
10-11-03 © 2003 United Feature Syndicate, Inc.
DO YOU HAVE ANYTHING TO CANCEL OUT FEELINGS OF A WASTED HOUR?
HAVE YOU TRIED DESPAIR?

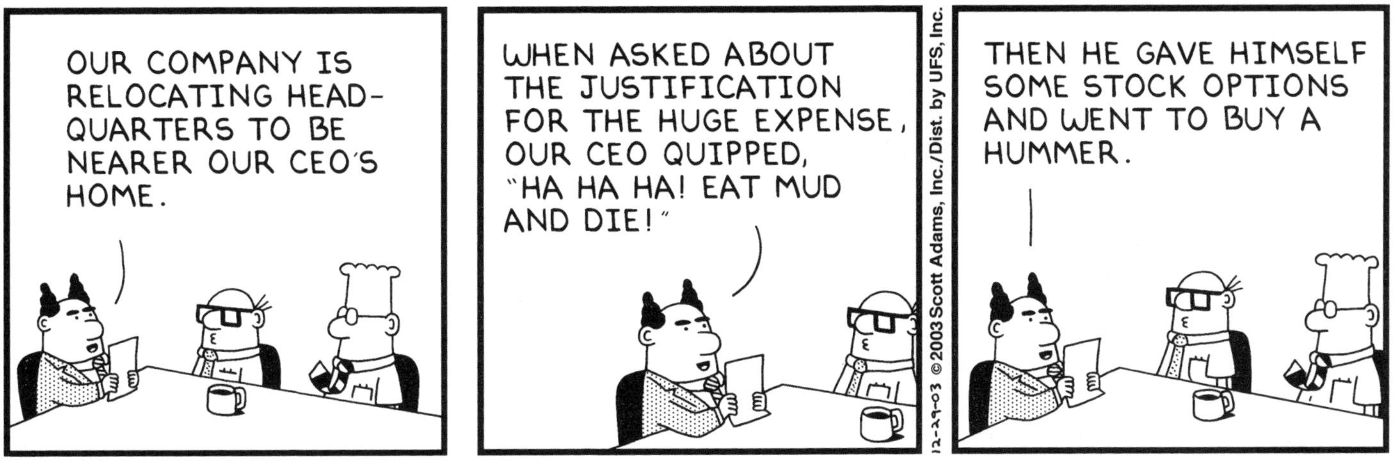
OUR COMPANY IS RELOCATING HEADQUARTERS TO BE NEARER OUR CEO'S HOME.
WHEN ASKED ABOUT THE JUSTIFICATION FOR THE HUGE EXPENSE, OUR CEO QUIPPED, "HA HA HA! EAT MUD AND DIE!"
12-29-03 © 2003 Scott Adams, Inc./Dist. by UFS, Inc.
THEN HE GAVE HIMSELF SOME STOCK OPTIONS AND WENT TO BUY A HUMMER.

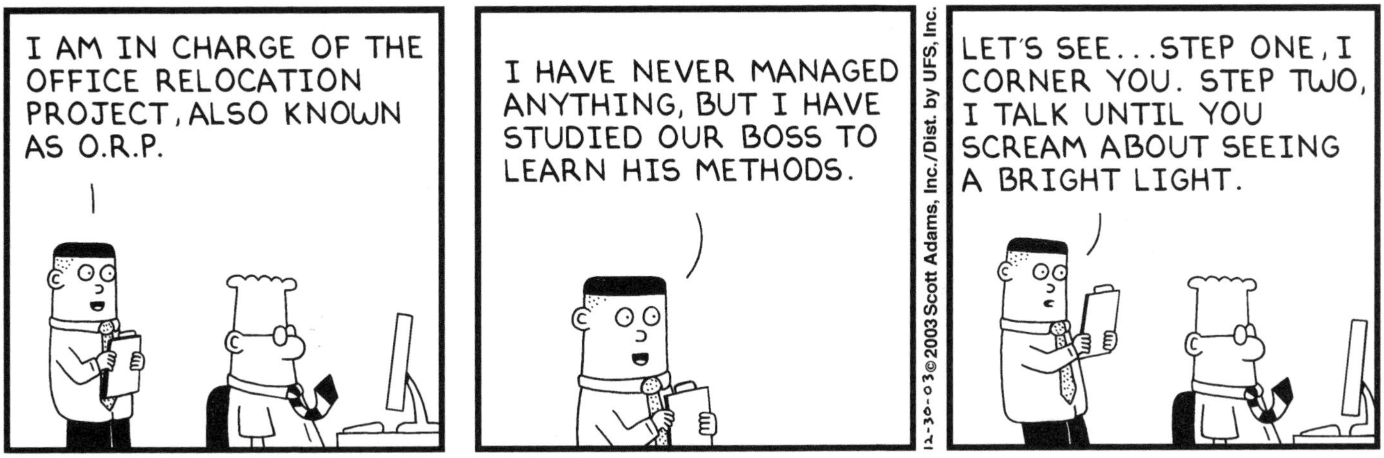
I AM IN CHARGE OF THE OFFICE RELOCATION PROJECT, ALSO KNOWN AS O.R.P.
I HAVE NEVER MANAGED ANYTHING, BUT I HAVE STUDIED OUR BOSS TO LEARN HIS METHODS.
12-30-03 © 2003 Scott Adams, Inc./Dist. by UFS, Inc.
LET'S SEE... STEP ONE, I CORNER YOU. STEP TWO, I TALK UNTIL YOU SCREAM ABOUT SEEING A BRIGHT LIGHT.

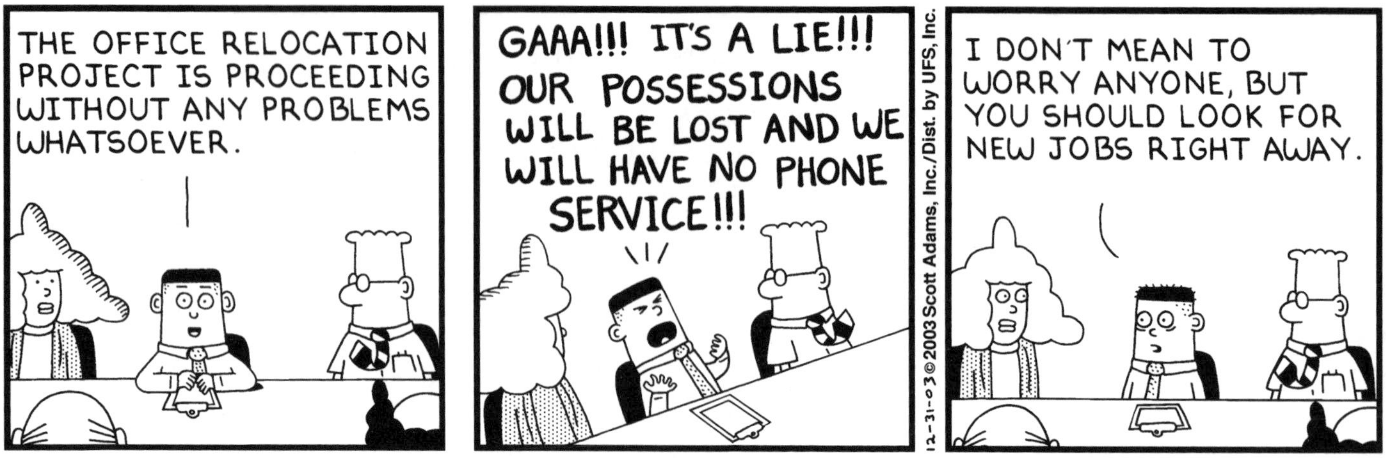
THE OFFICE RELOCATION PROJECT IS PROCEEDING WITHOUT ANY PROBLEMS WHATSOEVER.
GAAA!!! IT'S A LIE!!! OUR POSSESSIONS WILL BE LOST AND WE WILL HAVE NO PHONE SERVICE!!!
12-31-03 © 2003 Scott Adams, Inc./Dist. by UFS, Inc.
I DON'T MEAN TO WORRY ANYONE, BUT YOU SHOULD LOOK FOR NEW JOBS RIGHT AWAY.

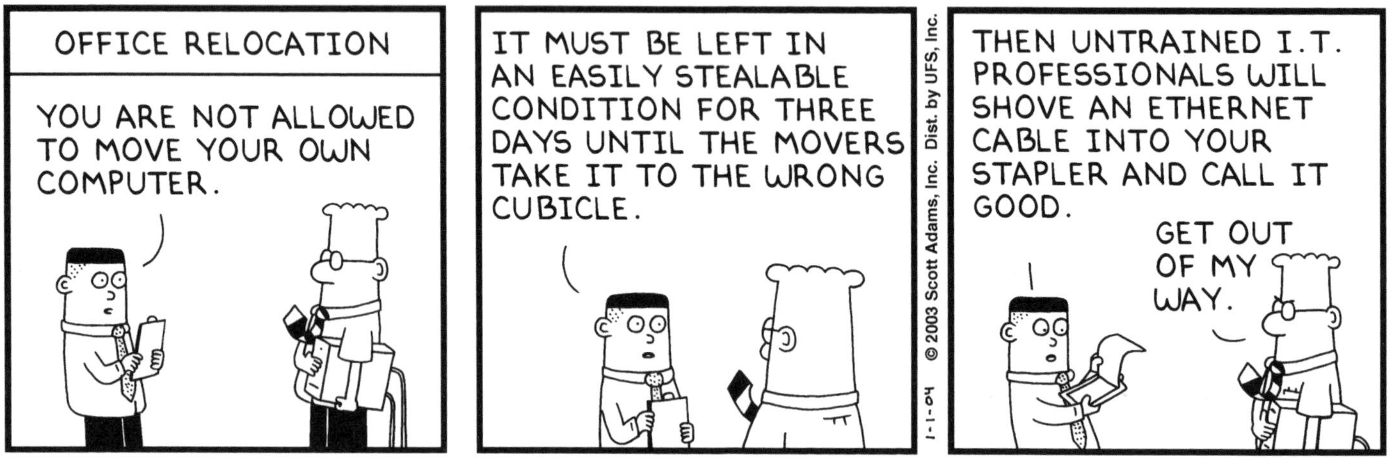
OFFICE RELOCATION
YOU ARE NOT ALLOWED TO MOVE YOUR OWN COMPUTER.
IT MUST BE LEFT IN AN EASILY STEALABLE CONDITION FOR THREE DAYS UNTIL THE MOVERS TAKE IT TO THE WRONG CUBICLE.
1-1-04 © 2003 Scott Adams, Inc. Dist. by UFS, Inc.
THEN UNTRAINED I.T. PROFESSIONALS WILL SHOVE AN ETHERNET CABLE INTO YOUR STAPLER AND CALL IT GOOD.
GET OUT OF MY WAY.

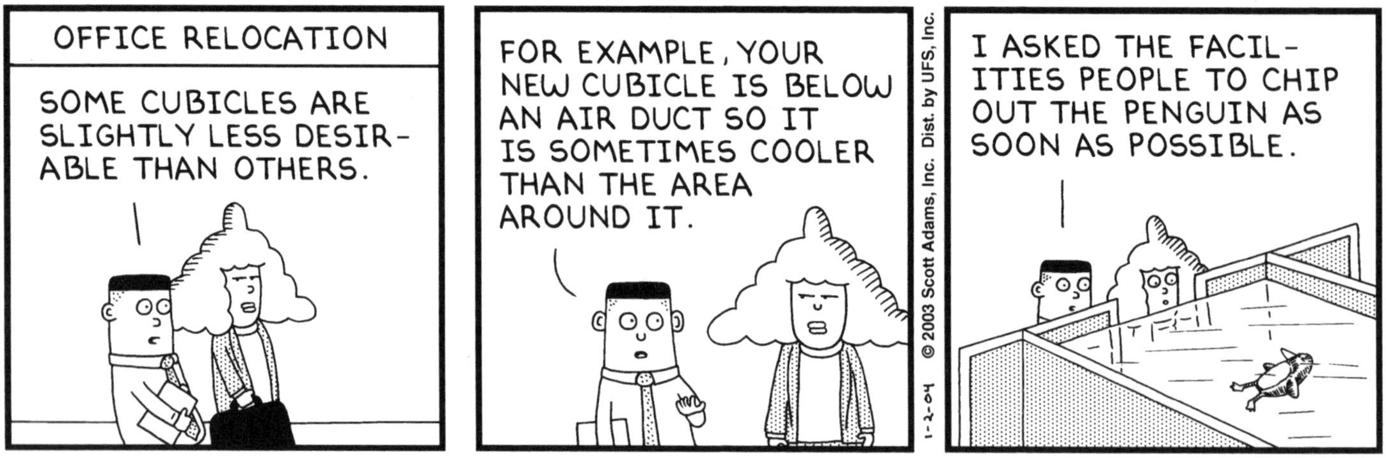
OFFICE RELOCATION
SOME CUBICLES ARE SLIGHTLY LESS DESIRABLE THAN OTHERS.
FOR EXAMPLE, YOUR NEW CUBICLE IS BELOW AN AIR DUCT SO IT IS SOMETIMES COOLER THAN THE AREA AROUND IT.
1-2-04 © 2003 Scott Adams, Inc. Dist. by UFS, Inc.
I ASKED THE FACILITIES PEOPLE TO CHIP OUT THE PENGUIN AS SOON AS POSSIBLE.

DOGBERT THE CEO
THE UNION WILL AGREE TO DEEP CUTS IF YOU AGREE TO WORK FOR ONE DOLLAR PER YEAR.
I AGREE, AS LONG AS I GET MY PAY IN ADVANCE AND THE MANDATORY RETIRE-MENT AGE IS WAIVED.
FINE.
3-28-09 © 2009 Scott Adams, Inc./Dist. by UFS, Inc.
CALL PAYROLL AND TELL THEM TO CUT A CHECK FOR MY NEXT TEN BILLION YEARS OF SERVICE.

DOGBERT THE CEO
THE NEW MOTIVATIONAL POSTERS ARE IN.
AS YOU REQUESTED, I BOUGHT THE LEAST EXPENSIVE ONES.
EXCUSE ME WHILE I STRETCH MY WAGGER.
4-8-09 © 2009 Scott Adams, Inc./Dist. by UFS, Inc.
IF ALL ELSE FAILS...
YOUR COWORKERS ARE EDIBLE

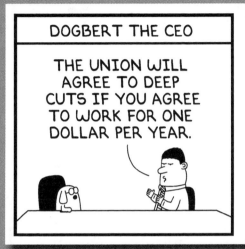

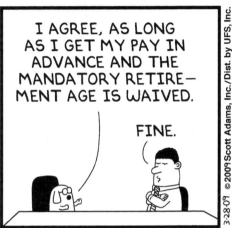

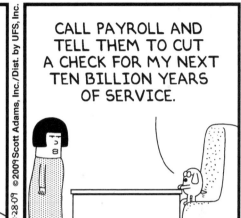

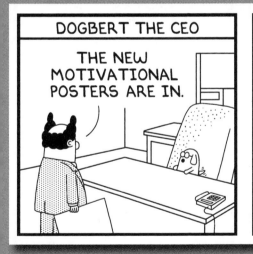

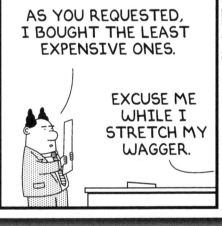

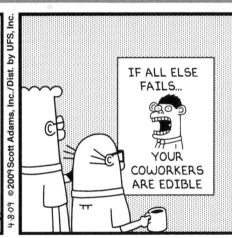

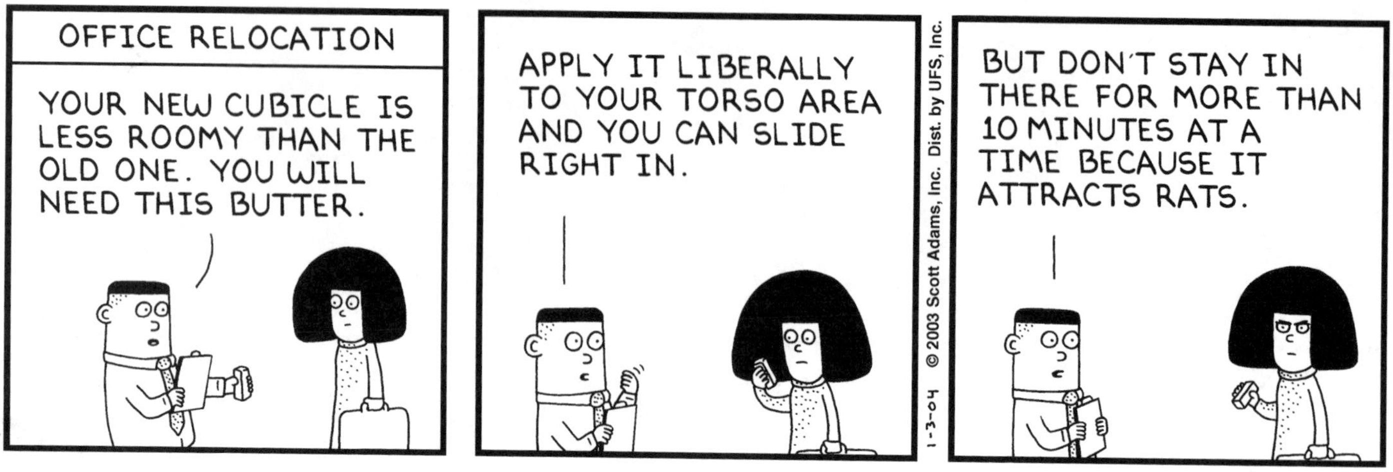
OFFICE RELOCATION
YOUR NEW CUBICLE IS LESS ROOMY THAN THE OLD ONE. YOU WILL NEED THIS BUTTER.
APPLY IT LIBERALLY TO YOUR TORSO AREA AND YOU CAN SLIDE RIGHT IN.
1-3-04 © 2003 Scott Adams, Inc. Dist. by UFS, Inc.
BUT DON'T STAY IN THERE FOR MORE THAN 10 MINUTES AT A TIME BECAUSE IT ATTRACTS RATS.

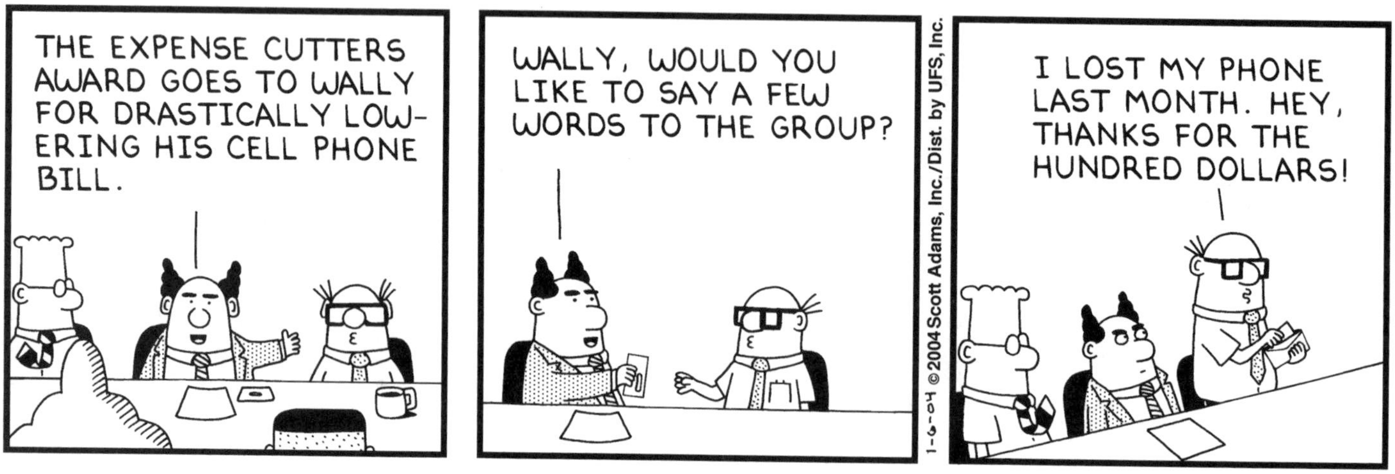
THE EXPENSE CUTTERS AWARD GOES TO WALLY FOR DRASTICALLY LOW-ERING HIS CELL PHONE BILL.
WALLY, WOULD YOU LIKE TO SAY A FEW WORDS TO THE GROUP?
1-6-04 © 2004 Scott Adams, Inc./Dist. by UFS, Inc.
I LOST MY PHONE LAST MONTH. HEY, THANKS FOR THE HUNDRED DOLLARS!

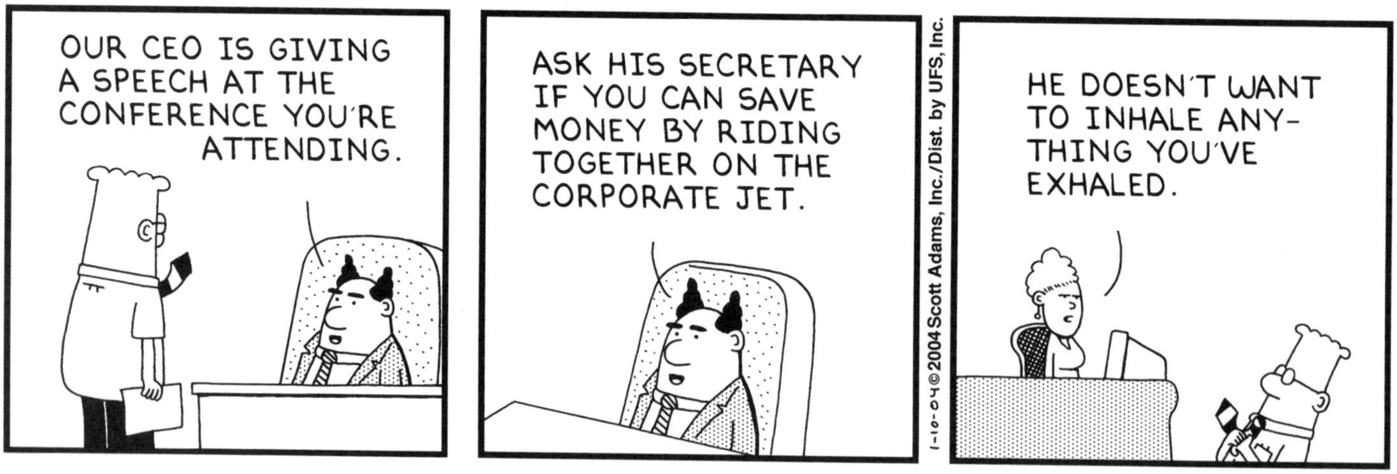
OUR CEO IS GIVING A SPEECH AT THE CONFERENCE YOU'RE ATTENDING.
ASK HIS SECRETARY IF YOU CAN SAVE MONEY BY RIDING TOGETHER ON THE CORPORATE JET.
1-10-04 © 2004 Scott Adams, Inc./Dist. by UFS, Inc.
HE DOESN'T WANT TO INHALE ANY-THING YOU'VE EXHALED.

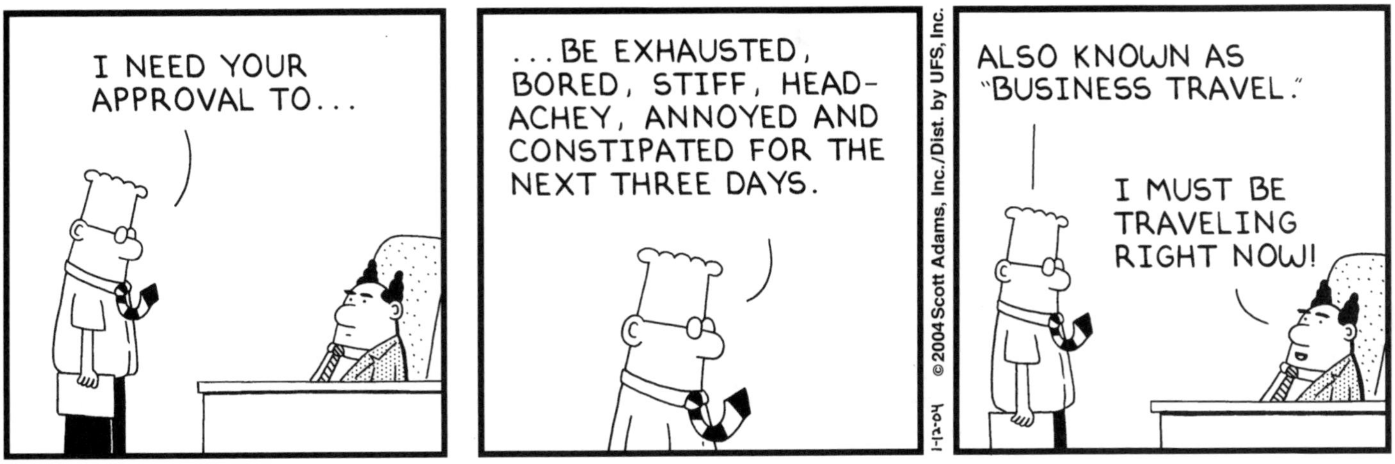
I NEED YOUR APPROVAL TO...
...BE EXHAUSTED, BORED, STIFF, HEAD-ACHEY, ANNOYED AND CONSTIPATED FOR THE NEXT THREE DAYS.
1-12-04 © 2004 Scott Adams, Inc./Dist. by UFS, Inc.
ALSO KNOWN AS "BUSINESS TRAVEL."
I MUST BE TRAVELING RIGHT NOW!

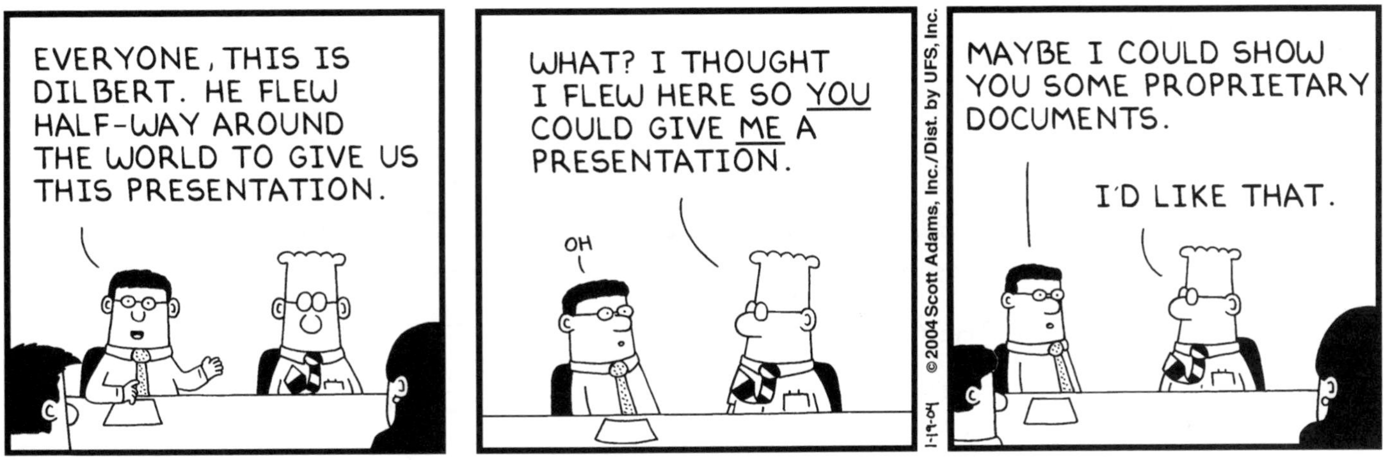
EVERYONE, THIS IS DILBERT. HE FLEW HALF-WAY AROUND THE WORLD TO GIVE US THIS PRESENTATION.
WHAT? I THOUGHT I FLEW HERE SO YOU COULD GIVE ME A PRESENTATION.
OH
1-19-04 © 2004 Scott Adams, Inc./Dist. by UFS, Inc.
MAYBE I COULD SHOW YOU SOME PROPRIETARY DOCUMENTS.
I'D LIKE THAT.

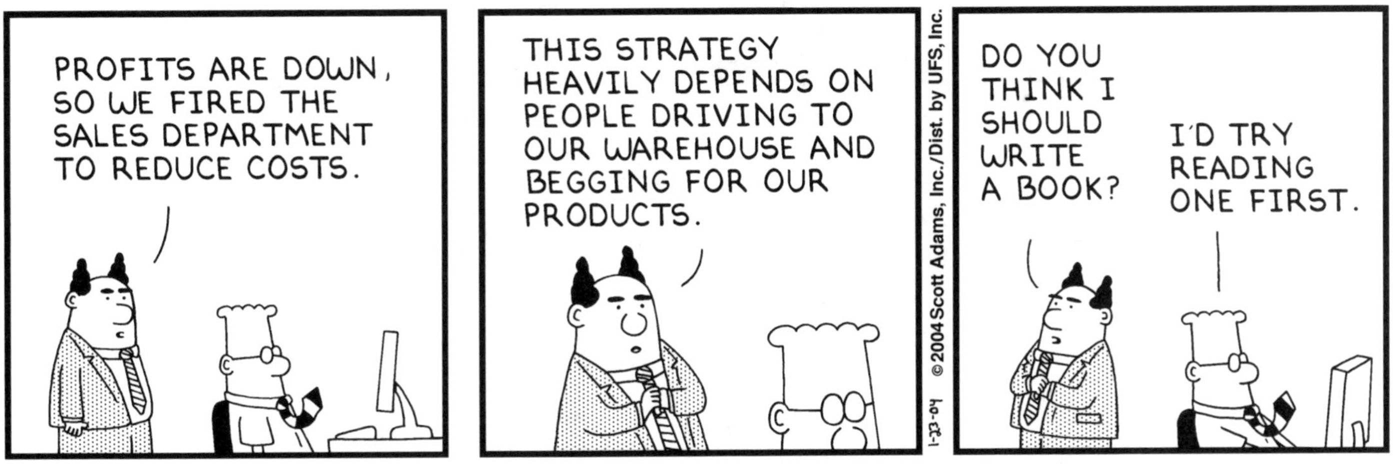
PROFITS ARE DOWN, SO WE FIRED THE SALES DEPARTMENT TO REDUCE COSTS.
THIS STRATEGY HEAVILY DEPENDS ON PEOPLE DRIVING TO OUR WAREHOUSE AND BEGGING FOR OUR PRODUCTS.
1-23-04 © 2004 Scott Adams, Inc./Dist. by UFS, Inc.
DO YOU THINK I SHOULD WRITE A BOOK?
I'D TRY READING ONE FIRST.

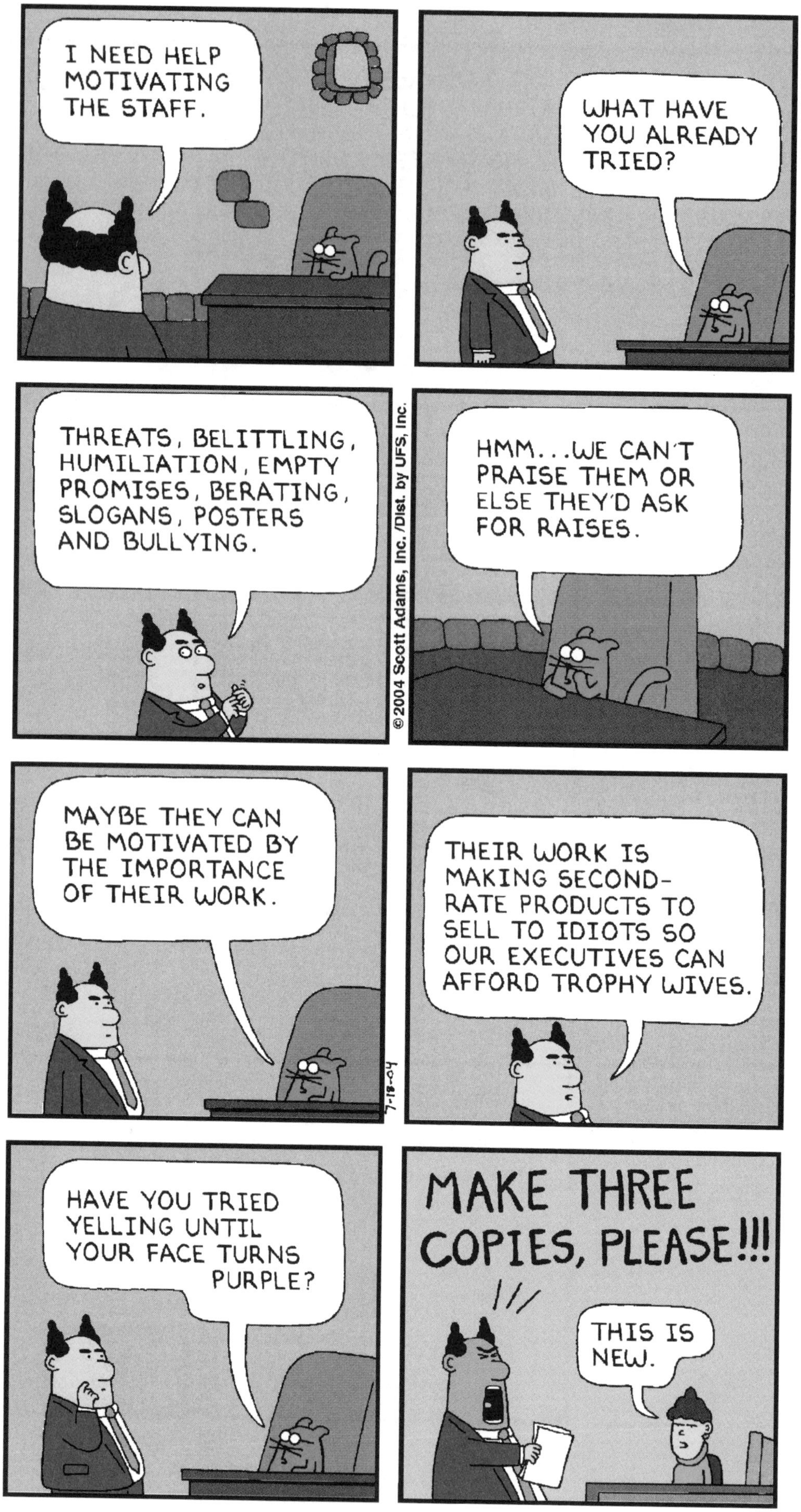
I NEED HELP MOTIVATING THE STAFF.
WHAT HAVE YOU ALREADY TRIED?
THREATS, BELITTLING, HUMILIATION, EMPTY PROMISES, BERATING, SLOGANS, POSTERS AND BULLYING.
©2004 Scott Adams, Inc./Dist. by UFS, Inc.
HMM...WE CAN'T PRAISE THEM OR ELSE THEY'D ASK FOR RAISES.
MAYBE THEY CAN BE MOTIVATED BY THE IMPORTANCE OF THEIR WORK.
7-18-04
THEIR WORK IS MAKING SECOND-RATE PRODUCTS TO SELL TO IDIOTS SO OUR EXECUTIVES CAN AFFORD TROPHY WIVES.
HAVE YOU TRIED YELLING UNTIL YOUR FACE TURNS PURPLE?
MAKE THREE COPIES, PLEASE!!!
THIS IS NEW.

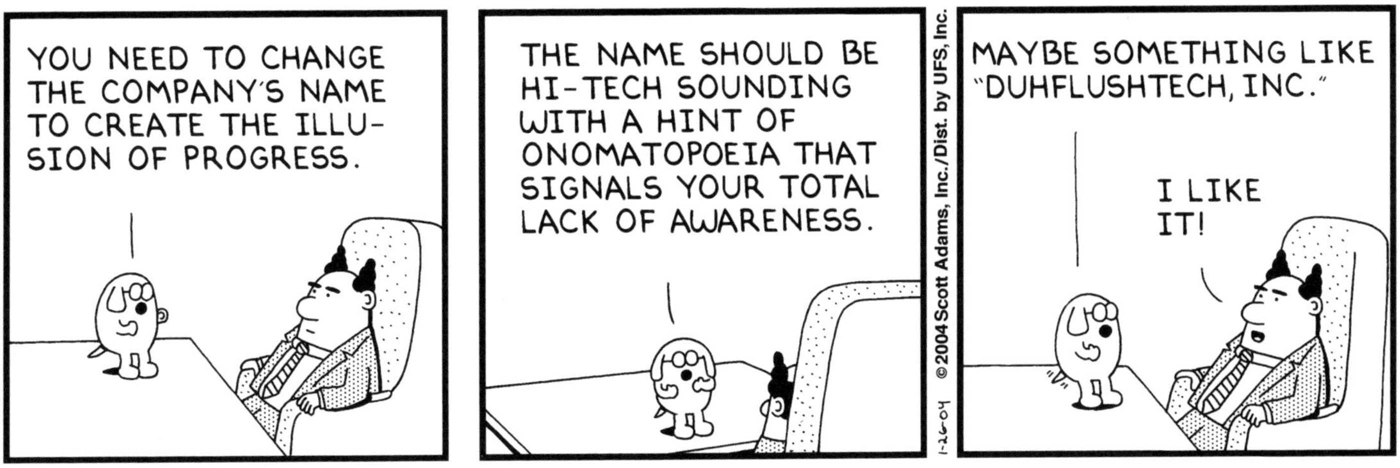
YOU NEED TO CHANGE THE COMPANY'S NAME TO CREATE THE ILLUSION OF PROGRESS.
THE NAME SHOULD BE HI-TECH SOUNDING WITH A HINT OF ONOMATOPOEIA THAT SIGNALS YOUR TOTAL LACK OF AWARENESS.
©2004 Scott Adams, Inc./Dist. by UFS, Inc.
1-26-04
MAYBE SOMETHING LIKE "DUHFLUSHTECH, INC."
I LIKE IT!

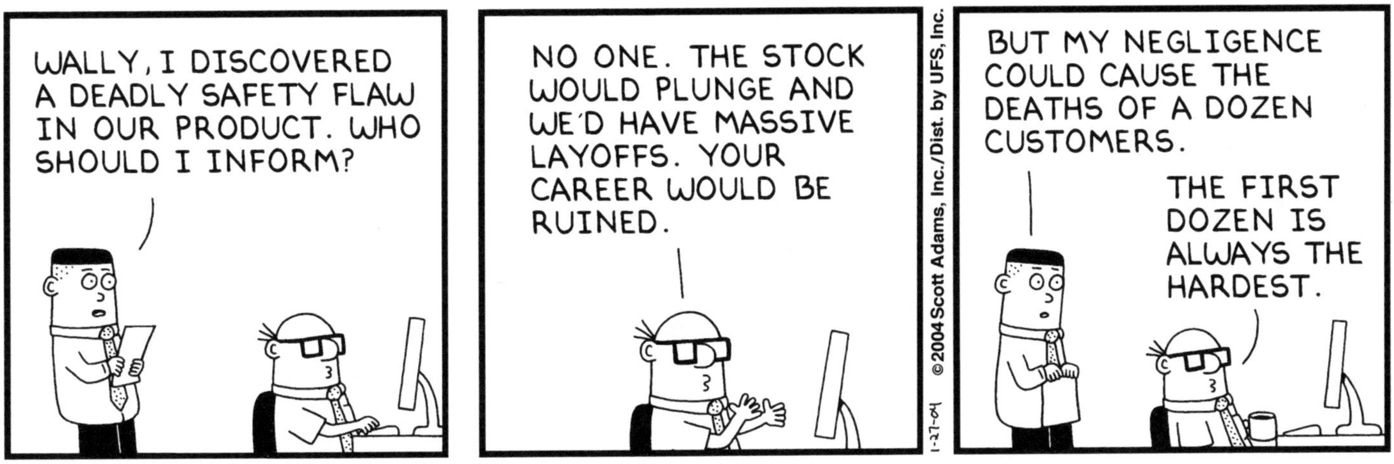
WALLY, I DISCOVERED A DEADLY SAFETY FLAW IN OUR PRODUCT. WHO SHOULD I INFORM?
NO ONE. THE STOCK WOULD PLUNGE AND WE'D HAVE MASSIVE LAYOFFS. YOUR CAREER WOULD BE RUINED.
©2004 Scott Adams, Inc./Dist. by UFS, Inc.
1-27-04
BUT MY NEGLIGENCE COULD CAUSE THE DEATHS OF A DOZEN CUSTOMERS.
THE FIRST DOZEN IS ALWAYS THE HARDEST.

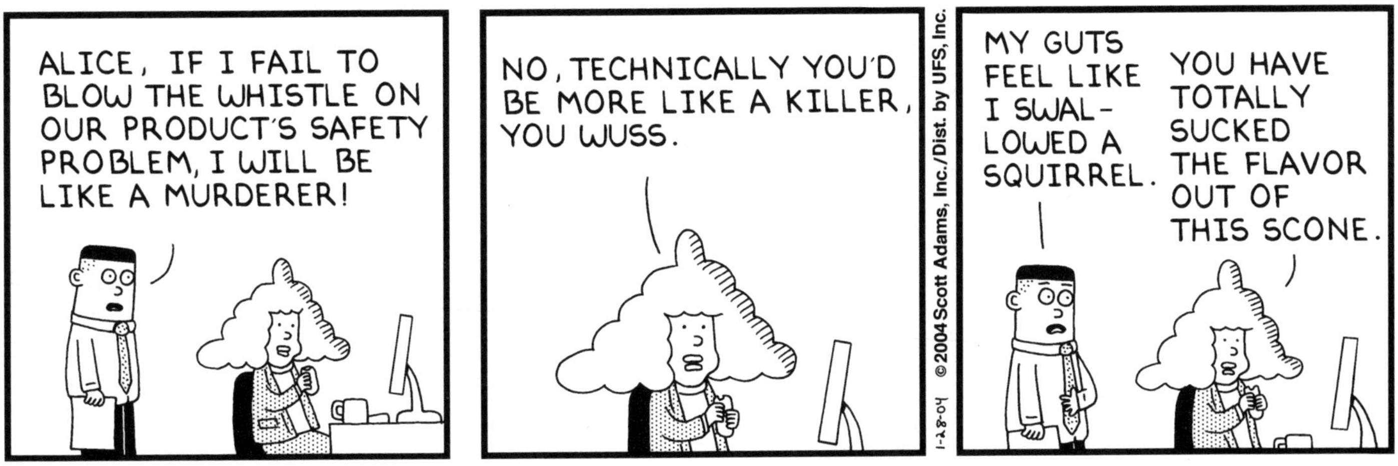
ALICE, IF I FAIL TO BLOW THE WHISTLE ON OUR PRODUCT'S SAFETY PROBLEM, I WILL BE LIKE A MURDERER!
NO, TECHNICALLY YOU'D BE MORE LIKE A KILLER, YOU WUSS.
©2004 Scott Adams, Inc./Dist. by UFS, Inc.
1-28-04
MY GUTS FEEL LIKE I SWALLOWED A SQUIRREL.
YOU HAVE TOTALLY SUCKED THE FLAVOR OUT OF THIS SCONE.

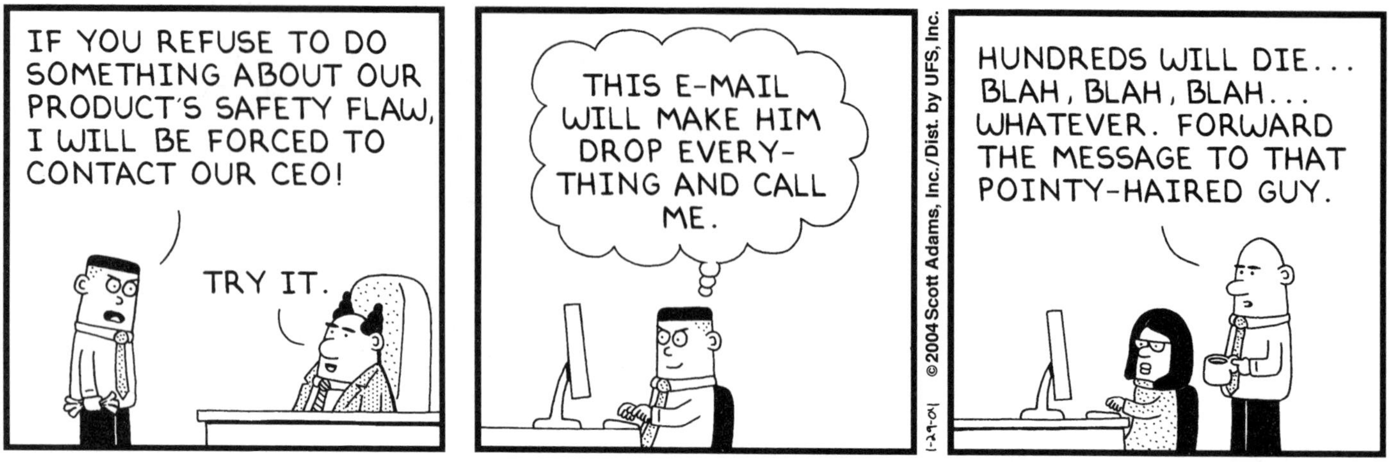
IF YOU REFUSE TO DO SOMETHING ABOUT OUR PRODUCT'S SAFETY FLAW, I WILL BE FORCED TO CONTACT OUR CEO!
TRY IT.
THIS E-MAIL WILL MAKE HIM DROP EVERY-THING AND CALL ME.
©2004 Scott Adams, Inc./Dist. by UFS, Inc.
HUNDREDS WILL DIE... BLAH, BLAH, BLAH... WHATEVER. FORWARD THE MESSAGE TO THAT POINTY-HAIRED GUY.

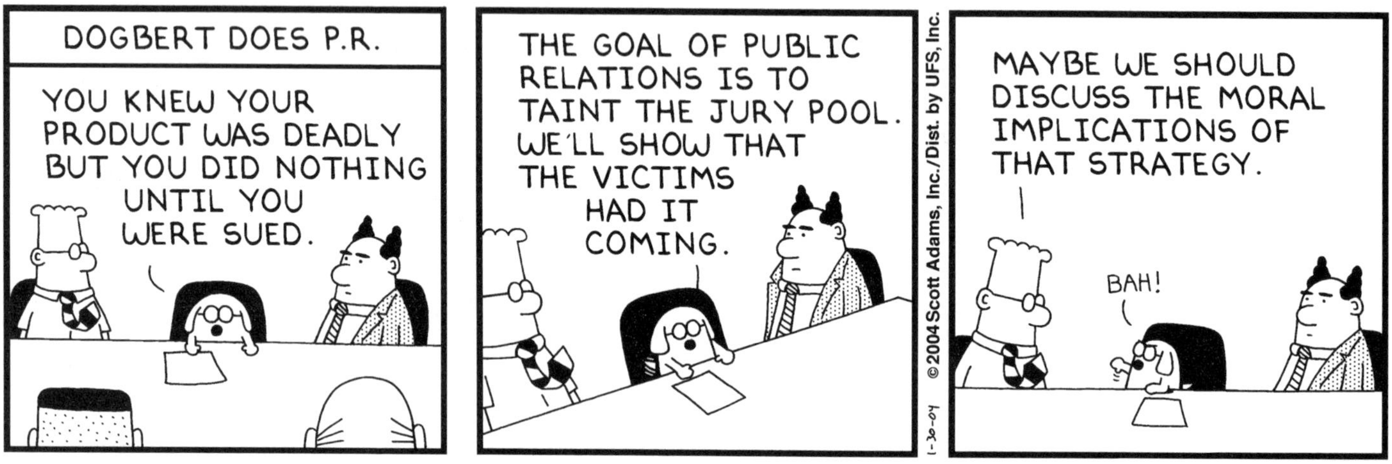
DOGBERT DOES P.R.
YOU KNEW YOUR PRODUCT WAS DEADLY BUT YOU DID NOTHING UNTIL YOU WERE SUED.
THE GOAL OF PUBLIC RELATIONS IS TO TAINT THE JURY POOL. WE'LL SHOW THAT THE VICTIMS HAD IT COMING.
©2004 Scott Adams, Inc./Dist. by UFS, Inc.
MAYBE WE SHOULD DISCUSS THE MORAL IMPLICATIONS OF THAT STRATEGY.
BAH!

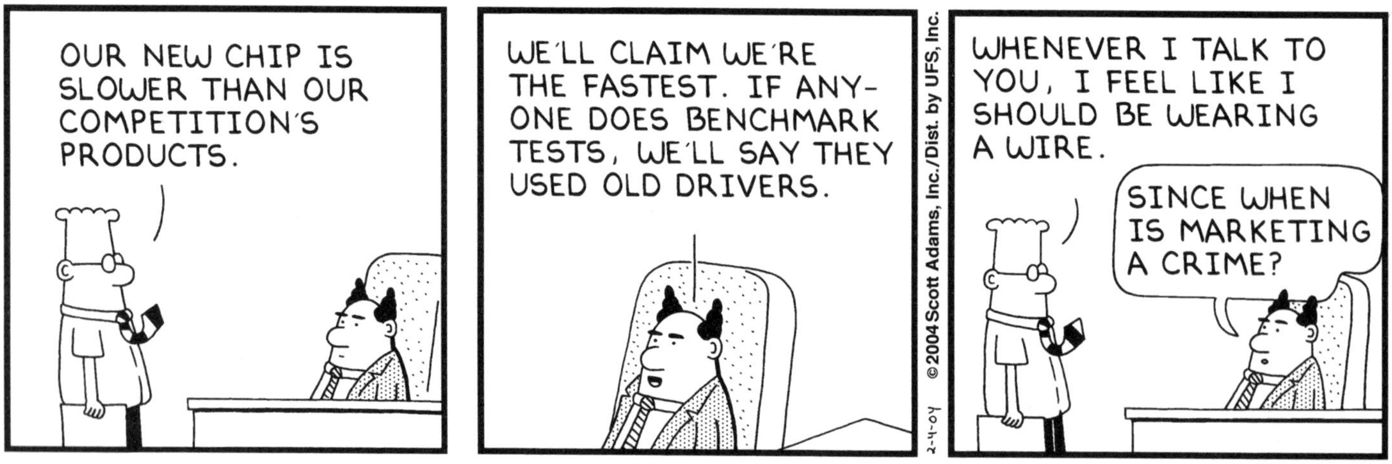
OUR NEW CHIP IS SLOWER THAN OUR COMPETITION'S PRODUCTS.
WE'LL CLAIM WE'RE THE FASTEST. IF ANY-ONE DOES BENCHMARK TESTS, WE'LL SAY THEY USED OLD DRIVERS.
©2004 Scott Adams, Inc./Dist. by UFS, Inc.
WHENEVER I TALK TO YOU, I FEEL LIKE I SHOULD BE WEARING A WIRE.
SINCE WHEN IS MARKETING A CRIME?

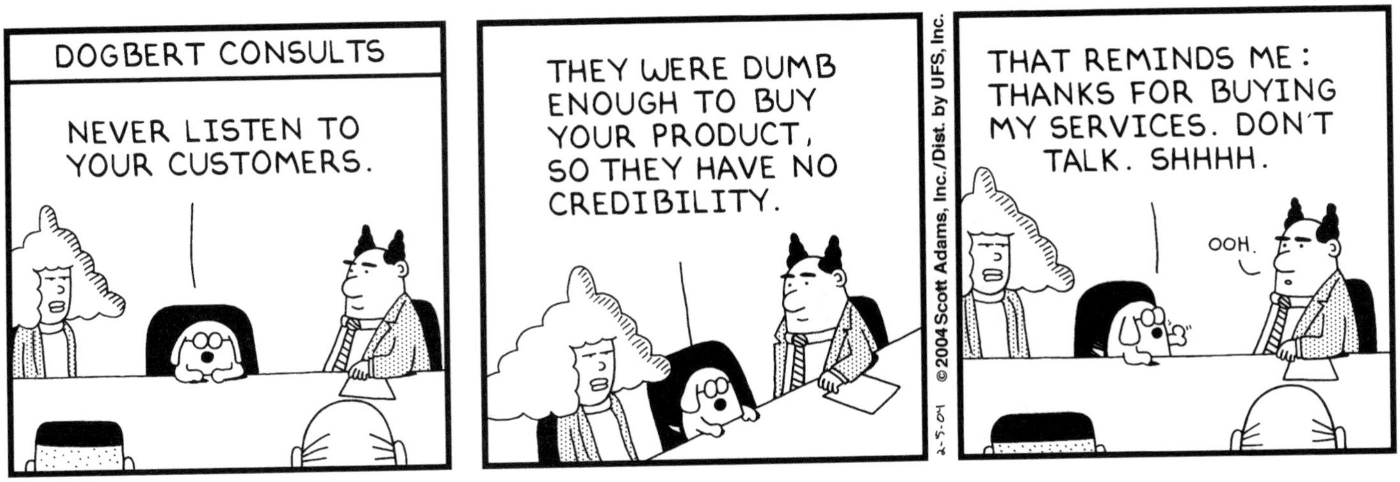
DOGBERT CONSULTS
NEVER LISTEN TO YOUR CUSTOMERS.
THEY WERE DUMB ENOUGH TO BUY YOUR PRODUCT, SO THEY HAVE NO CREDIBILITY.
THAT REMINDS ME: THANKS FOR BUYING MY SERVICES. DON'T TALK. SHHHH.
OOH.
© 2004 Scott Adams, Inc./Dist. by UFS, Inc.
2-5-04

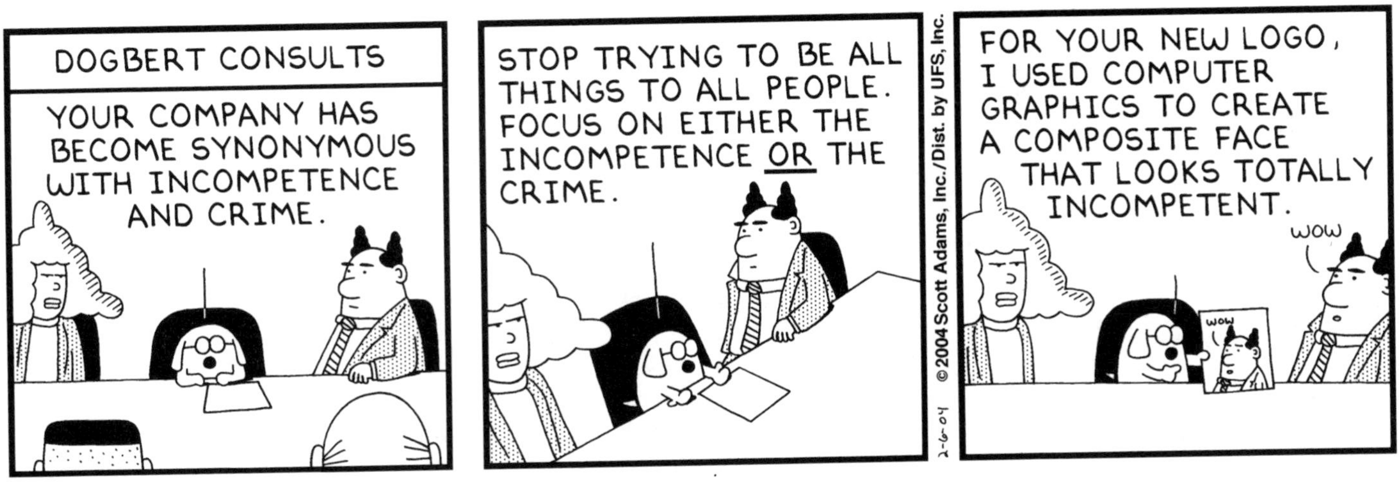
DOGBERT CONSULTS
YOUR COMPANY HAS BECOME SYNONYMOUS WITH INCOMPETENCE AND CRIME.
STOP TRYING TO BE ALL THINGS TO ALL PEOPLE. FOCUS ON EITHER THE INCOMPETENCE OR THE CRIME.
FOR YOUR NEW LOGO, I USED COMPUTER GRAPHICS TO CREATE A COMPOSITE FACE THAT LOOKS TOTALLY INCOMPETENT.
WOW
WOW
© 2004 Scott Adams, Inc./Dist. by UFS, Inc.
2-6-04

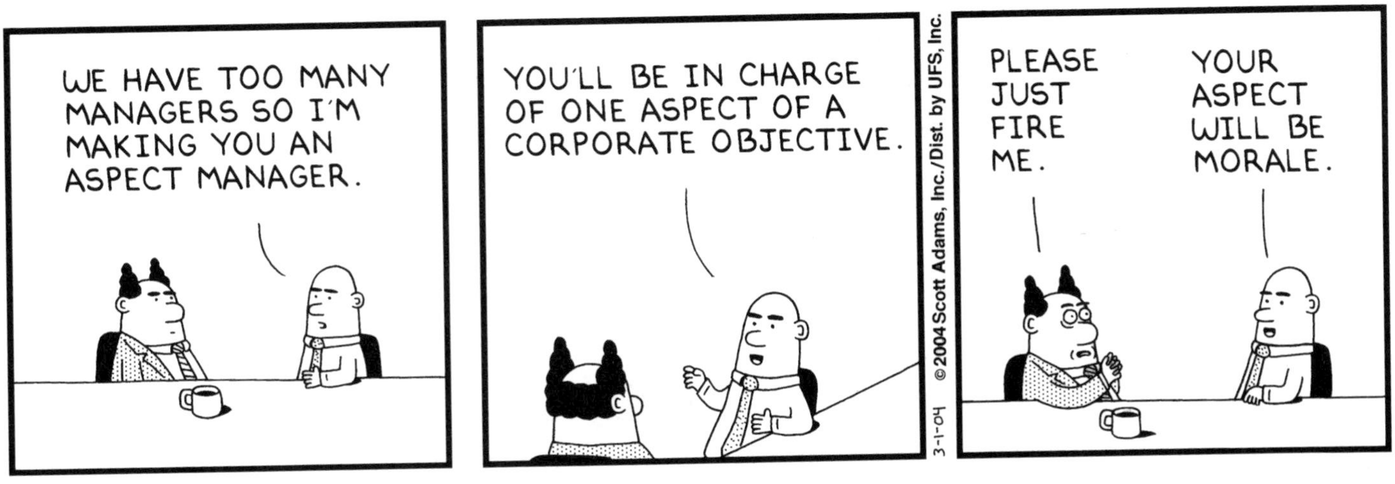
WE HAVE TOO MANY MANAGERS SO I'M MAKING YOU AN ASPECT MANAGER.
YOU'LL BE IN CHARGE OF ONE ASPECT OF A CORPORATE OBJECTIVE.
PLEASE JUST FIRE ME.
YOUR ASPECT WILL BE MORALE.
© 2004 Scott Adams, Inc./Dist. by UFS, Inc.
3-1-04

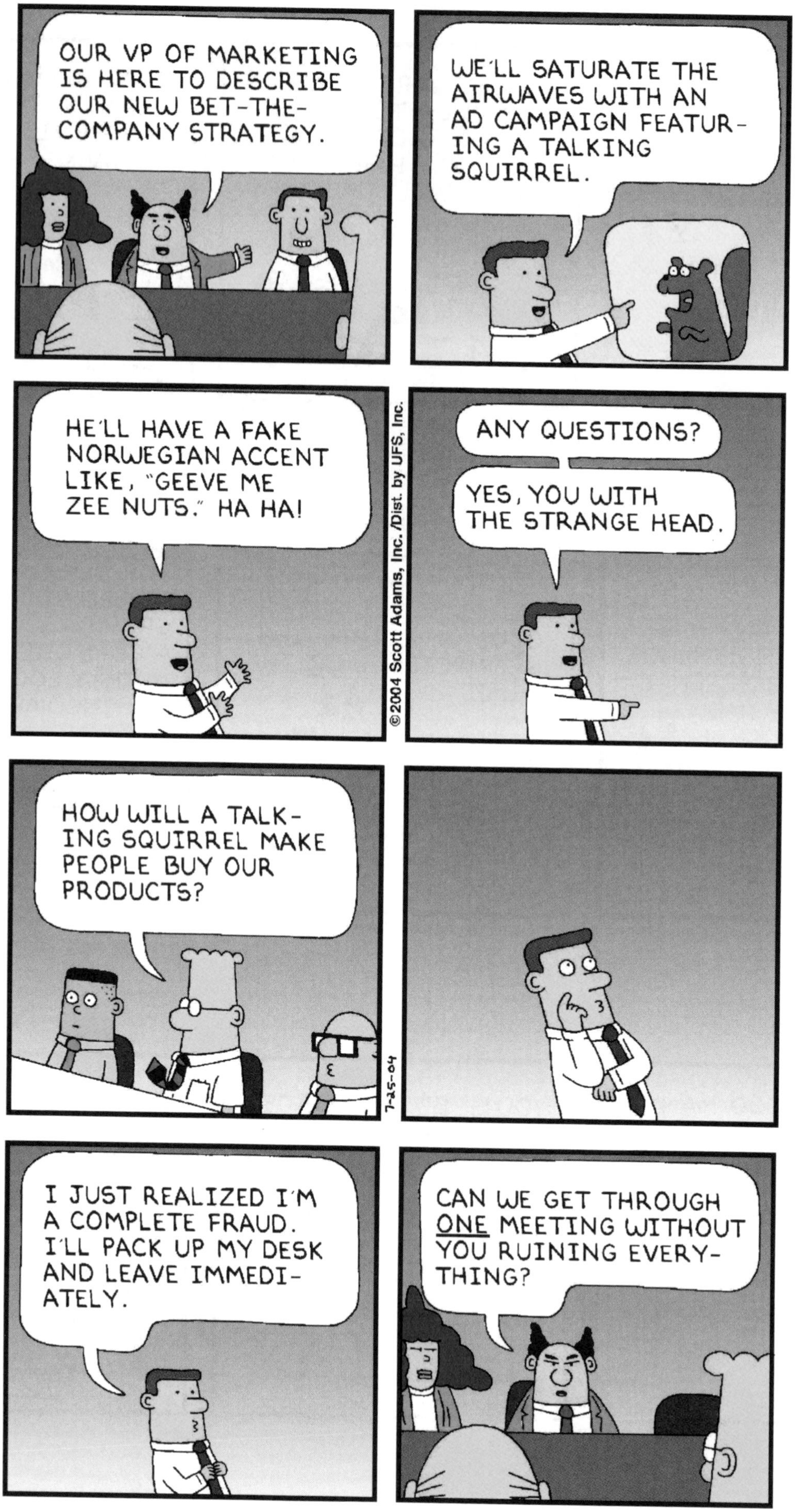
OUR VP OF MARKETING IS HERE TO DESCRIBE OUR NEW BET-THE-COMPANY STRATEGY.
WE'LL SATURATE THE AIRWAVES WITH AN AD CAMPAIGN FEATURING A TALKING SQUIRREL.
HE'LL HAVE A FAKE NORWEGIAN ACCENT LIKE, "GEEVE ME ZEE NUTS." HA HA!
ANY QUESTIONS?
YES, YOU WITH THE STRANGE HEAD.
HOW WILL A TALKING SQUIRREL MAKE PEOPLE BUY OUR PRODUCTS?
I JUST REALIZED I'M A COMPLETE FRAUD. I'LL PACK UP MY DESK AND LEAVE IMMEDIATELY.
CAN WE GET THROUGH ONE MEETING WITHOUT YOU RUINING EVERYTHING?
©2004 Scott Adams, Inc. /Dist. by UFS, Inc.
7-25-04

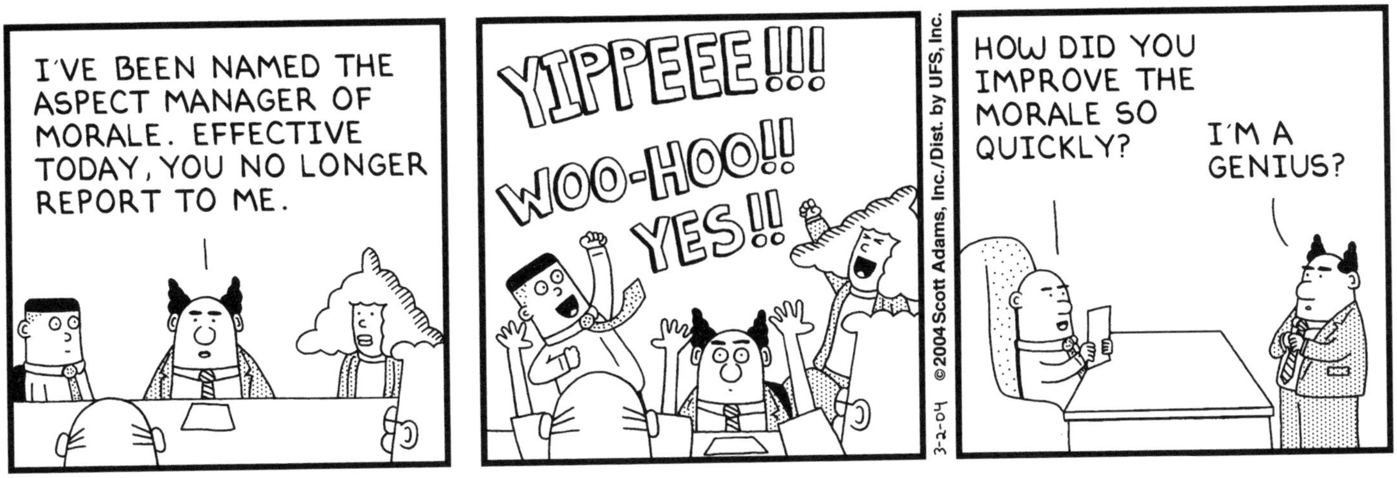
I'VE BEEN NAMED THE ASPECT MANAGER OF MORALE. EFFECTIVE TODAY, YOU NO LONGER REPORT TO ME.
YIPPEEE!!!
WOO-HOO!!
YES!!
3-2-04 ©2004 Scott Adams, Inc./Dist. by UFS, Inc.
HOW DID YOU IMPROVE THE MORALE SO QUICKLY?
I'M A GENIUS?

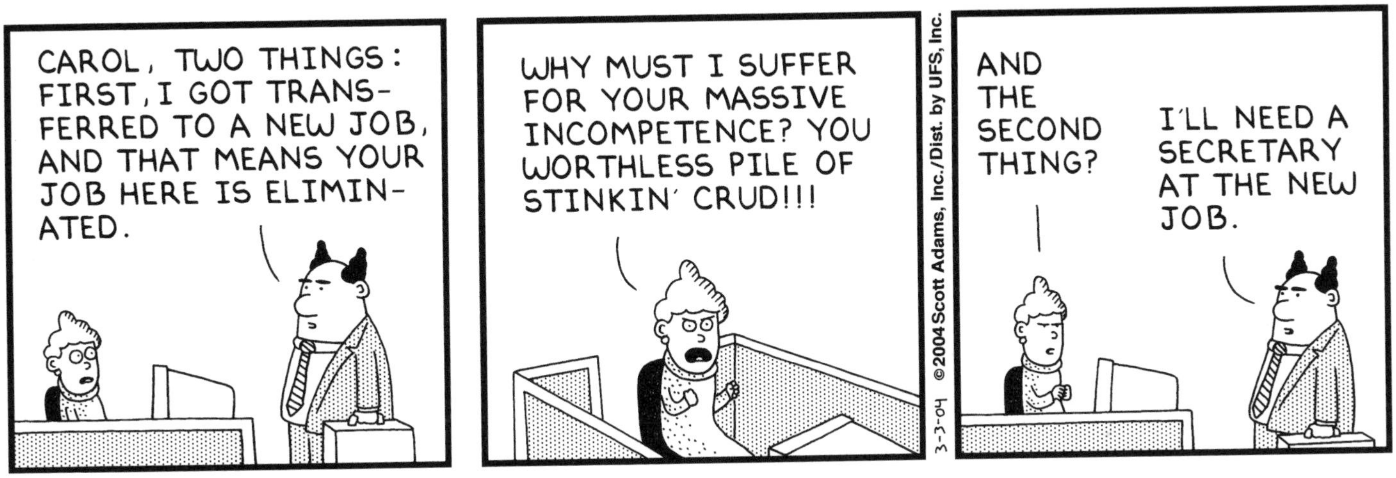
CAROL, TWO THINGS: FIRST, I GOT TRANSFERRED TO A NEW JOB, AND THAT MEANS YOUR JOB HERE IS ELIMINATED.
WHY MUST I SUFFER FOR YOUR MASSIVE INCOMPETENCE? YOU WORTHLESS PILE OF STINKIN' CRUD!!!
3-3-04 ©2004 Scott Adams, Inc./Dist. by UFS, Inc.
AND THE SECOND THING?
I'LL NEED A SECRETARY AT THE NEW JOB.

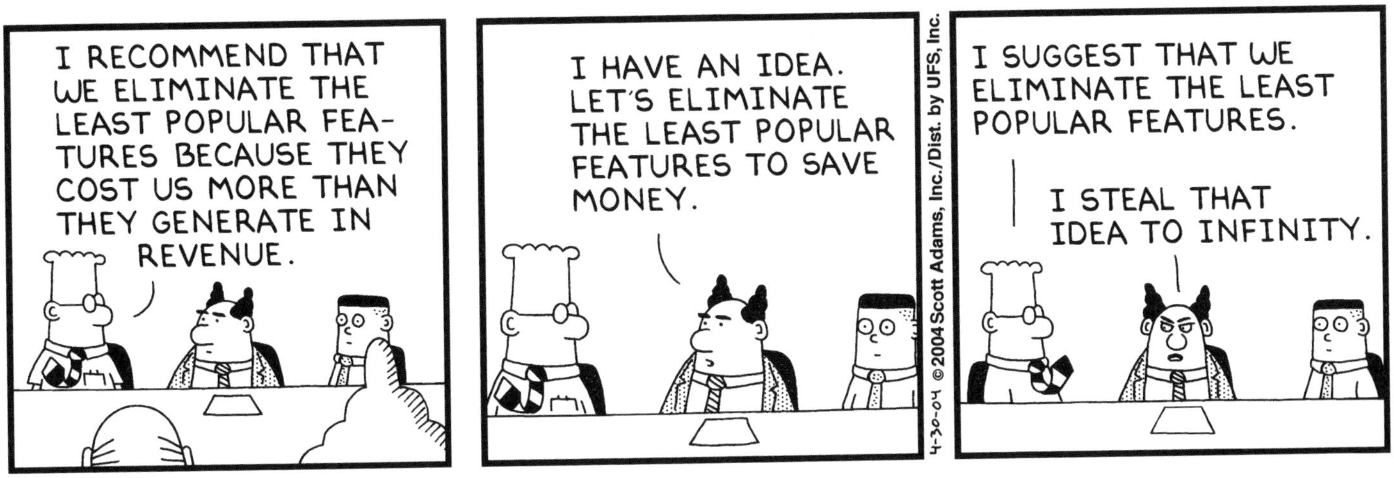
I RECOMMEND THAT WE ELIMINATE THE LEAST POPULAR FEATURES BECAUSE THEY COST US MORE THAN THEY GENERATE IN REVENUE.
I HAVE AN IDEA. LET'S ELIMINATE THE LEAST POPULAR FEATURES TO SAVE MONEY.
4-30-04 ©2004 Scott Adams, Inc./Dist. by UFS, Inc.
I SUGGEST THAT WE ELIMINATE THE LEAST POPULAR FEATURES.
I STEAL THAT IDEA TO INFINITY.

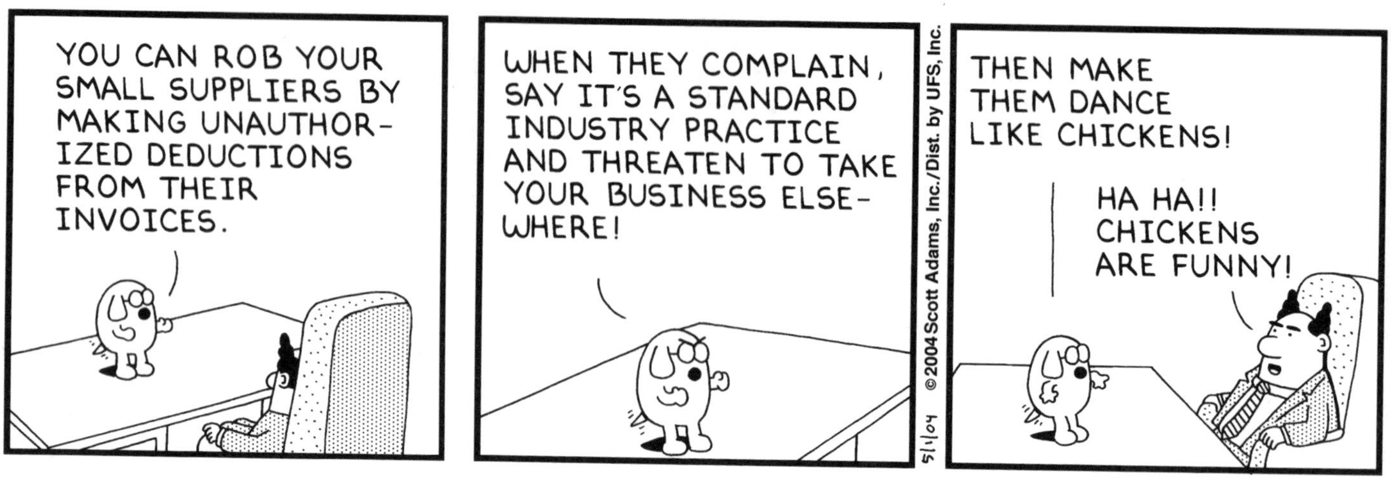
YOU CAN ROB YOUR SMALL SUPPLIERS BY MAKING UNAUTHOR-IZED DEDUCTIONS FROM THEIR INVOICES.
WHEN THEY COMPLAIN, SAY IT'S A STANDARD INDUSTRY PRACTICE AND THREATEN TO TAKE YOUR BUSINESS ELSE-WHERE!
THEN MAKE THEM DANCE LIKE CHICKENS!
HA HA!! CHICKENS ARE FUNNY!
5/1/04
© 2004 Scott Adams, Inc./Dist. by UFS, Inc.

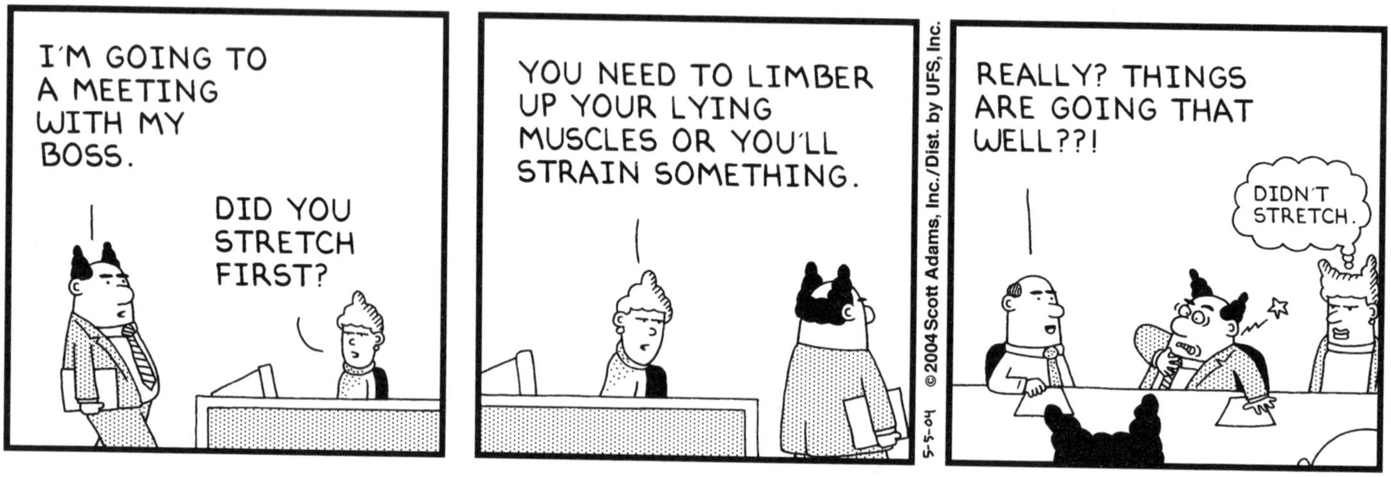
I'M GOING TO A MEETING WITH MY BOSS.
DID YOU STRETCH FIRST?
YOU NEED TO LIMBER UP YOUR LYING MUSCLES OR YOU'LL STRAIN SOMETHING.
REALLY? THINGS ARE GOING THAT WELL??!
DIDN'T STRETCH.
5-5-04
© 2004 Scott Adams, Inc./Dist. by UFS, Inc.

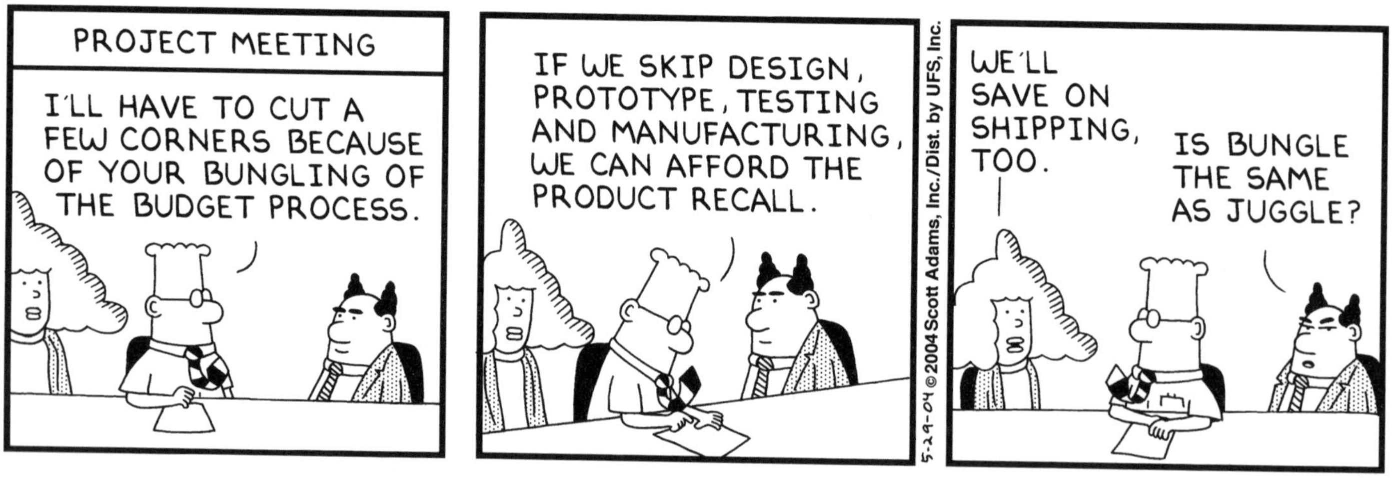
PROJECT MEETING
I'LL HAVE TO CUT A FEW CORNERS BECAUSE OF YOUR BUNGLING OF THE BUDGET PROCESS.
IF WE SKIP DESIGN, PROTOTYPE, TESTING AND MANUFACTURING, WE CAN AFFORD THE PRODUCT RECALL.
WE'LL SAVE ON SHIPPING, TOO.
IS BUNGLE THE SAME AS JUGGLE?
5-29-04
© 2004 Scott Adams, Inc./Dist. by UFS, Inc.

DOGBERT THE CEO VERSUS THE MBA
MY ANALYSIS DOESN'T SUPPORT YOUR STRATEGY.
MY ANALYSIS SAYS I CAN HIRE THREE HIGH SCHOOL DROP-OUTS TO SLAP YOU UNTIL IT DOES.
NO... PLEASE, NOT DROP-OUTS!
THEY WILL KICK YOUR AS-SUMPTIONS.
5-23-09 ©2009 Scott Adams, Inc./Dist. by UFS, Inc.

DOGBERT THE CEO
WE'LL EXECUTE OUR STRATEGY IN THE USUAL WAY.
THE POWERFUL WILL DELEGATE TO THE UNTALENTED UNTIL FAILURE IS ACHIEVED.
HOW LONG WILL THAT TAKE?
WE JUST FINISHED.
6-11-09 ©2009 Scott Adams, Inc./Dist. by UFS, Inc.

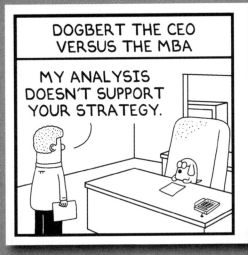

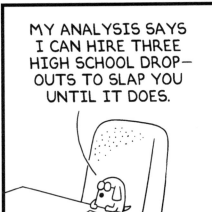

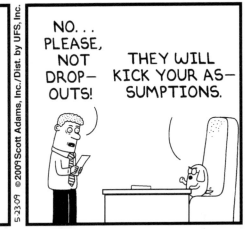

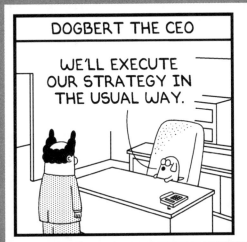

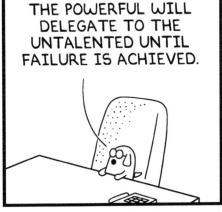

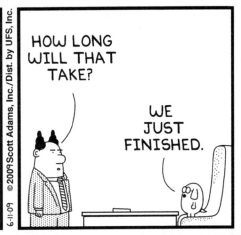

I OWN A SMALL BUSINESS.

IT'S IMPERATIVE THAT YOU PAY US ON TIME OR ELSE WE'LL GO OUT OF BUSINESS.

AND THEN YOU WOULDN'T EVER NEED TO PAY...

OH, DEAR LORD, WHAT HAVE I SAID?!!

NOW THAT OUR PROFITS ARE IMPROVING, CAN I HAVE A RAISE?

IF I START GIVING PEOPLE RAISES, THEN PROFITS WILL PLUMMET AND WE'LL BE NOWHERE.

DOES YOUR BONUS DEPEND ON HOW EFFECTIVELY YOU OPPRESS ME?

IF YOU DON'T LIKE IT, TRY COMMUNISM.

THE LEADERSHIP TEAM CAN'T DECIDE WHERE TO MAKE THE DEEPEST BUDGET CUTS.

BUT DON'T WORRY. I OFFERED TO BRING A SYSTEMATIC, DATA-DRIVEN FOCUS TO THE PROCESS.

A DEATH SPIRAL GOES CLOCKWISE NORTH OF THE EQUATOR.

BUDGET CUTS

RESEARCH
DESIGN
MARCOM
SALES

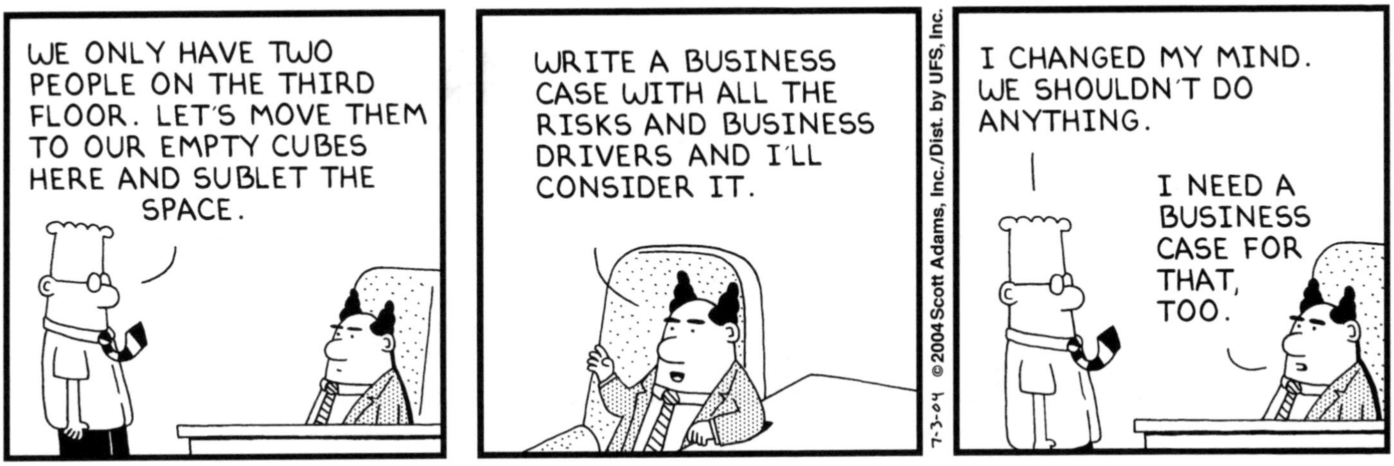
WE ONLY HAVE TWO PEOPLE ON THE THIRD FLOOR. LET'S MOVE THEM TO OUR EMPTY CUBES HERE AND SUBLET THE SPACE.
WRITE A BUSINESS CASE WITH ALL THE RISKS AND BUSINESS DRIVERS AND I'LL CONSIDER IT.
7-3-04 © 2004 Scott Adams, Inc./Dist. by UFS, Inc.
I CHANGED MY MIND. WE SHOULDN'T DO ANYTHING.
I NEED A BUSINESS CASE FOR THAT, TOO.

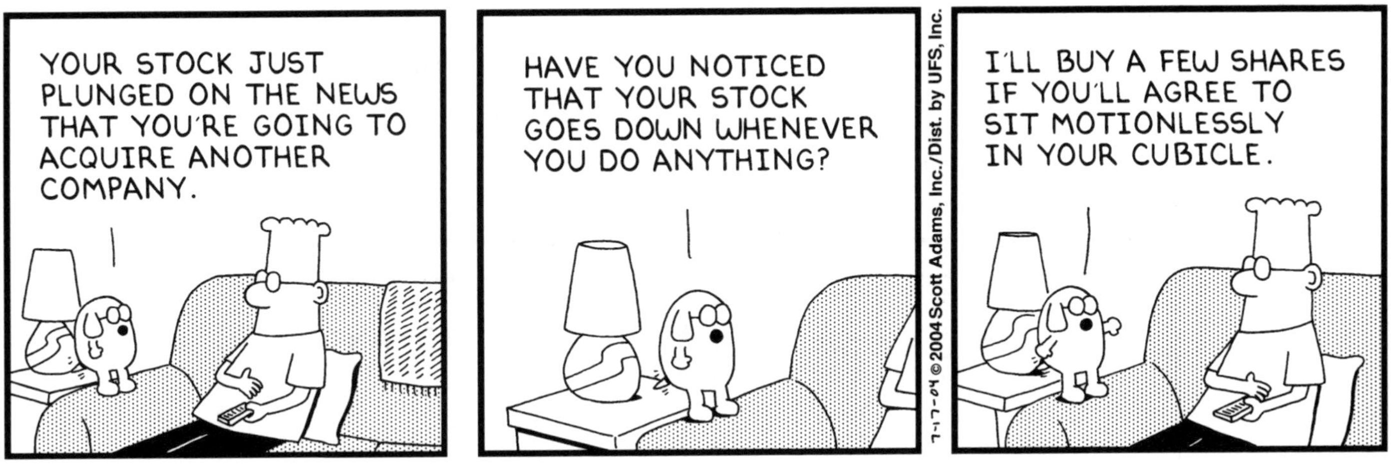
YOUR STOCK JUST PLUNGED ON THE NEWS THAT YOU'RE GOING TO ACQUIRE ANOTHER COMPANY.
HAVE YOU NOTICED THAT YOUR STOCK GOES DOWN WHENEVER YOU DO ANYTHING?
7-17-04 © 2004 Scott Adams, Inc./Dist. by UFS, Inc.
I'LL BUY A FEW SHARES IF YOU'LL AGREE TO SIT MOTIONLESSLY IN YOUR CUBICLE.

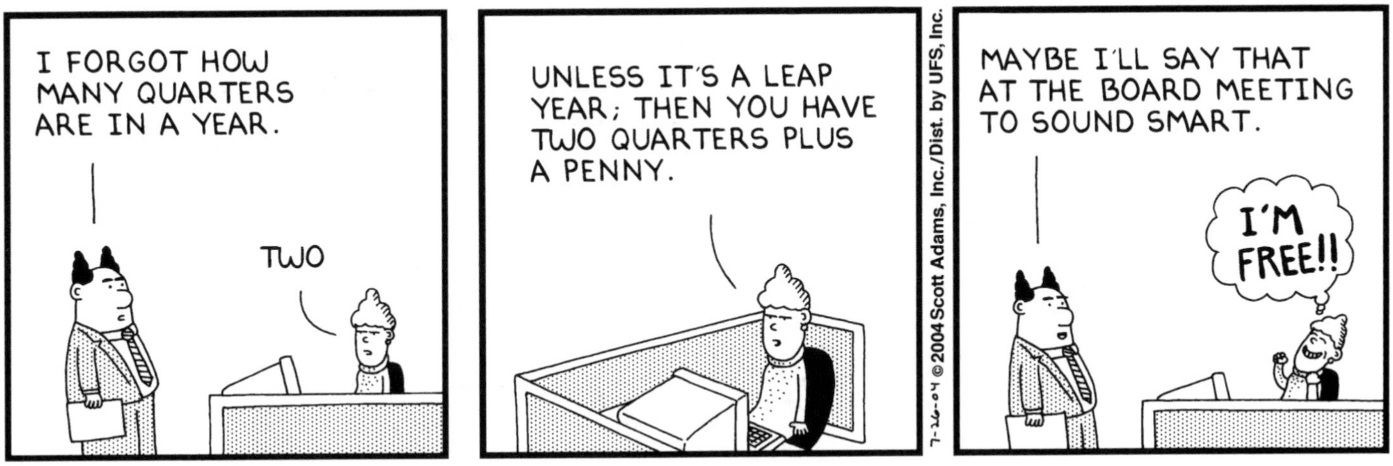
I FORGOT HOW MANY QUARTERS ARE IN A YEAR.
TWO
UNLESS IT'S A LEAP YEAR; THEN YOU HAVE TWO QUARTERS PLUS A PENNY.
7-26-04 © 2004 Scott Adams, Inc./Dist. by UFS, Inc.
MAYBE I'LL SAY THAT AT THE BOARD MEETING TO SOUND SMART.
I'M FREE!!

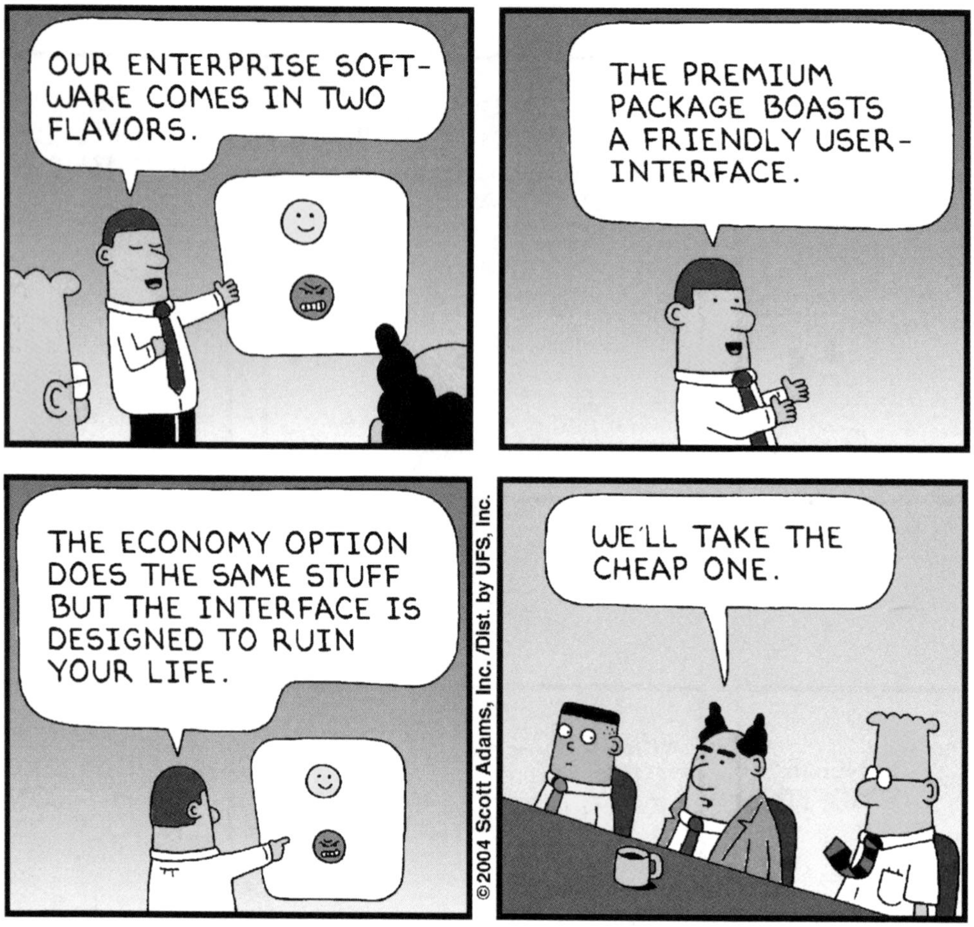
OUR ENTERPRISE SOFT-WARE COMES IN TWO FLAVORS.
THE PREMIUM PACKAGE BOASTS A FRIENDLY USER-INTERFACE.
THE ECONOMY OPTION DOES THE SAME STUFF BUT THE INTERFACE IS DESIGNED TO RUIN YOUR LIFE.
WE'LL TAKE THE CHEAP ONE.
©2004 Scott Adams, Inc. /Dist. by UFS, Inc.

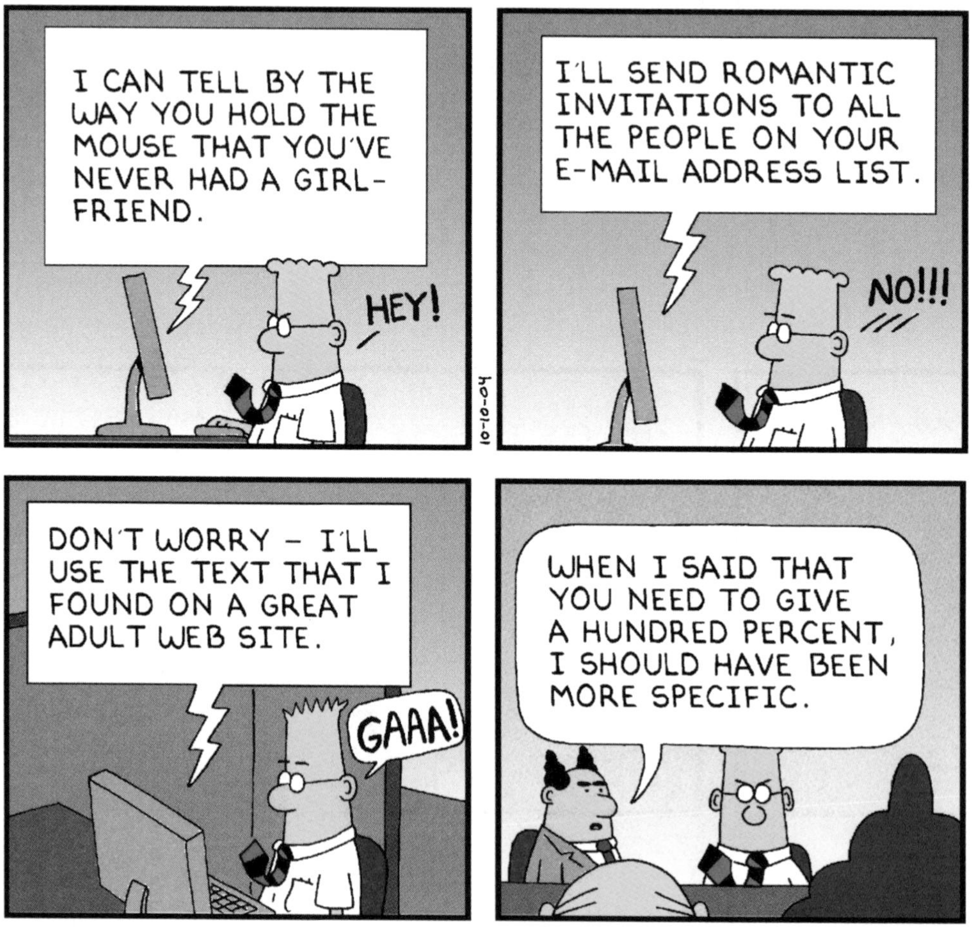
I CAN TELL BY THE WAY YOU HOLD THE MOUSE THAT YOU'VE NEVER HAD A GIRL-FRIEND.
HEY!
10-10-04
I'LL SEND ROMANTIC INVITATIONS TO ALL THE PEOPLE ON YOUR E-MAIL ADDRESS LIST.
NO!!!
DON'T WORRY – I'LL USE THE TEXT THAT I FOUND ON A GREAT ADULT WEB SITE.
GAAA!
WHEN I SAID THAT YOU NEED TO GIVE A HUNDRED PERCENT, I SHOULD HAVE BEEN MORE SPECIFIC.

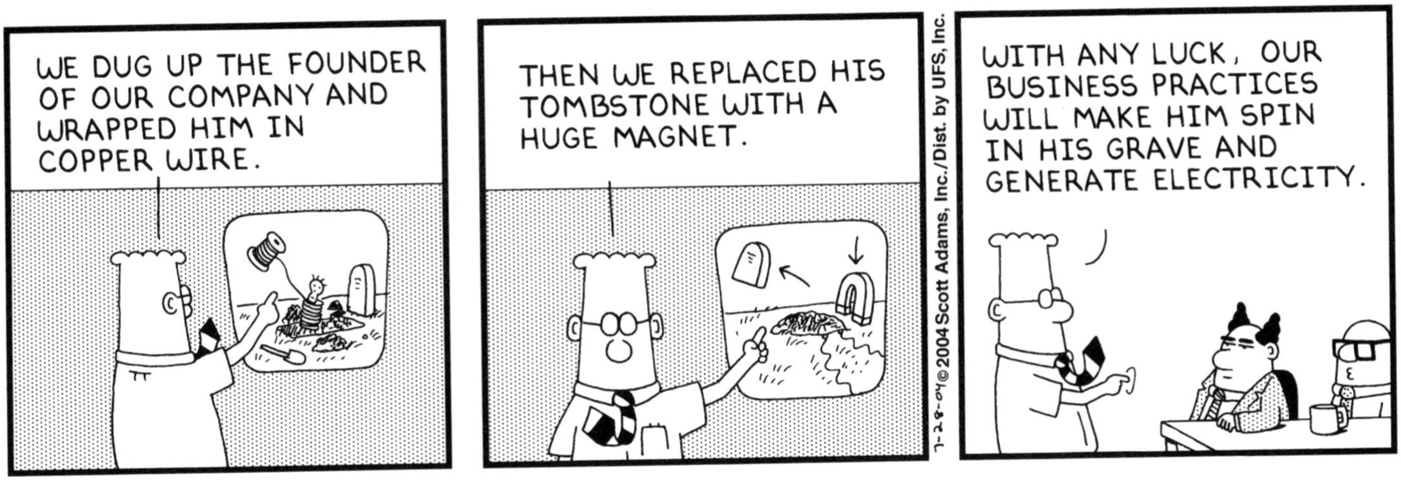
WE DUG UP THE FOUNDER OF OUR COMPANY AND WRAPPED HIM IN COPPER WIRE.
THEN WE REPLACED HIS TOMBSTONE WITH A HUGE MAGNET.
7-28-04 © 2004 Scott Adams, Inc./Dist. by UFS, Inc.
WITH ANY LUCK, OUR BUSINESS PRACTICES WILL MAKE HIM SPIN IN HIS GRAVE AND GENERATE ELECTRICITY.

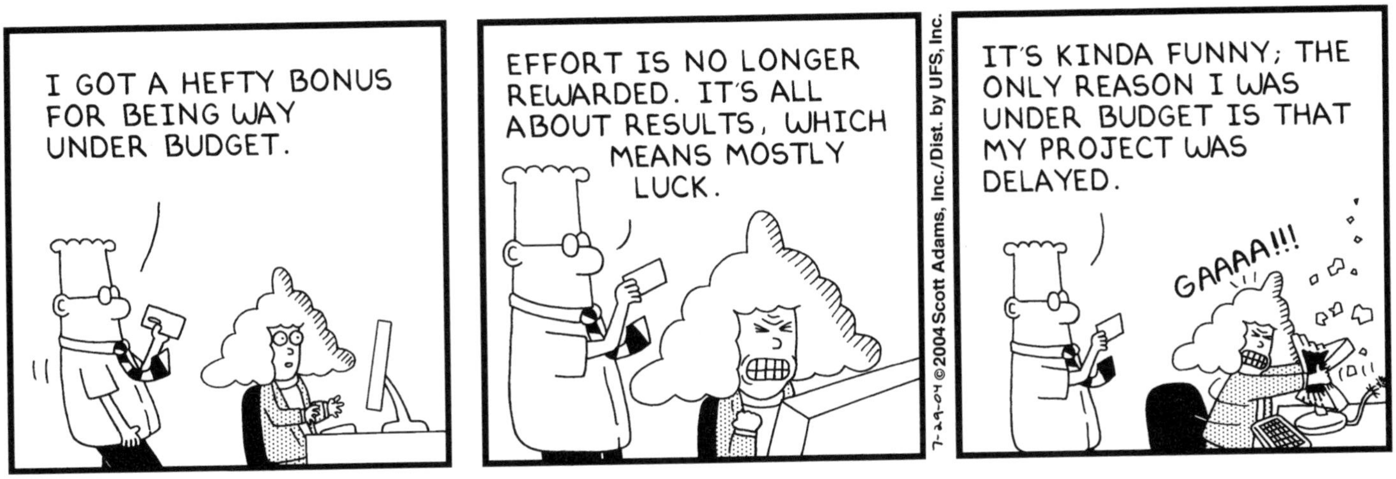
I GOT A HEFTY BONUS FOR BEING WAY UNDER BUDGET.
EFFORT IS NO LONGER REWARDED. IT'S ALL ABOUT RESULTS, WHICH MEANS MOSTLY LUCK.
7-29-04 © 2004 Scott Adams, Inc./Dist. by UFS, Inc.
IT'S KINDA FUNNY; THE ONLY REASON I WAS UNDER BUDGET IS THAT MY PROJECT WAS DELAYED.
GAAAA!!!

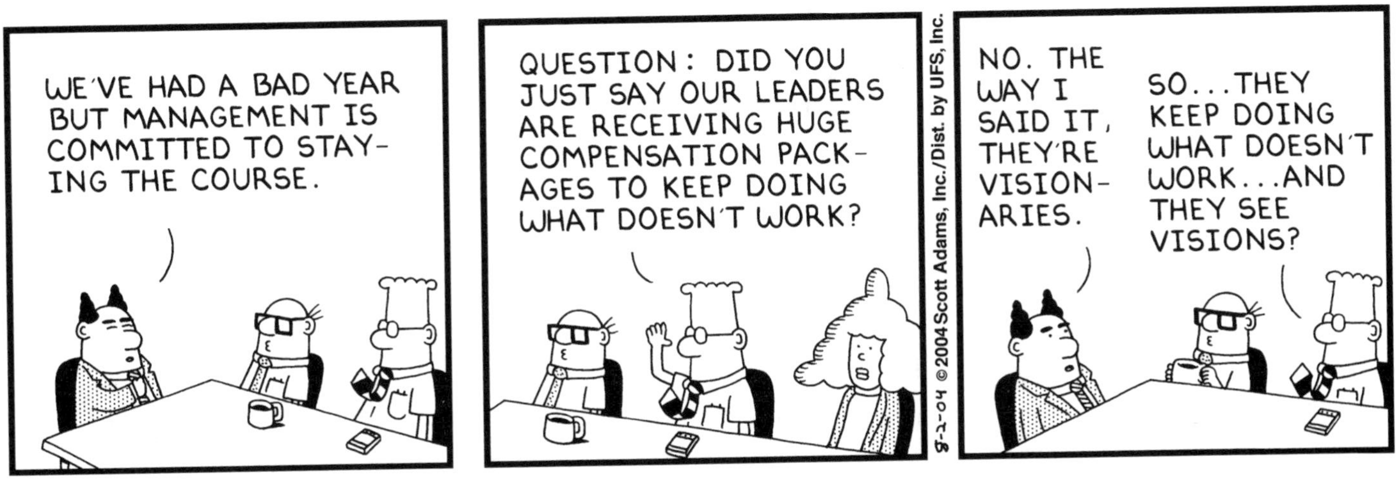
WE'VE HAD A BAD YEAR BUT MANAGEMENT IS COMMITTED TO STAYING THE COURSE.
QUESTION: DID YOU JUST SAY OUR LEADERS ARE RECEIVING HUGE COMPENSATION PACKAGES TO KEEP DOING WHAT DOESN'T WORK?
8-2-04 © 2004 Scott Adams, Inc./Dist. by UFS, Inc.
NO. THE WAY I SAID IT, THEY'RE VISIONARIES.
SO...THEY KEEP DOING WHAT DOESN'T WORK...AND THEY SEE VISIONS?

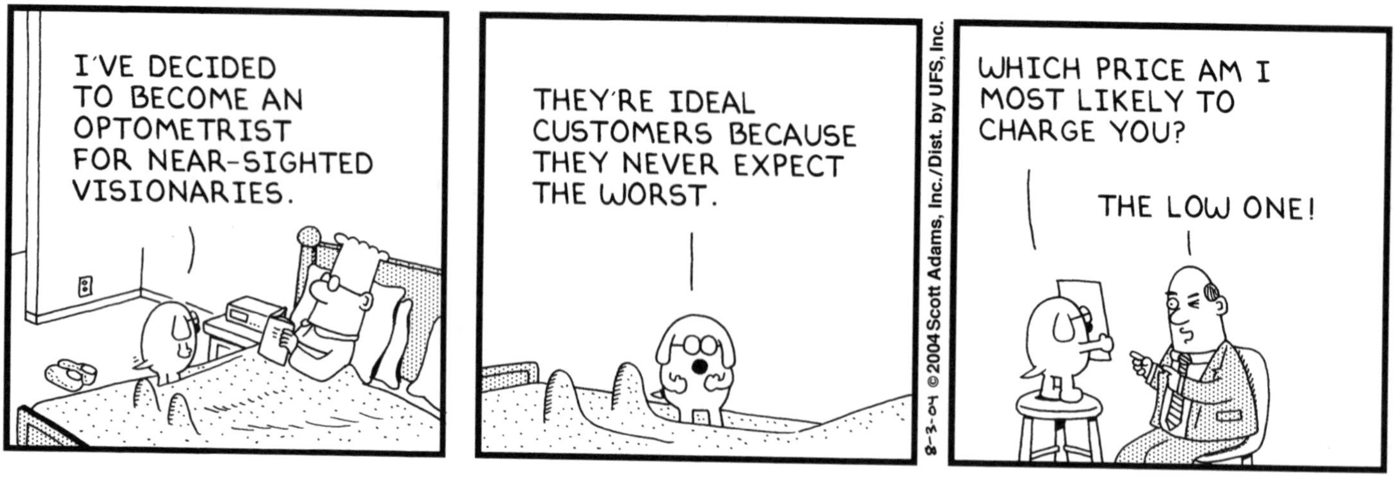
I'VE DECIDED TO BECOME AN OPTOMETRIST FOR NEAR-SIGHTED VISIONARIES.
THEY'RE IDEAL CUSTOMERS BECAUSE THEY NEVER EXPECT THE WORST.
8-3-04 © 2004 Scott Adams, Inc./Dist. by UFS, Inc.
WHICH PRICE AM I MOST LIKELY TO CHARGE YOU?
THE LOW ONE!

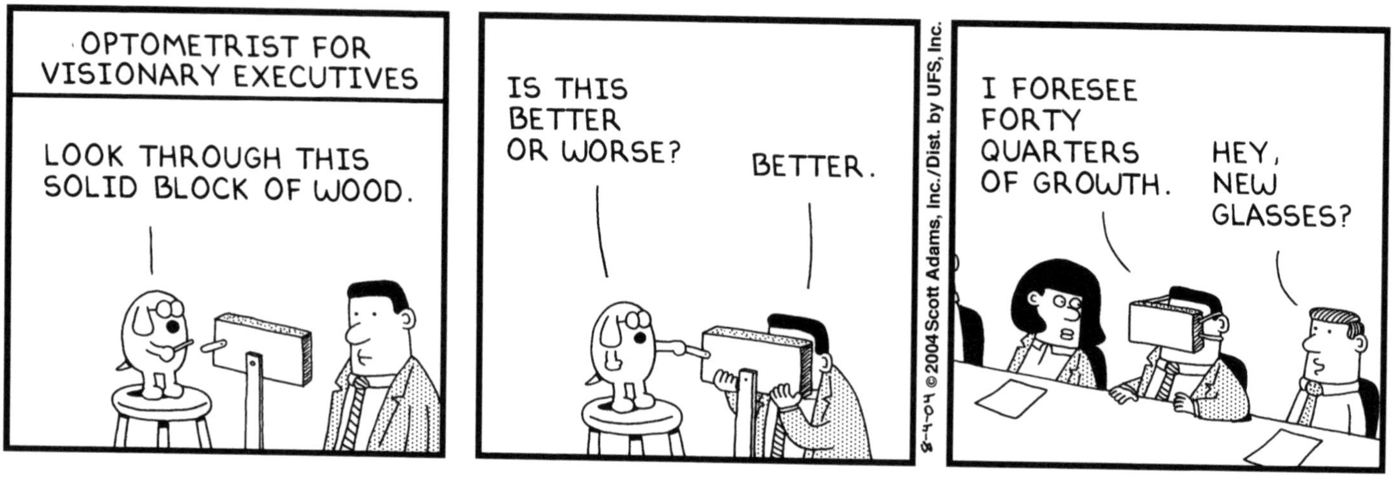
OPTOMETRIST FOR VISIONARY EXECUTIVES
LOOK THROUGH THIS SOLID BLOCK OF WOOD.
IS THIS BETTER OR WORSE?
BETTER.
8-4-04 © 2004 Scott Adams, Inc./Dist. by UFS, Inc.
I FORESEE FORTY QUARTERS OF GROWTH.
HEY, NEW GLASSES?

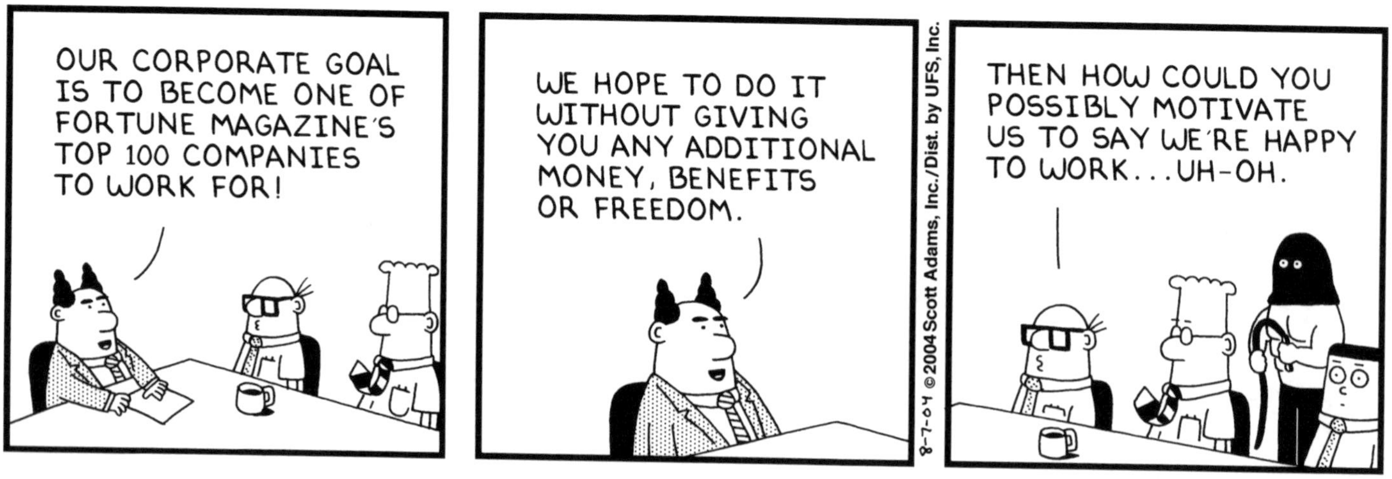
OUR CORPORATE GOAL IS TO BECOME ONE OF FORTUNE MAGAZINE'S TOP 100 COMPANIES TO WORK FOR!
WE HOPE TO DO IT WITHOUT GIVING YOU ANY ADDITIONAL MONEY, BENEFITS OR FREEDOM.
8-7-04 © 2004 Scott Adams, Inc./Dist. by UFS, Inc.
THEN HOW COULD YOU POSSIBLY MOTIVATE US TO SAY WE'RE HAPPY TO WORK...UH-OH.

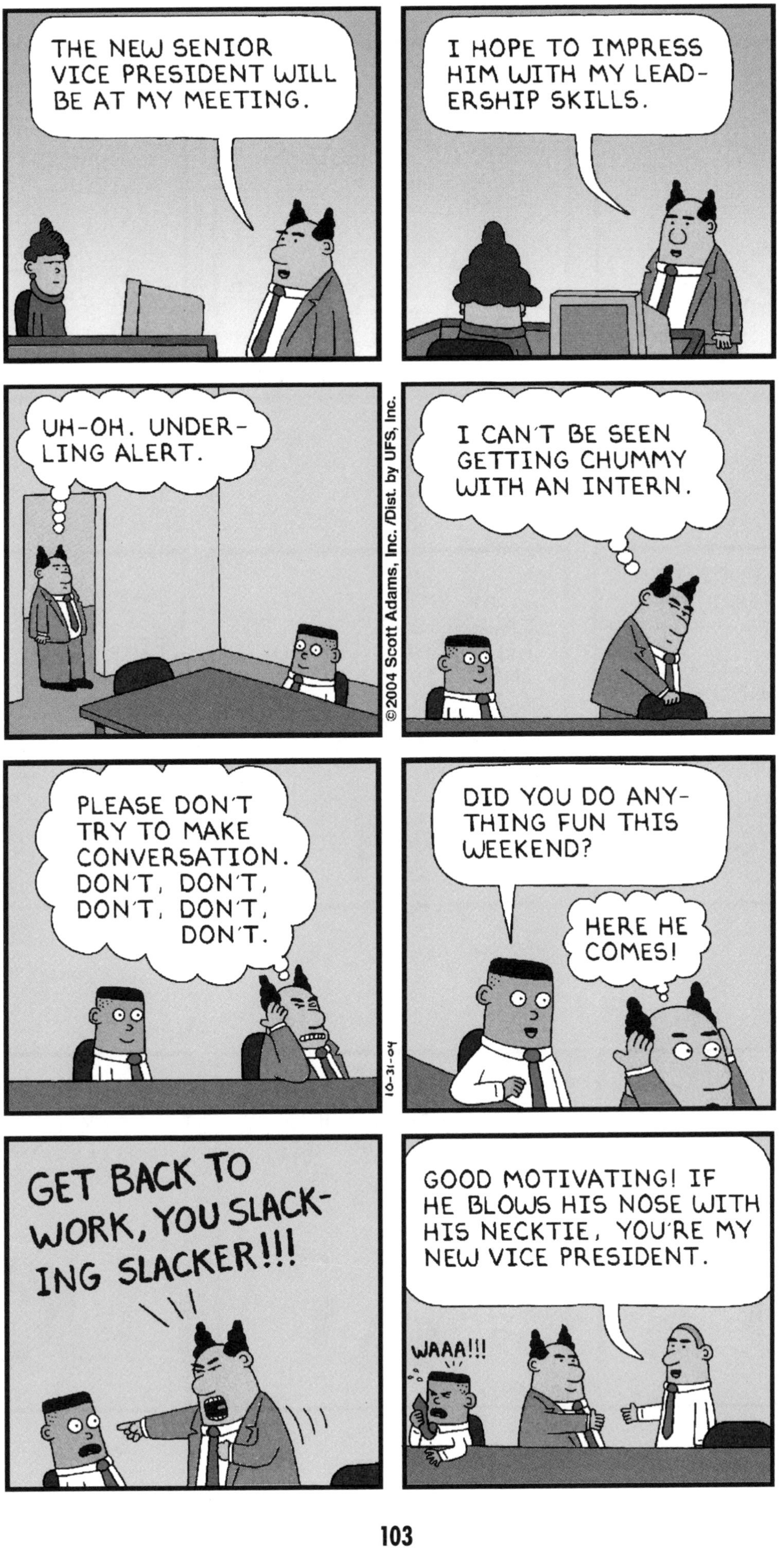
THE NEW SENIOR VICE PRESIDENT WILL BE AT MY MEETING.
I HOPE TO IMPRESS HIM WITH MY LEAD-ERSHIP SKILLS.
UH-OH. UNDER-LING ALERT.
©2004 Scott Adams, Inc./Dist. by UFS, Inc.
I CAN'T BE SEEN GETTING CHUMMY WITH AN INTERN.
PLEASE DON'T TRY TO MAKE CONVERSATION. DON'T, DON'T, DON'T, DON'T, DON'T.
10-31-04
DID YOU DO ANY-THING FUN THIS WEEKEND?
HERE HE COMES!
GET BACK TO WORK, YOU SLACK-ING SLACKER!!!
GOOD MOTIVATING! IF HE BLOWS HIS NOSE WITH HIS NECKTIE, YOU'RE MY NEW VICE PRESIDENT.
WAAA!!!

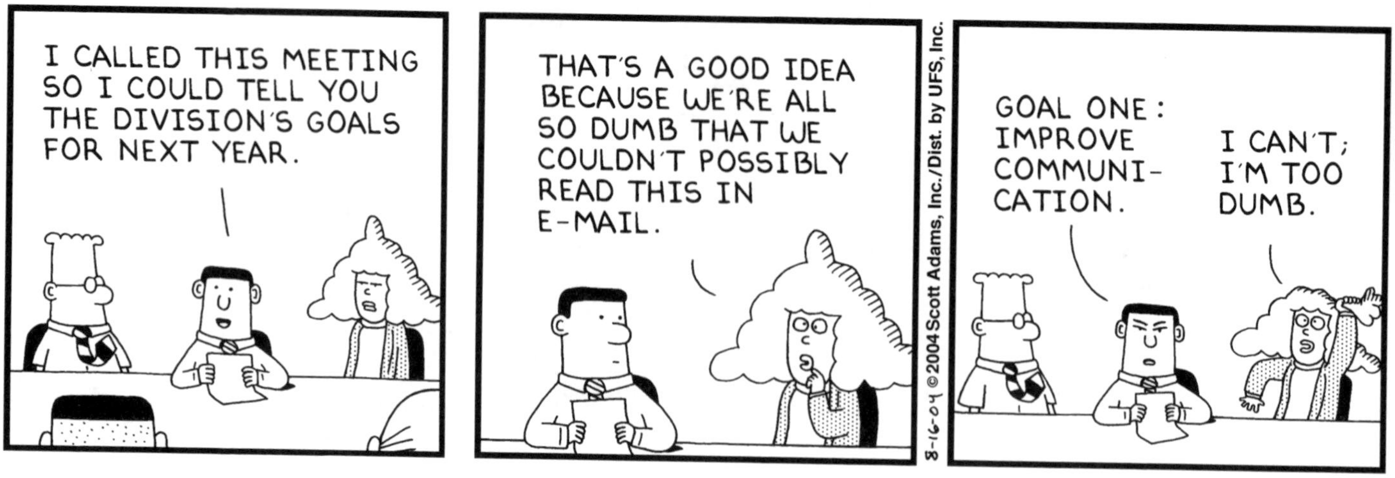
I CALLED THIS MEETING SO I COULD TELL YOU THE DIVISION'S GOALS FOR NEXT YEAR.
THAT'S A GOOD IDEA BECAUSE WE'RE ALL SO DUMB THAT WE COULDN'T POSSIBLY READ THIS IN E-MAIL.
8-16-04 © 2004 Scott Adams, Inc./Dist. by UFS, Inc.
GOAL ONE: IMPROVE COMMUNI-CATION.
I CAN'T; I'M TOO DUMB.

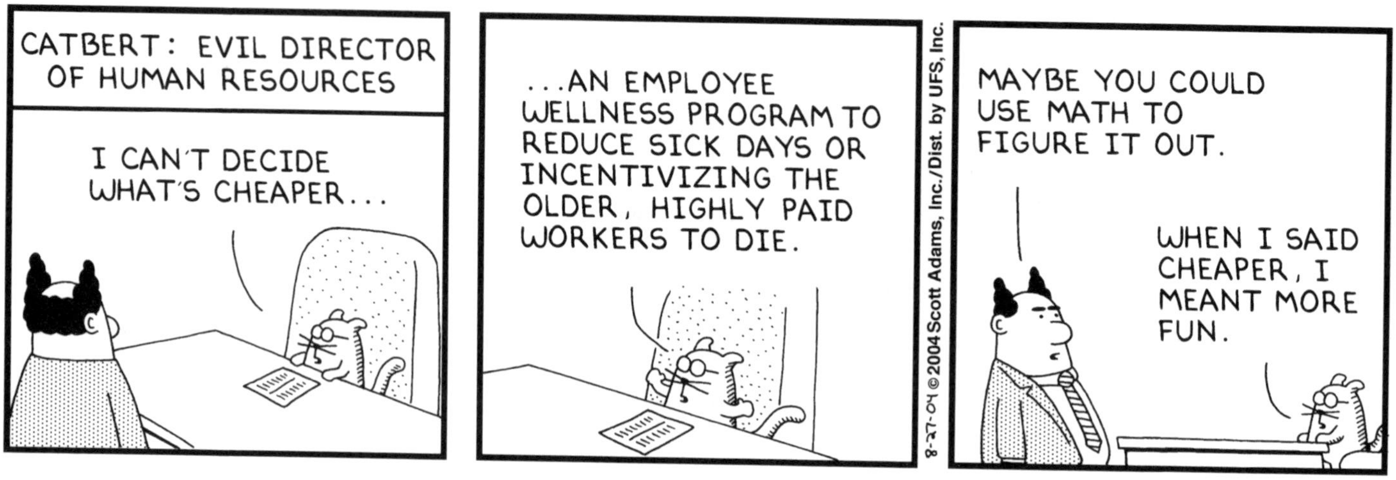
CATBERT: EVIL DIRECTOR OF HUMAN RESOURCES
I CAN'T DECIDE WHAT'S CHEAPER...
...AN EMPLOYEE WELLNESS PROGRAM TO REDUCE SICK DAYS OR INCENTIVIZING THE OLDER, HIGHLY PAID WORKERS TO DIE.
8-27-04 © 2004 Scott Adams, Inc./Dist. by UFS, Inc.
MAYBE YOU COULD USE MATH TO FIGURE IT OUT.
WHEN I SAID CHEAPER, I MEANT MORE FUN.

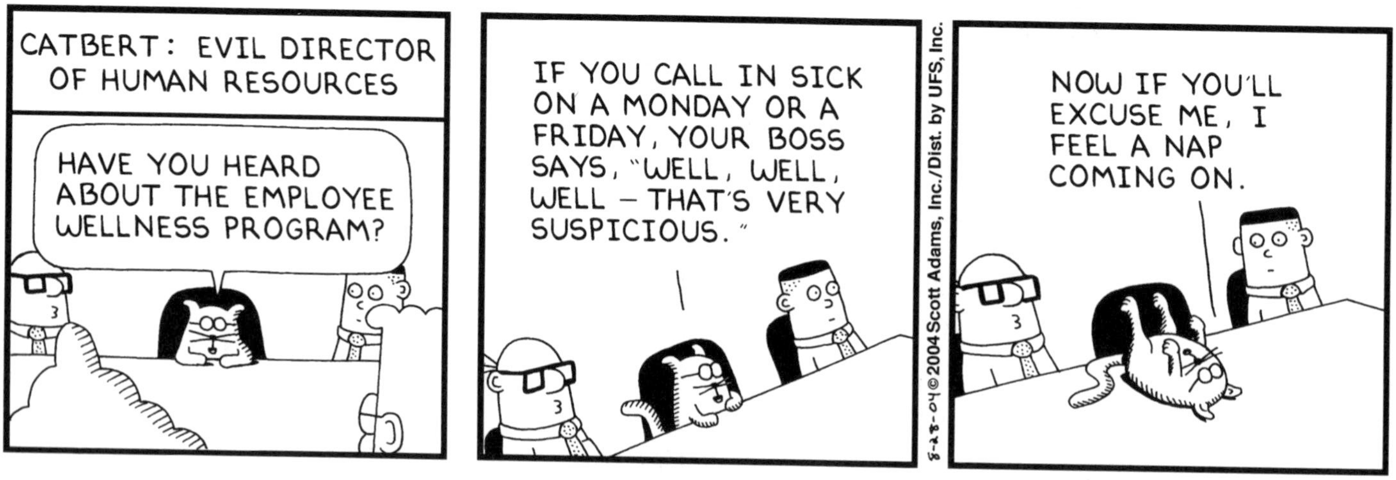
CATBERT: EVIL DIRECTOR OF HUMAN RESOURCES
HAVE YOU HEARD ABOUT THE EMPLOYEE WELLNESS PROGRAM?
IF YOU CALL IN SICK ON A MONDAY OR A FRIDAY, YOUR BOSS SAYS, "WELL, WELL, WELL – THAT'S VERY SUSPICIOUS."
8-28-04 © 2004 Scott Adams, Inc./Dist. by UFS, Inc.
NOW IF YOU'LL EXCUSE ME, I FEEL A NAP COMING ON.

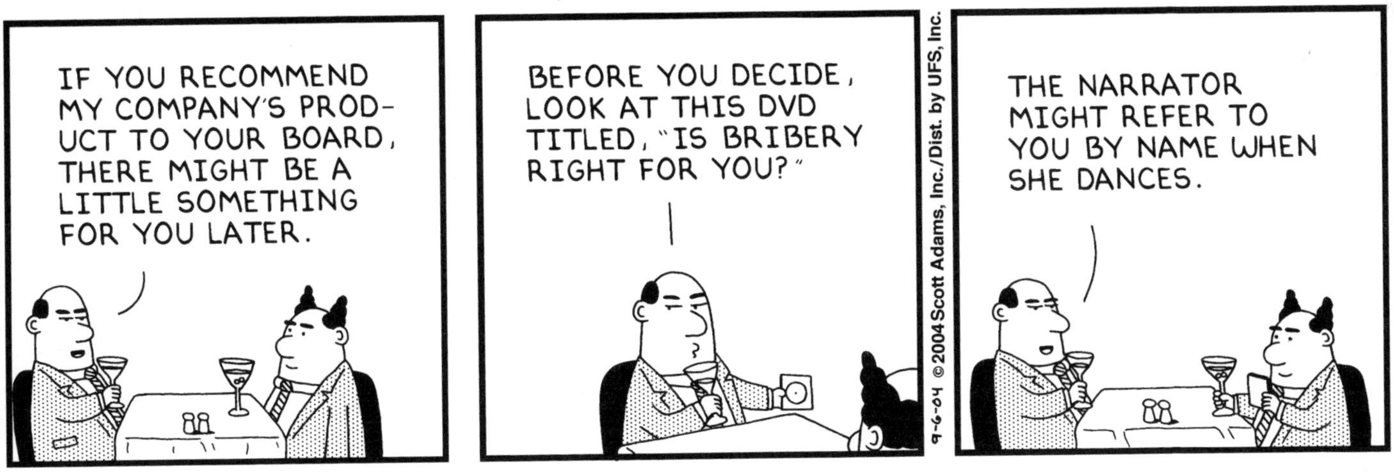
IF YOU RECOMMEND MY COMPANY'S PROD-UCT TO YOUR BOARD, THERE MIGHT BE A LITTLE SOMETHING FOR YOU LATER.
BEFORE YOU DECIDE, LOOK AT THIS DVD TITLED, "IS BRIBERY RIGHT FOR YOU?"
9-6-04 © 2004 Scott Adams, Inc./Dist. by UFS, Inc.
THE NARRATOR MIGHT REFER TO YOU BY NAME WHEN SHE DANCES.

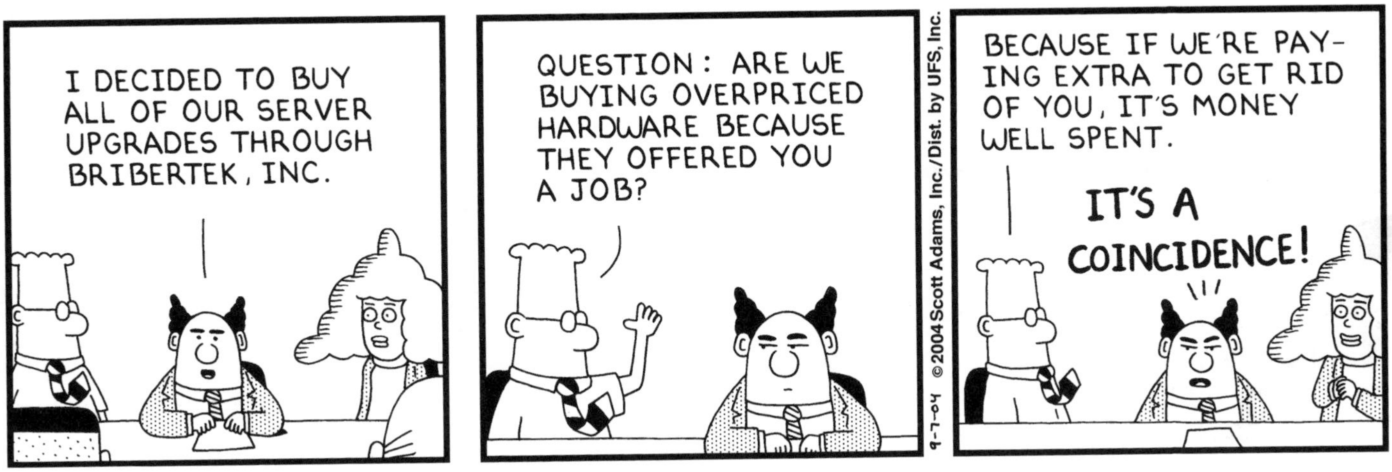
I DECIDED TO BUY ALL OF OUR SERVER UPGRADES THROUGH BRIBERTEK, INC.
QUESTION: ARE WE BUYING OVERPRICED HARDWARE BECAUSE THEY OFFERED YOU A JOB?
9-7-04 © 2004 Scott Adams, Inc./Dist. by UFS, Inc.
BECAUSE IF WE'RE PAY-ING EXTRA TO GET RID OF YOU, IT'S MONEY WELL SPENT.
IT'S A COINCIDENCE!

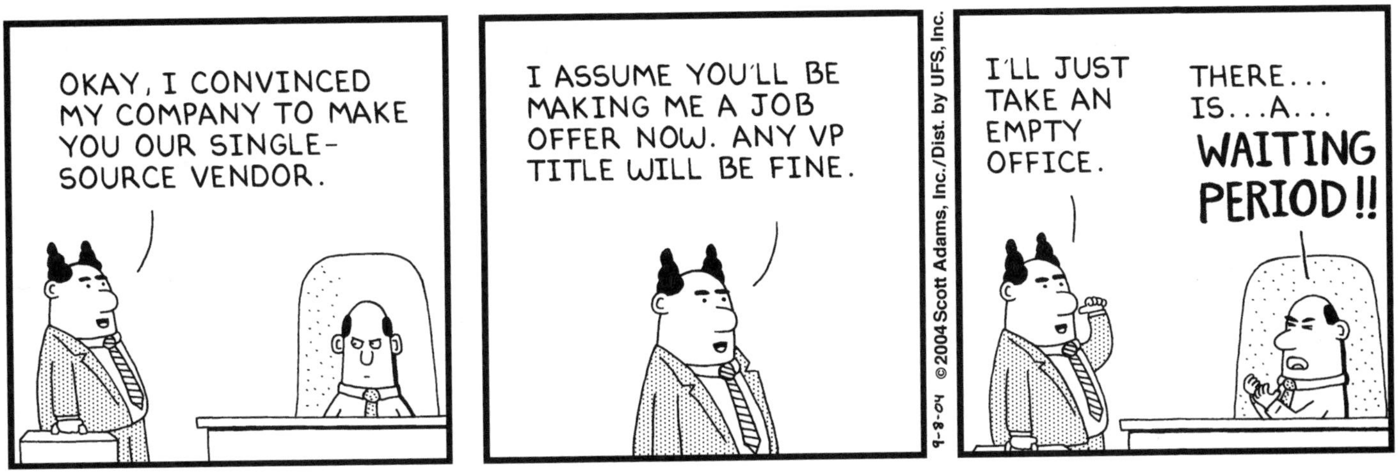
OKAY, I CONVINCED MY COMPANY TO MAKE YOU OUR SINGLE-SOURCE VENDOR.
I ASSUME YOU'LL BE MAKING ME A JOB OFFER NOW. ANY VP TITLE WILL BE FINE.
9-8-04 © 2004 Scott Adams, Inc./Dist. by UFS, Inc.
I'LL JUST TAKE AN EMPTY OFFICE.
THERE... IS... A... WAITING PERIOD!!

DOGBERT THE CEO
RATBERT, YOU'RE MY NEW VP OF SALES.
YOUR JOB IS TO SET IMPOSSIBLE GOALS FOR THE SALESPEOPLE AND PUNISH THEM FOR FAILING.
YAY! I ALWAYS WANTED TO BE A SADIST!
DREAMS DO COME TRUE.
6-3-09 © 2009 Scott Adams, Inc./Dist. by UFS, Inc.

DOGBERT THE CEO
EMPLOYEES ARE SO IMPORTANT TO ME THAT OUR HEAD OF HUMAN RESOURCES WILL GET A C-LEVEL TITLE.
EDNA WILL BE OUR CPO, OR CHIEF PEOPLE OFFICER.
TAKE A SEAT OVER THERE BY THE CHIEF ARTIFICIAL COFFEE CREAMER OFFICER.
11-21-09 © 2009 Scott Adams, Inc./Dist. by UFS, Inc.

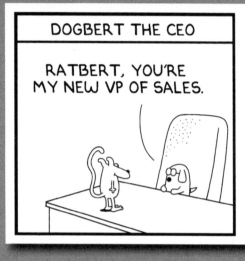

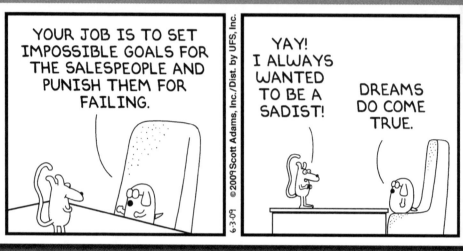

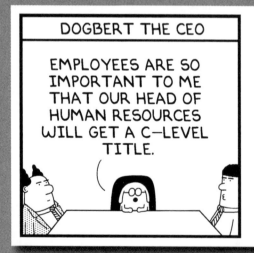

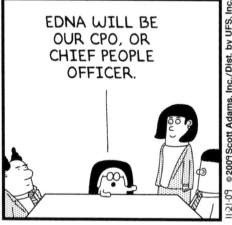

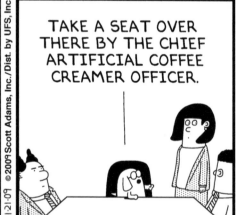

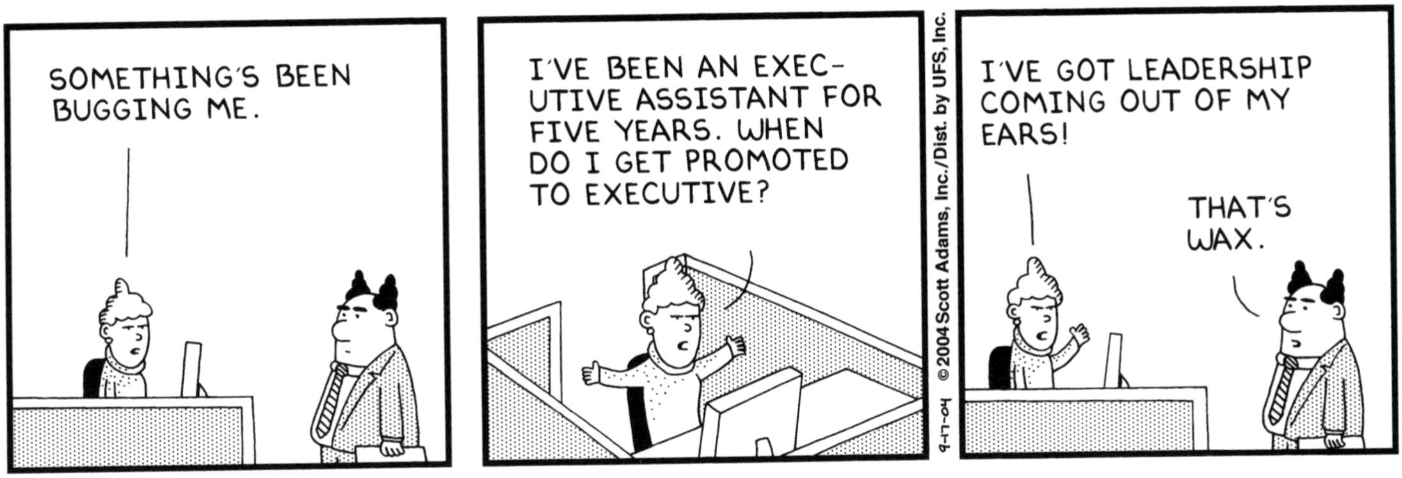
SOMETHING'S BEEN BUGGING ME.
I'VE BEEN AN EXECUTIVE ASSISTANT FOR FIVE YEARS. WHEN DO I GET PROMOTED TO EXECUTIVE?
I'VE GOT LEADERSHIP COMING OUT OF MY EARS!
THAT'S WAX.
9-17-04 © 2004 Scott Adams, Inc./Dist. by UFS, Inc.

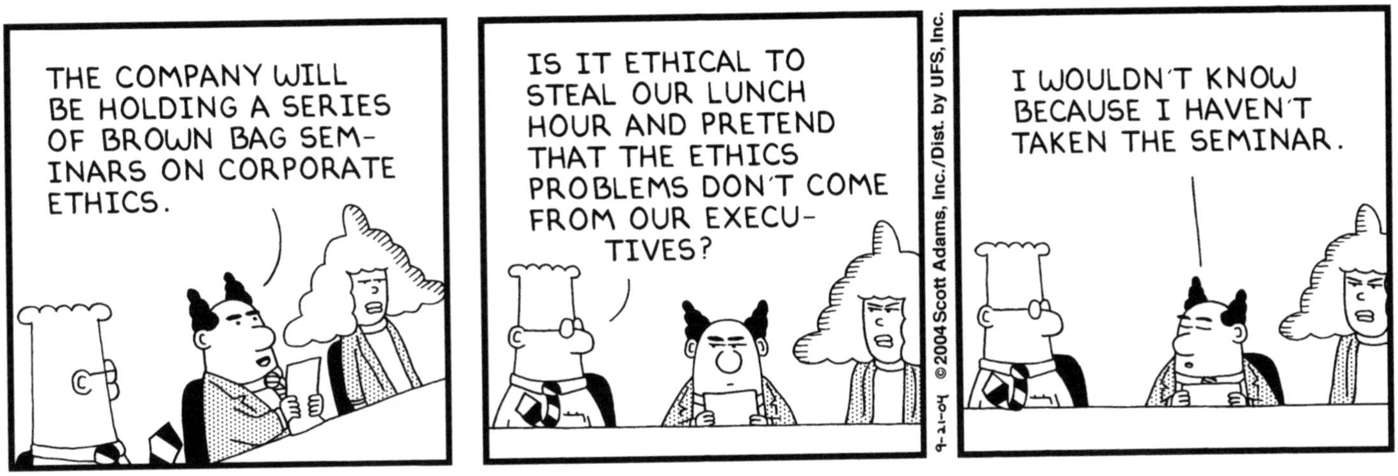
THE COMPANY WILL BE HOLDING A SERIES OF BROWN BAG SEMINARS ON CORPORATE ETHICS.
IS IT ETHICAL TO STEAL OUR LUNCH HOUR AND PRETEND THAT THE ETHICS PROBLEMS DON'T COME FROM OUR EXECUTIVES?
I WOULDN'T KNOW BECAUSE I HAVEN'T TAKEN THE SEMINAR.
9-21-04 © 2004 Scott Adams, Inc./Dist. by UFS, Inc.

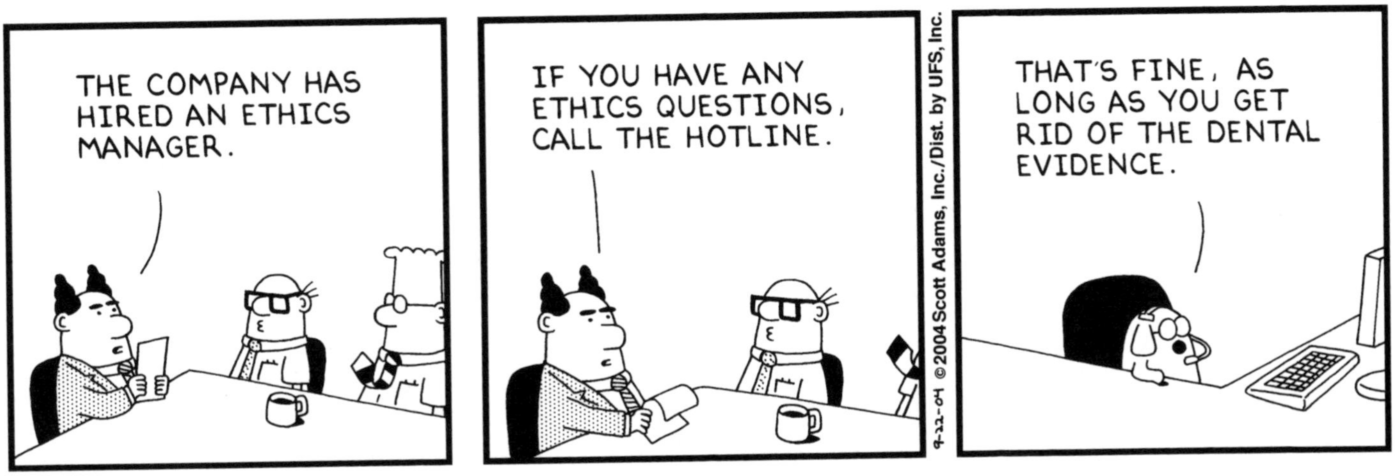
THE COMPANY HAS HIRED AN ETHICS MANAGER.
IF YOU HAVE ANY ETHICS QUESTIONS, CALL THE HOTLINE.
THAT'S FINE, AS LONG AS YOU GET RID OF THE DENTAL EVIDENCE.
9-22-04 © 2004 Scott Adams, Inc./Dist. by UFS, Inc.

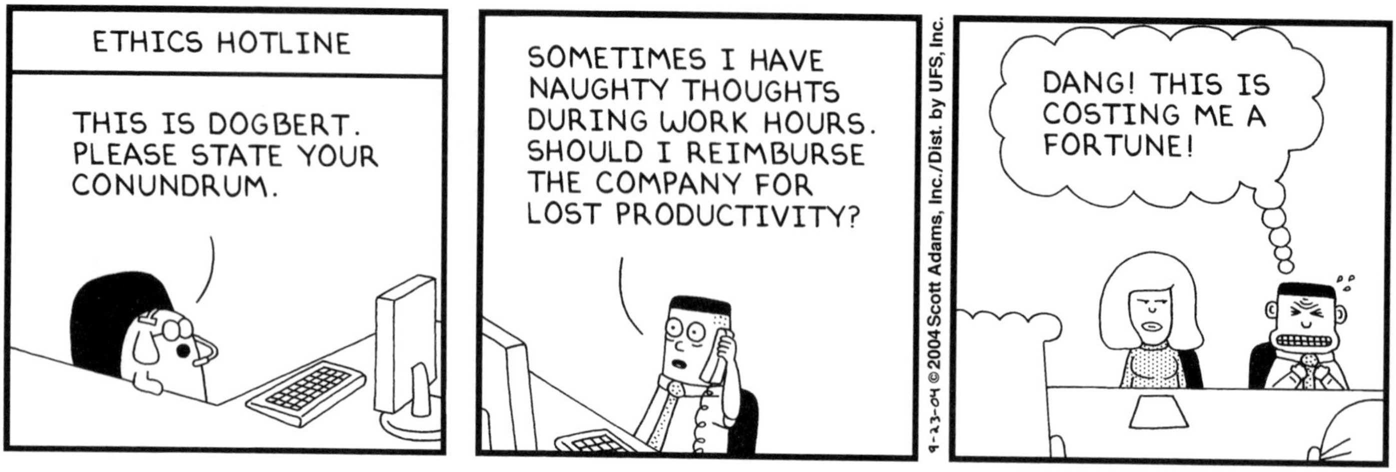
ETHICS HOTLINE
THIS IS DOGBERT. PLEASE STATE YOUR CONUNDRUM.
SOMETIMES I HAVE NAUGHTY THOUGHTS DURING WORK HOURS. SHOULD I REIMBURSE THE COMPANY FOR LOST PRODUCTIVITY?
9-23-04 © 2004 Scott Adams, Inc./Dist. by UFS, Inc.
DANG! THIS IS COSTING ME A FORTUNE!

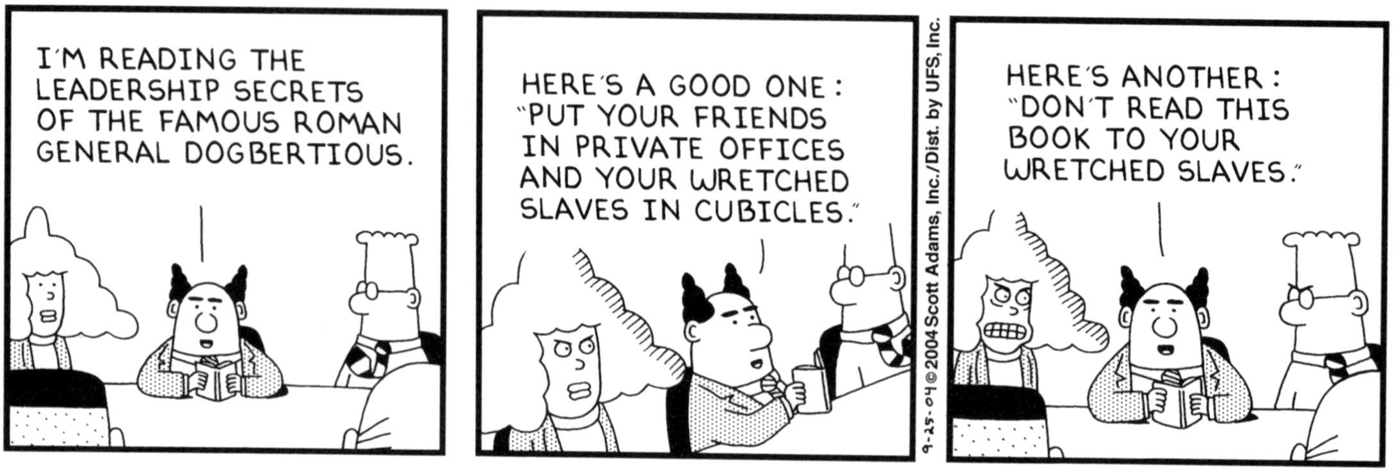
I'M READING THE LEADERSHIP SECRETS OF THE FAMOUS ROMAN GENERAL DOGBERTIOUS.
HERE'S A GOOD ONE: "PUT YOUR FRIENDS IN PRIVATE OFFICES AND YOUR WRETCHED SLAVES IN CUBICLES."
9-25-04 © 2004 Scott Adams, Inc./Dist. by UFS, Inc.
HERE'S ANOTHER: "DON'T READ THIS BOOK TO YOUR WRETCHED SLAVES."

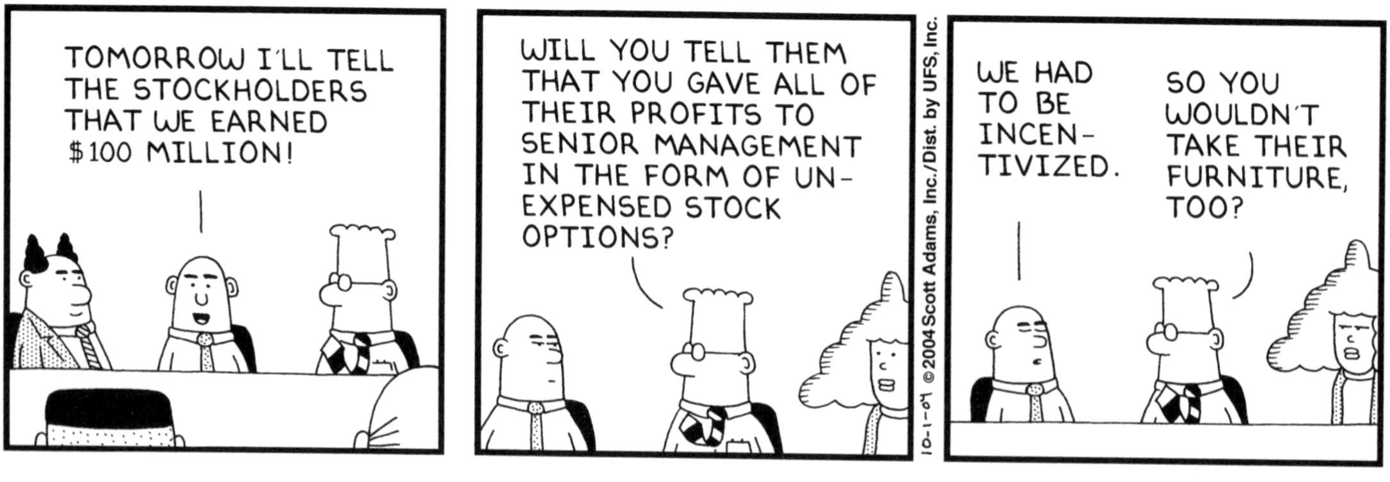
TOMORROW I'LL TELL THE STOCKHOLDERS THAT WE EARNED $100 MILLION!
WILL YOU TELL THEM THAT YOU GAVE ALL OF THEIR PROFITS TO SENIOR MANAGEMENT IN THE FORM OF UN-EXPENSED STOCK OPTIONS?
10-1-04 © 2004 Scott Adams, Inc./Dist. by UFS, Inc.
WE HAD TO BE INCEN-TIVIZED.
SO YOU WOULDN'T TAKE THEIR FURNITURE, TOO?

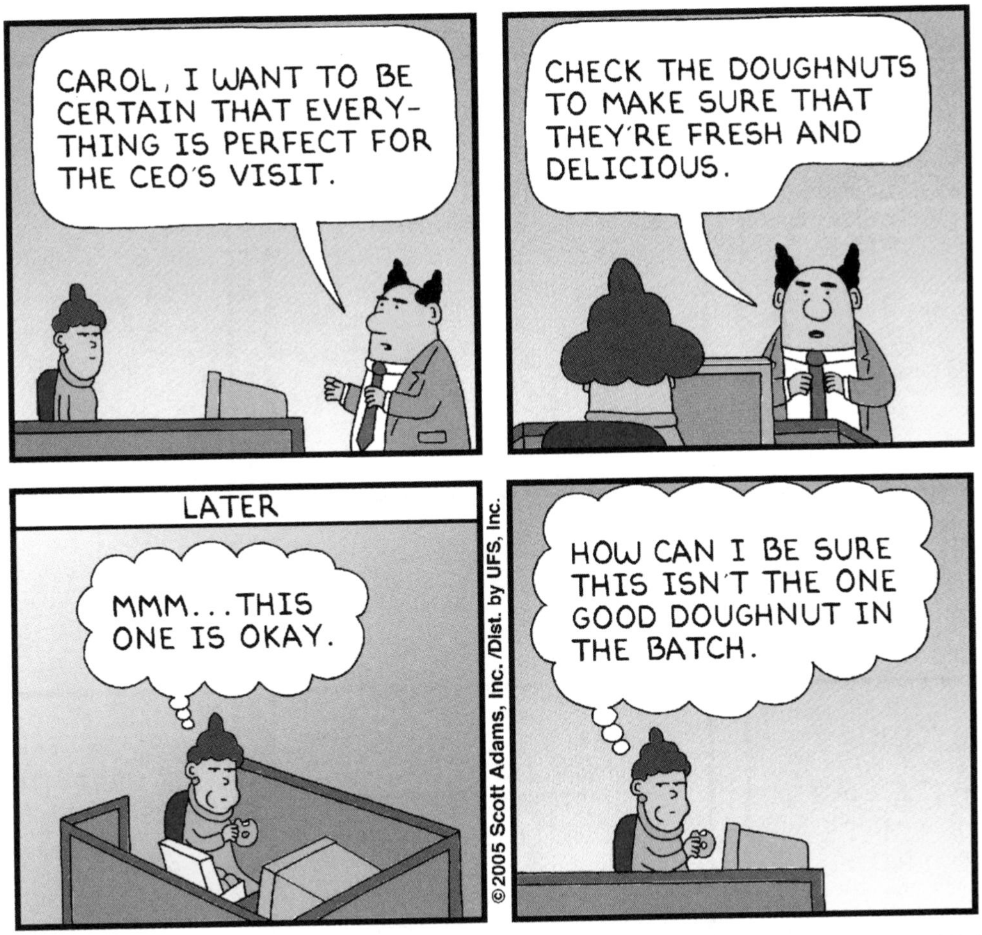
CAROL, I WANT TO BE CERTAIN THAT EVERYTHING IS PERFECT FOR THE CEO'S VISIT.
CHECK THE DOUGHNUTS TO MAKE SURE THAT THEY'RE FRESH AND DELICIOUS.
LATER
MMM...THIS ONE IS OKAY.
HOW CAN I BE SURE THIS ISN'T THE ONE GOOD DOUGHNUT IN THE BATCH.
©2005 Scott Adams, Inc./Dist. by UFS, Inc.

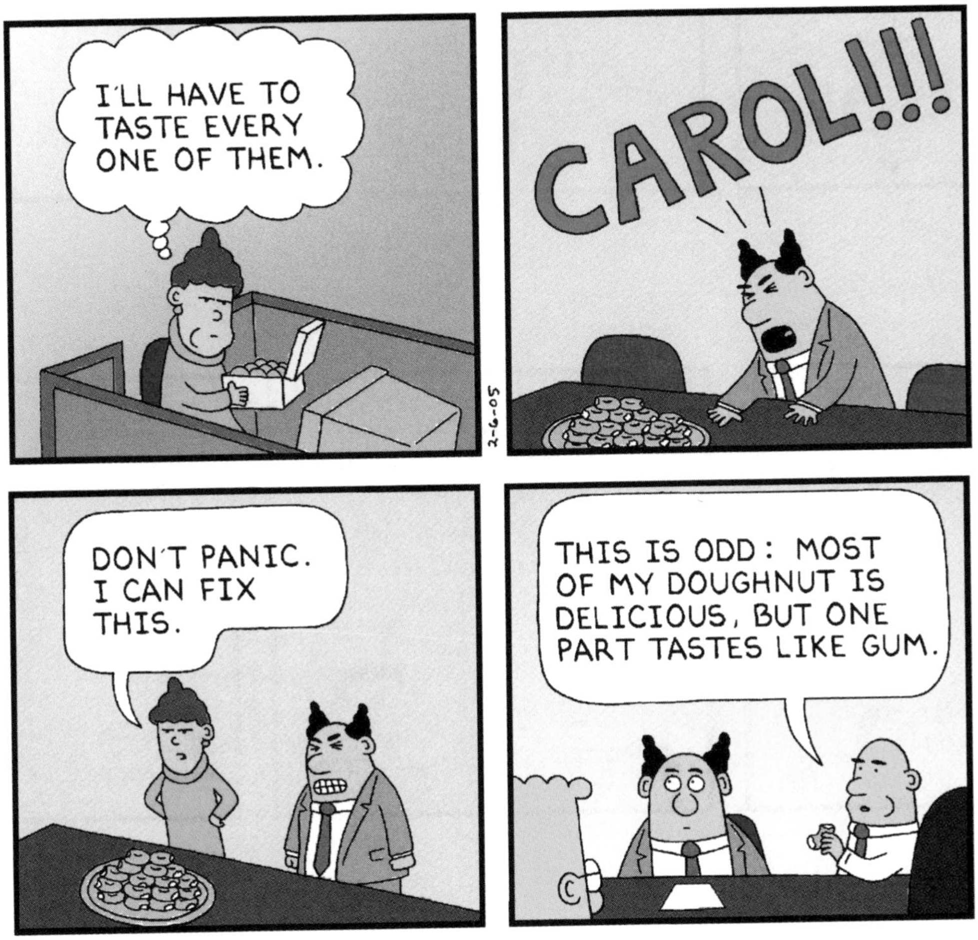
I'LL HAVE TO TASTE EVERY ONE OF THEM.
2-6-05
CAROL!!!
DON'T PANIC. I CAN FIX THIS.
THIS IS ODD: MOST OF MY DOUGHNUT IS DELICIOUS, BUT ONE PART TASTES LIKE GUM.

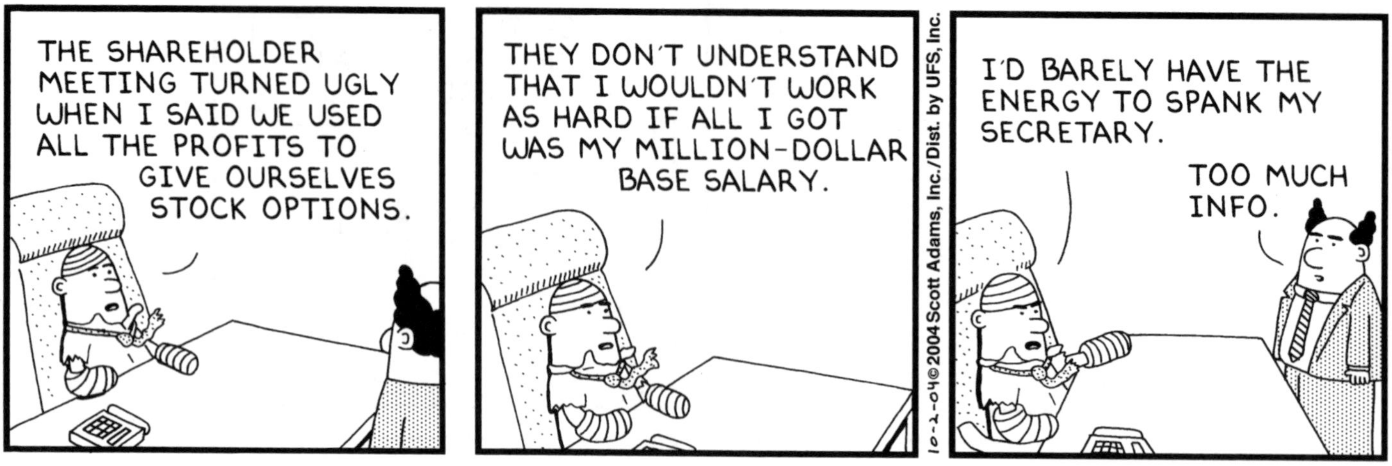
THE SHAREHOLDER MEETING TURNED UGLY WHEN I SAID WE USED ALL THE PROFITS TO GIVE OURSELVES STOCK OPTIONS.
THEY DON'T UNDERSTAND THAT I WOULDN'T WORK AS HARD IF ALL I GOT WAS MY MILLION-DOLLAR BASE SALARY.
10-2-04 © 2004 Scott Adams, Inc./Dist. by UFS, Inc.
I'D BARELY HAVE THE ENERGY TO SPANK MY SECRETARY.
TOO MUCH INFO.

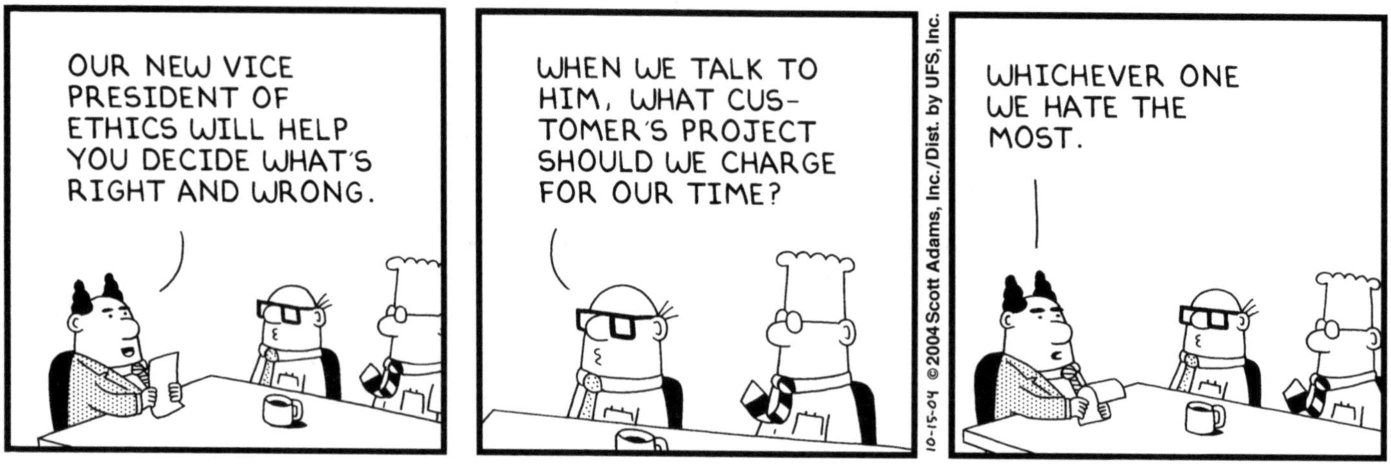
OUR NEW VICE PRESIDENT OF ETHICS WILL HELP YOU DECIDE WHAT'S RIGHT AND WRONG.
WHEN WE TALK TO HIM, WHAT CUS-TOMER'S PROJECT SHOULD WE CHARGE FOR OUR TIME?
10-15-04 © 2004 Scott Adams, Inc./Dist. by UFS, Inc.
WHICHEVER ONE WE HATE THE MOST.

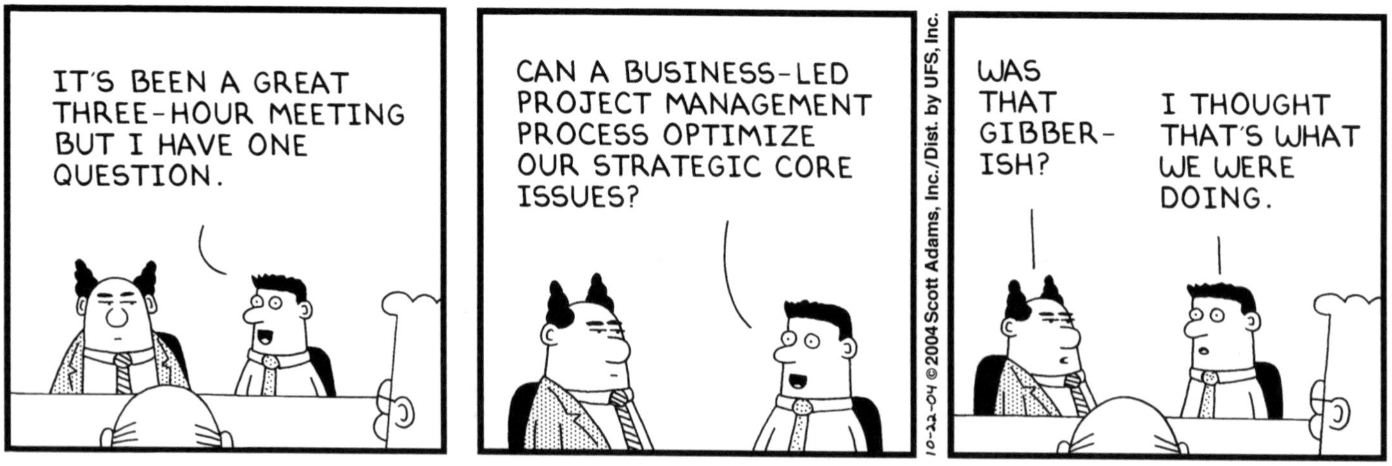
IT'S BEEN A GREAT THREE-HOUR MEETING BUT I HAVE ONE QUESTION.
CAN A BUSINESS-LED PROJECT MANAGEMENT PROCESS OPTIMIZE OUR STRATEGIC CORE ISSUES?
10-22-04 © 2004 Scott Adams, Inc./Dist. by UFS, Inc.
WAS THAT GIBBER-ISH?
I THOUGHT THAT'S WHAT WE WERE DOING.

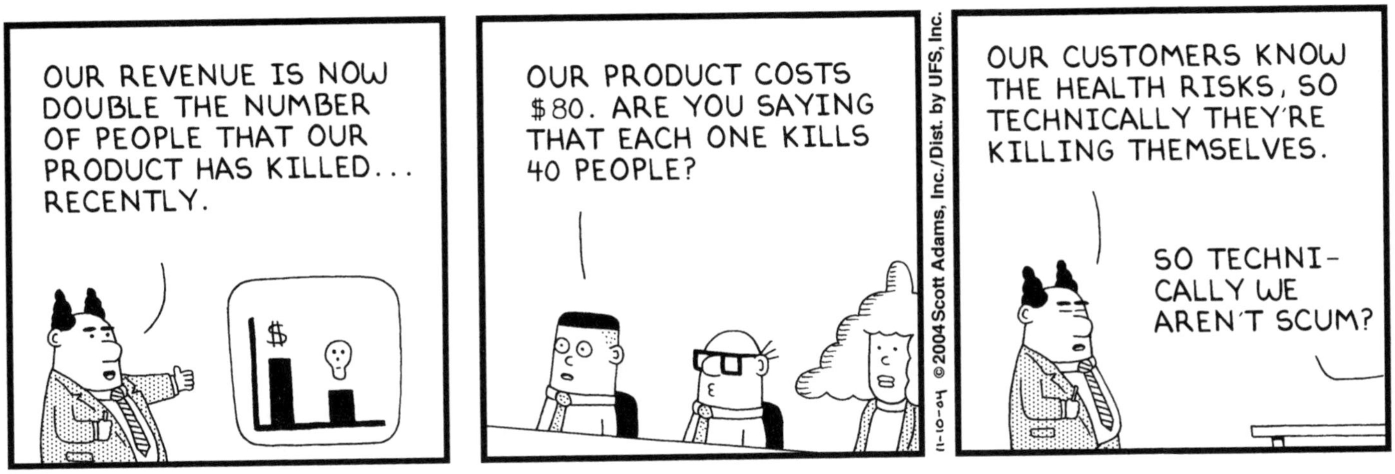
OUR REVENUE IS NOW DOUBLE THE NUMBER OF PEOPLE THAT OUR PRODUCT HAS KILLED... RECENTLY.
$
OUR PRODUCT COSTS $80. ARE YOU SAYING THAT EACH ONE KILLS 40 PEOPLE?
11-10-04 ©2004 Scott Adams, Inc./Dist. by UFS, Inc.
OUR CUSTOMERS KNOW THE HEALTH RISKS, SO TECHNICALLY THEY'RE KILLING THEMSELVES.
SO TECHNI- CALLY WE AREN'T SCUM?

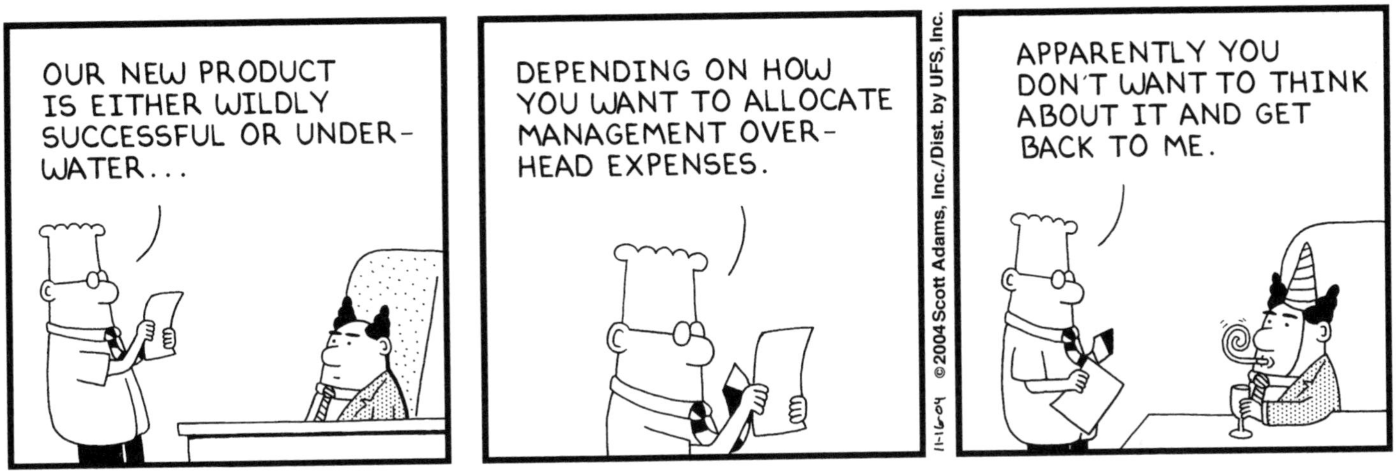
OUR NEW PRODUCT IS EITHER WILDLY SUCCESSFUL OR UNDER- WATER...
DEPENDING ON HOW YOU WANT TO ALLOCATE MANAGEMENT OVER- HEAD EXPENSES.
11-16-04 ©2004 Scott Adams, Inc./Dist. by UFS, Inc.
APPARENTLY YOU DON'T WANT TO THINK ABOUT IT AND GET BACK TO ME.

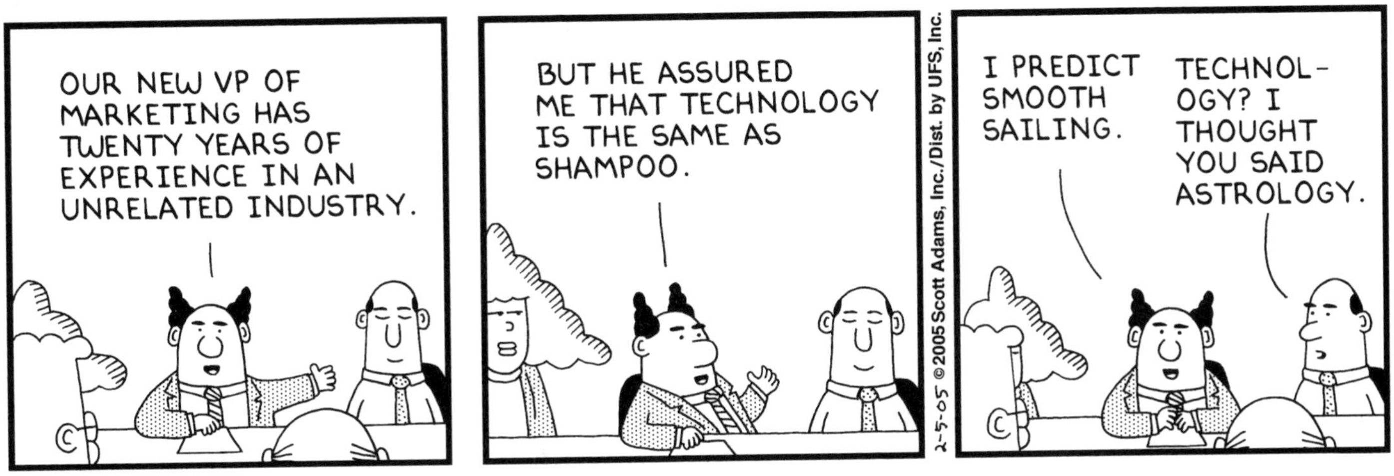
OUR NEW VP OF MARKETING HAS TWENTY YEARS OF EXPERIENCE IN AN UNRELATED INDUSTRY.
BUT HE ASSURED ME THAT TECHNOLOGY IS THE SAME AS SHAMPOO.
2-5-05 ©2005 Scott Adams, Inc./Dist. by UFS, Inc.
I PREDICT SMOOTH SAILING.
TECHNOL- OGY? I THOUGHT YOU SAID ASTROLOGY.

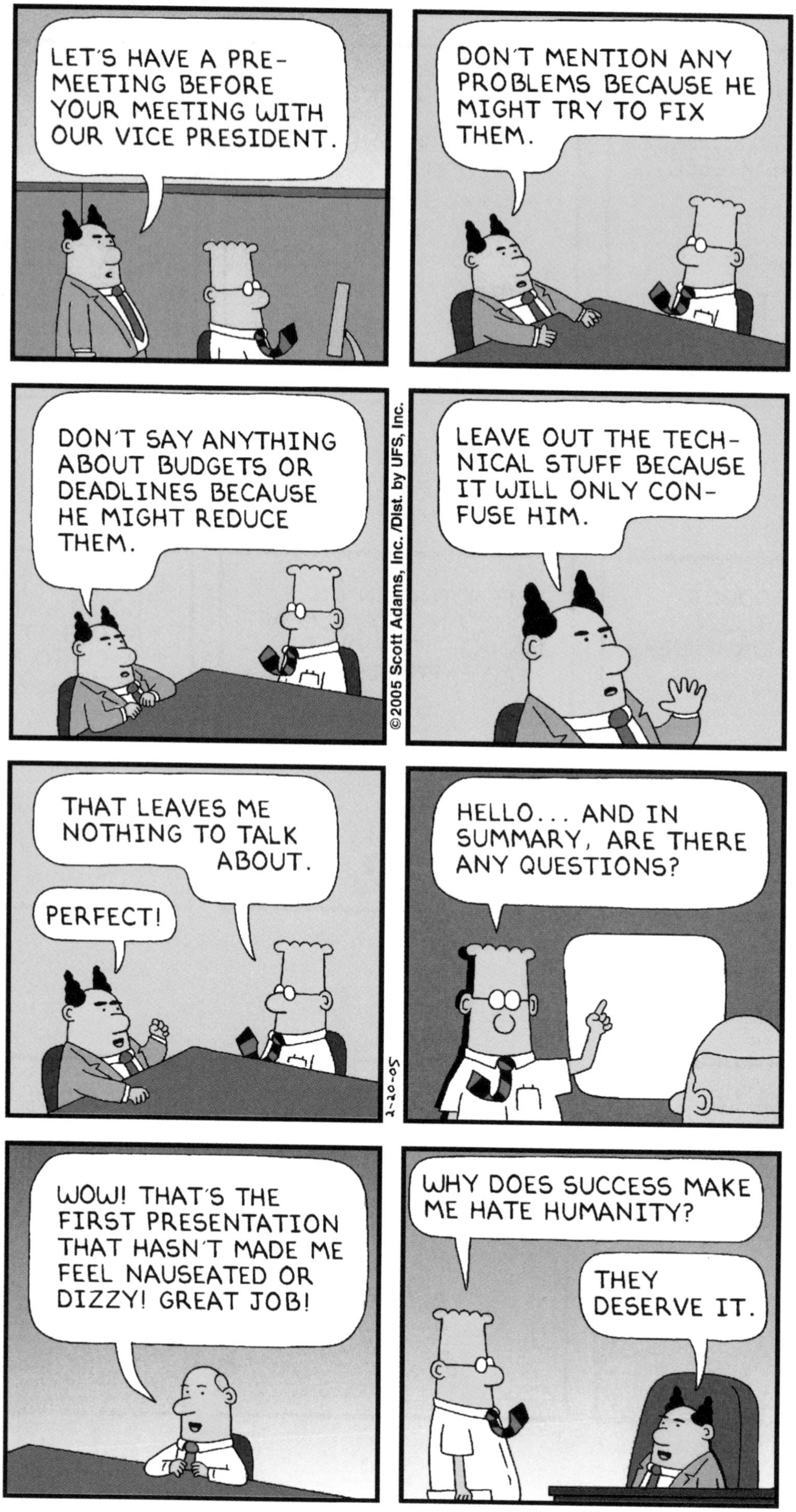
LET'S HAVE A PRE-MEETING BEFORE YOUR MEETING WITH OUR VICE PRESIDENT.
DON'T MENTION ANY PROBLEMS BECAUSE HE MIGHT TRY TO FIX THEM.
DON'T SAY ANYTHING ABOUT BUDGETS OR DEADLINES BECAUSE HE MIGHT REDUCE THEM.
©2005 Scott Adams, Inc. /Dist. by UFS, Inc.
LEAVE OUT THE TECHNICAL STUFF BECAUSE IT WILL ONLY CONFUSE HIM.
THAT LEAVES ME NOTHING TO TALK ABOUT.
PERFECT!
2-20-05
HELLO... AND IN SUMMARY, ARE THERE ANY QUESTIONS?
WOW! THAT'S THE FIRST PRESENTATION THAT HASN'T MADE ME FEEL NAUSEATED OR DIZZY! GREAT JOB!
WHY DOES SUCCESS MAKE ME HATE HUMANITY?
THEY DESERVE IT.

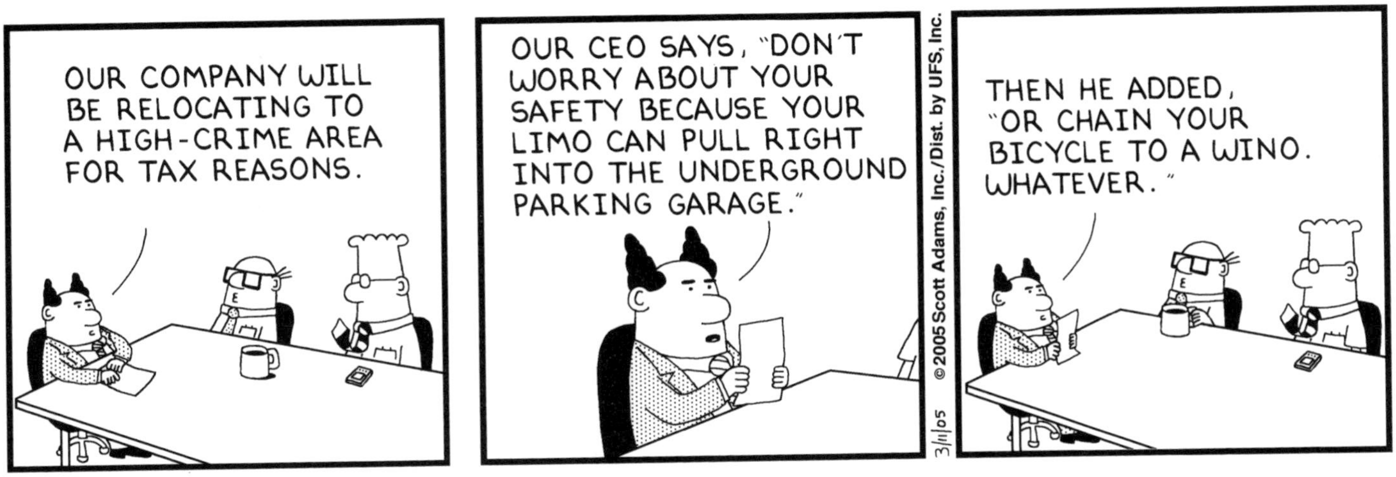
OUR COMPANY WILL BE RELOCATING TO A HIGH-CRIME AREA FOR TAX REASONS.
OUR CEO SAYS, "DON'T WORRY ABOUT YOUR SAFETY BECAUSE YOUR LIMO CAN PULL RIGHT INTO THE UNDERGROUND PARKING GARAGE."
3/11/05 © 2005 Scott Adams, Inc./Dist. by UFS, Inc.
THEN HE ADDED, "OR CHAIN YOUR BICYCLE TO A WINO. WHATEVER."

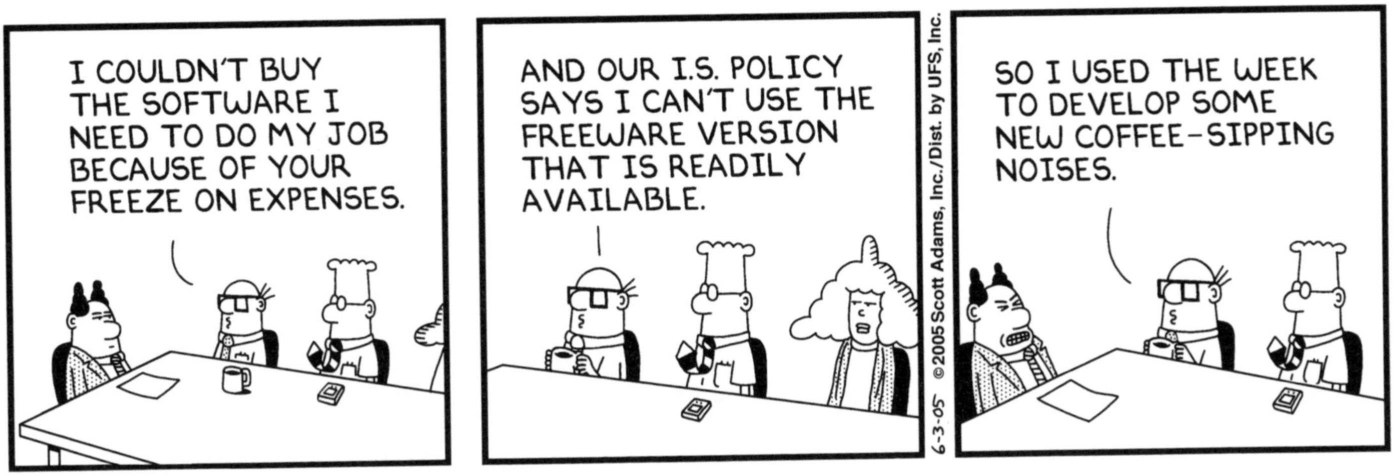
I COULDN'T BUY THE SOFTWARE I NEED TO DO MY JOB BECAUSE OF YOUR FREEZE ON EXPENSES.
AND OUR I.S. POLICY SAYS I CAN'T USE THE FREEWARE VERSION THAT IS READILY AVAILABLE.
6-3-05 © 2005 Scott Adams, Inc./Dist. by UFS, Inc.
SO I USED THE WEEK TO DEVELOP SOME NEW COFFEE-SIPPING NOISES.

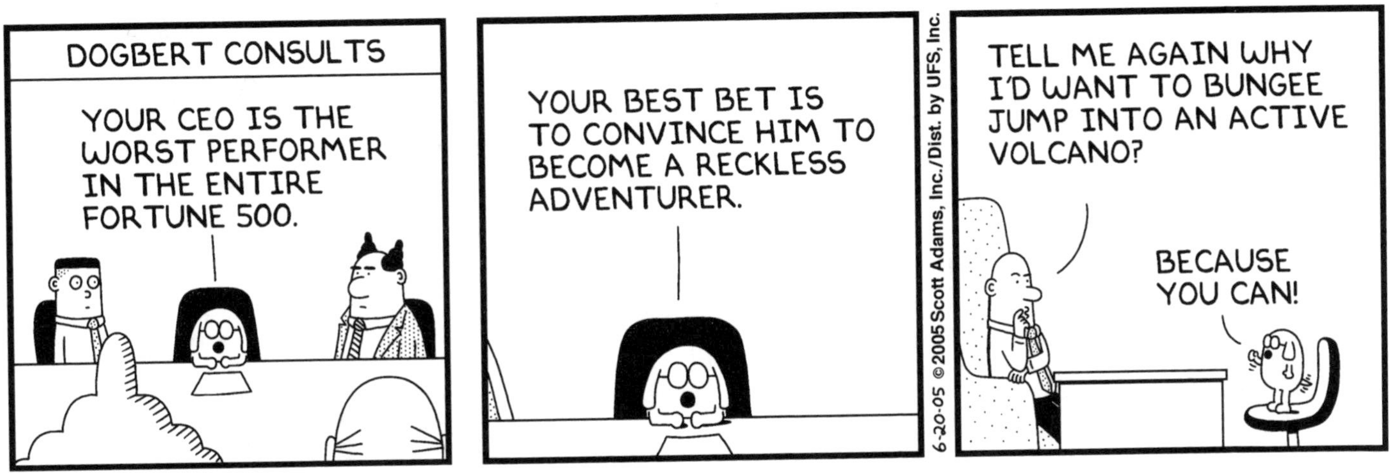
DOGBERT CONSULTS
YOUR CEO IS THE WORST PERFORMER IN THE ENTIRE FORTUNE 500.
YOUR BEST BET IS TO CONVINCE HIM TO BECOME A RECKLESS ADVENTURER.
6-20-05 © 2005 Scott Adams, Inc./Dist. by UFS, Inc.
TELL ME AGAIN WHY I'D WANT TO BUNGEE JUMP INTO AN ACTIVE VOLCANO?
BECAUSE YOU CAN!

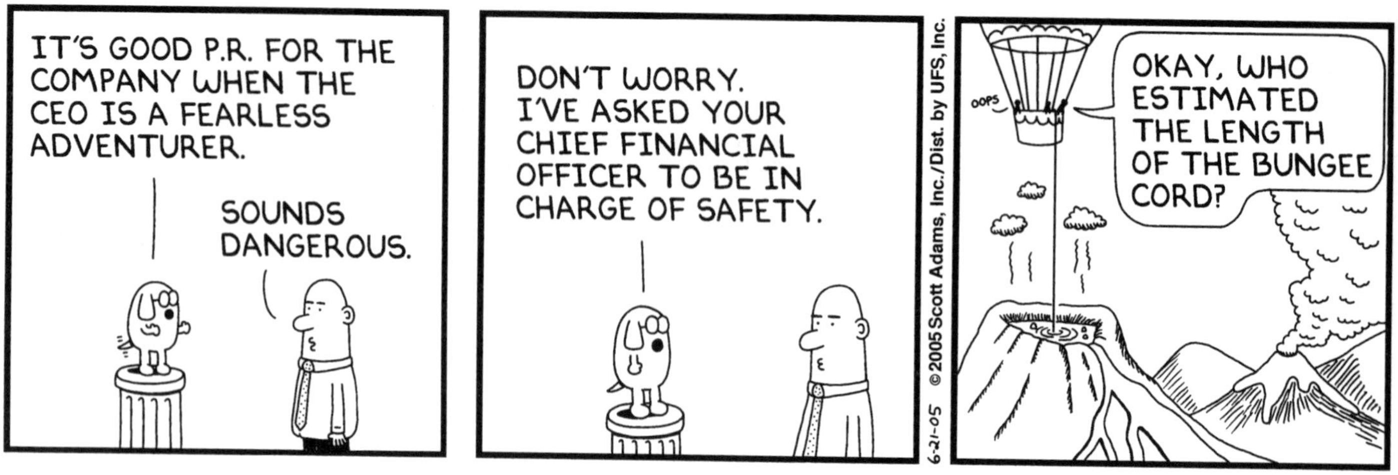
IT'S GOOD P.R. FOR THE COMPANY WHEN THE CEO IS A FEARLESS ADVENTURER.
SOUNDS DANGEROUS.
DON'T WORRY. I'VE ASKED YOUR CHIEF FINANCIAL OFFICER TO BE IN CHARGE OF SAFETY.
6-21-05 © 2005 Scott Adams, Inc./Dist. by UFS, Inc.
OOPS
OKAY, WHO ESTIMATED THE LENGTH OF THE BUNGEE CORD?

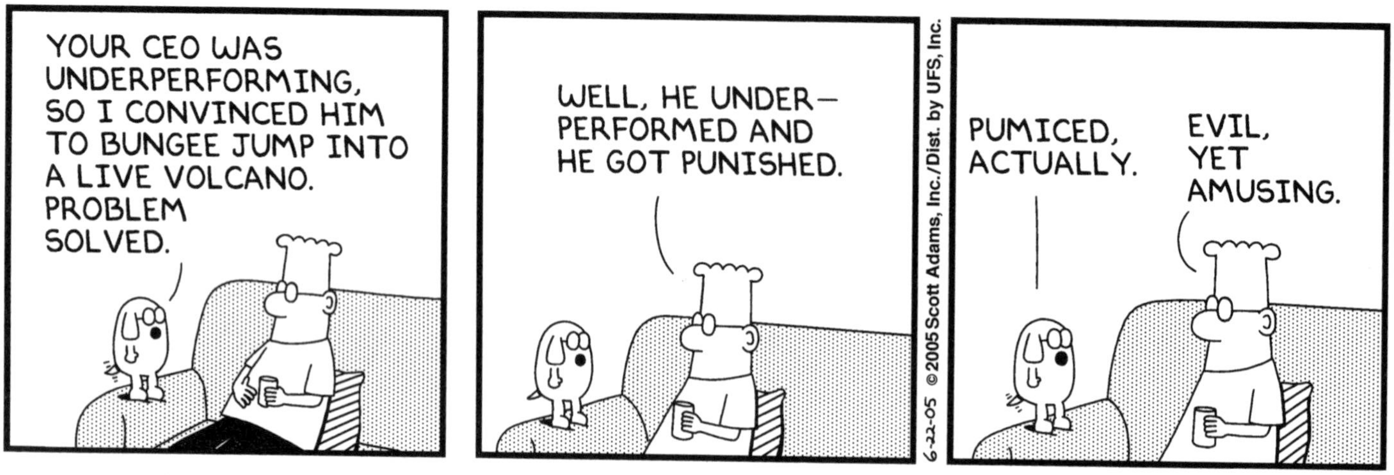
YOUR CEO WAS UNDERPERFORMING, SO I CONVINCED HIM TO BUNGEE JUMP INTO A LIVE VOLCANO. PROBLEM SOLVED.
WELL, HE UNDER-PERFORMED AND HE GOT PUNISHED.
6-22-05 © 2005 Scott Adams, Inc./Dist. by UFS, Inc.
PUMICED, ACTUALLY.
EVIL, YET AMUSING.

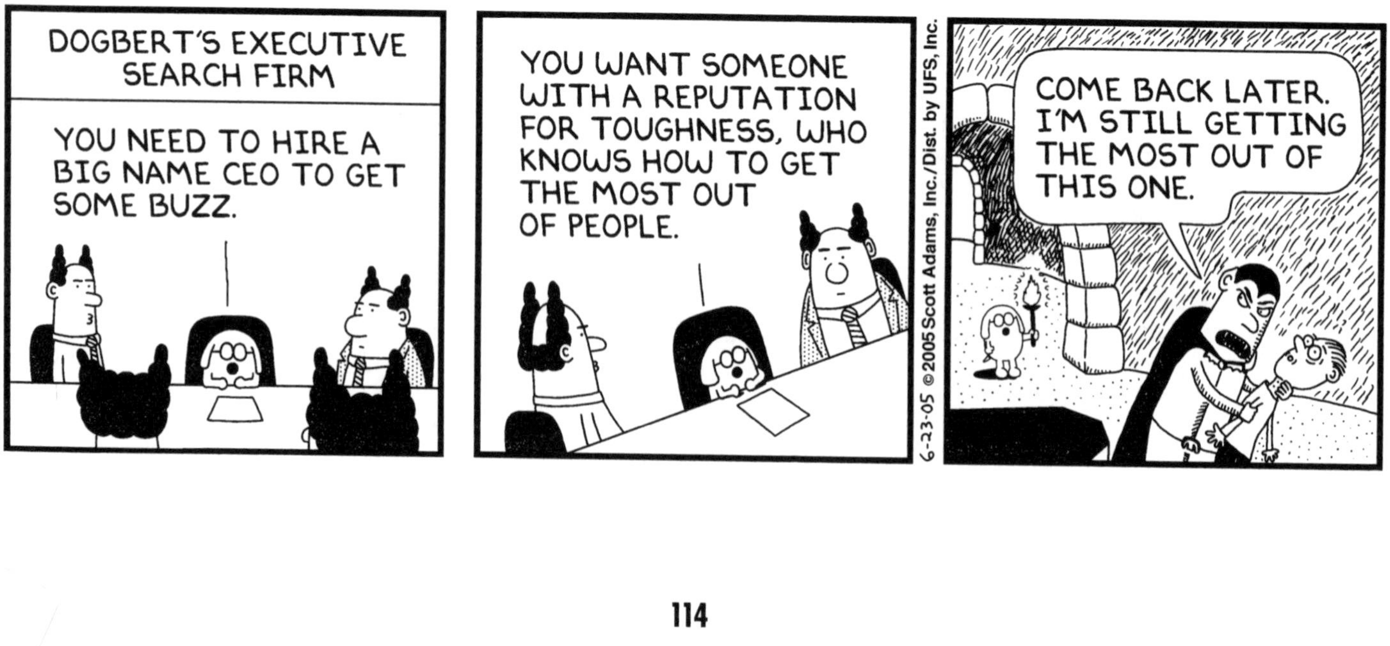
DOGBERT'S EXECUTIVE SEARCH FIRM
YOU NEED TO HIRE A BIG NAME CEO TO GET SOME BUZZ.
YOU WANT SOMEONE WITH A REPUTATION FOR TOUGHNESS, WHO KNOWS HOW TO GET THE MOST OUT OF PEOPLE.
6-23-05 © 2005 Scott Adams, Inc./Dist. by UFS, Inc.
COME BACK LATER. I'M STILL GETTING THE MOST OUT OF THIS ONE.

DOGBERT THE CEO
MY BASE PAY WILL BE ONE DOLLAR PER YEAR. THE REST WILL BE STOCK INCENTIVES.
THAT GUARANTEES YOU WILL REAP OBSCENE PROFITS WHEN THE OVERALL STOCK MARKET IMPROVES, NO MATTER WHAT YOU DO.
PRETEND YOU DON'T KNOW THAT.
6-12-09 ©2009 Scott Adams, Inc./Dist. by UFS, Inc.

DOGBERT THE CEO
YOU TWO ARE MY EXECUTIVE COMPENSATION COMMITTEE.
I LIVE TO SERVE YOU, MY LORD AND MASTER!
DIAL IT BACK JUST A LITTLE.
ARE WE ALLOWED TO KNEEL?
6-13-09 ©2009 Scott Adams, Inc./Dist. by UFS, Inc.

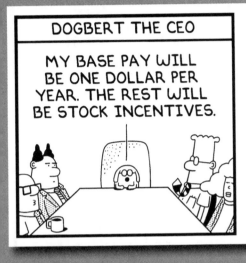

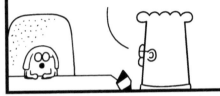

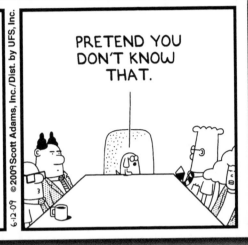

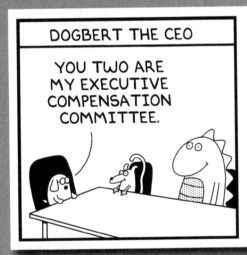

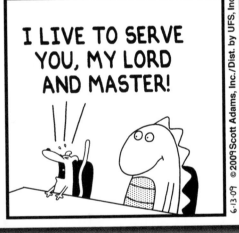

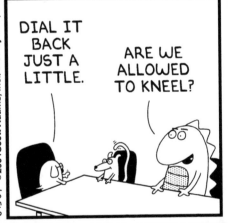

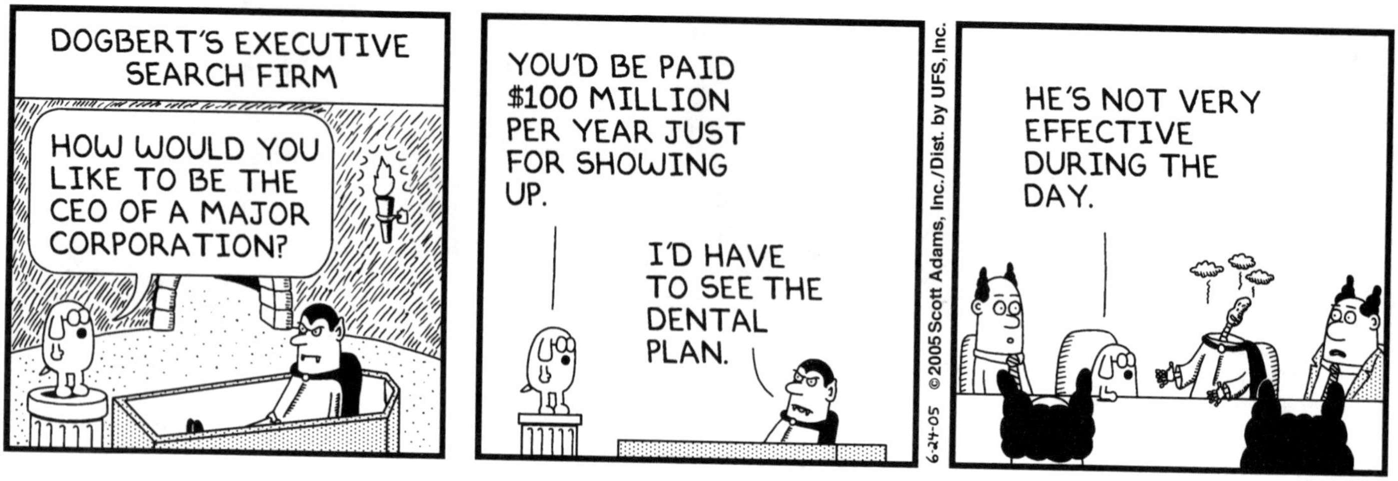
DOGBERT'S EXECUTIVE SEARCH FIRM
HOW WOULD YOU LIKE TO BE THE CEO OF A MAJOR CORPORATION?
YOU'D BE PAID $100 MILLION PER YEAR JUST FOR SHOWING UP.
I'D HAVE TO SEE THE DENTAL PLAN.
6-24-05 © 2005 Scott Adams, Inc./Dist. by UFS, Inc.
HE'S NOT VERY EFFECTIVE DURING THE DAY.

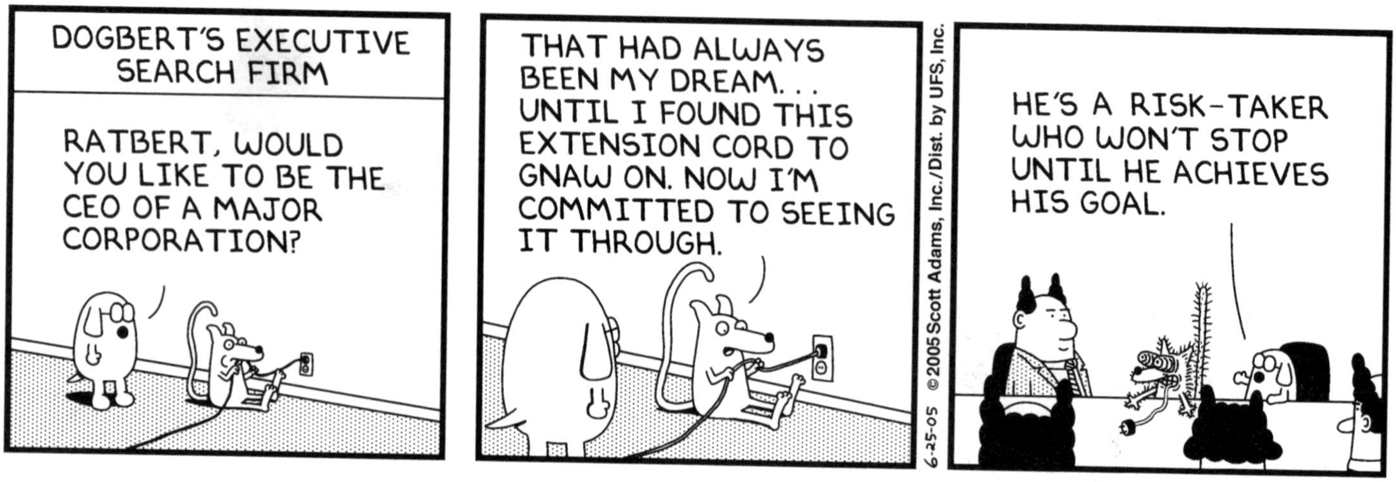
DOGBERT'S EXECUTIVE SEARCH FIRM
RATBERT, WOULD YOU LIKE TO BE THE CEO OF A MAJOR CORPORATION?
THAT HAD ALWAYS BEEN MY DREAM... UNTIL I FOUND THIS EXTENSION CORD TO GNAW ON. NOW I'M COMMITTED TO SEEING IT THROUGH.
6-25-05 © 2005 Scott Adams, Inc./Dist. by UFS, Inc.
HE'S A RISK-TAKER WHO WON'T STOP UNTIL HE ACHIEVES HIS GOAL.

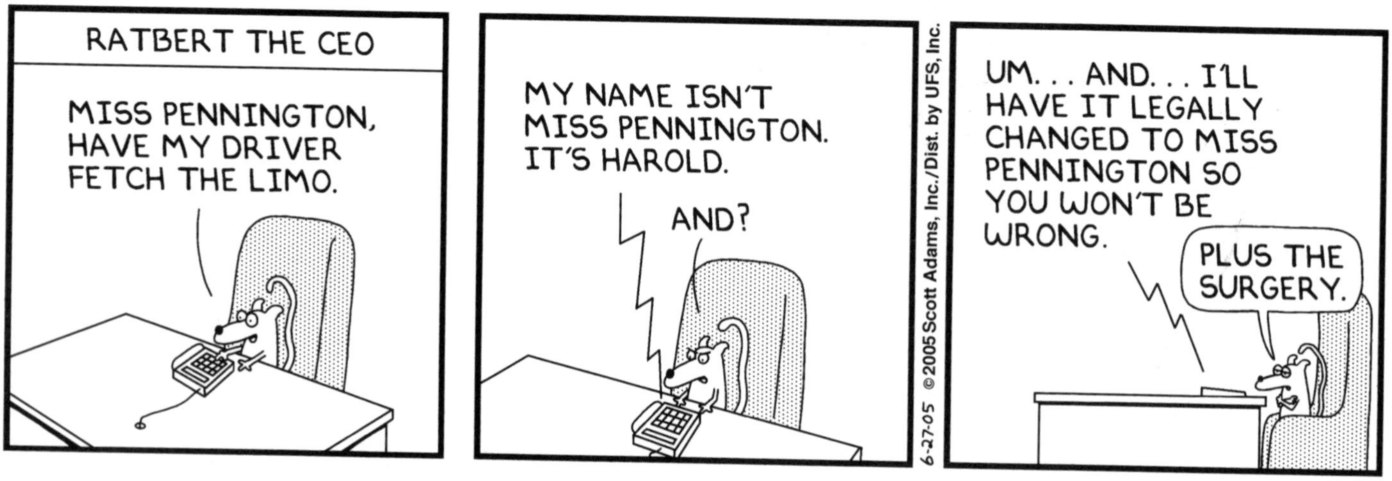
RATBERT THE CEO
MISS PENNINGTON, HAVE MY DRIVER FETCH THE LIMO.
MY NAME ISN'T MISS PENNINGTON. IT'S HAROLD.
AND?
6-27-05 © 2005 Scott Adams, Inc./Dist. by UFS, Inc.
UM... AND... I'LL HAVE IT LEGALLY CHANGED TO MISS PENNINGTON SO YOU WON'T BE WRONG.
PLUS THE SURGERY.

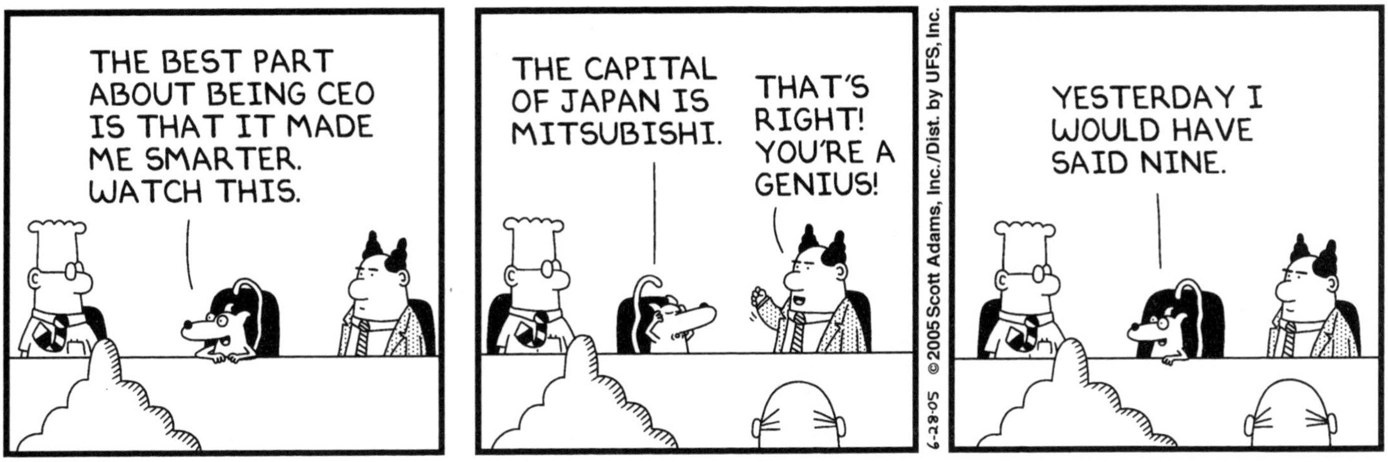
THE BEST PART ABOUT BEING CEO IS THAT IT MADE ME SMARTER. WATCH THIS.
THE CAPITAL OF JAPAN IS MITSUBISHI.
THAT'S RIGHT! YOU'RE A GENIUS!
6-28-05 ©2005 Scott Adams, Inc./Dist. by UFS, Inc.
YESTERDAY I WOULD HAVE SAID NINE.

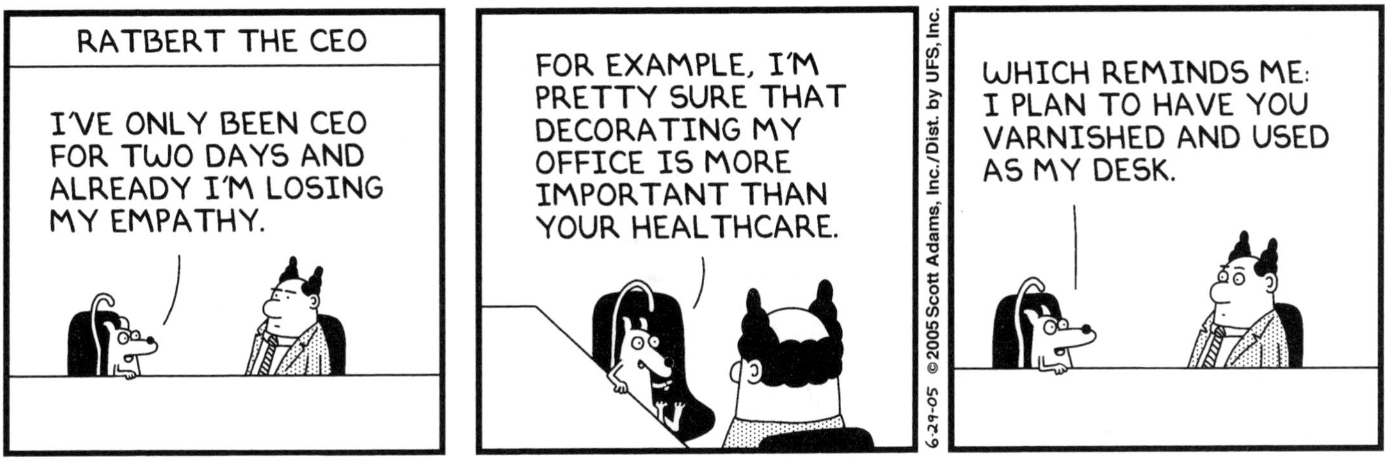
RATBERT THE CEO
I'VE ONLY BEEN CEO FOR TWO DAYS AND ALREADY I'M LOSING MY EMPATHY.
FOR EXAMPLE, I'M PRETTY SURE THAT DECORATING MY OFFICE IS MORE IMPORTANT THAN YOUR HEALTHCARE.
6-29-05 ©2005 Scott Adams, Inc./Dist. by UFS, Inc.
WHICH REMINDS ME: I PLAN TO HAVE YOU VARNISHED AND USED AS MY DESK.

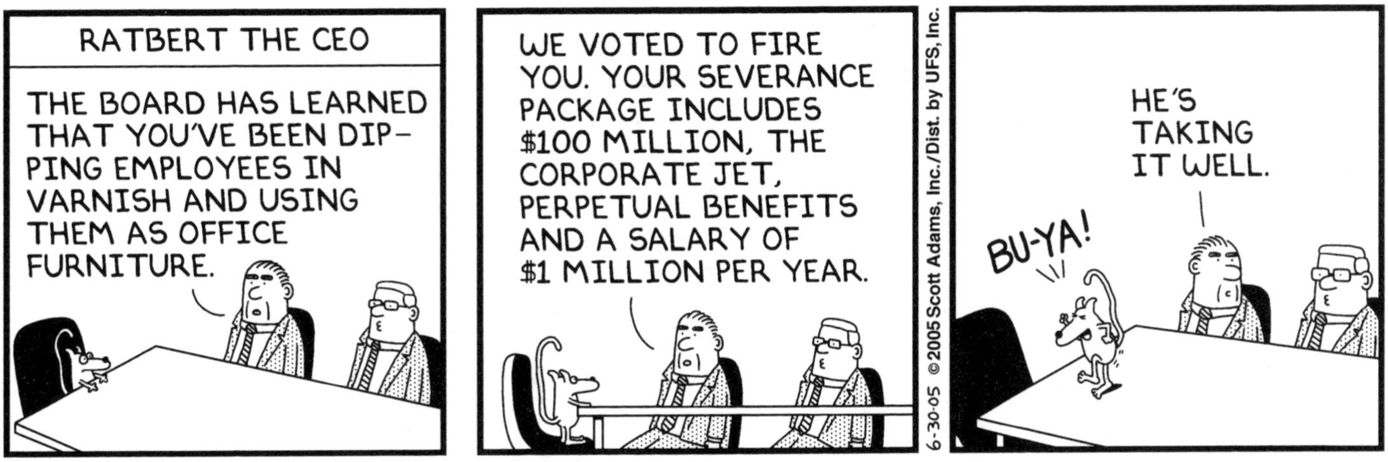
RATBERT THE CEO
THE BOARD HAS LEARNED THAT YOU'VE BEEN DIP-PING EMPLOYEES IN VARNISH AND USING THEM AS OFFICE FURNITURE.
WE VOTED TO FIRE YOU. YOUR SEVERANCE PACKAGE INCLUDES $100 MILLION, THE CORPORATE JET, PERPETUAL BENEFITS AND A SALARY OF $1 MILLION PER YEAR.
6-30-05 ©2005 Scott Adams, Inc./Dist. by UFS, Inc.
BU-YA!
HE'S TAKING IT WELL.

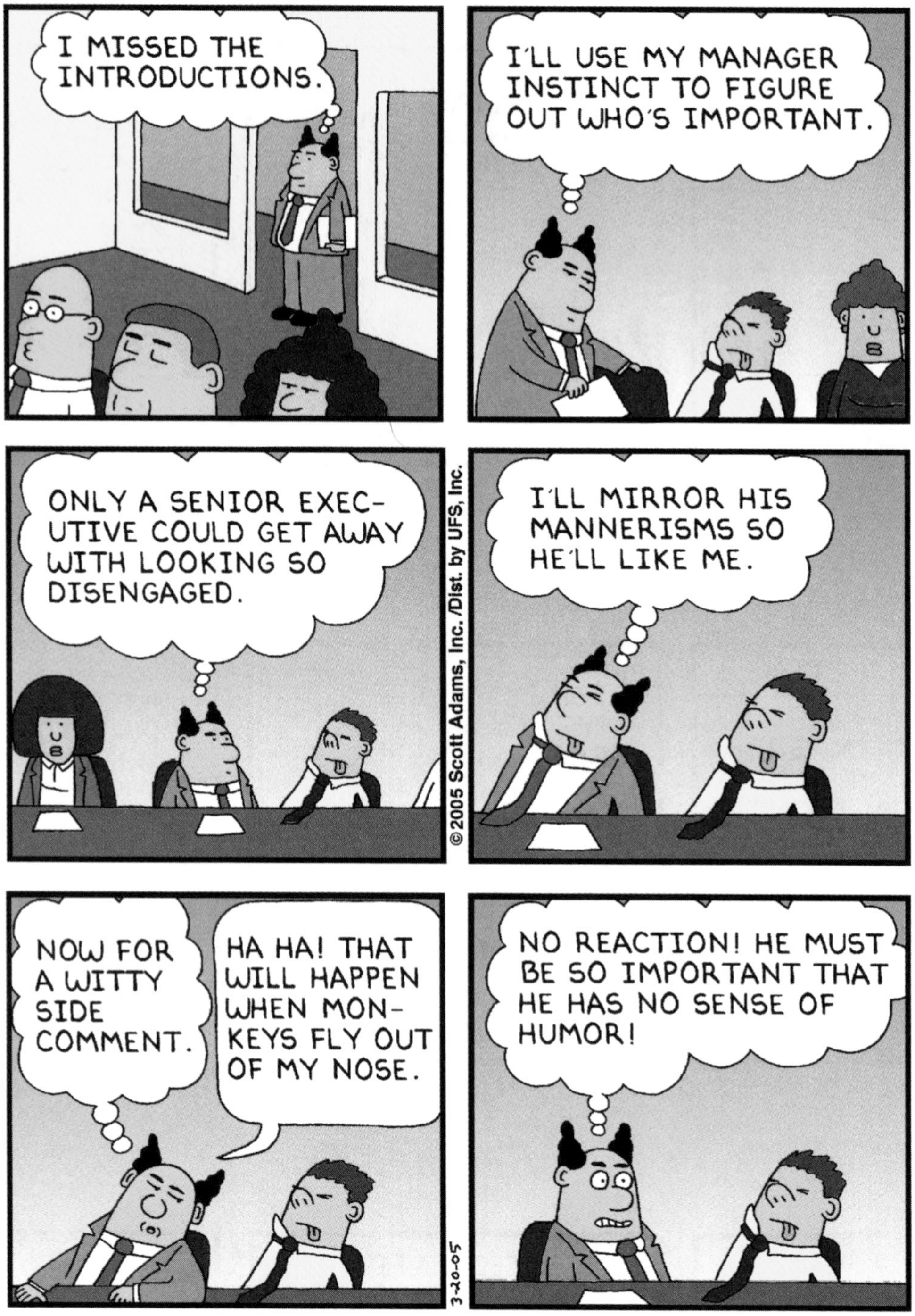
I MISSED THE INTRODUCTIONS.
I'LL USE MY MANAGER INSTINCT TO FIGURE OUT WHO'S IMPORTANT.
ONLY A SENIOR EXECUTIVE COULD GET AWAY WITH LOOKING SO DISENGAGED.
I'LL MIRROR HIS MANNERISMS SO HE'LL LIKE ME.
NOW FOR A WITTY SIDE COMMENT.
HA HA! THAT WILL HAPPEN WHEN MONKEYS FLY OUT OF MY NOSE.
NO REACTION! HE MUST BE SO IMPORTANT THAT HE HAS NO SENSE OF HUMOR!
©2005 Scott Adams, Inc./Dist. by UFS, Inc.
3-20-05

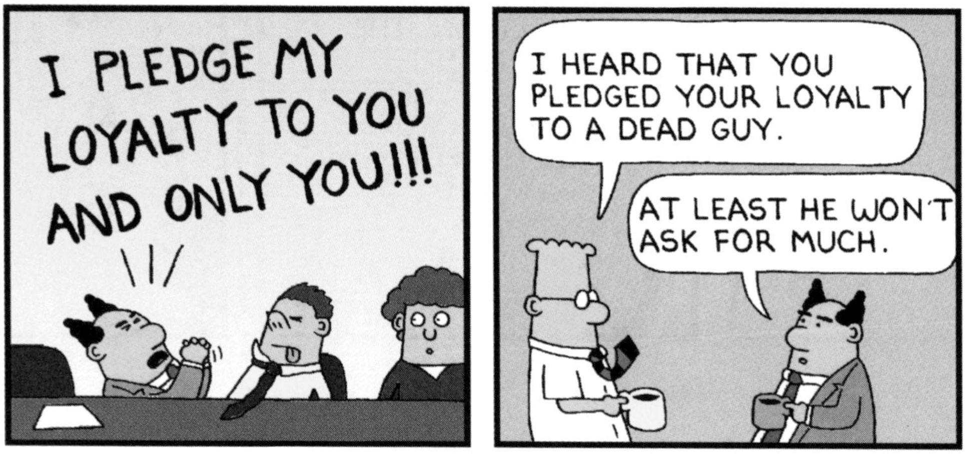
I PLEDGE MY LOYALTY TO YOU AND ONLY YOU!!!
I HEARD THAT YOU PLEDGED YOUR LOYALTY TO A DEAD GUY.
AT LEAST HE WON'T ASK FOR MUCH.

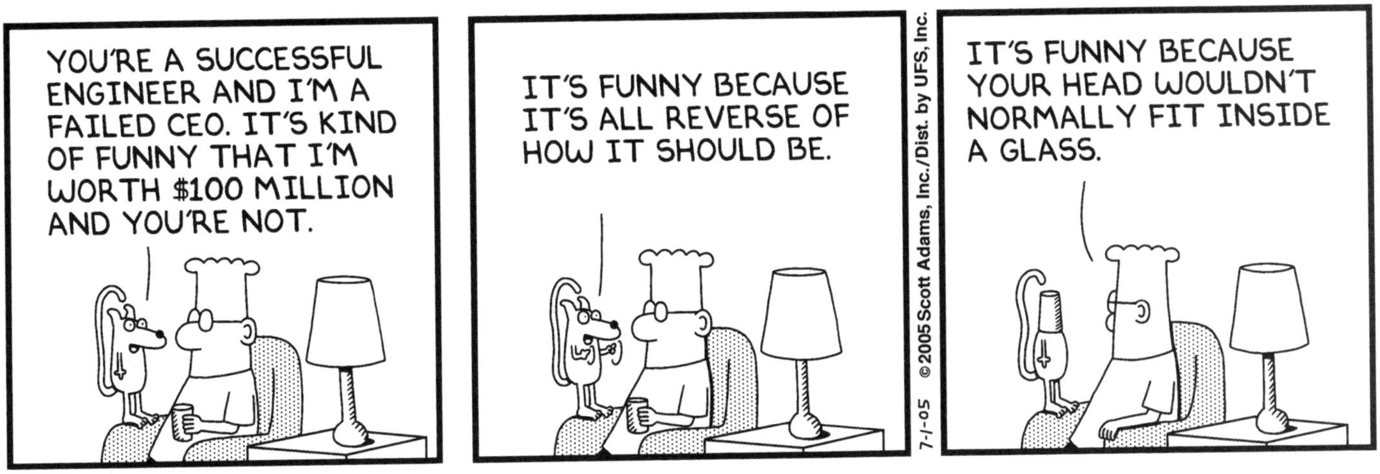
YOU'RE A SUCCESSFUL ENGINEER AND I'M A FAILED CEO. IT'S KIND OF FUNNY THAT I'M WORTH $100 MILLION AND YOU'RE NOT.
IT'S FUNNY BECAUSE IT'S ALL REVERSE OF HOW IT SHOULD BE.
IT'S FUNNY BECAUSE YOUR HEAD WOULDN'T NORMALLY FIT INSIDE A GLASS.
7-1-05 © 2005 Scott Adams, Inc./Dist. by UFS, Inc.

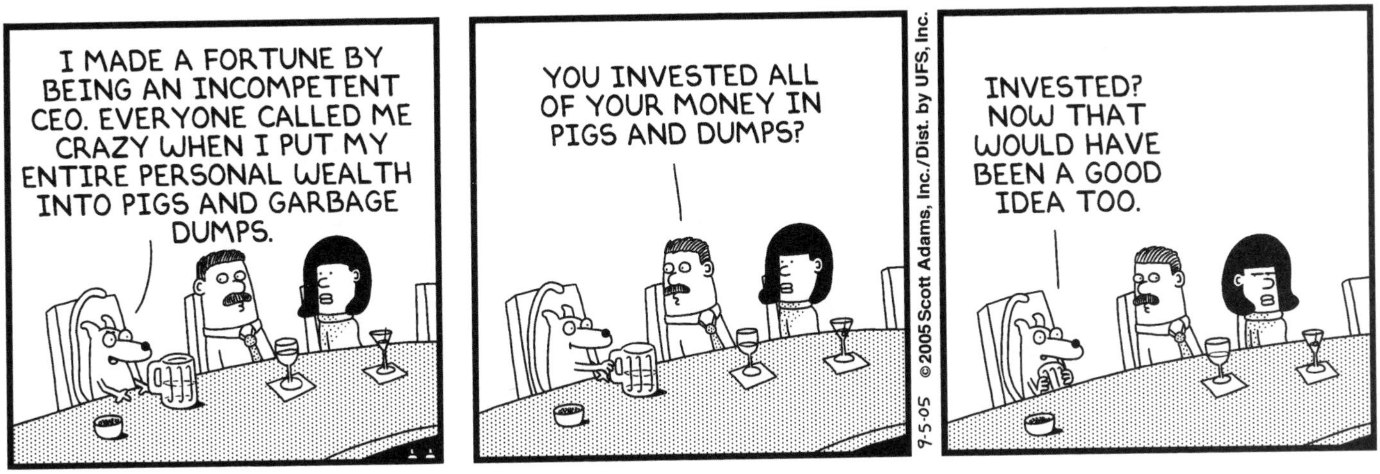
I MADE A FORTUNE BY BEING AN INCOMPETENT CEO. EVERYONE CALLED ME CRAZY WHEN I PUT MY ENTIRE PERSONAL WEALTH INTO PIGS AND GARBAGE DUMPS.
YOU INVESTED ALL OF YOUR MONEY IN PIGS AND DUMPS?
INVESTED? NOW THAT WOULD HAVE BEEN A GOOD IDEA TOO.
9-5-05 © 2005 Scott Adams, Inc./Dist. by UFS, Inc.

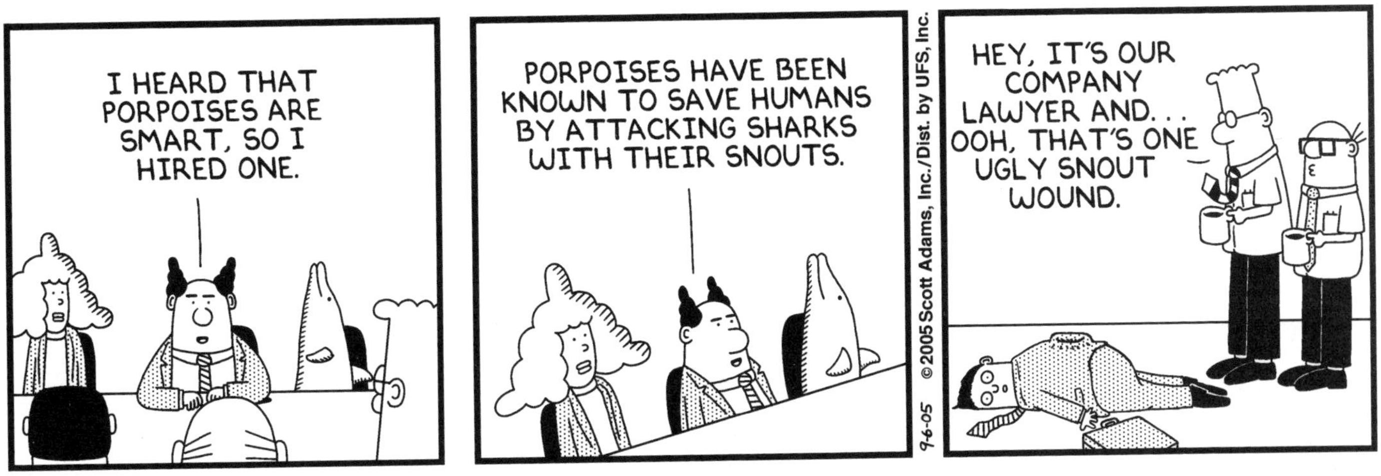
I HEARD THAT PORPOISES ARE SMART, SO I HIRED ONE.
PORPOISES HAVE BEEN KNOWN TO SAVE HUMANS BY ATTACKING SHARKS WITH THEIR SNOUTS.
HEY, IT'S OUR COMPANY LAWYER AND... OOH, THAT'S ONE UGLY SNOUT WOUND.
9-6-05 © 2005 Scott Adams, Inc./Dist. by UFS, Inc.

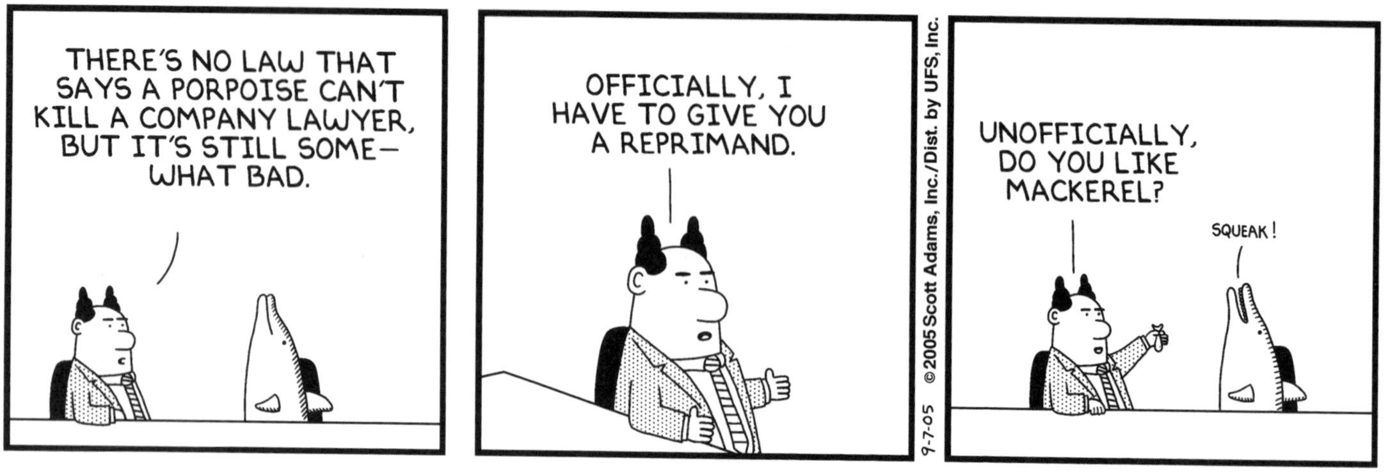
THERE'S NO LAW THAT SAYS A PORPOISE CAN'T KILL A COMPANY LAWYER, BUT IT'S STILL SOME-WHAT BAD.
OFFICIALLY, I HAVE TO GIVE YOU A REPRIMAND.
9-7-05 ©2005 Scott Adams, Inc./Dist. by UFS, Inc.
UNOFFICIALLY, DO YOU LIKE MACKEREL?
SQUEAK!

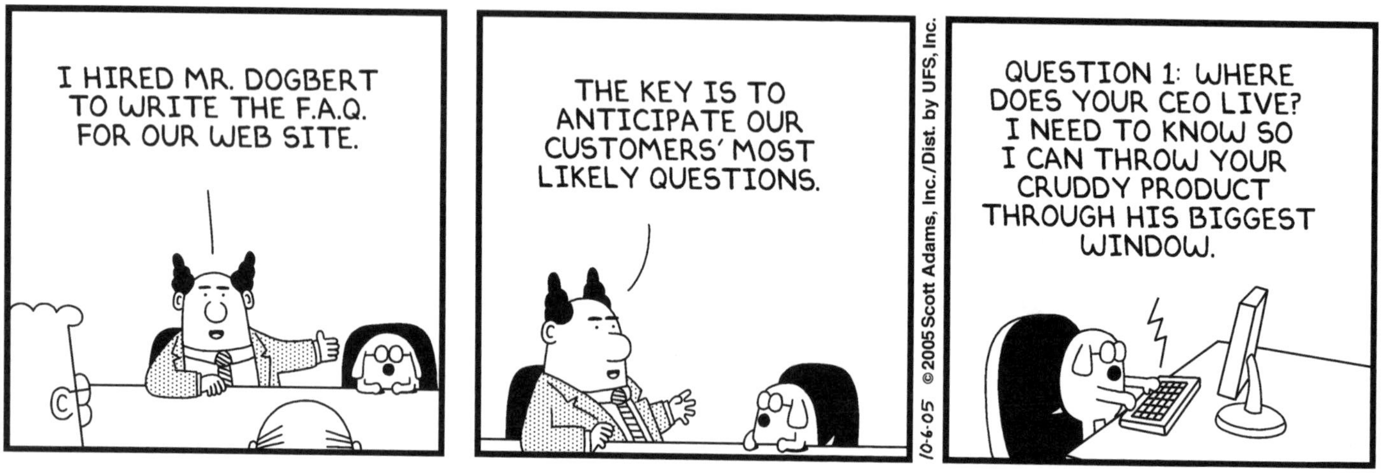
I HIRED MR. DOGBERT TO WRITE THE F.A.Q. FOR OUR WEB SITE.
THE KEY IS TO ANTICIPATE OUR CUSTOMERS' MOST LIKELY QUESTIONS.
10-6-05 ©2005 Scott Adams, Inc./Dist. by UFS, Inc.
QUESTION 1: WHERE DOES YOUR CEO LIVE? I NEED TO KNOW SO I CAN THROW YOUR CRUDDY PRODUCT THROUGH HIS BIGGEST WINDOW.

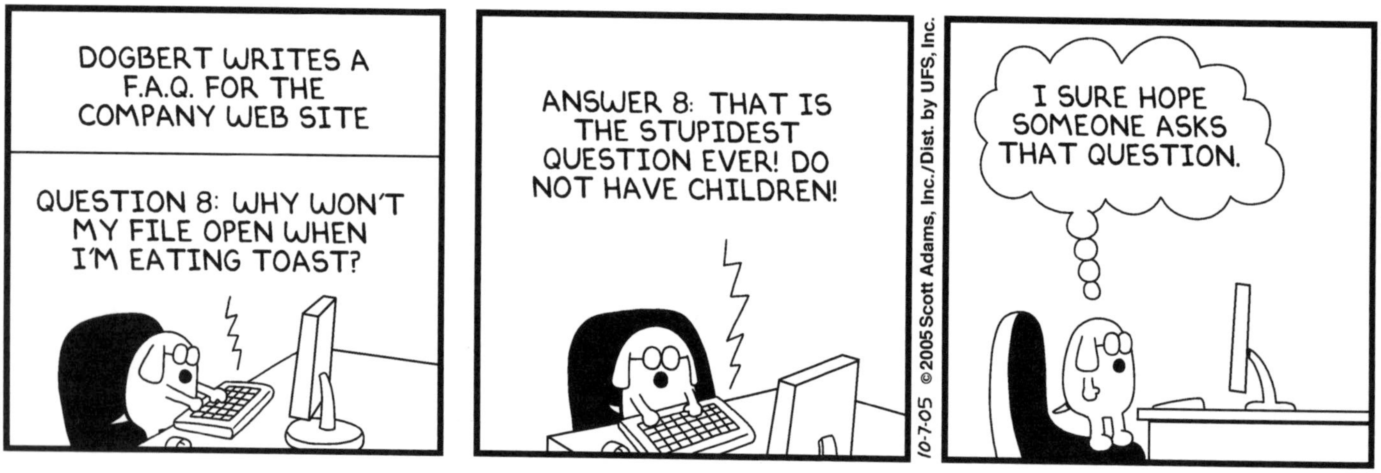
DOGBERT WRITES A F.A.Q. FOR THE COMPANY WEB SITE
QUESTION 8: WHY WON'T MY FILE OPEN WHEN I'M EATING TOAST?
ANSWER 8: THAT IS THE STUPIDEST QUESTION EVER! DO NOT HAVE CHILDREN!
10-7-05 ©2005 Scott Adams, Inc./Dist. by UFS, Inc.
I SURE HOPE SOMEONE ASKS THAT QUESTION.

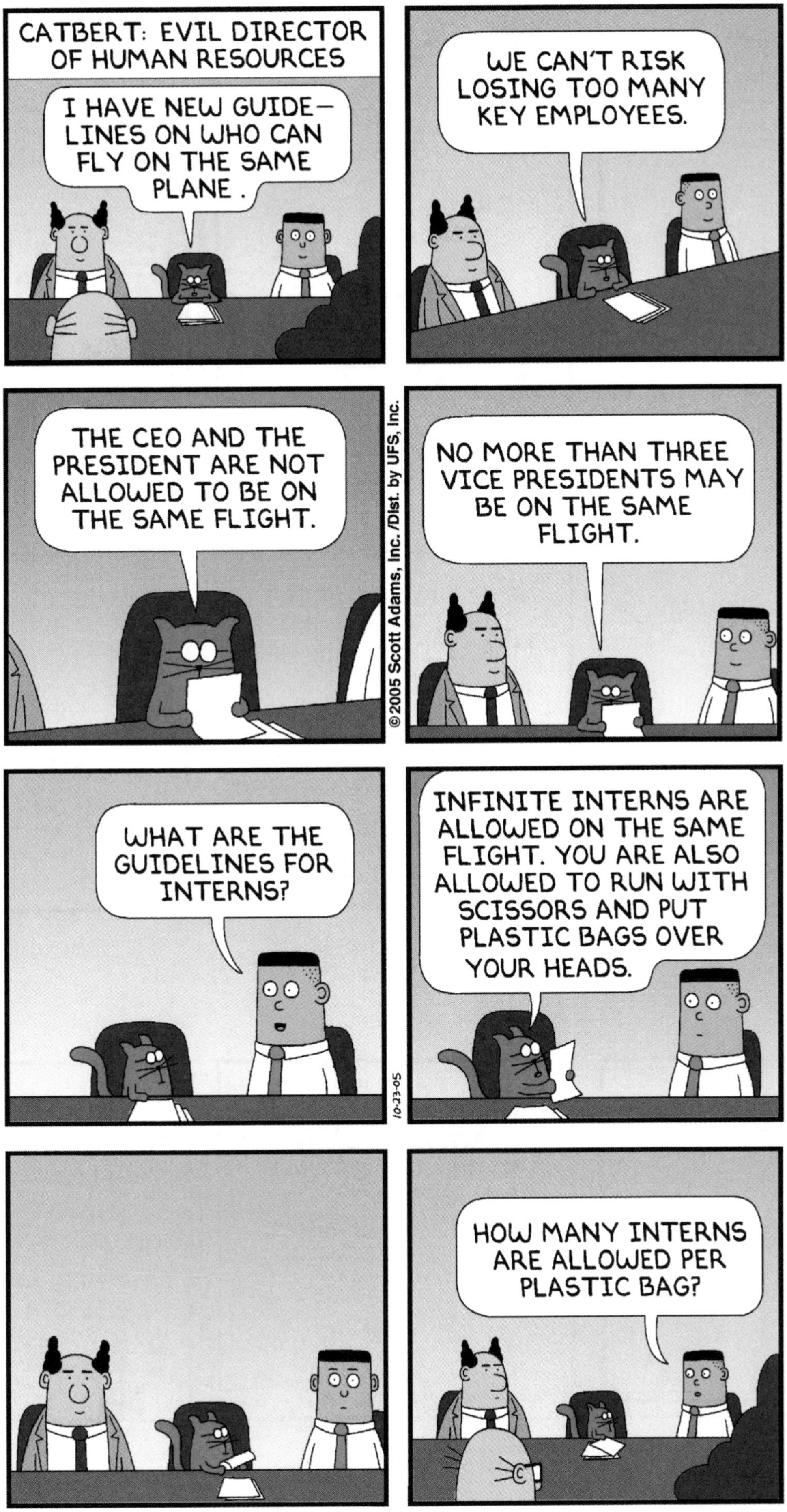
CATBERT: EVIL DIRECTOR OF HUMAN RESOURCES
I HAVE NEW GUIDE-LINES ON WHO CAN FLY ON THE SAME PLANE.
WE CAN'T RISK LOSING TOO MANY KEY EMPLOYEES.
THE CEO AND THE PRESIDENT ARE NOT ALLOWED TO BE ON THE SAME FLIGHT.
NO MORE THAN THREE VICE PRESIDENTS MAY BE ON THE SAME FLIGHT.
©2005 Scott Adams, Inc./Dist. by UFS, Inc.
WHAT ARE THE GUIDELINES FOR INTERNS?
INFINITE INTERNS ARE ALLOWED ON THE SAME FLIGHT. YOU ARE ALSO ALLOWED TO RUN WITH SCISSORS AND PUT PLASTIC BAGS OVER YOUR HEADS.
10-23-05
HOW MANY INTERNS ARE ALLOWED PER PLASTIC BAG?

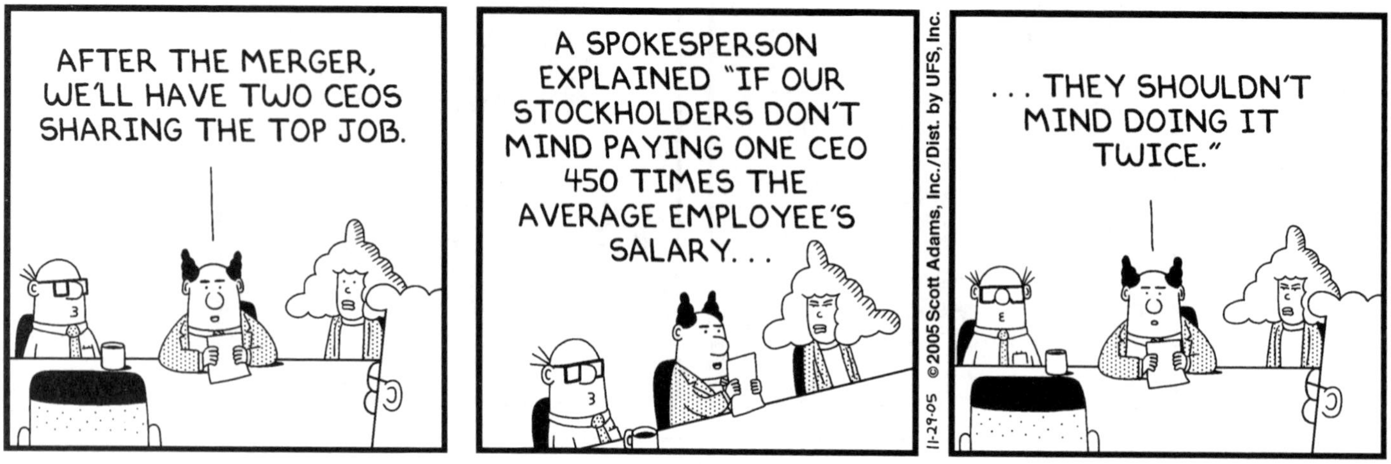
AFTER THE MERGER, WE'LL HAVE TWO CEOS SHARING THE TOP JOB.
A SPOKESPERSON EXPLAINED "IF OUR STOCKHOLDERS DON'T MIND PAYING ONE CEO 450 TIMES THE AVERAGE EMPLOYEE'S SALARY...
... THEY SHOULDN'T MIND DOING IT TWICE."
11-29-05 ©2005 Scott Adams, Inc./Dist. by UFS, Inc.

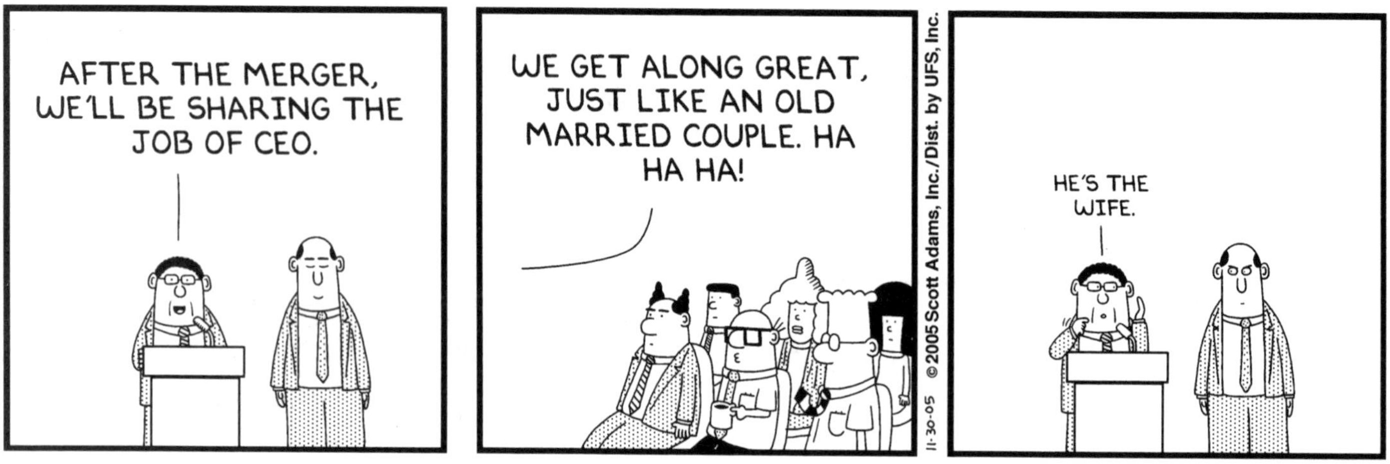
AFTER THE MERGER, WE'LL BE SHARING THE JOB OF CEO.
WE GET ALONG GREAT, JUST LIKE AN OLD MARRIED COUPLE. HA HA HA!
HE'S THE WIFE.
11-30-05 ©2005 Scott Adams, Inc./Dist. by UFS, Inc.

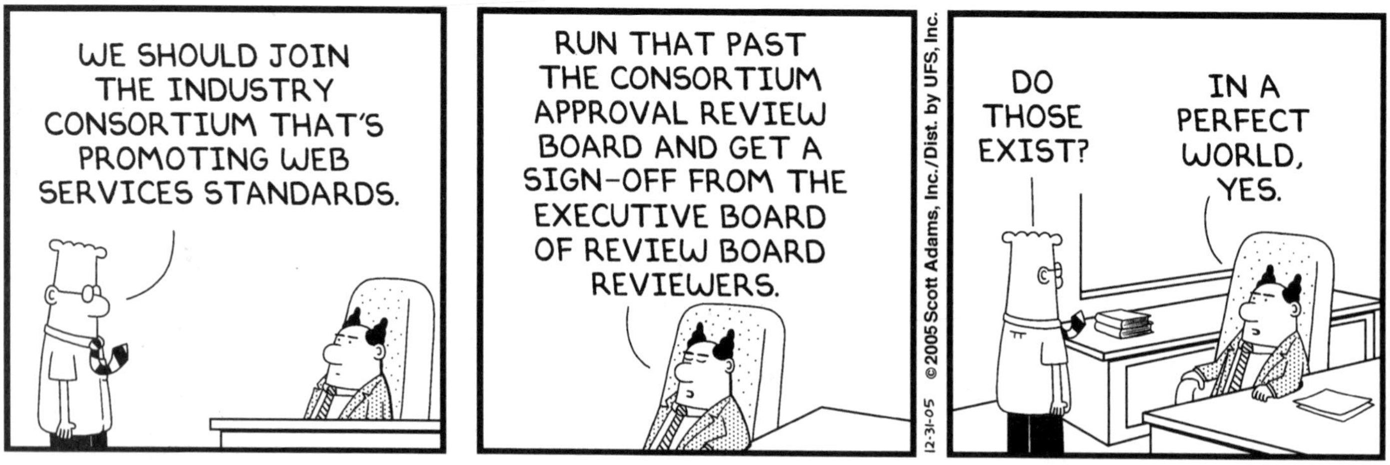
WE SHOULD JOIN THE INDUSTRY CONSORTIUM THAT'S PROMOTING WEB SERVICES STANDARDS.
RUN THAT PAST THE CONSORTIUM APPROVAL REVIEW BOARD AND GET A SIGN-OFF FROM THE EXECUTIVE BOARD OF REVIEW BOARD REVIEWERS.
DO THOSE EXIST?
IN A PERFECT WORLD, YES.
12-31-05 ©2005 Scott Adams, Inc./Dist. by UFS, Inc.

DOGBERT THE CEO
I'M THINKING OF BECOMING A SOMALIAN PIRATE.
I'D STILL GET TO STEAL FROM STOCK-HOLDERS, BUT MY BOOTY WOULDN'T BE TAXED.
AND WHO DOESN'T LIKE GRENADE LAUNCHERS?
KA-POW!
MOM? CANCEL YOUR CRUISE.
6-15-09
© 2009 Scott Adams, Inc./Dist. by UFS, Inc.

DOGBERT THE CEO
I'M TAKING A SIDE JOB AS A PIRATE.
I'LL KIDNAP EMPLOYEES AND AUTHORIZE HUGE RANSOM PAYMENTS TO MYSELF FOR THEIR RETURN.
THEN YOU'LL RETURN THEM SAFELY?
THAT'S A DIFFERENT BUSINESS MODEL.
6-16-09
© 2009 Scott Adams, Inc./Dist. by UFS, Inc.

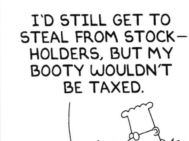

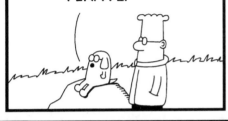

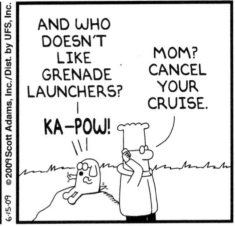

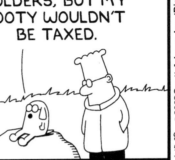

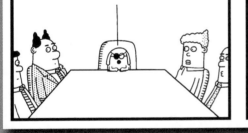

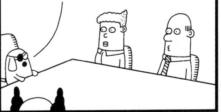

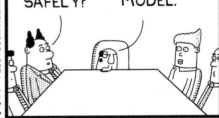

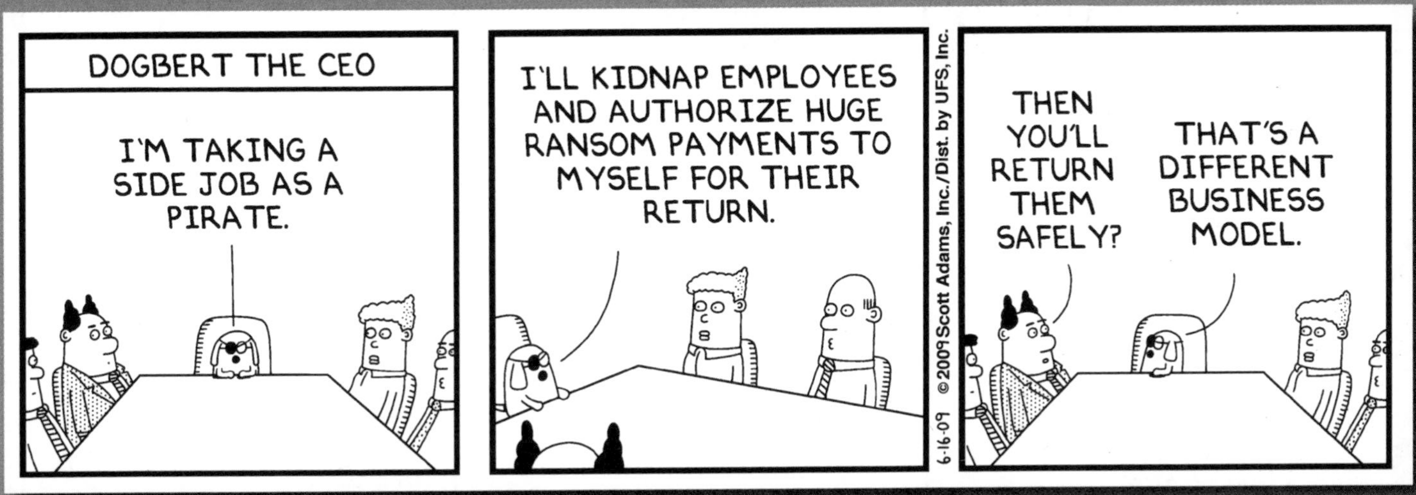

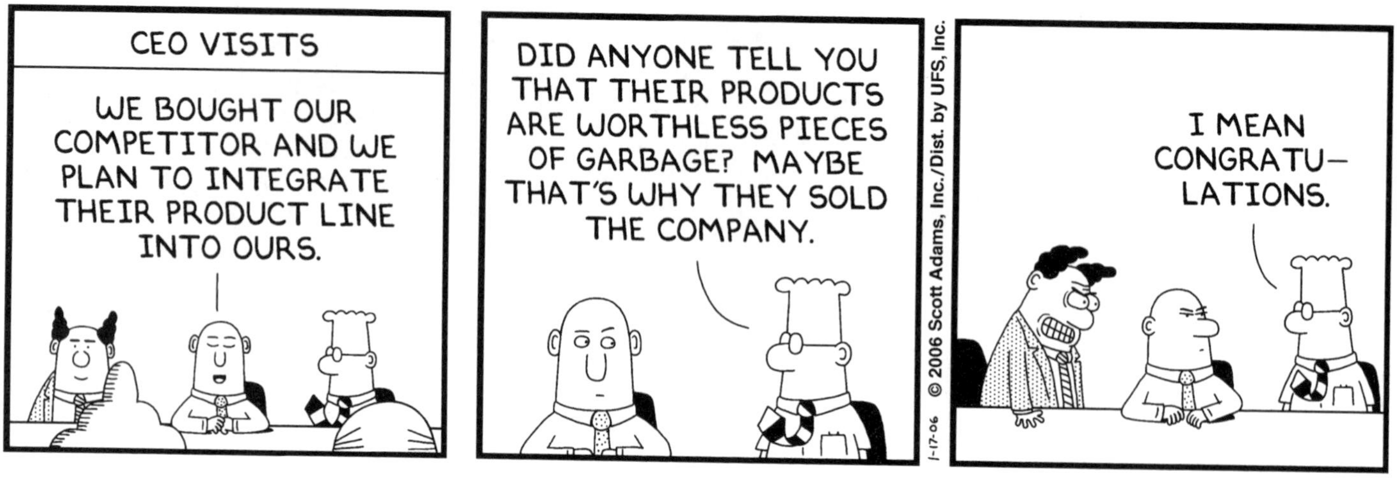
CEO VISITS
WE BOUGHT OUR COMPETITOR AND WE PLAN TO INTEGRATE THEIR PRODUCT LINE INTO OURS.
DID ANYONE TELL YOU THAT THEIR PRODUCTS ARE WORTHLESS PIECES OF GARBAGE? MAYBE THAT'S WHY THEY SOLD THE COMPANY.
© 2006 Scott Adams, Inc./Dist. by UFS, Inc.
1-17-06
I MEAN CONGRATU-LATIONS.

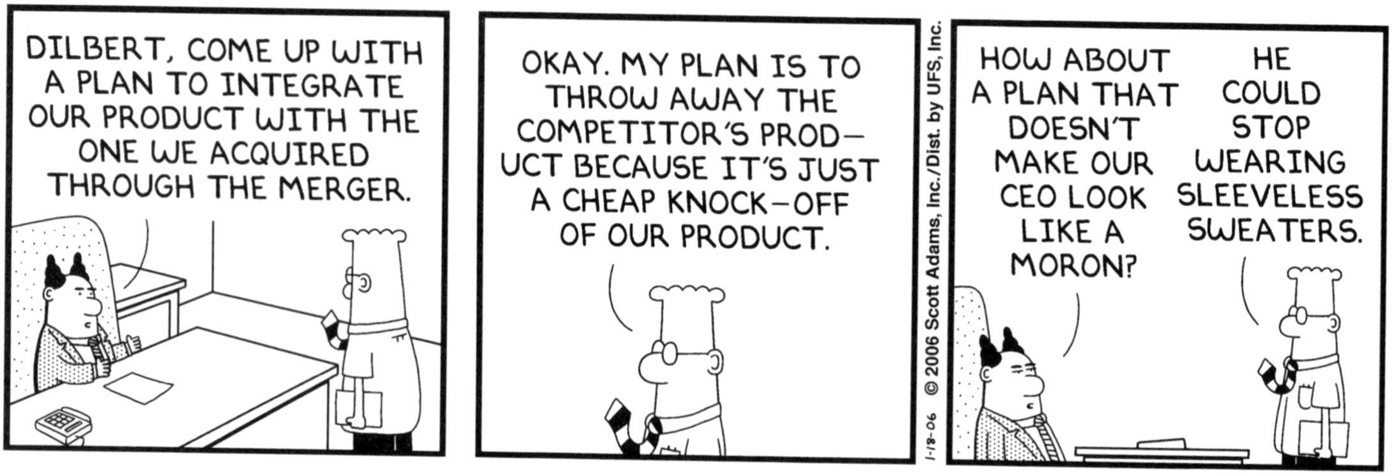
DILBERT, COME UP WITH A PLAN TO INTEGRATE OUR PRODUCT WITH THE ONE WE ACQUIRED THROUGH THE MERGER.
OKAY. MY PLAN IS TO THROW AWAY THE COMPETITOR'S PROD-UCT BECAUSE IT'S JUST A CHEAP KNOCK-OFF OF OUR PRODUCT.
© 2006 Scott Adams, Inc./Dist. by UFS, Inc.
1-18-06
HOW ABOUT A PLAN THAT DOESN'T MAKE OUR CEO LOOK LIKE A MORON?
HE COULD STOP WEARING SLEEVELESS SWEATERS.

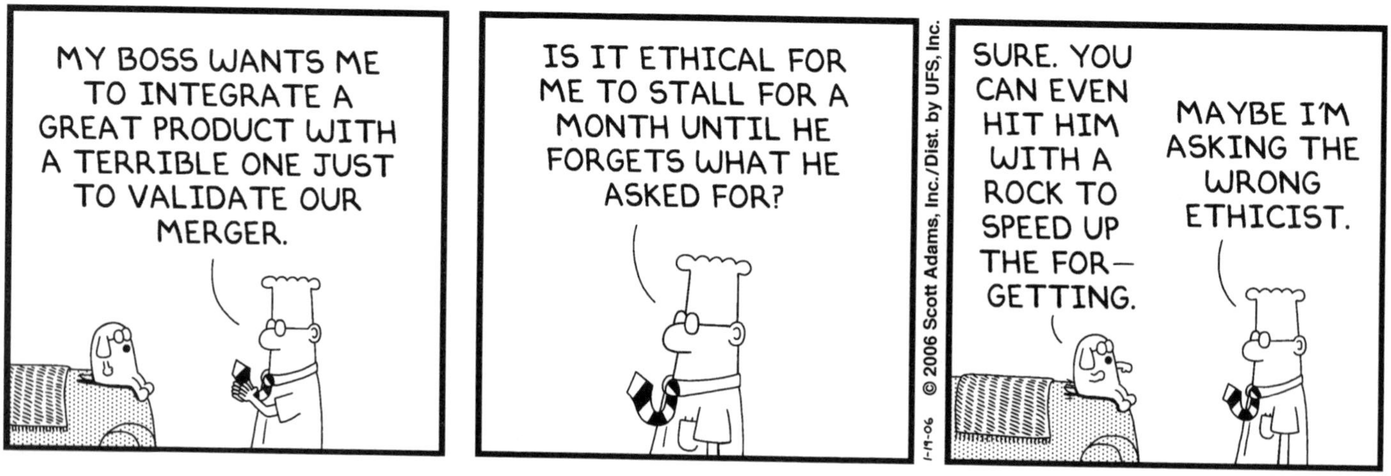
MY BOSS WANTS ME TO INTEGRATE A GREAT PRODUCT WITH A TERRIBLE ONE JUST TO VALIDATE OUR MERGER.
IS IT ETHICAL FOR ME TO STALL FOR A MONTH UNTIL HE FORGETS WHAT HE ASKED FOR?
© 2006 Scott Adams, Inc./Dist. by UFS, Inc.
1-19-06
SURE. YOU CAN EVEN HIT HIM WITH A ROCK TO SPEED UP THE FOR-GETTING.
MAYBE I'M ASKING THE WRONG ETHICIST.

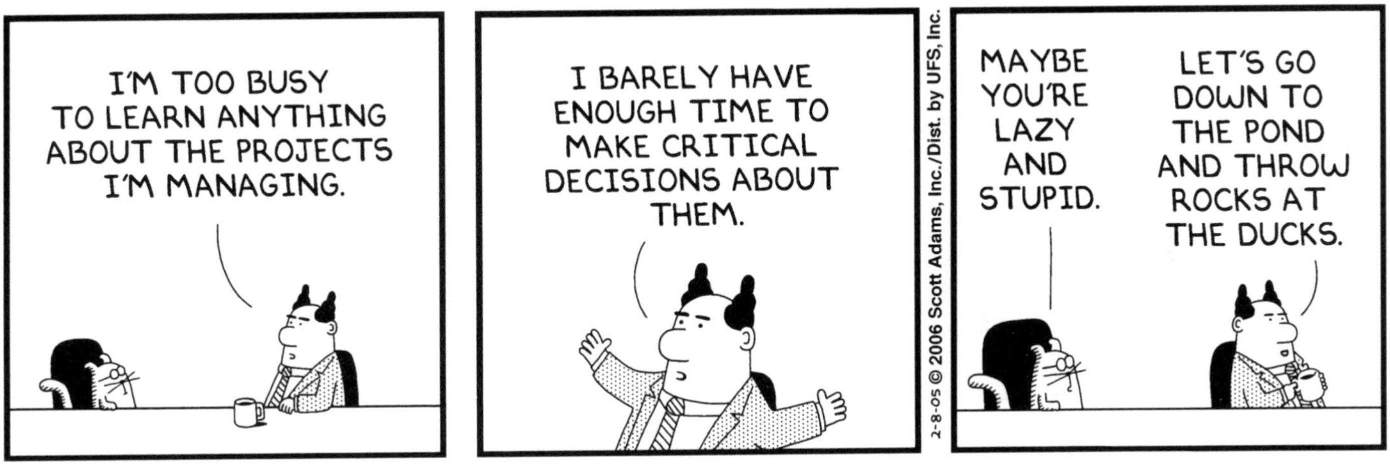
I'M TOO BUSY TO LEARN ANYTHING ABOUT THE PROJECTS I'M MANAGING.
I BARELY HAVE ENOUGH TIME TO MAKE CRITICAL DECISIONS ABOUT THEM.
2-8-05 © 2006 Scott Adams, Inc./Dist. by UFS, Inc.
MAYBE YOU'RE LAZY AND STUPID.
LET'S GO DOWN TO THE POND AND THROW ROCKS AT THE DUCKS.

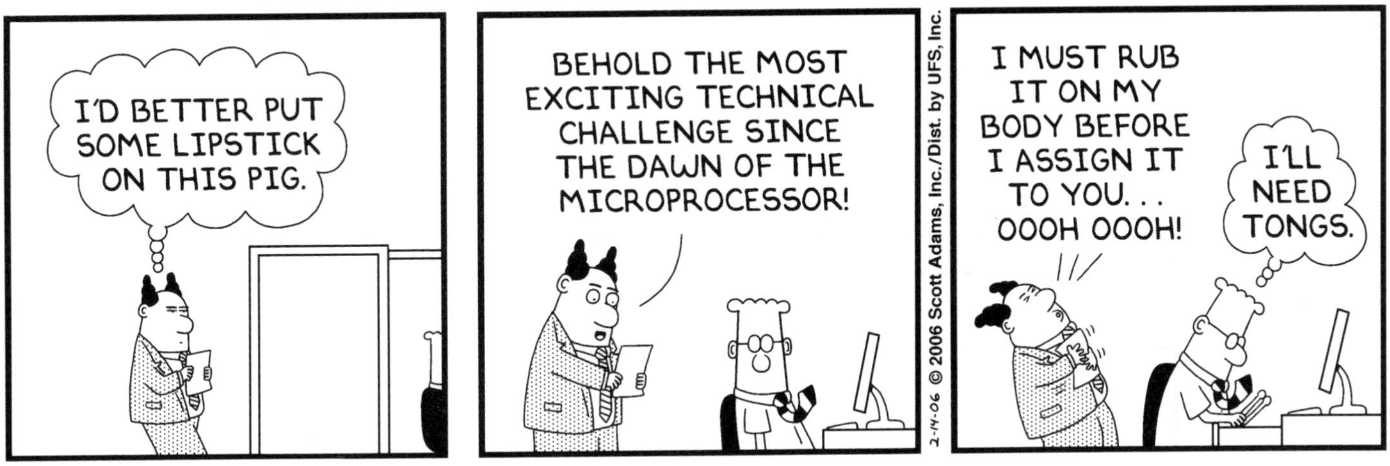
I'D BETTER PUT SOME LIPSTICK ON THIS PIG.
BEHOLD THE MOST EXCITING TECHNICAL CHALLENGE SINCE THE DAWN OF THE MICROPROCESSOR!
2-14-06 © 2006 Scott Adams, Inc./Dist. by UFS, Inc.
I MUST RUB IT ON MY BODY BEFORE I ASSIGN IT TO YOU. . . OOOH OOOH!
I'LL NEED TONGS.

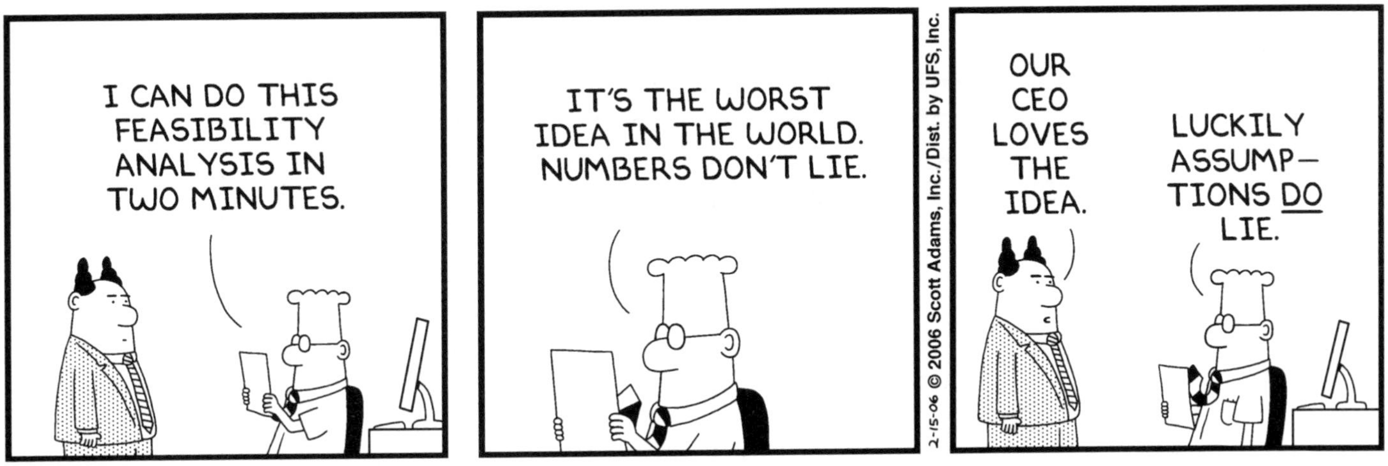
I CAN DO THIS FEASIBILITY ANALYSIS IN TWO MINUTES.
IT'S THE WORST IDEA IN THE WORLD. NUMBERS DON'T LIE.
2-15-06 © 2006 Scott Adams, Inc./Dist. by UFS, Inc.
OUR CEO LOVES THE IDEA.
LUCKILY ASSUMP-TIONS DO LIE.

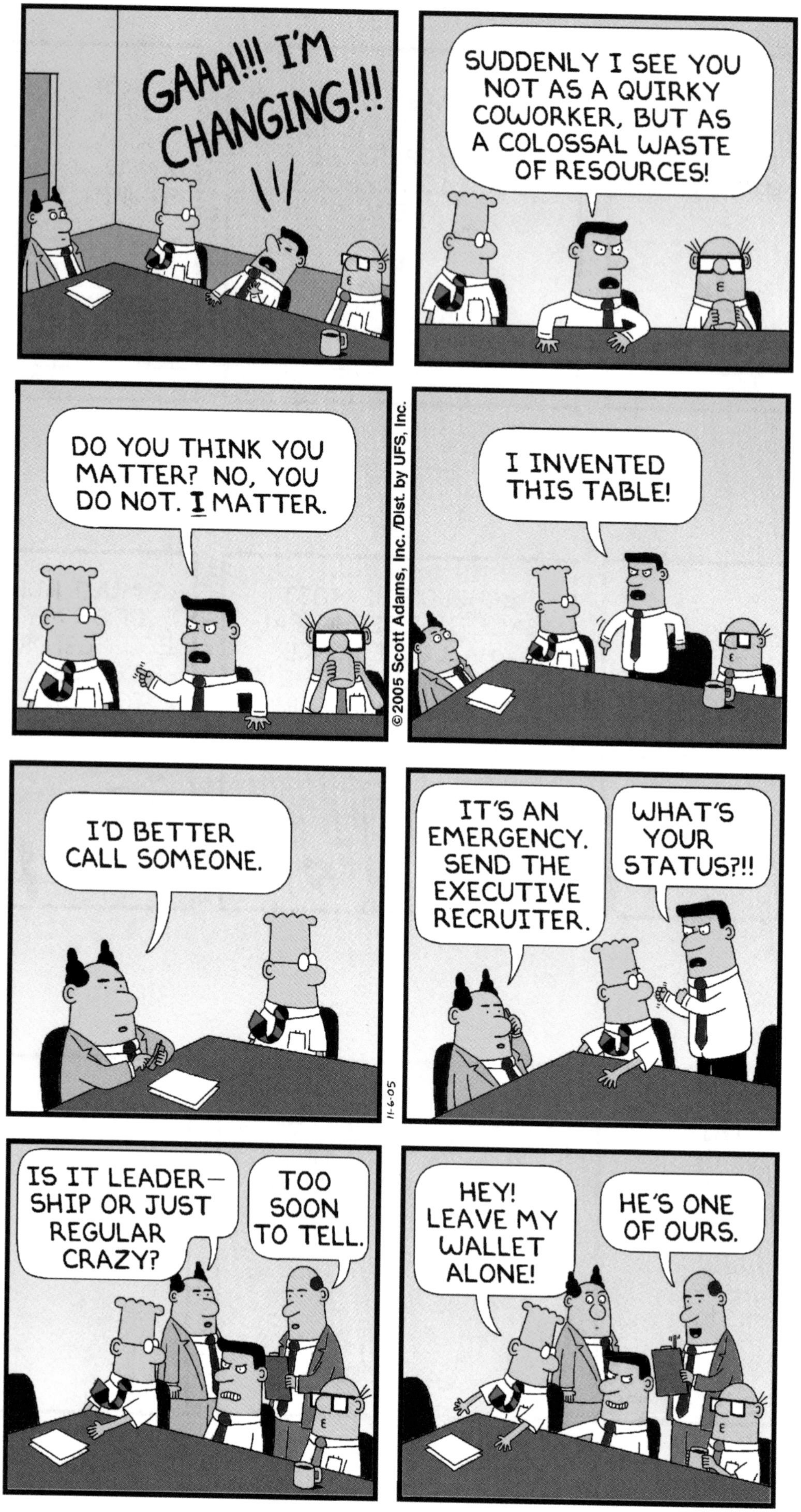
GAAA!!! I'M CHANGING!!!
SUDDENLY I SEE YOU NOT AS A QUIRKY COWORKER, BUT AS A COLOSSAL WASTE OF RESOURCES!
DO YOU THINK YOU MATTER? NO, YOU DO NOT. I MATTER.
©2005 Scott Adams, Inc. /Dist. by UFS, Inc.
I INVENTED THIS TABLE!
I'D BETTER CALL SOMEONE.
11-6-05
IT'S AN EMERGENCY. SEND THE EXECUTIVE RECRUITER.
WHAT'S YOUR STATUS?!!
IS IT LEADER-SHIP OR JUST REGULAR CRAZY?
TOO SOON TO TELL.
HEY! LEAVE MY WALLET ALONE!
HE'S ONE OF OURS.

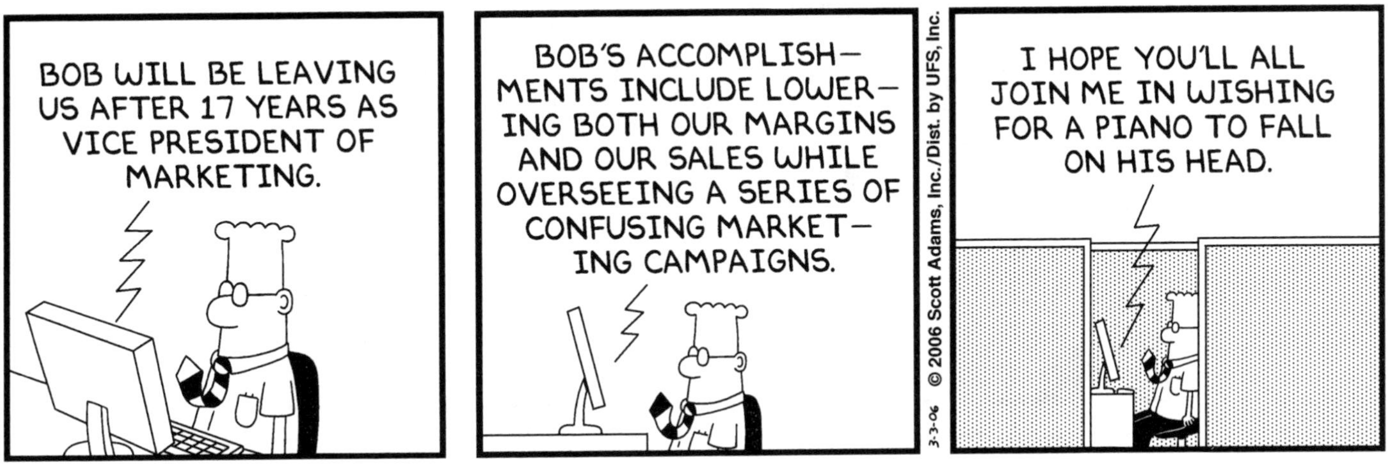
BOB WILL BE LEAVING US AFTER 17 YEARS AS VICE PRESIDENT OF MARKETING.
BOB'S ACCOMPLISH-MENTS INCLUDE LOWER-ING BOTH OUR MARGINS AND OUR SALES WHILE OVERSEEING A SERIES OF CONFUSING MARKET-ING CAMPAIGNS.
3-3-06 © 2006 Scott Adams, Inc./Dist. by UFS, Inc.
I HOPE YOU'LL ALL JOIN ME IN WISHING FOR A PIANO TO FALL ON HIS HEAD.

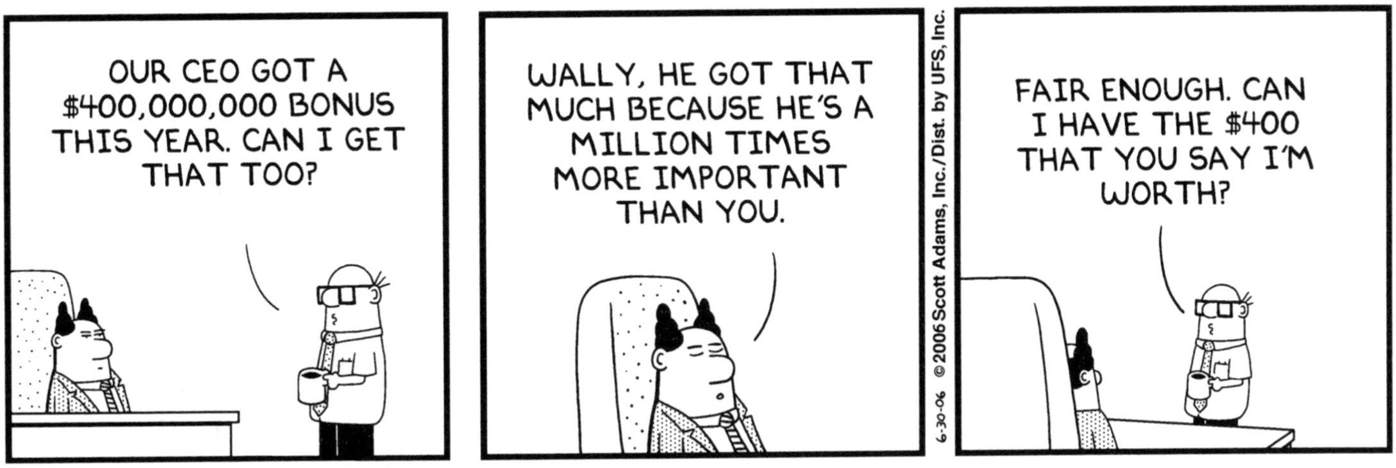
OUR CEO GOT A $400,000,000 BONUS THIS YEAR. CAN I GET THAT TOO?
WALLY, HE GOT THAT MUCH BECAUSE HE'S A MILLION TIMES MORE IMPORTANT THAN YOU.
6-30-06 © 2006 Scott Adams, Inc./Dist. by UFS, Inc.
FAIR ENOUGH. CAN I HAVE THE $400 THAT YOU SAY I'M WORTH?

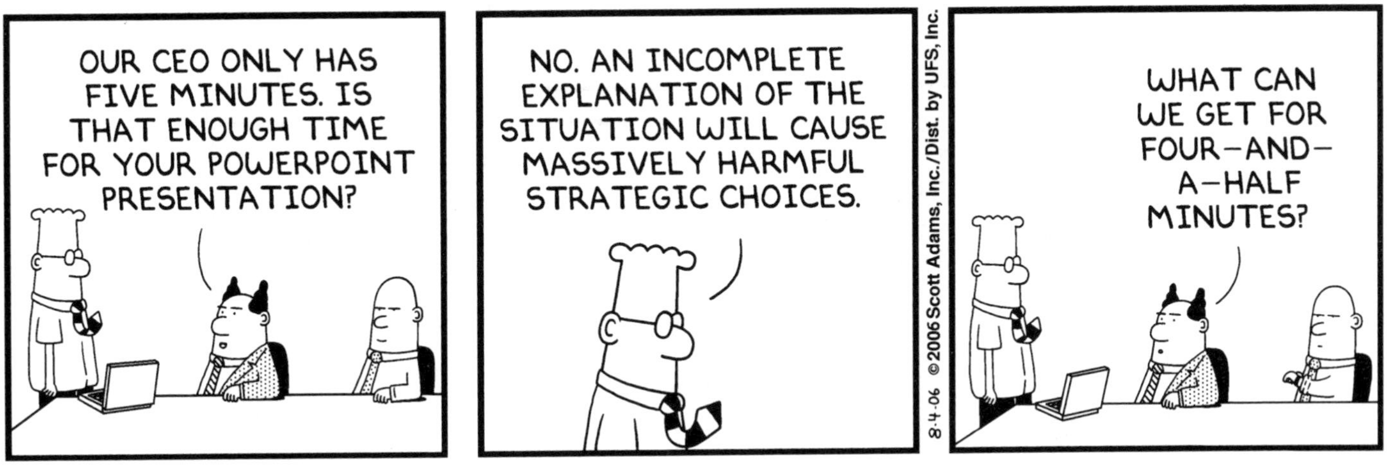
OUR CEO ONLY HAS FIVE MINUTES. IS THAT ENOUGH TIME FOR YOUR POWERPOINT PRESENTATION?
NO. AN INCOMPLETE EXPLANATION OF THE SITUATION WILL CAUSE MASSIVELY HARMFUL STRATEGIC CHOICES.
8-4-06 © 2006 Scott Adams, Inc./Dist. by UFS, Inc.
WHAT CAN WE GET FOR FOUR-AND-A-HALF MINUTES?

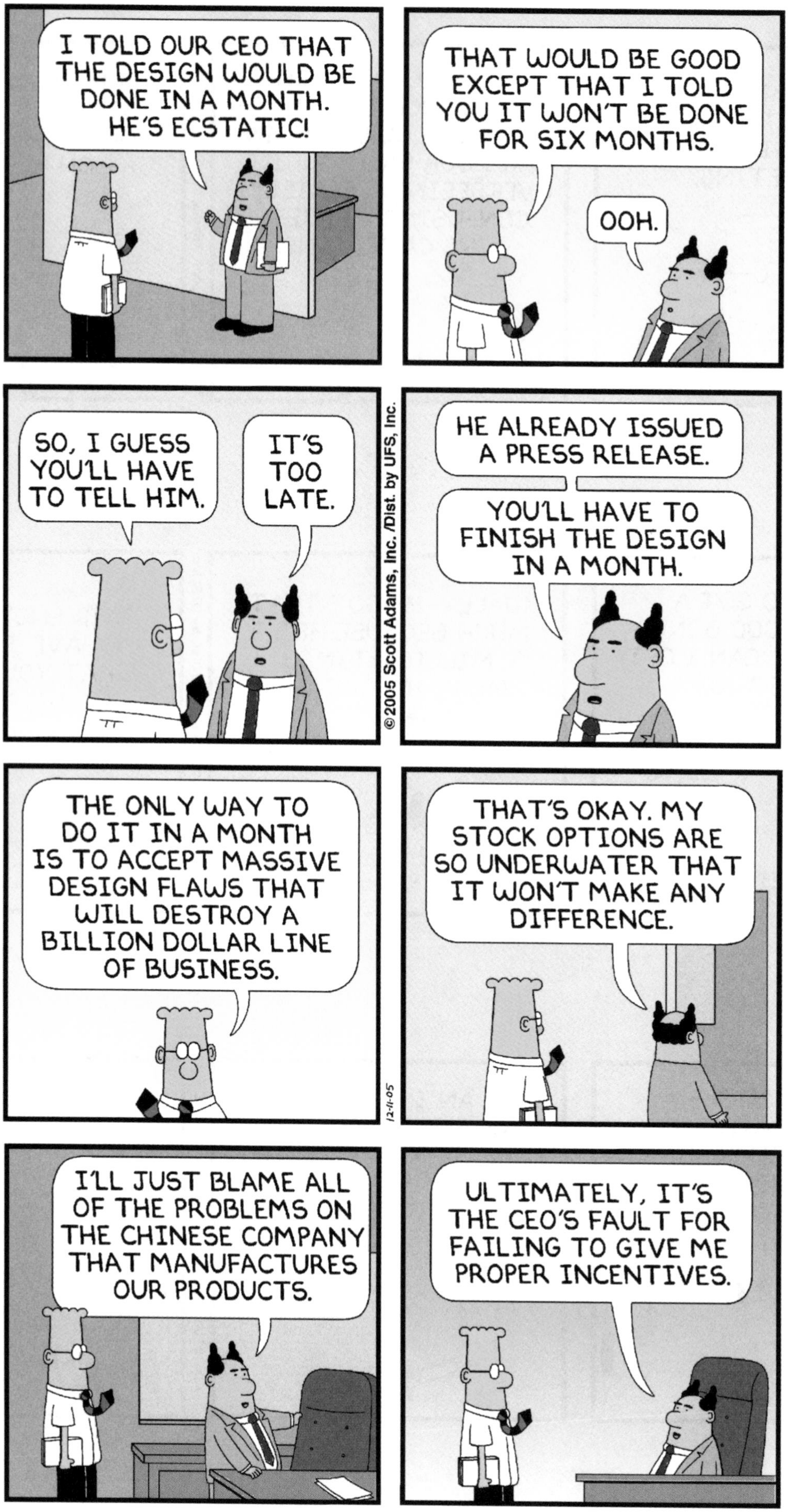
I TOLD OUR CEO THAT THE DESIGN WOULD BE DONE IN A MONTH. HE'S ECSTATIC!
THAT WOULD BE GOOD EXCEPT THAT I TOLD YOU IT WON'T BE DONE FOR SIX MONTHS.
OOH.
SO, I GUESS YOU'LL HAVE TO TELL HIM.
IT'S TOO LATE.
HE ALREADY ISSUED A PRESS RELEASE.
YOU'LL HAVE TO FINISH THE DESIGN IN A MONTH.
THE ONLY WAY TO DO IT IN A MONTH IS TO ACCEPT MASSIVE DESIGN FLAWS THAT WILL DESTROY A BILLION DOLLAR LINE OF BUSINESS.
THAT'S OKAY. MY STOCK OPTIONS ARE SO UNDERWATER THAT IT WON'T MAKE ANY DIFFERENCE.
I'LL JUST BLAME ALL OF THE PROBLEMS ON THE CHINESE COMPANY THAT MANUFACTURES OUR PRODUCTS.
ULTIMATELY, IT'S THE CEO'S FAULT FOR FAILING TO GIVE ME PROPER INCENTIVES.
©2005 Scott Adams, Inc./Dist. by UFS, Inc.
12-11-05

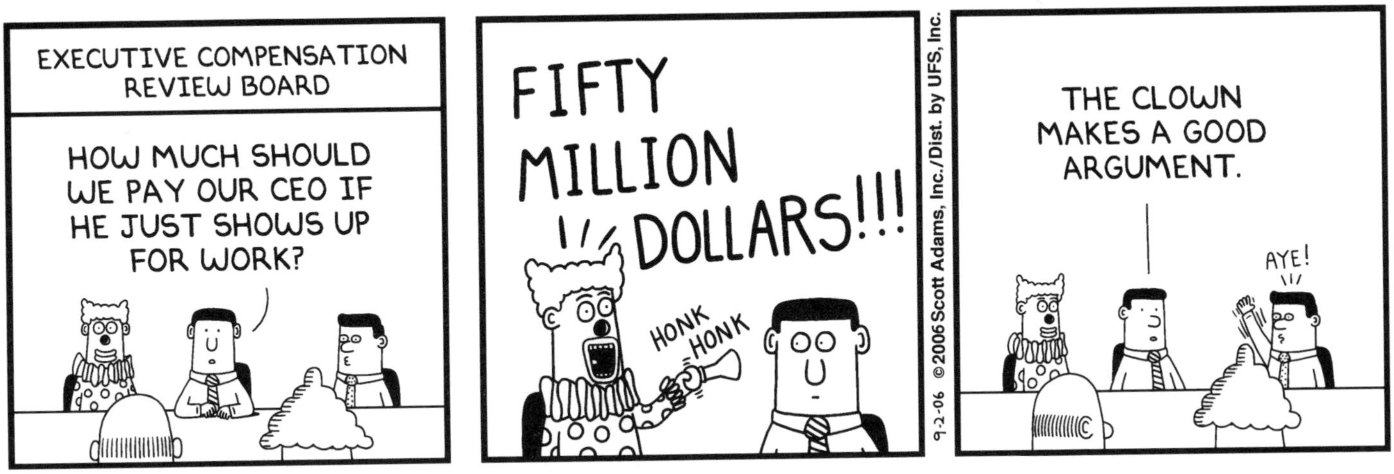
EXECUTIVE COMPENSATION REVIEW BOARD
HOW MUCH SHOULD WE PAY OUR CEO IF HE JUST SHOWS UP FOR WORK?
FIFTY MILLION DOLLARS!!!
HONK HONK
9-2-06 ©2006 Scott Adams, Inc./Dist. by UFS, Inc.
THE CLOWN MAKES A GOOD ARGUMENT.
AYE!

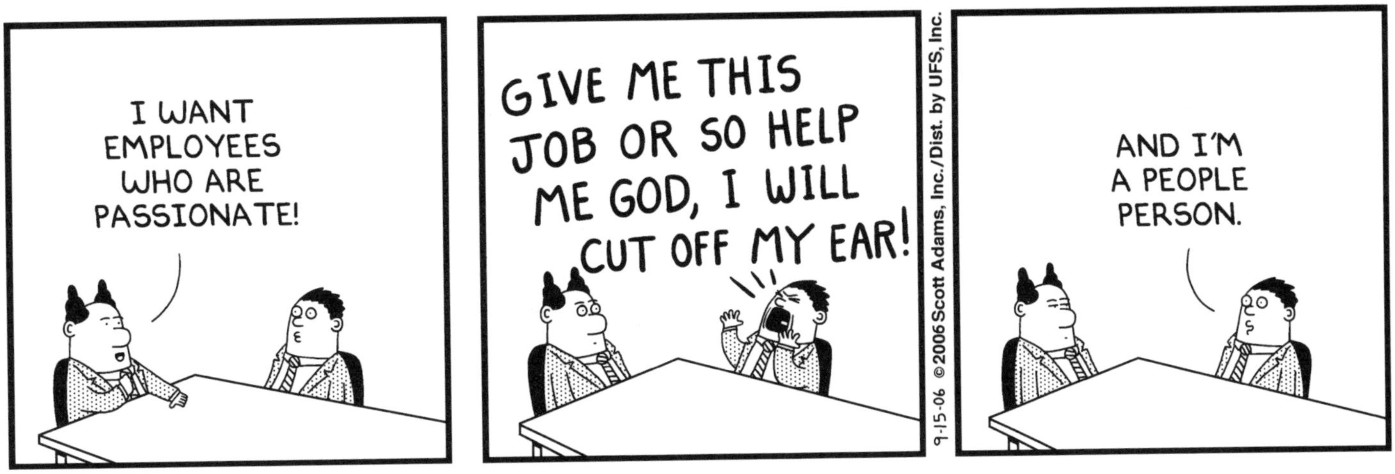
I WANT EMPLOYEES WHO ARE PASSIONATE!
GIVE ME THIS JOB OR SO HELP ME GOD, I WILL CUT OFF MY EAR!
9-15-06 ©2006 Scott Adams, Inc./Dist. by UFS, Inc.
AND I'M A PEOPLE PERSON.

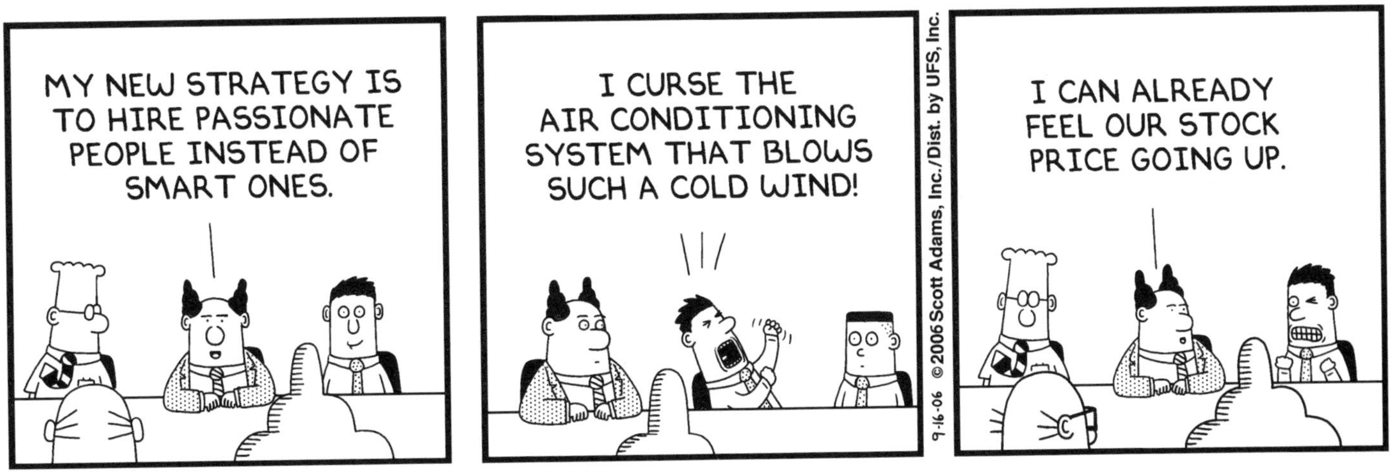
MY NEW STRATEGY IS TO HIRE PASSIONATE PEOPLE INSTEAD OF SMART ONES.
I CURSE THE AIR CONDITIONING SYSTEM THAT BLOWS SUCH A COLD WIND!
9-16-06 ©2006 Scott Adams, Inc./Dist. by UFS, Inc.
I CAN ALREADY FEEL OUR STOCK PRICE GOING UP.

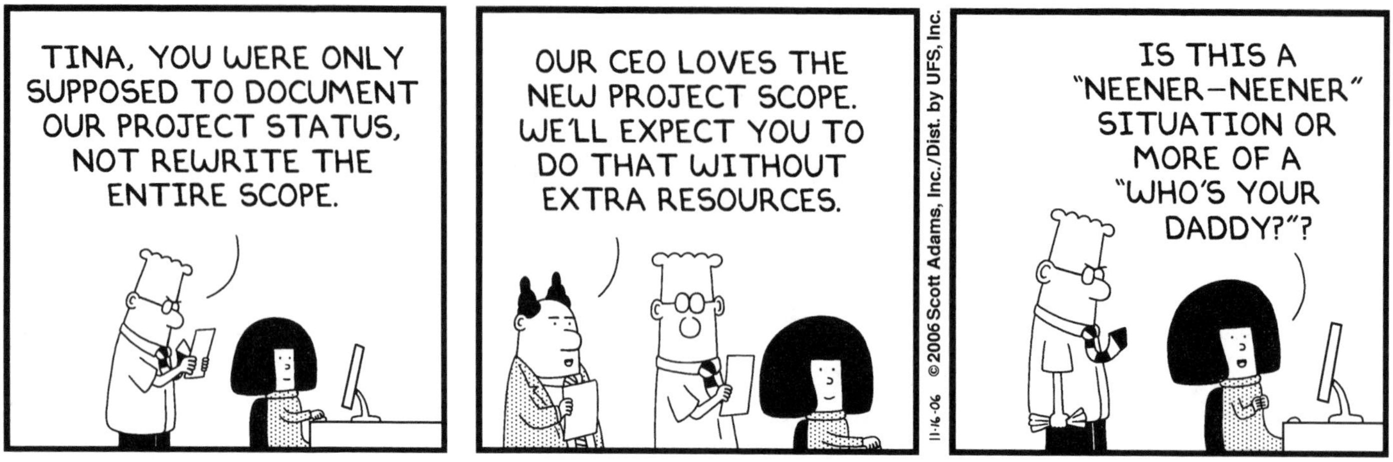
TINA, YOU WERE ONLY SUPPOSED TO DOCUMENT OUR PROJECT STATUS, NOT REWRITE THE ENTIRE SCOPE.
OUR CEO LOVES THE NEW PROJECT SCOPE. WE'LL EXPECT YOU TO DO THAT WITHOUT EXTRA RESOURCES.
11-16-06 ©2006 Scott Adams, Inc./Dist. by UFS, Inc.
IS THIS A "NEENER-NEENER" SITUATION OR MORE OF A "WHO'S YOUR DADDY?"?

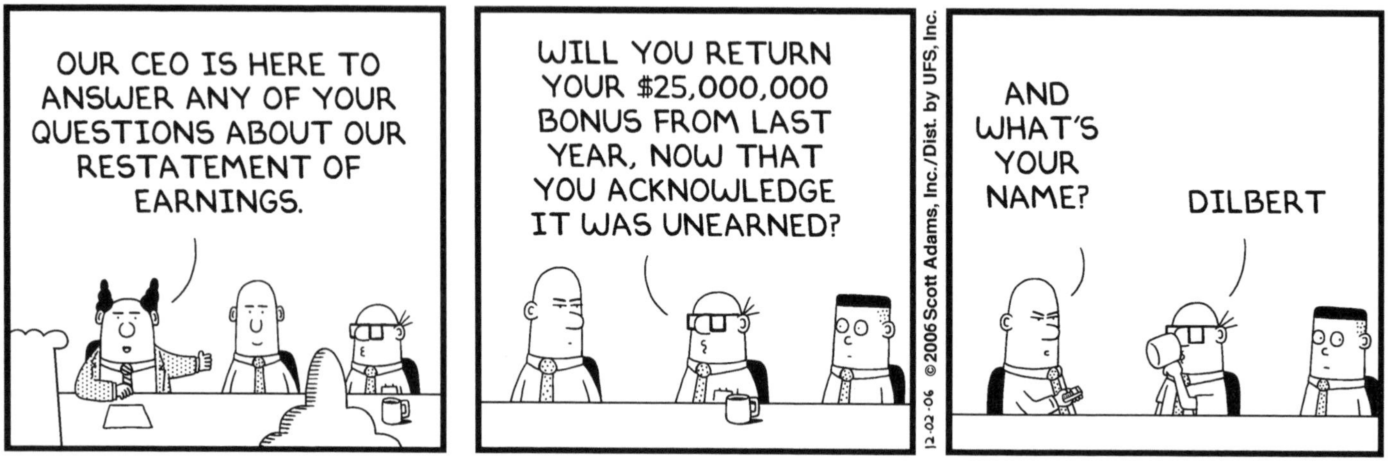
OUR CEO IS HERE TO ANSWER ANY OF YOUR QUESTIONS ABOUT OUR RESTATEMENT OF EARNINGS.
WILL YOU RETURN YOUR $25,000,000 BONUS FROM LAST YEAR, NOW THAT YOU ACKNOWLEDGE IT WAS UNEARNED?
12-02-06 ©2006 Scott Adams, Inc./Dist. by UFS, Inc.
AND WHAT'S YOUR NAME?
DILBERT

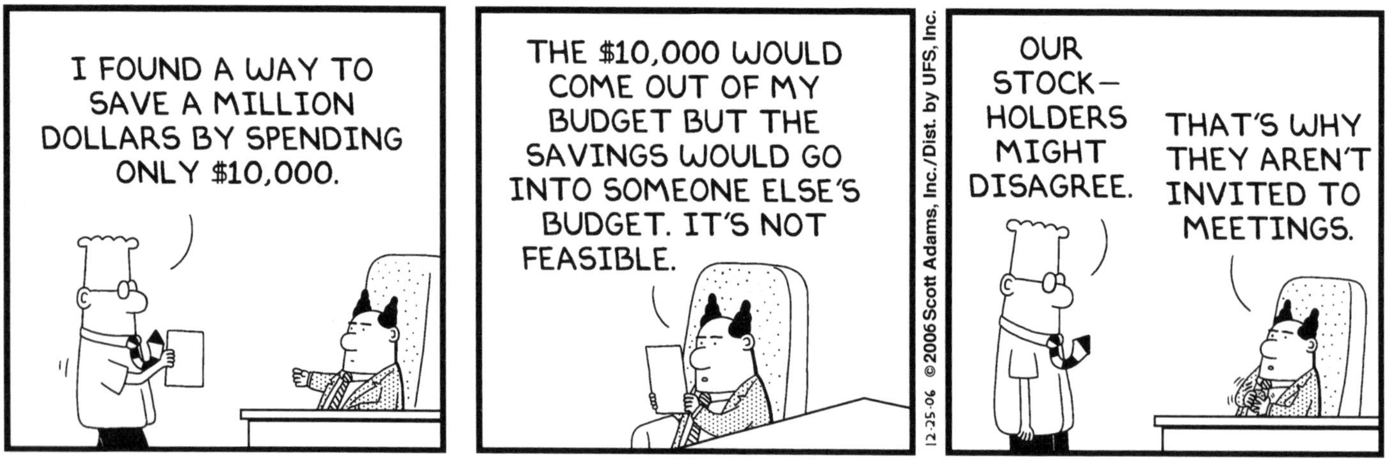
I FOUND A WAY TO SAVE A MILLION DOLLARS BY SPENDING ONLY $10,000.
THE $10,000 WOULD COME OUT OF MY BUDGET BUT THE SAVINGS WOULD GO INTO SOMEONE ELSE'S BUDGET. IT'S NOT FEASIBLE.
12-25-06 ©2006 Scott Adams, Inc./Dist. by UFS, Inc.
OUR STOCK-HOLDERS MIGHT DISAGREE.
THAT'S WHY THEY AREN'T INVITED TO MEETINGS.

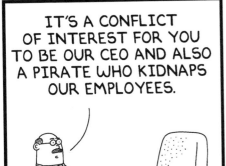

IT'S A CONFLICT OF INTEREST FOR YOU TO BE OUR CEO AND ALSO A PIRATE WHO KIDNAPS OUR EMPLOYEES.
THE EXECUTIVE COMPENSATION COMMITTEE APPROVED THIS ARRANGEMENT. IT'S ALL SPELLED OUT IN MY EMPLOYMENT AGREEMENT.
SO IT IS.
WAIT HERE WHILE I CALL MYSELF AND RANSOM YOU BACK TO YOUR OFFICE.
6-17-09 © 2009 Scott Adams, Inc./Dist. by UFS, Inc.

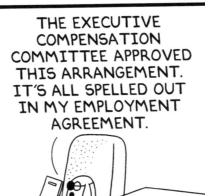

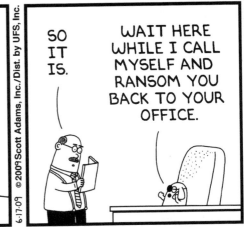

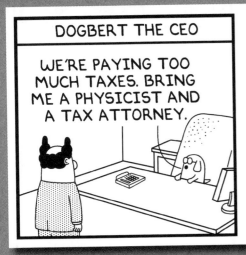

DOGBERT THE CEO
WE'RE PAYING TOO MUCH TAXES. BRING ME A PHYSICIST AND A TAX ATTORNEY.
I WANT TO INCORPORATE IN ANOTHER DIMENSION. MAKE IT HAPPEN.
SOMEWHERE IN THE MULTIVERSE IT'S ALREADY DONE.
I LIKE YOU. THE LAWYER GUY IS FIRED.
6-23-09 © 2009 Scott Adams, Inc./Dist. by UFS, Inc.

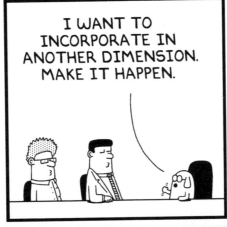

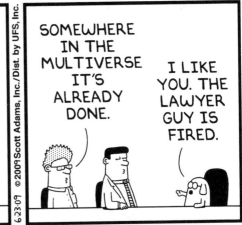

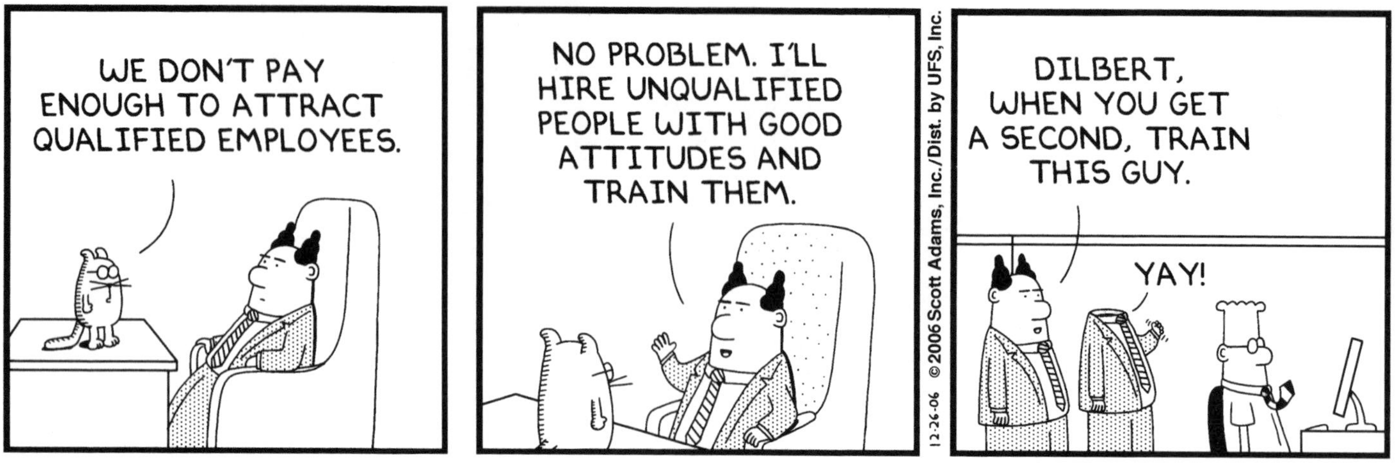
WE DON'T PAY ENOUGH TO ATTRACT QUALIFIED EMPLOYEES.
NO PROBLEM. I'LL HIRE UNQUALIFIED PEOPLE WITH GOOD ATTITUDES AND TRAIN THEM.
12-26-06 © 2006 Scott Adams, Inc./Dist. by UFS, Inc.
DILBERT, WHEN YOU GET A SECOND, TRAIN THIS GUY.
YAY!

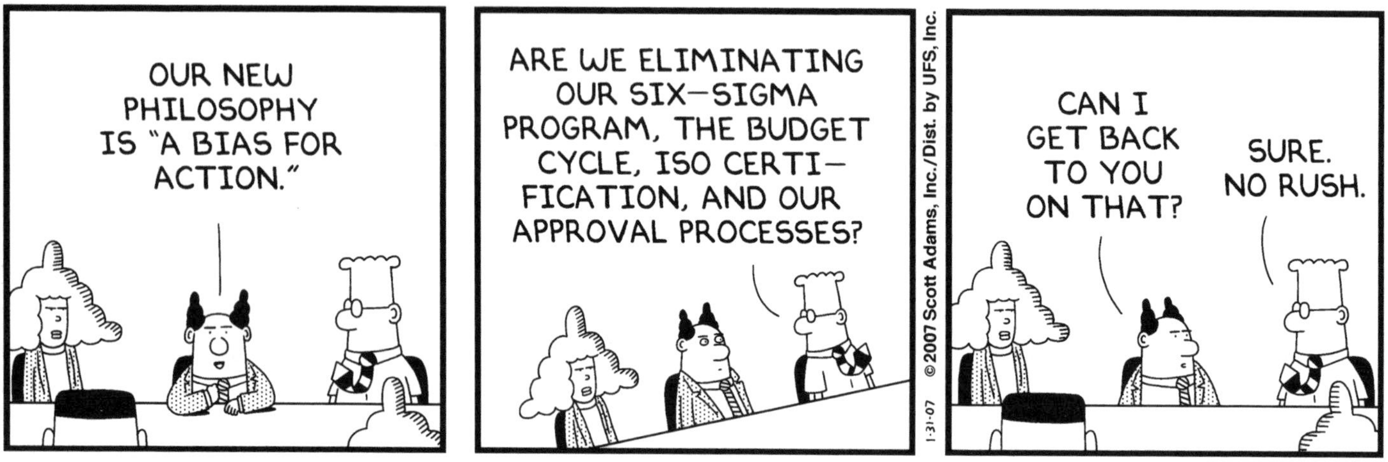
OUR NEW PHILOSOPHY IS "A BIAS FOR ACTION."
ARE WE ELIMINATING OUR SIX-SIGMA PROGRAM, THE BUDGET CYCLE, ISO CERTI-FICATION, AND OUR APPROVAL PROCESSES?
1-31-07 © 2007 Scott Adams, Inc./Dist. by UFS, Inc.
CAN I GET BACK TO YOU ON THAT?
SURE. NO RUSH.

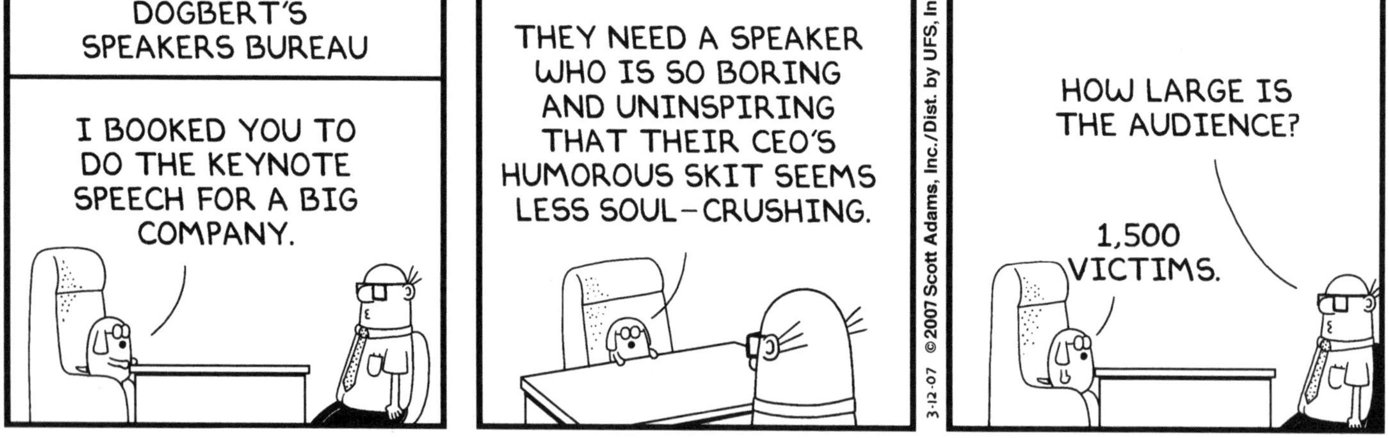
DOGBERT'S SPEAKERS BUREAU
I BOOKED YOU TO DO THE KEYNOTE SPEECH FOR A BIG COMPANY.
THEY NEED A SPEAKER WHO IS SO BORING AND UNINSPIRING THAT THEIR CEO'S HUMOROUS SKIT SEEMS LESS SOUL-CRUSHING.
3-12-07 © 2007 Scott Adams, Inc./Dist. by UFS, Inc.
HOW LARGE IS THE AUDIENCE?
1,500 VICTIMS.

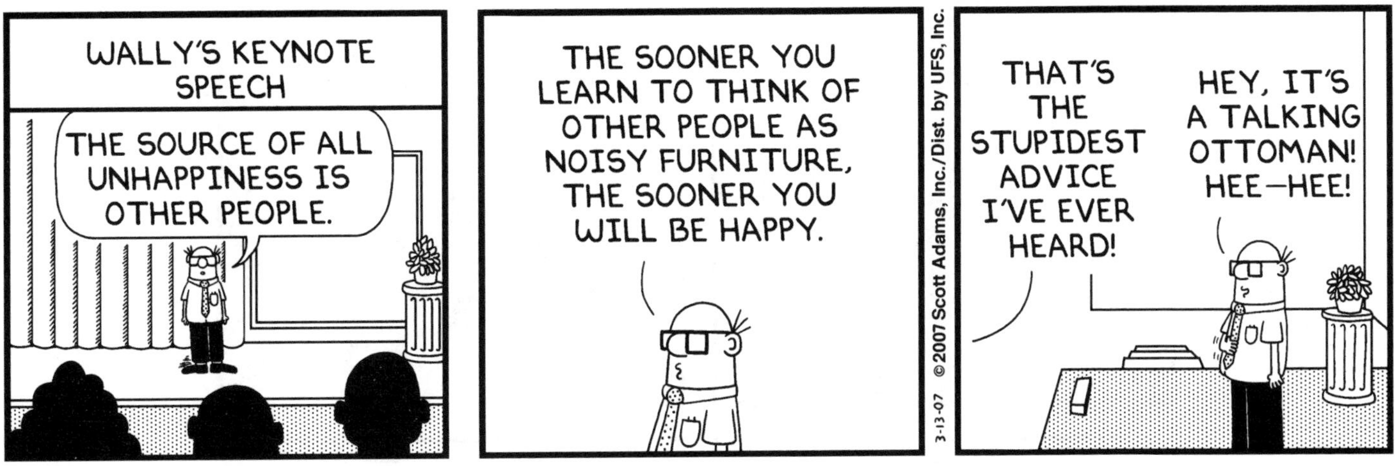
WALLY'S KEYNOTE SPEECH
THE SOURCE OF ALL UNHAPPINESS IS OTHER PEOPLE.
THE SOONER YOU LEARN TO THINK OF OTHER PEOPLE AS NOISY FURNITURE, THE SOONER YOU WILL BE HAPPY.
3-13-07 © 2007 Scott Adams, Inc./Dist. by UFS, Inc.
THAT'S THE STUPIDEST ADVICE I'VE EVER HEARD!
HEY, IT'S A TALKING OTTOMAN! HEE—HEE!

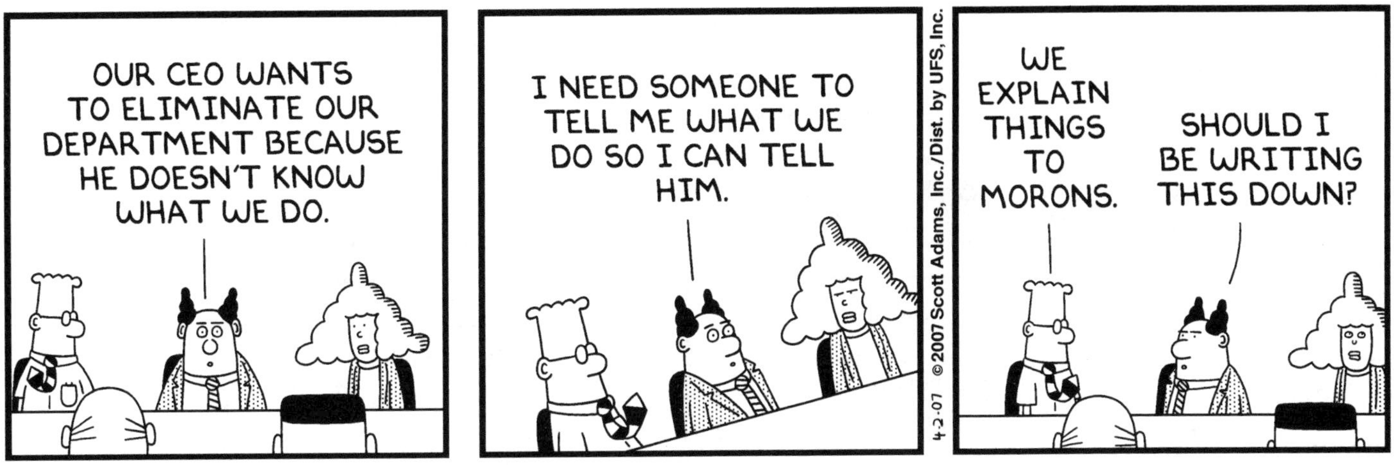
OUR CEO WANTS TO ELIMINATE OUR DEPARTMENT BECAUSE HE DOESN'T KNOW WHAT WE DO.
I NEED SOMEONE TO TELL ME WHAT WE DO SO I CAN TELL HIM.
4-2-07 © 2007 Scott Adams, Inc./Dist. by UFS, Inc.
WE EXPLAIN THINGS TO MORONS.
SHOULD I BE WRITING THIS DOWN?

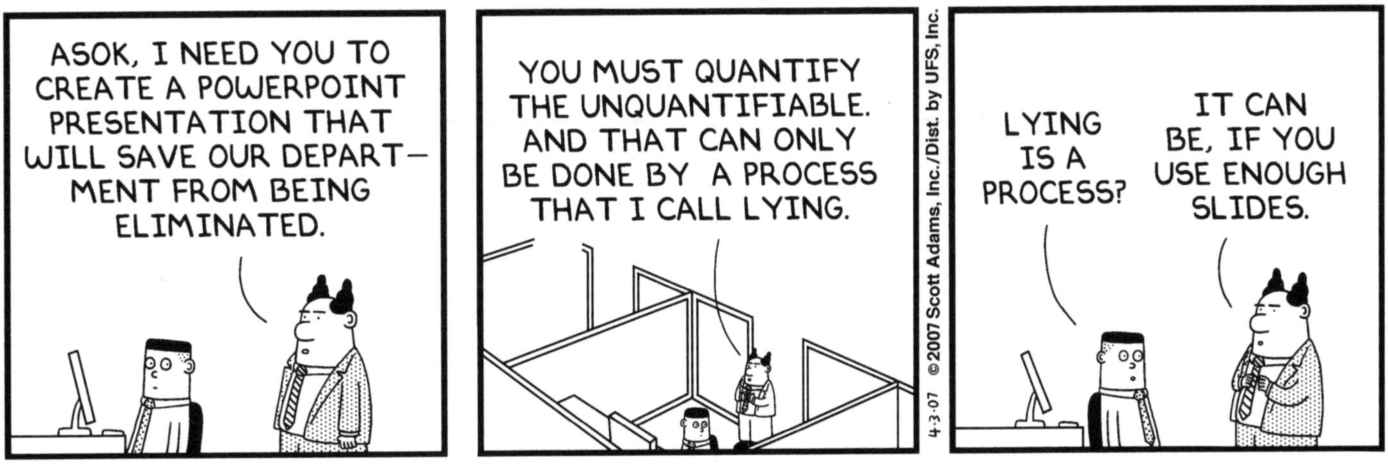
ASOK, I NEED YOU TO CREATE A POWERPOINT PRESENTATION THAT WILL SAVE OUR DEPART-MENT FROM BEING ELIMINATED.
YOU MUST QUANTIFY THE UNQUANTIFIABLE. AND THAT CAN ONLY BE DONE BY A PROCESS THAT I CALL LYING.
4-3-07 © 2007 Scott Adams, Inc./Dist. by UFS, Inc.
LYING IS A PROCESS?
IT CAN BE, IF YOU USE ENOUGH SLIDES.

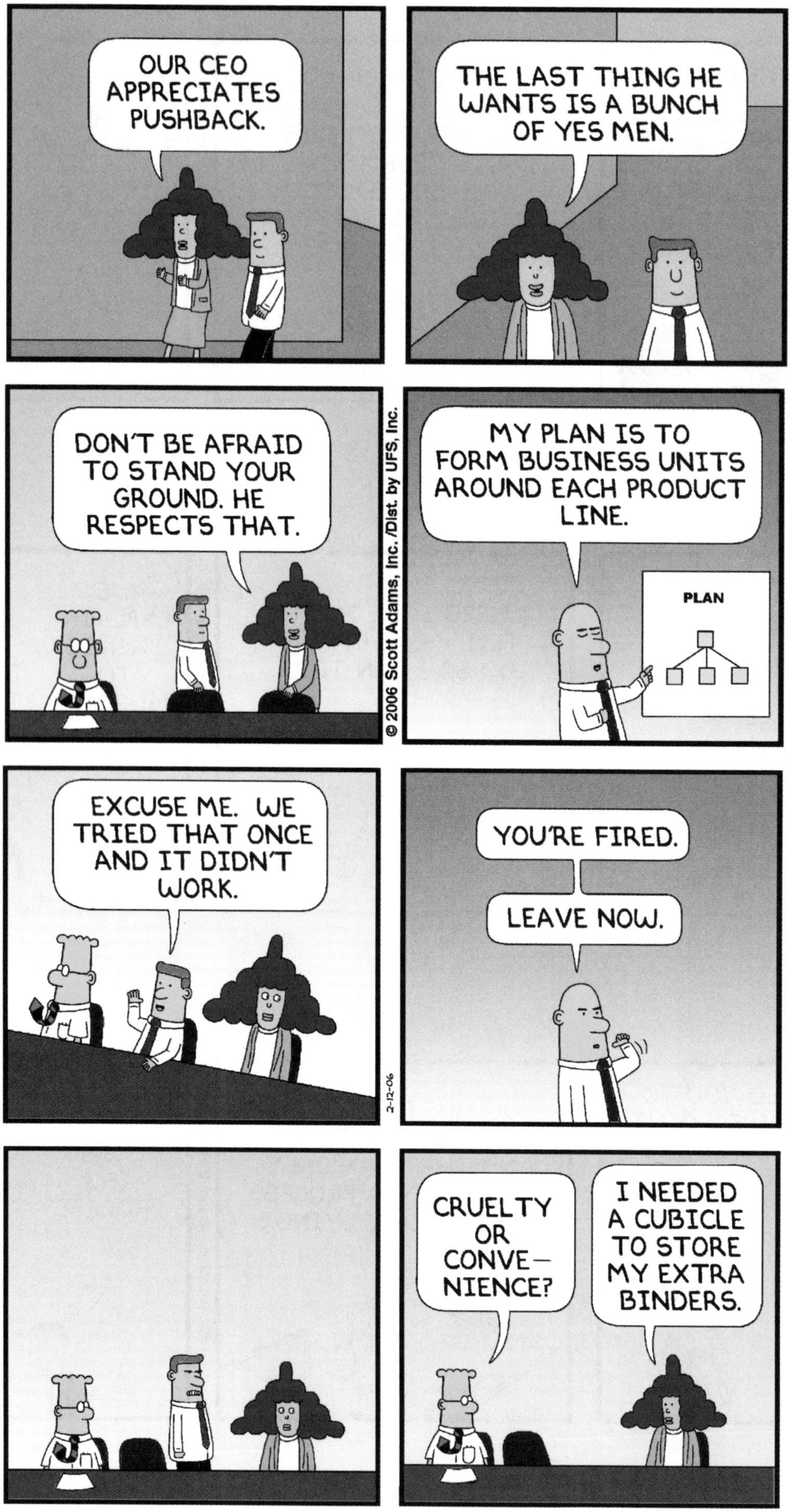
OUR CEO APPRECIATES PUSHBACK.
THE LAST THING HE WANTS IS A BUNCH OF YES MEN.
DON'T BE AFRAID TO STAND YOUR GROUND. HE RESPECTS THAT.
© 2006 Scott Adams, Inc. /Dist. by UFS, Inc.
MY PLAN IS TO FORM BUSINESS UNITS AROUND EACH PRODUCT LINE.
PLAN
EXCUSE ME. WE TRIED THAT ONCE AND IT DIDN'T WORK.
2-12-06
YOU'RE FIRED.
LEAVE NOW.
CRUELTY OR CONVE—NIENCE?
I NEEDED A CUBICLE TO STORE MY EXTRA BINDERS.

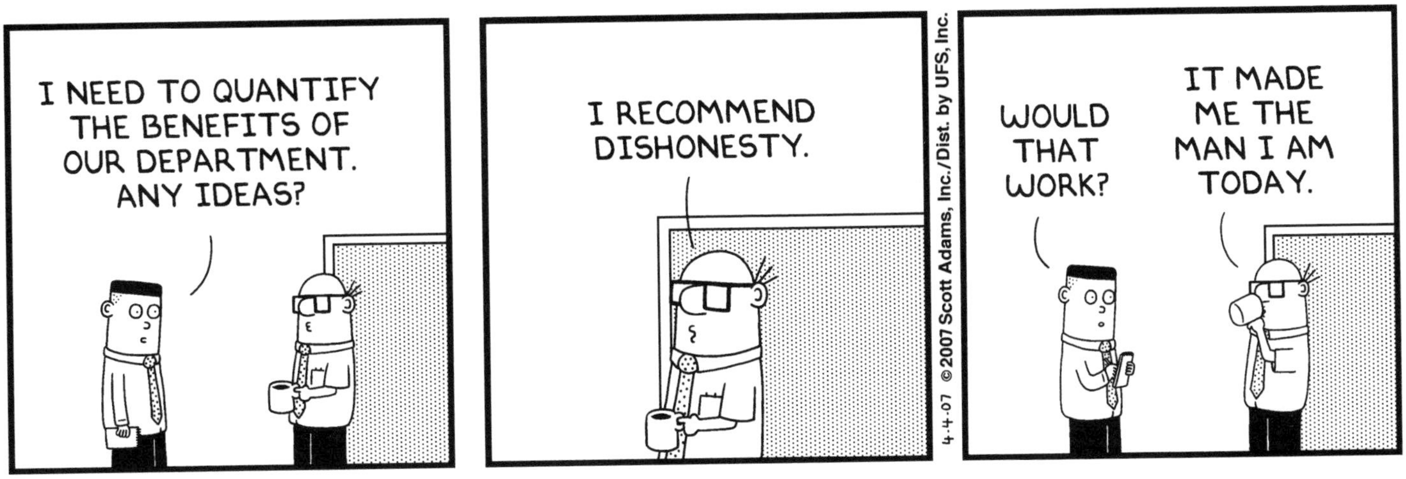
I NEED TO QUANTIFY THE BENEFITS OF OUR DEPARTMENT. ANY IDEAS?
I RECOMMEND DISHONESTY.
4-4-07 ©2007 Scott Adams, Inc./Dist. by UFS, Inc.
WOULD THAT WORK?
IT MADE ME THE MAN I AM TODAY.

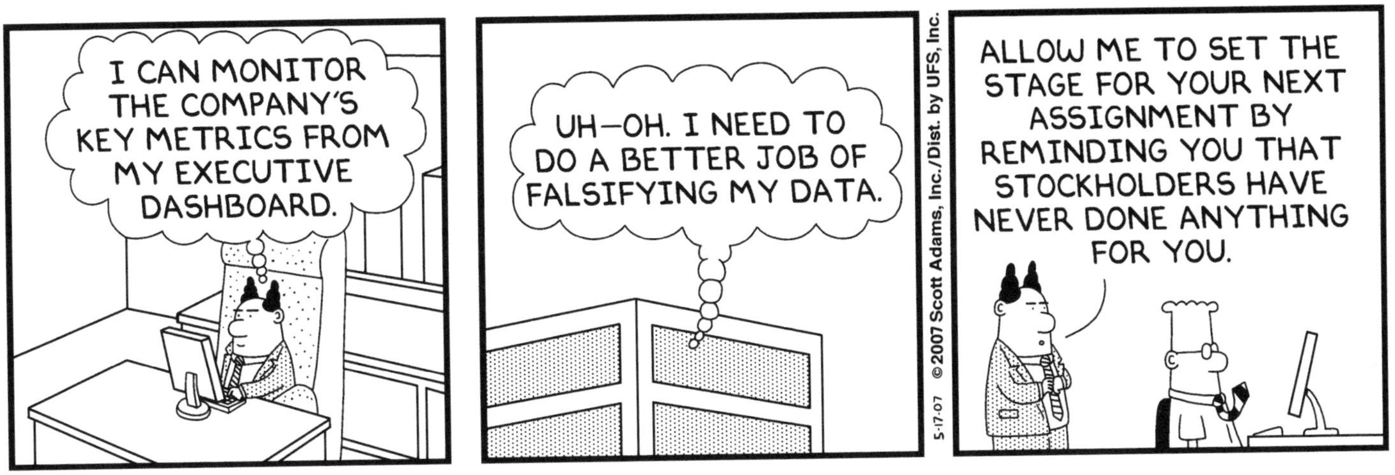
I CAN MONITOR THE COMPANY'S KEY METRICS FROM MY EXECUTIVE DASHBOARD.
UH-OH. I NEED TO DO A BETTER JOB OF FALSIFYING MY DATA.
5-17-07 ©2007 Scott Adams, Inc./Dist. by UFS, Inc.
ALLOW ME TO SET THE STAGE FOR YOUR NEXT ASSIGNMENT BY REMINDING YOU THAT STOCKHOLDERS HAVE NEVER DONE ANYTHING FOR YOU.

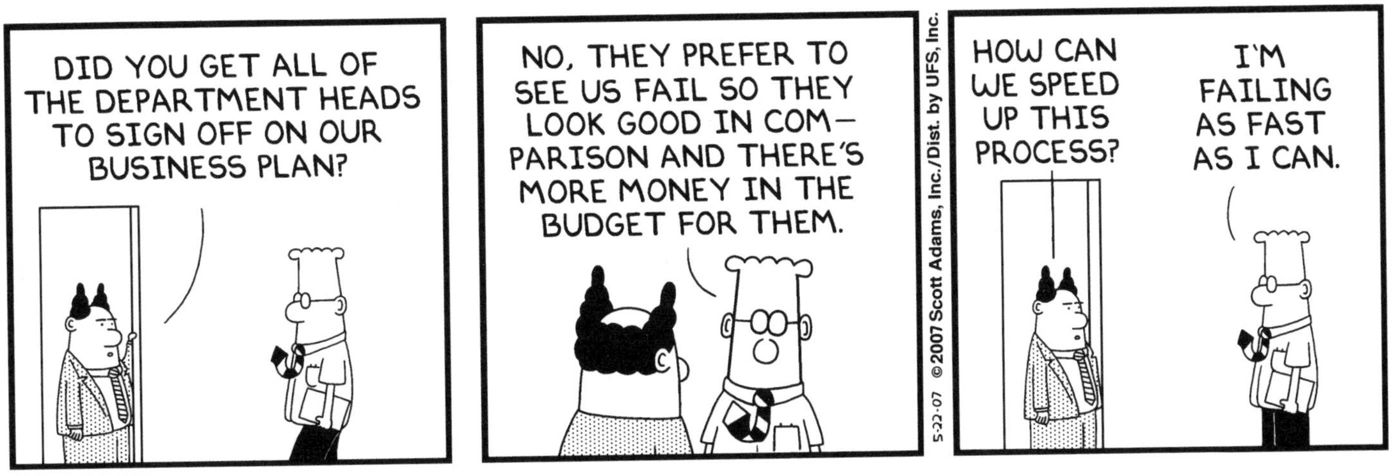
DID YOU GET ALL OF THE DEPARTMENT HEADS TO SIGN OFF ON OUR BUSINESS PLAN?
NO, THEY PREFER TO SEE US FAIL SO THEY LOOK GOOD IN COM-PARISON AND THERE'S MORE MONEY IN THE BUDGET FOR THEM.
5-22-07 ©2007 Scott Adams, Inc./Dist. by UFS, Inc.
HOW CAN WE SPEED UP THIS PROCESS?
I'M FAILING AS FAST AS I CAN.

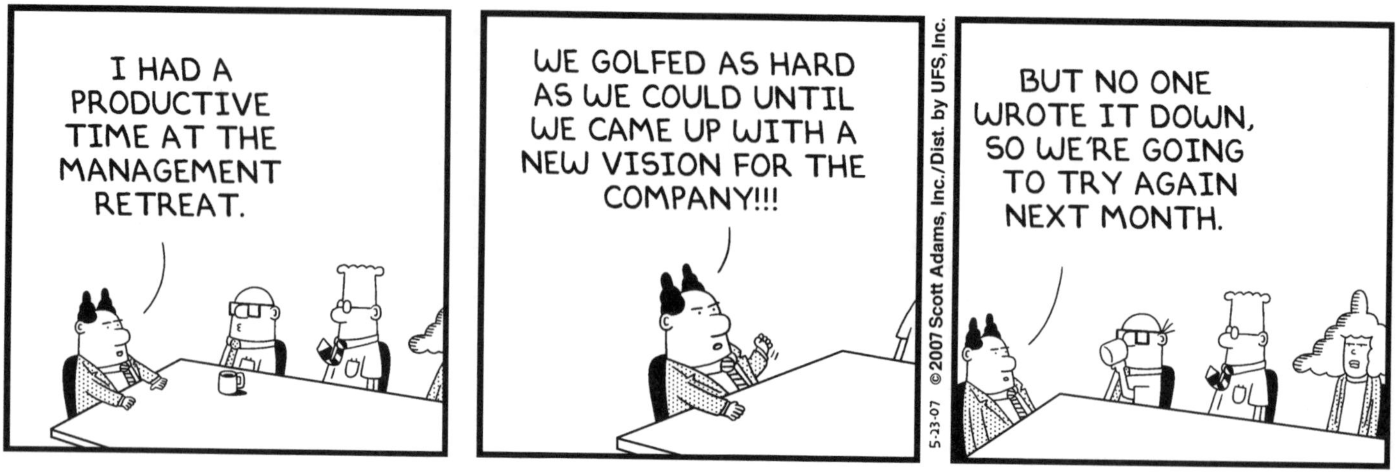
I HAD A PRODUCTIVE TIME AT THE MANAGEMENT RETREAT.
WE GOLFED AS HARD AS WE COULD UNTIL WE CAME UP WITH A NEW VISION FOR THE COMPANY!!!
5-23-07 ©2007 Scott Adams, Inc./Dist. by UFS, Inc.
BUT NO ONE WROTE IT DOWN, SO WE'RE GOING TO TRY AGAIN NEXT MONTH.

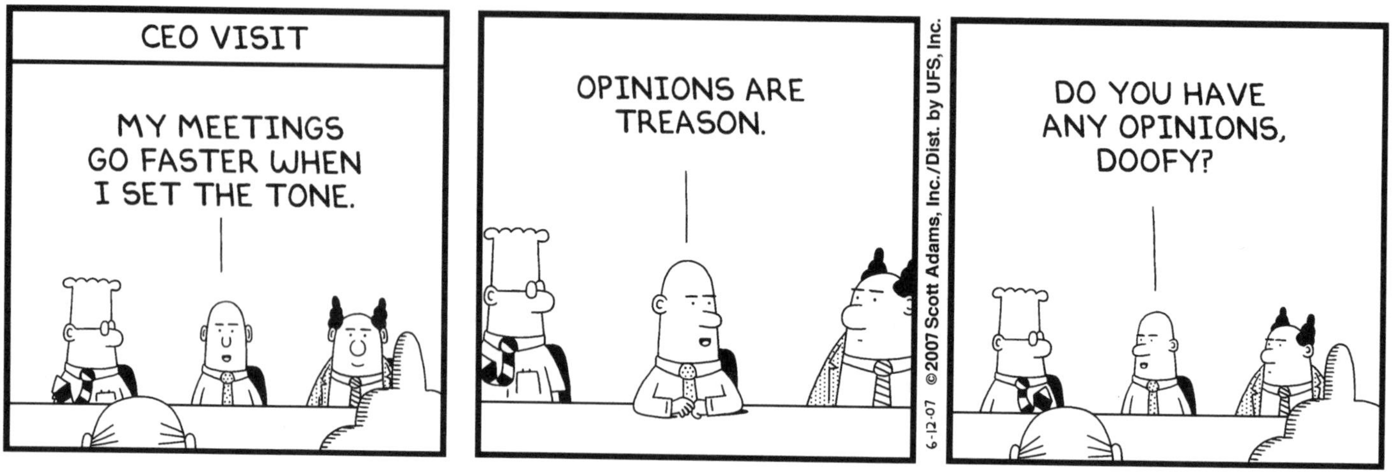
CEO VISIT
MY MEETINGS GO FASTER WHEN I SET THE TONE.
OPINIONS ARE TREASON.
6-12-07 ©2007 Scott Adams, Inc./Dist. by UFS, Inc.
DO YOU HAVE ANY OPINIONS, DOOFY?

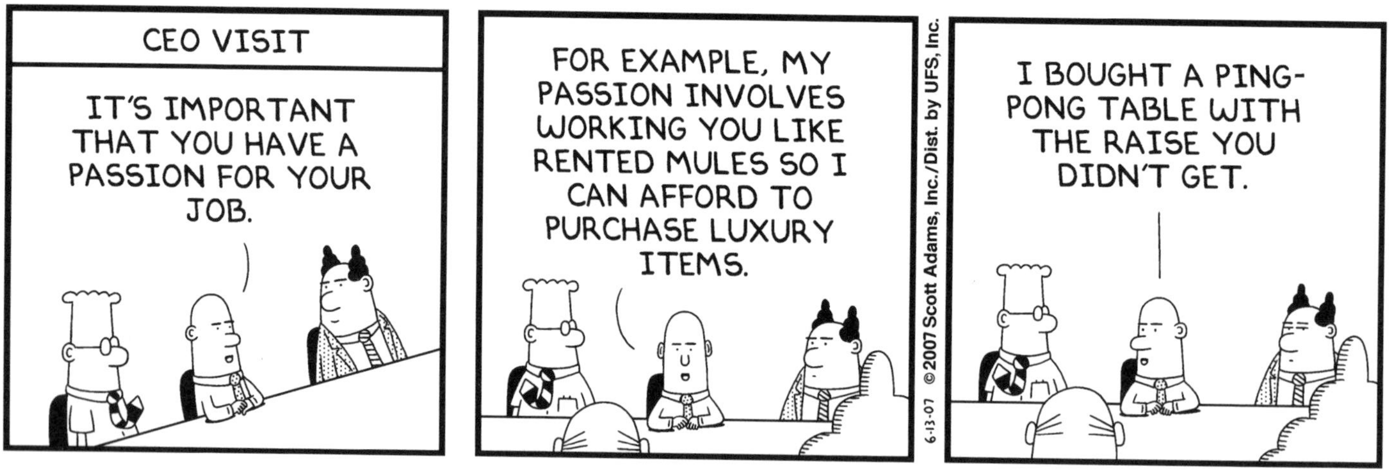
CEO VISIT
IT'S IMPORTANT THAT YOU HAVE A PASSION FOR YOUR JOB.
FOR EXAMPLE, MY PASSION INVOLVES WORKING YOU LIKE RENTED MULES SO I CAN AFFORD TO PURCHASE LUXURY ITEMS.
6-13-07 ©2007 Scott Adams, Inc./Dist. by UFS, Inc.
I BOUGHT A PING-PONG TABLE WITH THE RAISE YOU DIDN'T GET.

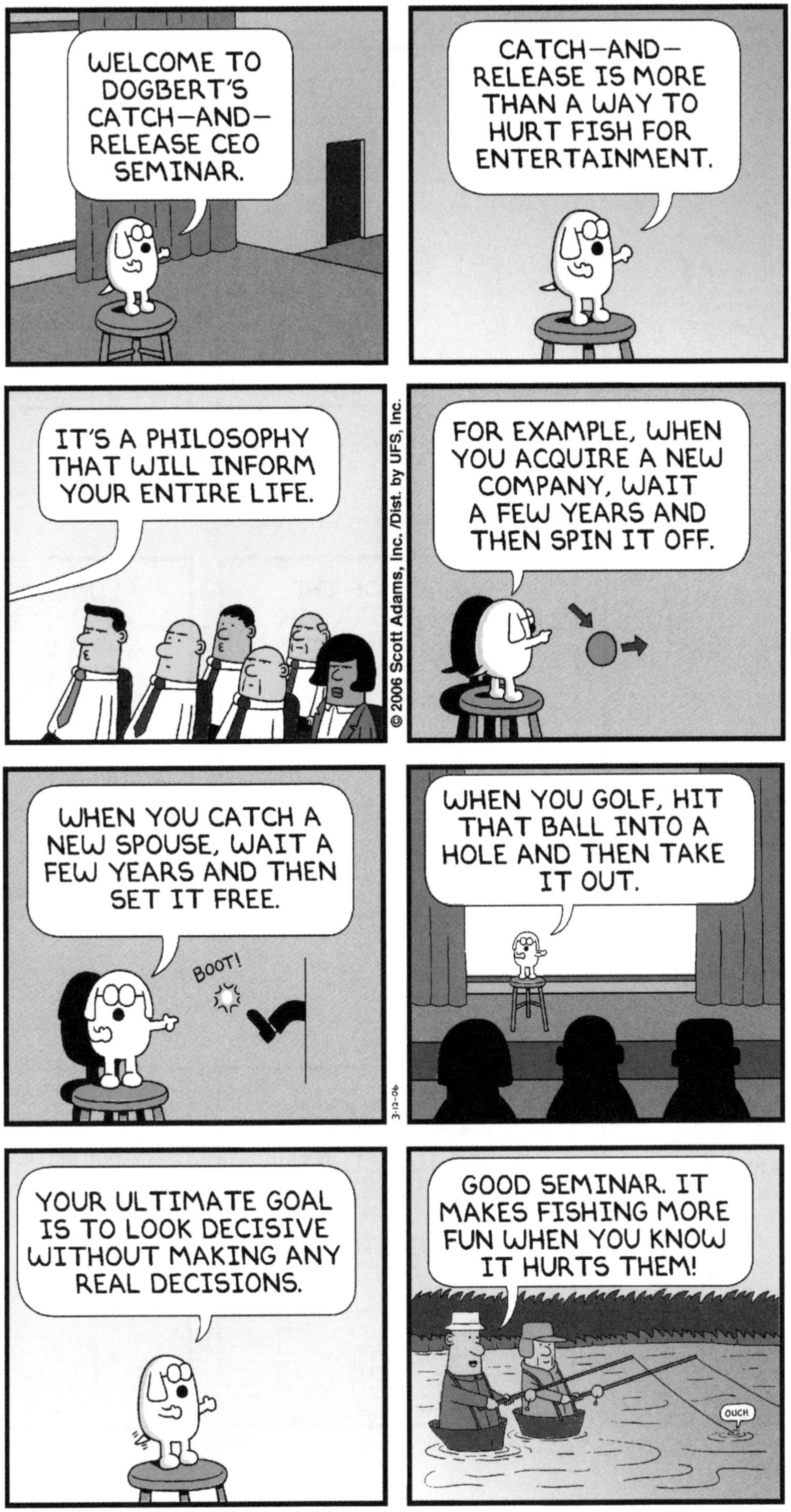
WELCOME TO DOGBERT'S CATCH-AND-RELEASE CEO SEMINAR.
CATCH-AND-RELEASE IS MORE THAN A WAY TO HURT FISH FOR ENTERTAINMENT.
IT'S A PHILOSOPHY THAT WILL INFORM YOUR ENTIRE LIFE.
FOR EXAMPLE, WHEN YOU ACQUIRE A NEW COMPANY, WAIT A FEW YEARS AND THEN SPIN IT OFF.
WHEN YOU CATCH A NEW SPOUSE, WAIT A FEW YEARS AND THEN SET IT FREE.
BOOT!
WHEN YOU GOLF, HIT THAT BALL INTO A HOLE AND THEN TAKE IT OUT.
YOUR ULTIMATE GOAL IS TO LOOK DECISIVE WITHOUT MAKING ANY REAL DECISIONS.
GOOD SEMINAR. IT MAKES FISHING MORE FUN WHEN YOU KNOW IT HURTS THEM!
OUCH
© 2006 Scott Adams, Inc. /Dist. by UFS, Inc.
3-12-06

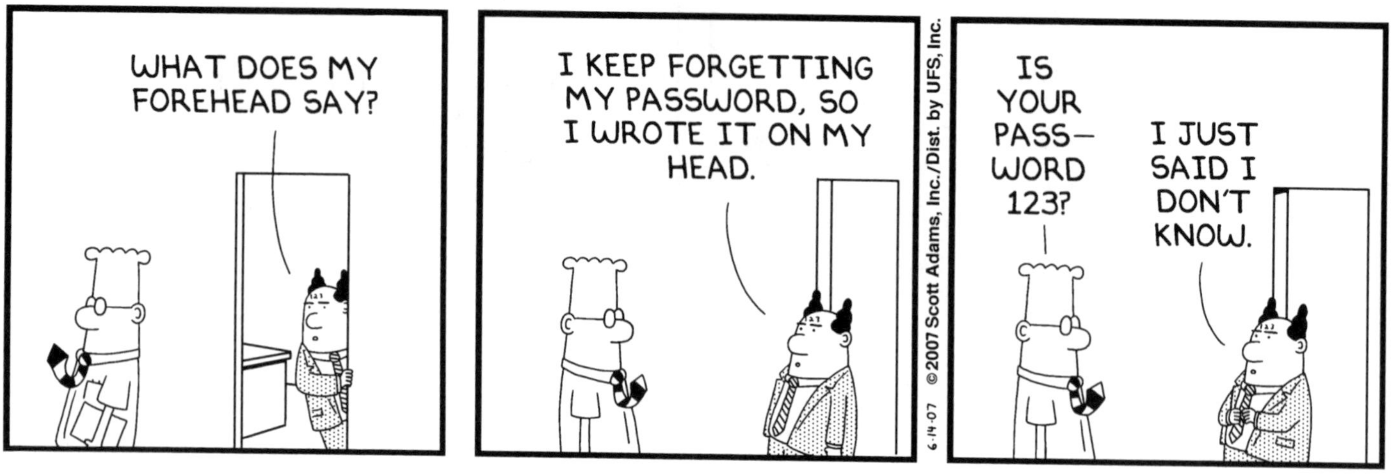
WHAT DOES MY FOREHEAD SAY?
I KEEP FORGETTING MY PASSWORD, SO I WROTE IT ON MY HEAD.
6-14-07 © 2007 Scott Adams, Inc./Dist. by UFS, Inc.
IS YOUR PASS—WORD 123?
I JUST SAID I DON'T KNOW.

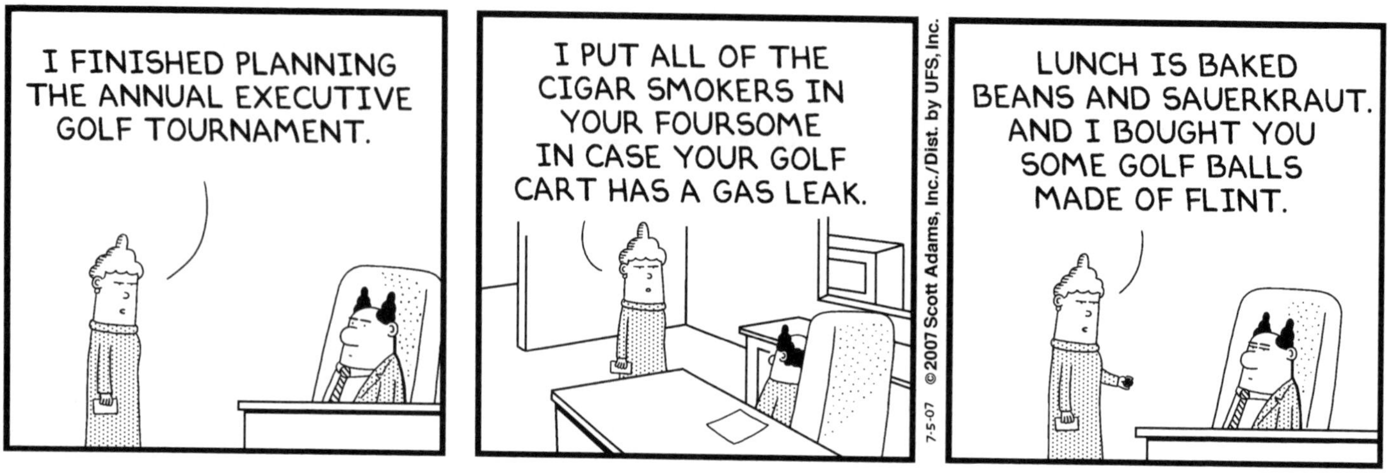
I FINISHED PLANNING THE ANNUAL EXECUTIVE GOLF TOURNAMENT.
I PUT ALL OF THE CIGAR SMOKERS IN YOUR FOURSOME IN CASE YOUR GOLF CART HAS A GAS LEAK.
7-5-07 © 2007 Scott Adams, Inc./Dist. by UFS, Inc.
LUNCH IS BAKED BEANS AND SAUERKRAUT. AND I BOUGHT YOU SOME GOLF BALLS MADE OF FLINT.

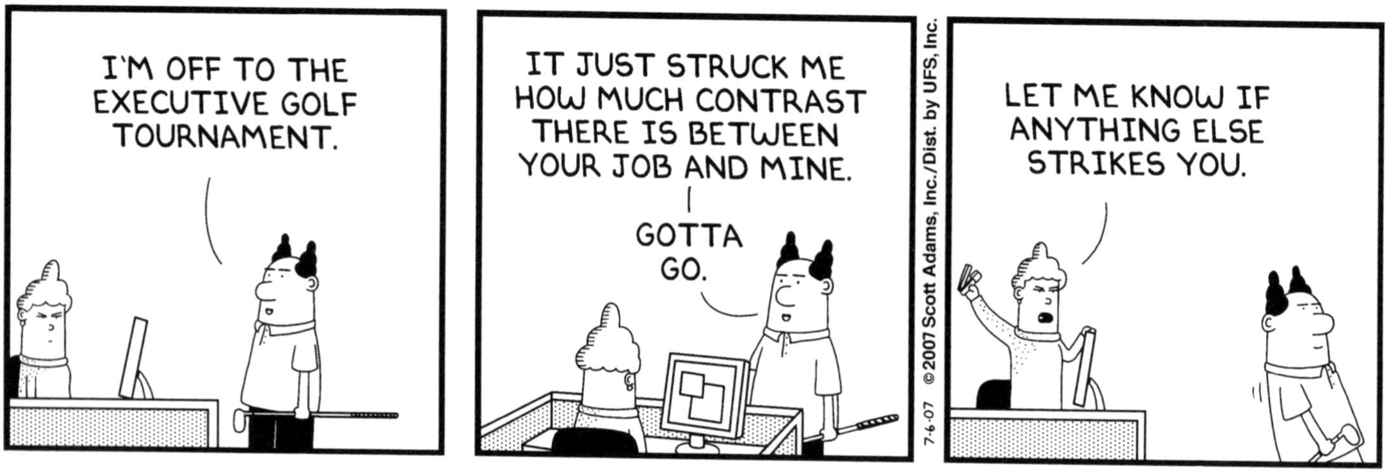
I'M OFF TO THE EXECUTIVE GOLF TOURNAMENT.
IT JUST STRUCK ME HOW MUCH CONTRAST THERE IS BETWEEN YOUR JOB AND MINE.
GOTTA GO.
7-6-07 © 2007 Scott Adams, Inc./Dist. by UFS, Inc.
LET ME KNOW IF ANYTHING ELSE STRIKES YOU.

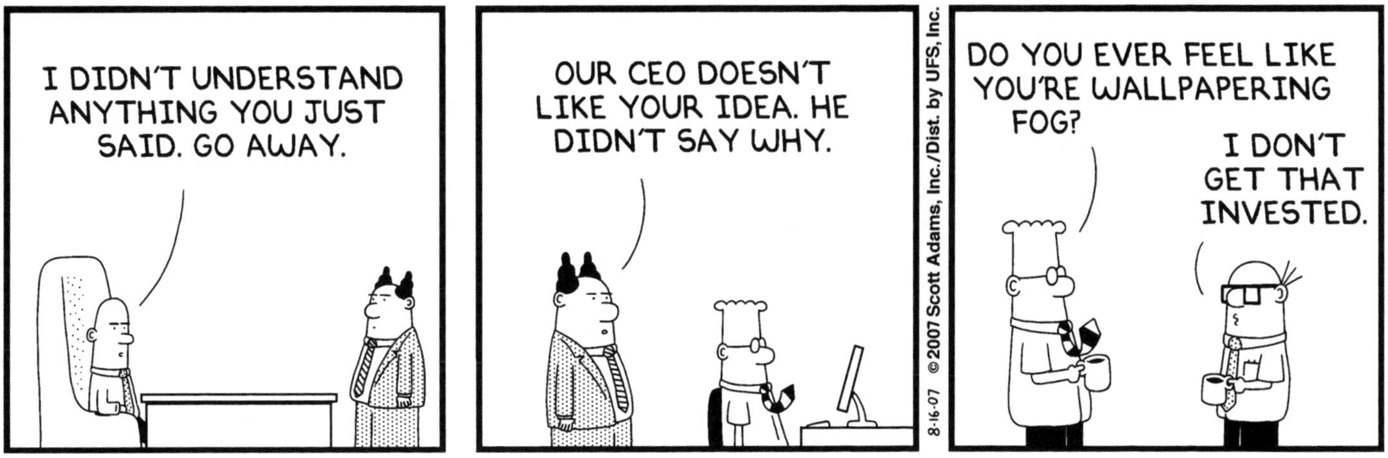
I DIDN'T UNDERSTAND ANYTHING YOU JUST SAID. GO AWAY.
OUR CEO DOESN'T LIKE YOUR IDEA. HE DIDN'T SAY WHY.
8-16-07 © 2007 Scott Adams, Inc./Dist. by UFS, Inc.
DO YOU EVER FEEL LIKE YOU'RE WALLPAPERING FOG?
I DON'T GET THAT INVESTED.

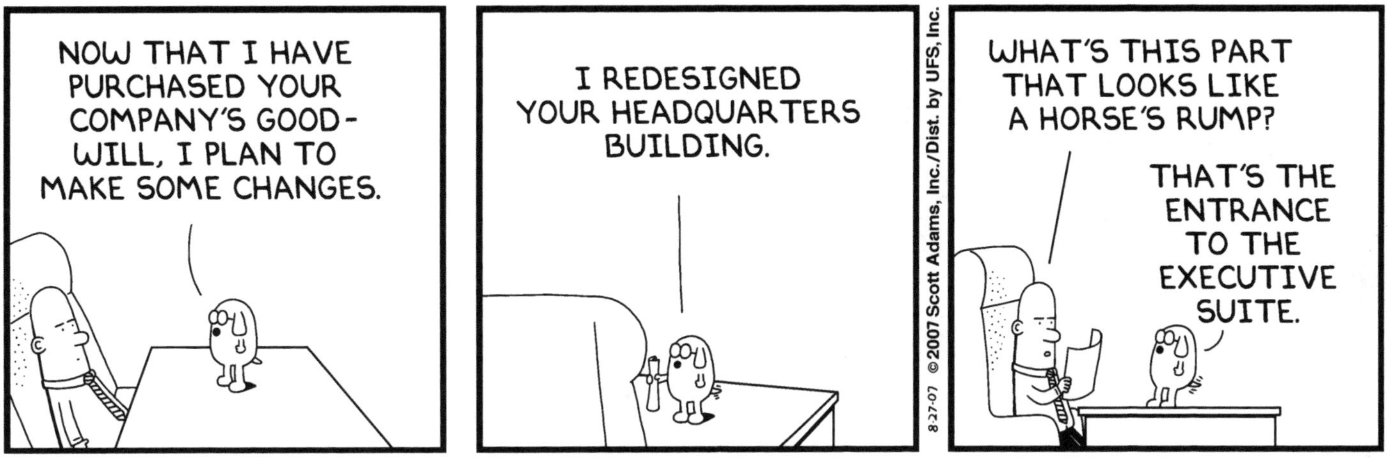
NOW THAT I HAVE PURCHASED YOUR COMPANY'S GOOD-WILL, I PLAN TO MAKE SOME CHANGES.
I REDESIGNED YOUR HEADQUARTERS BUILDING.
8-27-07 © 2007 Scott Adams, Inc./Dist. by UFS, Inc.
WHAT'S THIS PART THAT LOOKS LIKE A HORSE'S RUMP?
THAT'S THE ENTRANCE TO THE EXECUTIVE SUITE.

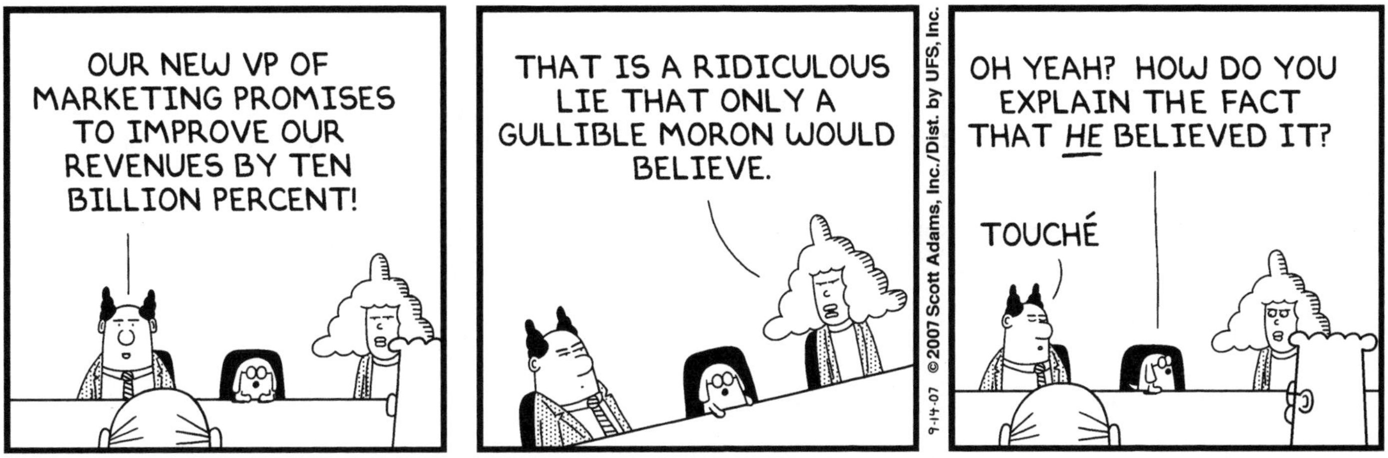
OUR NEW VP OF MARKETING PROMISES TO IMPROVE OUR REVENUES BY TEN BILLION PERCENT!
THAT IS A RIDICULOUS LIE THAT ONLY A GULLIBLE MORON WOULD BELIEVE.
9-14-07 © 2007 Scott Adams, Inc./Dist. by UFS, Inc.
OH YEAH? HOW DO YOU EXPLAIN THE FACT THAT HE BELIEVED IT?
TOUCHÉ

DOGBERT THE CEO
I'M HERE TO DO A TAX AUDIT OF YOUR COMPANY.
HOW'S THAT WORK?
I LOOK FOR REASONS TO TRANSFER MONEY FROM SMALL, DISREPU- TABLE ENTITIES TO A LARGER ONE.
6-24-09 © 2009 Scott Adams, Inc./Dist. by UFS, Inc.
I CALL MY SALARY VIGORISH, BUT IT'S NOT AS IRONIC AS IT ONCE WAS.

DOGBERT THE CEO
WE'LL BUILD A FACTORY IN EVERY STATE.
POLITICIANS WILL VOTE TO THROW HUGE PORK PROJECTS OUR WAY TO BENEFIT THEIR HOME STATES.
7-6-09 © 2009 Scott Adams, Inc./Dist. by UFS, Inc.
YOU'RE TURNING CAPITALISM AGAINST DEMOCRACY.
YOU SAY WEINER, I SAY WINNER.

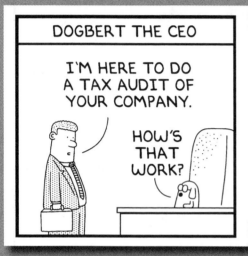

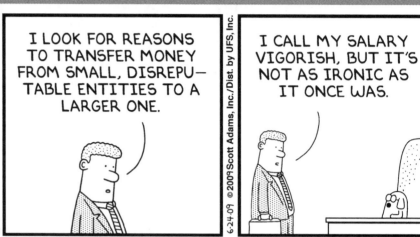

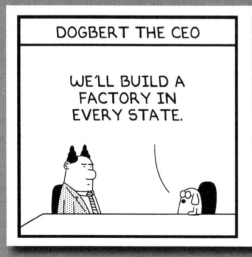

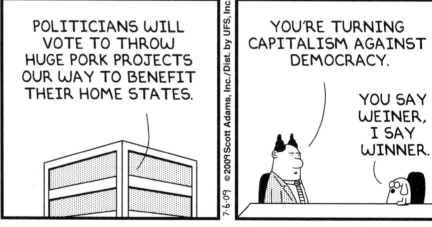

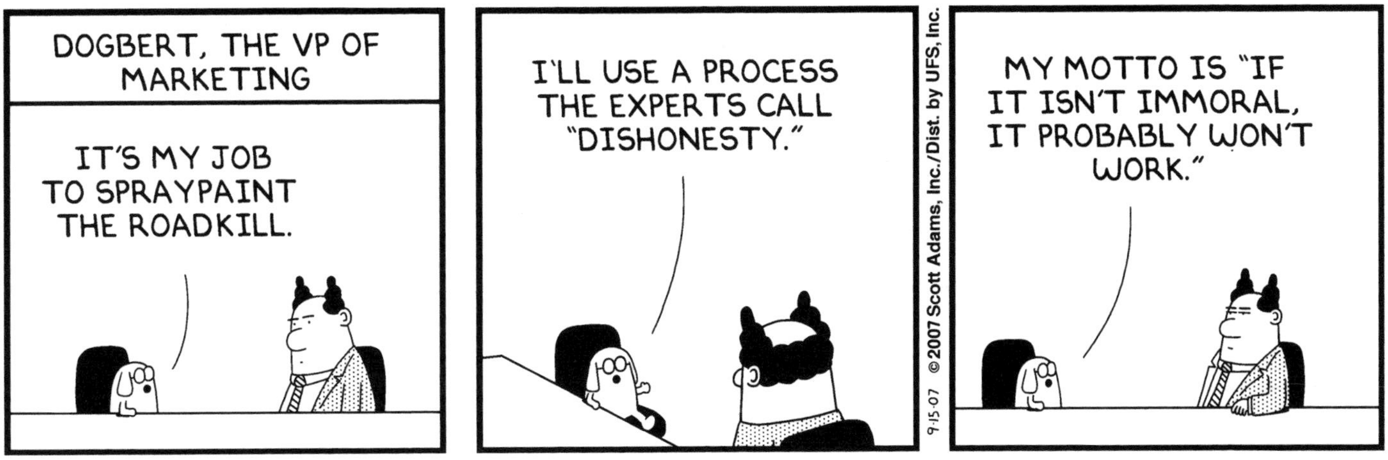
DOGBERT, THE VP OF MARKETING
IT'S MY JOB TO SPRAYPAINT THE ROADKILL.
I'LL USE A PROCESS THE EXPERTS CALL "DISHONESTY."
MY MOTTO IS "IF IT ISN'T IMMORAL, IT PROBABLY WON'T WORK."
9-15-07 © 2007 Scott Adams, Inc./Dist. by UFS, Inc.

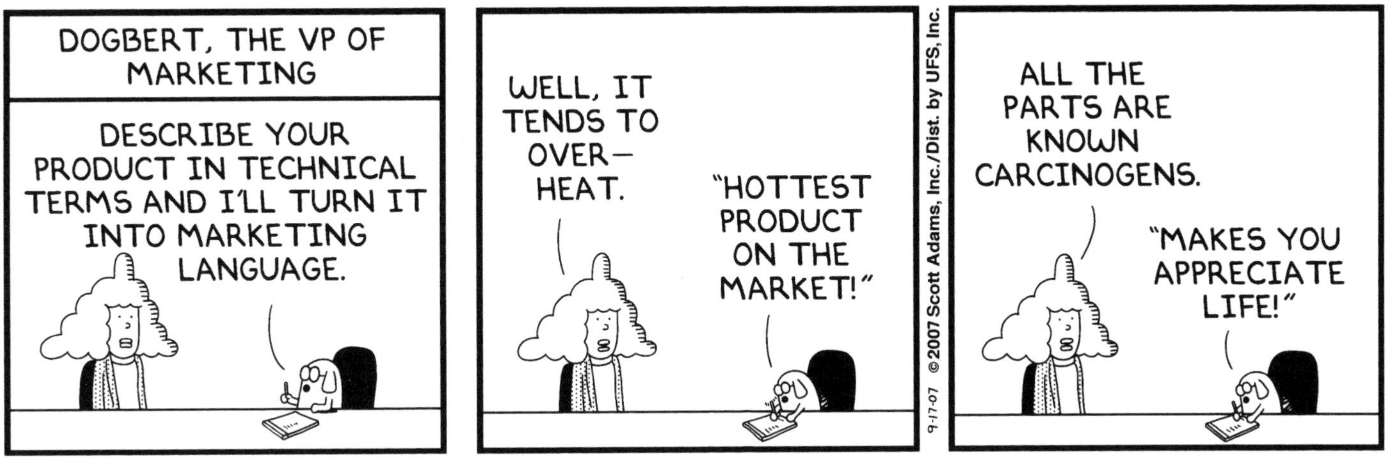
DOGBERT, THE VP OF MARKETING
DESCRIBE YOUR PRODUCT IN TECHNICAL TERMS AND I'LL TURN IT INTO MARKETING LANGUAGE.
WELL, IT TENDS TO OVER-HEAT.
"HOTTEST PRODUCT ON THE MARKET!"
ALL THE PARTS ARE KNOWN CARCINOGENS.
"MAKES YOU APPRECIATE LIFE!"
9-17-07 © 2007 Scott Adams, Inc./Dist. by UFS, Inc.

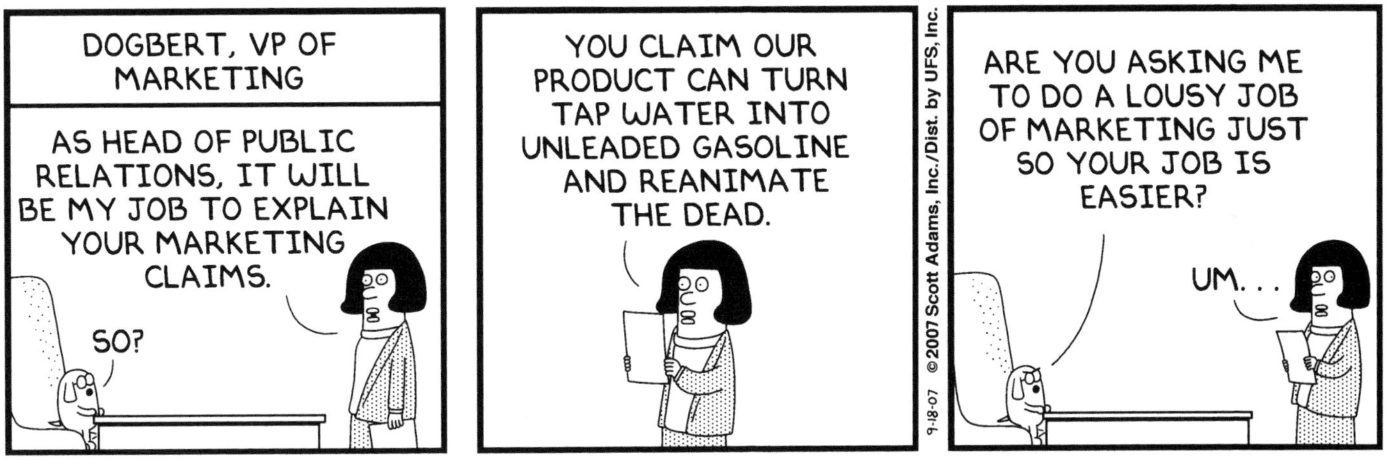
DOGBERT, VP OF MARKETING
AS HEAD OF PUBLIC RELATIONS, IT WILL BE MY JOB TO EXPLAIN YOUR MARKETING CLAIMS.
SO?
YOU CLAIM OUR PRODUCT CAN TURN TAP WATER INTO UNLEADED GASOLINE AND REANIMATE THE DEAD.
ARE YOU ASKING ME TO DO A LOUSY JOB OF MARKETING JUST SO YOUR JOB IS EASIER?
UM. . .
9-18-07 © 2007 Scott Adams, Inc./Dist. by UFS, Inc.

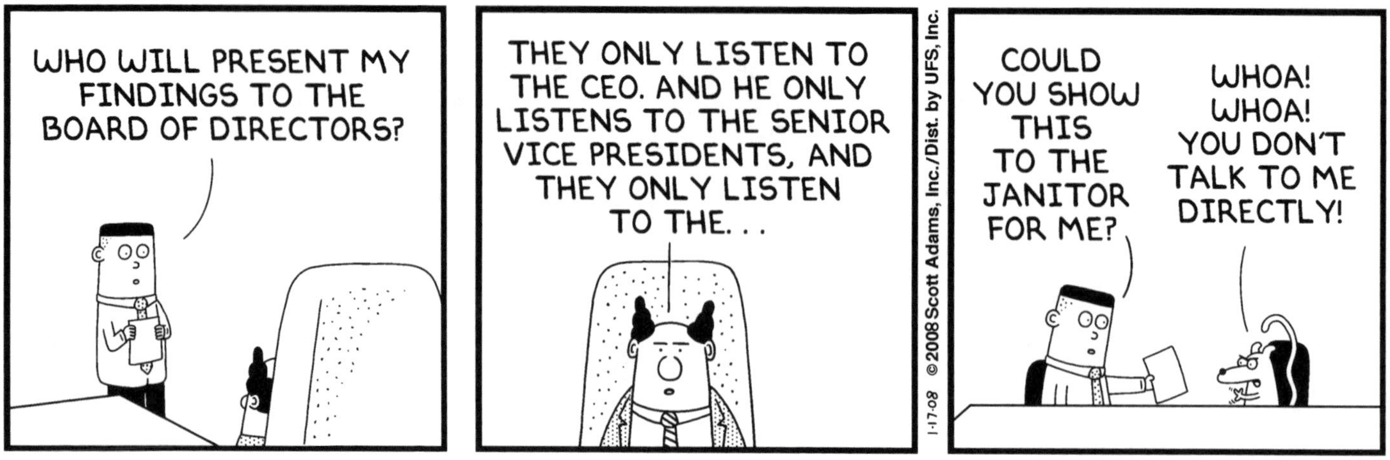
WHO WILL PRESENT MY FINDINGS TO THE BOARD OF DIRECTORS?
THEY ONLY LISTEN TO THE CEO. AND HE ONLY LISTENS TO THE SENIOR VICE PRESIDENTS, AND THEY ONLY LISTEN TO THE. . .
COULD YOU SHOW THIS TO THE JANITOR FOR ME?
WHOA! WHOA! YOU DON'T TALK TO ME DIRECTLY!
1-17-08 © 2008 Scott Adams, Inc./Dist. by UFS, Inc.

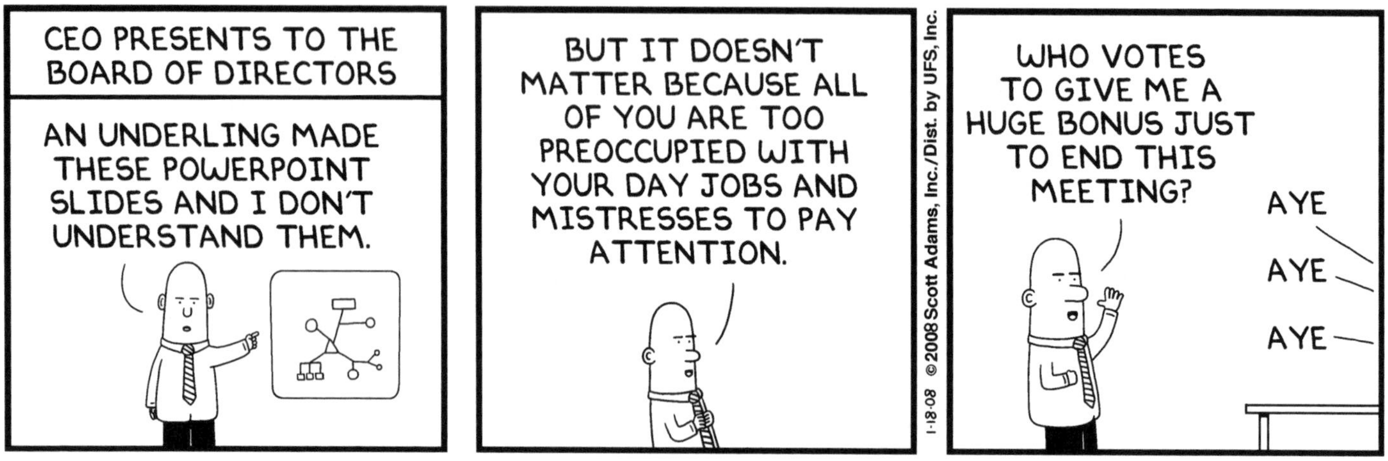
CEO PRESENTS TO THE BOARD OF DIRECTORS
AN UNDERLING MADE THESE POWERPOINT SLIDES AND I DON'T UNDERSTAND THEM.
BUT IT DOESN'T MATTER BECAUSE ALL OF YOU ARE TOO PREOCCUPIED WITH YOUR DAY JOBS AND MISTRESSES TO PAY ATTENTION.
WHO VOTES TO GIVE ME A HUGE BONUS JUST TO END THIS MEETING?
AYE
AYE
AYE
1-18-08 © 2008 Scott Adams, Inc./Dist. by UFS, Inc.

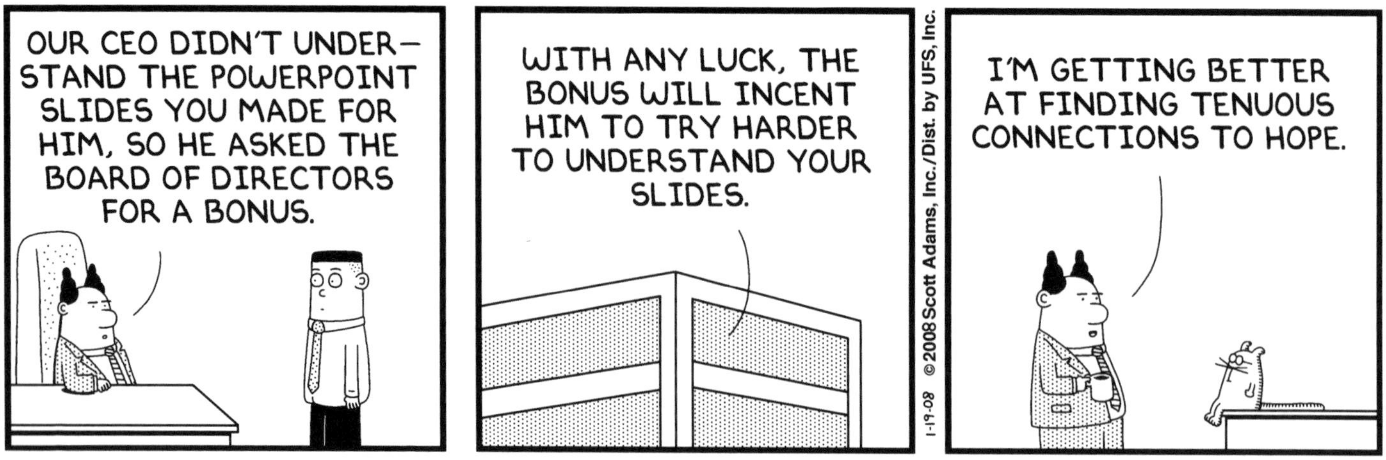
OUR CEO DIDN'T UNDER-STAND THE POWERPOINT SLIDES YOU MADE FOR HIM, SO HE ASKED THE BOARD OF DIRECTORS FOR A BONUS.
WITH ANY LUCK, THE BONUS WILL INCENT HIM TO TRY HARDER TO UNDERSTAND YOUR SLIDES.
I'M GETTING BETTER AT FINDING TENUOUS CONNECTIONS TO HOPE.
1-19-08 © 2008 Scott Adams, Inc./Dist. by UFS, Inc.

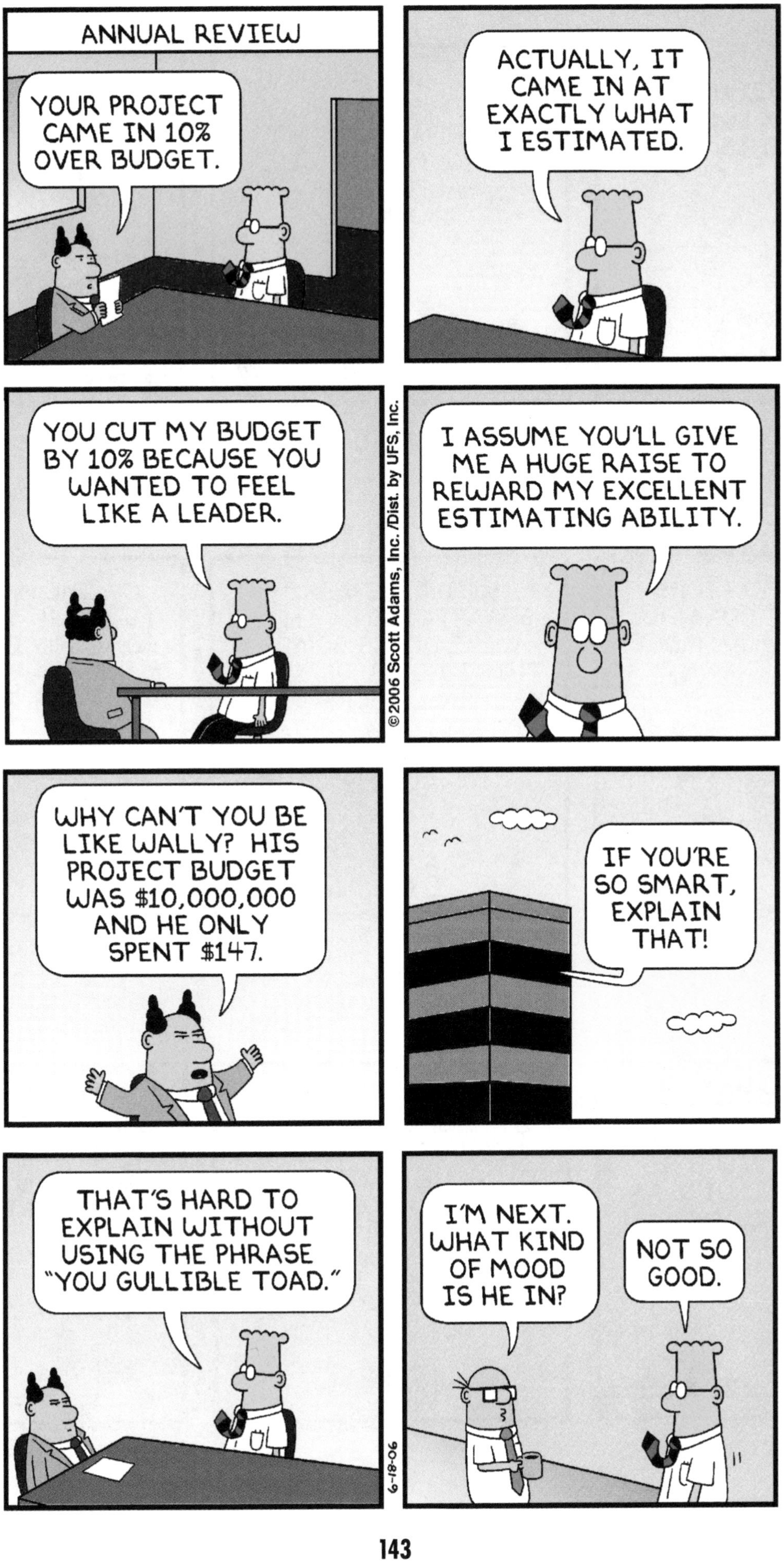
ANNUAL REVIEW
YOUR PROJECT CAME IN 10% OVER BUDGET.
ACTUALLY, IT CAME IN AT EXACTLY WHAT I ESTIMATED.
YOU CUT MY BUDGET BY 10% BECAUSE YOU WANTED TO FEEL LIKE A LEADER.
I ASSUME YOU'LL GIVE ME A HUGE RAISE TO REWARD MY EXCELLENT ESTIMATING ABILITY.
WHY CAN'T YOU BE LIKE WALLY? HIS PROJECT BUDGET WAS $10,000,000 AND HE ONLY SPENT $147.
IF YOU'RE SO SMART, EXPLAIN THAT!
THAT'S HARD TO EXPLAIN WITHOUT USING THE PHRASE "YOU GULLIBLE TOAD."
I'M NEXT. WHAT KIND OF MOOD IS HE IN?
NOT SO GOOD.
©2006 Scott Adams, Inc. /Dist. by UFS, Inc.
6-18-06

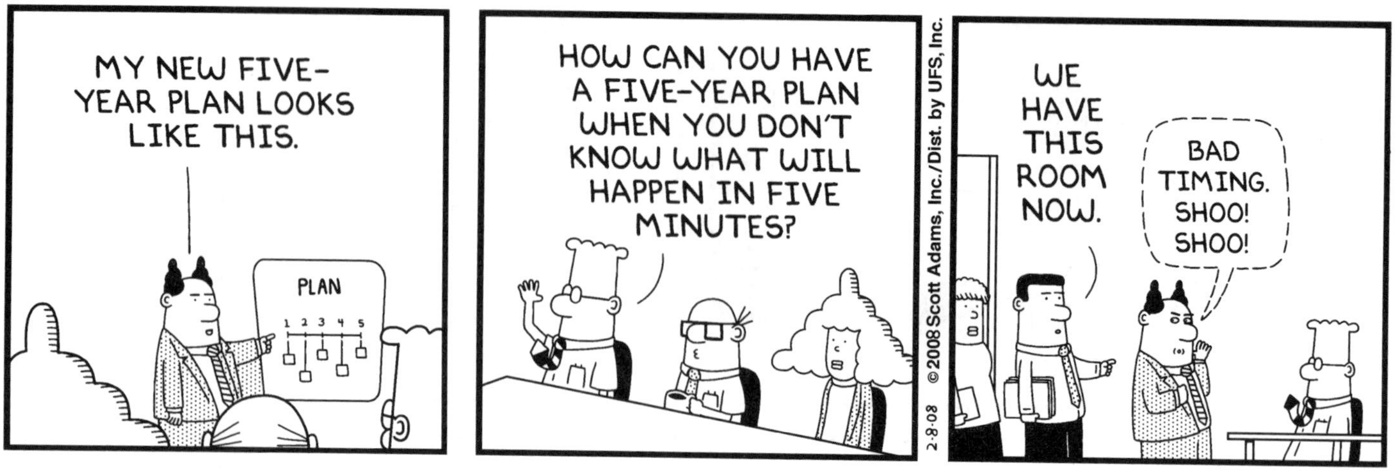
MY NEW FIVE-YEAR PLAN LOOKS LIKE THIS.
PLAN
1 2 3 4 5
HOW CAN YOU HAVE A FIVE-YEAR PLAN WHEN YOU DON'T KNOW WHAT WILL HAPPEN IN FIVE MINUTES?
2-8-08 © 2008 Scott Adams, Inc./Dist. by UFS, Inc.
WE HAVE THIS ROOM NOW.
BAD TIMING. SHOO! SHOO!

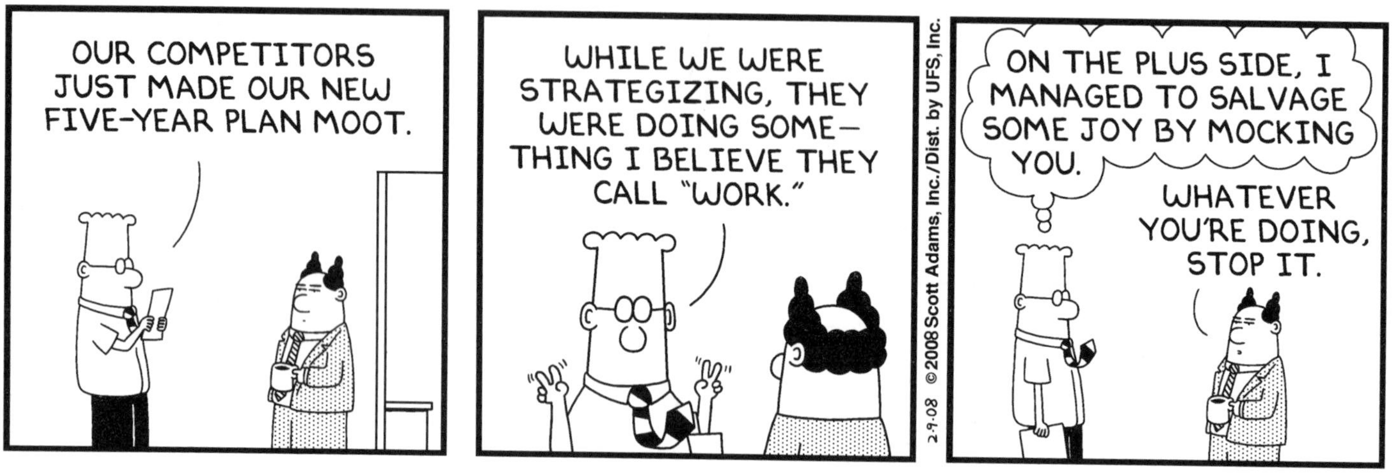
OUR COMPETITORS JUST MADE OUR NEW FIVE-YEAR PLAN MOOT.
WHILE WE WERE STRATEGIZING, THEY WERE DOING SOME-THING I BELIEVE THEY CALL "WORK."
2-9-08 © 2008 Scott Adams, Inc./Dist. by UFS, Inc.
ON THE PLUS SIDE, I MANAGED TO SALVAGE SOME JOY BY MOCKING YOU.
WHATEVER YOU'RE DOING, STOP IT.

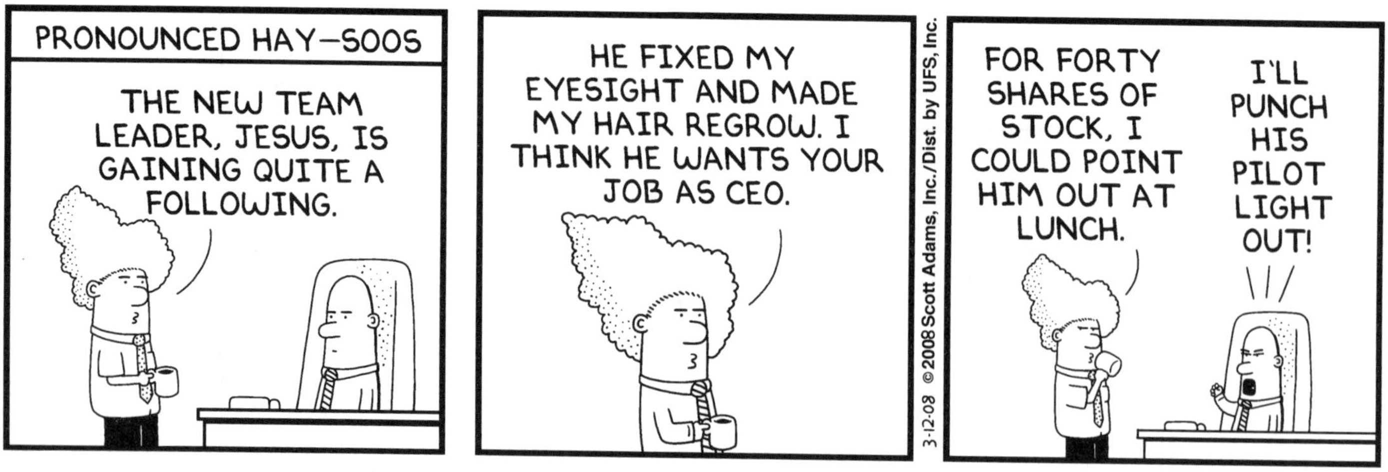
PRONOUNCED HAY-SOOS
THE NEW TEAM LEADER, JESUS, IS GAINING QUITE A FOLLOWING.
HE FIXED MY EYESIGHT AND MADE MY HAIR REGROW. I THINK HE WANTS YOUR JOB AS CEO.
3-12-08 © 2008 Scott Adams, Inc./Dist. by UFS, Inc.
FOR FORTY SHARES OF STOCK, I COULD POINT HIM OUT AT LUNCH.
I'LL PUNCH HIS PILOT LIGHT OUT!

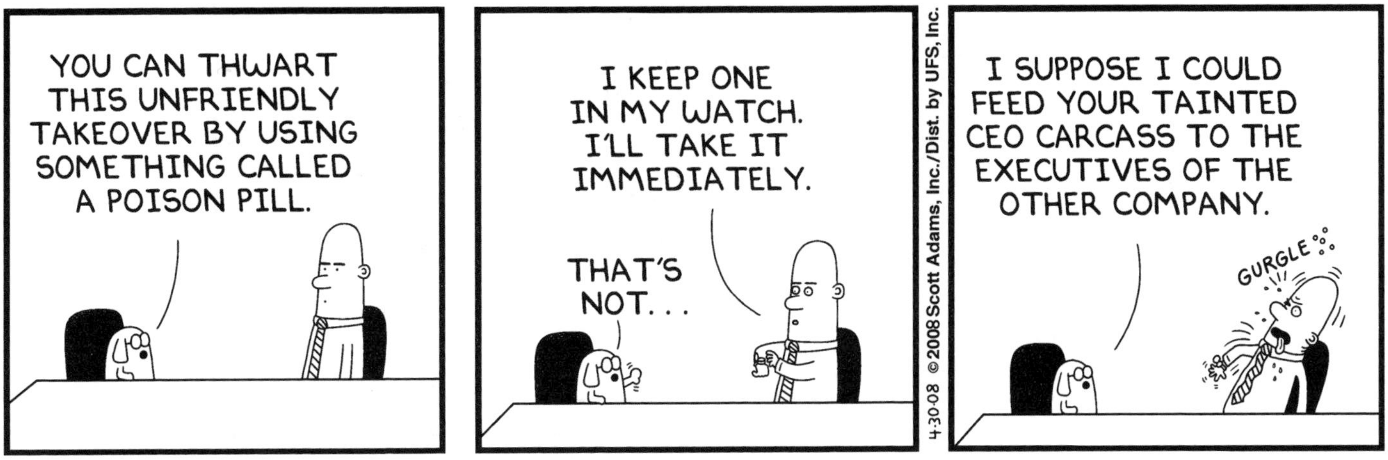
YOU CAN THWART THIS UNFRIENDLY TAKEOVER BY USING SOMETHING CALLED A POISON PILL.
I KEEP ONE IN MY WATCH. I'LL TAKE IT IMMEDIATELY.
THAT'S NOT. . .
4-30-08 ©2008 Scott Adams, Inc./Dist. by UFS, Inc.
I SUPPOSE I COULD FEED YOUR TAINTED CEO CARCASS TO THE EXECUTIVES OF THE OTHER COMPANY.
GURGLE

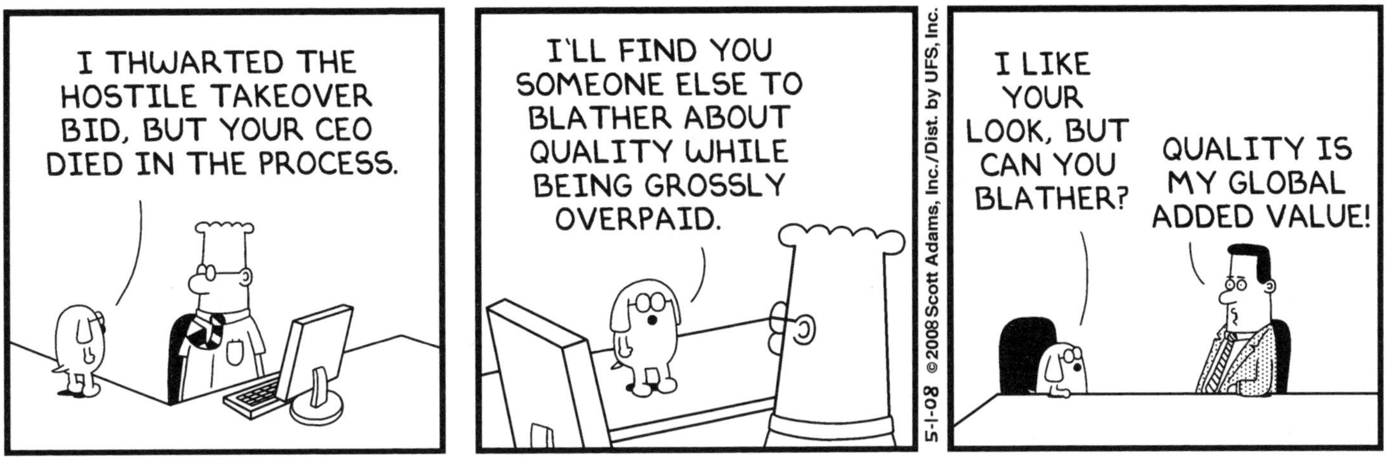
I THWARTED THE HOSTILE TAKEOVER BID, BUT YOUR CEO DIED IN THE PROCESS.
I'LL FIND YOU SOMEONE ELSE TO BLATHER ABOUT QUALITY WHILE BEING GROSSLY OVERPAID.
5-1-08 ©2008 Scott Adams, Inc./Dist. by UFS, Inc.
I LIKE YOUR LOOK, BUT CAN YOU BLATHER?
QUALITY IS MY GLOBAL ADDED VALUE!

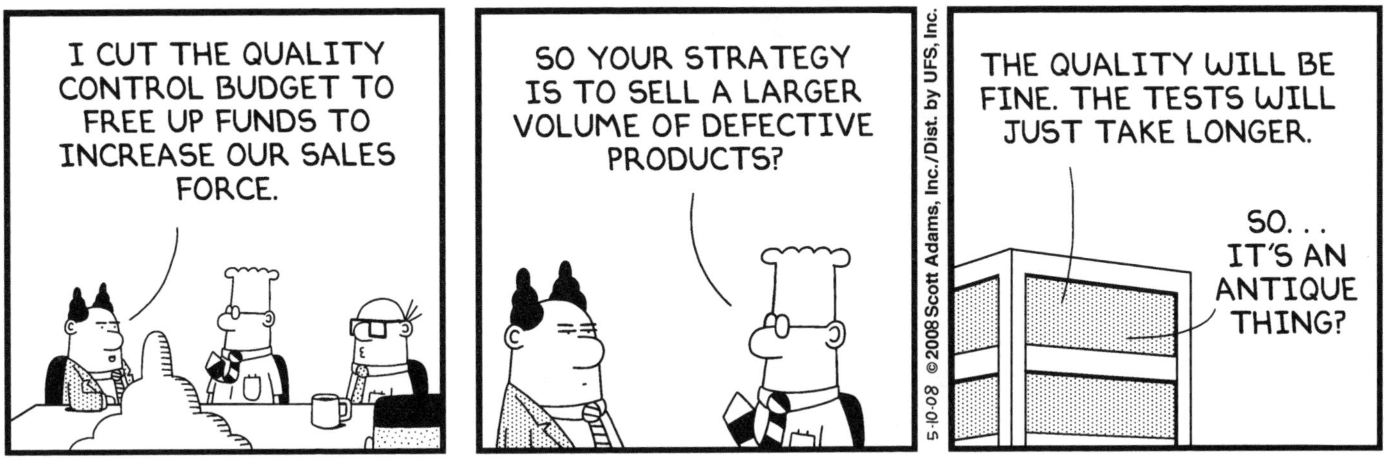
I CUT THE QUALITY CONTROL BUDGET TO FREE UP FUNDS TO INCREASE OUR SALES FORCE.
SO YOUR STRATEGY IS TO SELL A LARGER VOLUME OF DEFECTIVE PRODUCTS?
5-10-08 ©2008 Scott Adams, Inc./Dist. by UFS, Inc.
THE QUALITY WILL BE FINE. THE TESTS WILL JUST TAKE LONGER.
SO. . . IT'S AN ANTIQUE THING?

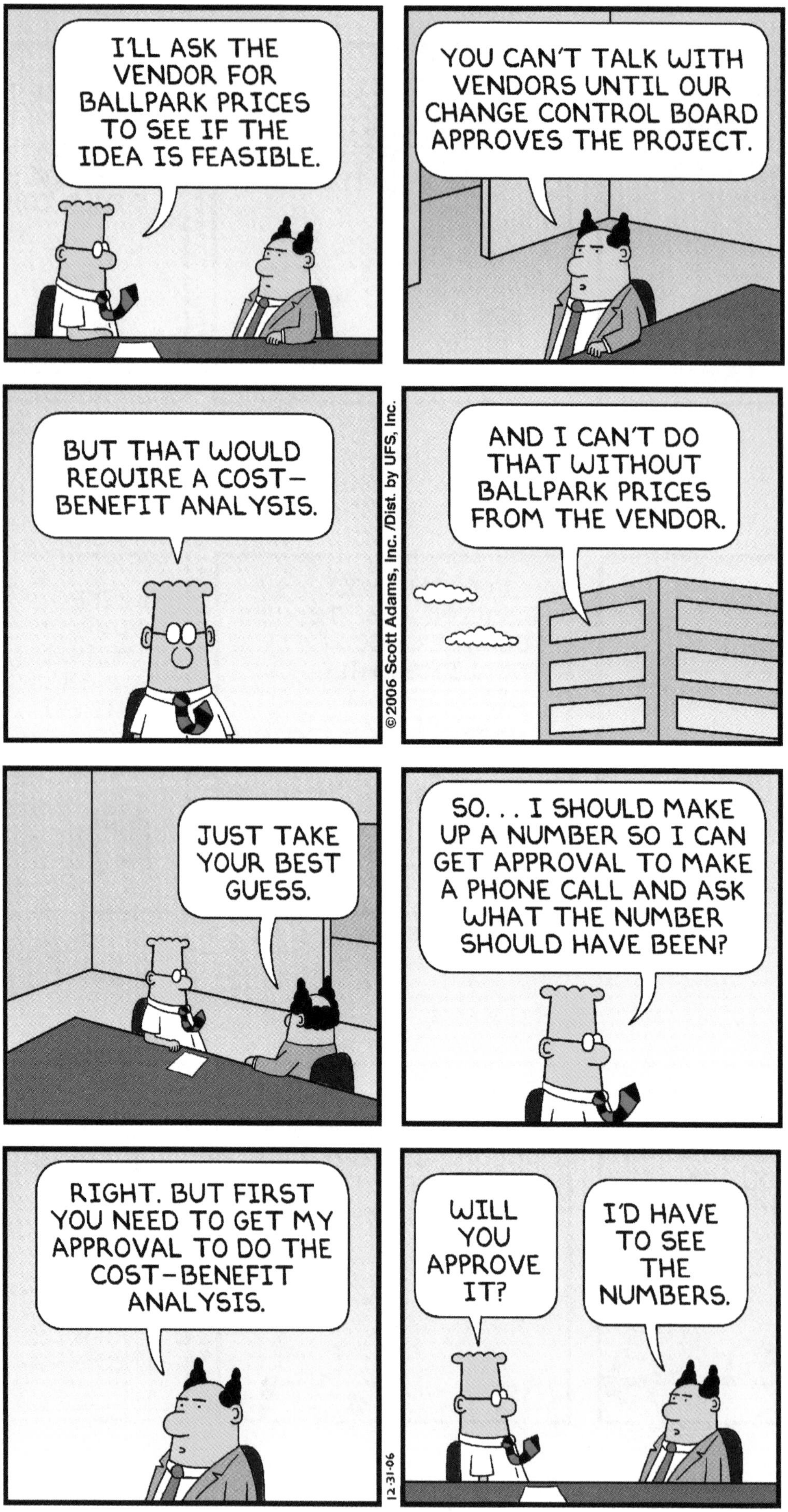
I'LL ASK THE VENDOR FOR BALLPARK PRICES TO SEE IF THE IDEA IS FEASIBLE.
YOU CAN'T TALK WITH VENDORS UNTIL OUR CHANGE CONTROL BOARD APPROVES THE PROJECT.
BUT THAT WOULD REQUIRE A COST–BENEFIT ANALYSIS.
AND I CAN'T DO THAT WITHOUT BALLPARK PRICES FROM THE VENDOR.
JUST TAKE YOUR BEST GUESS.
SO. . . I SHOULD MAKE UP A NUMBER SO I CAN GET APPROVAL TO MAKE A PHONE CALL AND ASK WHAT THE NUMBER SHOULD HAVE BEEN?
RIGHT. BUT FIRST YOU NEED TO GET MY APPROVAL TO DO THE COST–BENEFIT ANALYSIS.
WILL YOU APPROVE IT?
I'D HAVE TO SEE THE NUMBERS.
©2006 Scott Adams, Inc./Dist. by UFS, Inc.
12-31-06

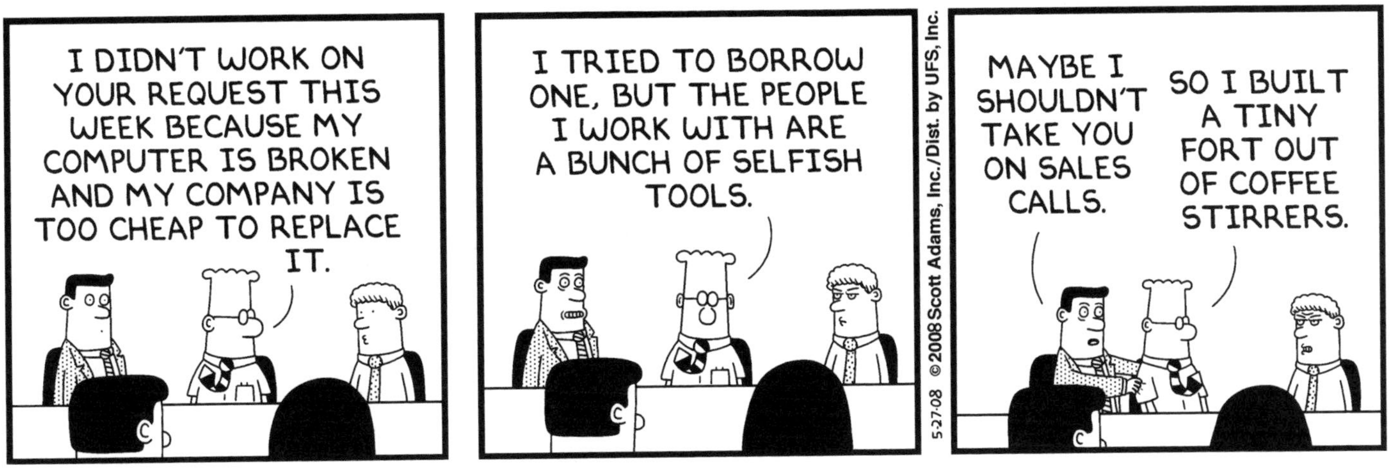
I DIDN'T WORK ON YOUR REQUEST THIS WEEK BECAUSE MY COMPUTER IS BROKEN AND MY COMPANY IS TOO CHEAP TO REPLACE IT.
I TRIED TO BORROW ONE, BUT THE PEOPLE I WORK WITH ARE A BUNCH OF SELFISH TOOLS.
5-27-08 ©2008 Scott Adams, Inc./Dist. by UFS, Inc.
MAYBE I SHOULDN'T TAKE YOU ON SALES CALLS.
SO I BUILT A TINY FORT OUT OF COFFEE STIRRERS.

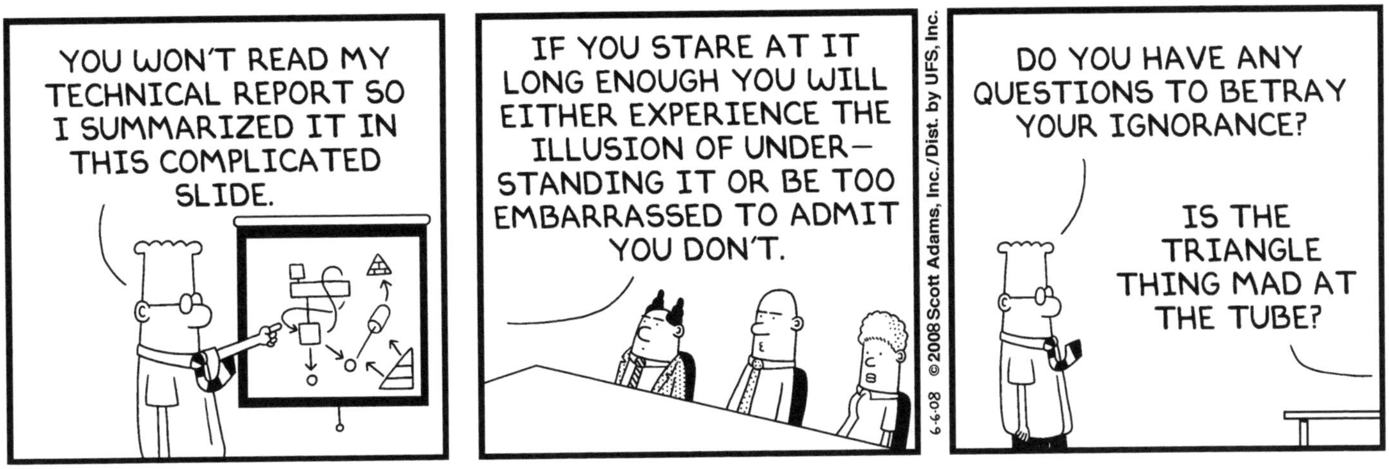
YOU WON'T READ MY TECHNICAL REPORT SO I SUMMARIZED IT IN THIS COMPLICATED SLIDE.
IF YOU STARE AT IT LONG ENOUGH YOU WILL EITHER EXPERIENCE THE ILLUSION OF UNDER-STANDING IT OR BE TOO EMBARRASSED TO ADMIT YOU DON'T.
6-6-08 ©2008 Scott Adams, Inc./Dist. by UFS, Inc.
DO YOU HAVE ANY QUESTIONS TO BETRAY YOUR IGNORANCE?
IS THE TRIANGLE THING MAD AT THE TUBE?

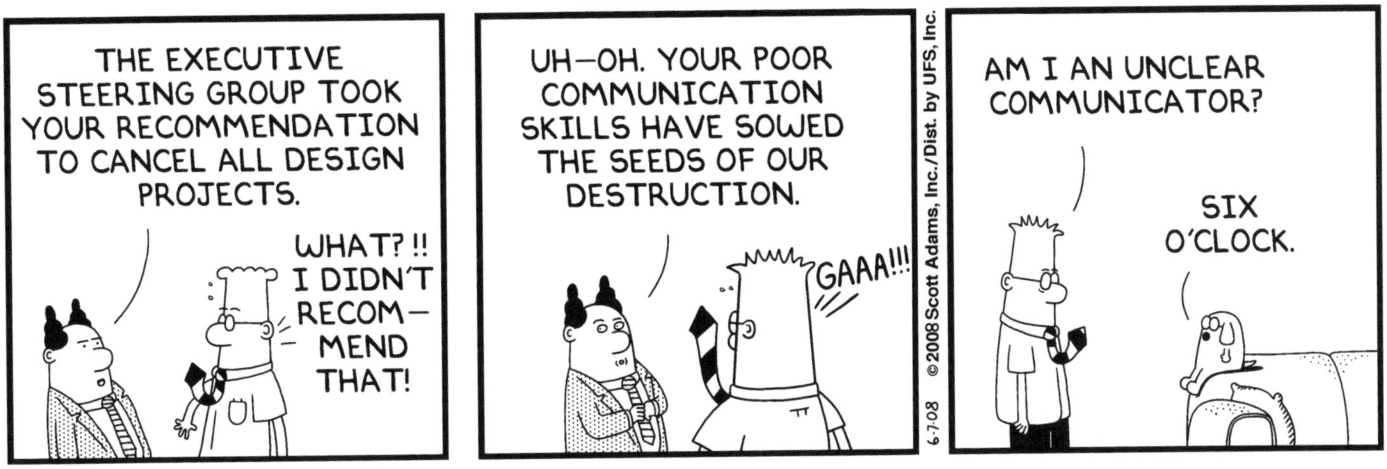
THE EXECUTIVE STEERING GROUP TOOK YOUR RECOMMENDATION TO CANCEL ALL DESIGN PROJECTS.
WHAT? !! I DIDN'T RECOM-MEND THAT!
UH-OH. YOUR POOR COMMUNICATION SKILLS HAVE SOWED THE SEEDS OF OUR DESTRUCTION.
GAAA!!!
6-7-08 ©2008 Scott Adams, Inc./Dist. by UFS, Inc.
AM I AN UNCLEAR COMMUNICATOR?
SIX O'CLOCK.

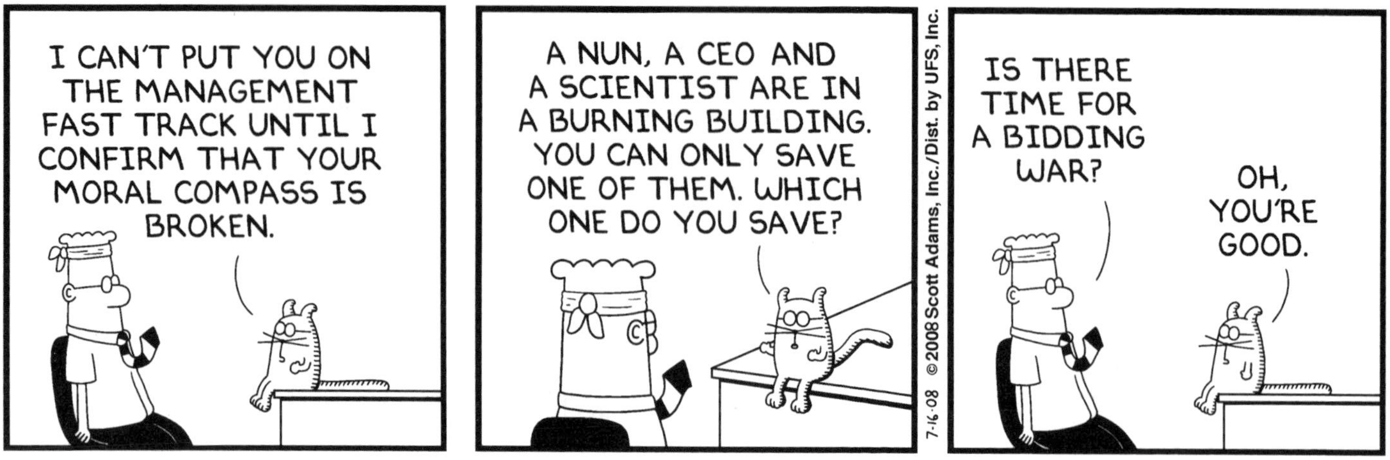
I CAN'T PUT YOU ON THE MANAGEMENT FAST TRACK UNTIL I CONFIRM THAT YOUR MORAL COMPASS IS BROKEN.
A NUN, A CEO AND A SCIENTIST ARE IN A BURNING BUILDING. YOU CAN ONLY SAVE ONE OF THEM. WHICH ONE DO YOU SAVE?
7-16-08 © 2008 Scott Adams, Inc./Dist. by UFS, Inc.
IS THERE TIME FOR A BIDDING WAR?
OH, YOU'RE GOOD.

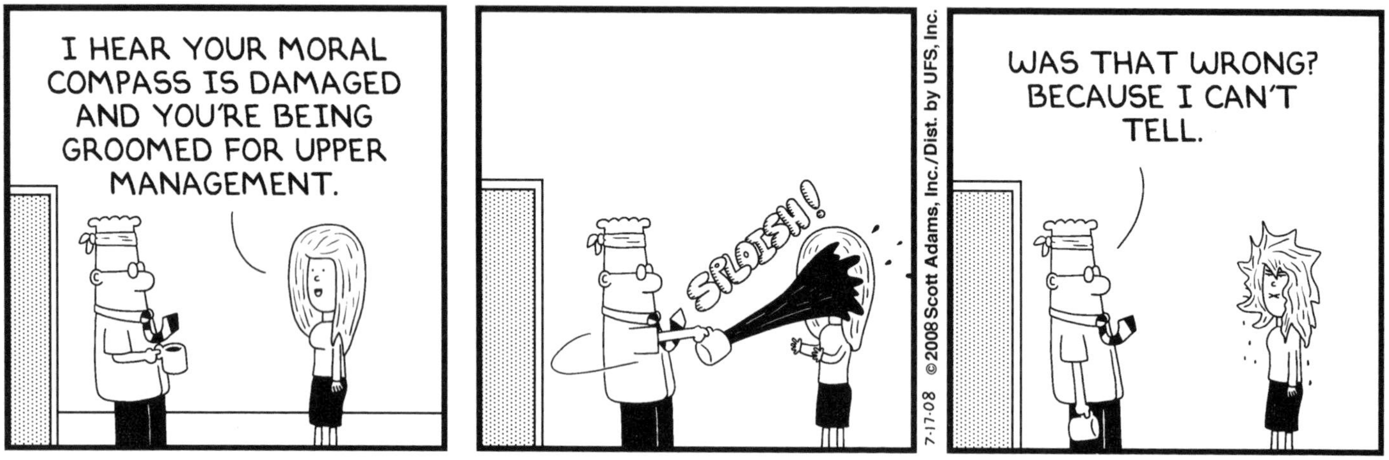
I HEAR YOUR MORAL COMPASS IS DAMAGED AND YOU'RE BEING GROOMED FOR UPPER MANAGEMENT.
SPLOOSH!
7-17-08 © 2008 Scott Adams, Inc./Dist. by UFS, Inc.
WAS THAT WRONG? BECAUSE I CAN'T TELL.

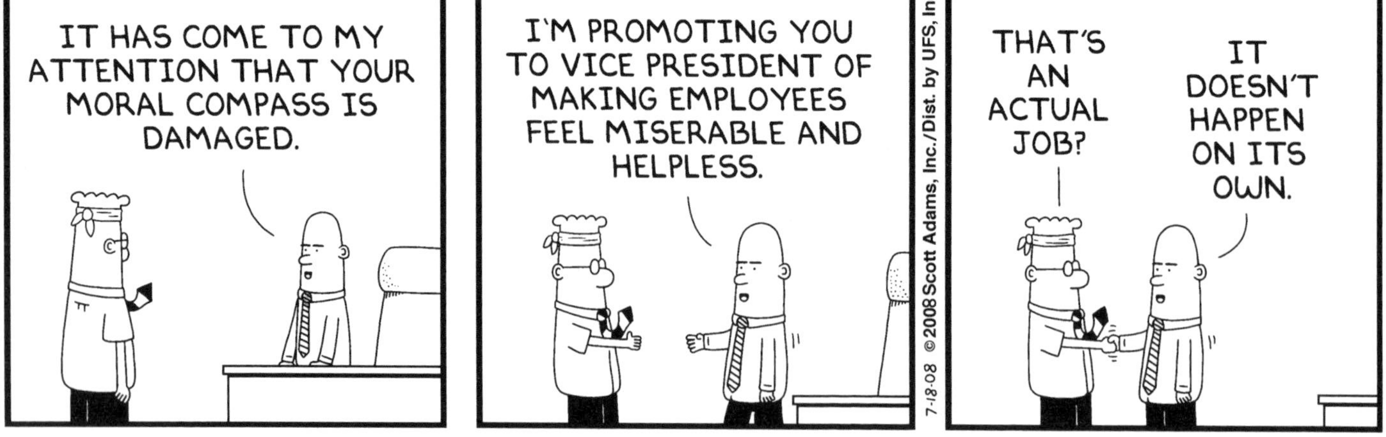
IT HAS COME TO MY ATTENTION THAT YOUR MORAL COMPASS IS DAMAGED.
I'M PROMOTING YOU TO VICE PRESIDENT OF MAKING EMPLOYEES FEEL MISERABLE AND HELPLESS.
7-18-08 © 2008 Scott Adams, Inc./Dist. by UFS, Inc.
THAT'S AN ACTUAL JOB?
IT DOESN'T HAPPEN ON ITS OWN.

DOGBERT THE CEO
I'M NEARING RETIREMENT, SO FIRE THE RESEARCH AND DEVELOPMENT GROUP.
THE COST CUTTING WILL GOOSE MY STOCK OPTIONS SO I CAN CASH OUT BEFORE THE DEATH SPIRAL.
7-28-09 © 2009 Scott Adams, Inc./Dist. by UFS, Inc.
PLEASE DON'T MAKE THE NOISE.
TOO LATE!
CHA-CHING!

DOGBERT THE CEO
GAS UP THE COMPANY JET, FLUNKY. I'M GOING SKIING IN ASPEN.
USING THE CORPORATE JET FOR A VACATION SENDS THE WRONG MESSAGE.
8-15-09 © 2009 Scott Adams, Inc./Dist. by UFS, Inc.
AND YOU CAN'T SKI IN THE SUMMER.
WHAT MESSAGE DO FORTY PLANELOADS OF SNOW SEND?

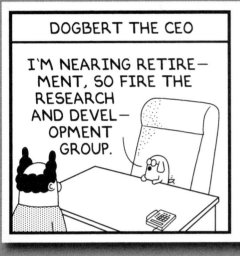

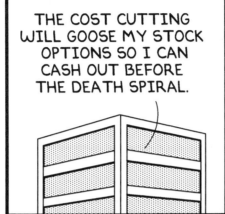

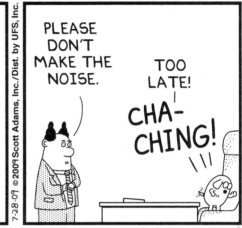

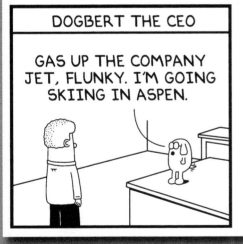

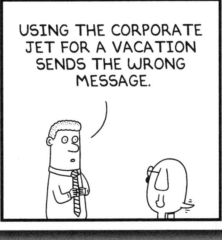

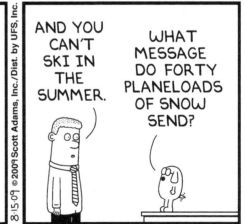

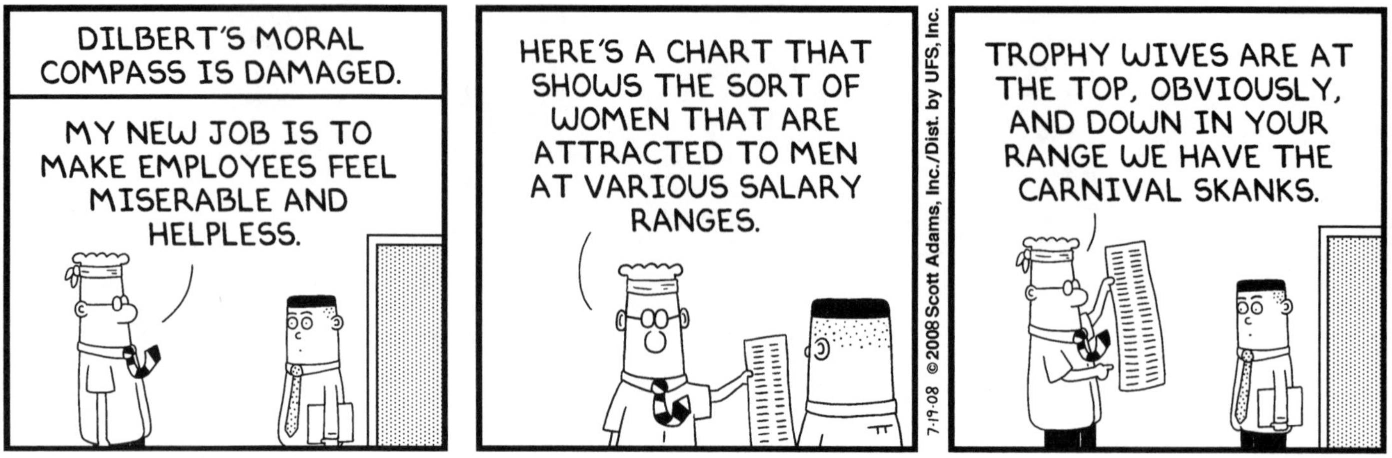
DILBERT'S MORAL COMPASS IS DAMAGED.
MY NEW JOB IS TO MAKE EMPLOYEES FEEL MISERABLE AND HELPLESS.
HERE'S A CHART THAT SHOWS THE SORT OF WOMEN THAT ARE ATTRACTED TO MEN AT VARIOUS SALARY RANGES.
7-19-08 © 2008 Scott Adams, Inc./Dist. by UFS, Inc.
TROPHY WIVES ARE AT THE TOP, OBVIOUSLY, AND DOWN IN YOUR RANGE WE HAVE THE CARNIVAL SKANKS.

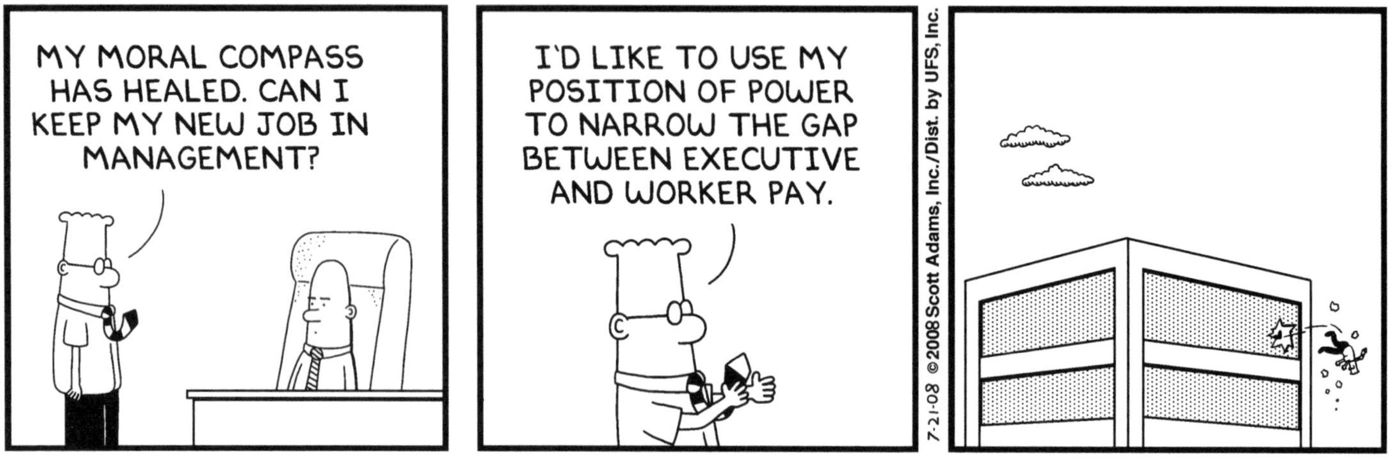
MY MORAL COMPASS HAS HEALED. CAN I KEEP MY NEW JOB IN MANAGEMENT?
I'D LIKE TO USE MY POSITION OF POWER TO NARROW THE GAP BETWEEN EXECUTIVE AND WORKER PAY.
7-21-08 © 2008 Scott Adams, Inc./Dist. by UFS, Inc.

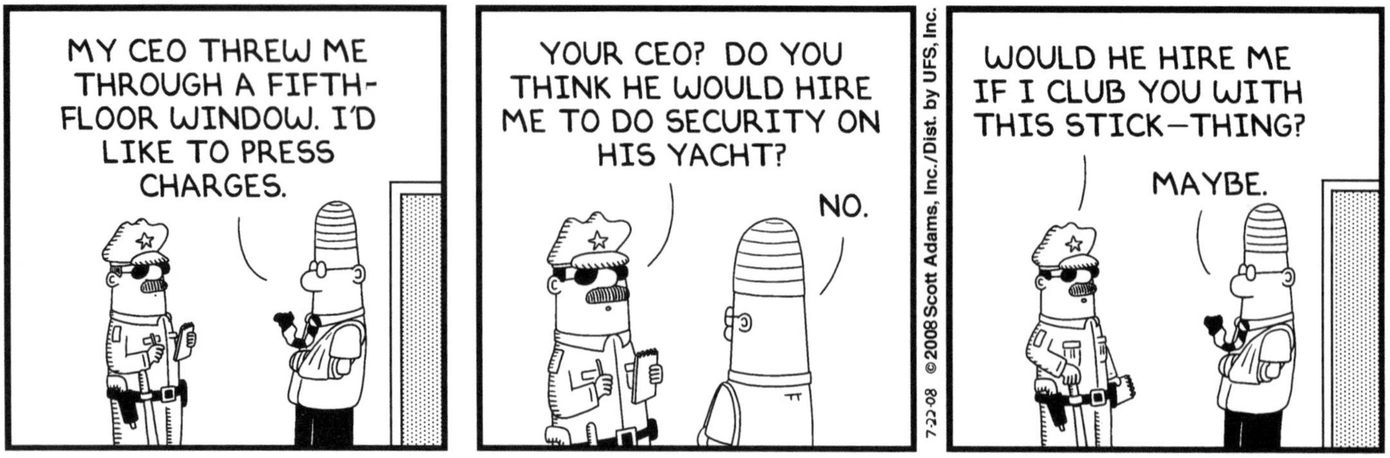
MY CEO THREW ME THROUGH A FIFTH-FLOOR WINDOW. I'D LIKE TO PRESS CHARGES.
YOUR CEO? DO YOU THINK HE WOULD HIRE ME TO DO SECURITY ON HIS YACHT?
NO.
7-22-08 © 2008 Scott Adams, Inc./Dist. by UFS, Inc.
WOULD HE HIRE ME IF I CLUB YOU WITH THIS STICK—THING?
MAYBE.

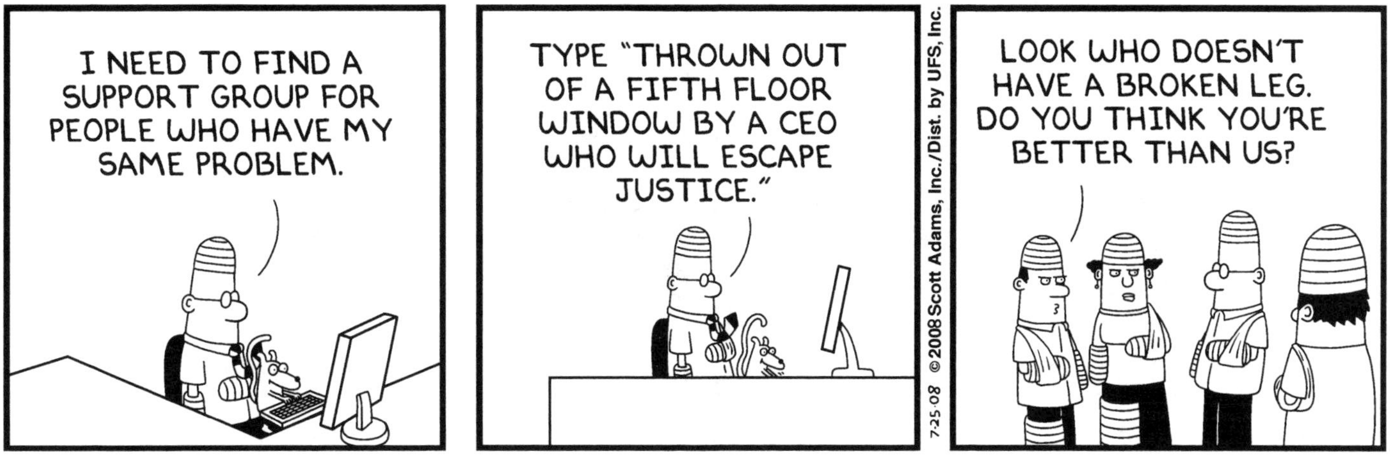
I NEED TO FIND A SUPPORT GROUP FOR PEOPLE WHO HAVE MY SAME PROBLEM.
TYPE "THROWN OUT OF A FIFTH FLOOR WINDOW BY A CEO WHO WILL ESCAPE JUSTICE."
7-25-08 © 2008 Scott Adams, Inc./Dist. by UFS, Inc.
LOOK WHO DOESN'T HAVE A BROKEN LEG. DO YOU THINK YOU'RE BETTER THAN US?

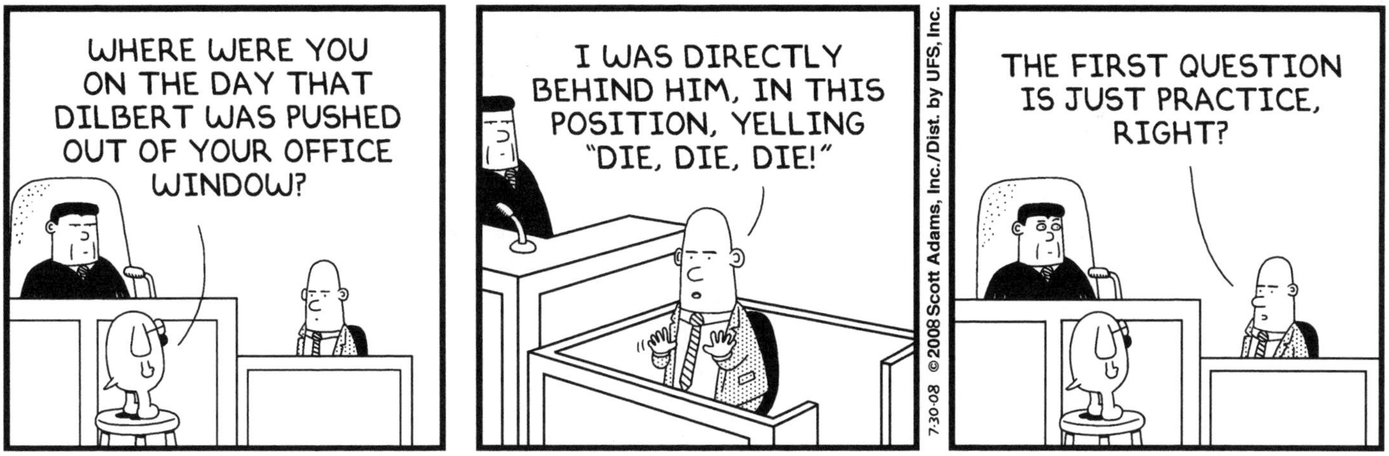
WHERE WERE YOU ON THE DAY THAT DILBERT WAS PUSHED OUT OF YOUR OFFICE WINDOW?
I WAS DIRECTLY BEHIND HIM, IN THIS POSITION, YELLING "DIE, DIE, DIE!"
7-30-08 © 2008 Scott Adams, Inc./Dist. by UFS, Inc.
THE FIRST QUESTION IS JUST PRACTICE, RIGHT?

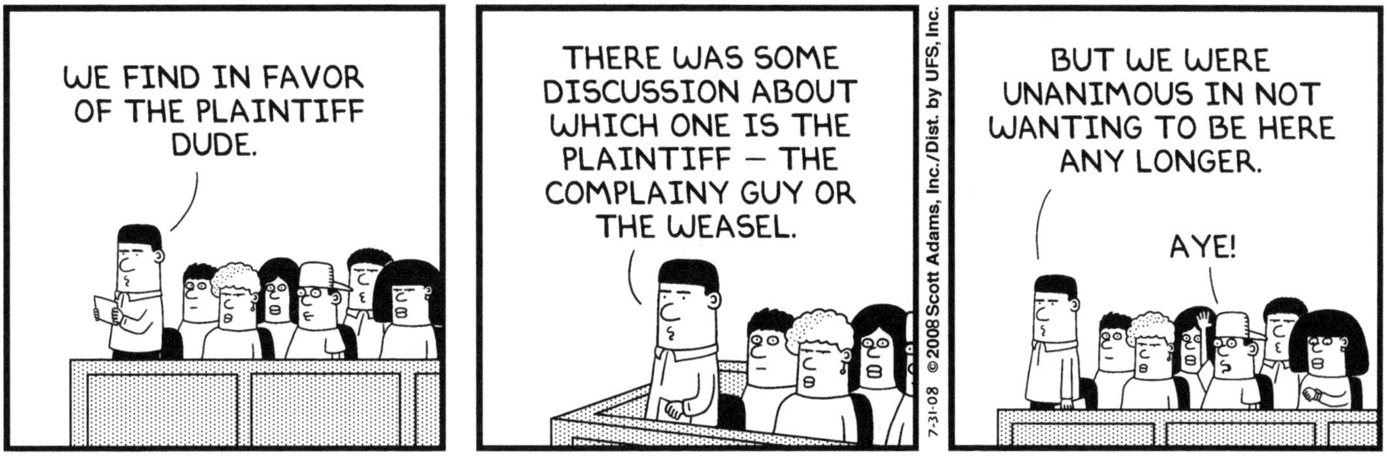
WE FIND IN FAVOR OF THE PLAINTIFF DUDE.
THERE WAS SOME DISCUSSION ABOUT WHICH ONE IS THE PLAINTIFF — THE COMPLAINY GUY OR THE WEASEL.
7-31-08 © 2008 Scott Adams, Inc./Dist. by UFS, Inc.
BUT WE WERE UNANIMOUS IN NOT WANTING TO BE HERE ANY LONGER.
AYE!

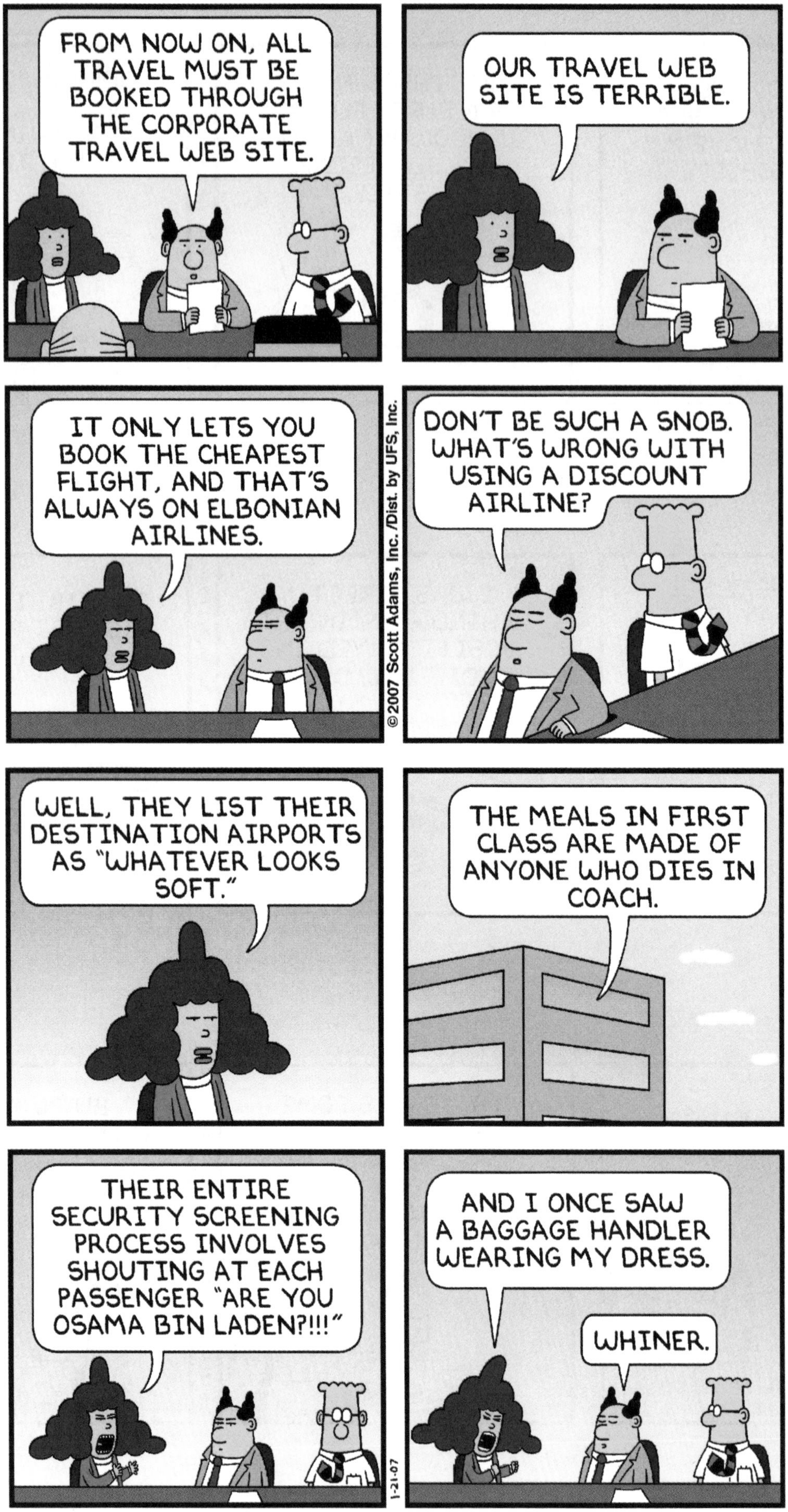
FROM NOW ON, ALL TRAVEL MUST BE BOOKED THROUGH THE CORPORATE TRAVEL WEB SITE.
OUR TRAVEL WEB SITE IS TERRIBLE.
IT ONLY LETS YOU BOOK THE CHEAPEST FLIGHT, AND THAT'S ALWAYS ON ELBONIAN AIRLINES.
DON'T BE SUCH A SNOB. WHAT'S WRONG WITH USING A DISCOUNT AIRLINE?
WELL, THEY LIST THEIR DESTINATION AIRPORTS AS "WHATEVER LOOKS SOFT."
THE MEALS IN FIRST CLASS ARE MADE OF ANYONE WHO DIES IN COACH.
THEIR ENTIRE SECURITY SCREENING PROCESS INVOLVES SHOUTING AT EACH PASSENGER "ARE YOU OSAMA BIN LADEN?!!!"
AND I ONCE SAW A BAGGAGE HANDLER WEARING MY DRESS.
WHINER.
©2007 Scott Adams, Inc./Dist. by UFS, Inc.
1-21-07

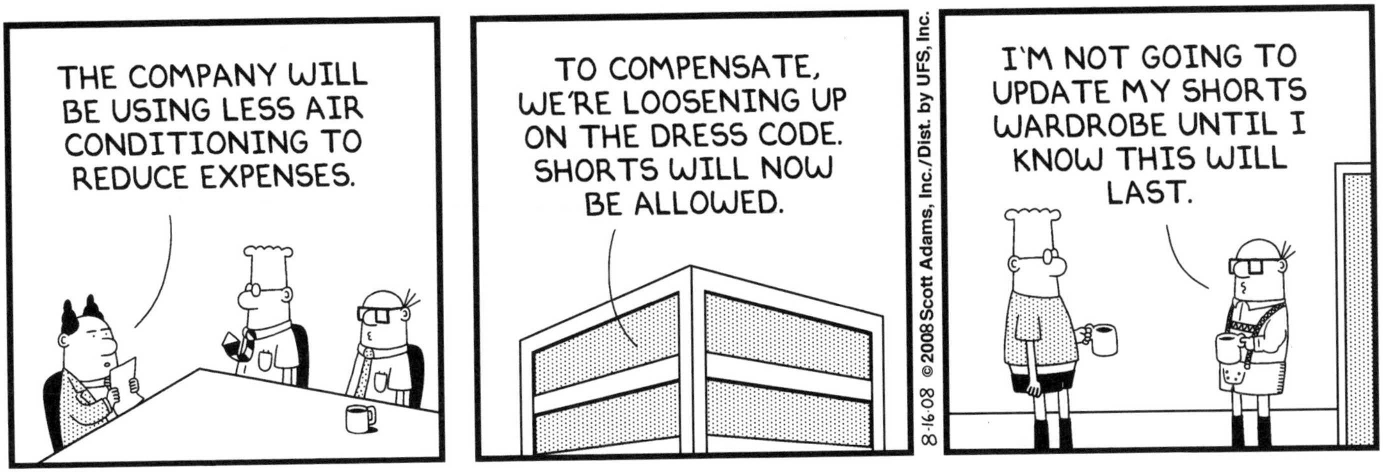
THE COMPANY WILL BE USING LESS AIR CONDITIONING TO REDUCE EXPENSES.
TO COMPENSATE, WE'RE LOOSENING UP ON THE DRESS CODE. SHORTS WILL NOW BE ALLOWED.
8-16-08 ©2008 Scott Adams, Inc./Dist. by UFS, Inc.
I'M NOT GOING TO UPDATE MY SHORTS WARDROBE UNTIL I KNOW THIS WILL LAST.

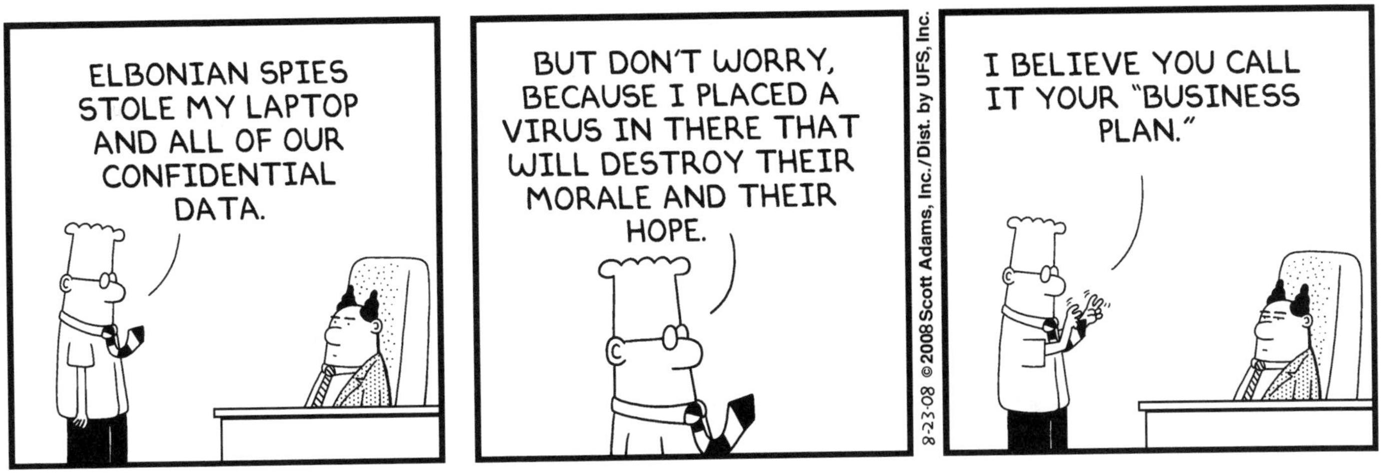
ELBONIAN SPIES STOLE MY LAPTOP AND ALL OF OUR CONFIDENTIAL DATA.
BUT DON'T WORRY, BECAUSE I PLACED A VIRUS IN THERE THAT WILL DESTROY THEIR MORALE AND THEIR HOPE.
8-23-08 ©2008 Scott Adams, Inc./Dist. by UFS, Inc.
I BELIEVE YOU CALL IT YOUR "BUSINESS PLAN."

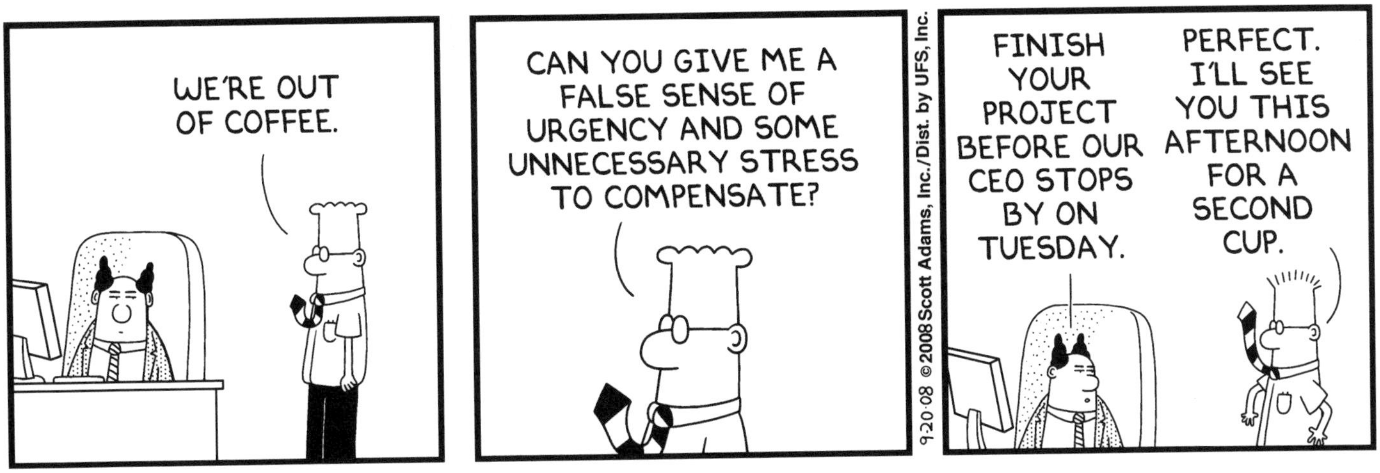
WE'RE OUT OF COFFEE.
CAN YOU GIVE ME A FALSE SENSE OF URGENCY AND SOME UNNECESSARY STRESS TO COMPENSATE?
9-20-08 ©2008 Scott Adams, Inc./Dist. by UFS, Inc.
FINISH YOUR PROJECT BEFORE OUR CEO STOPS BY ON TUESDAY.
PERFECT. I'LL SEE YOU THIS AFTERNOON FOR A SECOND CUP.

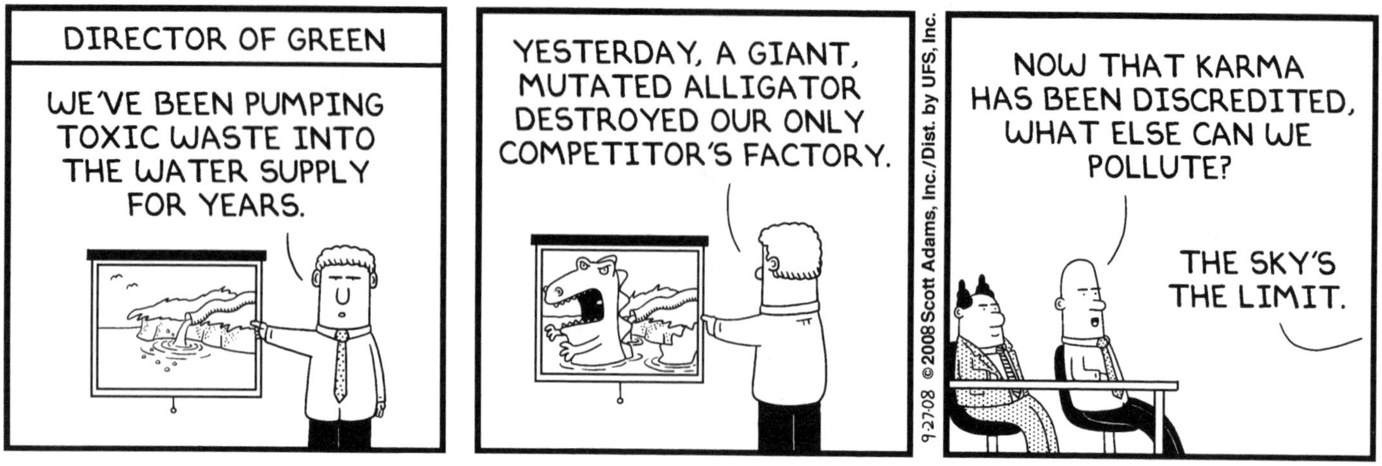
DIRECTOR OF GREEN
WE'VE BEEN PUMPING TOXIC WASTE INTO THE WATER SUPPLY FOR YEARS.
YESTERDAY, A GIANT, MUTATED ALLIGATOR DESTROYED OUR ONLY COMPETITOR'S FACTORY.
9-27-08 © 2008 Scott Adams, Inc./Dist. by UFS, Inc.
NOW THAT KARMA HAS BEEN DISCREDITED, WHAT ELSE CAN WE POLLUTE?
THE SKY'S THE LIMIT.

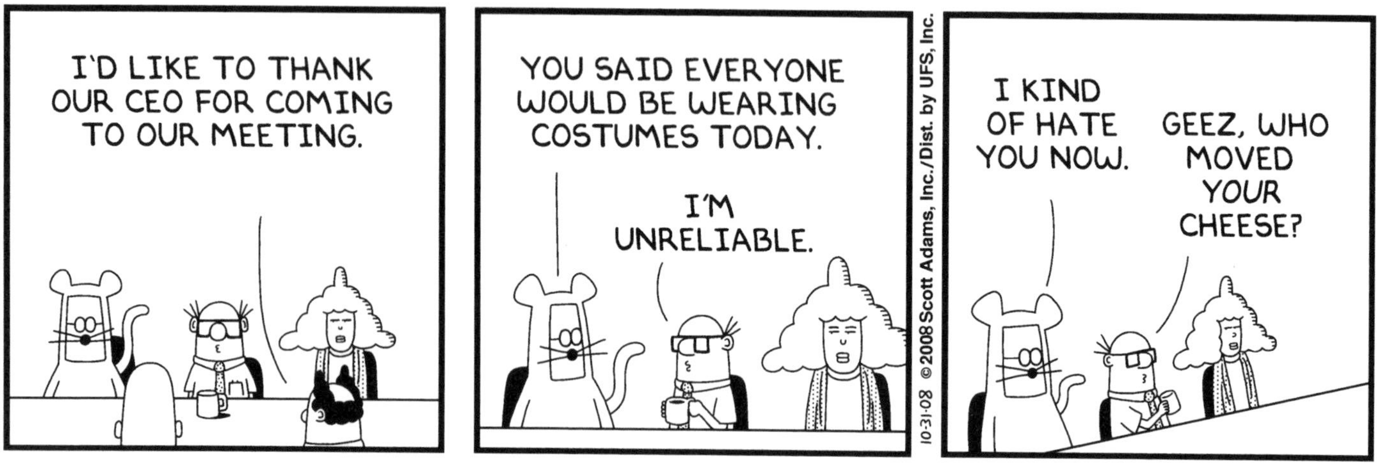
I'D LIKE TO THANK OUR CEO FOR COMING TO OUR MEETING.
YOU SAID EVERYONE WOULD BE WEARING COSTUMES TODAY.
I'M UNRELIABLE.
10-31-08 © 2008 Scott Adams, Inc./Dist. by UFS, Inc.
I KIND OF HATE YOU NOW.
GEEZ, WHO MOVED *YOUR* CHEESE?

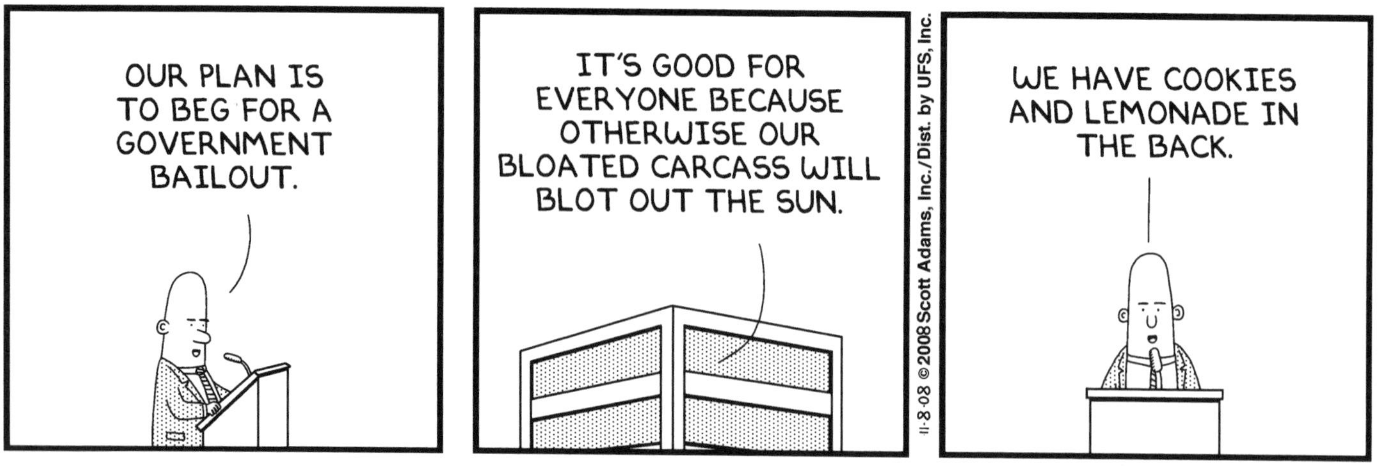
OUR PLAN IS TO BEG FOR A GOVERNMENT BAILOUT.
IT'S GOOD FOR EVERYONE BECAUSE OTHERWISE OUR BLOATED CARCASS WILL BLOT OUT THE SUN.
11-8-08 © 2008 Scott Adams, Inc./Dist. by UFS, Inc.
WE HAVE COOKIES AND LEMONADE IN THE BACK.

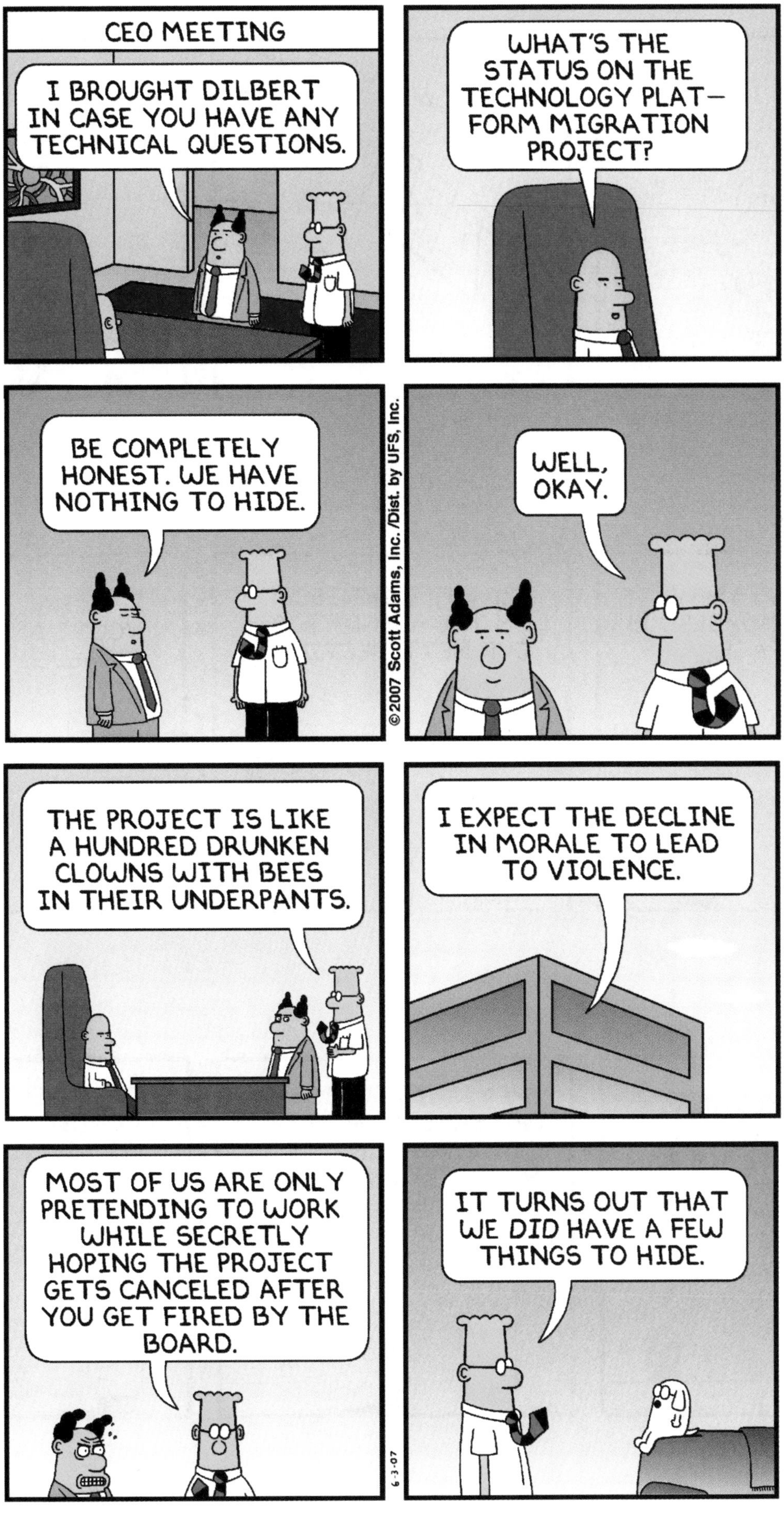
CEO MEETING
I BROUGHT DILBERT IN CASE YOU HAVE ANY TECHNICAL QUESTIONS.
WHAT'S THE STATUS ON THE TECHNOLOGY PLAT-FORM MIGRATION PROJECT?
BE COMPLETELY HONEST. WE HAVE NOTHING TO HIDE.
©2007 Scott Adams, Inc. /Dist. by UFS, Inc.
WELL, OKAY.
THE PROJECT IS LIKE A HUNDRED DRUNKEN CLOWNS WITH BEES IN THEIR UNDERPANTS.
I EXPECT THE DECLINE IN MORALE TO LEAD TO VIOLENCE.
MOST OF US ARE ONLY PRETENDING TO WORK WHILE SECRETLY HOPING THE PROJECT GETS CANCELED AFTER YOU GET FIRED BY THE BOARD.
6-3-07
IT TURNS OUT THAT WE *DID* HAVE A FEW THINGS TO HIDE.

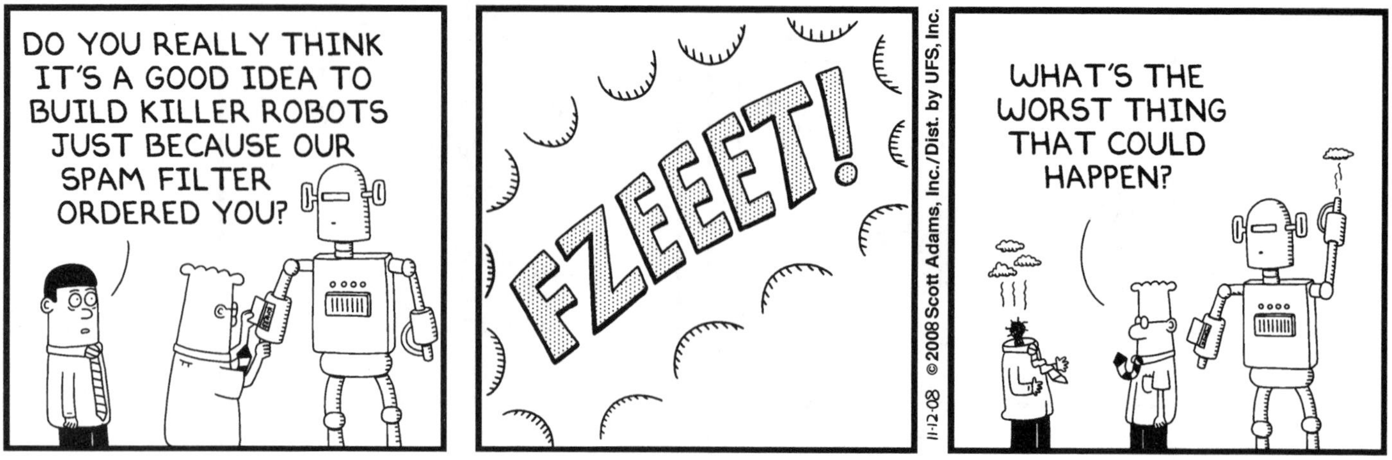
DO YOU REALLY THINK IT'S A GOOD IDEA TO BUILD KILLER ROBOTS JUST BECAUSE OUR SPAM FILTER ORDERED YOU?
FZEEET!
11-12-08 ©2008 Scott Adams, Inc./Dist. by UFS, Inc.
WHAT'S THE WORST THING THAT COULD HAPPEN?

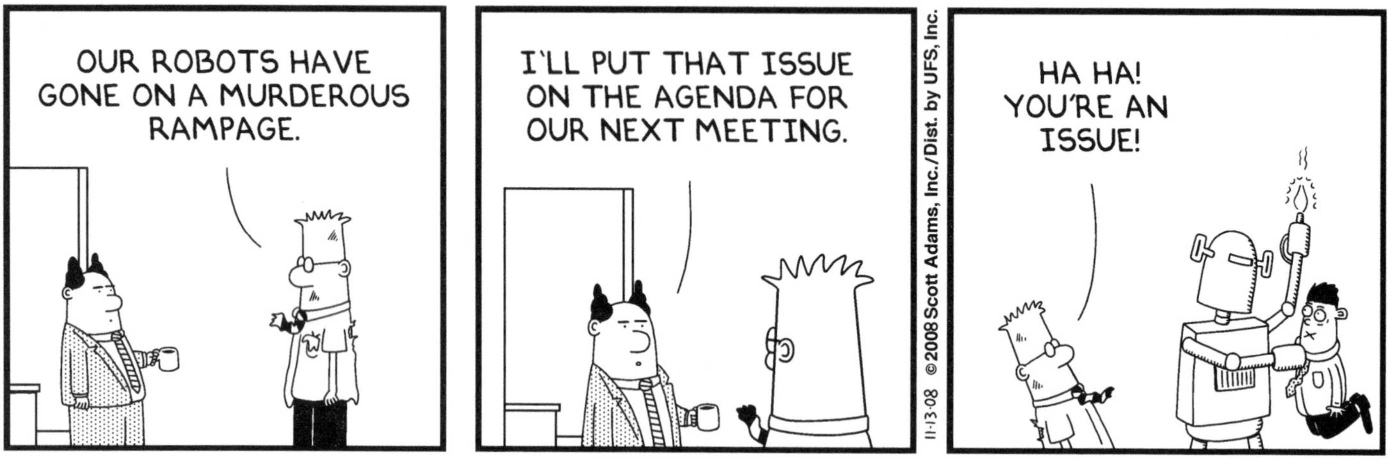
OUR ROBOTS HAVE GONE ON A MURDEROUS RAMPAGE.
I'LL PUT THAT ISSUE ON THE AGENDA FOR OUR NEXT MEETING.
11-13-08 ©2008 Scott Adams, Inc./Dist. by UFS, Inc.
HA HA! YOU'RE AN ISSUE!

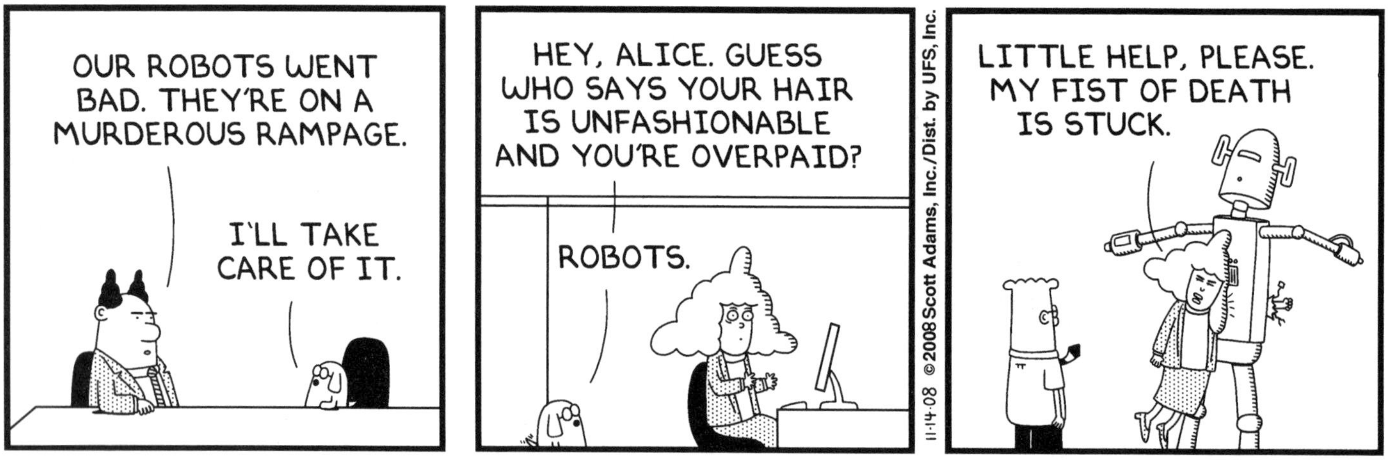
OUR ROBOTS WENT BAD. THEY'RE ON A MURDEROUS RAMPAGE.
I'LL TAKE CARE OF IT.
HEY, ALICE. GUESS WHO SAYS YOUR HAIR IS UNFASHIONABLE AND YOU'RE OVERPAID?
ROBOTS.
11-14-08 ©2008 Scott Adams, Inc./Dist. by UFS, Inc.
LITTLE HELP, PLEASE. MY FIST OF DEATH IS STUCK.

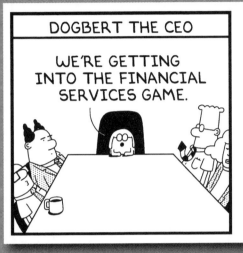

DOGBERT THE CEO
WE'RE GETTING INTO THE FINANCIAL SERVICES GAME.
THAT WAY ALL OF OUR PRODUCTS CAN BE IMAGINARY.
CAN YOU GIVE ME RELIABLE INVEST-MENT ADVICE?
YES, AS FAR AS YOU KNOW.
8-21-09 © 2009 Scott Adams, Inc./Dist. by UFS, Inc.

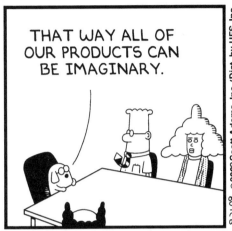

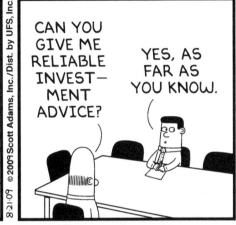

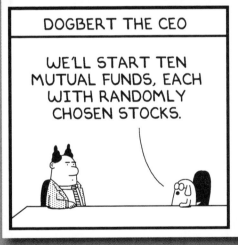

DOGBERT THE CEO
WE'LL START TEN MUTUAL FUNDS, EACH WITH RANDOMLY CHOSEN STOCKS.
LATER WE'LL BUILD OUR ADVERTISEMENTS AROUND WHICHEVER ONE DOES THE BEST PURELY BY CHANCE.
MY GOAL IS TO BE THE PREMIER PROVIDER OF IMAGINARY EXPERTISE.
WAG! WAG!
8-22-09 © 2009 Scott Adams, Inc./Dist. by UFS, Inc.

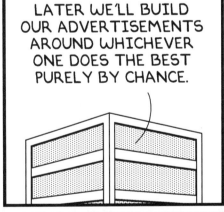

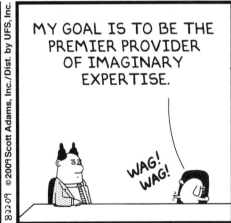

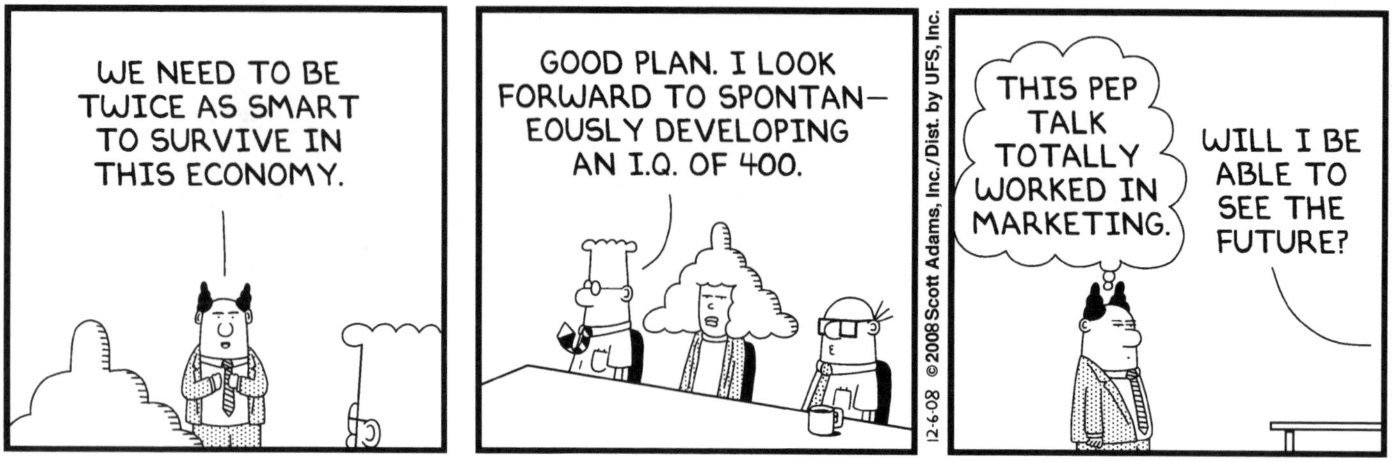
WE NEED TO BE TWICE AS SMART TO SURVIVE IN THIS ECONOMY.
GOOD PLAN. I LOOK FORWARD TO SPONTANEOUSLY DEVELOPING AN I.Q. OF 400.
12-6-08 ©2008 Scott Adams, Inc./Dist. by UFS, Inc.
THIS PEP TALK TOTALLY WORKED IN MARKETING.
WILL I BE ABLE TO SEE THE FUTURE?

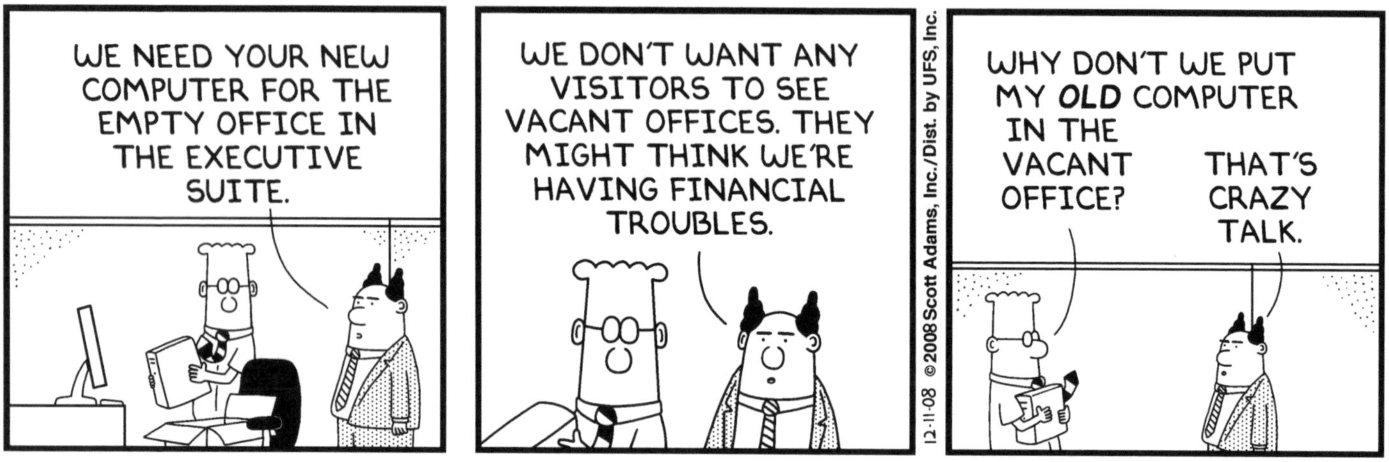
WE NEED YOUR NEW COMPUTER FOR THE EMPTY OFFICE IN THE EXECUTIVE SUITE.
WE DON'T WANT ANY VISITORS TO SEE VACANT OFFICES. THEY MIGHT THINK WE'RE HAVING FINANCIAL TROUBLES.
12-11-08 ©2008 Scott Adams, Inc./Dist. by UFS, Inc.
WHY DON'T WE PUT MY OLD COMPUTER IN THE VACANT OFFICE?
THAT'S CRAZY TALK.

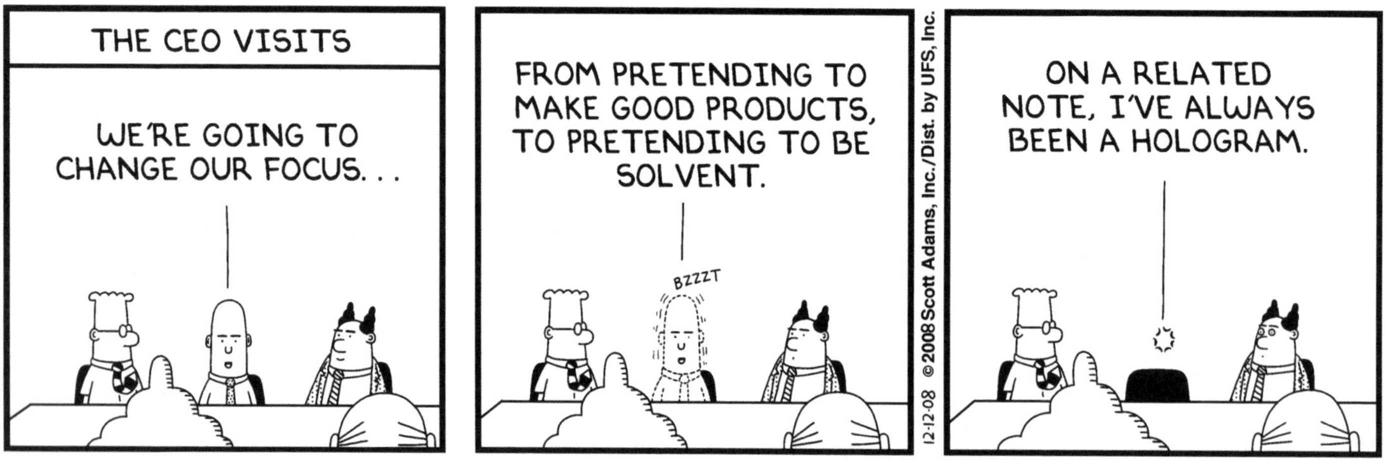
THE CEO VISITS
WE'RE GOING TO CHANGE OUR FOCUS. . .
FROM PRETENDING TO MAKE GOOD PRODUCTS, TO PRETENDING TO BE SOLVENT.
BZZZT
12-12-08 ©2008 Scott Adams, Inc./Dist. by UFS, Inc.
ON A RELATED NOTE, I'VE ALWAYS BEEN A HOLOGRAM.

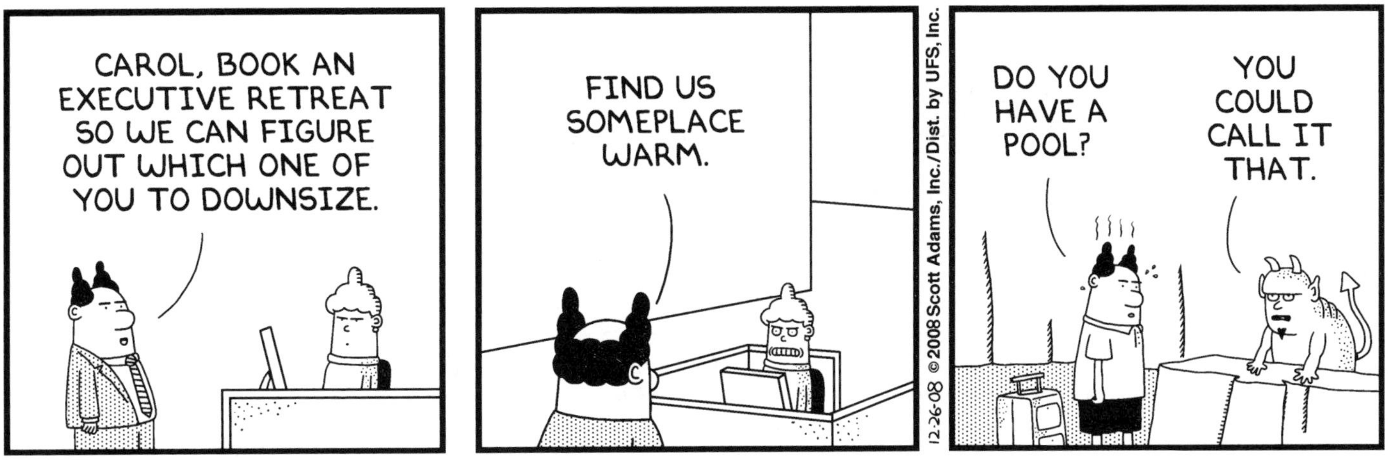
CAROL, BOOK AN EXECUTIVE RETREAT SO WE CAN FIGURE OUT WHICH ONE OF YOU TO DOWNSIZE.
FIND US SOMEPLACE WARM.
12-26-08 © 2008 Scott Adams, Inc./Dist. by UFS, Inc.
DO YOU HAVE A POOL?
YOU COULD CALL IT THAT.

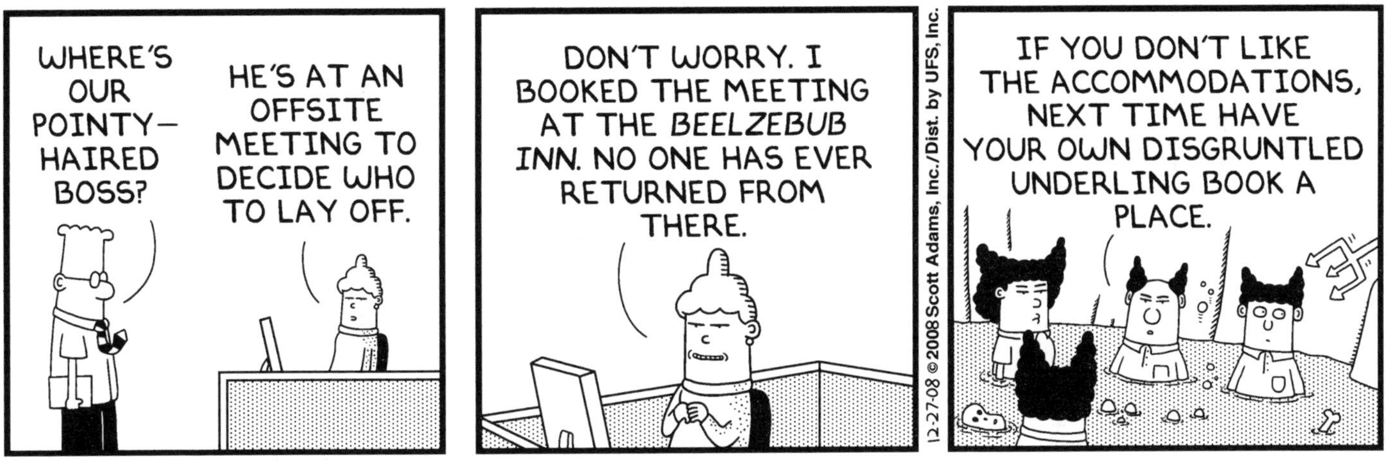
WHERE'S OUR POINTY-HAIRED BOSS?
HE'S AT AN OFFSITE MEETING TO DECIDE WHO TO LAY OFF.
DON'T WORRY. I BOOKED THE MEETING AT THE *BEELZEBUB INN*. NO ONE HAS EVER RETURNED FROM THERE.
12-27-08 © 2008 Scott Adams, Inc./Dist. by UFS, Inc.
IF YOU DON'T LIKE THE ACCOMMODATIONS, NEXT TIME HAVE YOUR OWN DISGRUNTLED UNDERLING BOOK A PLACE.

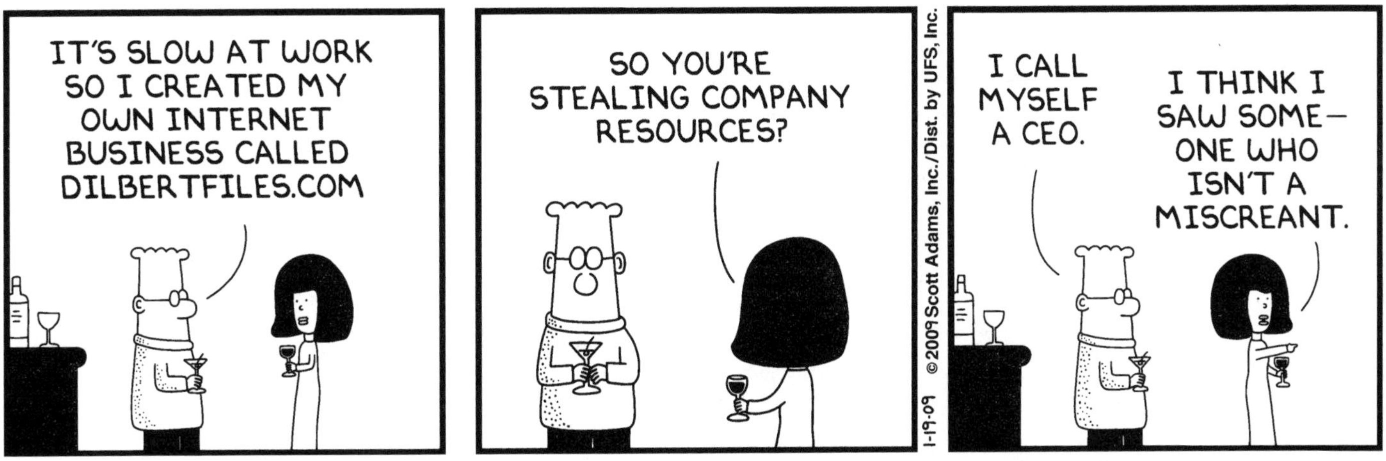
IT'S SLOW AT WORK SO I CREATED MY OWN INTERNET BUSINESS CALLED DILBERTFILES.COM
SO YOU'RE STEALING COMPANY RESOURCES?
1-19-09 © 2009 Scott Adams, Inc./Dist. by UFS, Inc.
I CALL MYSELF A CEO.
I THINK I SAW SOME-ONE WHO ISN'T A MISCREANT.

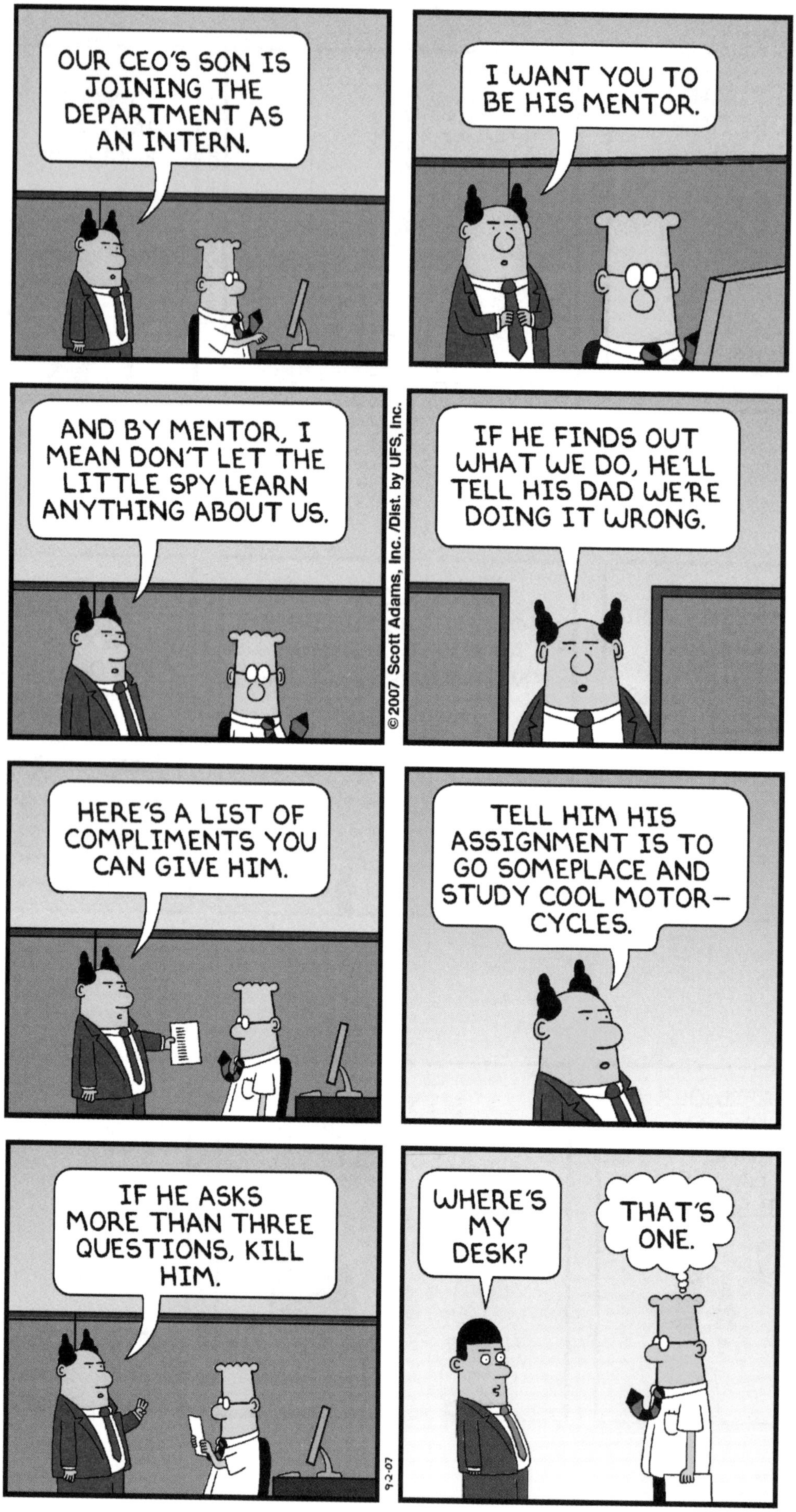
OUR CEO'S SON IS JOINING THE DEPARTMENT AS AN INTERN.
I WANT YOU TO BE HIS MENTOR.
AND BY MENTOR, I MEAN DON'T LET THE LITTLE SPY LEARN ANYTHING ABOUT US.
©2007 Scott Adams, Inc. /Dist. by UFS, Inc.
IF HE FINDS OUT WHAT WE DO, HE'LL TELL HIS DAD WE'RE DOING IT WRONG.
HERE'S A LIST OF COMPLIMENTS YOU CAN GIVE HIM.
TELL HIM HIS ASSIGNMENT IS TO GO SOMEPLACE AND STUDY COOL MOTOR-CYCLES.
IF HE ASKS MORE THAN THREE QUESTIONS, KILL HIM.
9-2-07
WHERE'S MY DESK?
THAT'S ONE.

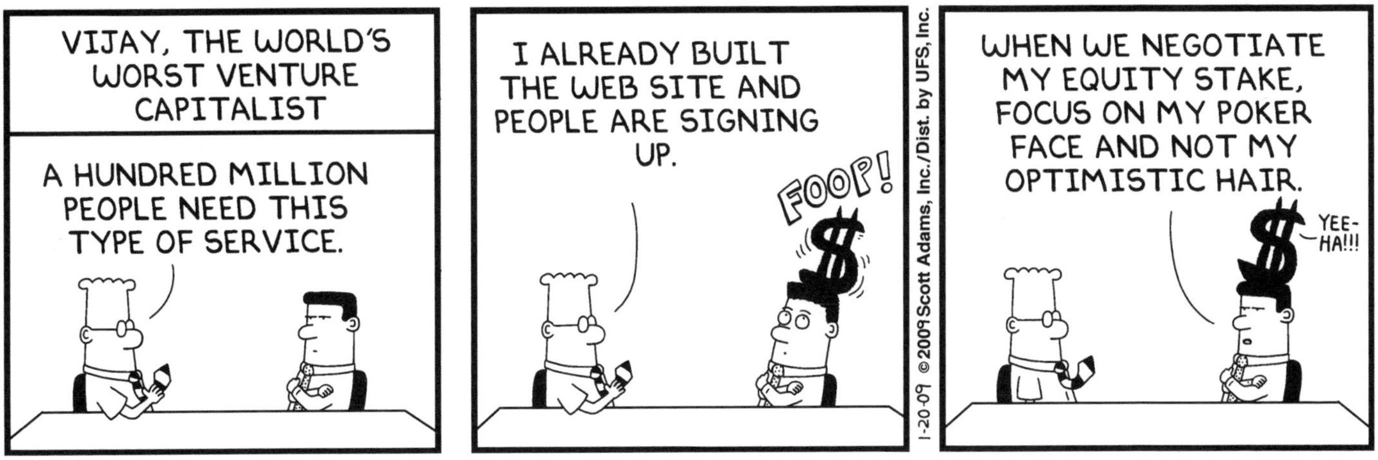
VIJAY, THE WORLD'S WORST VENTURE CAPITALIST
A HUNDRED MILLION PEOPLE NEED THIS TYPE OF SERVICE.
I ALREADY BUILT THE WEB SITE AND PEOPLE ARE SIGNING UP.
FOOP!
1-20-09 © 2009 Scott Adams, Inc./Dist. by UFS, Inc.
WHEN WE NEGOTIATE MY EQUITY STAKE, FOCUS ON MY POKER FACE AND NOT MY OPTIMISTIC HAIR.
YEE-HA!!!

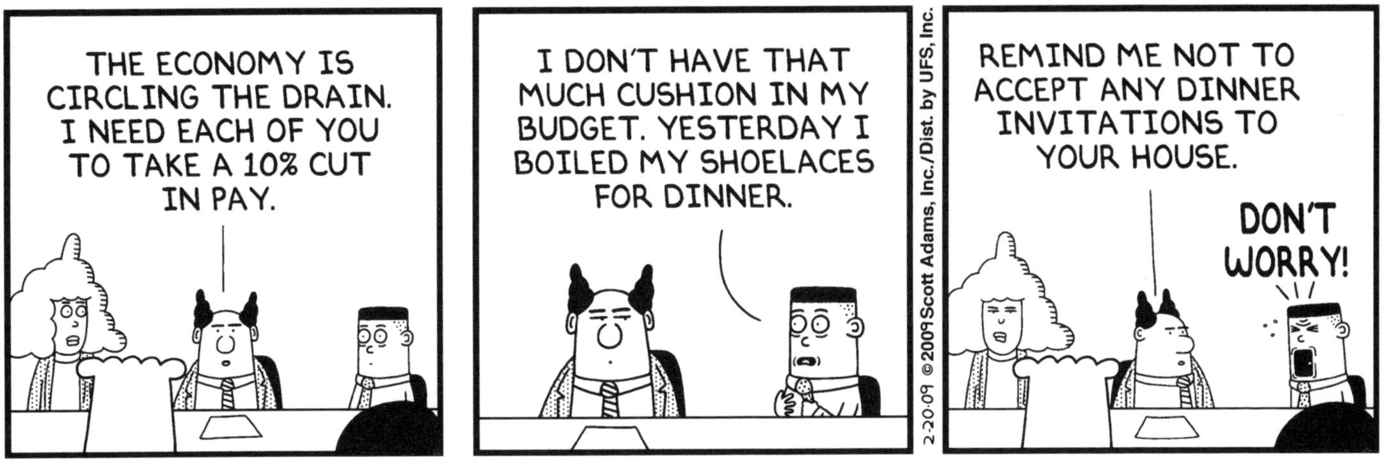
THE ECONOMY IS CIRCLING THE DRAIN. I NEED EACH OF YOU TO TAKE A 10% CUT IN PAY.
I DON'T HAVE THAT MUCH CUSHION IN MY BUDGET. YESTERDAY I BOILED MY SHOELACES FOR DINNER.
2-20-09 © 2009 Scott Adams, Inc./Dist. by UFS, Inc.
REMIND ME NOT TO ACCEPT ANY DINNER INVITATIONS TO YOUR HOUSE.
DON'T WORRY!

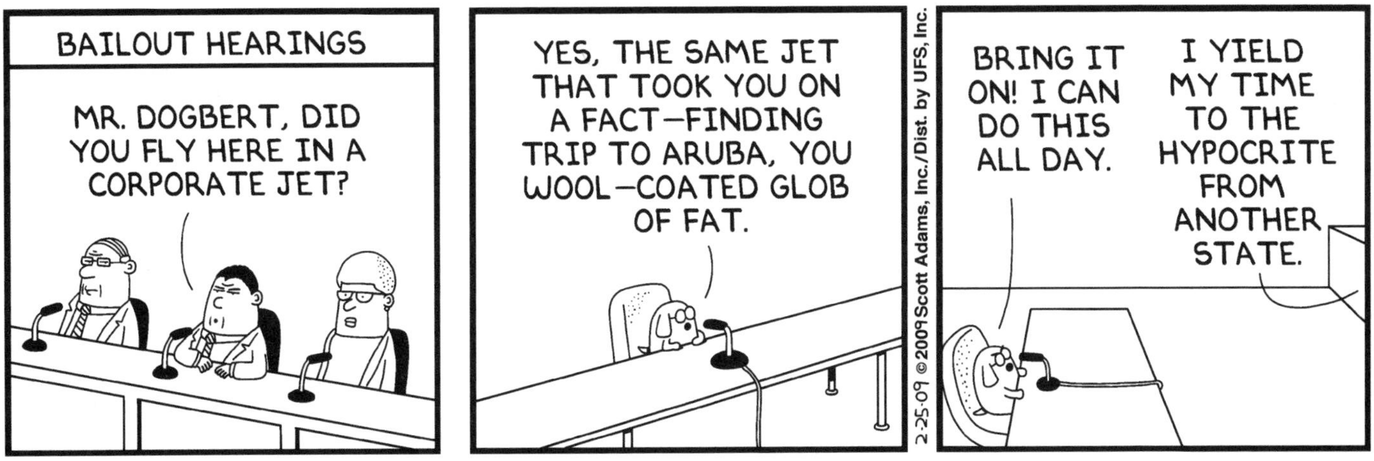
BAILOUT HEARINGS
MR. DOGBERT, DID YOU FLY HERE IN A CORPORATE JET?
YES, THE SAME JET THAT TOOK YOU ON A FACT-FINDING TRIP TO ARUBA, YOU WOOL-COATED GLOB OF FAT.
2-25-09 © 2009 Scott Adams, Inc./Dist. by UFS, Inc.
BRING IT ON! I CAN DO THIS ALL DAY.
I YIELD MY TIME TO THE HYPOCRITE FROM ANOTHER STATE.

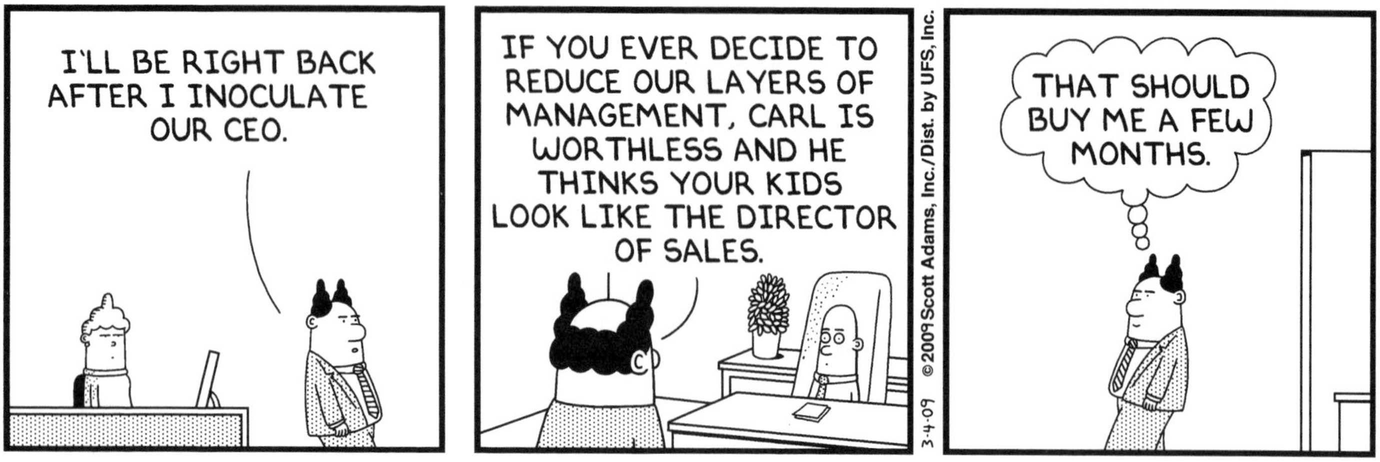
I'LL BE RIGHT BACK AFTER I INOCULATE OUR CEO.
IF YOU EVER DECIDE TO REDUCE OUR LAYERS OF MANAGEMENT, CARL IS WORTHLESS AND HE THINKS YOUR KIDS LOOK LIKE THE DIRECTOR OF SALES.
3-4-09 ©2009 Scott Adams, Inc./Dist. by UFS, Inc.
THAT SHOULD BUY ME A FEW MONTHS.

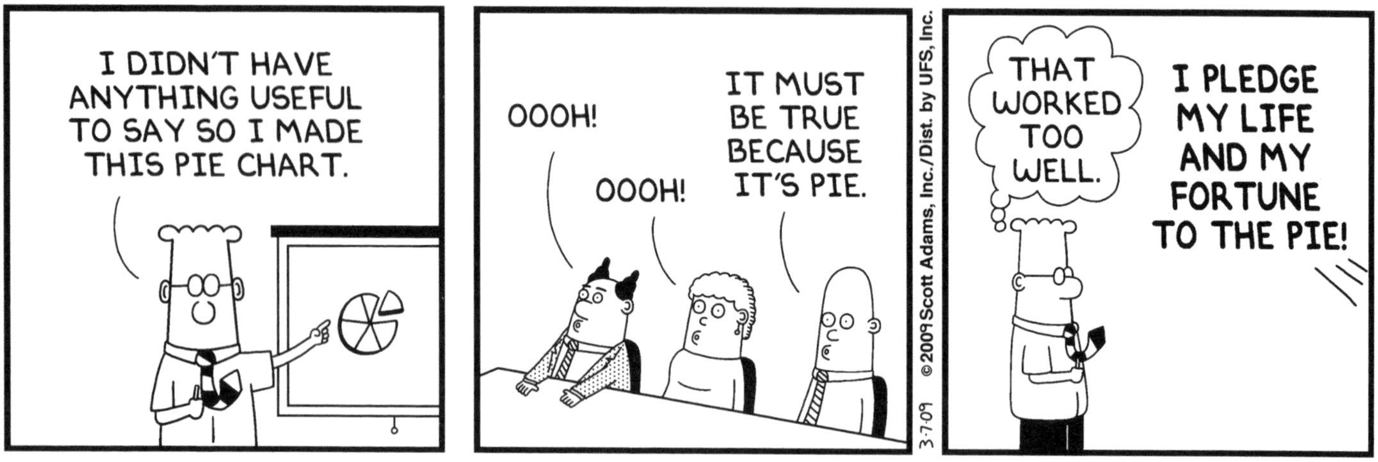
I DIDN'T HAVE ANYTHING USEFUL TO SAY SO I MADE THIS PIE CHART.
OOOH!
OOOH!
IT MUST BE TRUE BECAUSE IT'S PIE.
3-7-09 ©2009 Scott Adams, Inc./Dist. by UFS, Inc.
THAT WORKED TOO WELL.
I PLEDGE MY LIFE AND MY FORTUNE TO THE PIE!

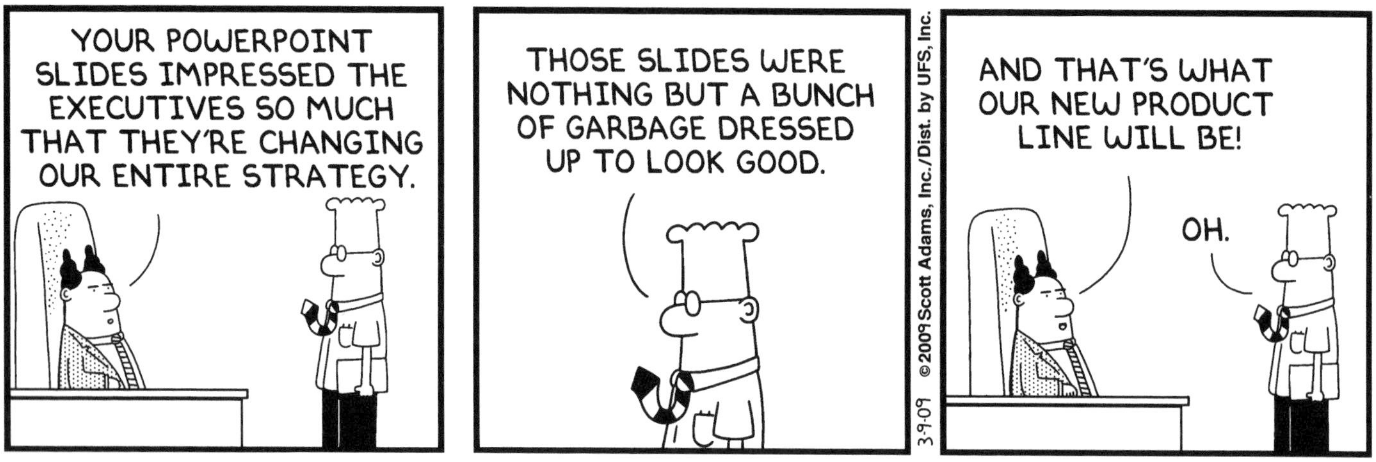
YOUR POWERPOINT SLIDES IMPRESSED THE EXECUTIVES SO MUCH THAT THEY'RE CHANGING OUR ENTIRE STRATEGY.
THOSE SLIDES WERE NOTHING BUT A BUNCH OF GARBAGE DRESSED UP TO LOOK GOOD.
3-9-09 ©2009 Scott Adams, Inc./Dist. by UFS, Inc.
AND THAT'S WHAT OUR NEW PRODUCT LINE WILL BE!
OH.

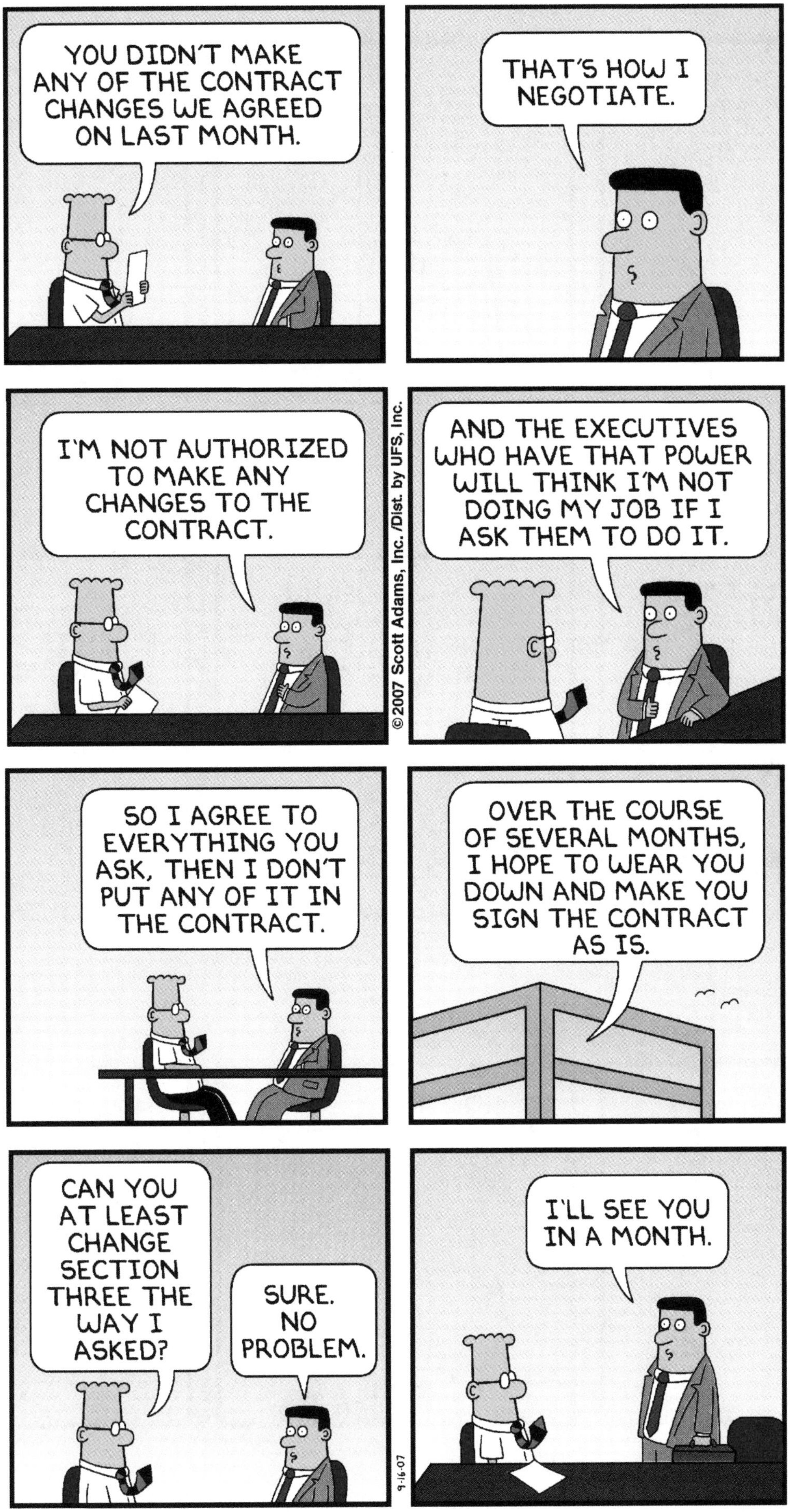
YOU DIDN'T MAKE ANY OF THE CONTRACT CHANGES WE AGREED ON LAST MONTH.
THAT'S HOW I NEGOTIATE.
I'M NOT AUTHORIZED TO MAKE ANY CHANGES TO THE CONTRACT.
AND THE EXECUTIVES WHO HAVE THAT POWER WILL THINK I'M NOT DOING MY JOB IF I ASK THEM TO DO IT.
SO I AGREE TO EVERYTHING YOU ASK, THEN I DON'T PUT ANY OF IT IN THE CONTRACT.
OVER THE COURSE OF SEVERAL MONTHS, I HOPE TO WEAR YOU DOWN AND MAKE YOU SIGN THE CONTRACT AS IS.
CAN YOU AT LEAST CHANGE SECTION THREE THE WAY I ASKED?
SURE. NO PROBLEM.
I'LL SEE YOU IN A MONTH.
© 2007 Scott Adams, Inc. /Dist. by UFS, Inc.
9-16-07

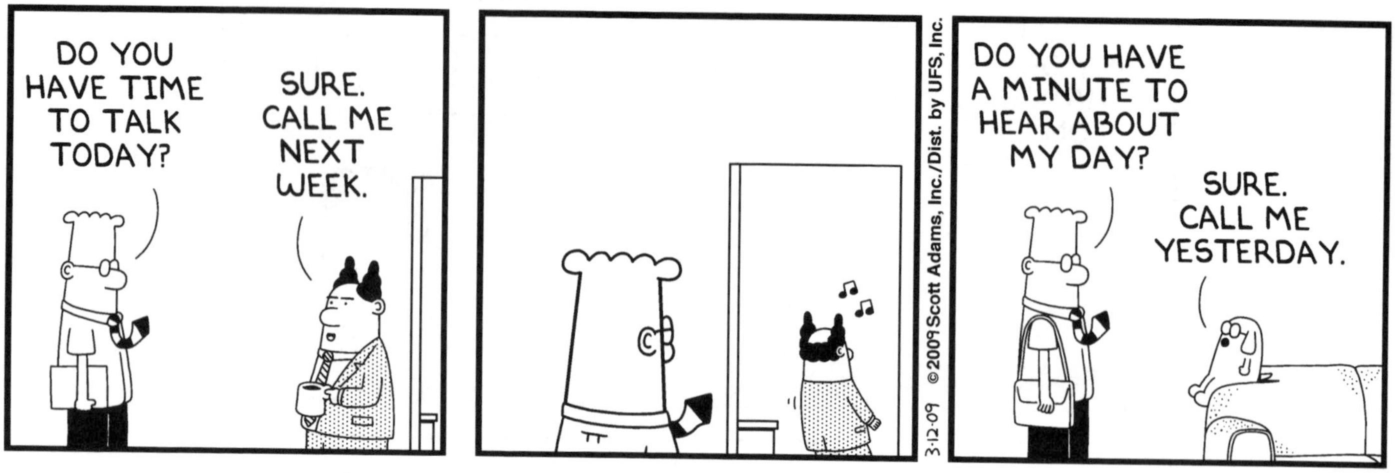
DO YOU HAVE TIME TO TALK TODAY?
SURE. CALL ME NEXT WEEK.
3-12-09 © 2009 Scott Adams, Inc./Dist. by UFS, Inc.
DO YOU HAVE A MINUTE TO HEAR ABOUT MY DAY?
SURE. CALL ME YESTERDAY.

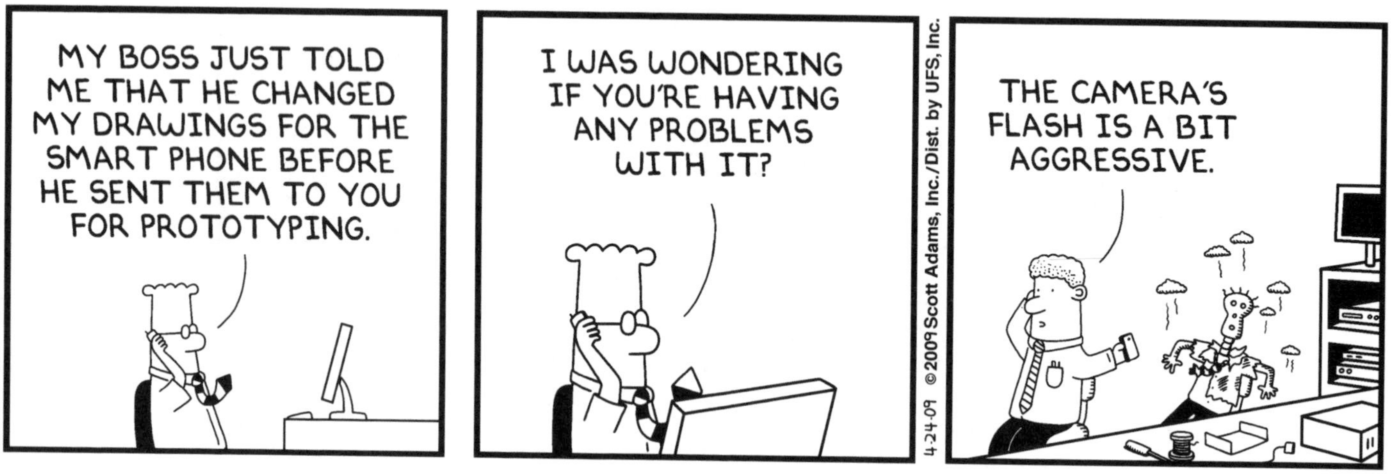
MY BOSS JUST TOLD ME THAT HE CHANGED MY DRAWINGS FOR THE SMART PHONE BEFORE HE SENT THEM TO YOU FOR PROTOTYPING.
I WAS WONDERING IF YOU'RE HAVING ANY PROBLEMS WITH IT?
4-24-09 © 2009 Scott Adams, Inc./Dist. by UFS, Inc.
THE CAMERA'S FLASH IS A BIT AGGRESSIVE.

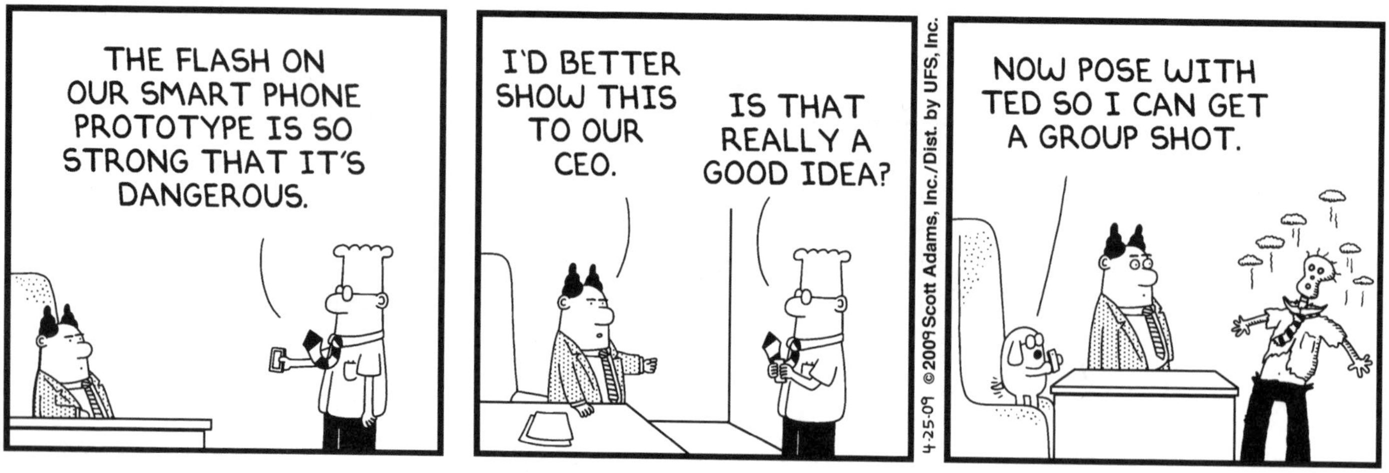
THE FLASH ON OUR SMART PHONE PROTOTYPE IS SO STRONG THAT IT'S DANGEROUS.
I'D BETTER SHOW THIS TO OUR CEO.
IS THAT REALLY A GOOD IDEA?
4-25-09 © 2009 Scott Adams, Inc./Dist. by UFS, Inc.
NOW POSE WITH TED SO I CAN GET A GROUP SHOT.

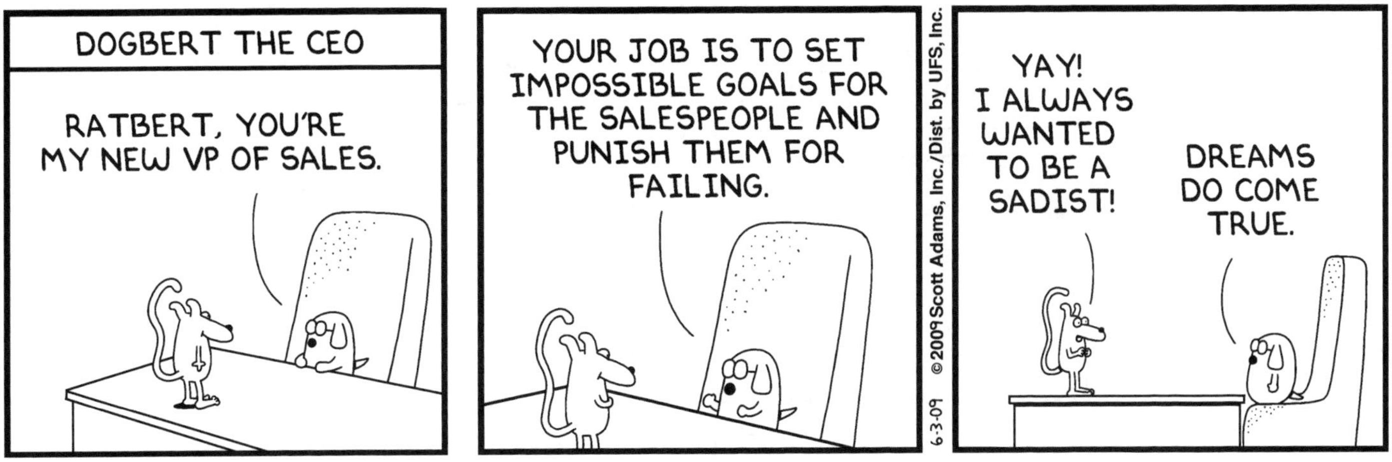
DOGBERT THE CEO
RATBERT, YOU'RE MY NEW VP OF SALES.
YOUR JOB IS TO SET IMPOSSIBLE GOALS FOR THE SALESPEOPLE AND PUNISH THEM FOR FAILING.
YAY! I ALWAYS WANTED TO BE A SADIST!
DREAMS DO COME TRUE.
6-3-09 © 2009 Scott Adams, Inc./Dist. by UFS, Inc.

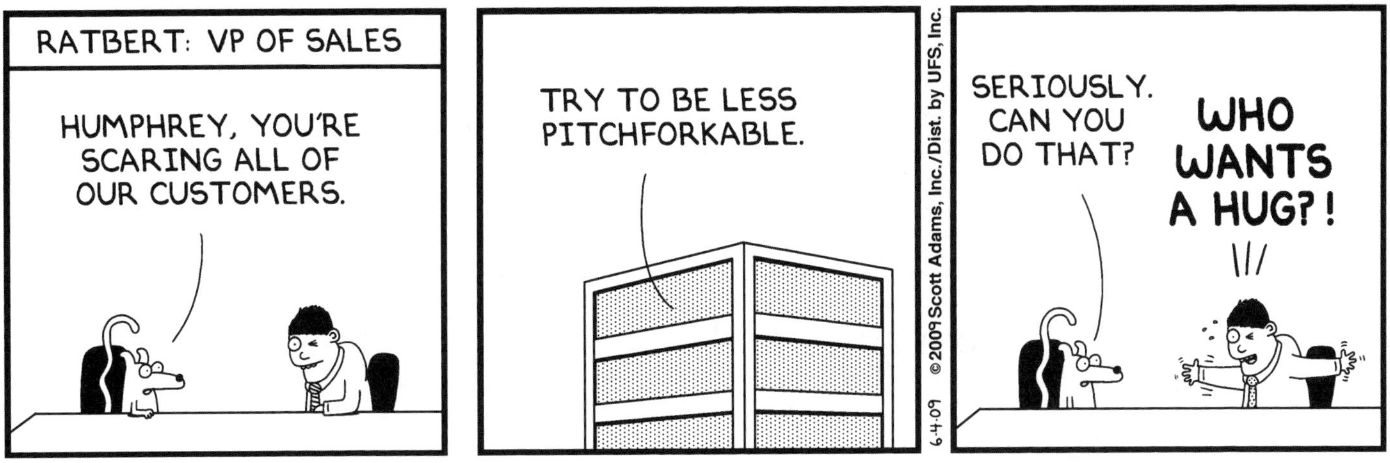
RATBERT: VP OF SALES
HUMPHREY, YOU'RE SCARING ALL OF OUR CUSTOMERS.
TRY TO BE LESS PITCHFORKABLE.
SERIOUSLY. CAN YOU DO THAT?
WHO WANTS A HUG?!
6-4-09 © 2009 Scott Adams, Inc./Dist. by UFS, Inc.

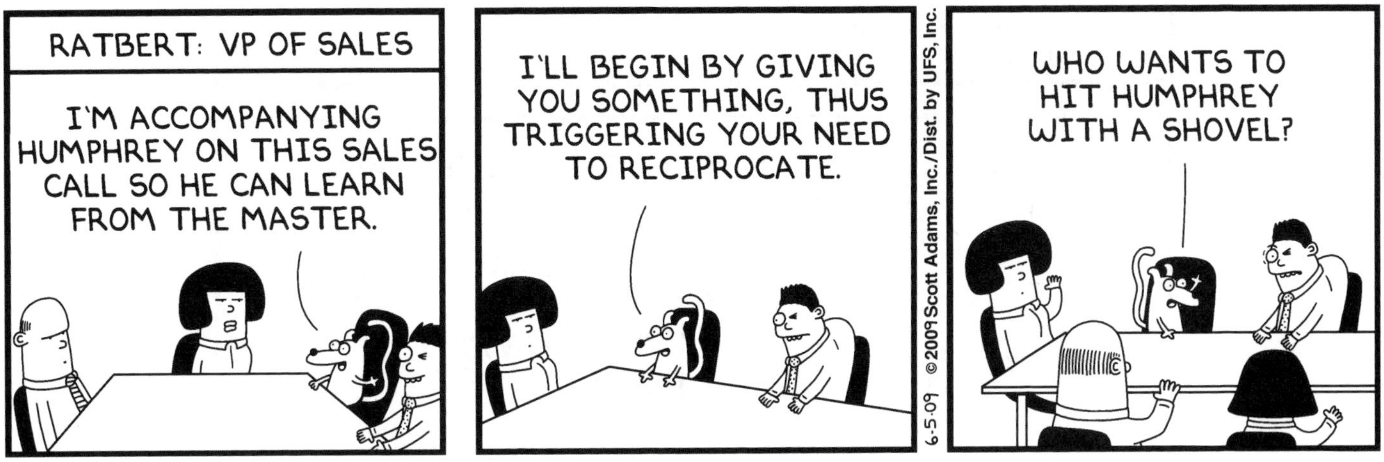
RATBERT: VP OF SALES
I'M ACCOMPANYING HUMPHREY ON THIS SALES CALL SO HE CAN LEARN FROM THE MASTER.
I'LL BEGIN BY GIVING YOU SOMETHING, THUS TRIGGERING YOUR NEED TO RECIPROCATE.
WHO WANTS TO HIT HUMPHREY WITH A SHOVEL?
6-5-09 © 2009 Scott Adams, Inc./Dist. by UFS, Inc.

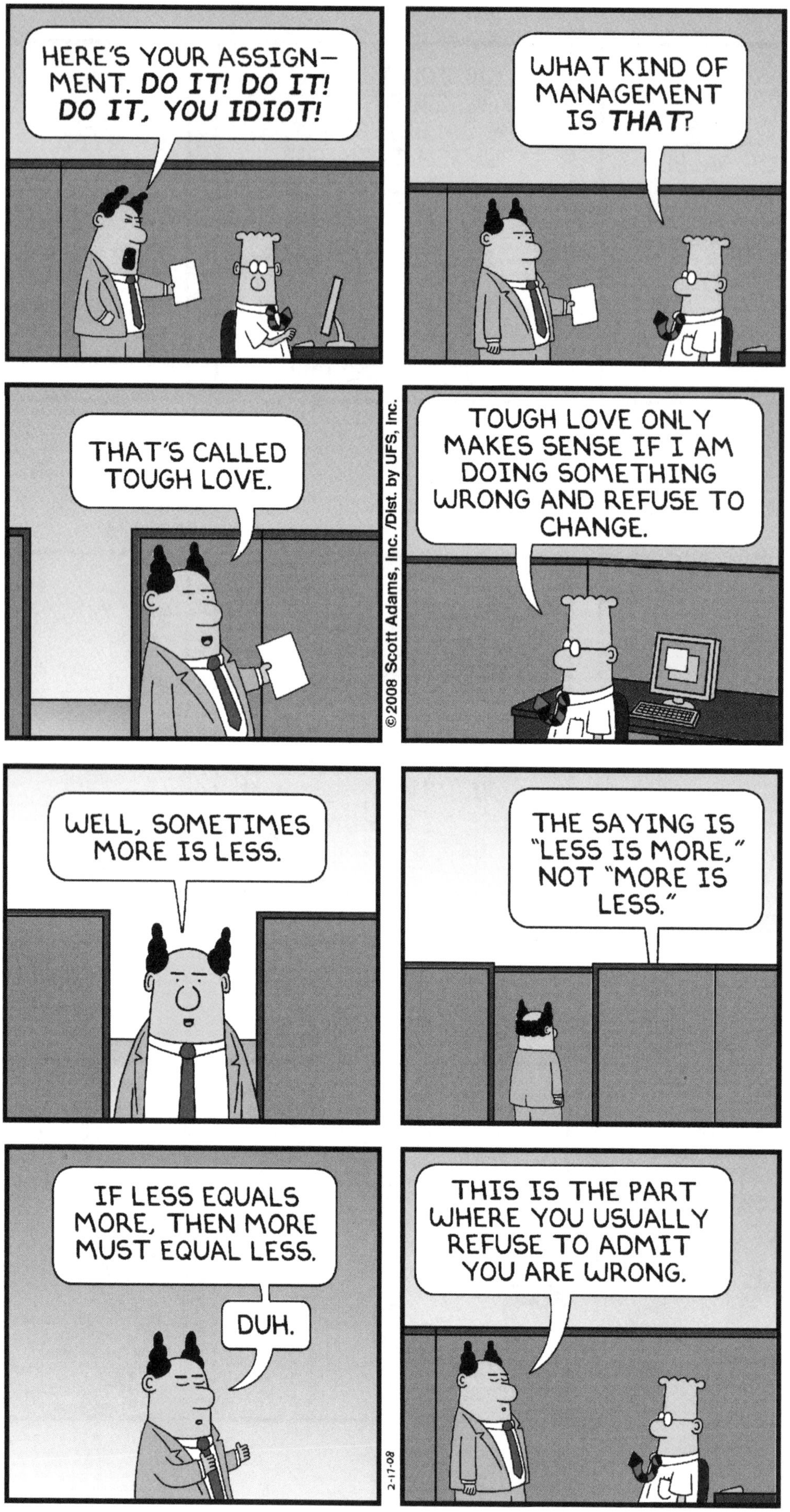
HERE'S YOUR ASSIGN-MENT. DO IT! DO IT! DO IT, YOU IDIOT!
WHAT KIND OF MANAGEMENT IS THAT?
THAT'S CALLED TOUGH LOVE.
TOUGH LOVE ONLY MAKES SENSE IF I AM DOING SOMETHING WRONG AND REFUSE TO CHANGE.
WELL, SOMETIMES MORE IS LESS.
THE SAYING IS "LESS IS MORE," NOT "MORE IS LESS."
IF LESS EQUALS MORE, THEN MORE MUST EQUAL LESS.
DUH.
THIS IS THE PART WHERE YOU USUALLY REFUSE TO ADMIT YOU ARE WRONG.
©2008 Scott Adams, Inc. /Dist. by UFS, Inc.
2-17-08

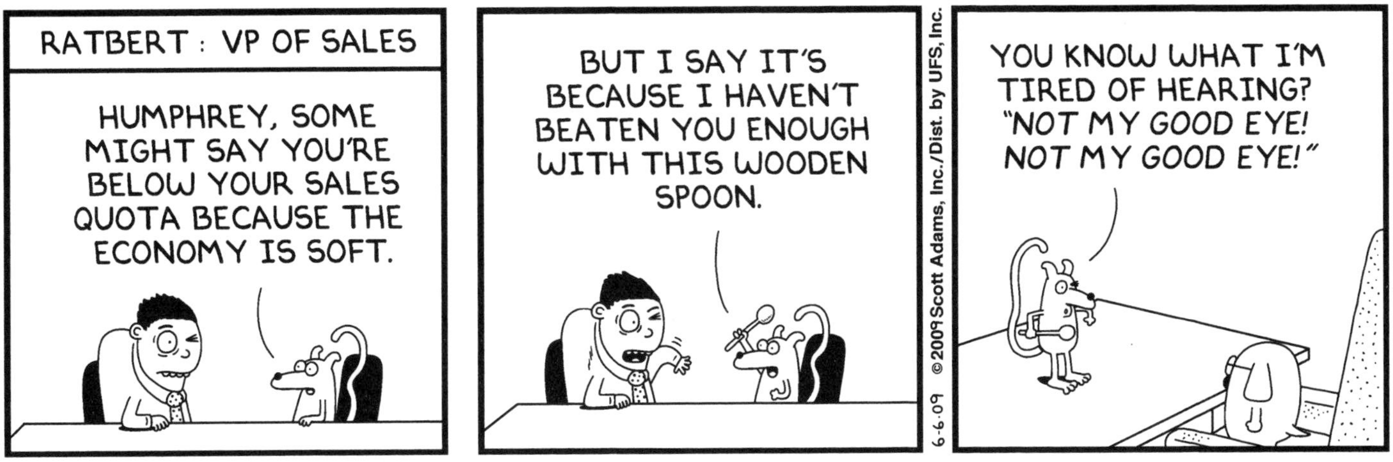
RATBERT : VP OF SALES
HUMPHREY, SOME MIGHT SAY YOU'RE BELOW YOUR SALES QUOTA BECAUSE THE ECONOMY IS SOFT.
BUT I SAY IT'S BECAUSE I HAVEN'T BEATEN YOU ENOUGH WITH THIS WOODEN SPOON.
YOU KNOW WHAT I'M TIRED OF HEARING? "NOT MY GOOD EYE! NOT MY GOOD EYE!"
6-6-09 ©2009 Scott Adams, Inc./Dist. by UFS, Inc.

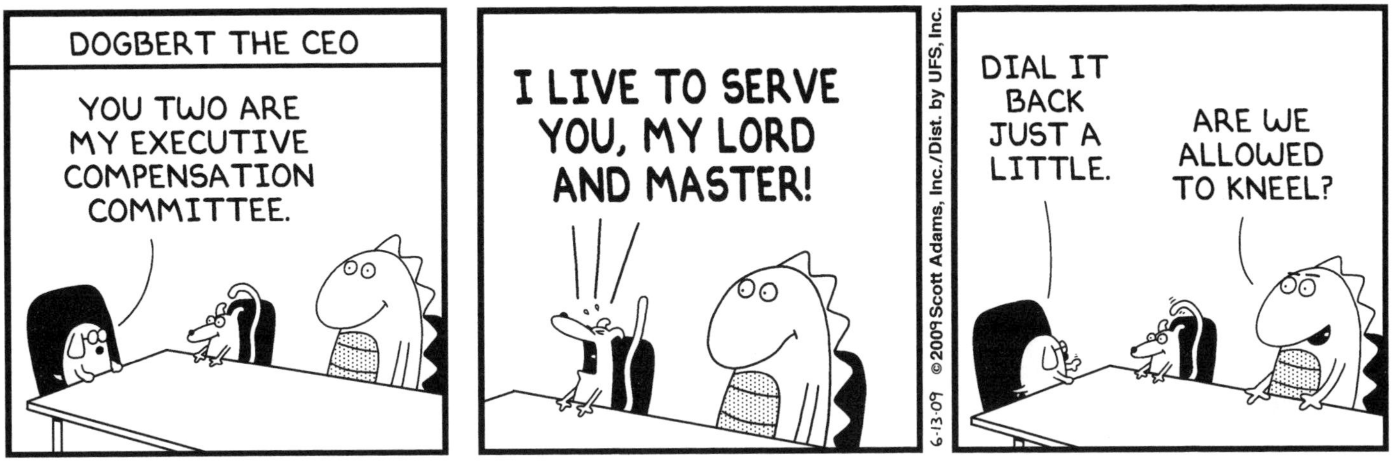
DOGBERT THE CEO
YOU TWO ARE MY EXECUTIVE COMPENSATION COMMITTEE.
I LIVE TO SERVE YOU, MY LORD AND MASTER!
DIAL IT BACK JUST A LITTLE.
ARE WE ALLOWED TO KNEEL?
6-13-09 ©2009 Scott Adams, Inc./Dist. by UFS, Inc.

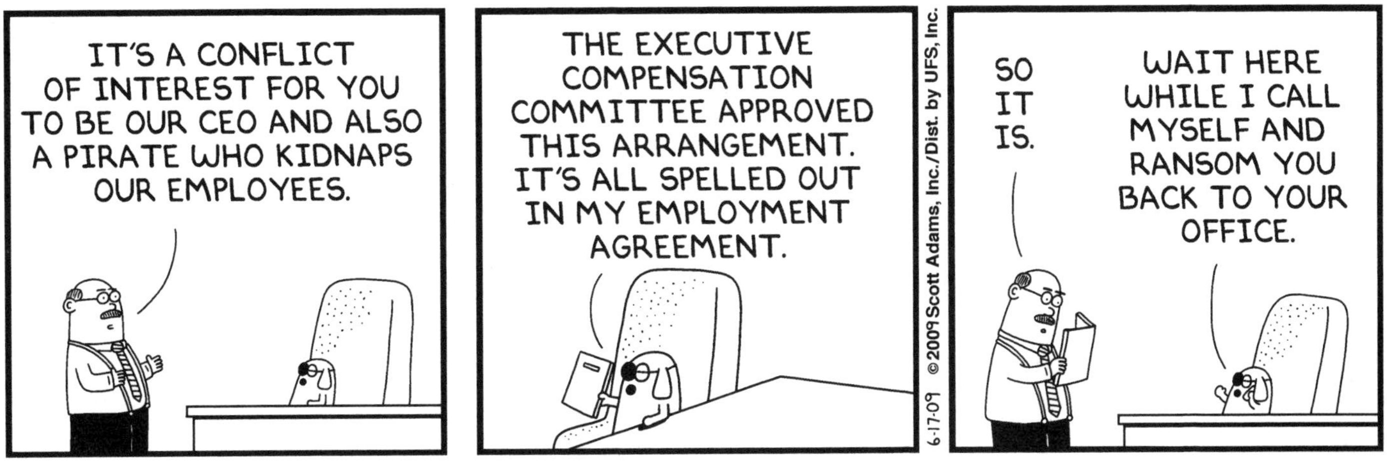
IT'S A CONFLICT OF INTEREST FOR YOU TO BE OUR CEO AND ALSO A PIRATE WHO KIDNAPS OUR EMPLOYEES.
THE EXECUTIVE COMPENSATION COMMITTEE APPROVED THIS ARRANGEMENT. IT'S ALL SPELLED OUT IN MY EMPLOYMENT AGREEMENT.
SO IT IS.
WAIT HERE WHILE I CALL MYSELF AND RANSOM YOU BACK TO YOUR OFFICE.
6-17-09 ©2009 Scott Adams, Inc./Dist. by UFS, Inc.

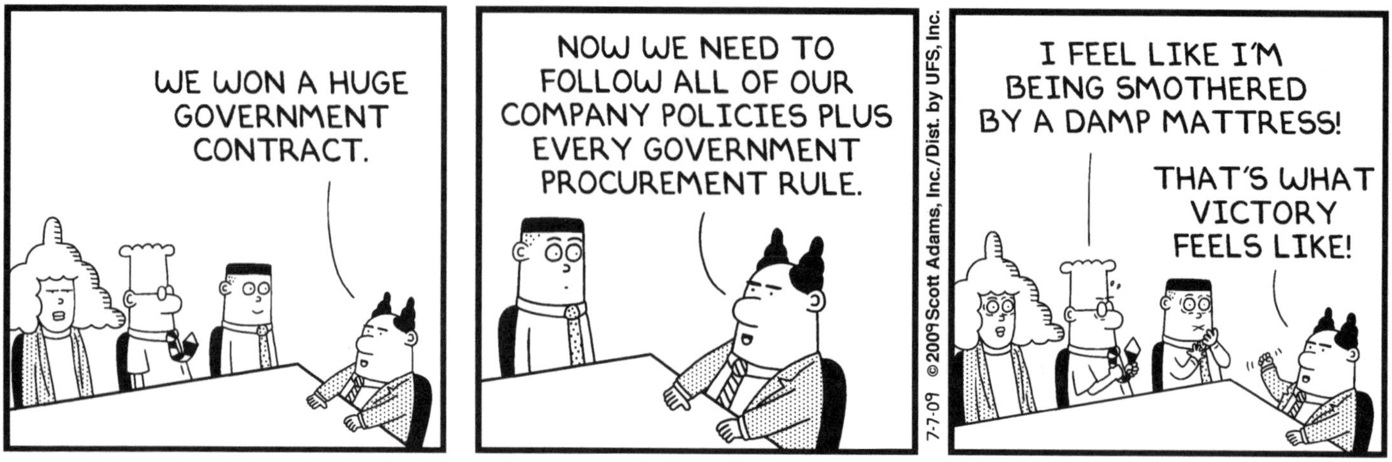
WE WON A HUGE GOVERNMENT CONTRACT.
NOW WE NEED TO FOLLOW ALL OF OUR COMPANY POLICIES PLUS EVERY GOVERNMENT PROCUREMENT RULE.
I FEEL LIKE I'M BEING SMOTHERED BY A DAMP MATTRESS!
THAT'S WHAT VICTORY FEELS LIKE!
7-7-09 © 2009 Scott Adams, Inc./Dist. by UFS, Inc.

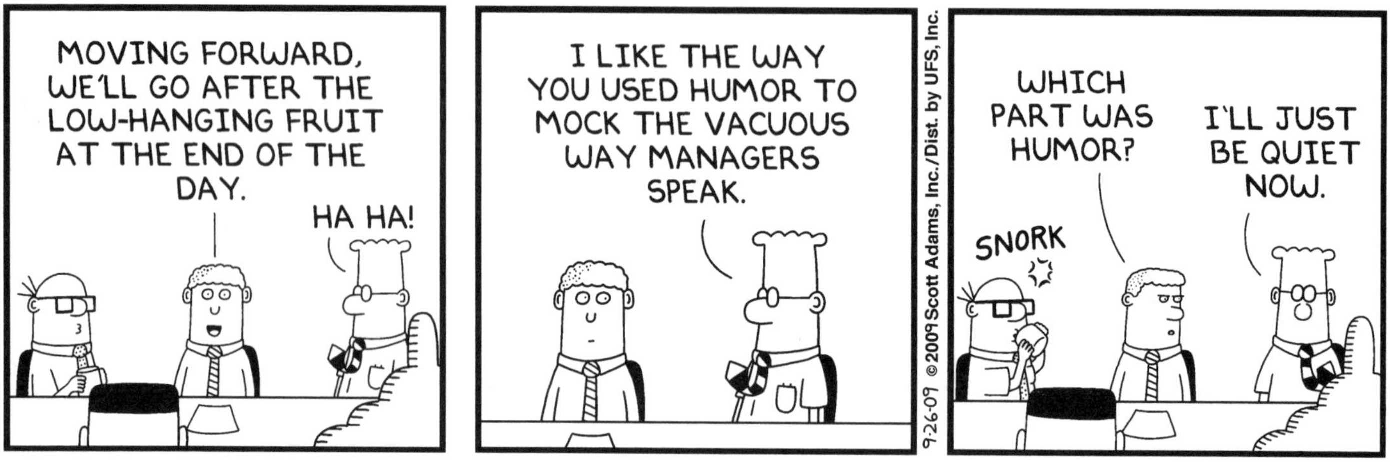
MOVING FORWARD, WE'LL GO AFTER THE LOW-HANGING FRUIT AT THE END OF THE DAY.
HA HA!
I LIKE THE WAY YOU USED HUMOR TO MOCK THE VACUOUS WAY MANAGERS SPEAK.
SNORK
WHICH PART WAS HUMOR?
I'LL JUST BE QUIET NOW.
9-26-09 © 2009 Scott Adams, Inc./Dist. by UFS, Inc.

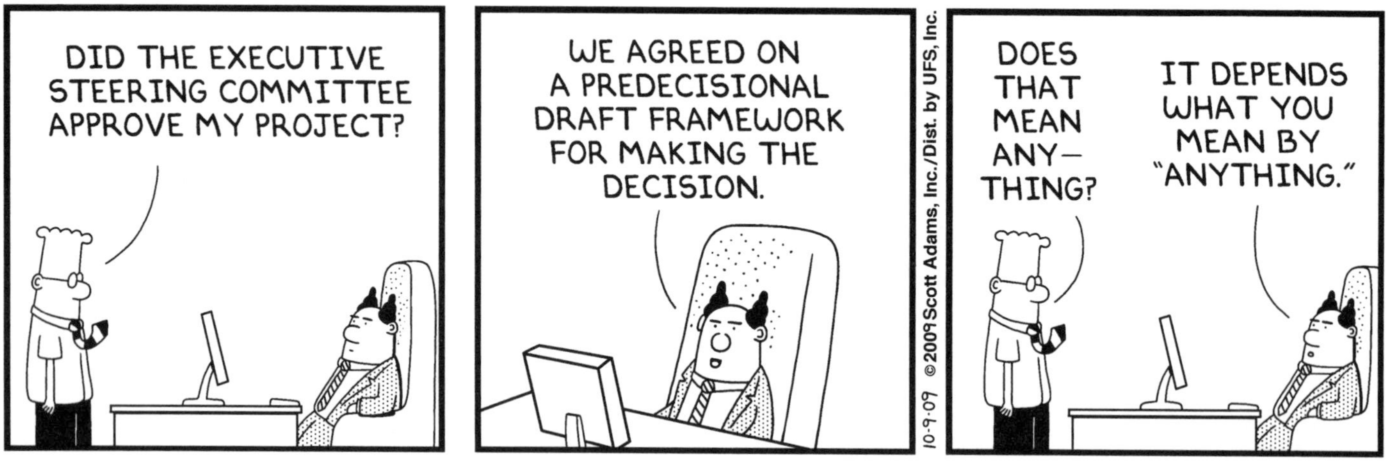
DID THE EXECUTIVE STEERING COMMITTEE APPROVE MY PROJECT?
WE AGREED ON A PREDECISIONAL DRAFT FRAMEWORK FOR MAKING THE DECISION.
DOES THAT MEAN ANY-THING?
IT DEPENDS WHAT YOU MEAN BY "ANYTHING."
10-9-09 © 2009 Scott Adams, Inc./Dist. by UFS, Inc.

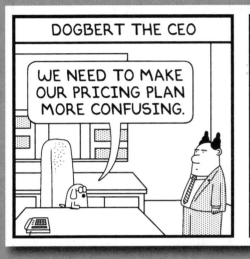

DOGBERT THE CEO
WE NEED TO MAKE OUR PRICING PLAN MORE CONFUSING.
AND CHANGE OUR PACKAGING TO THAT HARD PLASTIC THAT ALWAYS CUTS THE CONSUMERS' HANDS.
I'VE BEEN IN A BAD MOOD SINCE EVERYONE STARTED TALKING ABOUT CAPPING MY EXCESSIVE PAY.
9-14-09 © 2009 Scott Adams, Inc./Dist. by UFS, Inc.

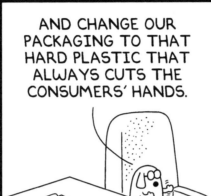

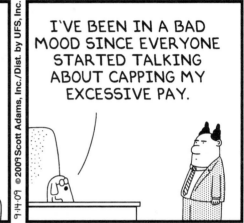

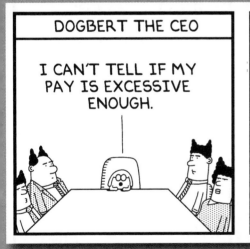

DOGBERT THE CEO
I CAN'T TELL IF MY PAY IS EXCESSIVE ENOUGH.
SO I CREATED A LAB TO TEST THE REACTION OF HOBOS TO MY DIFFERENT PAY SCENARIOS.
IT'S YOUR TURN TO FIND THE NEXT HOBO.
9-15-09 © 2009 Scott Adams, Inc./Dist. by UFS, Inc.

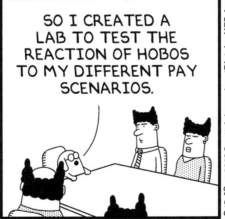

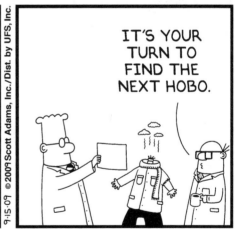

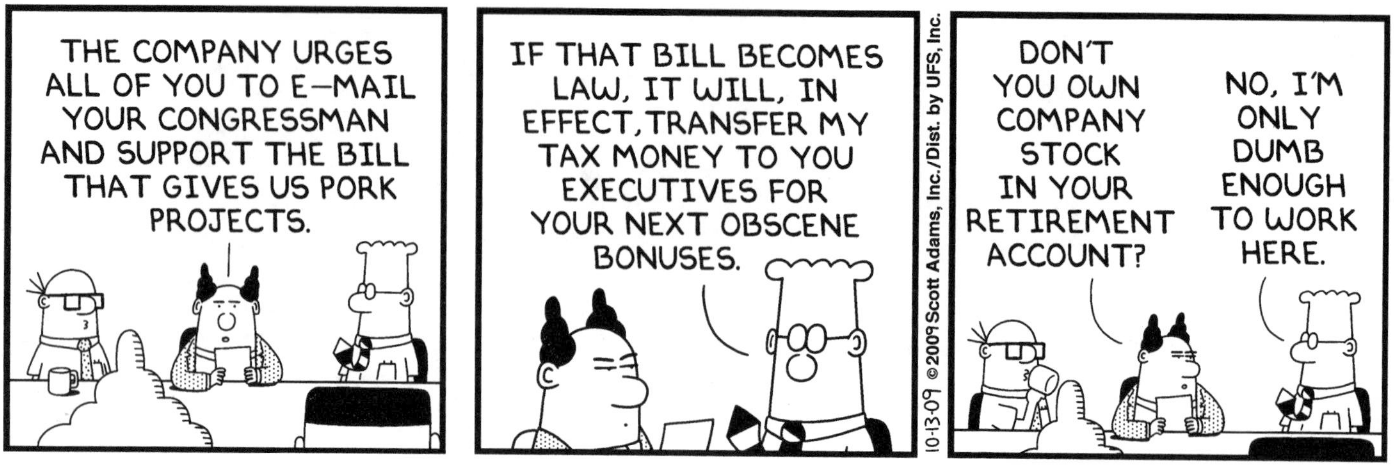
THE COMPANY URGES ALL OF YOU TO E-MAIL YOUR CONGRESSMAN AND SUPPORT THE BILL THAT GIVES US PORK PROJECTS.
IF THAT BILL BECOMES LAW, IT WILL, IN EFFECT, TRANSFER MY TAX MONEY TO YOU EXECUTIVES FOR YOUR NEXT OBSCENE BONUSES.
10-13-09 ©2009 Scott Adams, Inc./Dist. by UFS, Inc.
DON'T YOU OWN COMPANY STOCK IN YOUR RETIREMENT ACCOUNT?
NO, I'M ONLY DUMB ENOUGH TO WORK HERE.

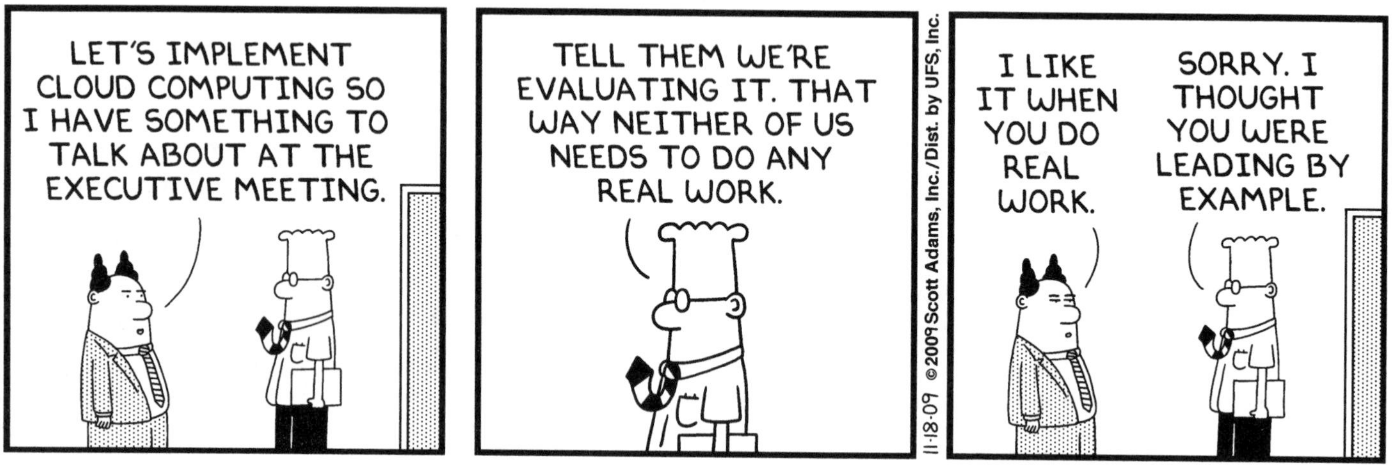
LET'S IMPLEMENT CLOUD COMPUTING SO I HAVE SOMETHING TO TALK ABOUT AT THE EXECUTIVE MEETING.
TELL THEM WE'RE EVALUATING IT. THAT WAY NEITHER OF US NEEDS TO DO ANY REAL WORK.
11-18-09 ©2009 Scott Adams, Inc./Dist. by UFS, Inc.
I LIKE IT WHEN YOU DO REAL WORK.
SORRY. I THOUGHT YOU WERE LEADING BY EXAMPLE.

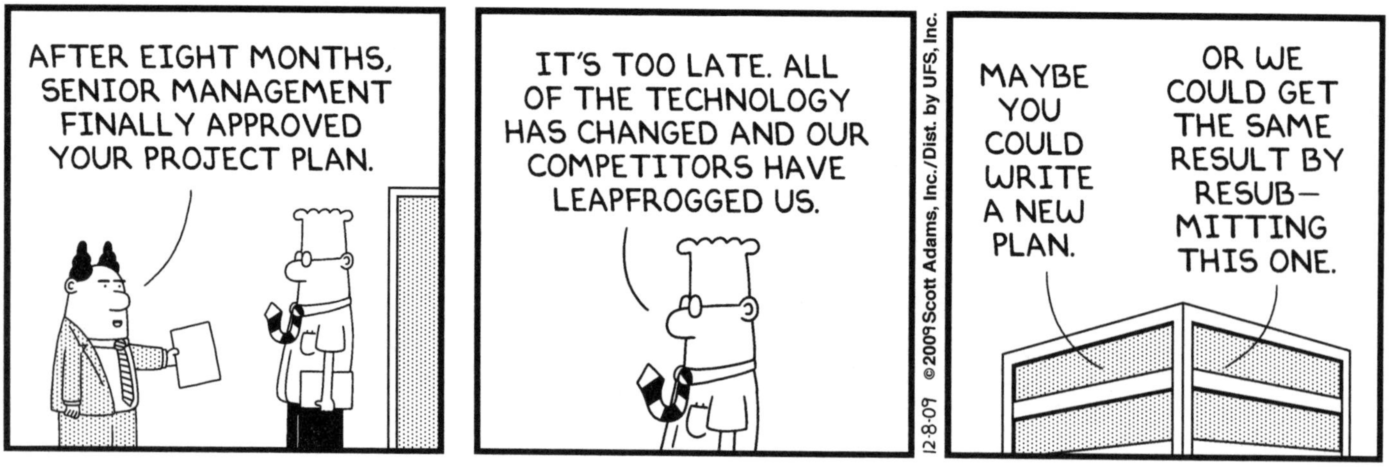
AFTER EIGHT MONTHS, SENIOR MANAGEMENT FINALLY APPROVED YOUR PROJECT PLAN.
IT'S TOO LATE. ALL OF THE TECHNOLOGY HAS CHANGED AND OUR COMPETITORS HAVE LEAPFROGGED US.
12-8-09 ©2009 Scott Adams, Inc./Dist. by UFS, Inc.
MAYBE YOU COULD WRITE A NEW PLAN.
OR WE COULD GET THE SAME RESULT BY RESUB-MITTING THIS ONE.

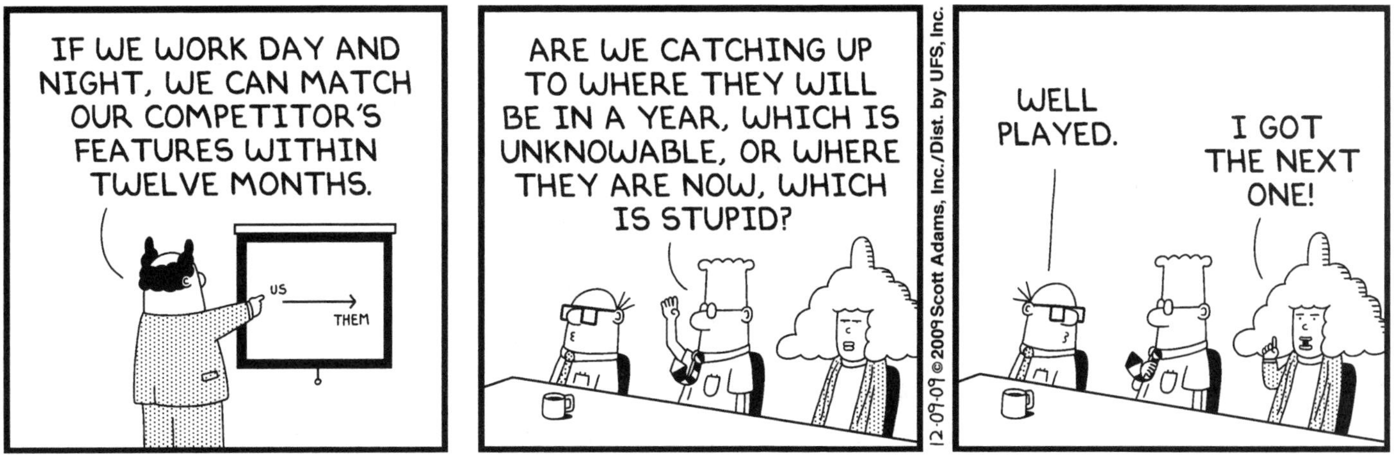
IF WE WORK DAY AND NIGHT, WE CAN MATCH OUR COMPETITOR'S FEATURES WITHIN TWELVE MONTHS.
US
THEM
ARE WE CATCHING UP TO WHERE THEY WILL BE IN A YEAR, WHICH IS UNKNOWABLE, OR WHERE THEY ARE NOW, WHICH IS STUPID?
12-09-09 ©2009 Scott Adams, Inc./Dist. by UFS, Inc.
WELL PLAYED.
I GOT THE NEXT ONE!

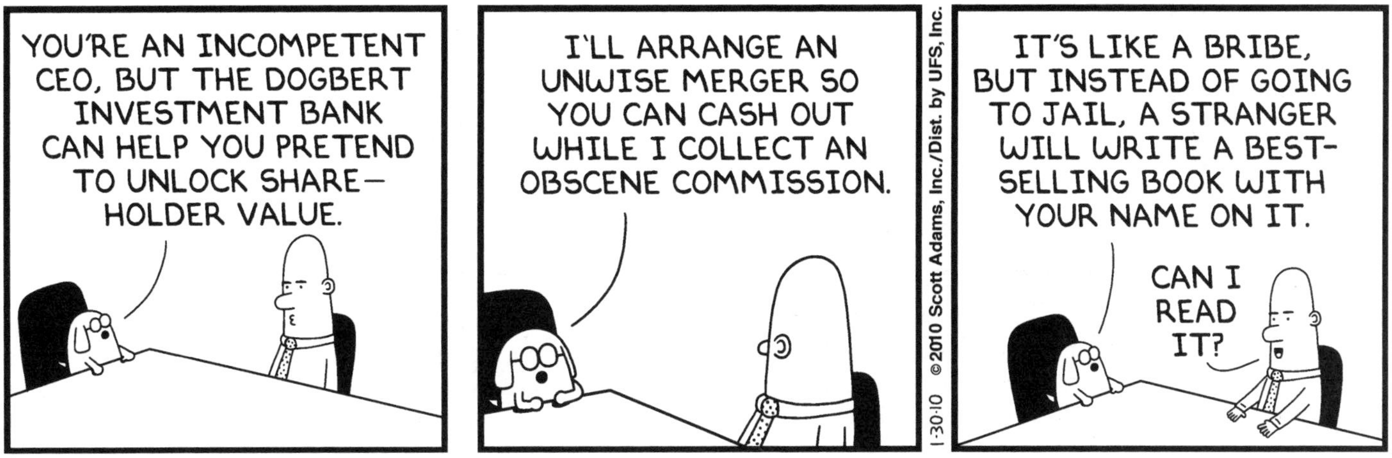
YOU'RE AN INCOMPETENT CEO, BUT THE DOGBERT INVESTMENT BANK CAN HELP YOU PRETEND TO UNLOCK SHARE-HOLDER VALUE.
I'LL ARRANGE AN UNWISE MERGER SO YOU CAN CASH OUT WHILE I COLLECT AN OBSCENE COMMISSION.
1-30-10 ©2010 Scott Adams, Inc./Dist. by UFS, Inc.
IT'S LIKE A BRIBE, BUT INSTEAD OF GOING TO JAIL, A STRANGER WILL WRITE A BEST-SELLING BOOK WITH YOUR NAME ON IT.
CAN I READ IT?

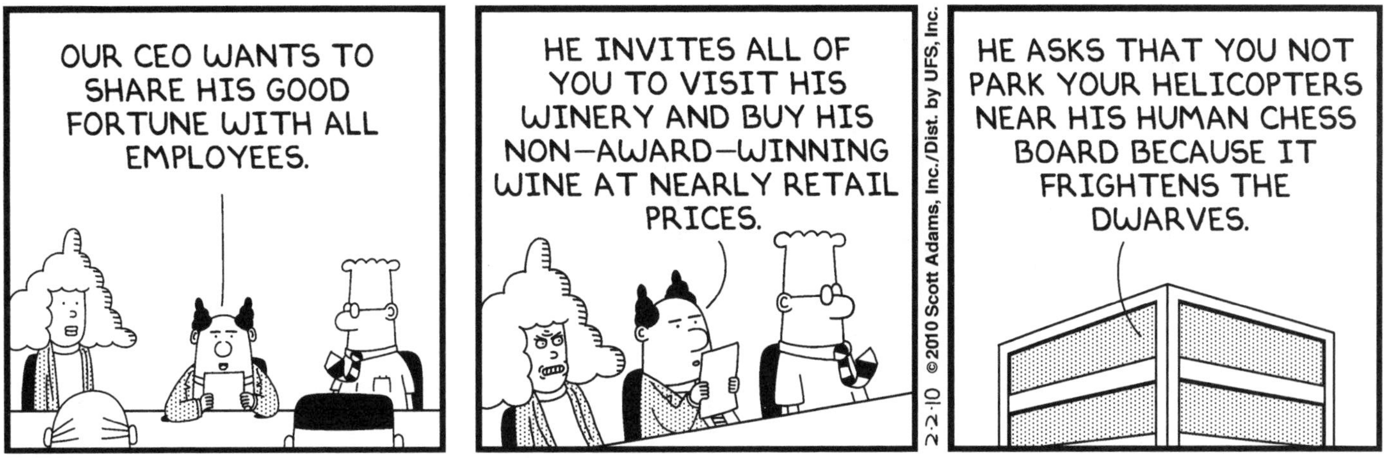
OUR CEO WANTS TO SHARE HIS GOOD FORTUNE WITH ALL EMPLOYEES.
HE INVITES ALL OF YOU TO VISIT HIS WINERY AND BUY HIS NON-AWARD-WINNING WINE AT NEARLY RETAIL PRICES.
2-2-10 ©2010 Scott Adams, Inc./Dist. by UFS, Inc.
HE ASKS THAT YOU NOT PARK YOUR HELICOPTERS NEAR HIS HUMAN CHESS BOARD BECAUSE IT FRIGHTENS THE DWARVES.

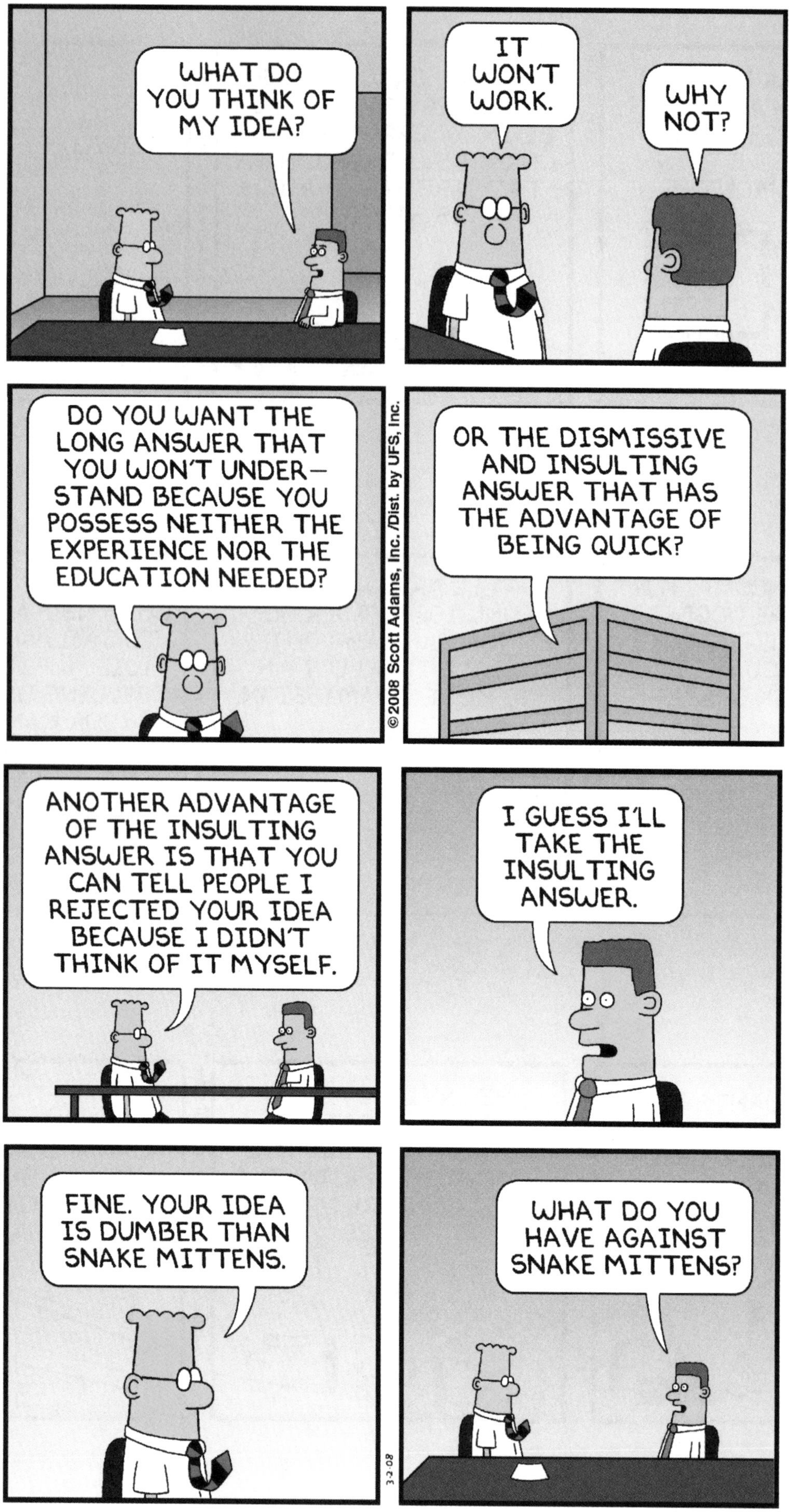
WHAT DO YOU THINK OF MY IDEA?
IT WON'T WORK.
WHY NOT?
DO YOU WANT THE LONG ANSWER THAT YOU WON'T UNDER-STAND BECAUSE YOU POSSESS NEITHER THE EXPERIENCE NOR THE EDUCATION NEEDED?
©2008 Scott Adams, Inc. /Dist. by UFS, Inc.
OR THE DISMISSIVE AND INSULTING ANSWER THAT HAS THE ADVANTAGE OF BEING QUICK?
ANOTHER ADVANTAGE OF THE INSULTING ANSWER IS THAT YOU CAN TELL PEOPLE I REJECTED YOUR IDEA BECAUSE I DIDN'T THINK OF IT MYSELF.
I GUESS I'LL TAKE THE INSULTING ANSWER.
FINE. YOUR IDEA IS DUMBER THAN SNAKE MITTENS.
3-2-08
WHAT DO YOU HAVE AGAINST SNAKE MITTENS?

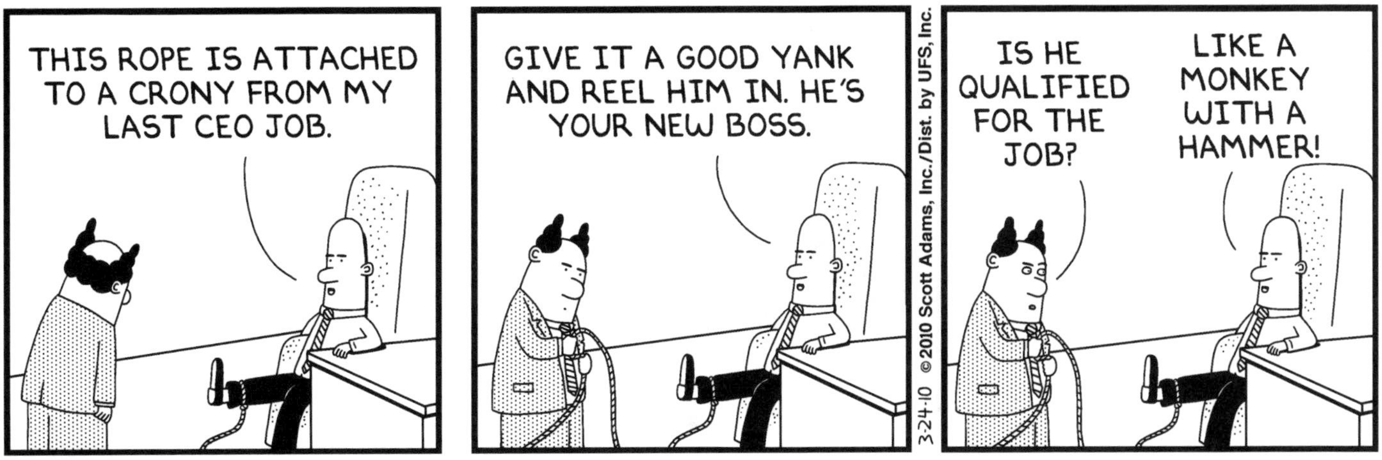
THIS ROPE IS ATTACHED TO A CRONY FROM MY LAST CEO JOB.
GIVE IT A GOOD YANK AND REEL HIM IN. HE'S YOUR NEW BOSS.
3-24-10 ©2010 Scott Adams, Inc./Dist. by UFS, Inc.
IS HE QUALIFIED FOR THE JOB?
LIKE A MONKEY WITH A HAMMER!

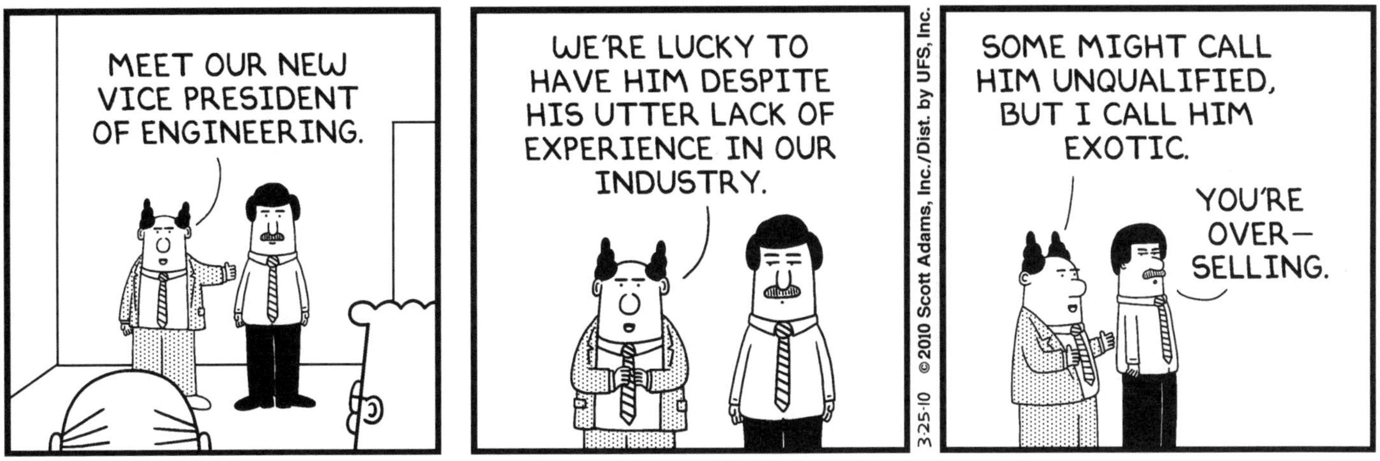
MEET OUR NEW VICE PRESIDENT OF ENGINEERING.
WE'RE LUCKY TO HAVE HIM DESPITE HIS UTTER LACK OF EXPERIENCE IN OUR INDUSTRY.
3-25-10 ©2010 Scott Adams, Inc./Dist. by UFS, Inc.
SOME MIGHT CALL HIM UNQUALIFIED, BUT I CALL HIM EXOTIC.
YOU'RE OVER—SELLING.

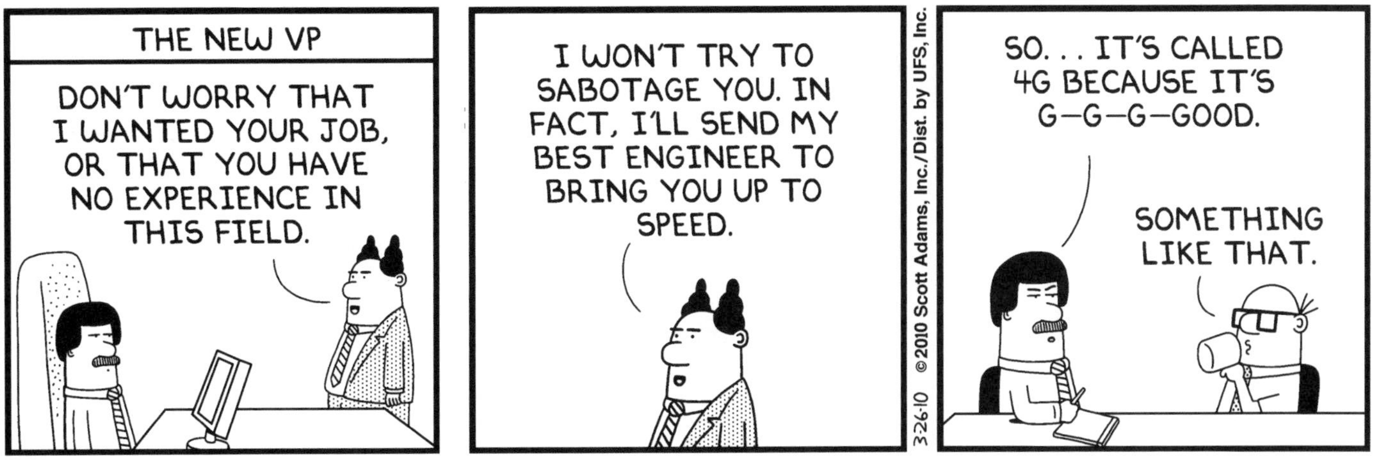
THE NEW VP
DON'T WORRY THAT I WANTED YOUR JOB, OR THAT YOU HAVE NO EXPERIENCE IN THIS FIELD.
I WON'T TRY TO SABOTAGE YOU. IN FACT, I'LL SEND MY BEST ENGINEER TO BRING YOU UP TO SPEED.
3-26-10 ©2010 Scott Adams, Inc./Dist. by UFS, Inc.
SO. . . IT'S CALLED 4G BECAUSE IT'S G—G—G—GOOD.
SOMETHING LIKE THAT.

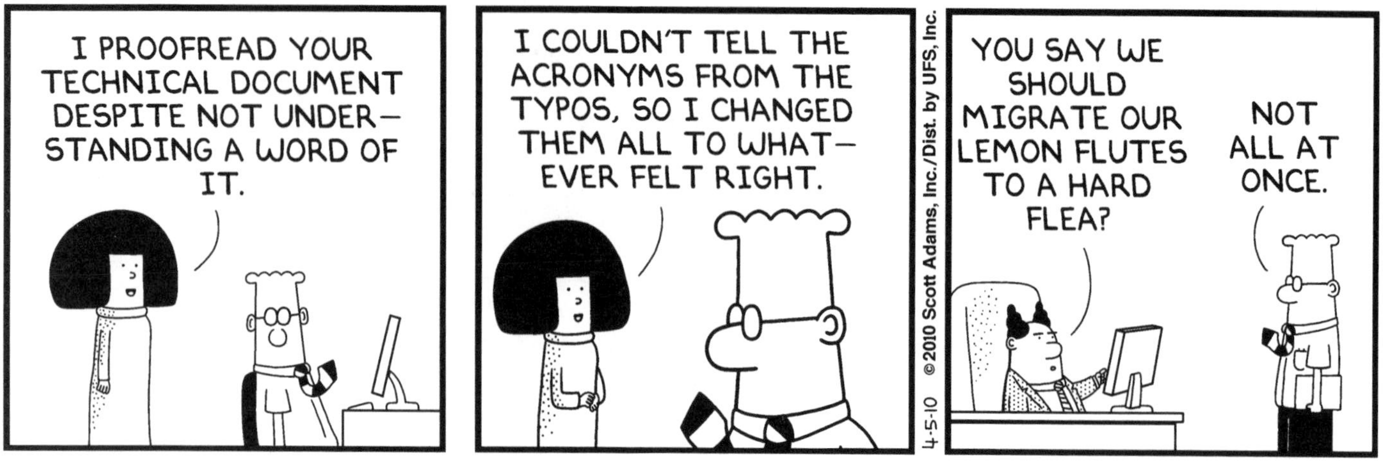
I PROOFREAD YOUR TECHNICAL DOCUMENT DESPITE NOT UNDER-STANDING A WORD OF IT.
I COULDN'T TELL THE ACRONYMS FROM THE TYPOS, SO I CHANGED THEM ALL TO WHAT-EVER FELT RIGHT.
4-5-10 ©2010 Scott Adams, Inc./Dist. by UFS, Inc.
YOU SAY WE SHOULD MIGRATE OUR LEMON FLUTES TO A HARD FLEA?
NOT ALL AT ONCE.

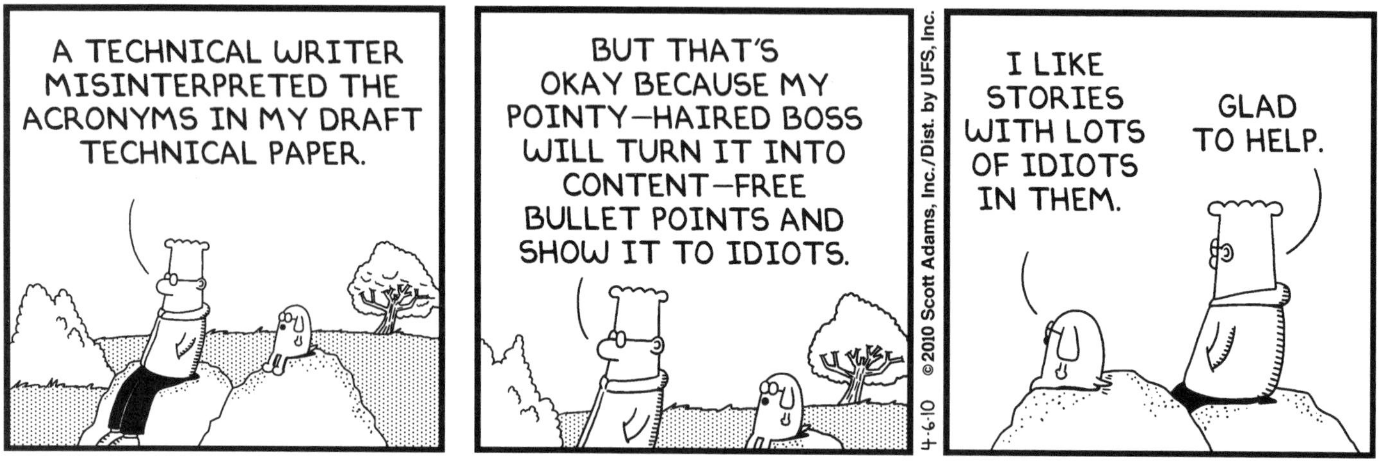
A TECHNICAL WRITER MISINTERPRETED THE ACRONYMS IN MY DRAFT TECHNICAL PAPER.
BUT THAT'S OKAY BECAUSE MY POINTY-HAIRED BOSS WILL TURN IT INTO CONTENT-FREE BULLET POINTS AND SHOW IT TO IDIOTS.
4-6-10 ©2010 Scott Adams, Inc./Dist. by UFS, Inc.
I LIKE STORIES WITH LOTS OF IDIOTS IN THEM.
GLAD TO HELP.

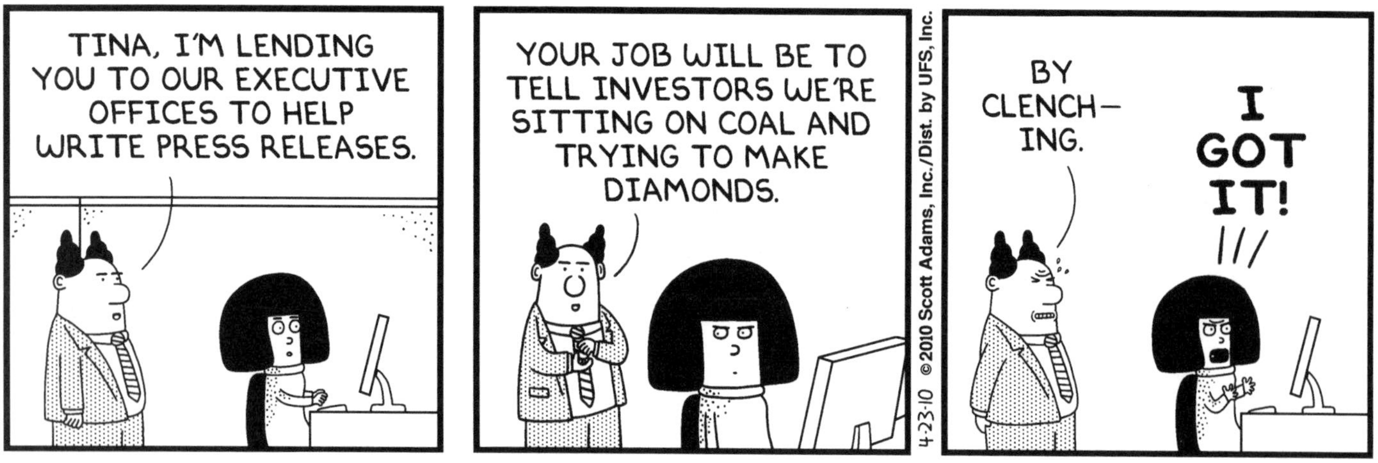
TINA, I'M LENDING YOU TO OUR EXECUTIVE OFFICES TO HELP WRITE PRESS RELEASES.
YOUR JOB WILL BE TO TELL INVESTORS WE'RE SITTING ON COAL AND TRYING TO MAKE DIAMONDS.
4-23-10 ©2010 Scott Adams, Inc./Dist. by UFS, Inc.
BY CLENCH-ING.
I GOT IT!

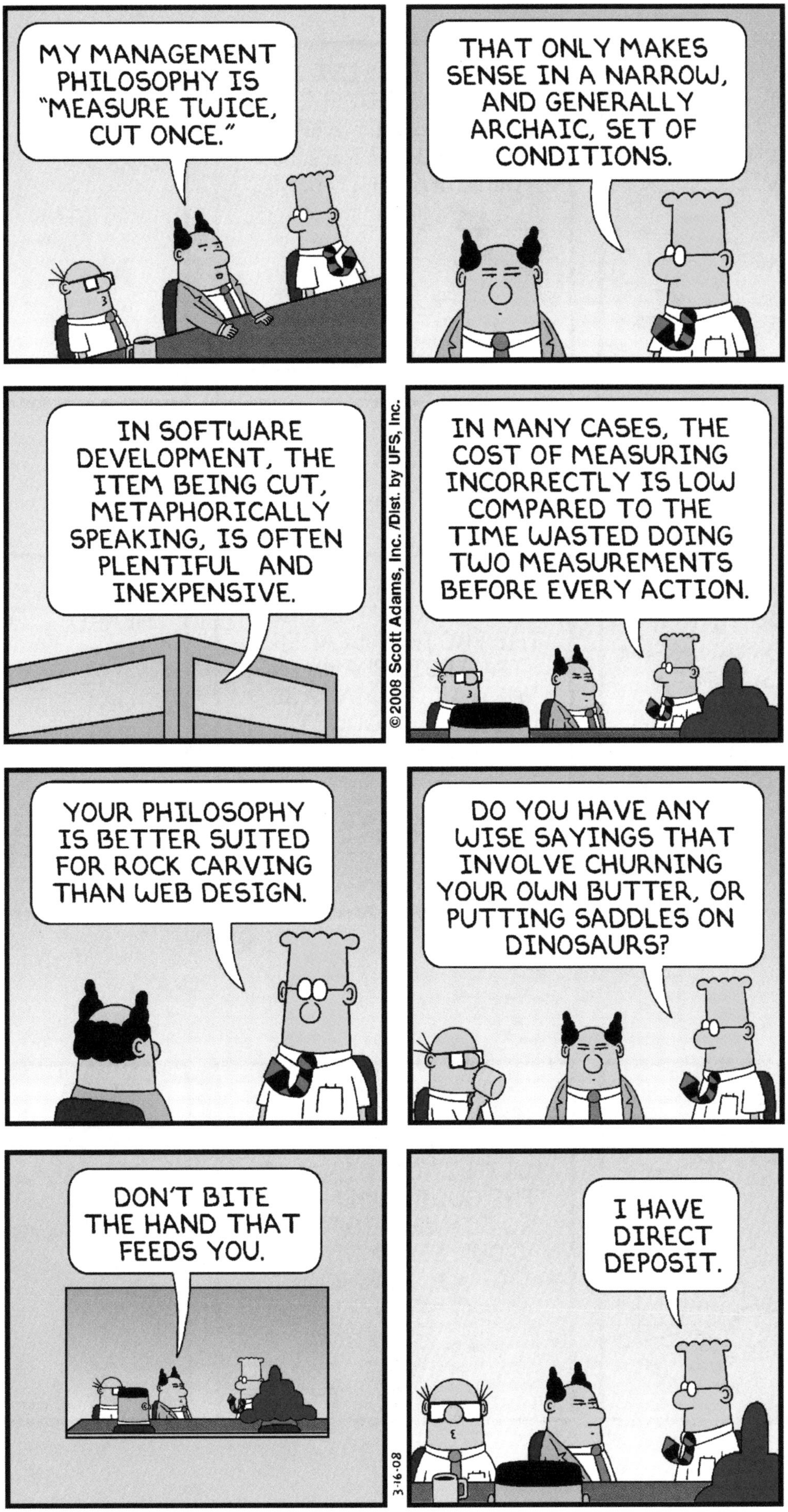
MY MANAGEMENT PHILOSOPHY IS "MEASURE TWICE, CUT ONCE."
THAT ONLY MAKES SENSE IN A NARROW, AND GENERALLY ARCHAIC, SET OF CONDITIONS.
IN SOFTWARE DEVELOPMENT, THE ITEM BEING CUT, METAPHORICALLY SPEAKING, IS OFTEN PLENTIFUL AND INEXPENSIVE.
©2008 Scott Adams, Inc. /Dist. by UFS, Inc.
IN MANY CASES, THE COST OF MEASURING INCORRECTLY IS LOW COMPARED TO THE TIME WASTED DOING TWO MEASUREMENTS BEFORE EVERY ACTION.
YOUR PHILOSOPHY IS BETTER SUITED FOR ROCK CARVING THAN WEB DESIGN.
DO YOU HAVE ANY WISE SAYINGS THAT INVOLVE CHURNING YOUR OWN BUTTER, OR PUTTING SADDLES ON DINOSAURS?
DON'T BITE THE HAND THAT FEEDS YOU.
3-16-08
I HAVE DIRECT DEPOSIT.

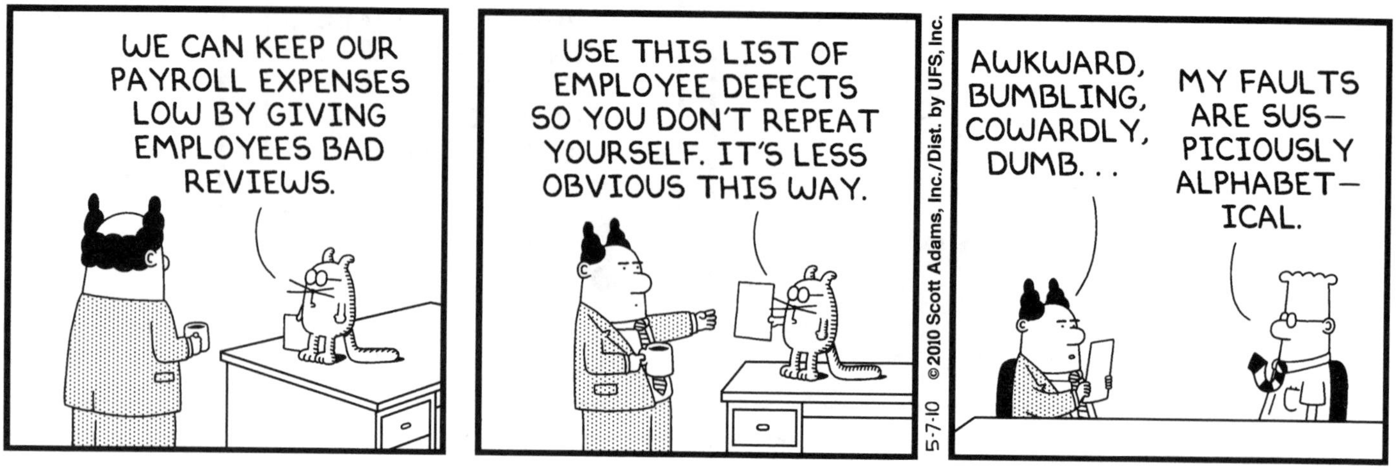
WE CAN KEEP OUR PAYROLL EXPENSES LOW BY GIVING EMPLOYEES BAD REVIEWS.
USE THIS LIST OF EMPLOYEE DEFECTS SO YOU DON'T REPEAT YOURSELF. IT'S LESS OBVIOUS THIS WAY.
AWKWARD, BUMBLING, COWARDLY, DUMB. . .
MY FAULTS ARE SUS– PICIOUSLY ALPHABET– ICAL.
5-7-10 © 2010 Scott Adams, Inc./Dist. by UFS, Inc.

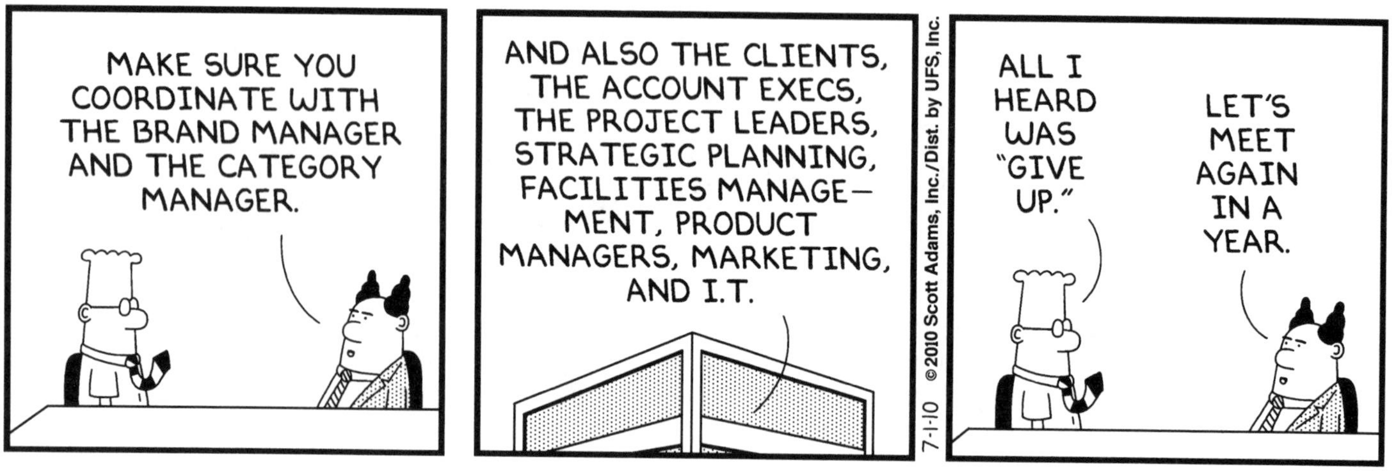
MAKE SURE YOU COORDINATE WITH THE BRAND MANAGER AND THE CATEGORY MANAGER.
AND ALSO THE CLIENTS, THE ACCOUNT EXECS, THE PROJECT LEADERS, STRATEGIC PLANNING, FACILITIES MANAGE– MENT, PRODUCT MANAGERS, MARKETING, AND I.T.
ALL I HEARD WAS "GIVE UP."
LET'S MEET AGAIN IN A YEAR.
7-1-10 © 2010 Scott Adams, Inc./Dist. by UFS, Inc.

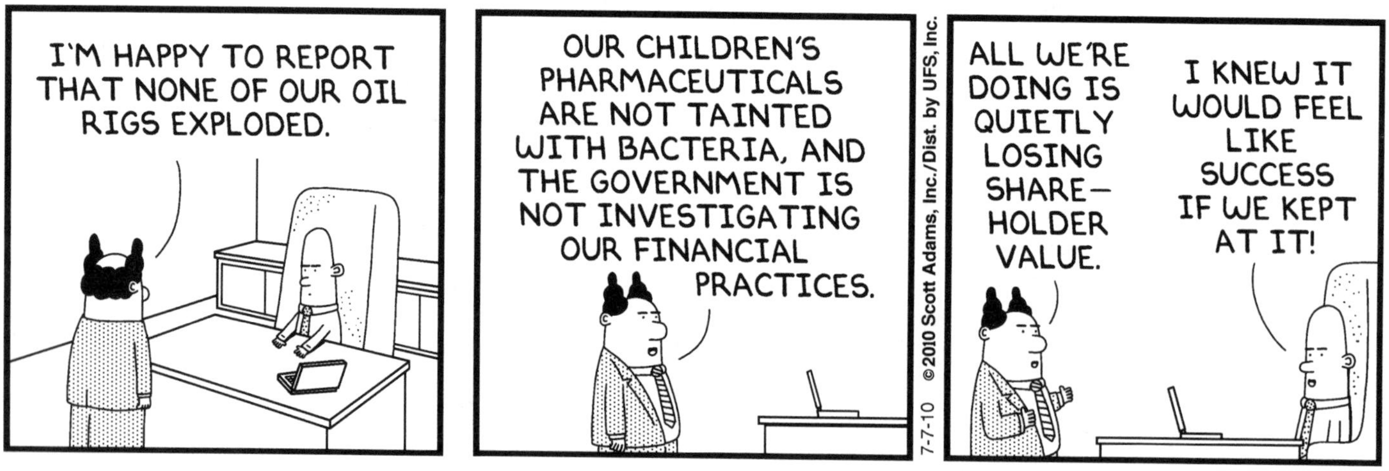
I'M HAPPY TO REPORT THAT NONE OF OUR OIL RIGS EXPLODED.
OUR CHILDREN'S PHARMACEUTICALS ARE NOT TAINTED WITH BACTERIA, AND THE GOVERNMENT IS NOT INVESTIGATING OUR FINANCIAL PRACTICES.
ALL WE'RE DOING IS QUIETLY LOSING SHARE– HOLDER VALUE.
I KNEW IT WOULD FEEL LIKE SUCCESS IF WE KEPT AT IT!
7-7-10 © 2010 Scott Adams, Inc./Dist. by UFS, Inc.

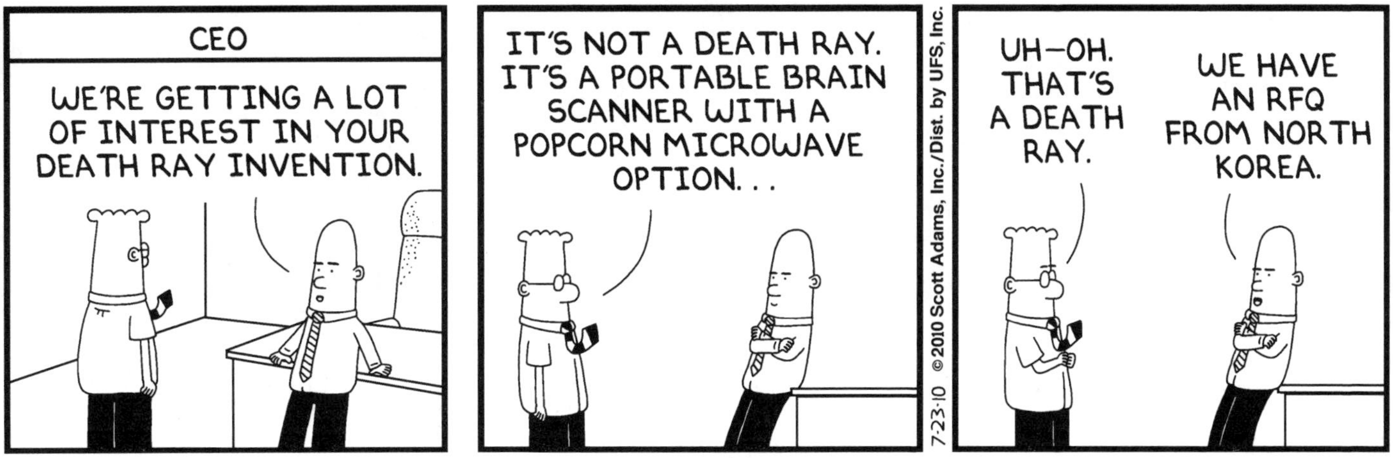
CEO
WE'RE GETTING A LOT OF INTEREST IN YOUR DEATH RAY INVENTION.
IT'S NOT A DEATH RAY. IT'S A PORTABLE BRAIN SCANNER WITH A POPCORN MICROWAVE OPTION. . .
UH-OH. THAT'S A DEATH RAY.
WE HAVE AN RFQ FROM NORTH KOREA.
7-23-10 © 2010 Scott Adams, Inc./Dist. by UFS, Inc.

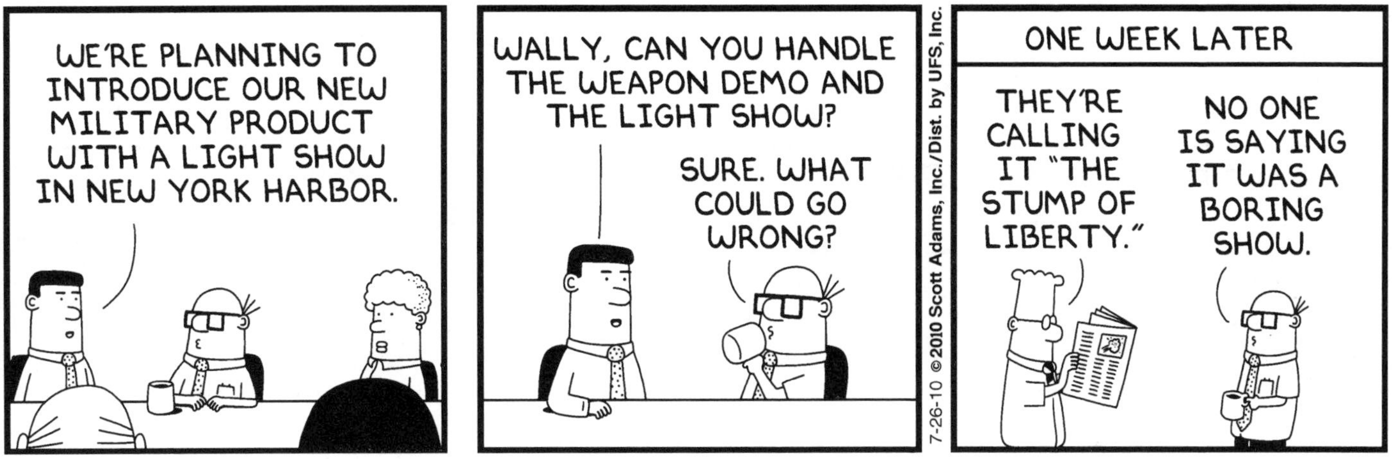
WE'RE PLANNING TO INTRODUCE OUR NEW MILITARY PRODUCT WITH A LIGHT SHOW IN NEW YORK HARBOR.
WALLY, CAN YOU HANDLE THE WEAPON DEMO AND THE LIGHT SHOW?
SURE. WHAT COULD GO WRONG?
ONE WEEK LATER
THEY'RE CALLING IT "THE STUMP OF LIBERTY."
NO ONE IS SAYING IT WAS A BORING SHOW.
7-26-10 © 2010 Scott Adams, Inc./Dist. by UFS, Inc.

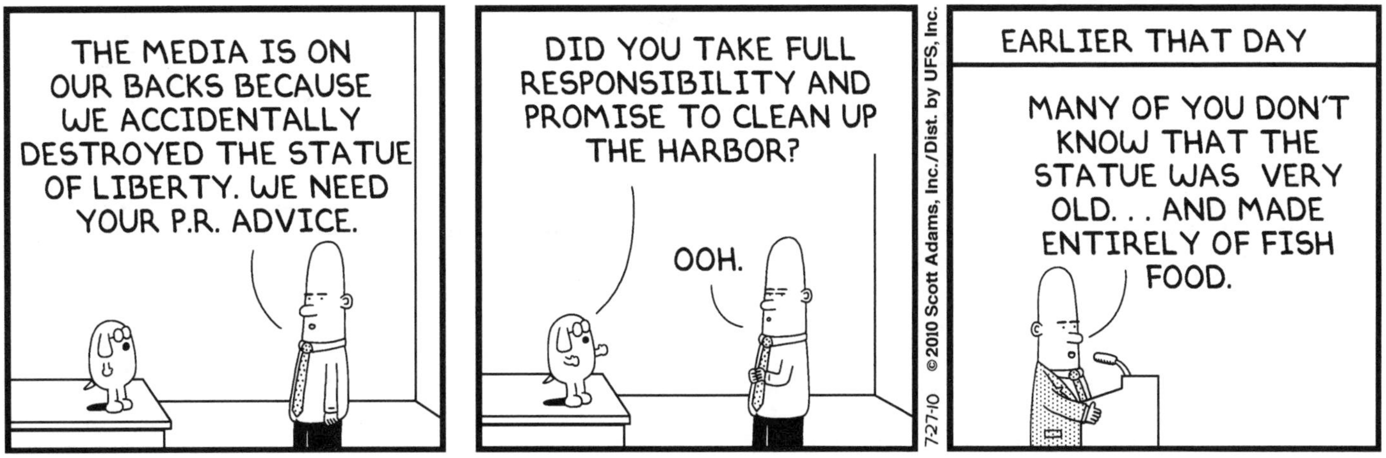
THE MEDIA IS ON OUR BACKS BECAUSE WE ACCIDENTALLY DESTROYED THE STATUE OF LIBERTY. WE NEED YOUR P.R. ADVICE.
DID YOU TAKE FULL RESPONSIBILITY AND PROMISE TO CLEAN UP THE HARBOR?
OOH.
EARLIER THAT DAY
MANY OF YOU DON'T KNOW THAT THE STATUE WAS VERY OLD. . . AND MADE ENTIRELY OF FISH FOOD.
7-27-10 © 2010 Scott Adams, Inc./Dist. by UFS, Inc.

CEO SUMMIT
OBVIOUSLY IT'S ILLEGAL FOR COMPANIES TO RIG BIDS.
BUT INTERESTINGLY, THE CRIME IS NEARLY IMPOSSIBLE TO PROVE WHEN NOTHING IS WRITTEN DOWN.
I'D LIKE YOU TO MEET EDDIE. PAY CLOSE ATTENTION TO HOW MANY TIMES HE STOMPS HIS HOOF.
9-18-09 ©2009 Scott Adams, Inc./Dist. by UFS, Inc.

CEO SUMMIT
DO YOU COLLUDE?
SOME–TIMES.
ARE YOU COLLUDING WITH ANYONE NOW, BECAUSE I'D SURE LIKE TO COLLUDE WITH YOU.
WHAT ARE YOU INTO? MAYBE A LITTLE PRICE–FIXING?
THIS IS ALL HAPPENING SO FAST.
9-19-09 ©2009 Scott Adams, Inc./Dist. by UFS, Inc.

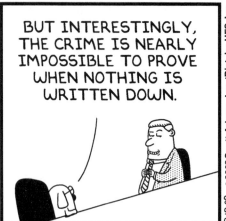

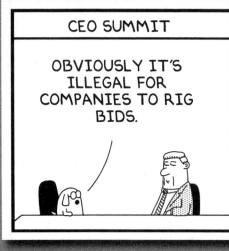

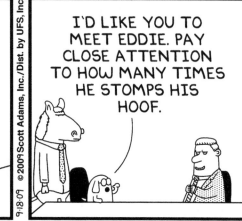

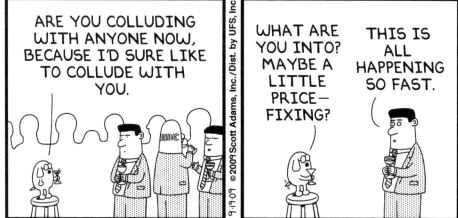

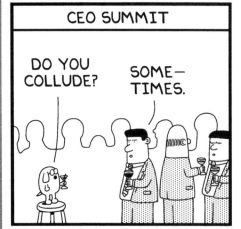

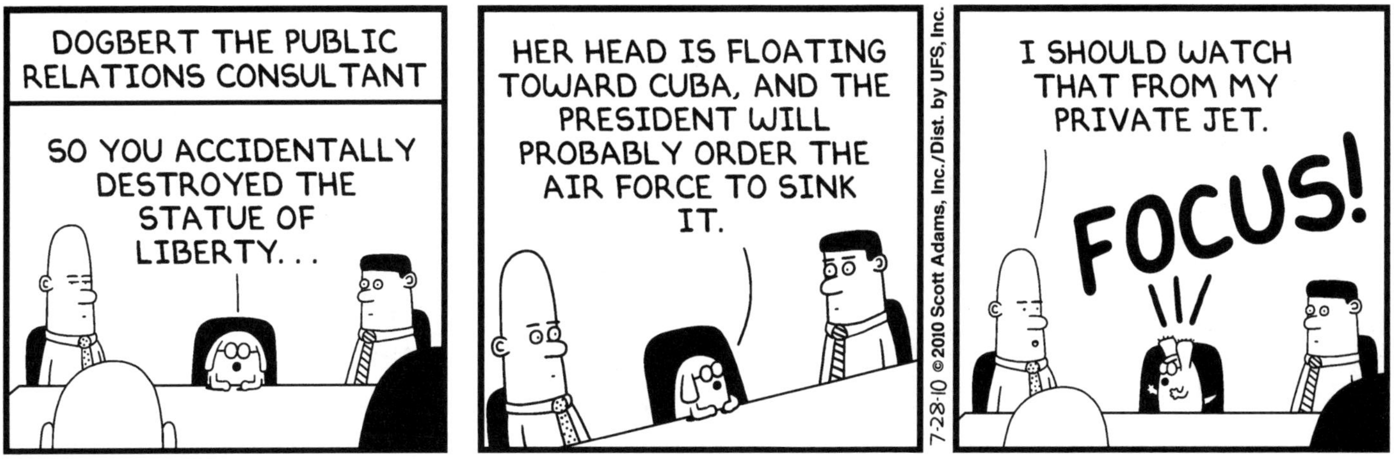
DOGBERT THE PUBLIC RELATIONS CONSULTANT
SO YOU ACCIDENTALLY DESTROYED THE STATUE OF LIBERTY...
HER HEAD IS FLOATING TOWARD CUBA, AND THE PRESIDENT WILL PROBABLY ORDER THE AIR FORCE TO SINK IT.
I SHOULD WATCH THAT FROM MY PRIVATE JET.
FOCUS!
7-28-10 © 2010 Scott Adams, Inc./Dist. by UFS, Inc.

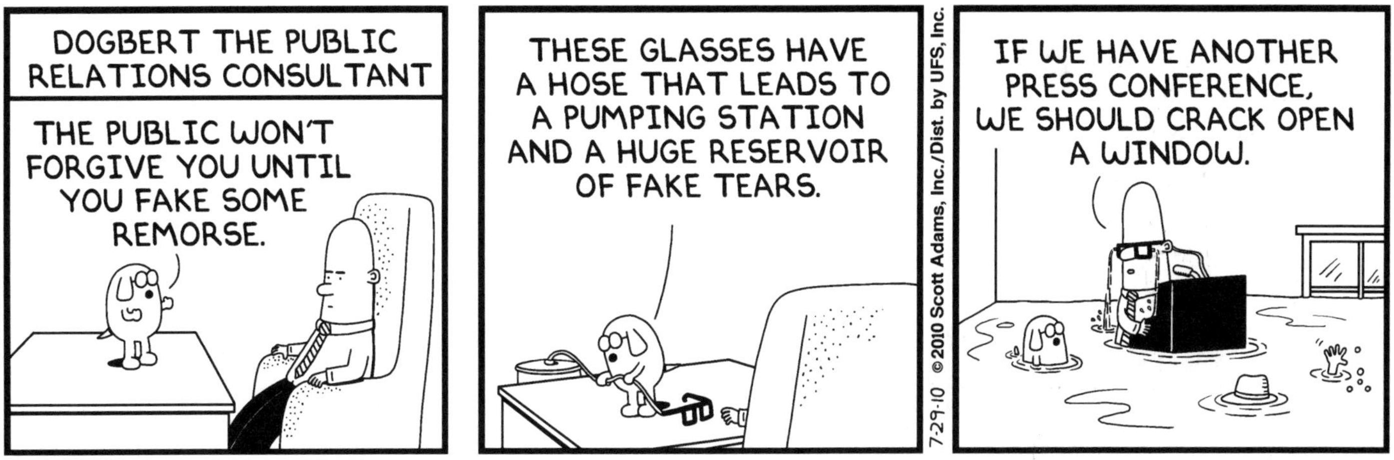
DOGBERT THE PUBLIC RELATIONS CONSULTANT
THE PUBLIC WON'T FORGIVE YOU UNTIL YOU FAKE SOME REMORSE.
THESE GLASSES HAVE A HOSE THAT LEADS TO A PUMPING STATION AND A HUGE RESERVOIR OF FAKE TEARS.
IF WE HAVE ANOTHER PRESS CONFERENCE, WE SHOULD CRACK OPEN A WINDOW.
7-29-10 © 2010 Scott Adams, Inc./Dist. by UFS, Inc.

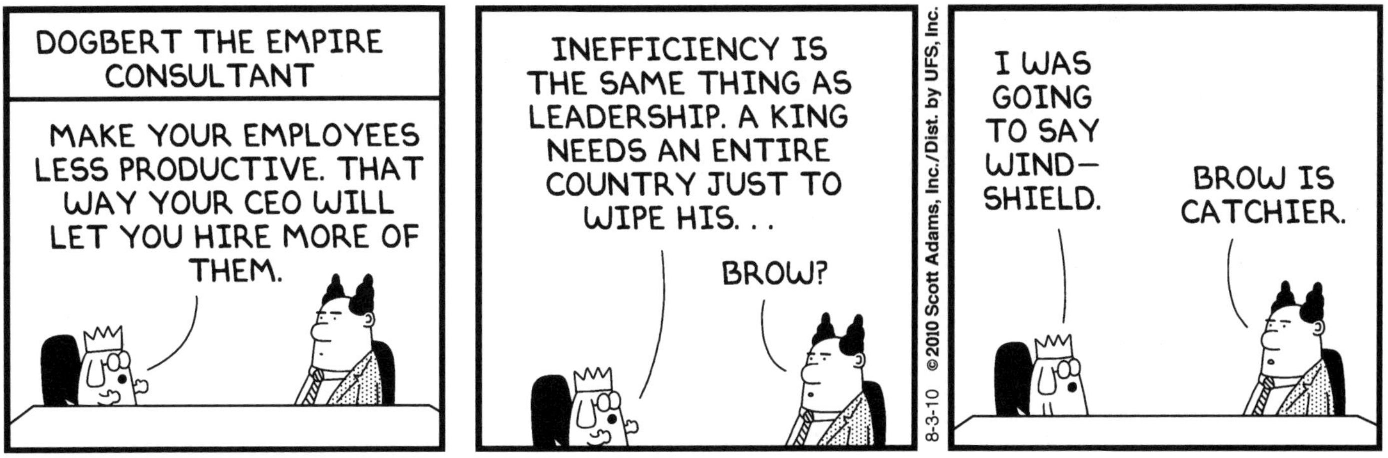
DOGBERT THE EMPIRE CONSULTANT
MAKE YOUR EMPLOYEES LESS PRODUCTIVE. THAT WAY YOUR CEO WILL LET YOU HIRE MORE OF THEM.
INEFFICIENCY IS THE SAME THING AS LEADERSHIP. A KING NEEDS AN ENTIRE COUNTRY JUST TO WIPE HIS...
BROW?
I WAS GOING TO SAY WIND-SHIELD.
BROW IS CATCHIER.
8-3-10 © 2010 Scott Adams, Inc./Dist. by UFS, Inc.

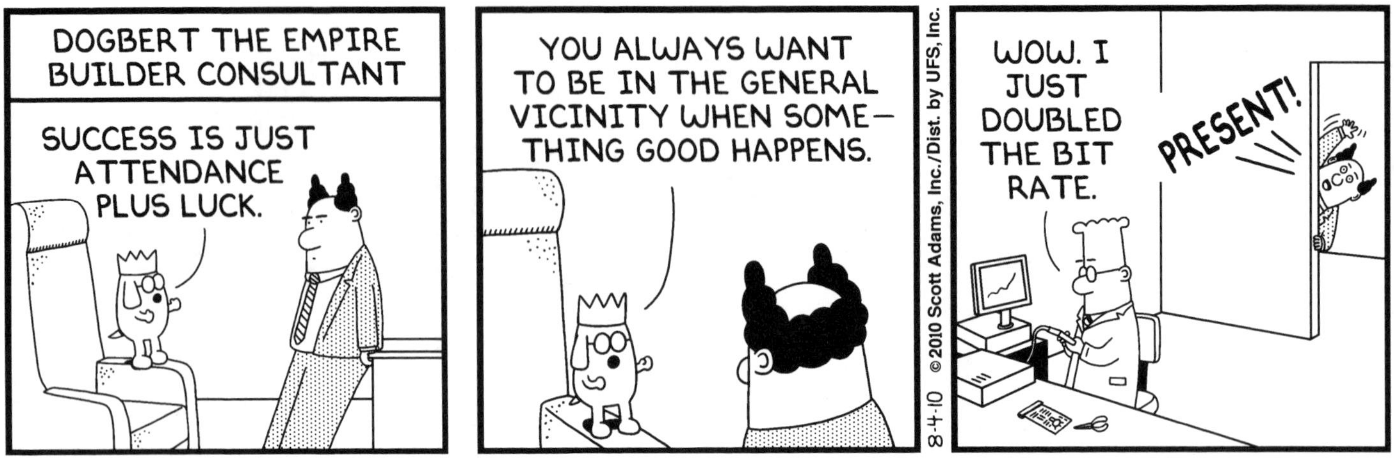
DOGBERT THE EMPIRE BUILDER CONSULTANT
SUCCESS IS JUST ATTENDANCE PLUS LUCK.
YOU ALWAYS WANT TO BE IN THE GENERAL VICINITY WHEN SOME-THING GOOD HAPPENS.
8-4-10 © 2010 Scott Adams, Inc./Dist. by UFS, Inc.
WOW. I JUST DOUBLED THE BIT RATE.
PRESENT!

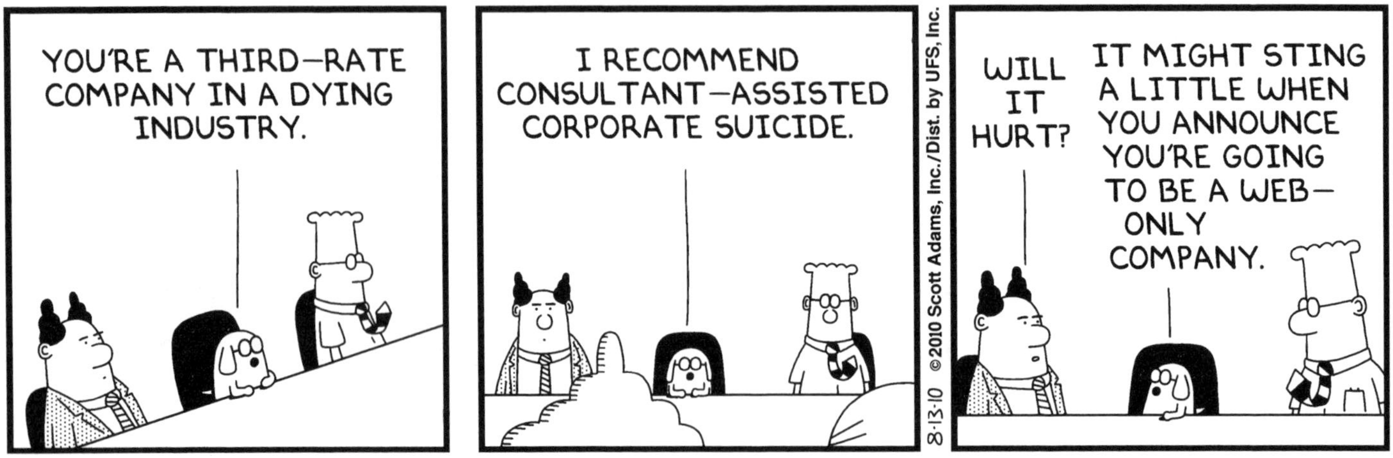
YOU'RE A THIRD-RATE COMPANY IN A DYING INDUSTRY.
I RECOMMEND CONSULTANT-ASSISTED CORPORATE SUICIDE.
8-13-10 © 2010 Scott Adams, Inc./Dist. by UFS, Inc.
WILL IT HURT?
IT MIGHT STING A LITTLE WHEN YOU ANNOUNCE YOU'RE GOING TO BE A WEB-ONLY COMPANY.

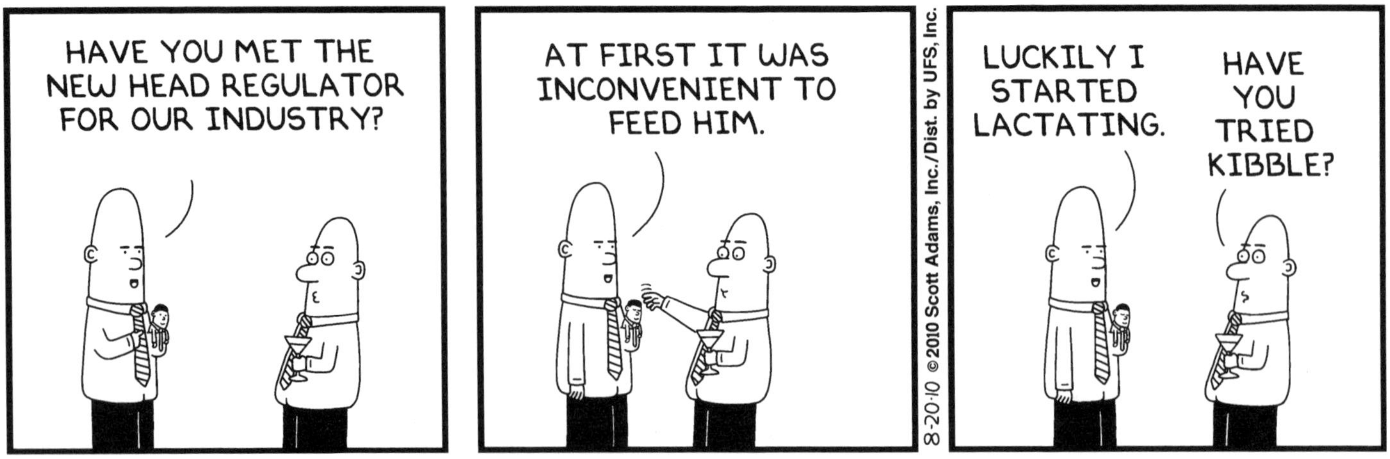
HAVE YOU MET THE NEW HEAD REGULATOR FOR OUR INDUSTRY?
AT FIRST IT WAS INCONVENIENT TO FEED HIM.
8-20-10 © 2010 Scott Adams, Inc./Dist. by UFS, Inc.
LUCKILY I STARTED LACTATING.
HAVE YOU TRIED KIBBLE?

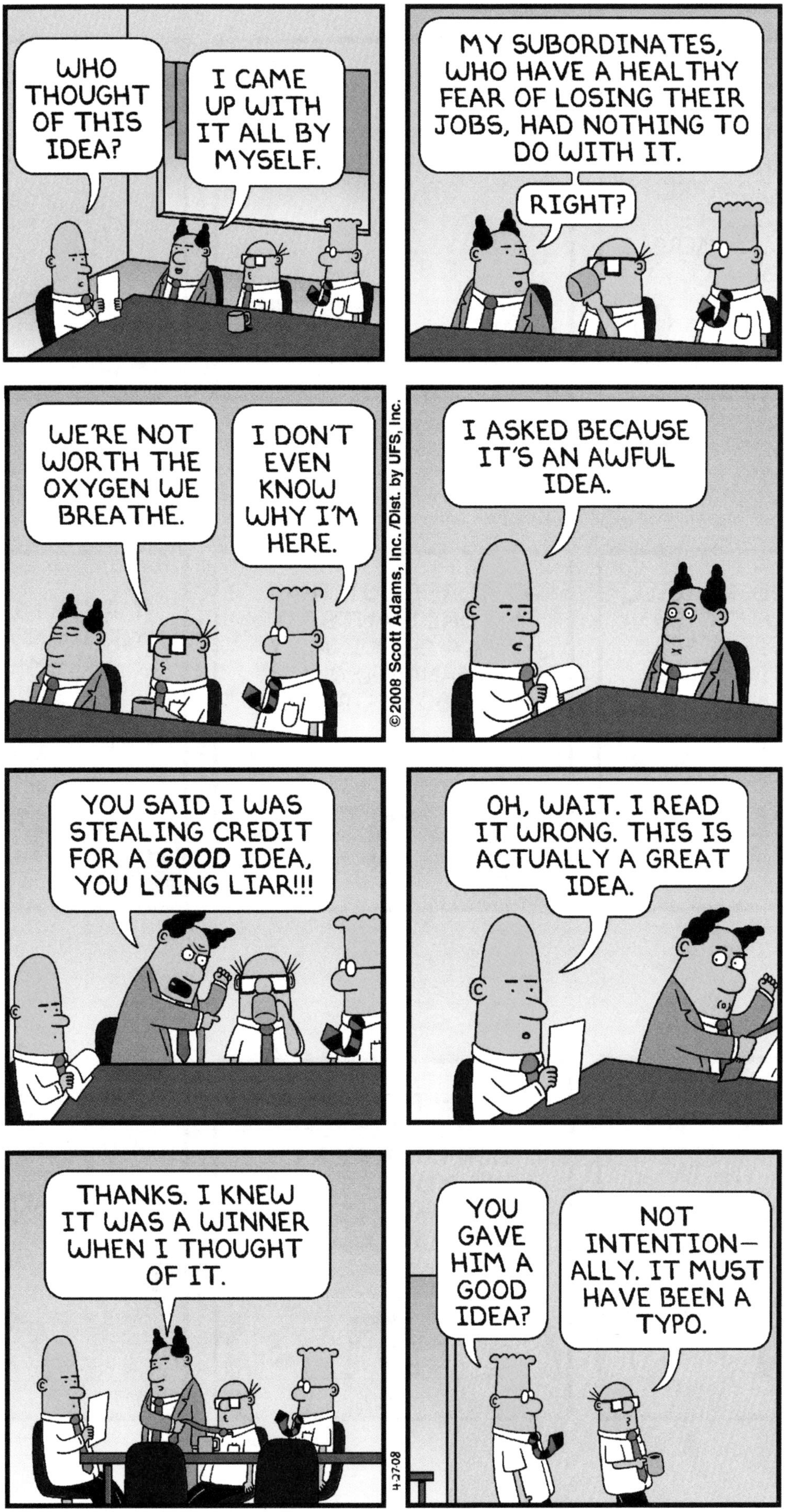
WHO THOUGHT OF THIS IDEA?
I CAME UP WITH IT ALL BY MYSELF.
MY SUBORDINATES, WHO HAVE A HEALTHY FEAR OF LOSING THEIR JOBS, HAD NOTHING TO DO WITH IT.
RIGHT?
WE'RE NOT WORTH THE OXYGEN WE BREATHE.
I DON'T EVEN KNOW WHY I'M HERE.
© 2008 Scott Adams, Inc./Dist. by UFS, Inc.
I ASKED BECAUSE IT'S AN AWFUL IDEA.
YOU SAID I WAS STEALING CREDIT FOR A *GOOD* IDEA, YOU LYING LIAR!!!
OH, WAIT. I READ IT WRONG. THIS IS ACTUALLY A GREAT IDEA.
THANKS. I KNEW IT WAS A WINNER WHEN I THOUGHT OF IT.
4-27-08
YOU GAVE HIM A GOOD IDEA?
NOT INTENTION-ALLY. IT MUST HAVE BEEN A TYPO.

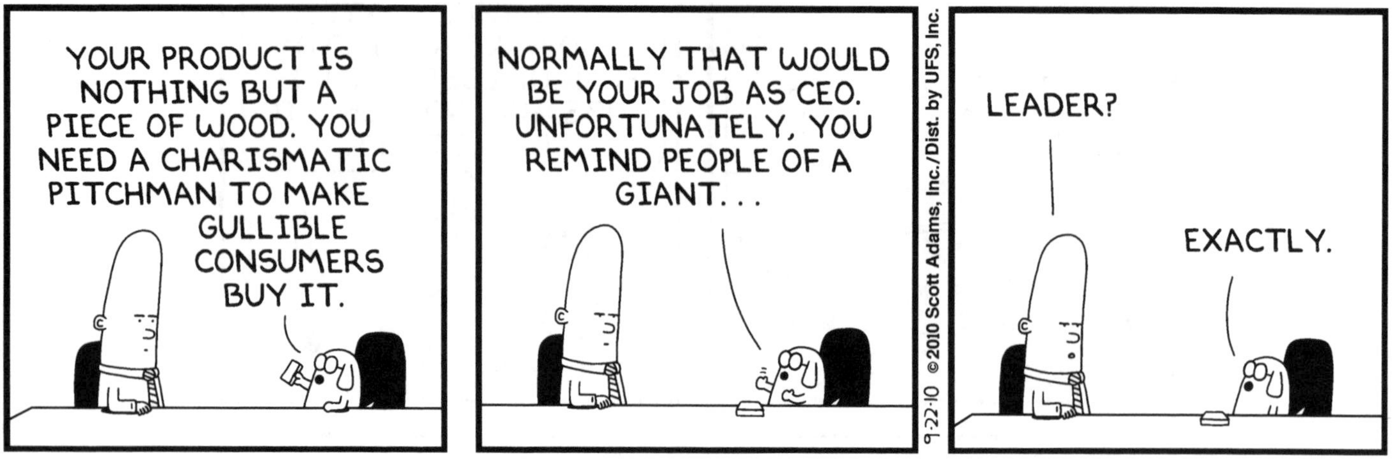
YOUR PRODUCT IS NOTHING BUT A PIECE OF WOOD. YOU NEED A CHARISMATIC PITCHMAN TO MAKE GULLIBLE CONSUMERS BUY IT.
NORMALLY THAT WOULD BE YOUR JOB AS CEO. UNFORTUNATELY, YOU REMIND PEOPLE OF A GIANT...
LEADER?
EXACTLY.
9-22-10 ©2010 Scott Adams, Inc./Dist. by UFS, Inc.

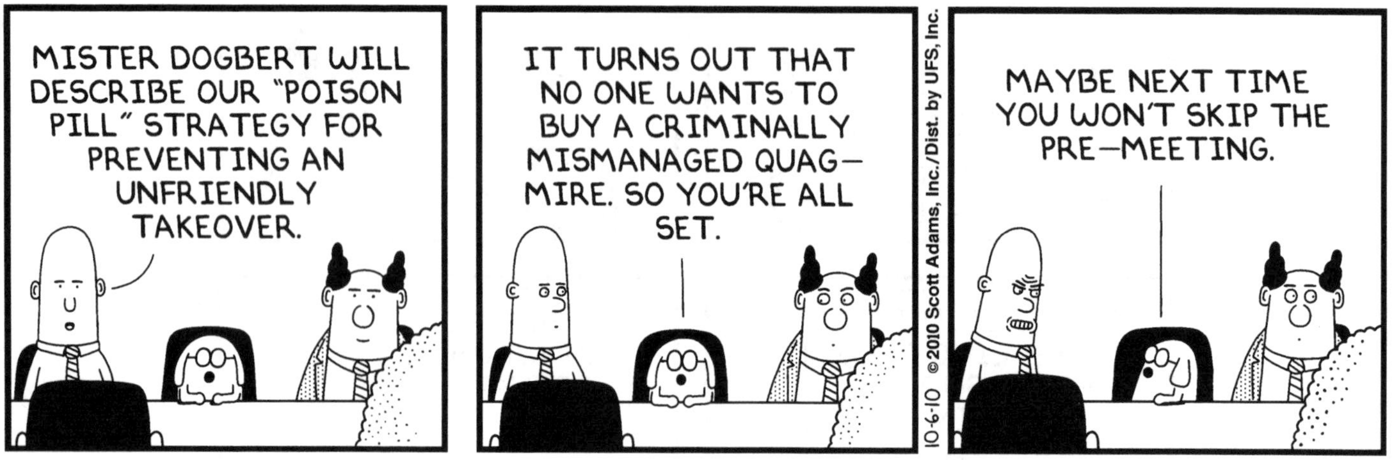
MISTER DOGBERT WILL DESCRIBE OUR "POISON PILL" STRATEGY FOR PREVENTING AN UNFRIENDLY TAKEOVER.
IT TURNS OUT THAT NO ONE WANTS TO BUY A CRIMINALLY MISMANAGED QUAG-MIRE. SO YOU'RE ALL SET.
MAYBE NEXT TIME YOU WON'T SKIP THE PRE-MEETING.
10-6-10 ©2010 Scott Adams, Inc./Dist. by UFS, Inc.

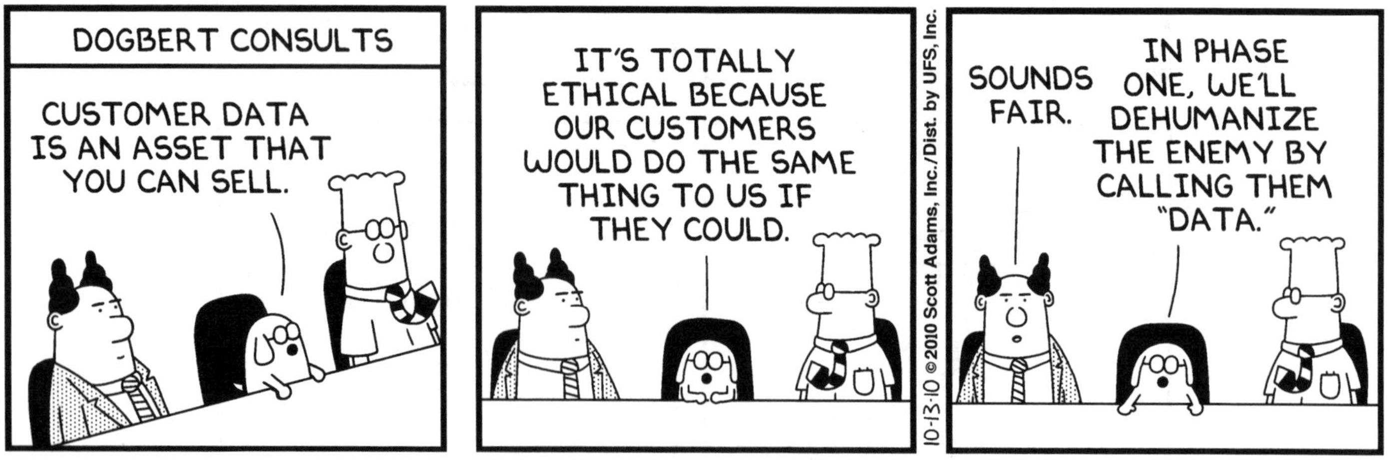
DOGBERT CONSULTS
CUSTOMER DATA IS AN ASSET THAT YOU CAN SELL.
IT'S TOTALLY ETHICAL BECAUSE OUR CUSTOMERS WOULD DO THE SAME THING TO US IF THEY COULD.
SOUNDS FAIR.
IN PHASE ONE, WE'LL DEHUMANIZE THE ENEMY BY CALLING THEM "DATA."
10-13-10 ©2010 Scott Adams, Inc./Dist. by UFS, Inc.

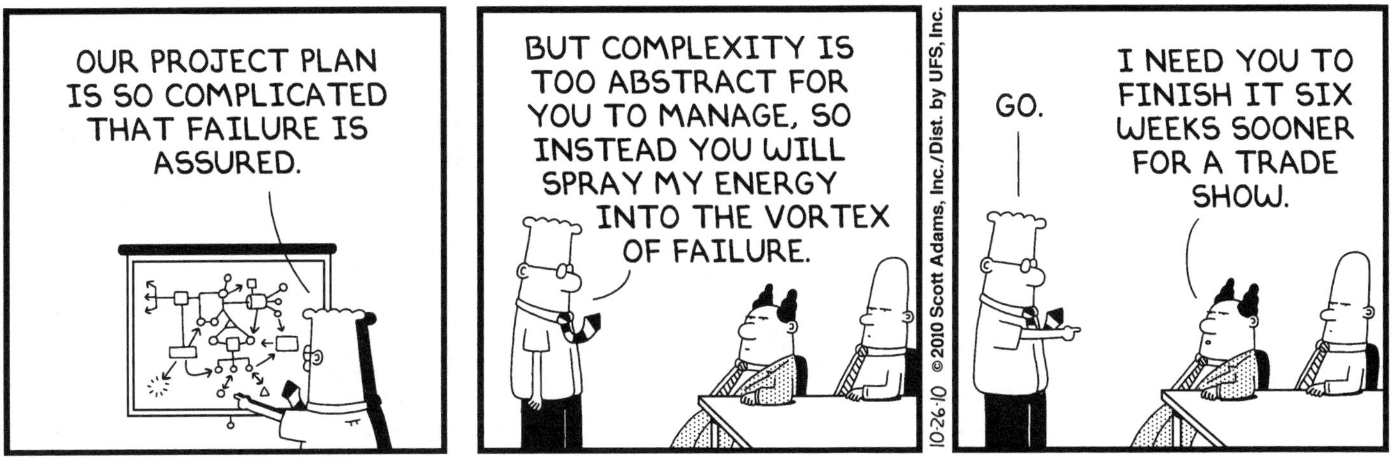
OUR PROJECT PLAN IS SO COMPLICATED THAT FAILURE IS ASSURED.
BUT COMPLEXITY IS TOO ABSTRACT FOR YOU TO MANAGE, SO INSTEAD YOU WILL SPRAY MY ENERGY INTO THE VORTEX OF FAILURE.
10-26-10 ©2010 Scott Adams, Inc./Dist. by UFS, Inc.
GO.
I NEED YOU TO FINISH IT SIX WEEKS SOONER FOR A TRADE SHOW.

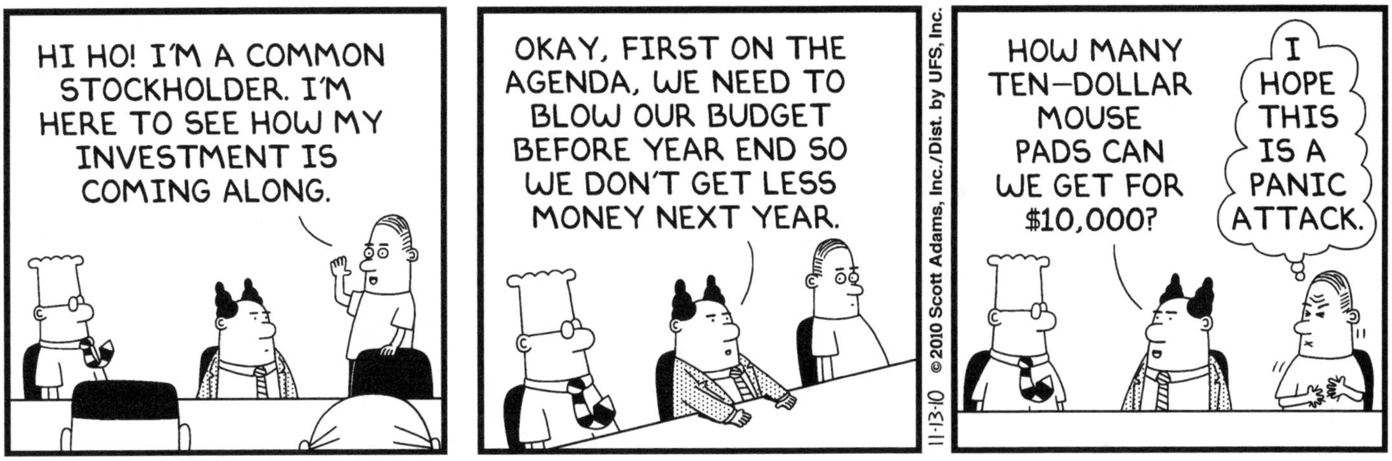
HI HO! I'M A COMMON STOCKHOLDER. I'M HERE TO SEE HOW MY INVESTMENT IS COMING ALONG.
OKAY, FIRST ON THE AGENDA, WE NEED TO BLOW OUR BUDGET BEFORE YEAR END SO WE DON'T GET LESS MONEY NEXT YEAR.
11-13-10 ©2010 Scott Adams, Inc./Dist. by UFS, Inc.
HOW MANY TEN-DOLLAR MOUSE PADS CAN WE GET FOR $10,000?
I HOPE THIS IS A PANIC ATTACK.

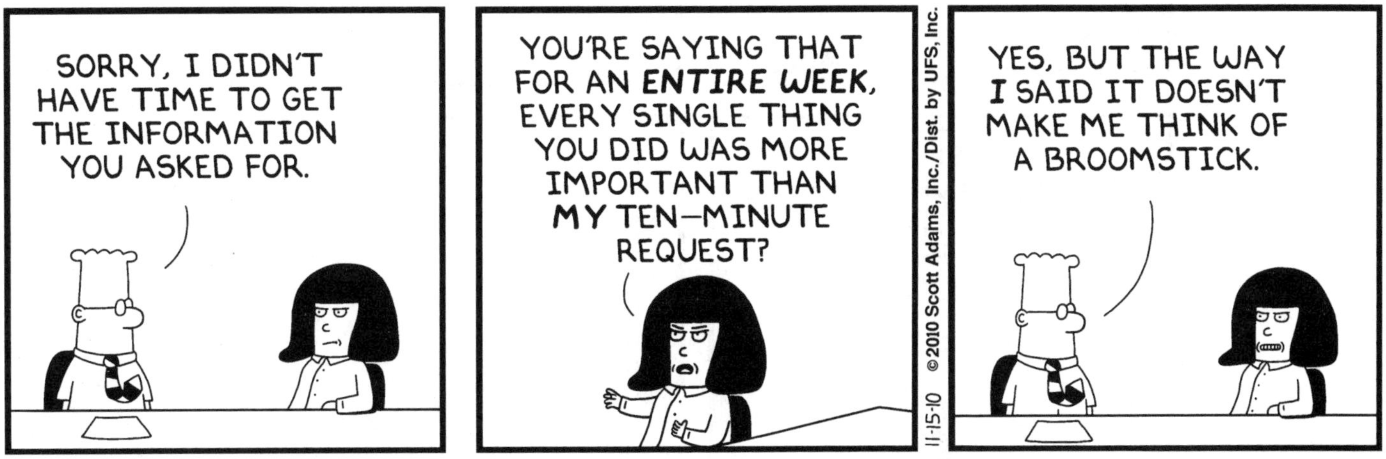
SORRY, I DIDN'T HAVE TIME TO GET THE INFORMATION YOU ASKED FOR.
YOU'RE SAYING THAT FOR AN ENTIRE WEEK, EVERY SINGLE THING YOU DID WAS MORE IMPORTANT THAN MY TEN-MINUTE REQUEST?
11-15-10 ©2010 Scott Adams, Inc./Dist. by UFS, Inc.
YES, BUT THE WAY I SAID IT DOESN'T MAKE ME THINK OF A BROOMSTICK.

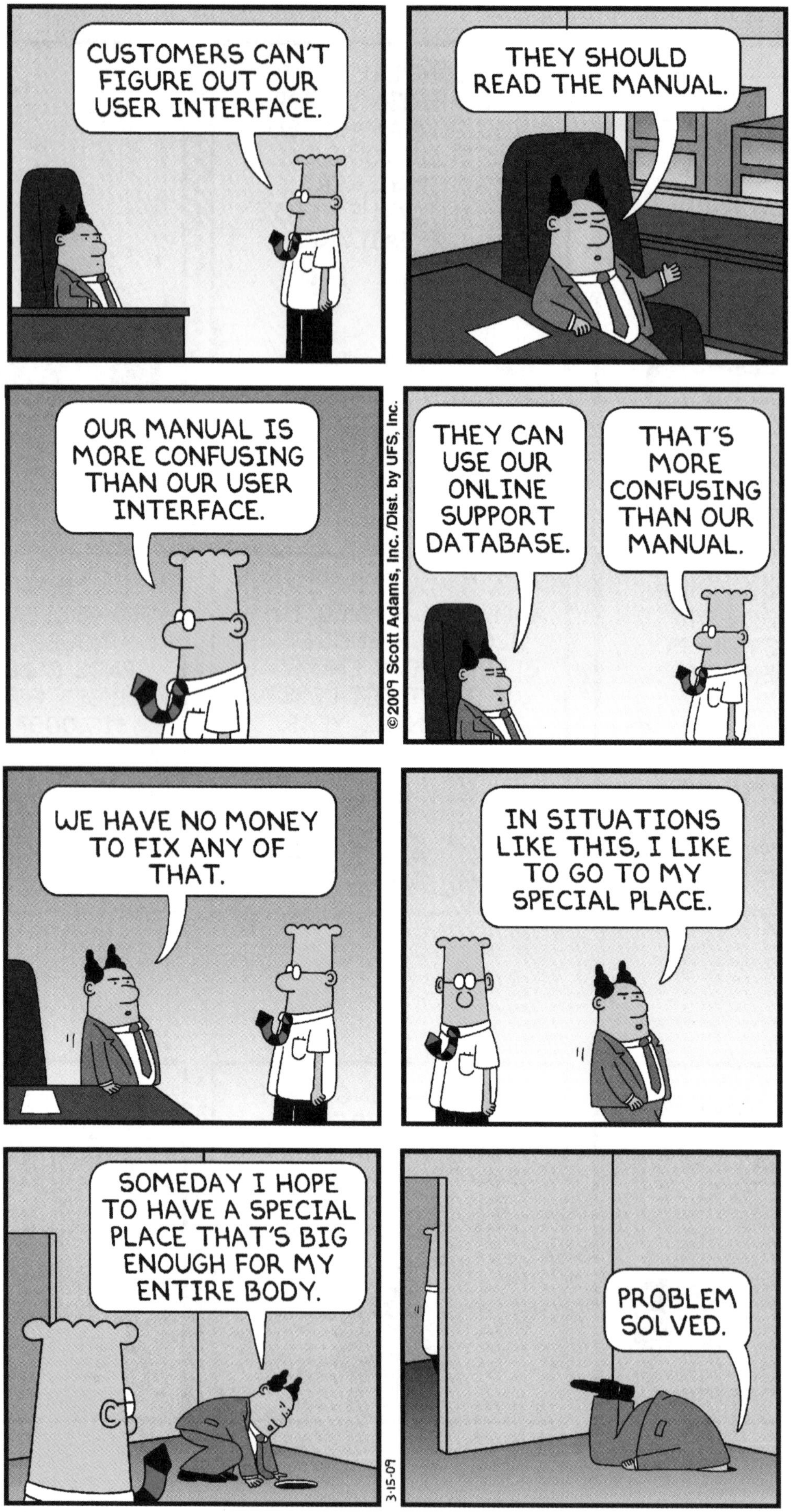
CUSTOMERS CAN'T FIGURE OUT OUR USER INTERFACE.
THEY SHOULD READ THE MANUAL.
OUR MANUAL IS MORE CONFUSING THAN OUR USER INTERFACE.
© 2009 Scott Adams, Inc. /Dist. by UFS, Inc.
THEY CAN USE OUR ONLINE SUPPORT DATABASE.
THAT'S MORE CONFUSING THAN OUR MANUAL.
WE HAVE NO MONEY TO FIX ANY OF THAT.
IN SITUATIONS LIKE THIS, I LIKE TO GO TO MY SPECIAL PLACE.
SOMEDAY I HOPE TO HAVE A SPECIAL PLACE THAT'S BIG ENOUGH FOR MY ENTIRE BODY.
3-15-09
PROBLEM SOLVED.

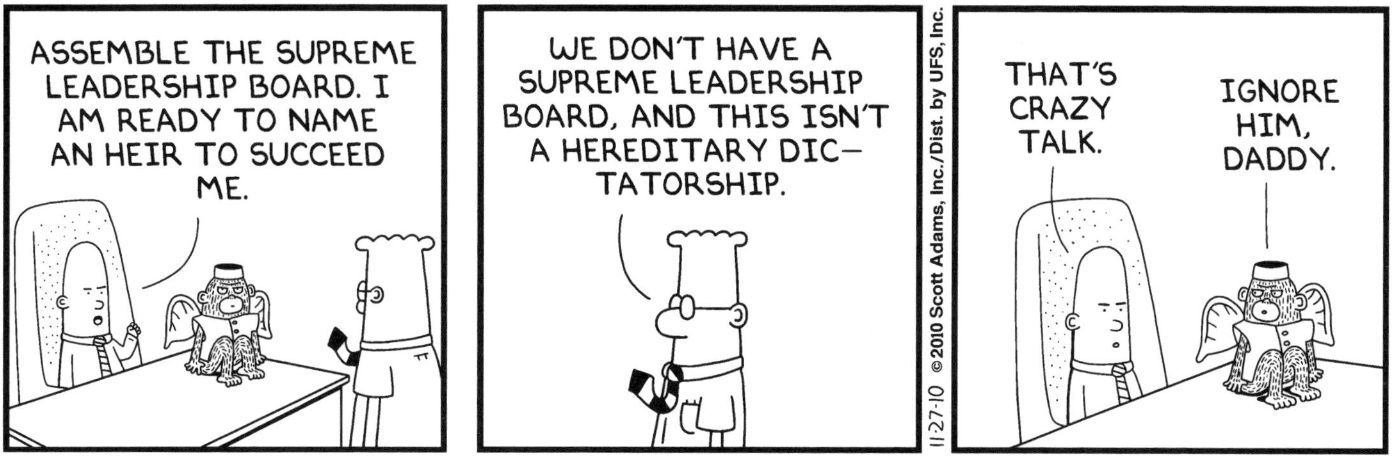
ASSEMBLE THE SUPREME LEADERSHIP BOARD. I AM READY TO NAME AN HEIR TO SUCCEED ME.
WE DON'T HAVE A SUPREME LEADERSHIP BOARD, AND THIS ISN'T A HEREDITARY DIC— TATORSHIP.
11-27-10 ©2010 Scott Adams, Inc./Dist. by UFS, Inc.
THAT'S CRAZY TALK.
IGNORE HIM, DADDY.

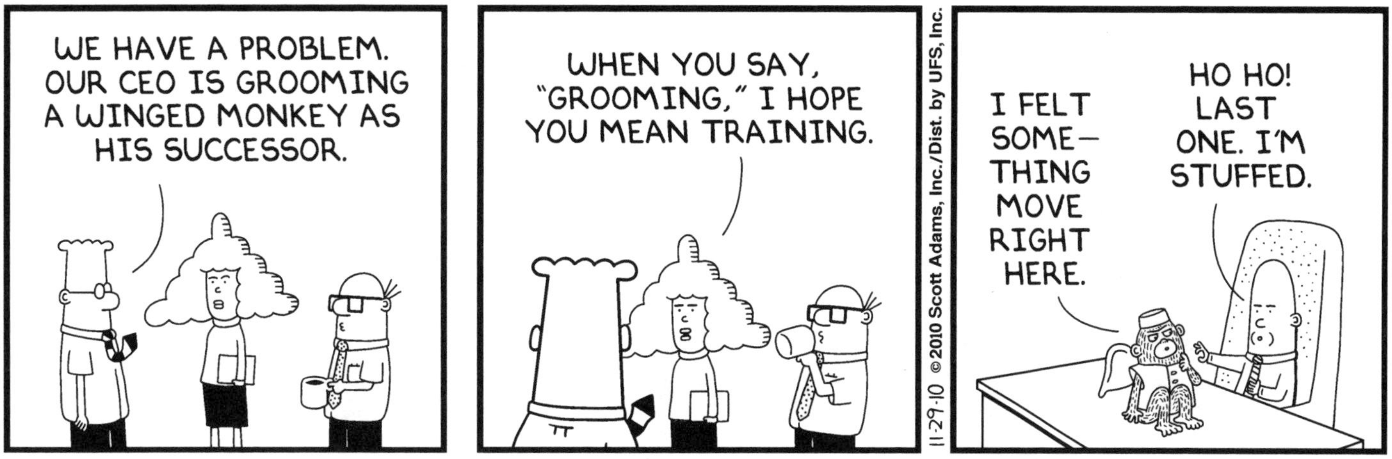
WE HAVE A PROBLEM. OUR CEO IS GROOMING A WINGED MONKEY AS HIS SUCCESSOR.
WHEN YOU SAY, "GROOMING," I HOPE YOU MEAN TRAINING.
11-29-10 ©2010 Scott Adams, Inc./Dist. by UFS, Inc.
I FELT SOME— THING MOVE RIGHT HERE.
HO HO! LAST ONE. I'M STUFFED.

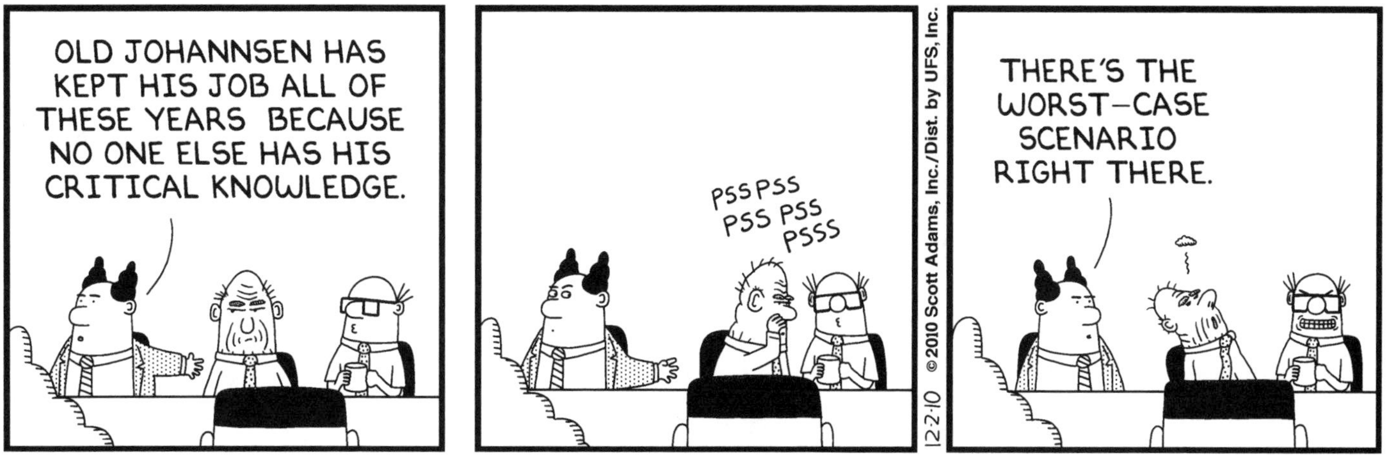
OLD JOHANNSEN HAS KEPT HIS JOB ALL OF THESE YEARS BECAUSE NO ONE ELSE HAS HIS CRITICAL KNOWLEDGE.
PSSPSS PSS PSS PSSS
12-2-10 ©2010 Scott Adams, Inc./Dist. by UFS, Inc.
THERE'S THE WORST—CASE SCENARIO RIGHT THERE.

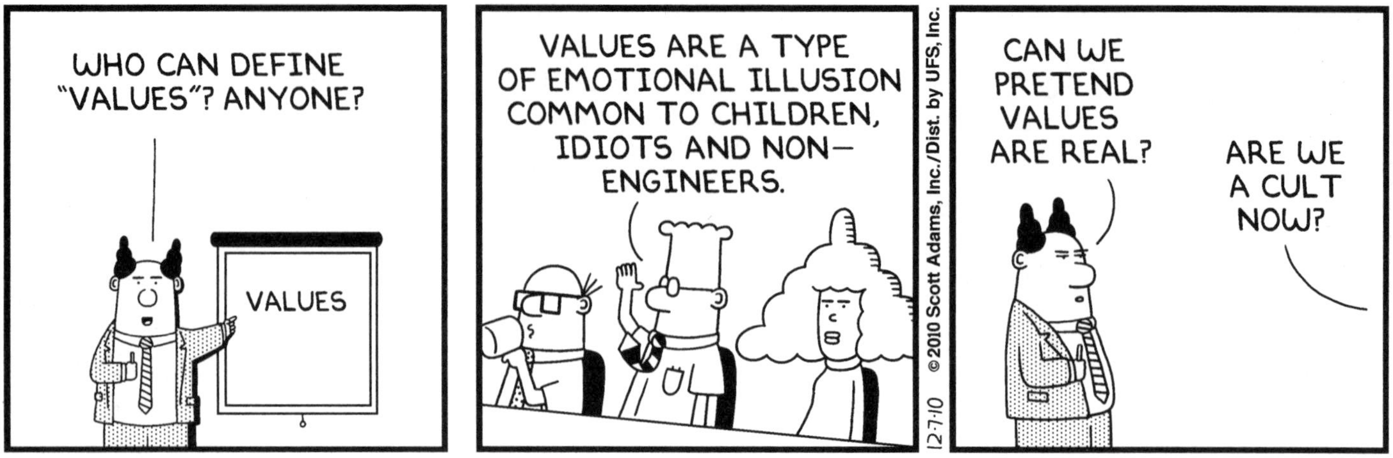
WHO CAN DEFINE "VALUES"? ANYONE?
VALUES
VALUES ARE A TYPE OF EMOTIONAL ILLUSION COMMON TO CHILDREN, IDIOTS AND NON-ENGINEERS.
© 2010 Scott Adams, Inc./Dist. by UFS, Inc.
12-7-10
CAN WE PRETEND VALUES ARE REAL?
ARE WE A CULT NOW?

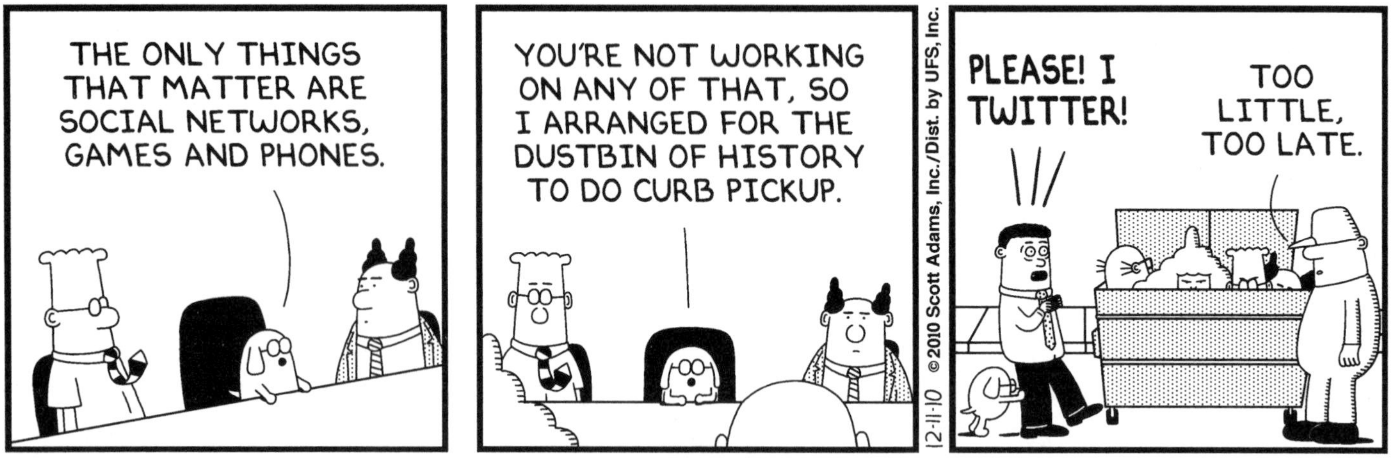
THE ONLY THINGS THAT MATTER ARE SOCIAL NETWORKS, GAMES AND PHONES.
YOU'RE NOT WORKING ON ANY OF THAT, SO I ARRANGED FOR THE DUSTBIN OF HISTORY TO DO CURB PICKUP.
© 2010 Scott Adams, Inc./Dist. by UFS, Inc.
12-11-10
PLEASE! I TWITTER!
TOO LITTLE, TOO LATE.

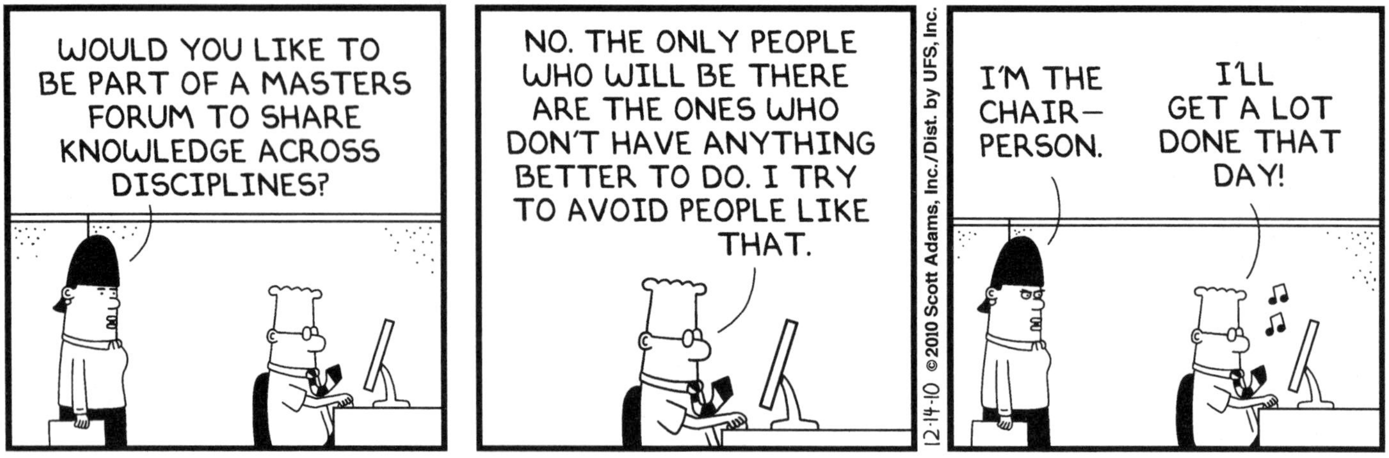
WOULD YOU LIKE TO BE PART OF A MASTERS FORUM TO SHARE KNOWLEDGE ACROSS DISCIPLINES?
NO. THE ONLY PEOPLE WHO WILL BE THERE ARE THE ONES WHO DON'T HAVE ANYTHING BETTER TO DO. I TRY TO AVOID PEOPLE LIKE THAT.
© 2010 Scott Adams, Inc./Dist. by UFS, Inc.
12-14-10
I'M THE CHAIR-PERSON.
I'LL GET A LOT DONE THAT DAY!

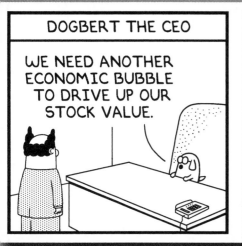

DOGBERT THE CEO
WE NEED ANOTHER ECONOMIC BUBBLE TO DRIVE UP OUR STOCK VALUE.
ASSEMBLE THE ILLUMINATI!
10-3-09 © 2009 Scott Adams, Inc./Dist. by UFS, Inc.
AS USUAL, I'LL CREATE THE MEDIA FRENZY, DOGBERT WILL MANIPULATE PRICES, AND IXPU WILL VAPORIZE THE WHISTLE-BLOWERS.

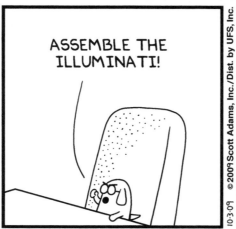

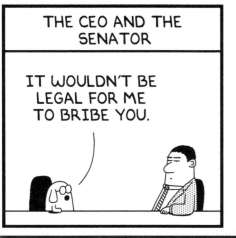

THE CEO AND THE SENATOR
IT WOULDN'T BE LEGAL FOR ME TO BRIBE YOU.
SO I HIRED YOUR WIFE AS A CONSULTANT DESPITE THE FACT THAT SHE THINKS "PRESENT VALUE" IS SOME SORT OF GIFT CARD.
10-14-09 © 2009 Scott Adams, Inc./Dist. by UFS, Inc.
AND I WROTE SOME LEGISLATION FOR YOU BECAUSE YOU'RE A LAZY THIEF.
HA HA! LET'S CALL THAT "ACCESS."

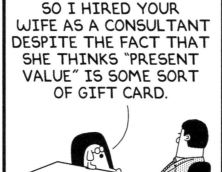

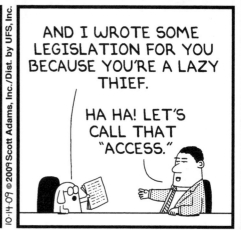

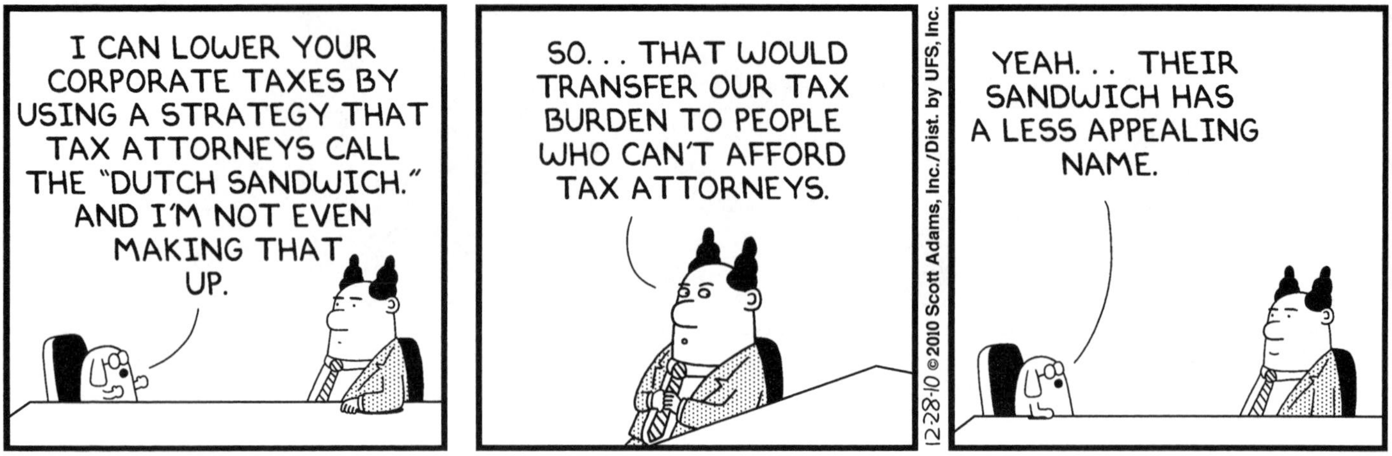
I CAN LOWER YOUR CORPORATE TAXES BY USING A STRATEGY THAT TAX ATTORNEYS CALL THE "DUTCH SANDWICH." AND I'M NOT EVEN MAKING THAT UP.
SO. . . THAT WOULD TRANSFER OUR TAX BURDEN TO PEOPLE WHO CAN'T AFFORD TAX ATTORNEYS.
12-28-10 © 2010 Scott Adams, Inc./Dist. by UFS, Inc.
YEAH. . . THEIR SANDWICH HAS A LESS APPEALING NAME.

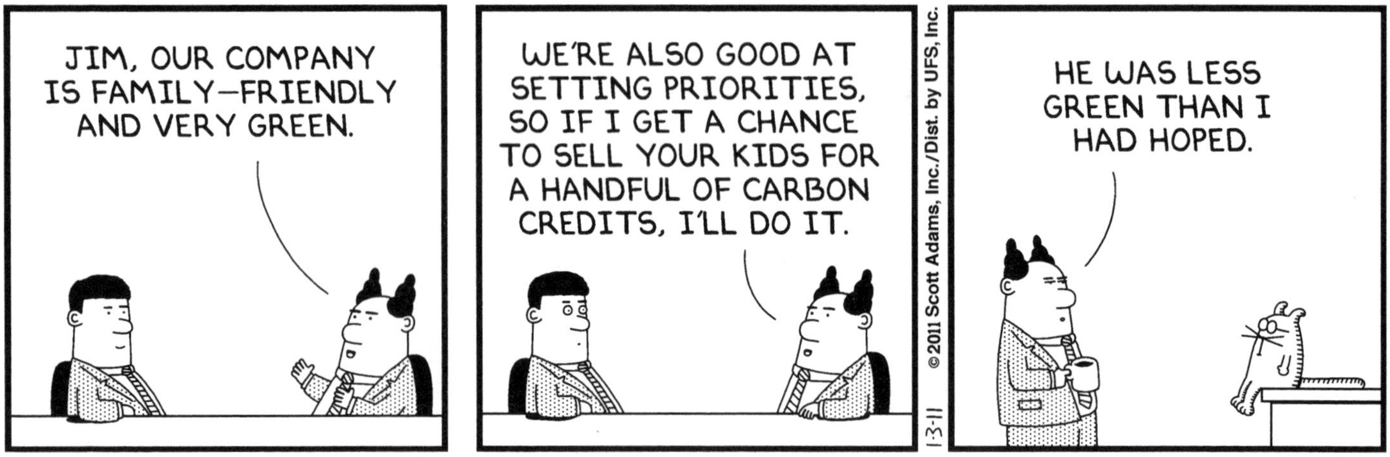
JIM, OUR COMPANY IS FAMILY-FRIENDLY AND VERY GREEN.
WE'RE ALSO GOOD AT SETTING PRIORITIES, SO IF I GET A CHANCE TO SELL YOUR KIDS FOR A HANDFUL OF CARBON CREDITS, I'LL DO IT.
1-3-11 © 2011 Scott Adams, Inc./Dist. by UFS, Inc.
HE WAS LESS GREEN THAN I HAD HOPED.

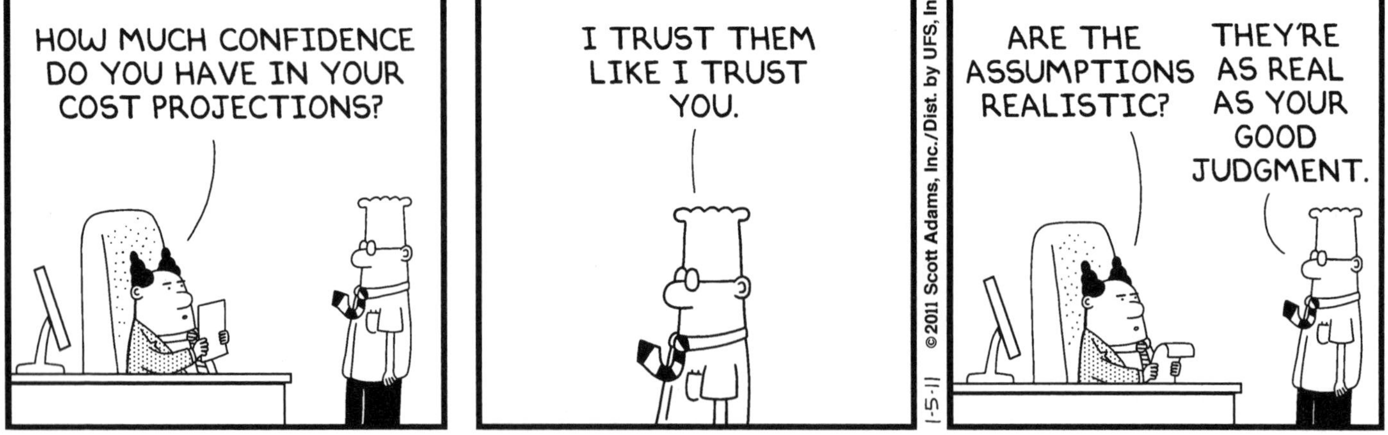
HOW MUCH CONFIDENCE DO YOU HAVE IN YOUR COST PROJECTIONS?
I TRUST THEM LIKE I TRUST YOU.
1-5-11 © 2011 Scott Adams, Inc./Dist. by UFS, Inc.
ARE THE ASSUMPTIONS REALISTIC?
THEY'RE AS REAL AS YOUR GOOD JUDGMENT.

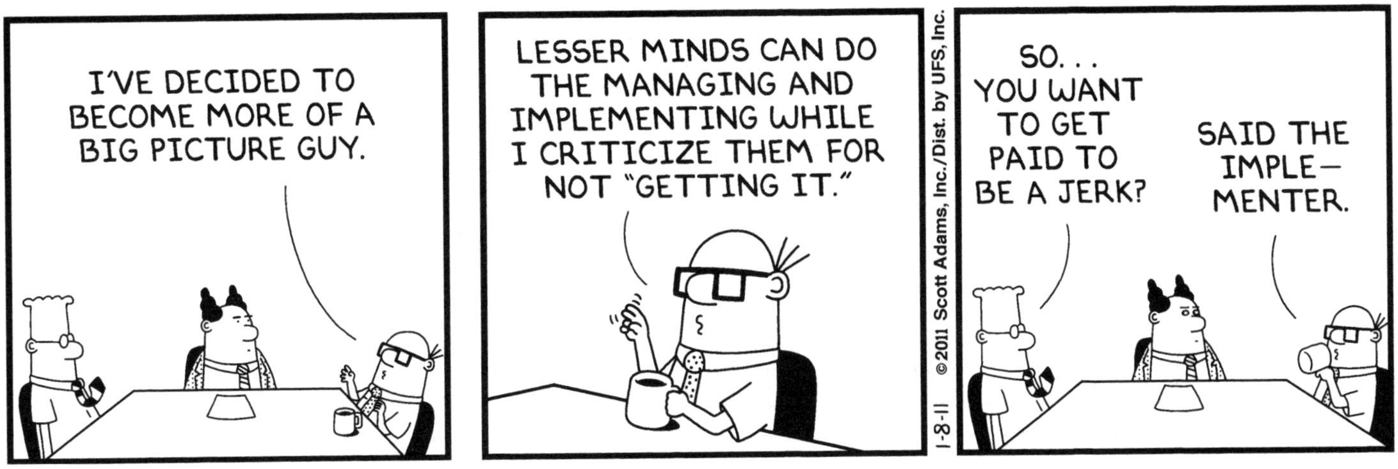
I'VE DECIDED TO BECOME MORE OF A BIG PICTURE GUY.
LESSER MINDS CAN DO THE MANAGING AND IMPLEMENTING WHILE I CRITICIZE THEM FOR NOT "GETTING IT."
SO. . . YOU WANT TO GET PAID TO BE A JERK?
SAID THE IMPLE– MENTER.
1-8-11
©2011 Scott Adams, Inc./Dist. by UFS, Inc.

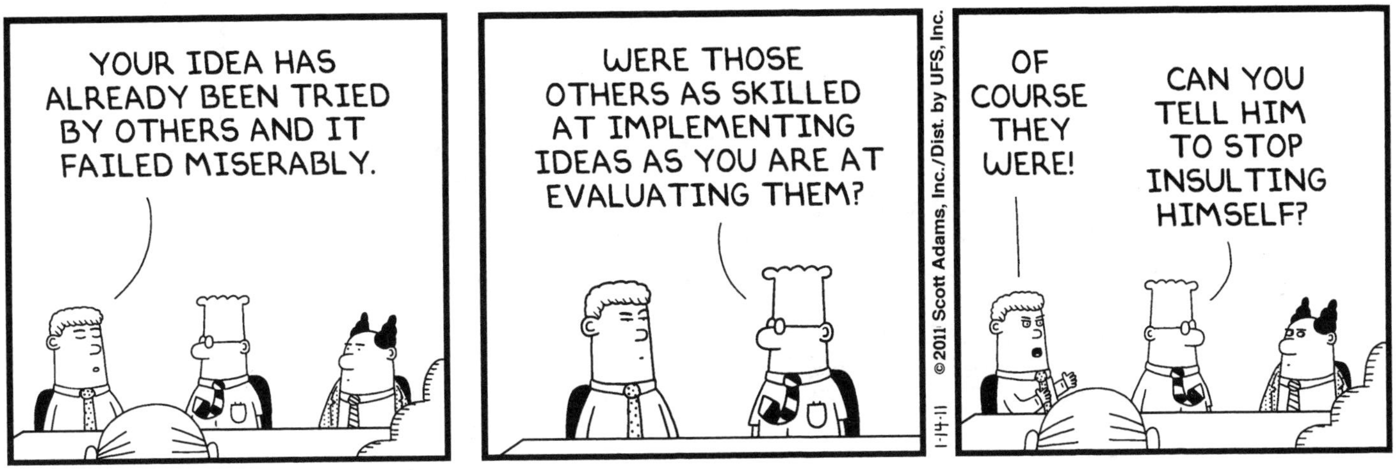
YOUR IDEA HAS ALREADY BEEN TRIED BY OTHERS AND IT FAILED MISERABLY.
WERE THOSE OTHERS AS SKILLED AT IMPLEMENTING IDEAS AS YOU ARE AT EVALUATING THEM?
OF COURSE THEY WERE!
CAN YOU TELL HIM TO STOP INSULTING HIMSELF?
1-14-11
©2011 Scott Adams, Inc./Dist. by UFS, Inc.

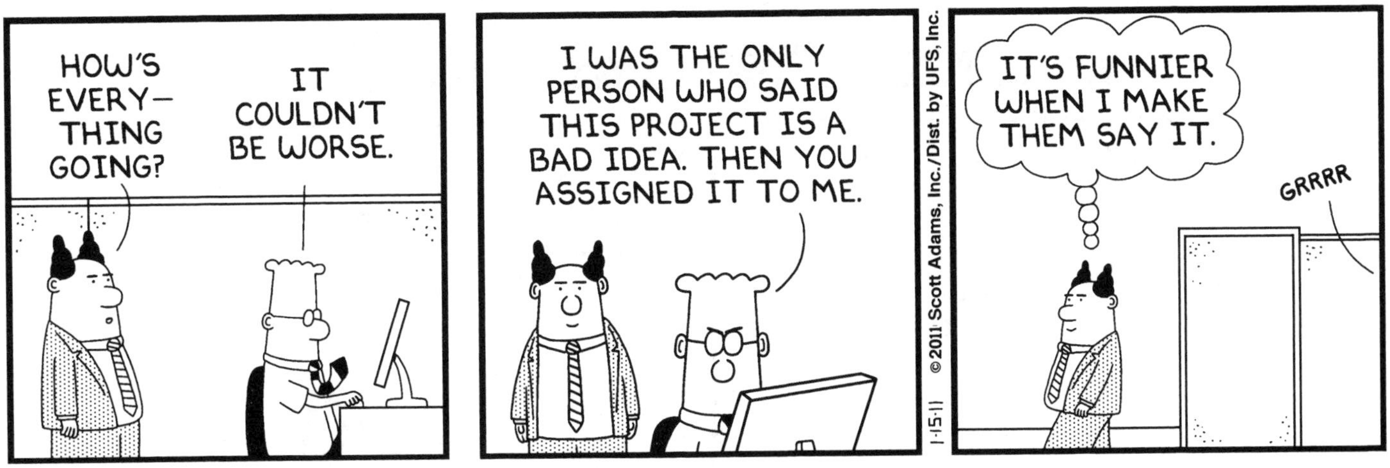
HOW'S EVERY– THING GOING?
IT COULDN'T BE WORSE.
I WAS THE ONLY PERSON WHO SAID THIS PROJECT IS A BAD IDEA. THEN YOU ASSIGNED IT TO ME.
IT'S FUNNIER WHEN I MAKE THEM SAY IT.
GRRRR
1-15-11
©2011 Scott Adams, Inc./Dist. by UFS, Inc.

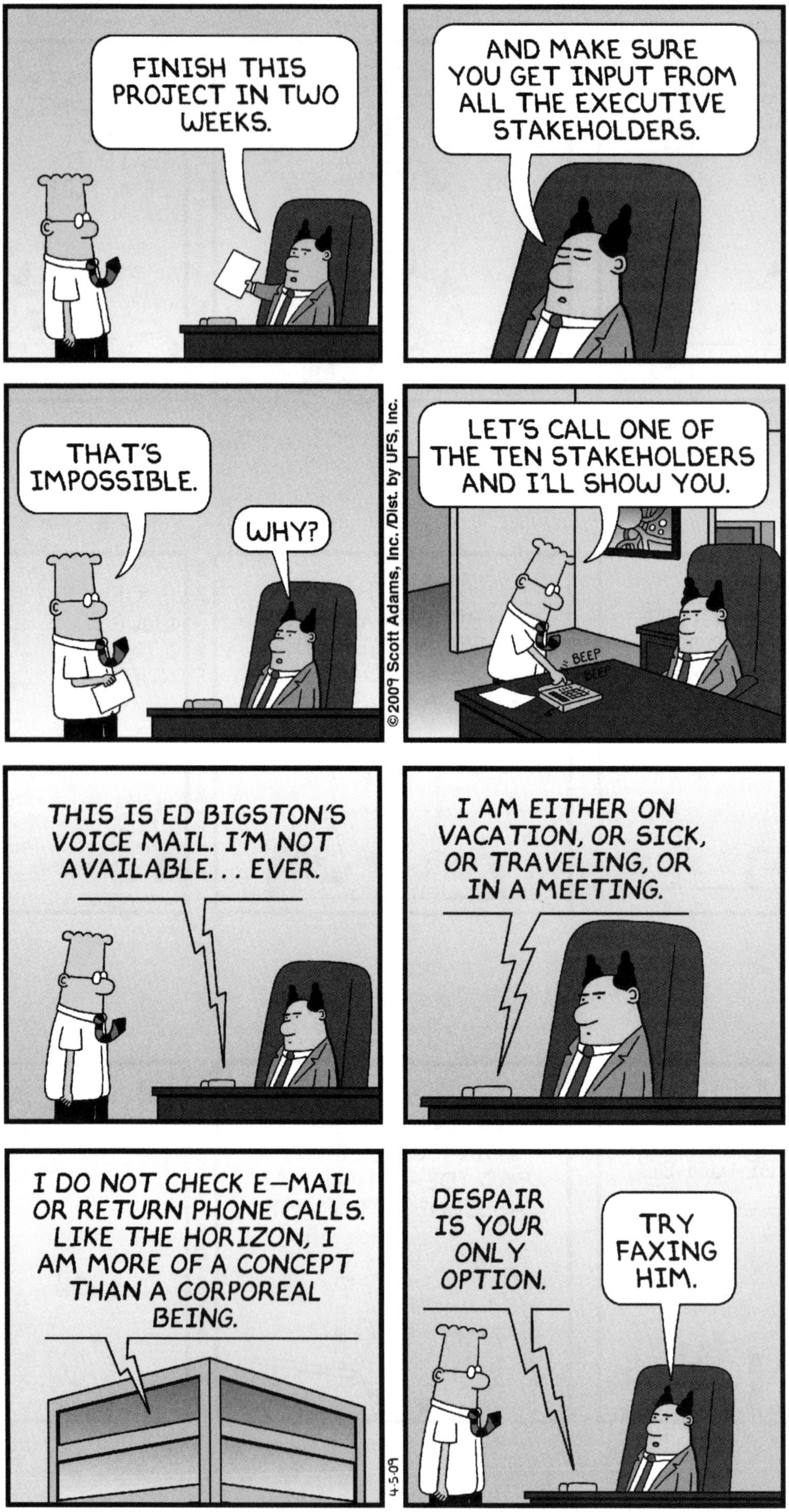
FINISH THIS PROJECT IN TWO WEEKS.
AND MAKE SURE YOU GET INPUT FROM ALL THE EXECUTIVE STAKEHOLDERS.
THAT'S IMPOSSIBLE.
WHY?
©2009 Scott Adams, Inc./Dist. by UFS, Inc.
LET'S CALL ONE OF THE TEN STAKEHOLDERS AND I'LL SHOW YOU.
BEEP
BEEP
THIS IS ED BIGSTON'S VOICE MAIL. I'M NOT AVAILABLE. . . EVER.
I AM EITHER ON VACATION, OR SICK, OR TRAVELING, OR IN A MEETING.
I DO NOT CHECK E-MAIL OR RETURN PHONE CALLS. LIKE THE HORIZON, I AM MORE OF A CONCEPT THAN A CORPOREAL BEING.
4-5-09
DESPAIR IS YOUR ONLY OPTION.
TRY FAXING HIM.

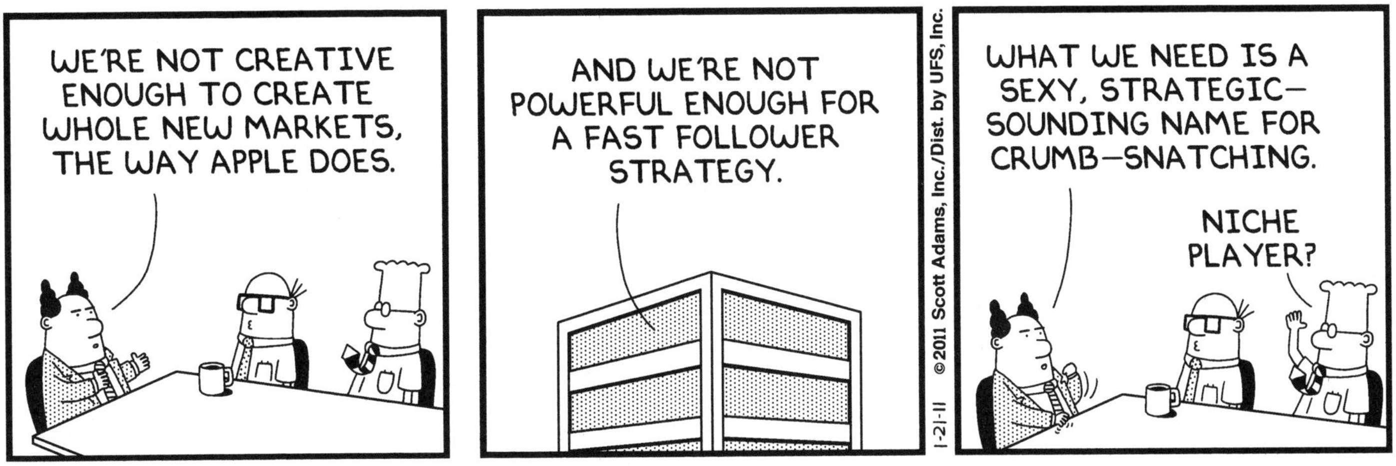
WE'RE NOT CREATIVE ENOUGH TO CREATE WHOLE NEW MARKETS, THE WAY APPLE DOES.
AND WE'RE NOT POWERFUL ENOUGH FOR A FAST FOLLOWER STRATEGY.
1-21-11 ©2011 Scott Adams, Inc./Dist. by UFS, Inc.
WHAT WE NEED IS A SEXY, STRATEGIC–SOUNDING NAME FOR CRUMB–SNATCHING.
NICHE PLAYER?

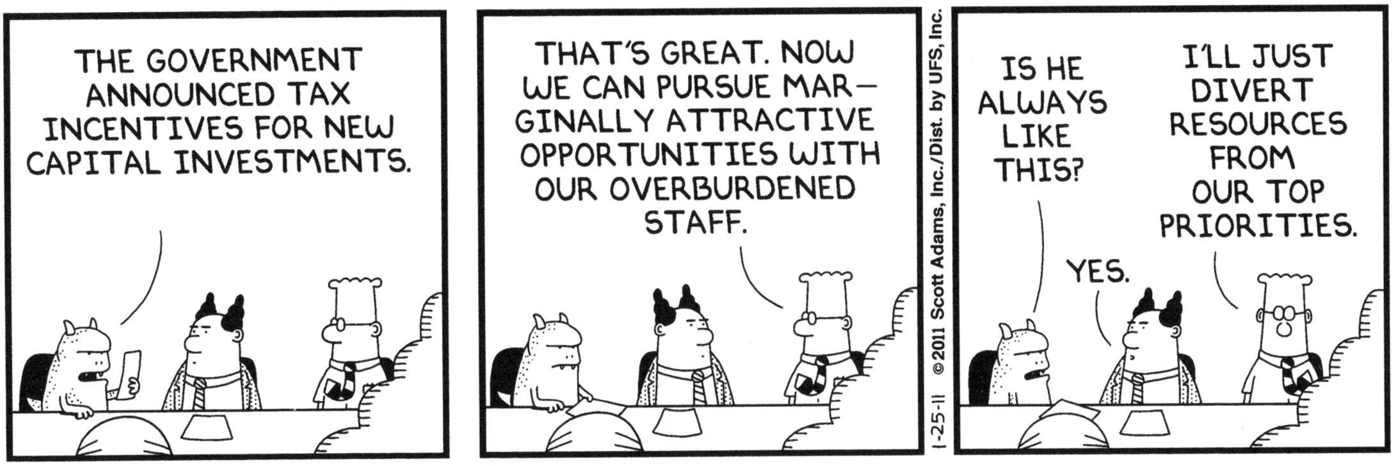
THE GOVERNMENT ANNOUNCED TAX INCENTIVES FOR NEW CAPITAL INVESTMENTS.
THAT'S GREAT. NOW WE CAN PURSUE MAR–GINALLY ATTRACTIVE OPPORTUNITIES WITH OUR OVERBURDENED STAFF.
1-25-11 ©2011 Scott Adams, Inc./Dist. by UFS, Inc.
IS HE ALWAYS LIKE THIS?
YES.
I'LL JUST DIVERT RESOURCES FROM OUR TOP PRIORITIES.

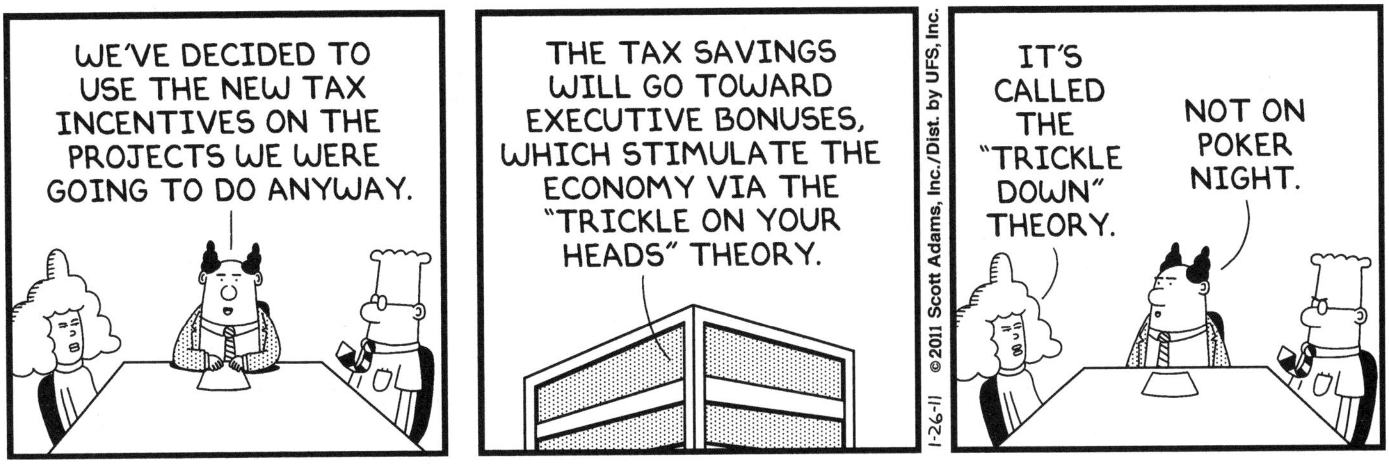
WE'VE DECIDED TO USE THE NEW TAX INCENTIVES ON THE PROJECTS WE WERE GOING TO DO ANYWAY.
THE TAX SAVINGS WILL GO TOWARD EXECUTIVE BONUSES, WHICH STIMULATE THE ECONOMY VIA THE "TRICKLE ON YOUR HEADS" THEORY.
1-26-11 ©2011 Scott Adams, Inc./Dist. by UFS, Inc.
IT'S CALLED THE "TRICKLE DOWN" THEORY.
NOT ON POKER NIGHT.

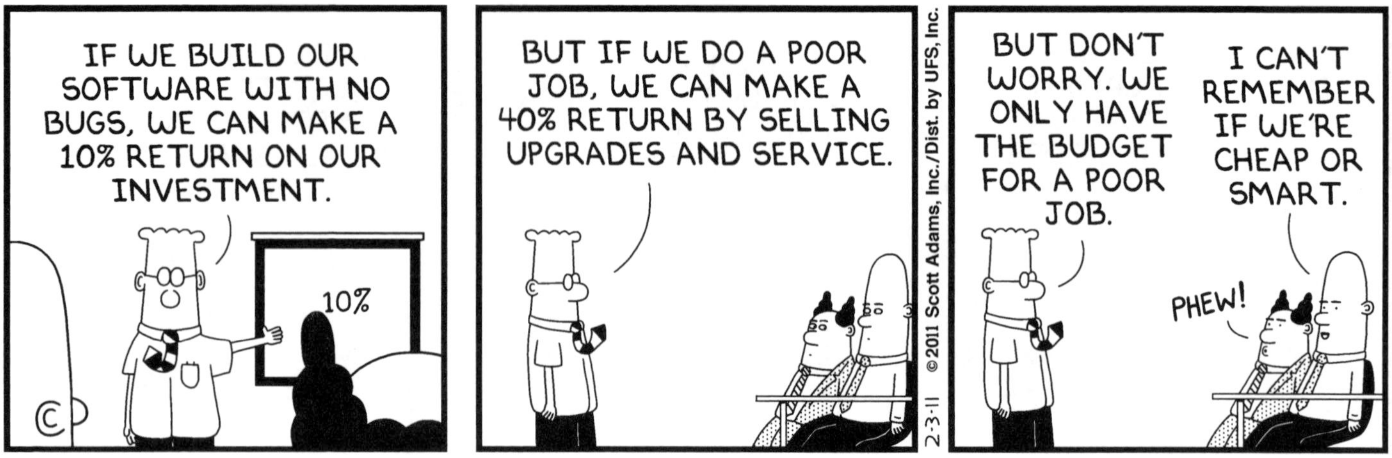
IF WE BUILD OUR SOFTWARE WITH NO BUGS, WE CAN MAKE A 10% RETURN ON OUR INVESTMENT.
10%
BUT IF WE DO A POOR JOB, WE CAN MAKE A 40% RETURN BY SELLING UPGRADES AND SERVICE.
2-3-11 © 2011 Scott Adams, Inc./Dist. by UFS, Inc.
BUT DON'T WORRY. WE ONLY HAVE THE BUDGET FOR A POOR JOB.
I CAN'T REMEMBER IF WE'RE CHEAP OR SMART.
PHEW!

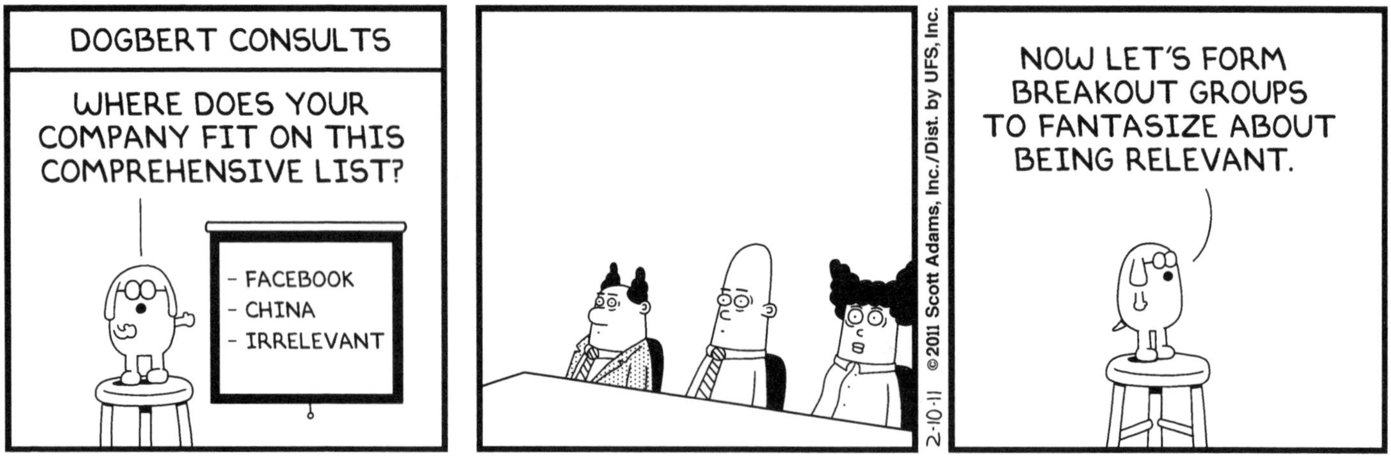
DOGBERT CONSULTS
WHERE DOES YOUR COMPANY FIT ON THIS COMPREHENSIVE LIST?
- FACEBOOK
- CHINA
- IRRELEVANT
2-10-11 © 2011 Scott Adams, Inc./Dist. by UFS, Inc.
NOW LET'S FORM BREAKOUT GROUPS TO FANTASIZE ABOUT BEING RELEVANT.

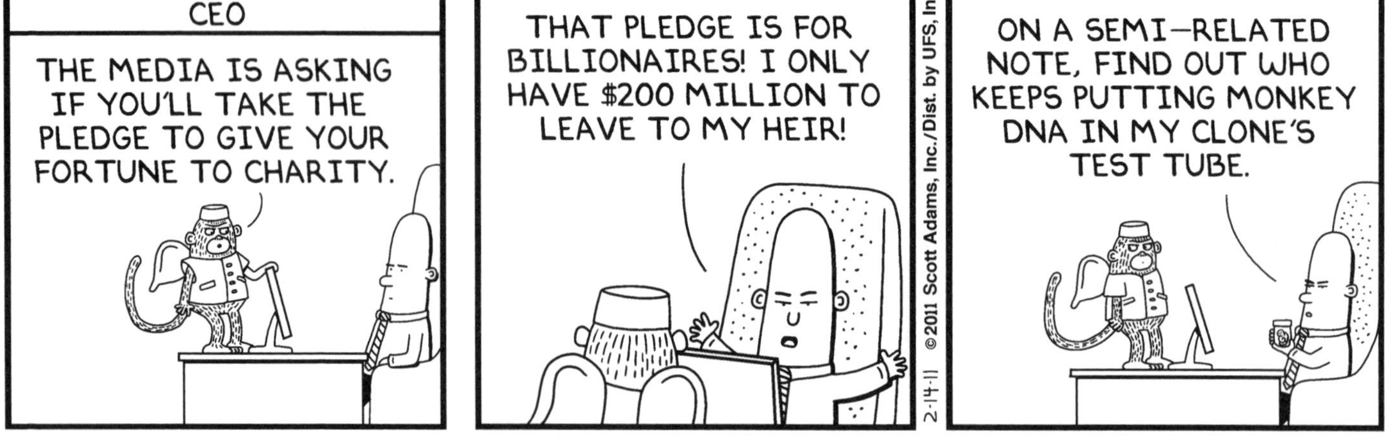
CEO
THE MEDIA IS ASKING IF YOU'LL TAKE THE PLEDGE TO GIVE YOUR FORTUNE TO CHARITY.
THAT PLEDGE IS FOR BILLIONAIRES! I ONLY HAVE $200 MILLION TO LEAVE TO MY HEIR!
2-14-11 © 2011 Scott Adams, Inc./Dist. by UFS, Inc.
ON A SEMI–RELATED NOTE, FIND OUT WHO KEEPS PUTTING MONKEY DNA IN MY CLONE'S TEST TUBE.

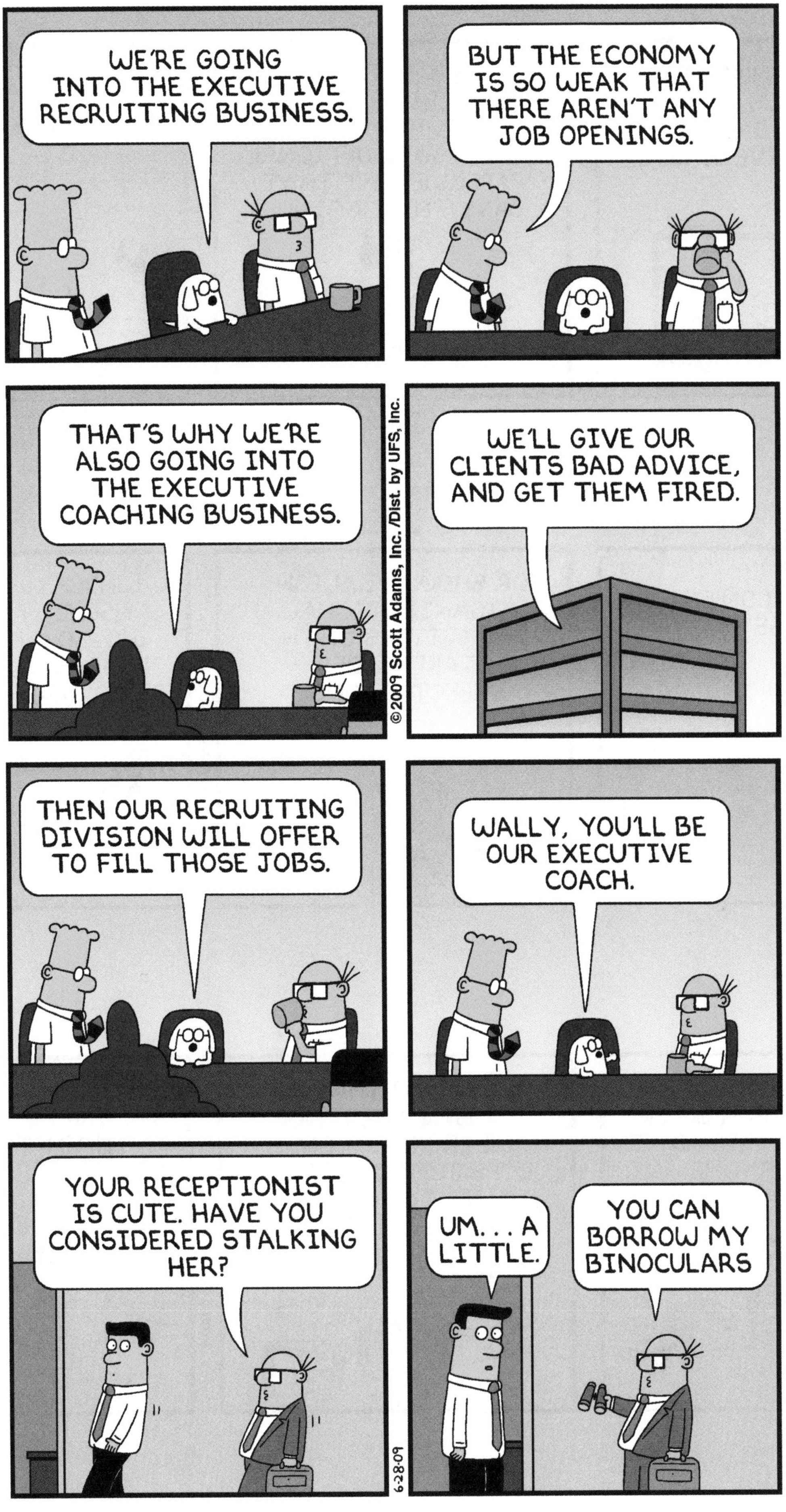
WE'RE GOING INTO THE EXECUTIVE RECRUITING BUSINESS.
BUT THE ECONOMY IS SO WEAK THAT THERE AREN'T ANY JOB OPENINGS.
THAT'S WHY WE'RE ALSO GOING INTO THE EXECUTIVE COACHING BUSINESS.
WE'LL GIVE OUR CLIENTS BAD ADVICE, AND GET THEM FIRED.
THEN OUR RECRUITING DIVISION WILL OFFER TO FILL THOSE JOBS.
WALLY, YOU'LL BE OUR EXECUTIVE COACH.
YOUR RECEPTIONIST IS CUTE. HAVE YOU CONSIDERED STALKING HER?
UM. . . A LITTLE.
YOU CAN BORROW MY BINOCULARS
©2009 Scott Adams, Inc./Dist. by UFS, Inc.
6-28-09

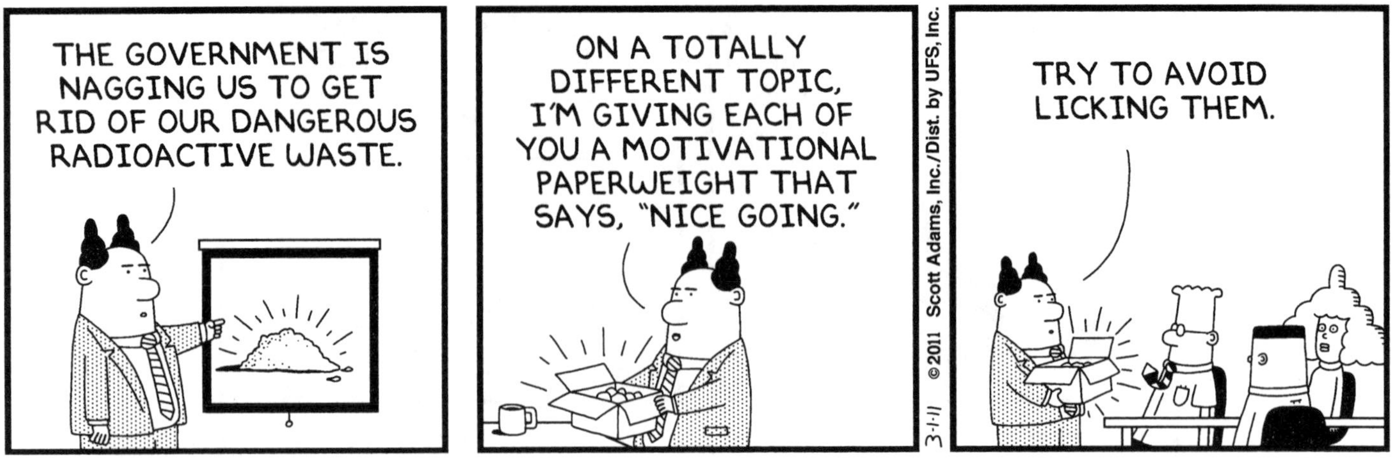
THE GOVERNMENT IS NAGGING US TO GET RID OF OUR DANGEROUS RADIOACTIVE WASTE.
ON A TOTALLY DIFFERENT TOPIC, I'M GIVING EACH OF YOU A MOTIVATIONAL PAPERWEIGHT THAT SAYS, "NICE GOING."
3-1-11 ©2011 Scott Adams, Inc./Dist. by UFS, Inc.
TRY TO AVOID LICKING THEM.

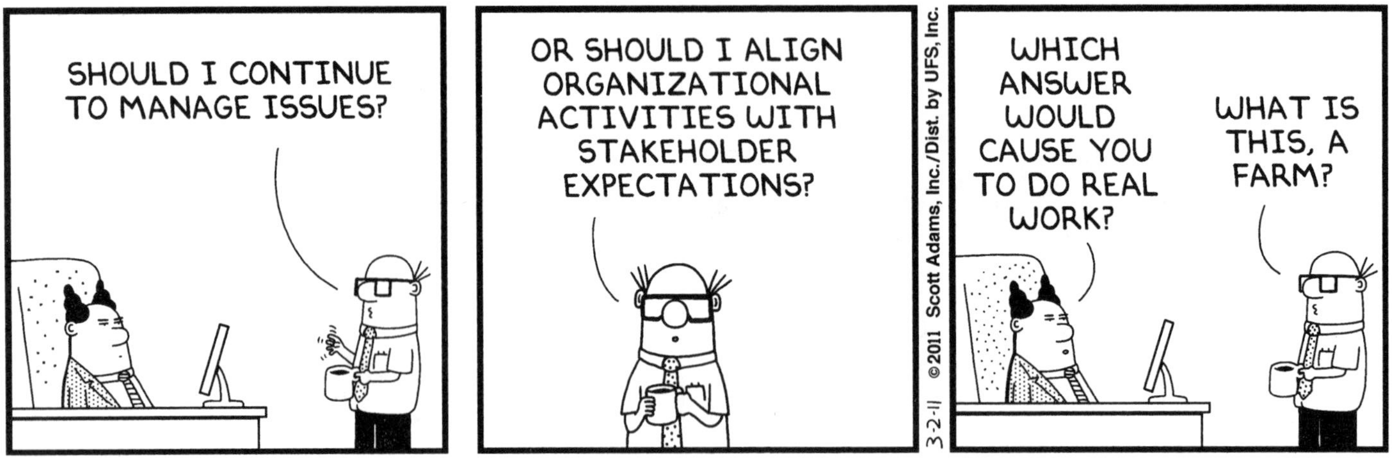
SHOULD I CONTINUE TO MANAGE ISSUES?
OR SHOULD I ALIGN ORGANIZATIONAL ACTIVITIES WITH STAKEHOLDER EXPECTATIONS?
3-2-11 ©2011 Scott Adams, Inc./Dist. by UFS, Inc.
WHICH ANSWER WOULD CAUSE YOU TO DO REAL WORK?
WHAT IS THIS, A FARM?

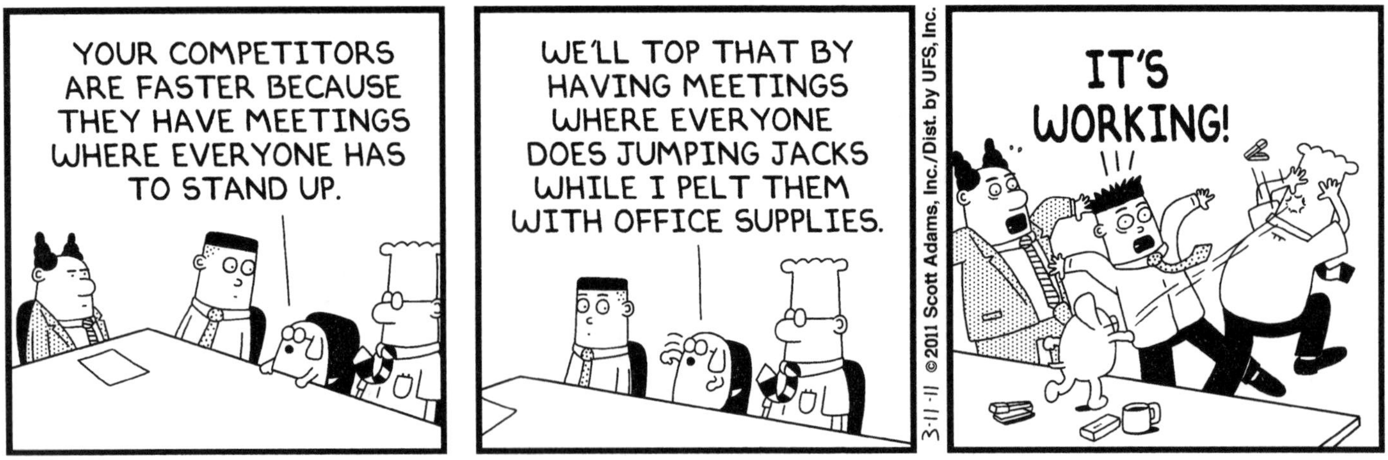
YOUR COMPETITORS ARE FASTER BECAUSE THEY HAVE MEETINGS WHERE EVERYONE HAS TO STAND UP.
WE'LL TOP THAT BY HAVING MEETINGS WHERE EVERYONE DOES JUMPING JACKS WHILE I PELT THEM WITH OFFICE SUPPLIES.
3-11-11 ©2011 Scott Adams, Inc./Dist. by UFS, Inc.
IT'S WORKING!

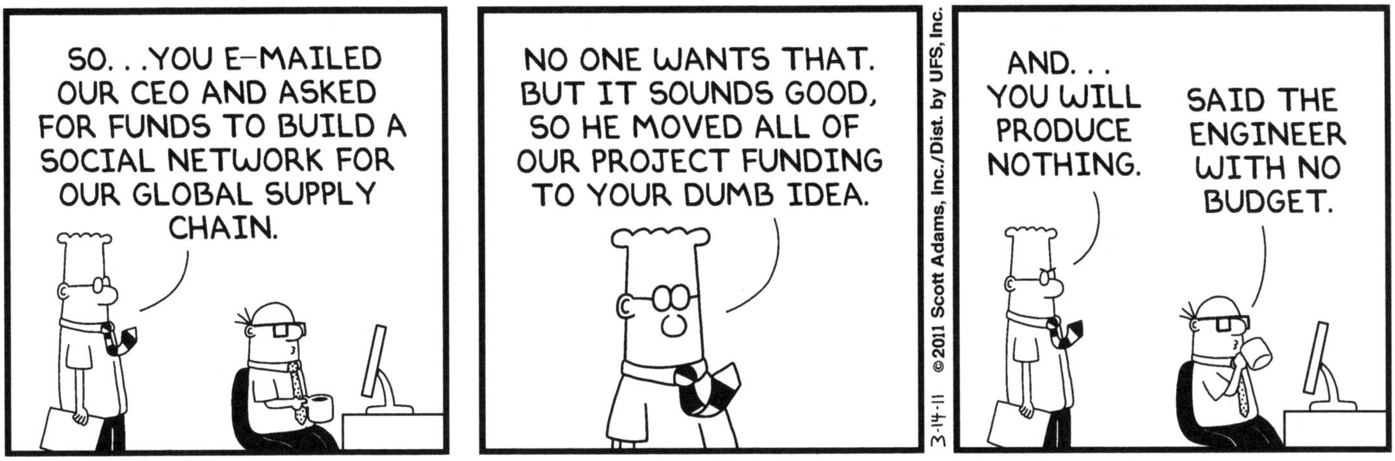
SO. . .YOU E-MAILED OUR CEO AND ASKED FOR FUNDS TO BUILD A SOCIAL NETWORK FOR OUR GLOBAL SUPPLY CHAIN.
NO ONE WANTS THAT. BUT IT SOUNDS GOOD, SO HE MOVED ALL OF OUR PROJECT FUNDING TO YOUR DUMB IDEA.
3-14-11 ©2011 Scott Adams, Inc./Dist. by UFS, Inc.
AND. . . YOU WILL PRODUCE NOTHING.
SAID THE ENGINEER WITH NO BUDGET.

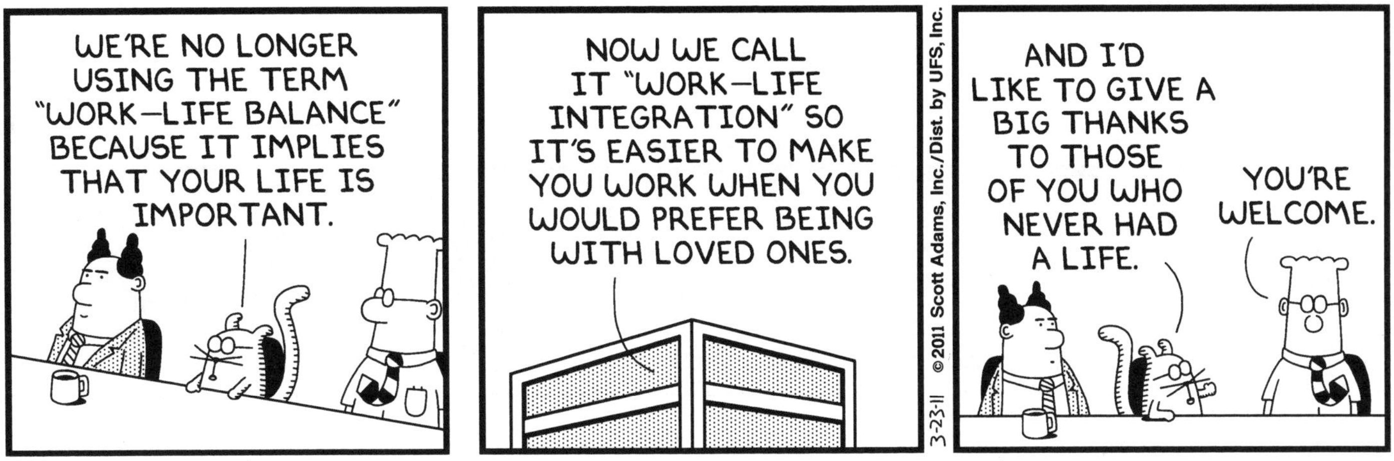
WE'RE NO LONGER USING THE TERM "WORK-LIFE BALANCE" BECAUSE IT IMPLIES THAT YOUR LIFE IS IMPORTANT.
NOW WE CALL IT "WORK-LIFE INTEGRATION" SO IT'S EASIER TO MAKE YOU WORK WHEN YOU WOULD PREFER BEING WITH LOVED ONES.
3-23-11 ©2011 Scott Adams, Inc./Dist. by UFS, Inc.
AND I'D LIKE TO GIVE A BIG THANKS TO THOSE OF YOU WHO NEVER HAD A LIFE.
YOU'RE WELCOME.

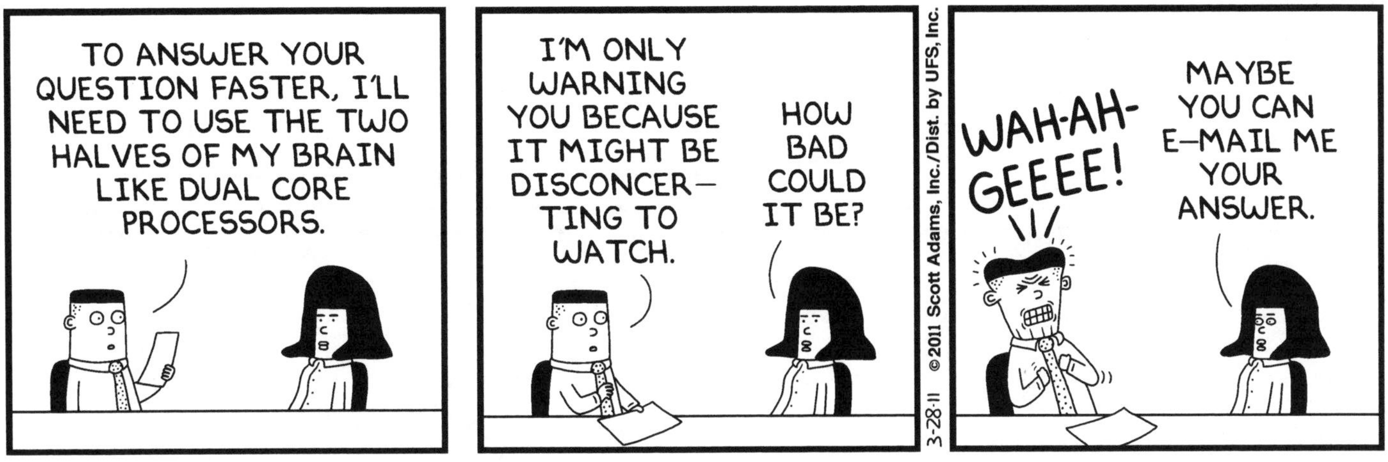
TO ANSWER YOUR QUESTION FASTER, I'LL NEED TO USE THE TWO HALVES OF MY BRAIN LIKE DUAL CORE PROCESSORS.
I'M ONLY WARNING YOU BECAUSE IT MIGHT BE DISCONCER-TING TO WATCH.
HOW BAD COULD IT BE?
3-28-11 ©2011 Scott Adams, Inc./Dist. by UFS, Inc.
WAH-AH-GEEEE!
MAYBE YOU CAN E-MAIL ME YOUR ANSWER.

DOGBERT THE CEO
CONSUMER CONFIDENCE IS UP, AND THAT MEANS MORE PEOPLE WILL BUY OUR PRODUCTS.
I'M OFF TO MAKE RANDOM MANAGEMENT CHANGES SO I CAN TAKE CREDIT FOR THE IMPROVED ECONOMY.
10-21-09 © 2009 Scott Adams, Inc./Dist. by UFS, Inc.
IT'S WORKING?
SALES ARE UP!

DOGBERT THE CEO
I WANT TO WIN A HUMANITARIAN AWARD.
BUT I DON'T WANT TO TOUCH ANYONE WHO IS SICK. OR POOR. OR UNATTRACTIVE.
10-22-09 © 2009 Scott Adams, Inc./Dist. by UFS, Inc.
DO YOU WANT TO DONATE YOUR TIME OR YOUR MONEY?
I'M HOPING TO DONATE *YOUR* TIME AND THE STOCK-HOLDERS' MONEY.

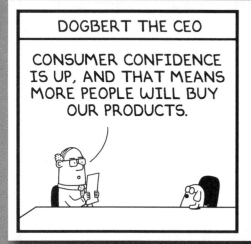

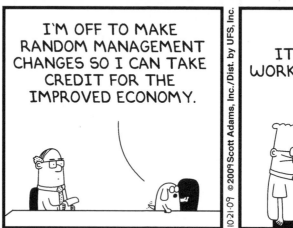

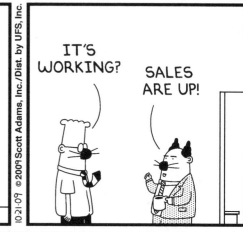

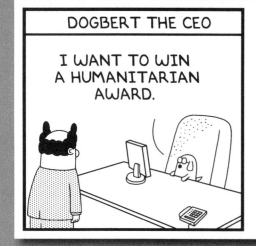

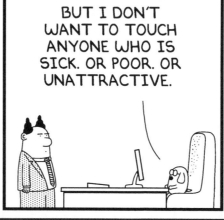

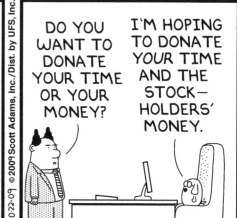

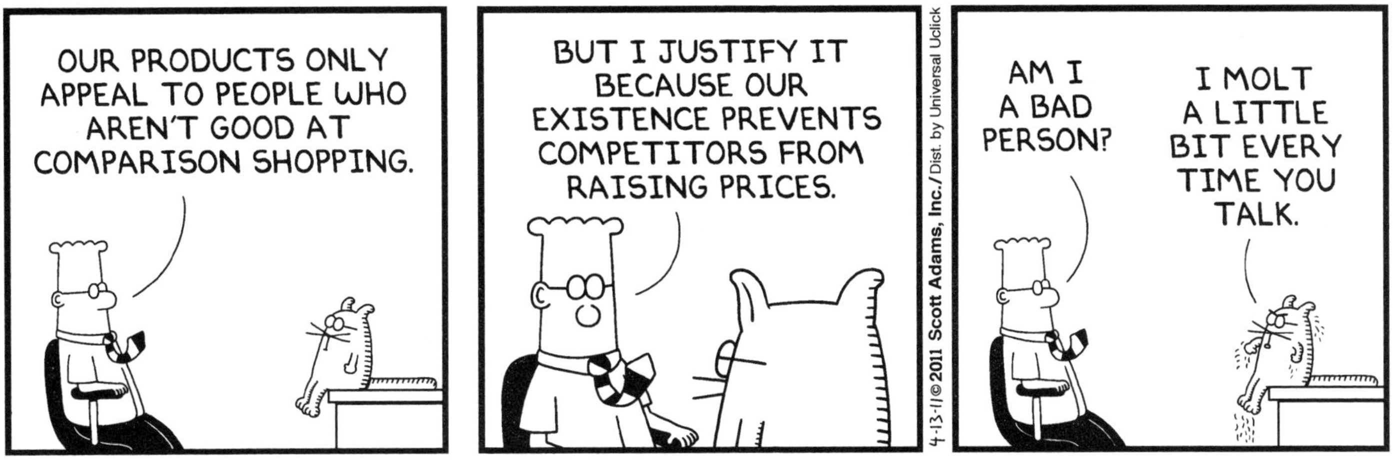
OUR PRODUCTS ONLY APPEAL TO PEOPLE WHO AREN'T GOOD AT COMPARISON SHOPPING.
BUT I JUSTIFY IT BECAUSE OUR EXISTENCE PREVENTS COMPETITORS FROM RAISING PRICES.
4-13-11 © 2011 Scott Adams, Inc./Dist. by Universal Uclick
AM I A BAD PERSON?
I MOLT A LITTLE BIT EVERY TIME YOU TALK.

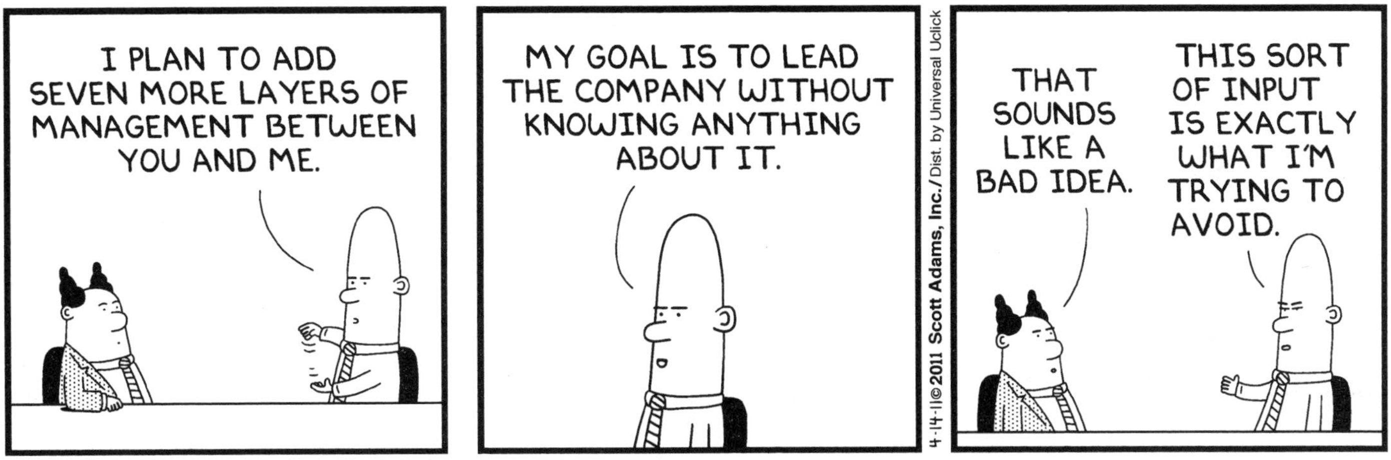
I PLAN TO ADD SEVEN MORE LAYERS OF MANAGEMENT BETWEEN YOU AND ME.
MY GOAL IS TO LEAD THE COMPANY WITHOUT KNOWING ANYTHING ABOUT IT.
4-14-11 © 2011 Scott Adams, Inc./Dist. by Universal Uclick
THAT SOUNDS LIKE A BAD IDEA.
THIS SORT OF INPUT IS EXACTLY WHAT I'M TRYING TO AVOID.

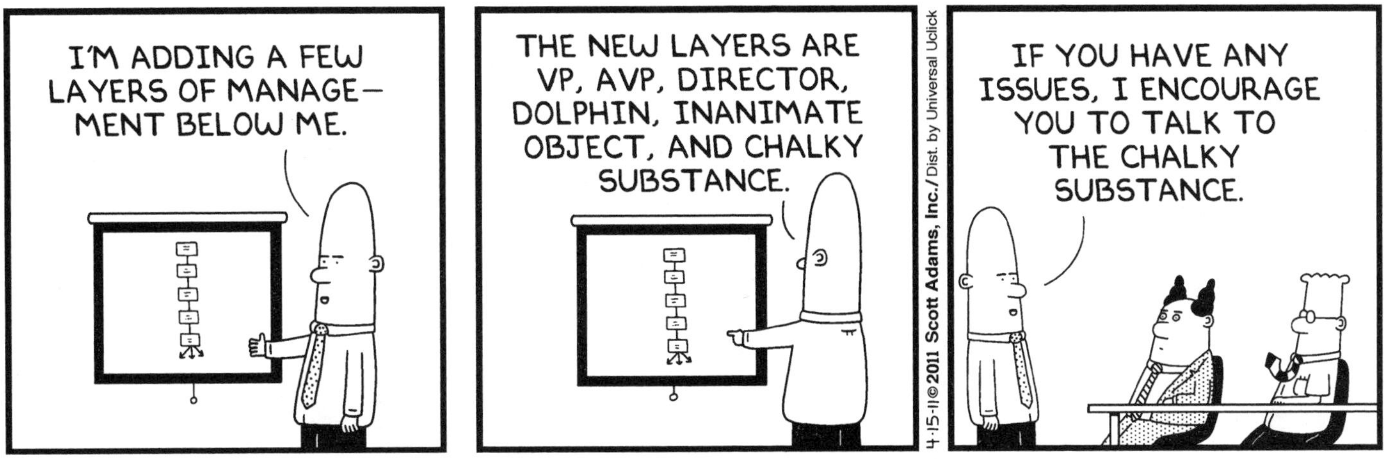
I'M ADDING A FEW LAYERS OF MANAGE-MENT BELOW ME.
THE NEW LAYERS ARE VP, AVP, DIRECTOR, DOLPHIN, INANIMATE OBJECT, AND CHALKY SUBSTANCE.
4-15-11 © 2011 Scott Adams, Inc./Dist. by Universal Uclick
IF YOU HAVE ANY ISSUES, I ENCOURAGE YOU TO TALK TO THE CHALKY SUBSTANCE.

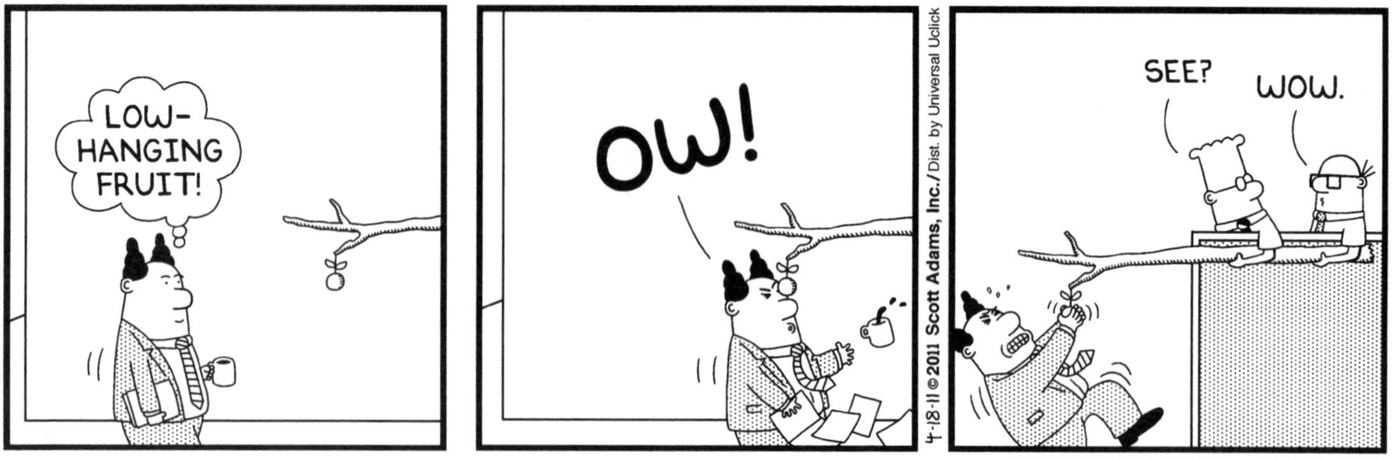
LOW-HANGING FRUIT!
OW!
SEE?
WOW.
4-18-11 © 2011 Scott Adams, Inc./Dist. by Universal Uclick

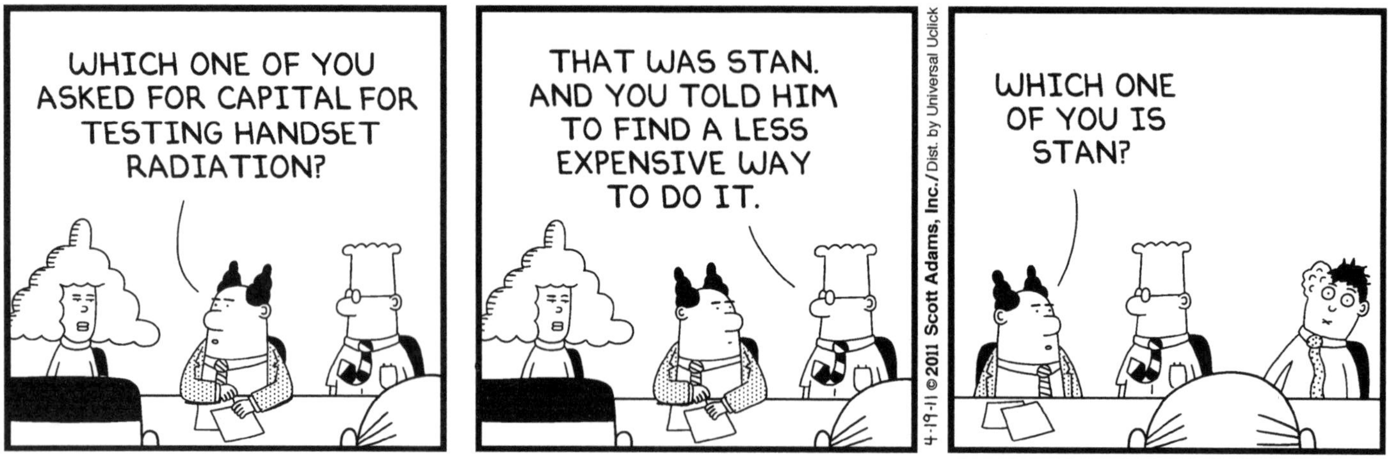
WHICH ONE OF YOU ASKED FOR CAPITAL FOR TESTING HANDSET RADIATION?
THAT WAS STAN. AND YOU TOLD HIM TO FIND A LESS EXPENSIVE WAY TO DO IT.
WHICH ONE OF YOU IS STAN?
4-19-11 © 2011 Scott Adams, Inc./Dist. by Universal Uclick

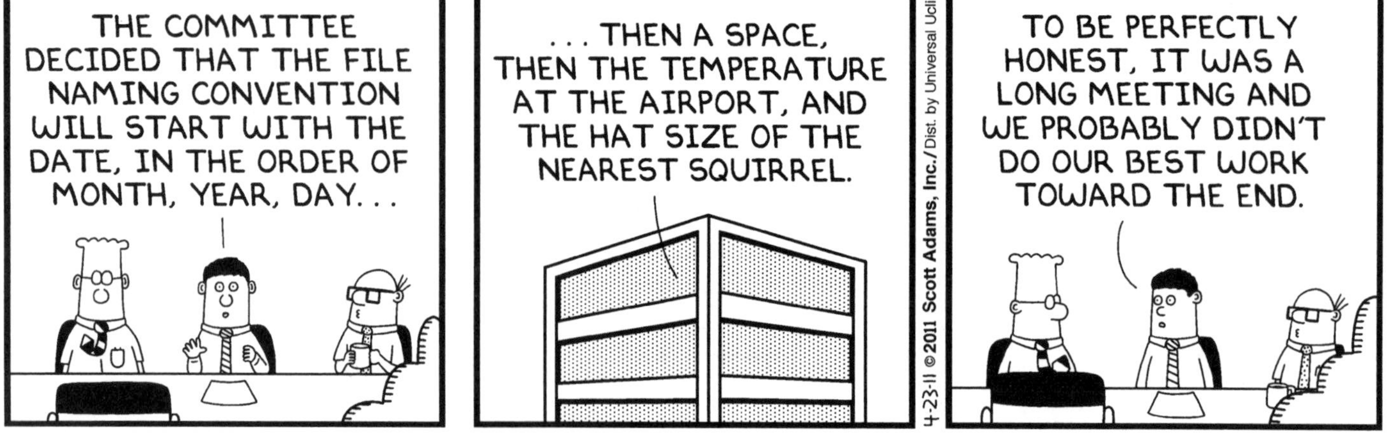
THE COMMITTEE DECIDED THAT THE FILE NAMING CONVENTION WILL START WITH THE DATE, IN THE ORDER OF MONTH, YEAR, DAY. . .
. . . THEN A SPACE, THEN THE TEMPERATURE AT THE AIRPORT, AND THE HAT SIZE OF THE NEAREST SQUIRREL.
TO BE PERFECTLY HONEST, IT WAS A LONG MEETING AND WE PROBABLY DIDN'T DO OUR BEST WORK TOWARD THE END.
4-23-11 © 2011 Scott Adams, Inc./Dist. by Universal Uclick

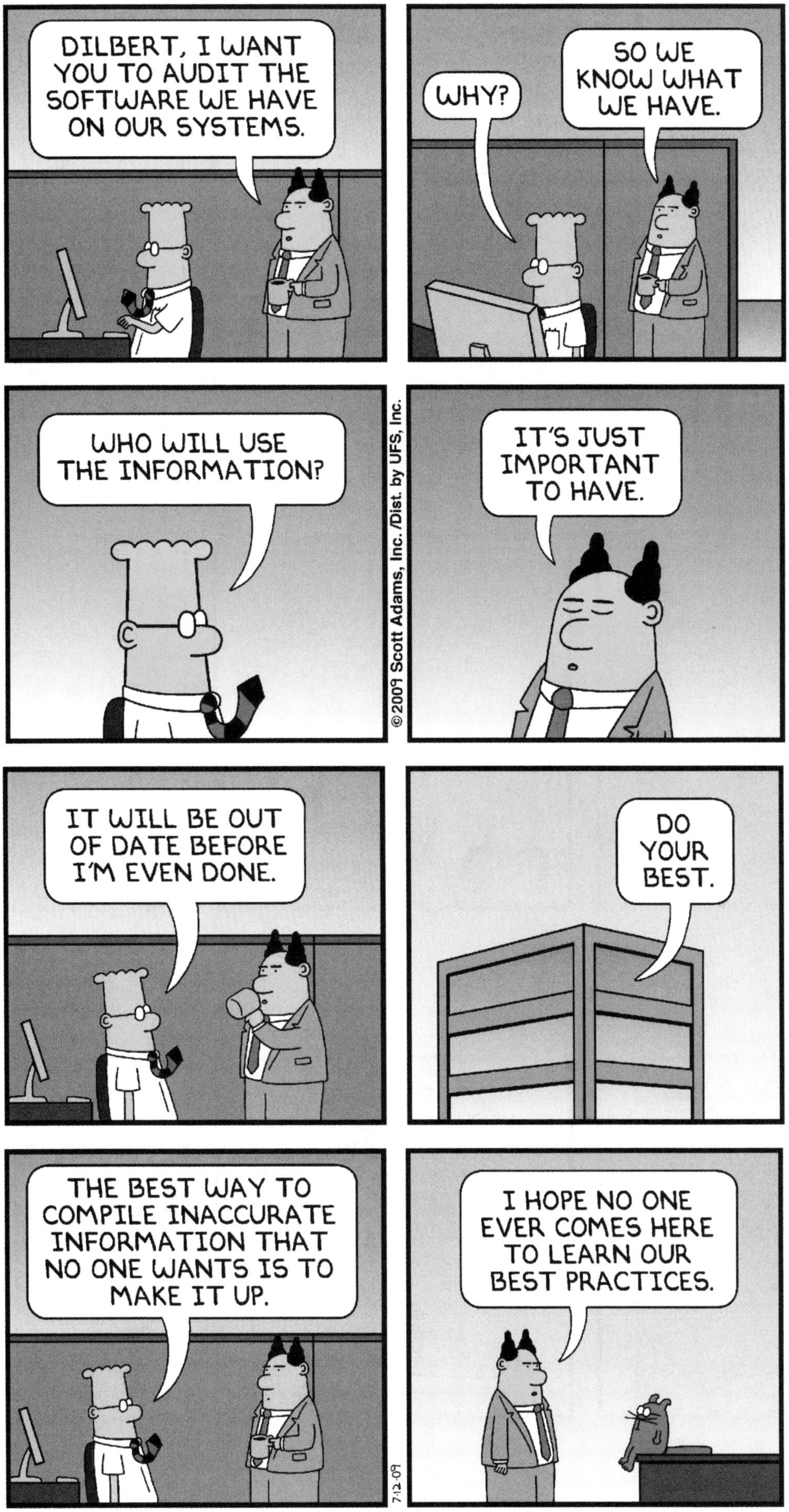
DILBERT, I WANT YOU TO AUDIT THE SOFTWARE WE HAVE ON OUR SYSTEMS.
WHY?
SO WE KNOW WHAT WE HAVE.
WHO WILL USE THE INFORMATION?
IT'S JUST IMPORTANT TO HAVE.
IT WILL BE OUT OF DATE BEFORE I'M EVEN DONE.
DO YOUR BEST.
THE BEST WAY TO COMPILE INACCURATE INFORMATION THAT NO ONE WANTS IS TO MAKE IT UP.
I HOPE NO ONE EVER COMES HERE TO LEARN OUR BEST PRACTICES.
©2009 Scott Adams, Inc. /Dist. by UFS, Inc.
7-12-09

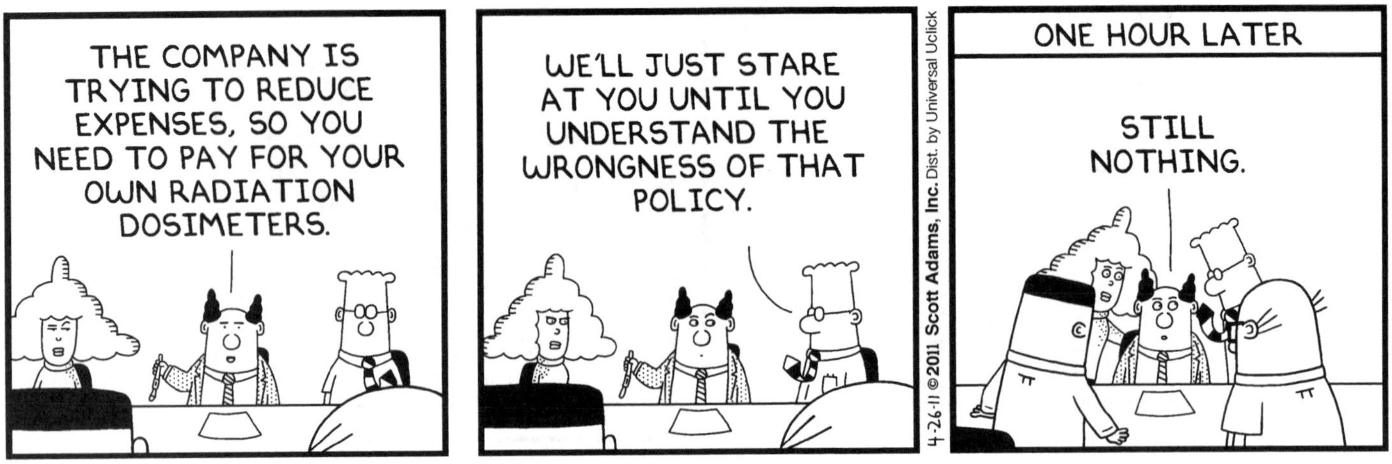
THE COMPANY IS TRYING TO REDUCE EXPENSES, SO YOU NEED TO PAY FOR YOUR OWN RADIATION DOSIMETERS.
WE'LL JUST STARE AT YOU UNTIL YOU UNDERSTAND THE WRONGNESS OF THAT POLICY.
4-26-11 © 2011 Scott Adams, Inc. Dist. by Universal Uclick
ONE HOUR LATER
STILL NOTHING.

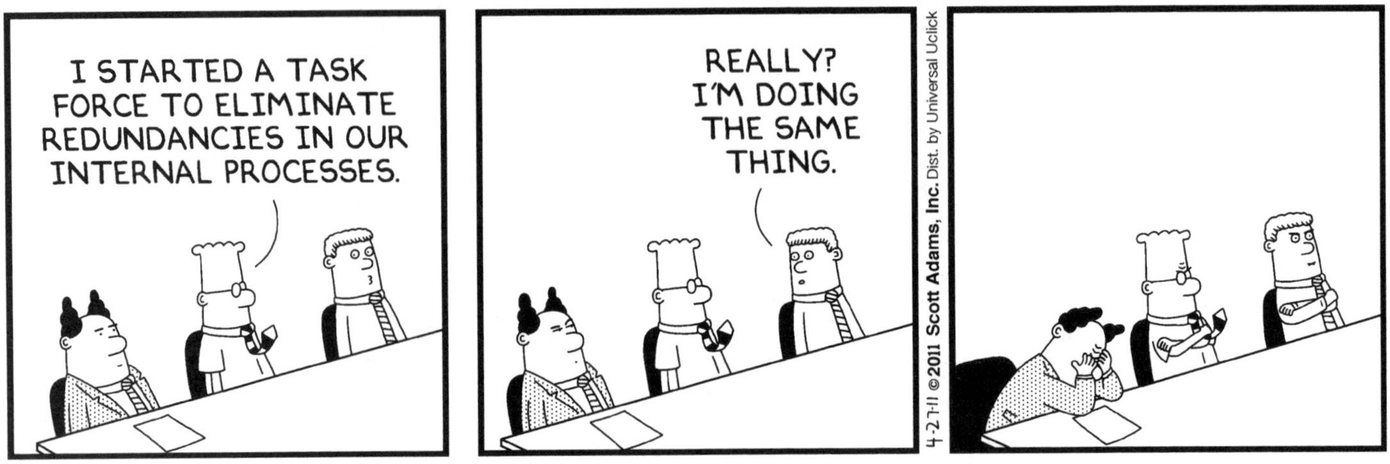
I STARTED A TASK FORCE TO ELIMINATE REDUNDANCIES IN OUR INTERNAL PROCESSES.
REALLY? I'M DOING THE SAME THING.
4-27-11 © 2011 Scott Adams, Inc. Dist. by Universal Uclick

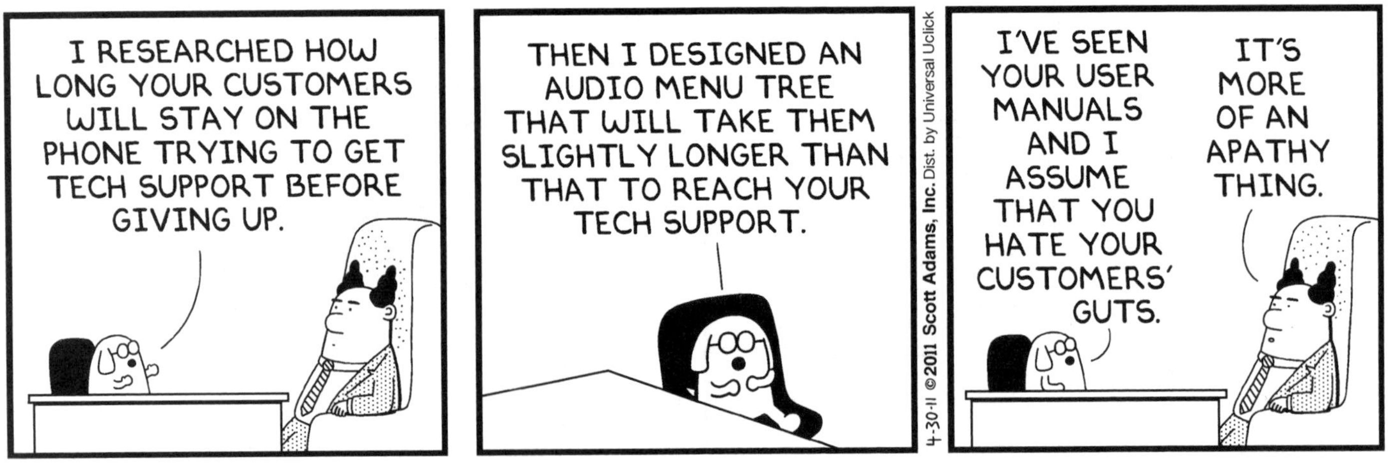
I RESEARCHED HOW LONG YOUR CUSTOMERS WILL STAY ON THE PHONE TRYING TO GET TECH SUPPORT BEFORE GIVING UP.
THEN I DESIGNED AN AUDIO MENU TREE THAT WILL TAKE THEM SLIGHTLY LONGER THAN THAT TO REACH YOUR TECH SUPPORT.
4-30-11 © 2011 Scott Adams, Inc. Dist. by Universal Uclick
I'VE SEEN YOUR USER MANUALS AND I ASSUME THAT YOU HATE YOUR CUSTOMERS' GUTS.
IT'S MORE OF AN APATHY THING.

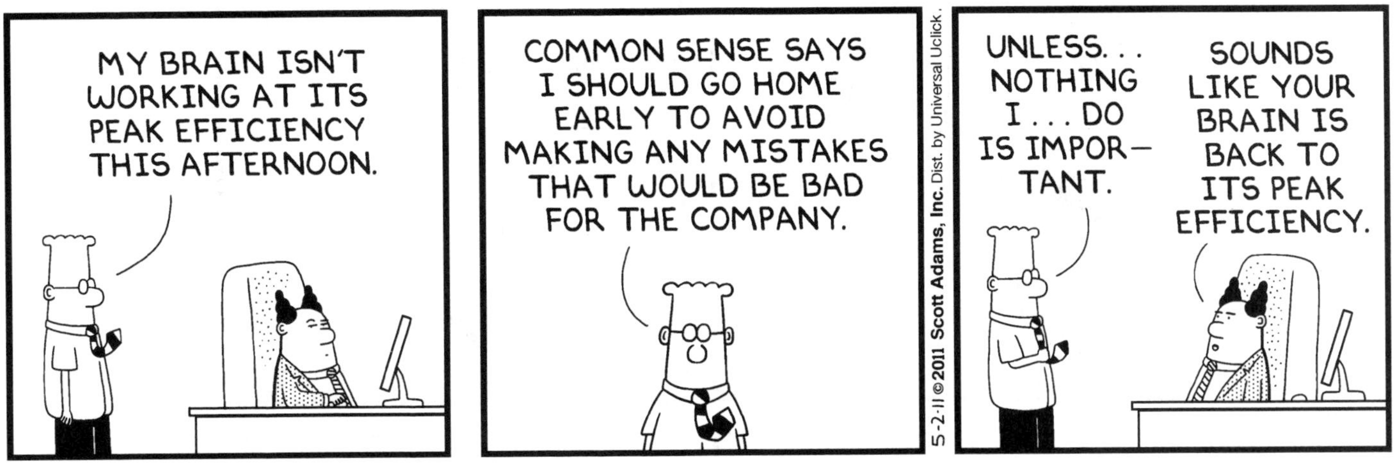
MY BRAIN ISN'T WORKING AT ITS PEAK EFFICIENCY THIS AFTERNOON.
COMMON SENSE SAYS I SHOULD GO HOME EARLY TO AVOID MAKING ANY MISTAKES THAT WOULD BE BAD FOR THE COMPANY.
5-2-11 ©2011 Scott Adams, Inc. Dist. by Universal Uclick.
UNLESS... NOTHING I... DO IS IMPOR-TANT.
SOUNDS LIKE YOUR BRAIN IS BACK TO ITS PEAK EFFICIENCY.

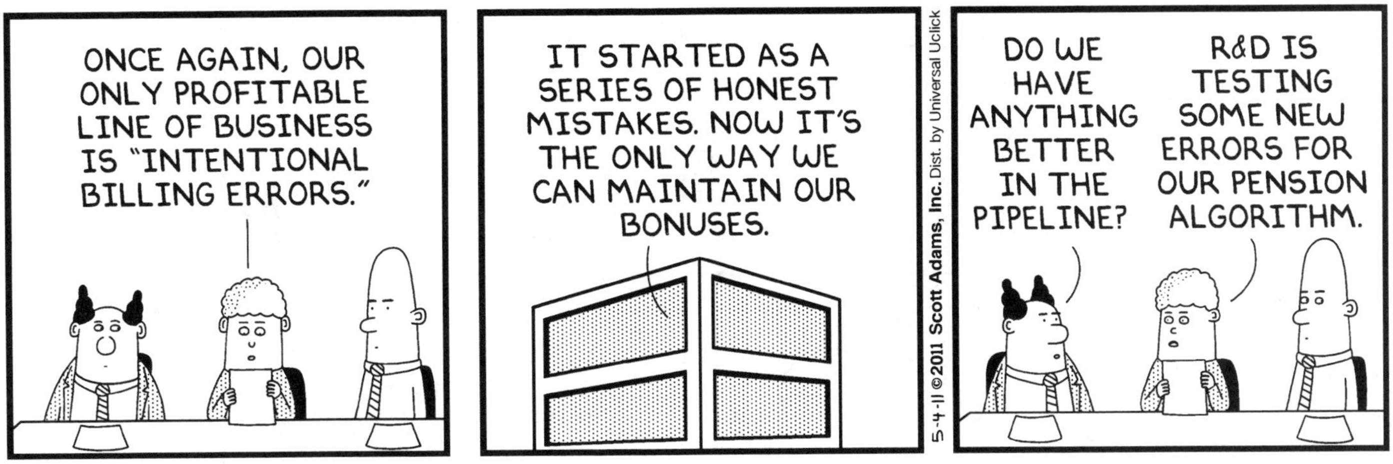
ONCE AGAIN, OUR ONLY PROFITABLE LINE OF BUSINESS IS "INTENTIONAL BILLING ERRORS."
IT STARTED AS A SERIES OF HONEST MISTAKES. NOW IT'S THE ONLY WAY WE CAN MAINTAIN OUR BONUSES.
5-4-11 ©2011 Scott Adams, Inc. Dist. by Universal Uclick
DO WE HAVE ANYTHING BETTER IN THE PIPELINE?
R&D IS TESTING SOME NEW ERRORS FOR OUR PENSION ALGORITHM.

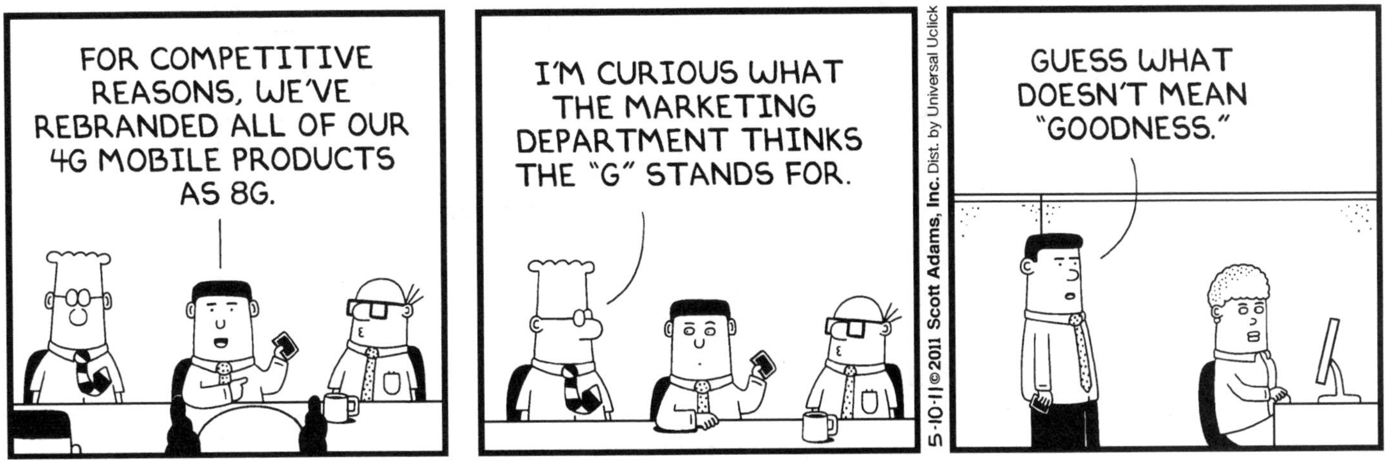
FOR COMPETITIVE REASONS, WE'VE REBRANDED ALL OF OUR 4G MOBILE PRODUCTS AS 8G.
I'M CURIOUS WHAT THE MARKETING DEPARTMENT THINKS THE "G" STANDS FOR.
5-10-11 ©2011 Scott Adams, Inc. Dist. by Universal Uclick
GUESS WHAT DOESN'T MEAN "GOODNESS."

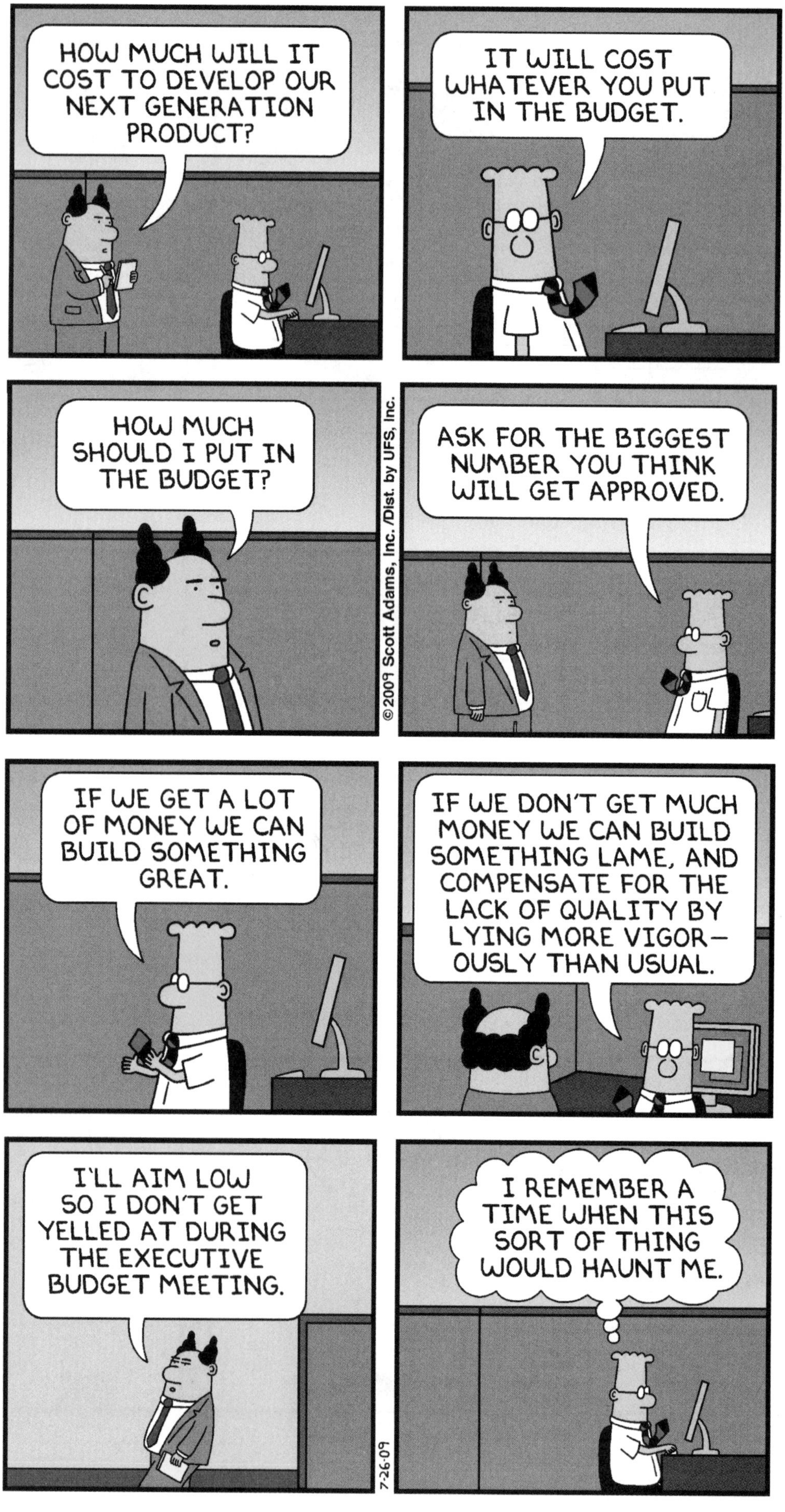
HOW MUCH WILL IT COST TO DEVELOP OUR NEXT GENERATION PRODUCT?
IT WILL COST WHATEVER YOU PUT IN THE BUDGET.
HOW MUCH SHOULD I PUT IN THE BUDGET?
ASK FOR THE BIGGEST NUMBER YOU THINK WILL GET APPROVED.
©2009 Scott Adams, Inc. /Dist. by UFS, Inc.
IF WE GET A LOT OF MONEY WE CAN BUILD SOMETHING GREAT.
IF WE DON'T GET MUCH MONEY WE CAN BUILD SOMETHING LAME, AND COMPENSATE FOR THE LACK OF QUALITY BY LYING MORE VIGOR-OUSLY THAN USUAL.
I'LL AIM LOW SO I DON'T GET YELLED AT DURING THE EXECUTIVE BUDGET MEETING.
I REMEMBER A TIME WHEN THIS SORT OF THING WOULD HAUNT ME.
7-26-09

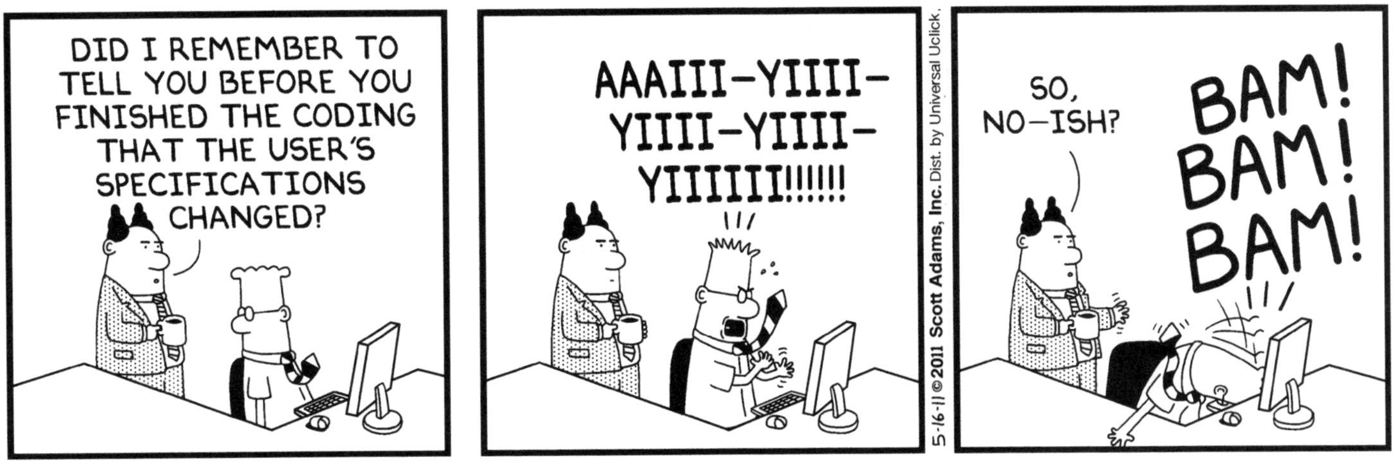
DID I REMEMBER TO TELL YOU BEFORE YOU FINISHED THE CODING THAT THE USER'S SPECIFICATIONS CHANGED?
AAAIII-YIIII-YIIII-YIIII-YIIIIII!!!!!!
SO, NO-ISH?
BAM! BAM! BAM!
5-16-11 ©2011 Scott Adams, Inc. Dist. by Universal Uclick.

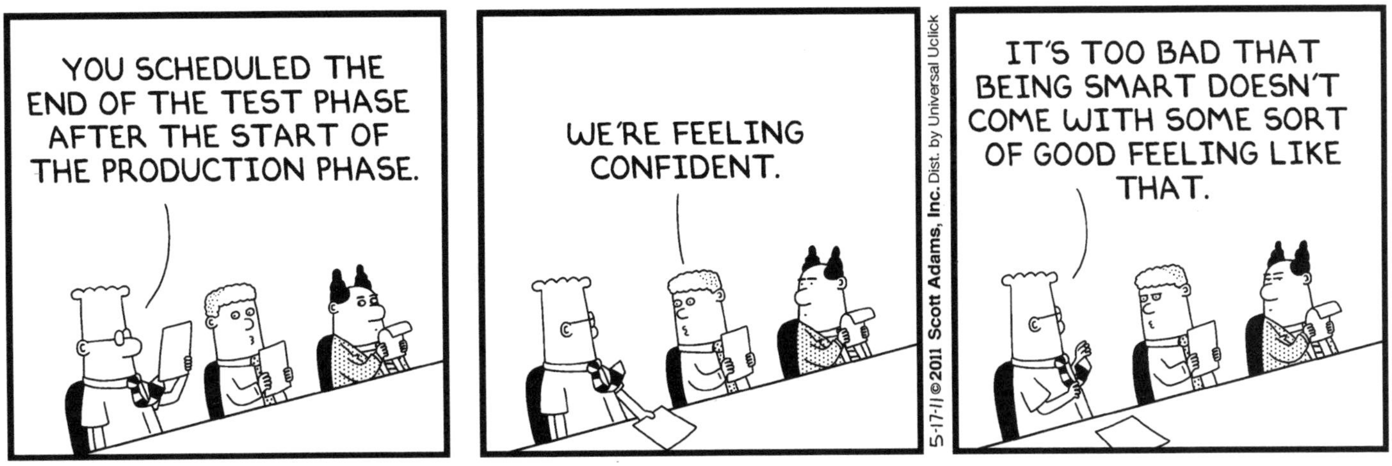
YOU SCHEDULED THE END OF THE TEST PHASE AFTER THE START OF THE PRODUCTION PHASE.
WE'RE FEELING CONFIDENT.
IT'S TOO BAD THAT BEING SMART DOESN'T COME WITH SOME SORT OF GOOD FEELING LIKE THAT.
5-17-11 ©2011 Scott Adams, Inc. Dist. by Universal Uclick

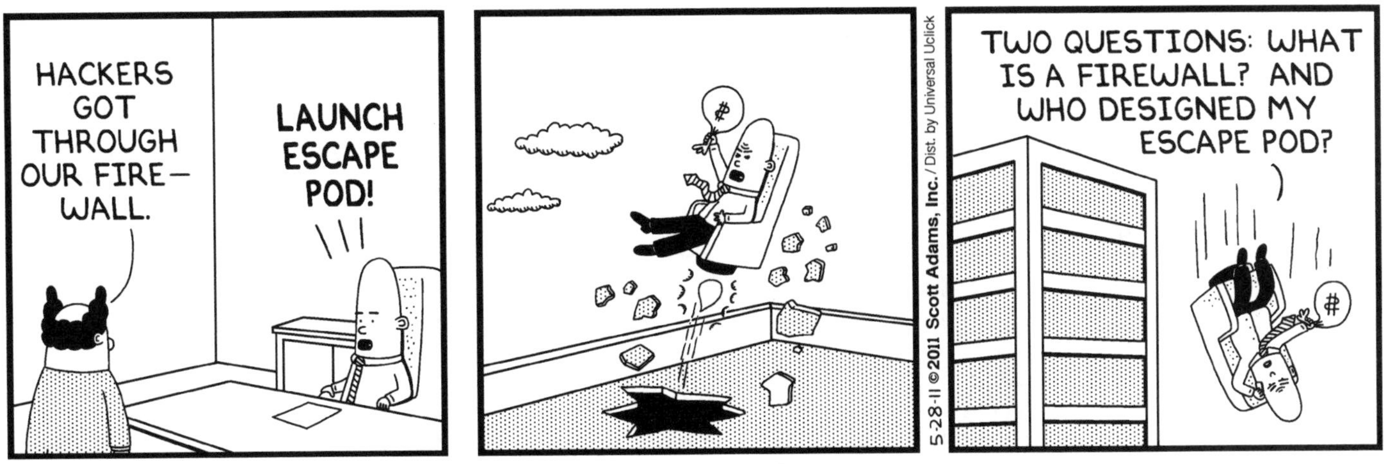
HACKERS GOT THROUGH OUR FIRE-WALL.
LAUNCH ESCAPE POD!
TWO QUESTIONS: WHAT IS A FIREWALL? AND WHO DESIGNED MY ESCAPE POD?
5-28-11 ©2011 Scott Adams, Inc./Dist. by Universal Uclick

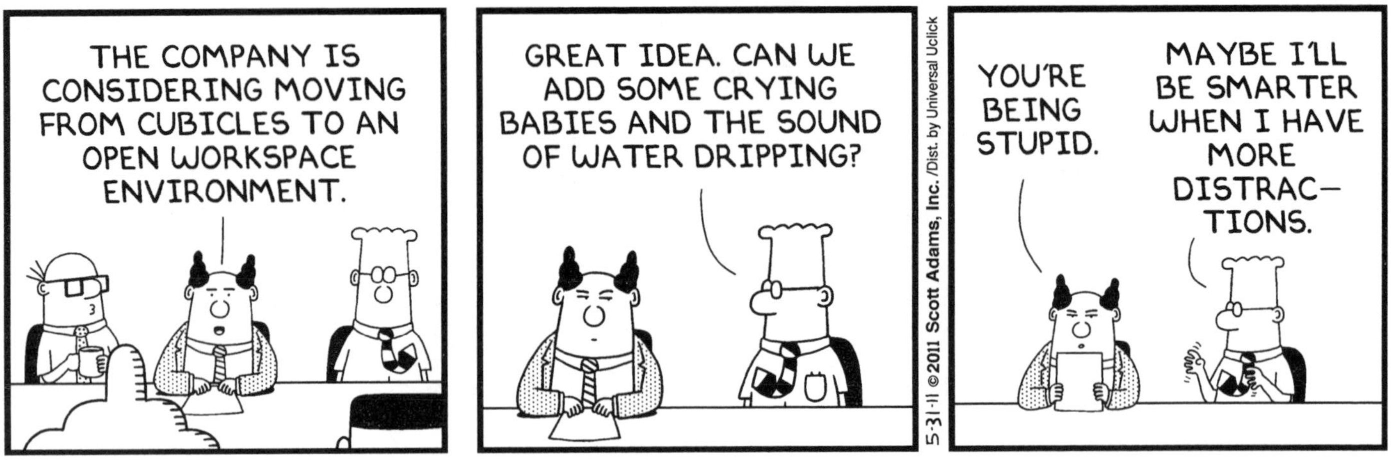
THE COMPANY IS CONSIDERING MOVING FROM CUBICLES TO AN OPEN WORKSPACE ENVIRONMENT.
GREAT IDEA. CAN WE ADD SOME CRYING BABIES AND THE SOUND OF WATER DRIPPING?
5-31-11 ©2011 Scott Adams, Inc. /Dist. by Universal Uclick
YOU'RE BEING STUPID.
MAYBE I'LL BE SMARTER WHEN I HAVE MORE DISTRAC-TIONS.

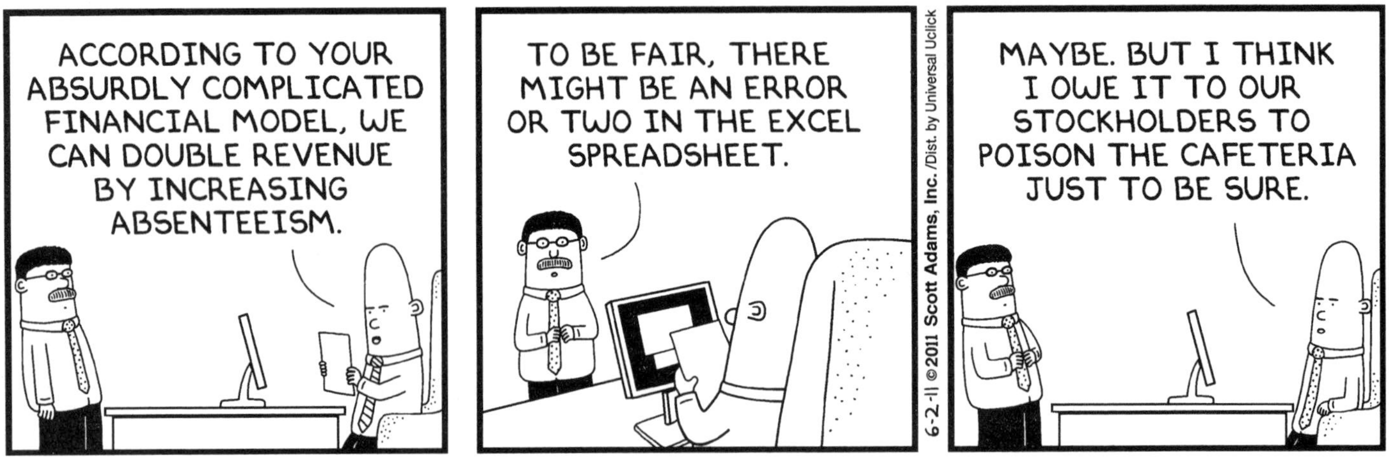
ACCORDING TO YOUR ABSURDLY COMPLICATED FINANCIAL MODEL, WE CAN DOUBLE REVENUE BY INCREASING ABSENTEEISM.
TO BE FAIR, THERE MIGHT BE AN ERROR OR TWO IN THE EXCEL SPREADSHEET.
6-2-11 ©2011 Scott Adams, Inc. /Dist. by Universal Uclick
MAYBE. BUT I THINK I OWE IT TO OUR STOCKHOLDERS TO POISON THE CAFETERIA JUST TO BE SURE.

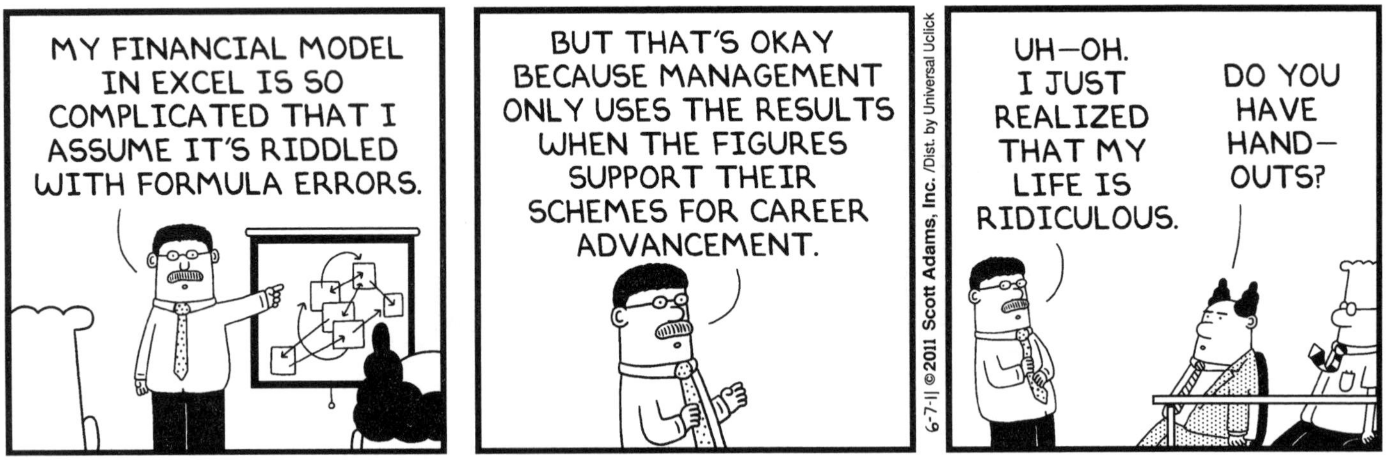
MY FINANCIAL MODEL IN EXCEL IS SO COMPLICATED THAT I ASSUME IT'S RIDDLED WITH FORMULA ERRORS.
BUT THAT'S OKAY BECAUSE MANAGEMENT ONLY USES THE RESULTS WHEN THE FIGURES SUPPORT THEIR SCHEMES FOR CAREER ADVANCEMENT.
6-7-11 ©2011 Scott Adams, Inc. /Dist. by Universal Uclick
UH-OH. I JUST REALIZED THAT MY LIFE IS RIDICULOUS.
DO YOU HAVE HAND-OUTS?

DOGBERT THE CEO
WE'RE GOING INTO THE INTERNET NEWS BUSINESS.
WE'RE HIRING REPORT-ERS?
NO, WE'LL SUMMARIZE STORIES FROM OTHER SITES AND PROVIDE LINKS.
11-17-09 © 2009 Scott Adams, Inc./Dist. by UFS, Inc.
SO... WE'LL BE PARA-SITES?
GO BUY A VINYL RECORD, GRANDPA.

DOGBERT THE CEO
FLOYD, I'M GIVING YOU A C-LEVEL TITLE.
YOU'LL BE THE CHIEF JANITORIAL OFFICER, IN CHARGE OF ALL DIRT, GERMS, DEAD CRITTERS AND PROBLEMATIC EXCRETIONS.
11-20-09 © 2009 Scott Adams, Inc./Dist. by UFS, Inc.
IS IT BECAUSE I'M SO IMPOR-TANT?
WHAT ANSWER WOULD MAKE YOU CLEAN UP POOP FASTER?

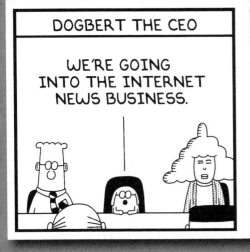

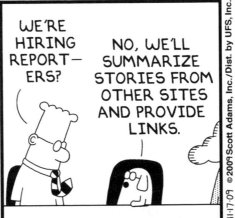

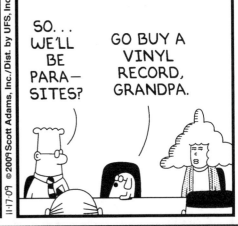

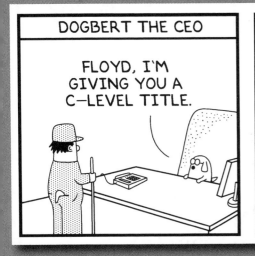

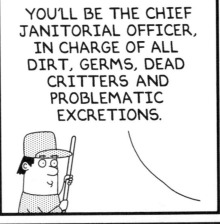

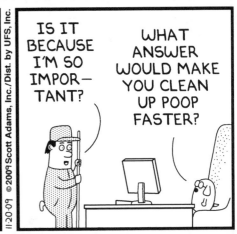

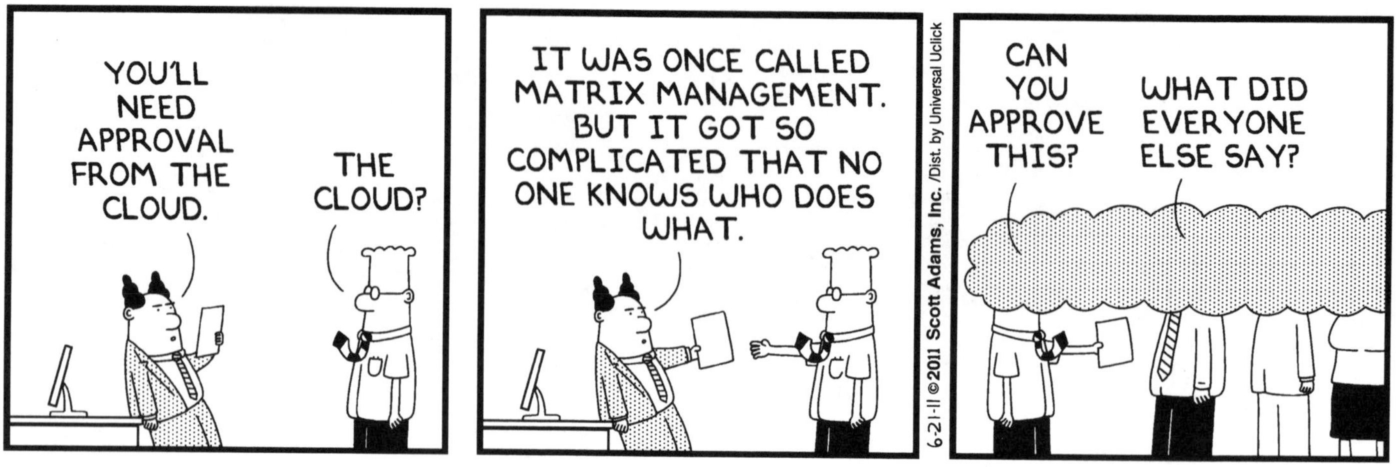
YOU'LL NEED APPROVAL FROM THE CLOUD.
THE CLOUD?
IT WAS ONCE CALLED MATRIX MANAGEMENT. BUT IT GOT SO COMPLICATED THAT NO ONE KNOWS WHO DOES WHAT.
6-21-11 © 2011 Scott Adams, Inc. /Dist. by Universal Uclick
CAN YOU APPROVE THIS?
WHAT DID EVERYONE ELSE SAY?

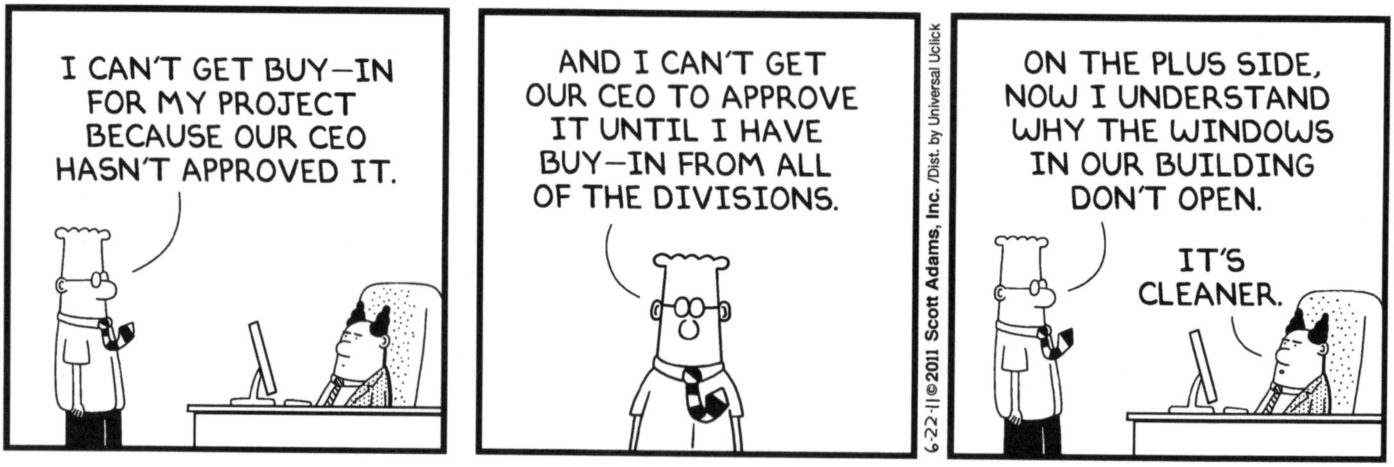
I CAN'T GET BUY—IN FOR MY PROJECT BECAUSE OUR CEO HASN'T APPROVED IT.
AND I CAN'T GET OUR CEO TO APPROVE IT UNTIL I HAVE BUY—IN FROM ALL OF THE DIVISIONS.
6-22-11 © 2011 Scott Adams, Inc. /Dist. by Universal Uclick
ON THE PLUS SIDE, NOW I UNDERSTAND WHY THE WINDOWS IN OUR BUILDING DON'T OPEN.
IT'S CLEANER.

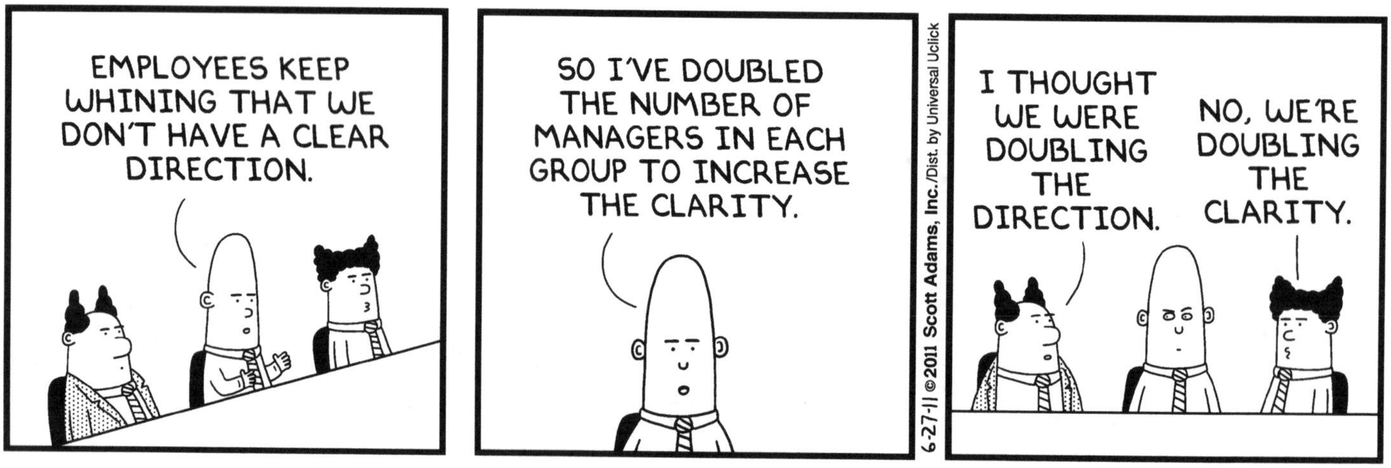
EMPLOYEES KEEP WHINING THAT WE DON'T HAVE A CLEAR DIRECTION.
SO I'VE DOUBLED THE NUMBER OF MANAGERS IN EACH GROUP TO INCREASE THE CLARITY.
6-27-11 © 2011 Scott Adams, Inc. /Dist. by Universal Uclick
I THOUGHT WE WERE DOUBLING THE DIRECTION.
NO, WE'RE DOUBLING THE CLARITY.

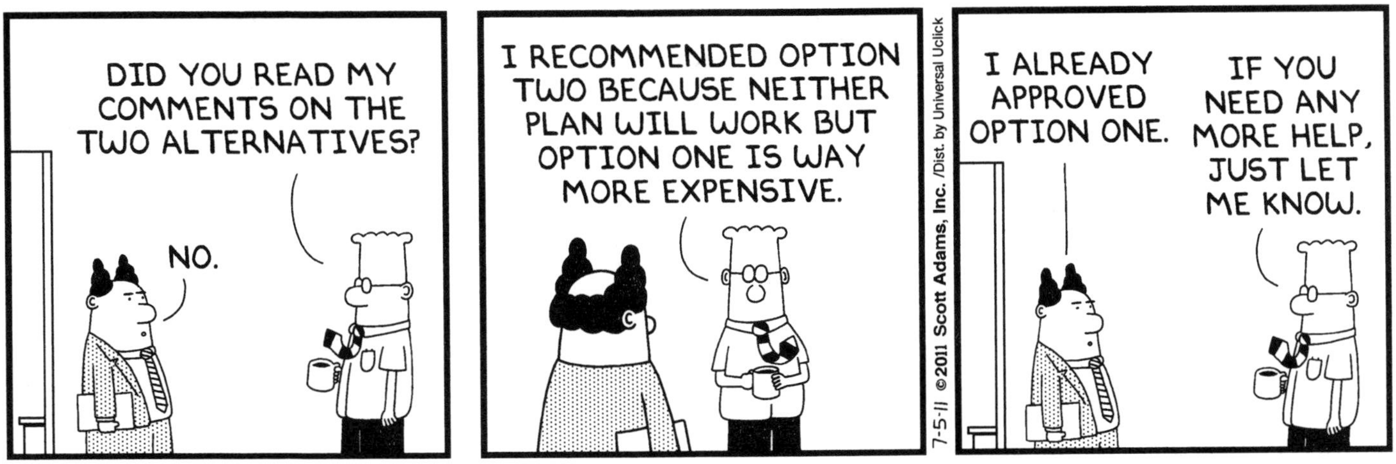
DID YOU READ MY COMMENTS ON THE TWO ALTERNATIVES?
NO.
I RECOMMENDED OPTION TWO BECAUSE NEITHER PLAN WILL WORK BUT OPTION ONE IS WAY MORE EXPENSIVE.
7-5-11 ©2011 Scott Adams, Inc. /Dist. by Universal Uclick
I ALREADY APPROVED OPTION ONE.
IF YOU NEED ANY MORE HELP, JUST LET ME KNOW.

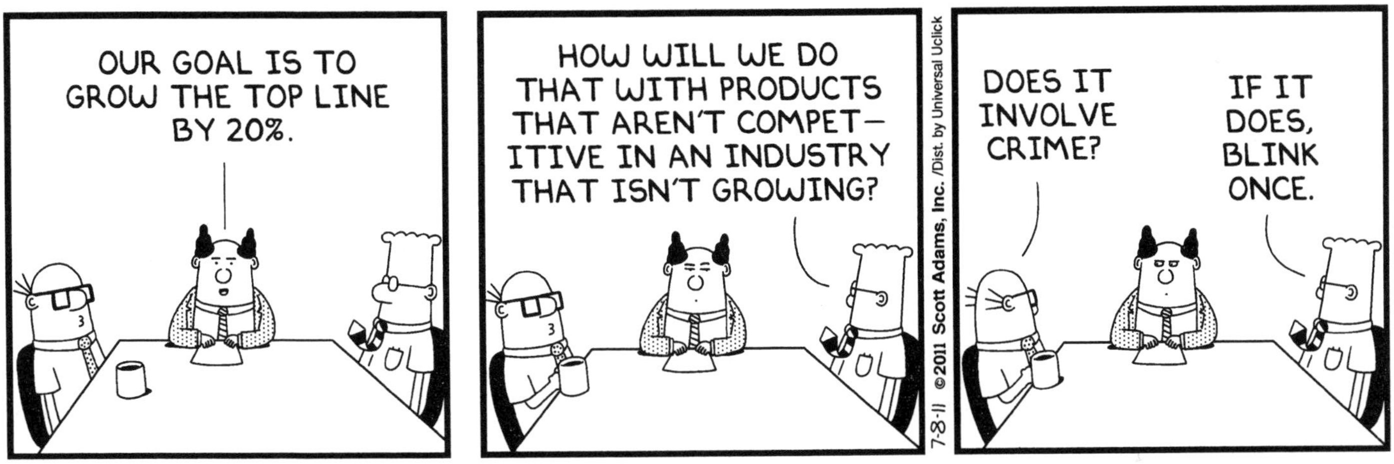
OUR GOAL IS TO GROW THE TOP LINE BY 20%.
HOW WILL WE DO THAT WITH PRODUCTS THAT AREN'T COMPET-ITIVE IN AN INDUSTRY THAT ISN'T GROWING?
7-8-11 ©2011 Scott Adams, Inc. /Dist. by Universal Uclick
DOES IT INVOLVE CRIME?
IF IT DOES, BLINK ONCE.

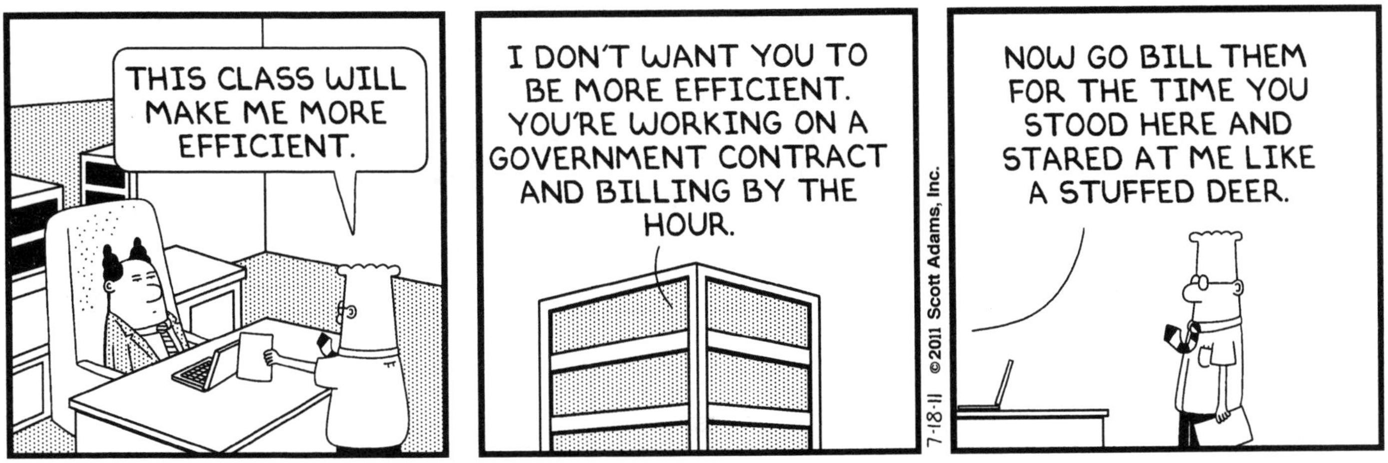
THIS CLASS WILL MAKE ME MORE EFFICIENT.
I DON'T WANT YOU TO BE MORE EFFICIENT. YOU'RE WORKING ON A GOVERNMENT CONTRACT AND BILLING BY THE HOUR.
7-18-11 ©2011 Scott Adams, Inc.
NOW GO BILL THEM FOR THE TIME YOU STOOD HERE AND STARED AT ME LIKE A STUFFED DEER.